Constitutional Courts in Post-Soviet States

STUDIES IN POLITICS, SECURITY AND SOCIETY

Edited by Stanisław Sulowski
Faculty of Political Science and International Studies
University of Warsaw

VOLUME 25

PETER LANG

Jacek Zaleśny (ed.)

Constitutional Courts in Post-Soviet States

Between the Model of a State of Law and Its Local Application

PETER LANG

Bibliographic Information published by the Deutsche Nationalbibliothek
The Deutsche Nationalbibliothek lists this publication in the Deutsche Nationalbibliografie; detailed bibliographic data is available in the internet at http://dnb.d-nb.de.

Library of Congress Cataloging-in-Publication Data
A CIP catalog record for this book has been applied for at the Library of Congress.

This monographic study is a result of research conducted by an international research team within the framework of the National Science Center (Poland) Constitutional courts in post-Soviet states: between the model of a state of law and its local application (No. 2016/23/B/HS5/03648).
The chief of the project: Jacek Zaleśny

This publication was financially supported by The Faculty of Political Sciences and International Studies at the University of Warsaw.

ISSN 2199-028X
ISBN 978-3-631-79308-4 (Print)
E-ISBN 978-3-631-79978-9 (E-PDF)
E-ISBN 978-3-631-79979-6 (EPUB)
E-ISBN 978-3-631-79980-2 (MOBI)
DOI 10.3726/b16045

Peter Lang Edition is an Imprint of Peter Lang GmbH.

Peter Lang – Frankfurt am Main · Bern · Bruxelles · New York · Oxford · Warszawa · Wien

This publication has been peer reviewed.

www.peterlang.com

This book is dedicated to Professor Tadeusz Mołdawa – a scholar and an educator of a several generations of Polish political scientists (Institute of Political Science, University of Warsaw).

Contents

Introduction

This monographic study is a result of research conducted by an international research team within the framework of the National Science Center (Poland) *Constitutional courts in post-Soviet states: between the model of a state of law and its local application* (No. 2016/23/B/HS5/03648).

The Scientific Objective of the Project

Constitutional courts in the countries of contemporary Europe are the key participants in legal and political relations. These courts now have a role, along with the political authorities, i.e. the head of state, the government and the parliament[1] in establishing the binding legal and political order. In accordance with the regulations of their binding documents, constitutional courts now determine the legal frameworks, and hence the political ones, of the activities of the bodies of state authorities, including above all the parliaments as the legislators. Independently of the effects of the states' membership in the European Union, parliaments are no longer sovereign authorities, which – by an act of their own will – could establish the content of legal and political relations occurring in their territory. Together with the development of constitutional courts and the strengthening of their jurisdiction, parliaments became a rationed and controlled power. Their acts, both legislative and the application of the law, are subject to constitutional review, and in case of a negative finding – they lose their binding force.

Constitutional courts can determine the course of key political events in a state. For example, in 2000 the Ukrainian Constitutional Court found two of the six questions set in the referendum by President Leonid Kuchma incompatible with the constitution. This finding halted the process of the extension of the President's power that would have occurred at the expense of the competences of the Supreme Council and its political marginalization. Another, radically different, example arose in Belarus in 1996, when the Belarusian Constitutional Court decreed the unconstitutionality of a referendum question prepared by President Alexander Lukashenko. In response, the President, by decree, declared

1 I leave out the actual influence of such entities as international concerns, interest groups, regulatory authorities or supra-national bodies and organizations on the binding legal and political relations.

the finding invalid and submitted the said question to the nation in the referendum. The Belarusian referendum of 1996 is considered the key example of non-constitutional extension of the competences of the head of state. The President of the Russian Federation, Boris Yeltsin, on the other hand, who was in conflict with the Supreme Council and did not agree with the jurisdiction of the Constitutional Court, dissolved the Court, thus removing the institutional obstacle that could prevent his law-making activity. These three examples taken from post-Soviet states suffice to show how radically different the influence of constitutional courts can be on adherence to the provisions of the constitution, ranging from its affirmation (in the Ukraine), through the court's finding being questioned by the President (in Belarus) to the dissolution of the constitutional court, depriving it of the competence to adjudicate in the sphere of constitutional issues (in the Russian Federation).

Against the background of these and other events that occurred with or without the participation of constitutional courts when that participation should have taken place, what has been the role of the organs of the constitutional review of law in shaping legal and political relations in the post-Soviet states? Lithuania, Latvia and Georgia chose the Euro-Atlantic option (a military alliance in the form of NATO and a political and economic alliance within EU or, in case of Georgia, orientation towards cooperation with EU and NATO). Of the rest, Armenia, Azerbaijan, Belarus, the Russian Federation, Kazakhstan, Kyrgyzstan, Moldova, Tajikistan, Ukraine and Uzbekistan all chose the model of judicial constitutional review of law. Only Turkmenistan chose the parliamentary model of the constitutional review of law, which is in fact the presidential model not so much of constitutionality but of law as such.

What role do the organs of constitutional review of law in these post-Soviet states have in creating legal and political relations? What legal solutions did the legislators of the various states in the region adopt? To what models did they refer? What were their expectations following the establishment of the constitutional courts? To what extent were the expectations an expression of each state's aspirations, and to what extent were they based on the experiences of other countries? Were those expectations fulfilled or not, and if not – why? What was lacking to realize the will of the legislator? What is the system of constitutional courts in particular states? What is its relation to the models of control of legal norms, i.e. the so-called American model of the control of legal norms and so-called Kelsen's model of constitutionality of legal norms? Which institutions of constitutional jurisdiction are an expression of the native specific character, political traditions or structure of political forces taking place during the process of the establishment of the constitutional court? What is the role of the organ of constitutional review of law in the reception of law and in making law the source of national law binding to the national law-making bodies and the bodies applying law? What was this process like in the less-than-democratic post-Soviet states? Was it affected by the special political position of the president in the majority of those countries as a guarantor of harmonious functioning and cooperation of the organs of state authorities and the post-Soviet mentality?

In the states of West and Central Europe the organs of constitutional review of law (like the Supreme Court in the United States) are regarded as participants in political relations who can show inclinations to dominate in the system of separated power and to enforce their views upon other participants. Does a similar phenomenon occur in post-Soviet states? Are the organs of the constitutional review of law competent to affect the content of the binding law by way of jurisdiction? To what degree are they still based on Kelsen's understanding of the constitutional court as the so-called negative law-maker, and to what degree – referring to the experiences of some countries of the European continent – do they go beyond this model and show a special kind of law-making competence, which – on the example of the Russian Federation – is highlighted by Grigorij Alieksiejewicz Wasiliewicz (Григорий Алексеевич Василевич) and Igor Juriewicz Ostapowicz (Игорь Юрьевич Остапович) in their latest monographic study (2016) entitled *Нормативность решений специализированных органов конституционного контроля в Российской Федерации, Республике Беларусь и Республике Казахстан: сравнительно-правовое исследование*? *("The normative power of the decisions of the bodies of constitutional review in the Russian Federation, the Republic of Belarus and the Republic of Kazakhstan: a comparative legal study").*

The example of Kyrgyzstan raised another research question. Like Kazakhstan, Kyrgyzstan gave up the idea of the Constitutional Court and replaced it with the Constitutional Chamber of the Supreme Court, which indicates that the issue of the constitutional court is also not indisputable in this region. Despite the relatively short experience in this respect, certain legislators consider the adopted model of the constitutional review of legal norms to be inadequate to the political needs of the state and they modify it, but to what effect? Was the desired effect of the change achieved or it is irrelevant, or, perhaps, does it not meet the law-maker's expectations? These are the next research questions addressed in this study.

To provide a complete picture of the studied institutions, a normative analysis must be supplemented with the analysis of selected elements of political practice. It can deviate from the model's assumptions and their articulation in the regulations of law. All the more, this issue calls for analysis in the states which do not have many centuries of parliamentary traditions. These states did not find themselves within the sphere of the influence of the doctrine of a state of law and the European legal culture until the end of the 20th century. This takes place through participation in international relations or membership of those countries (and their associations) in the Council of Europe, and the spread of the values of this international organization into their system of law.

The development of constitutional courts affects the understanding of the principle of a nation's sovereignty and the ways of expressing it in the political system of the nation. The organs of constitutional review of law are sometimes contested as they work to prevent other bodies with public power from expansion at the cost of constitutional values and freedoms and rights of the individual. That was the case at the end of the 18th century and in the later period, when – together with the birth of modern constitutions – a question began to be posed about its superior character in relation to the law, and this is the case now. In some countries of Europe, e.g. France, constitutional courts as for the arbiters of the ex-post control of the compatibility of laws with the constitution have not been established till now. They are perceived as bodies in opposition to the rule of the nation's sovereignty as expressed by the parliament. In France, despite the existence of the Constitutional Council and the extension of its competences in 2008 by constitutional amendment, it still does not have the features of a constitutional court according to the Austrian or German model. In other European countries, on the other hand, contesting constitutional courts can be seen as an obstacle in realizing the political will of the democratically elected parliament. The American model has been referred to as the "dictatorship of courts". The echo of perceiving the constitutional court as an organ limiting the principle of the nation's sovereignty as articulated by the political authorities is reflected in the construction of the Kazakh Constitutional Council, not only in its name but also the scope of its tasks which draw on the French Constitutional Council, and not to the German or Austrian constitutional courts seen by the majority of European countries as the model of constitutional law.

In most post-Soviet states the organs of constitutional review of law are perceived as ineffective, dependent on the political authorities and having no influence on the loss of the binding force of unconstitutional normative acts. These are serious concerns that require investigation and explanation: firstly, how do these features manifest themselves in the political systems of those countries and their normative acts (including constitutional ones)? If these objections reflect the legal and political reality, what are their origins? Is it a wrongly shaped state of law, the practice deviating from the former, or maybe a combination of faultily formulated legal regulations and political practice that is inadequate to the constitutional models? Are there common features that may be observed across former Soviet countries or, conversely, despite the many years of similar Soviet experiences, does the dynamics of their development vary?

There is a lack of research in the field of constitutional courts in post-Soviet states. This monograph, based on the analysis of normative acts, the circumstances and premises of their creation as well as the circumstances and way of their application, aims to establish the specific political character of the organs of constitutional review of law in post-Soviet states. It seeks to establish and explain the political character of the organs of the constitutional review of law, i.e. their role in the system of state authorities, and assess the tasks assigned to them, the way they were established, the course of their work, the legal force of their decisions, the legal status of their members, and to present conclusions on optimization of the political status of the organs of the constitutional review of law as the organs of the protection of the constitution.

To realize the above research aim, it will be necessary to:

- analyze the process of creation and development of the organs of constitutional review of law (bodies) in post-Soviet states in its historical context,
- establish the legal and constitutional character of these bodies,
- establish the political differences and similarities between the legal solutions and the practice in particular post-Soviet states (viz. Armenia, Azerbaijan, Belarus, Kazakhstan, Kyrgyzstan, the Russian Federation and Ukraine referred to here as "the studied states"),
- recognize the legal and constitutional status of the bodies in the studied states,
- analyze the legal and constitutional status of the members of the bodies in the studied states,
- establish and compare the tasks and competences of the bodies in the studied states,
- establish the characteristic features and the legal force of the decisions of the organs of constitutional review and analyze the relations of those decisions to the sources of law binding in these states,
- assess the effect of the bodies in the studied states on the process of protecting the primacy of the constitution,
- assess the problems and perspectives of the development of the constitutional review of law in the studied states.

The present monograph poses the following major research hypotheses:

1) The legal protection of the constitution in post-Soviet states is based on the so-called European model of the constitutional review of law, according

to which a specialized organ is formed within the frameworks of the systems of public power whose basic task is the legally binding constitutional review of law. Most frequently, it is called the "Constitutional Court". An exception among the post-Soviet states is Turkmenistan, where – on the Soviet model – there is no judicial constitutional review of law, and the organ supposed to ensure the compatibility laws with the constitution is formally the parliament, while in fact law is subordinated to the will of the president.

2) The fact that post-Soviet states refer to the model of a constitutional court separate from other state authorities has not led to the adoption of one formula (e.g. the Austrian or German models). Instead, there are different mutations of the European model. The differences concern not only the procedure of electing the persons composing the organs of the constitutional review of law and their legal status but also the scope of their competences, the procedure of executing those competences (including a preventive vs. a repressive constitutional review of law; a complaint from the subjects of private law), and the participants in the constitutional proceedings and the character of the decisions taken.
3) In post-Soviet states, the persons composing the bodies have the status of judges, similar to the legal status of court judges.
4) The organizational structure of the bodies in post-Soviet states is not uniform. Some of them allow for the establishment of chambers or boards of judges possessing the right to realize the competences in the name of the body. This non-uniform organizational structure is not a relevant feature and does not affect the quality of their jurisdiction in the system of the bodies of state authorities.
5) In post-Soviet states, the dilemma of a constitutional complaint as a measure to appeal against the unconstitutional regulations of law to which the non-public participants of legal relations are entitled is solved in varying ways. These variations are not particularly significant and do not influence the limited importance of the constitutional complaint within the system of the protection of constitutional freedoms and rights of persons and citizens.
6) Independently of the reference to the model solutions in European states, the bodies in the political practice of post-Soviet states are able to affect the compatibility of the created law with the constitution only occasionally and to a narrow extent. In principle, they affirm law-making decisions taken by the parliament and the president.

The Importance of the Research

Most analysis of the constitutional courts in post-Soviet states has been undertaken in the Russian language. Analyses were made on selected issues related to constitutional courts in particular countries of the region, as well as individual monographs on constitutional courts in some post-Soviet states. There are also studies devoted to constitutional courts in a few countries of the region, especially comparing the Russian Constitutional Court to the Kazakh Constitutional Council or the Ukrainian Constitutional Court. The major studies include (for example, considering the multitude of excellent publications on different aspects of constitutional courts in post-Soviet states) the monographs of such authors as A. Arseni, *Jurisdicţia constituţională a Republicii Moldova*, Chişinău 2000; Г.Г. Арутюнян, *Конституционный суд в системе государственной власти (сравнительный анализ)*, Ереван 1999; М.С. Бейбитов, *Институт конституционного контроля в Республике Казахстан: эволюция и проблемы модернизации*, Алматы 2005; Н.С. Бондарь, *Судебный конституционализм: доктрина и практика : монография*, Москва 2016; Т.О. Бринь, *Конституційний Суд України в механізмі захисту та забезпечення прав і свобод людини і громад янина*, Харків 2010; Г.А. Василевич, *Конституционное правосудие: учебное пособие для студентов учреждений высшего образования по специальности "Правоведение"*, Минск 2014; Г.А. Василевич, И.Ю. Остапович, *Нормативность решений специализированных органов конституционного контроля в Российской Федерации, Республике Беларусь и Республике Казахстан: сравнительно-правовое исследование*, Минск 2016; П.В. Волвенко, *Діяльність Конституційного Суду України щодо тлумачення Конституції України: теоретичний аспект*, Київ 2006; В.Д. Зорькин, *Конституционный Суд России: доктрина и практика: монография*, Москва 2017; А.А. Караев, *Конституционный контроль: Казахстан и зарубежный опыт: учеб. пособие*, Алматы. 2002; И.И. Рогов, В.А. Малиновский (ред.), *Конституционный контроль в Казахстане: доктрина и практика утвер ждения конституционализма: Монография*, Алматы 2015; Р.М. Мырзалим ов, *Вопросы конституционного правосудия в Кыргызстане*, Бишкек 2001; Р.М. Мырзалимов, *Конституционная юстиция в странах Центральной Азии*, Москва 2013; И.Ю. Остапович, *Конституционный Совет Республики Казахстан: вопросы теории и практики*, Усть – Каменогорск 2015; А.П. Ткачук, *Конституційний Суд у механізмі захисту основних прав і свобод людини: модельний підхід*, Київ 2012; К.Н. Холиков, *Конституционный Суд Республики Таджикистан: статус, организация и деятельность*,

Москва 2009; Ю.Л. Шульженко, *Конституционный контроль в России*, Москва 1995.

Although there are valuable publications (books, scientific articles as well as, importantly, dissertations prepared for scientific degrees) on constitutional courts in post-Soviet states, the present monograph fills the gap in the existing research by comparing the organs of constitutional review of law in post-Soviet states. Significantly, this study was prepared by an international team of researchers from the region. The organs of constitutional review in post-Soviet states have been studied earlier in time. However, most of the existing research did not include any monograph of a *sensu stricto* comparative character on this subject. There is no monograph by authors from different states of the region considering the many aspects of the studied research problem and analyzing constitutional courts in post-Soviet states. There is a lack of deep analysis of the constitutional review bodies in post-Soviet states, their effect on the perception of constitutional regulations, realization of the rule of separated powers or the protection of freedoms and rights of an individual, the constitutional status of the bodies, the practice of their activity and, consequently, the relation between the constitutional regulation of the bodies and their importance for political practice.

The development of the organs of constitutional review of law in post-Soviet states has been determined by the conditions in which those countries found themselves after the collapse of the USSR, the common history and the choice of similar models of political development. Nevertheless, because of different political, historical, economic and other conditions, constitutional courts in these countries have individual features; hence, the need to study and compare them. The various post-Soviet states took different approaches toward regulating the issues of the constitutional review of law, its functions, proceedings before it, the legal character of the decisions taken and the legal status of its members. Therefore a scientific reflection is needed on the political position of those organs, their role in the legal realization of the protection of the constitution, the protection of the constitutional system of the state and the freedoms and rights of individuals as well as securing the implementation of decisions. These issues are of key importance in guaranteeing the superior character of the constitution and the establishment – as proclaimed in those countries' constitutions – of the state of law. At the same time, the principle of a state of law adopted in post-Soviet states should be understood as related to another principle characteristic of the majority of post-Soviet states, and in some (Belarus, Kazakhstan, Russia, Tajikistan) directly expressed in the provisions of the constitution, according to which the president ensures a harmonious functioning and cooperation of the bodies of state authorities and he is the guarantor of the constitution and the rights and freedoms of individuals. He guarantees the realization of the main directions of interior and exterior policy. He undertakes activities to protect the state's sovereignty, its security and territorial integrity as well as securing its political and economic stability. The president's realization of the function of securing a harmonious functioning and cooperation of the bodies of state authorities is expressed in his relations with the constitutional court and the possibility of achieving the effects desired by him in the work of the constitutional court.

The above-outlined questions and problems determine the weight of the studies; in other words, the way of realizing the constitutional review of law. A comparative analysis of the states which have common Soviet experiences and which are both politically and economically related is needed. There is also a need to record and review those countries' search for an optimal and effective variant to realize the constitutional review of law, the procedure of the establishment and activity of the organs realizing it and the creation of the necessary guarantees ensuring the actual primacy of the constitution in the studied states.

A scientific novelty of this research is the introduction of new findings into the international state of research on constitutional courts and these were obtained as a result of studying the institution of constitutional courts in post-Soviet states by a research team of constitutional experts from this region.

Another novelty is the complex analysis of theoretical and legal issues concerning the constitutional review of law and problems of the formation of bodies realizing it, in addition to the establishment of similarities and differences as well as the legal and constitutional status of members of those bodies.

The conclusions and findings reported here extend and supplement the constitutional knowledge on the specific character of the political status of the bodies in post-Soviet states. The presented material enables a multi-dimensional recognition of particular theoretical and legal problems as well as the practice of the activity of the bodies. It can be used to draw conclusions on the specific features of the constitutional review of law in this group of states. Theoretical findings, conclusions and recommendations formulated as a results of these studies can be applied to change the mechanisms of the protection of constitutionality in post-Soviet states, or to show to the law-makers in other countries the consequences of adopting particular legal solutions.

Results of the studies can be used as comparative material in the process of establishing the political status of the organs of the constitutional review of law in contemporary states.

The formulated arguments and recommendations can also be used in the analysis of the rule of law in particular states of the region. In particular, this kind of analysis is required in the investment process in those countries in order to estimate the constitutional and political risk, predictability of law, its compatibility with the constitution in the context of assessing the investment risk and protecting from that risk.

Outstanding representatives of science in particular countries of the region participated in these international studies, ensuring the quality of the obtained research results, and its high intellectual and prognostic value.

Methodology of Research

This research studied the creation and functioning of the constitutional review of law in post-Soviet states. These states have similar historical experiences (dominated by the Soviet experience) and are characterized by similar constitutional values and a similar manner of realizing them as well as a similar legal and political culture. Most of them belong to one political and economic alliance, namely the Commonwealth of Independent States.

The present studies consider the legislation, juristic science and judicial decisions. The subject of the analysis includes not only the binding legislation but also the historical stages in the development of the organs of the constitutional review of law. This is necessary to get to know the dynamics of their change and understand the process of perfecting the legal constructions. A comprehensive analysis of all these elements at the same time makes it possible to describe and explain the creation and functioning of the constitutional review of law in post-Soviet states. This is why the subject of the research conducted comprises the analysis of constitutional norms referring to the organization and activity of the organs of constitutional review of law in post-Soviet states, the theories and ideas on their placement in the system of state authorities, statutory norms and the norms of other normative acts referring to the organs of the constitutional review of law and jurisprudence where the constitutional regulations of post-Soviet states that directly refer to the constitutional review of law are materialized.

The theoretical basis of the present studies consists of the analyses (monographs, scientific articles, dissertations prepared for scientific degrees, appearances at scientific conferences) by constitutional experts from post-Soviet states as well as experts from other countries in the field of constitutional courts of post-Soviet states, including the issues of the constitutional review of law, cognition of constitutional courts and history of the constitutional review of law. Besides, the theoretical basis of the research includes works devoted to the process of the constitutional review of law together with its conditions, importance and the legal character of the decisions of constitutional courts.

The empirical basis is made up of the texts of constitutions and laws of the states in the region relevant to the legal and constitutional status of the bodies charged with the constitutional review of law as well as internal acts of these bodies, official documents of the bodies of post-Soviet states and the jurisdiction of the bodies in post-Soviet states.

The present studies attach great importance to the choice of representatives of the doctrine of constitutional law who prepared reports on the establishment and functioning of the constitutional review of law in post-Soviet states. These are persons with significant scientific achievements who are representative for the doctrine of post-Soviet states. For this reason, constitutional experts from particular post-Soviet states – one from each country – were invited to participate in the project. The analyses were carried out by constitutional experts from the leading universities in the region who specialize in the issues of constitutional courts. The adopted manner of choosing the authors in the research project was expected to guarantee the highest possible quality of the analyses grounded in the specific constitutional character of particular countries. I hope this objective was successfully achieved.

Another outcome of this choice of authors is the building of an international research team, whose work is representative of the doctrine of constitutional law and adequate to be presented not only to readers from post-Soviet states but also from other regions of the world.

Representatives of the doctrine of constitutional law from particular post-Soviet states prepared reports on the constitutional courts in the studied states and this enabled a comparative study in the form of a general report. The latter selected and highlighted the most important tendencies in the dynamics of constitutional courts included in particular reports.

The choice of the analyzed systems of law and the aim of the research affected the choice of the applied research methods. The following research methods were used to realize the research tasks: scientific analysis, synthesis, a comparative legal method and a detailed method, formal-dogmatic, historical-legal and a system-based method, with special importance attached to the formal-dogmatic and comparative legal methods.

Applying the formal-dogmatic method provided an analysis of normative acts related to constitutional review of law in post-Soviet states and their interpretation. The comparative legal method, on the other hand, made it possible to determine the general and specific features in the bodies in the studied states. After the legal solutions and their application in the studied states were presented and analyzed, they were assessed, from the comparative perspective. The application of different research methods enabled the researchers to recognize the theoretical and practical aspects of the organs of the constitutional review of law in post-Soviet states.

***

I would like to thank all those who contributed to this monographic study. First of all, I wish to thank the authors of the research project *Constitutional courts in post-Soviet states: between the model of a state of law and its local application* (No. 2016/23/B/HS5/03648) for their professional approach in realizing their tasks and for the fruitful cooperation. I also thank the National Science Center (Poland) for financing the studies as well as its workers for their kindness and help in conducting them.

I wish to thank to Elena Belousova (the Department of State and Legal Disciplines, Moscow University for the Humanities, Russian Federation) and Svetlana Inkina (the Department of Public Policy, Higher School of Economics, Russian Federation) for their support.

I am very grateful to Professor Stanisław Sulowski – Dean of the Faculty of Political Science and International Studies, University of Warsaw, and Professor Ewa Maria Marciniak – Director of the Institute of Political Science, University of Warsaw for their kindness, support and understanding, thanks to which we were able to focus on what was the most important for us in this field, and that was realization of the research project in accordance with the adopted concept and research assumptions.

Jacek Zaleśny

Jarosław Szymanek

Constitutional Justice of Post-Soviet States against the Model Solutions in the Sphere of Non-parliamentary Constitutional Review of Law

Abstract: The subject of the analysis are constitutional courts in post-Soviet states against the background of the models of constitutional courts. Characteristic features of the models of legal norms review are analyzed. They are compared to the specific character of legal solutions adopted in the examined group of countries. It is argued that this group bases on the European model of reviewing the legal norms. The only exceptions are the cases of Kazakhstan, where French legal solutions are referred to, and Kyrgyzstan, where the control over the compatibility of legal norms with the constitution is assigned to a specially established chamber of the Highest Court.

Keywords: constitutional courts in post-Soviet states, the models of legal norms review, the European model of reviewing the legal norms, extra-parliamentary control of the constitutionality of law

Introduction

Non-parliamentary constitutional review of law has characterized the development of the constitutional doctrine and law of the last one hundred years. Across a variety of institutions and procedures of constitutional law, no other issue has changed the picture of contemporary constitutionalism so much as constitutional jurisprudence (broadly understood as a mechanism of assessing the compatibility of law with the constitution regardless of whether the organ that makes the assessment is or is not equipped with the formal status of a court). The point is not so much about a simple quantitative change, measured by the number of countries where different versions of non-parliamentary forms of examining the compatibility of law with the constitution were installed, but about a qualitative change, which – to a greater or lesser extent – has changed nearly everything that makes up the classic form of constitutional law. Clearly, constitutional jurisprudence has revolutionised the way of thinking about law (especially the constitution and the relation between national law and international law), political institutions (including the relations between them which are entangled in a broader context of the assessment of the constitutionality of the law) and, finally, the key principles and values (the foundation of the contemporary constitutional state). Constitutional jurisprudence – regardless of the form in which it is applied – changed almost everything that traditional constitutional law had previously built and explained (in the institutional, procedural, functional and axiological sense). So it can be said without any exaggeration that the non-parliamentary form of assessing the compatibility of law with the constitution finally created a new, or renewed, science of constitutional law[1].

Nevertheless, while non-parliamentary, and especially judicial constitutional review of law radically changed constitutional law (its letter, doctrine and – finally – practice), this review itself is far from being *constans*. It evolves, changing and slowly taking on a completely new meaning. In the beginning it focused, above all, on formal control (i.e. competence and procedural conformity of law-making), but later the material aspects of assessment (i.e. conformity of the content and substance of the norms assessed) acquired primary importance. Today, on the other hand, both the formal and material aspects are *de facto* treated as the output instrument for the axiological and teleological constitutional review of law, where the element of the protection of law and individual freedom comes to the front, which is supposed to be the principal *ratio essendi* of the constitution itself as well as the mechanisms of its protection[2]. Non-parliamentary constitutional review also changed in the sense that being a *stricte* legal institution, it gradually acquired – together with its development – the features of a political institution[3], so that it now has the form of a mixed institution, which to a greater or lesser degree has political (often far reaching) consequences even if the institution is not assumed to be of a political nature[4]. Hence, it is suggested – not

---

1 F. Delpérée, *Le renouveau du droit constitutionnel*, "Revue Française de Droit Costitutionnel" 2008, No. 2, pp. 227 ff. It should be emphasized that in the concept of the so-called new constitutionalism the idea of constitutional review of law occupies the foremost place. Cf M. Shapiro, A. Stone, *The New Constitutional Politics of Europe*, "Comparative Political Studies" 1994, No. 25, p. 397.

2 Cf. M. Florczak-Wątor, *Orzeczenia Trybunału Konstytucyjnego i ich skutki prawne*, Poznań 2006, pp. 15–16.

3 Which, after all, was a natural consequence of an increased importance of the constitutional review of law.

4 Which is exemplified by more and more frequent arguments concerning constitutional judiciary in such countries as USA, Italy, Germany, Poland or South Korea. These arguments have different origins but eventually they pose questions on a daily basis about the activism of the organs of constitutional jurisprudence, their increasingly political role and, finally, their relation to the classic rule of the separation of state power. Cf.: P. Laidler, *Prawno-polityczny spór wokół wyboru sędziego Sądu Najwyższego*

without a reason – that the contemporary constitutional court is neither a judicial or political organ but both at the same time[5]. This shows how much the picture of non-parliamentary constitutional review of law has changed in recent decades. Some time ago the belief about the political involvement of this review was referred exclusively to particular (i.e. non-judicial) organs of control, which were confronted with the kind of control directly called non-political and expertise executed by the judicial-type or *quasi*-judicial organs[6].

While changing themselves, the organs of non-parliamentary constitutional review of law simultaneously affected all other bodies of the state (which, by the way, was one of the reasons why they acquired the features of political organs, especially if political character is understood as the ability to affect the situation of other entities). This especially concerns legislature and judicature. Due to the procedures verifying compatibility of law with the constitution, the former was significantly limited, forever losing the attributes of non-limited power, treated – if not from the legal, certainly from the political point of view – as the major power (if only because it directly represented the sovereign, which was for years the starting point to increase its legal and political relevance). The judicature, on the other hand, was significantly revalued due to the constitutional review of law, independently of whether the organ of constitutional review of law was ultimately treated as a part of the judiciary or was located elsewhere. This is because since the times of Montesquieu the judiciary was treated as the power "in a sense, none". This resulted above all from its passive, reactive role and the fact that the judicature – like the executive – mainly executed the law, possessing its own specific instruments[7]. The center of gravity has always been in the relationship between the legislative and the executive branches of power. Constitutional review of law entrusted either with the organs of the judicature, or organs modeled on it, radically changed the state of affairs. In fact, the judiciary became the key power, which – while referring to the vertical relation between the norms of law – arranges the state's space in nearly all its areas (legal, organizational, functional, procedural and axiological ones). That was why the constitutional

---

USA po śmierci Antonina Scalii, "Przegląd Sejmowy" 2017, No. 3, pp. 21 ff.; J. Szymanek, *Trybunał Konstytucyjny de lege ferenda – propozycje nowelizacji ustawy w odpowiedzi na opinię Komisji Weneckiej*, "Przegląd Sejmowy" 2017, No. 4, pp. 43 ff.

5 S. Fabbrini, *Transatlantic Constitutionalism: Comparing the United States and the European Union*, "European Journal of Political Research" 2004, No. 4, p. 555.

6 M. Cappelletti, *Judicial Review in the Contemporary World*, Indianapolis 1971, *passim*.

7 Which is why in a number of other theoretical views it is treated as part of a much more broadly viewed executive power.

court, independently of whether it *de iure* is a court or an organ at most similar to it, changed the judicial power so much and this, in turn, changed the whole map of the state's constitutional bodies, thus irretrievably departing from its classic canon.

In this way the non-parliamentary constitutional review of law changed the rudiments of the constitutional order. It raised the meaning of the constitution and law in general and restituted the rules and values, thus changing the *stricte* positivist vision of law, fitting it in the significant axiological and teleological context[8]. It transformed traditional relations within Montesquieu's idea of the three powers, at the same time strongly exposing the judicature as a beneficiary of all changes, thus acquiring a clearly political character[9]. All the processes signaled above proceeded in parallel, regardless of the adopted concrete model of the control of the constitutionality of law. Geographical, cultural, legal, political and historical differences, which *summa summarum* generated the adoption of a variety of versions of constitutional jurisprudence, paradoxically brought the effect of synergy with a more or less homogeneous and thus more or less repeatable character. Therefore, the consequences of establishing the non-parliamentary constitutional review of law were roughly similar although the models of applying this control differed at times. There were differences at the starting point (the genesis of the institution of non-parliamentary review itself and different organizational and functional variants of controlling bodies) but now, at the present point of development of the mechanisms of the constitutional review of law, those differences became obliterated, at least in some aspects, and the constitutional review of law – regardless of the model differences – took the form of a more or less universal solution. The development of the non-parliamentary constitutional review of law led to a convergence of certain features and solutions characterizing the constitutional review of law. This, however, does not change the fact that this review was shaped according to different organizational and

8 Note that the 20th century, the age of radical growth in the importance of the constitutional review of law, and the interpretation of the constitution included in it, became the age of constitutional principles and values which became the basic criteria in settling conflicts between the hierarchically built norms of law. For more on this subject, see: T. Giaro, *Wartości w języku prawnym i dyskursie prawniczym*, [in:] *Preambuła Konstytucji Rzeczypospolitej Polskiej*, Warszawa 2009, pp. 13 ff.

9 Cf. P. Laidler, *Trzecia władza czy pierwsza władza? Rozważania na temat konstytucyjnej pozycji władzy sądowniczej w Stanach Zjednoczonych*, [in:] *Amerykomania. Księga jubileuszowa Profesora dra hab. Andrzeja Mani*, eds. W. Bernacki, A. Walaszek, Kraków 2009, vol. I, pp. 133 ff.

functional schemes and the so-called model solutions concerning it still shape the way of thinking about the non-parliamentary review of law and they, despite everything, still determine its specific character.

Model Solutions

Models of non-parliamentary constitutional review of law are always a matter of convention. Depending on the adopted assumptions, presented views, emphasis on definite features and seeing specific solutions as model ones, they can be viewed differently. Hence, the literature shows a large range of opinions on the number of model solutions in the sphere of establishing the non-parliamentary mechanism of constitutional review of law. A disputable issue is the very approach to the problem of understanding and, therefore, dividing the constitutional review as well as, for example, the problem of how to view such review in the institutional (subjective) or functional (objective) aspect. In the first case, the review is realized by specially appointed bodies, while in the second, it is a special kind of proceeding the aim of which is to establish the consistency or inconsistency of a given norm with the constitution. If in the institutional view, constitutional review is the activity of a special entity whose *ratio legis* is performing such control, in the functional approach, constitutional review is a special procedure, regardless of what entity realizes it[10]. Reviews may be divided into the *hard* type review of legal norms and the *soft* type review. The former is the real constitutional review of law (*hard constitutional review*), which means that there is an organ and/or procedures within which the issue of the constitutionality of law is settled. The latter is the so-called soft or semi-review of constitutionality (*soft*-, or *quasi*-constitutional review), where there is no institutionally or functionally established regime of review but such control is carried out *nolens volens*, outside the ordinary or normal mechanisms of review (an example of this kind of constitutional review of law is Great Britain)[11]. The range of the issue of the division, and then the sequence of some kind of modeling the non-parliamentary constitutional review is therefore quite big and there is no point in searching for a common thread in the presented concepts. The authors in fact agree only on two issues, namely that there is no problem in distinguishing two basic, but at the

10 Cf. B. Banaszak, *Porównawcze prawo konstytucyjne współczesnych państw demokratycznych*, Kraków 2004, p. 592.

11 Cf. M. Shapiro, *The Success of Judicial Review*, [in:] *Constitutional Dialogues in Comparative Perspectives*, eds. S.J. Kenney, W.M. Reisinger, J.C. Reitz, New York 1999, p. 202.

same time extremely general – if not vague – models of the constitutional review of law (i.e. the American and the European models), and – secondly – that the two models are far from exhausting the solutions in the sphere of institutionalization of the organs of constitutional review and they are general, organizing schemes rather than specific typology[12]. This especially concerns the so-called European model, which is internally so differentiated that in fact its key identifying role is being in opposition to the American model, and nothing else[13]. It comprises a number of smaller solutions that frequently differ from each other considerably. It remains an open question whether those other solutions can be called model ones, or if they should rather be perceived as variants of the two cases recognized as the model ones, questioning the latter to a greater or smaller extent. If they are considered to be sufficiently permanent and sufficiently separate solutions that at the same time have clearly endemic features, they should be considered as separate – different from the two basic models – variants of the constitutional review of law. If, on the other hand, we perceive them as only a sort of mutation, a bigger or smaller departure from them, then they are not assigned the features of a model and are seen as a specific sub-group of the two principal models (i.e. the American or European ones).

Independently of all disputes, the dual division into the American type review and the European type is the most spread (but also the clearest)[14]. Other names are sometimes used for it, e.g. the model of de-centralized or de-concentrated control (referring to the American model) and the model of centralized or concentrated control (referring to the European model)[15]; nevertheless, regardless of the name, it is regarded as the most classic but also the one which well shows the

---

12 Other divisions are definitely more rarely presented, such as, for example, the division into political review (realized by the organs that do not have the features of a court) and judicial review (also including *quasi*-judicial organs). Cf. M. Cappelletti, *Judicial Review…*, p. 2.

13 Cf. L. Favoreu, *Constitutional Review in Europe*, [in:] *Constitutionalism and Rights: The Influence of the United States Constitution Abroad*, eds. L. Henkin, A. Rosenthal, New York 1990, pp. 38 ff.

14 Sometimes, based on this division, review of the judicial review type (i.e. American type) and review of the constitutional courts type (characteristic of the European model) are indicated. Cf. A. Stone Sweet, *Constitutional Courts*, [in:] *The Oxford Handbook of Comparative constitutional Law*, eds. M. Rosenfeld, A. Sajó, Oxford 2012, pp. 816 ff.

15 Cf. A. Chen, M. Poiares Maduro, *The Judiciary and Constitutional Review*, [in:] *Routledge Handbook of Constitutional Law*, eds. M. Tushnet, T. Fleiner, Ch. Saunders, London and New York 2015, p. 97.

specific character of the approach to the constitutional review of law and hence reflects the most important features in which the model solutions differ. It is also always the starting point in constructing more detailed systematization of non-parliamentary judicial review.

The American (decentralized) model is the first historical way of assessing the compatibility of law with the constitution. It is, however, different from the European model not only because it was established first but also because this model was shaped by way of practice and then introduced into the doctrine. Moreover, till now it has been the model deprived of *expressis verbis* constitutional basis, which makes it possible to call the American review the implied review, as opposed to the review characteristic of the European model, which is a non-implied review, provided directly by the rules of constitutional significance[16]. Considering its origin, the American model might also be called a pragmatic model, as distinct from the model which with time appeared in Europe and which was characterized by a high degree of idealism and theoretical specificity. In the USA the constitutional review of law was from the very beginning treated not as a logical conclusion drawn from the constitution but a practical condition of its fruitful activity[17]. It seems that apart from the obviously broader cultural context, the differences in the genesis of the establishment of both model solutions lie at the basis of diametrically different ways of institutionalizing the constitutional review of law. It is these differences which were naturally translated into all the details characterizing the American and the European ways of the constitutional review of law.

The American model of the constitutional review of law (called 'judicial review', which name, with time, became a synonym of each non-parliamentary form of assessing the compatibility of law with the constitution) is far from being accidental. Its framework was based on the specific legal culture of *common law* type and the experiences of constitutionalism of the colonial period connected with it. In the case of the latter the accepted practice was the participation of courts in controlling the norms of law and assessing their compatibility with the norms of a higher rank. In a great majority of American colonies, courts participated in trials that assessed, for example, the compatibility of legal norms with the constitutions of particular colonies. Such a solution was considered to

16 A. Brewer-Carias, *Judicial Review in Comparative World*, New York 1989, p. 186. Nevertheless, this model, although implied and only derived from the USA constitution, is very strongly authorized by the latter. Cf. M. Tushnet, *Advanced Introduction to Comparative Constitutional Law*, Cheltenham – Northampton 2014, p. 41.

17 R.M. Małajny, *Amerykański prezydencjalizm*, Warszawa 2012, p. 540.

be a normal and obvious practice, integrally linked with the idea of rule of law, on the one hand, and the role of judicial law-making characterizing common law, on the other[18]. The establishment of the United States of America did not change the situation, in principle. A disputable question, ultimately solved in the famous Marbury *versus* Madison decision, was only whether earlier colonial solutions could be transferred to the level of federation, especially when the federal constitution did not say anything about it. The final settlement of the matter, for the benefit of the cognition of common courts in matters of constitutional review, including the Supreme Court of the USA, only confirmed the earlier experiences and transposed the solutions recognized as obvious in particular colonies (and later the American states) to the level of federation. Here, it should be emphasized that the Marbury *versus* Madison decision, which was a milestone in the development of federal judicial review, did not come from nowhere but was a consequence of the processes taking place over a longer period[19]. Its adoption only facilitated the silence of the constitution in this issue and the colonial experiences. The silence of the constitution, in particular, could not be seen as a sufficient argument against the introduction of judicial review at the level of the federation[20]. It was so, above all, because the constitution of the USA contained other regulations which – by way of creative interpretation – could provide the basis to derive the constitutional review of law[21], and secondly, because the USA constitution was created against a definite social and cultural background for which the role of courts in the sphere of settling the collision of norms was indisputable (and followed from certain laws being attributed the

18 Within the idea of the rule of law in the American common law, the idea of giving primacy to certain laws was strongly present, which invariably correlated with the system of effective guarantees of such special laws. Cf. M. Cappelletti, *Comparative Constitutional Law. Cases and Materials*, Indianapolis 1979, p. 16.

19 Cf. P. Mikuli, *Zdekoncentrowana sądowa kontrola konstytucyjności prawa. Stany Zjednoczone i państwa europejskie*, Kraków 2007, pp. 19 ff. For more on this subject, see:. S. Kubas, *Judicial review: geneza i rozwój*, [in:] *Konstytucja i sądowe gwarancje jej ochrony*, eds. P. Czarny et al., Kraków 2004, pp. 127 ff.

20 Cf. A. Bryk, *The Origins of Constitutional Government. Higher Law and the Sources of Judicial Review*, Kraków 1999, pp. 332 ff.

21 The point was mainly about two principal constitutional settlements, i.e. the so-called supremacy clause from art. VI, section 1 (saying that "the USA constitution (...) shall be the supreme law for the land") and the competence of the judicial power defined in art. III section 2 (where it was directly stated that "the judicial power shall extend onto all legal issues which can emerge in connection with the content of the Constitution").

features of fundamental laws[22]). Therefore, the Marbury *versus* Madison decision fitted the American legal culture, constituting the solution and development of the procedures that had been known and practiced for a long time already (especially on the level of colonies). Consequently, this settlement was well understood and explained *pro futuro* and would not encounter opposition where the Supreme Court would propose a solution being some kind of a principal *novum*. Without depreciating the sentence given in 1803 then, it should be emphasized that it corresponded very well with the earlier concepts that had not aroused any disagreements or discussions[23].

Despite everything, the importance of the decision from 1803 was, however, exceptional. Firstly, because while making the above settlement, it laid down – for the first time – the whole etiology of the judicial review in relation to the federal constitution by indicating the reasons why the constitutional review of law was not only admissible but necessary. Secondly, it definitely settled the status of the USA constitution as the constitution, which at that time was not so obvious[24] and which was the basic argument for the judicial review also used towards the federal constitution (and not only state constitutions).

22 Cf. M. Cappelletti, *Comparative Constitutional Law…*, p. 16.

23 Especially that the decision from 1803 was not the first settlement of the American Supreme Court in this issue, although it was the first to be so firm and the first where the Court recognized the federal law as contrary to the federal constitution. That court spoke in reference to the constitution already in 1795 in the case *Van Horne's Lessee versus Dorrance*, when the Supreme Court recognized the state law as incompatible with the constitution. In 1796 and 1798 it dealt with the issue of the constitutionality of laws in cases *Hylton versus United States* and *Hollingsworth versus Virginia*. In all those cases the Supreme Court upheld the Congress laws although they were blamed for being incompatible with the constitution; hence from the very beginning – despite a lack of the proper, clear constitutional basis – it considered itself competent in this matter. For more on the subject, see: R.M. Małajny, *Amerykański prezydencjalizm…*, p. 539.

24 For some time the name of Thomas Jefferson was strongly associated with the views perceiving the USA constitution as a kind of *sui generis* of an international agreement (which was supposed to be emphasized, for example, by the ratification procedure of the constitution and the revision procedure of the provisions of the American constitution). On the basis of the dispute about the constitutionality of the USA constitution, a relatively permanent division into federalists and anti-federalists was fairly quickly established. The importance of the decision of 1803 lay in the fact that the judges of the Supreme Court decisively spoke for treating the USA constitution as a constitution, and not, for instance, a specific kind of an international agreement.

Consequently, the elements of the 1803 decision created the final model of the American judicial review, which was later on only maintained, developed and refined in detail[25]. All those processes connected with the consolidation of judicial review were also accompanied by, sometimes very bitter, controversy concerning the judicial review of constitutionality of law. Their participants indicated either the unconstitutionality of this form of the federation's action, or – especially later on – a too strong position of courts whose interpretation of the constitution gained – against the ideas of the Founding Fathers – priority before all other kinds of interpretation, or the violence of balance between the powers and a disproportionally strong position of the judicative, or – finally – an open contradiction towards the idea of democracy and promotion of elitaristic concepts of the juristocracy[26].

The American model of constitutional review of law not only established the basis for other solutions in this sphere but it also opened the still-ongoing discussion on the non-parliamentary constitutional review of law and on the necessity to create its sensible form which would reconcile the requirement of the protection of the constitution with the rationality of the state's activity and the balance between all bodies. The discussion was made sharper by the establishment of an alternative European model of constitutional review. It is here that the originality and importance of the American form of judicial review lies. It not only established the basis for its opposing version, the so-called European model, but also opened the continuing discussion on the non-parliamentary constitutional review of law and on the necessity to create its optimal shape, which is now growing in vigour[27].

---

25 This process was strongly spaced out over time since the successive decision, which entirely sustained the Marbury *versus* Madison sentence, was not until 1867 in the Dred Scott *versus* Sanford case when the decentralized type of judicial review began to be realized in practice.

26 Cf. A. Lever, *Democracy and Judicial Review: Are They Really Incompatible*? "Perspectives on Politics" 2009, No. 4, pp. 805 ff. The danger of the *gouvernement des juges* syndrome in connection with the development of constitutional judiciary is also indicated in the French literature. Cf. F. Hamon, C. Wienner, *La justice constitutionnelle en France et à l'étranger*, Paris 2011, p. 15.

27 Also in the USA, where the voices of the advocates of so-called popular constitutionalism are increasingly louder, they argue that judicial review does not have its clear constitutional basis; within the 200 years of its existence, its has become a mechanism strengthening the position of the judicial power, thus contradicting the idea of the separation of powers; its has no democratic legitimation since the judges – as the only in the tripartition of powers – do not come from general election. For more on

The judicial review assumes a few characteristic elements. The first is a lack of a special body that would have an exclusive competence in matters concerning compatibility between law and the constitution. As a result, according to the disposition of article III, section 11 of the USA constitution, "the judicial power shall extend to all cases, in law and equity, arising under the Constitution". The judicial power, spoken about in article III, section II, is constituted – in accordance with the provisions of article III, section I – by "one supreme Court, and such inferior Courts as the Congress may from time to time ordain and establish". As a result, judicial review is realized by all courts, including the Supreme Court, which satisfies the criterion of de-concentrated (decentralized) review of compatibility between law and the constitution. This feature is the most characteristic of the American version of constitutional review of law and it stands in strong contrast with its European counterpart. It should be emphasized that the USA Supreme Court does not accumulate the function of adjudicating in constitutional matters. This function is realized by all common courts, which are subject to the natural judicial supervision by the Supreme Court, which – if only for this reason (as an appellate court) takes part in settling constitutional issues. The second element that clearly distinguishes judicial review from the model of constitutional courts[28] is a concrete character of the American constitutional process. This means that the question of the possible defectiveness of the incriminated constitutional norm can be raised only when a given norm is supposed to be applied. The situation when the entities applying the law (courts) reach for this norm is supposed to be the reason for doubts concerning compatibility of this norm with the law of higher order and, which follows from it, for starting the reviewing mechanism. In other words, it is not possible within the system of judicial review to start the verifying proceedings if the questioned legal norm is not to be applied in a specific, incidental case of law application. It is the act of law application that provides the basis for the so-called litigation exception, which means bringing the charge of non-constitutionality of a given norm (this can be done by each of the parties in the ongoing court proceedings).

The third element characterizing the American model is a lack of a separate procedure, dedicated specially to the needs of the constitutional process, of assessing compatibility of the law with the constitution. The court, in typical conditions of common law, acts in this case in accordance with the general rules,

---

this subject in the Polish literature, see: T. Wieciech, *Anglosaska formuła politycznego konstytucjonalizmu*, Kraków 2014, pp. 141 ff.

28 In accordance with the division by Alec Stone Sweet, cf. A. Stone Sweet *Constitutional Courts…*, p. 816.

having no exceptional instruments at its disposal reserved for this procedure. The constitutional process is always, for American court proceedings, secondary and subsidiary to the principal court proceedings, where a doubt concerning the constitutionality of the norm to be used in a given case arises. Therefore, when a doubt arises, the court suspends its main proceedings (e.g. penal or civil) and settles the problem of constitutionality of the norm being questioned, after which it returns to the main proceedings, issuing the decision considering the position taken in the subsidiary constitutional proceedings.

Another point of contrast between the American and European models, and perhaps the most important from the legal point of view, is the relative consequence of the decision of the American court on the unconstitutionality of the investigated legal norm. Following the settlement of the constitutional issue brought before the court, the court states either the compatibility of the questioned norm with the constitution or its incompatibility. If it is compatible, the norm is the basis to issue the decision in the ongoing main (penal or civil) proceedings, pending before the court. In the other case, the court refuses to apply the unconstitutional norm and issues the decision referring to another legal norm which is the nearest in terms of its content and which constitutes the basis of the decision, while the defective norm is simply treated as non-existent.

Significantly, the consequence of recognized unconstitutionality is only of *inter partes* nature, which means that it binds the parties of the court proceedings where the constitutional proceedings were started. As a consequence, from the point of view of compatibility with the constitution, the defective norm is not repealed, which means that it is still a part of the USA system of law and the only result of the court finding out its unconstitutionality is the fact that it is not applied by the court which earlier acknowledged its unconstitutionality (possibly, also by a subsequent court which may recognize it as a precedent, or arrive at the same conclusion). Obviously, such a settlement is the most serious shortcoming of the American model of the constitutional review of law and mainly due to this, another, alternative (assumed to be better) way of protecting the constitution was sought which was understood as a possibility of derogation (and not only its possible omission) of the norm affected by constitutional defectiveness. In the American model of the constitutional review of law the norm recognized as unconstitutional still remains a part of the system of law and the courts which acknowledge its incompatibility with the constitution only refuse to apply it, without being able to repeal it. This situation arouses the greatest controversy; firstly, because it contradicts the principle of coherence of the legal system (where the binding of unconstitutional norms is admissible); secondly, because it does not eliminate the possibility of applying the norm affected by constitutional defectiveness (if, for instance, neither party involved in a given case raises the charge of unconstitutionality); thirdly, because it does not guarantee judicial coherence of courts adjudging in matters of constitutionality (which can, after all, take different positions while assessing the same norm); fourthly, because a lack of coherence of courts can cause the ultimate effect of different treatment of legal and physical persons who defend their rights in court. Nevertheless, it should be remembered that the relative effect of the decision on unconstitutionality of a norm in the system of judicial review does not generate more serious problems. It is so because it follows from the same etiology of the establishment of the American version of the constitutional review of law and because it is well amortized by the elements of that legal culture and other mechanisms typical of common law.

As for the etiology, it should be remembered that constitutional review itself is not directly provided for in the American constitution and it was only derived from its provisions. This means that courts (including the Supreme Court) have competences to assess the compatibility of law with the constitution but they do not have the competences to derogate the defective legal norms, because such a competence – due to its relevance and legislative character – cannot be implied by any means but it has to be established *expressis verbis*. Besides, the American constitutional law strongly emphasizes the restrictive or orthodox rule of the separation of powers, which was adapted in the USA, which means that each of the separated powers has its own *imperium*, which can by no means be narrowed. As a consequence, the role of courts is only to settle legal conflicts (and this is realized by judicial review), but it is not to decide what is law and what is not (since this is within the exclusive competences of the Congress as the legislative power).

While settling legal conflicts according to general rules, the American courts can, therefore, investigate compatibility of law with the constitution but they cannot interfere into the legislative competences including, for example, derogation of a legal norm being *actus contrarius* of its establishment. As for the elements of the common law culture which protect against the problems resulting from the relative character of the decision on unconstitutionality, the role of the precedent secures against the judicial discrepancy of American courts (especially in constitutional matters) and the judicial supervision realized by higher courts, with the Supreme Court at the top. The decision of the Supreme Court sustaining the unconstitutionality of the incriminated norm – despite the fact that *de lege lata* still produces only *inter partes* effect – will be in practice respected by all courts, which *de facto* is a guarantee of the application of the norm which the Supreme Court decreed unconstitutional.

From what can be seen, the American model of the constitutional review of law is very specific[29]. What defines it in the greatest degree is practical realism and pragmatism. It was derived from the regulations of the constitution and established within the specific range that the constitution left between the determination of the role of courts and the supremacy clause. Judicial review filled this space by granting the common courts the right to investigate the compatibility of the law with the constitution and – if the need should arise – the possibility of refusing to apply the law which would stand in conflict with the constitution, but without the possibility of undertaking further actions. In this way the American version of the constitutional review of law satisfied the minimalist criteria (entrusting this review to common courts but without the possibility of derogation of those regulations recognized as unconstitutional). At the same time it satisfied maximalist criteria by interpreting the constitution and finding a place in it for the establishment of judicial review without the necessity of making a literal change to the content of the constitution. This is where the pragmatism of the American model of the constitutional review of law is reflected[30].

The so-called European model was created in opposition to the pragmatic American model of the constitutional review of law, which arose out of practice. It should be emphasized that the European model does not only have different names (*vide* the Austrian model, the model of the constitutional courts, the centralized model, the Kelsenian model) but it is also situated differently. Sometimes it comprises all ways to control the constitutionality of law different from judicial review, sometimes it is identified with constitutional courts, or other bodies, less or more similar to them. Finally, the European model is at times understood to be a very narrow model of review in the shape once proposed by Hans Kelsen, and practically applied in the Austrian constitution from 1920 (hence, it is sometimes called the Kelsenian or Austrian model). It can be seen, then, that the very concept of the European model is disputable so its particular definitional features must be even more disputable. In fact, the only issue that does not cause

29 However, this specific character was not disturbed by the reception of this model and not only in the countries with the common law culture, where this kind of measure would certainly be easier to undertake, but also countries with established law culture. The reception of judicial review was especially intensified in Latin America, in the 19th century in particular. Cf. M. Fromont, *Justice constitutionnelle comparée*, Paris 2013, pp. 19, 20.

30 This model of review can maximize the use of the potential created by the American, orthodox version of the separation of powers. Cf. A. Barak, *A Judge on Judging: The Role of a Supreme Court in a Democracy*, "Harvard Law Review" 2002, vol. 116, pp. 121 ff.

arguments is that the model was shaped in a complete opposition to the judicial review. The aforementioned opposition concerns both particular elements identifying this model and the way in which it was established. The American model was created through practice while the European model – without delving into what is understood by it – is the creation of theory which was practically verified only after some time (and led to corrections of the system, which is why it has such a very heterogeneous form now).

However, it should be emphasized that opposition to the American model does not mean that in Europe the system of the constitutional review of norms was built considering its American version. The resulting opposition was rather the effect of the different legal cultures of the USA and continental Europe and not the fact that judicial review was treated as the point of departure to create another model[31]. This is proved by the first, very shy, projects to arrange the mechanism of the constitutional review of law which appeared in France and which preceded the famous Marbury *versus* Madison decision. There is no doubt that chronologically the first was the constitutional court (*jury constitutionnaire*) proposed by Emmanuel Jospeha Sieyès[32]. He designed a separate and independent organ of the state that exclusively assessed the compatibility of laws with the constitution and was empowered to change constitutional norms (since from time to time the court was to formulate propositions of changing the constitution so that its full coherence was guaranteed). The principal form of Sieyès's constitutional court (as a separate body which – in accordance with the rule of exclusiveness – would assess the constitutionality of norms) is still retained today, and is one of the main elements characterizing the European model of the review of legal norms. Sieyès's concept was not only the first involving non-parliamentary verification of legislation[33] but it also pointed to significant issues

31 Although it is natural that beginning with the 19th century the practice of judicial review was carefully watched and assessed in Europe, for example in France, where it was even postulated to transpose the American model. More on this subject, see: A. Laquieze, *Le contrôle de constitutionnalite de la loi aux Etats-Unis vu par les penseurs liberaux français u XIXe siècle*, [in:] *Aux origines du contrôle de constitutionnalité XVIIIe-XXe siècle*, ed. D. Chagnollaud, Paris 2003, pp. 96 ff.

32 Cf. J. Szymanek, *Emmanuel-Joseph Sieyès, O sądzie konstytucyjnym: tezy projektu ustawy przedstawionego przez Emmanuela-Jospeha Sieyèsa podczas obrad Konwencji w dniu 18 Thermidora roku III* (tłumaczenie, opracowanie i komentarz). "Studia Prawnicze KUL" 2016, No. 2, pp. 193 ff.

33 Naturally, disregarding the experiences of American colonies where such control was not treated as some completely new sphere of the state's activity but rather an integral part of the activity of courts and the hierarchy of law typical of common law culture.

evoked by the activity of the constitutional court and which are connected with its largely political profile and activity composing the scope of the constituent power. Sieyès was aware that the review of legislation was not a typical judicial activity (hence, the organ which he proposed was by him called a jury and not a court) and that it is, at least partly, a political activity, without any doubt having political consequences and that it, in fact, was situated between the powers since it had the features of court, it concerns legislation and in its consequences impact the constitutional system, by changing the constitution (at least by way of interpretation). Sieyès's concept of a constitutional court has never been realized. Nevertheless, it has remained a testimony of the European thought, which was not necessarily developed as a simple answer to the American version of the non-parliamentary constitutional review of law.

The second European project aimed to establish the mechanism of constitutional review was an idea by Georg Jellinek. It was created nearly a hundred years after Abbot Sieyès presented his vision of the constitutional court. Jellinek started with what he considered the impossibility of granting common courts the right to assess the compatibility of laws with the constitution. He perceived the American judicial review as a thoroughly bad procedure that threatened the certainty and stability of the legal order. He also added that it was in some measure ineffective since it did not ultimately lead to the repeal of the norms recognized as incompatible with the constitution. Judicial review, in Jellinek's opinion, facilitated the mechanisms of law application but it did not interfere in the mechanism of its establishment, which seriously discredited it because unconstitutionality is an effect of the establishment of law, not its application. The non-application of an unconstitutional norm does not, therefore, eliminate the basic problem, which is the binding of the norm violating the vertical dependence and one norm resulting from another. At the same time, Jellinek was probably the first to point to a close relation of the constitutional review of law with the restriction of the parliament's power, and with the mechanism of the protection of minorities (which elements were absent in the American discussion on judicial review). He argued that the sense of constitutional review was to protect the *status quo*, and above all, to realize the idea of a moderate system. Ultimately, in 1885 Jellinek proposed the establishment of a constitutional tribunal (*Verfassungsgerichtshof*). The tribunal proposed by Jellinek was

---

The power of colonial courts to review the norms was derived from the law of nature and the natural right to disobedience towards bad laws, which were understood, for example, as laws that violate the higher law. Cf. M. Cappelletti, *Judicial Review...*, pp. 46 ff.

to act only according to the preventive procedure (prior review) on the initiative of the parliamentary minority (a group of deputies) which, before the controversial law came into life, could submit an application to have it examined from the angle of its compatibility with the constitution. Jellinek did not conceal the weaknesses of such review, for example indicating the political nature of the tribunal and a lack of the mechanism of controlling the reviewer, which he expressed in a concise idea of *quis custodiet custodes ipsos*[34]. Both projects, almost a hundred years distant from each other, differ in a number of aspects. Sieyès's *jury constitutionnaire* was supposed to work within the repressive (consecutive) procedure and it showed certain features of the constitutional power. Jellinek's *Verfassungsgerichtshof* was envisaged as an organ of preventive control started on the motion of the parliamentary minority and its judicial activity was supposed to be similar to the court, although it was not a court proper (the preventive character of the assessment suggested that it was rather treated as an organ of law-making, and not law application). Nevertheless, both those entities had certain features in common, above all including the fact that in the field of constitutional review they were supposed to have no competition and were appointed according to the rule of exclusiveness to realize the tasks of protecting the constitution with simultaneous exclusion of the cognition of other organs in this respect, especially the courts. The European model, which was slowly taking shape, or the way of the protection of the constitution, began to have permanent, repeatable features. Those features were sustained by the final author of the so-called European model, Hans Kelsen[35]. The Austrian theoretician of the state and law created the most mature concept of a constitutional court as an organ appointed for constitutional review of law. This concept is to a large extent defined as an antonym of the features identifying the American judicial review. Among other things, that is why the European model is treated as an opposition to the American model, which – however, does not take into consideration its genesis and the fact that it was largely shaped independently of the American solutions.

The European model of constitutional review of law, sometimes referred to as the Kelsenian model, is above all, the model of centralized (concentrated) review.

---

34 Cf. A. Dziadzio, *Idea Trybunału Konstytucyjnego Georga Jellinka*, [in:] *Ustroje. Historia i współczesność. Polska, Europa, Ameryka Łacińska. Księga jubileuszowa dedykowana Profesorowi Jackowi Czajowskiemu*, eds. M. Grzybowski, G. Kuca, P. Mikuli, Kraków 2013, pp. 180 ff.

35 For more on H. Kelsen's concept, see: H. Kelsen, *Istota i rozwój sądownictwa konstytucyjnego*, transl. B. Banaszkiewicz, Warszawa 2009, *passim*.

It provides for the existence of only one, central organ of the state that – in accordance with the principle of exclusiveness – is entrusted with the settlement of issues related to the compatibility of law with the constitution. Such an organ is most frequently called the constitutional court or the constitutional tribunal but despite the name it is not qualified as an organ of judicial power and it is placed across the traditional tri-partite division of powers. It is linked to the courts especially by the attribute of being separated and independent in its activity, which is expected to guarantee reliable performance of its tasks. Nowadays the European model of constitutional review is frequently understood just as the model of centralized review, independently of all other elements, which do not have to be in agreement with the canon of the constitutional courts, as envisaged by H. Kelsen. Hence, *nomen omen*, the multitude of approaches concerning how the very concept of the European model of constitutional review of law should be properly understood[36]. The constitutional court being separate from all other bodies of the state and – at the same time – its exclusiveness in adjudicating in the subject of the constitutionality of law are also often regarded as the principal features distinguishing the European model, regardless of all its other properties[37], even if they are relevant. This, among other things, is the reason why the European model is treated so flexibly, ranging from Kelsen's idea to each kind of review as long as it is assigned to one, separate organ of the state. It should be emphasized that this element is also connected with treating the European review as a definitely more political one. If, then, the controlling organ distinguished by Kelsen is not the court proper, nor is it a part of the administration of justice even in its broadest sense, then the review realized by such an organ must have a more political character[38].

The second element that characterizes the European model is the abstract character of the review by the constitutional court (tribunal). In the model of judicial review proceedings regarding the assessment of compatibility of law with the constitution can be initiated only by an incidental matter, which means a concrete case concerning the application of the norm that arouses doubts of a constitutional nature, while in the European model the process of constitutional review is detached from concrete cases of law application (e.g. is a court trial

36 Cf. A. Stone Sweet *Constitutional Courts…*, pp. 816 ff.

37 Cf.: F. Rouvillois, *Droit constitutionnel. Fondements et pratiques*, Paris 2005, p. 152; A. Stone Sweet *Constitutional Dialogues: Protecting Human Rights in France, Germany, Italy and Spain,* [in:] *Constitutional Dialogues in Comparative Perspectives…*, p. 10.

38 L. Favoreu, *Constitutional Review in Europe…*, p. 56. Cf. M. Tushnet, *Advanced Introduction…*, p. 49.

where a given norm is to be the basis of the decision). Therefore, the abstract character of review in the European model means that definite entities (usually, within a narrow range) can instigate verifying proceedings before the court regardless of the circumstances where the norm was applied in legal transactions. In other words, the reason to start verifying proceedings is not an incidental case of the application of the norm, but only the belief of the plaintiff that the legal norm might be burdened with the allegation of unconstitutionality. The essence of abstract review is then "detachment from concrete cases of law application"[39].

The abstract nature of review by the European organs of constitutional jurisdiction evoked the third distinguishing feature of the European model, which is the main or basic character of the European constitutional process. The proceedings before the court, or another, central organ of the protection of the constitution is not – like in the American model – the secondary and subsidiary proceedings but the primary proceedings for which a given organ was appointed. Usually, it proceeds according to a highly formalized and thoroughly defined procedure that in many points parallels the court proceedings proper. The main or basic character of the constitutional proceedings going on before an organ of constitutional jurisdiction is a natural consequence of centralization of the European model of the constitutional review of law and its abstract character, free from concrete circumstances of the application of the incriminated norm. The consequence is the issuing of a binding decision of the constitutional court (tribunal) regarding the compatibility or incompatibility of the examined norm with the constitution, which closes the proceedings[40].

Finally, from the constitutional point of view, the most important element of the European model of the protection of the constitution is the absolute effect of the decision issued by the organ of constitutional jurisdiction. The settlement by the constitutional court or tribunal has the *erga omnes* effect and, therefore, it concerns everybody (and not, like in the American model, only the parties of the constitutional proceedings going on before the court). In the case of an affirmative decision, which ascertains compatibility of the examined norm with the constitution, the legal state does not change. The norm is still binding and has the same legal consequences as before the verifying procedure was started (the initiation of the proceedings itself does not change its legal state due to the rule

39 L. Garlicki, *Sądownictwo konstytucyjne w Europie Zachodniej*, Warszawa 1987, p. 40.
40 Cf. A. Stone Sweet *Constitutional Dialogues…*, p. 10.

of presumption of compatibility with the constitution which protects it[41]). A negative decision, on the other hand, produces far-reaching legal consequences, without going into detailed solutions[42], since it means repealing the defective norm and, therefore, eliminating it from the system of the binding law with the *erga omnes* effect[43]. Hence, in the European model, recognition of the incriminated norm as defective causes its derogation, which – according to Kelsen – guaranteed a fully pure theory of law, where there was no place for binding of defective norms, that is, such norms which violate – formally or materially – the norms situated higher in the hierarchically built system of norms[44]. The non-parliamentary constitutional review of law produces a real, and above all expected result, removing from the system of norms such a norm, which brings shame for the principles of coherence and the hierarchical construction of law sources. At the same time, this effect redefines the position of the organ of constitutional jurisdiction in the highest degree since it is not a typical court or another organ of judicial power, although it certainly possesses certain judicial attributes (e.g. independence). Nor is it, as Kelsen particularly emphasized, a legislative power, although the effect of the decision ascertaining the defectiveness of the norm has a legislative effect *par excellence.* Derogation of the norm, which is a direct consequence of finding out its incompatibility with the constitution, is after all the *actus contrarius* of its establishment, and hence it is nothing else but the reverse of the law-maker's activity. Broadly understood, law-making contains two kinds of activity, the positive activity, whose effect is establishing a legal norm, and the negative activity, which comes down to removing the norms from the binding system of norms. The organ of constitutional jurisdiction constructed according to the European model is then *de facto* a negative legislator since the effect of its activity is derogation of legal norms affected by constitutional defectiveness.

One of the more serious problems evoked by the European model of the constitutional review of law is the organ's location. Its opposition towards the judicial review is the reason why the constitutional court is most frequently refused the character of the proper or typical court. At the same time, the thesis that it is a negative legislator is not accepted either, mainly due to its revolutionary character

41 This rule is also binding in the model of judicial review. More on this subject, see: T. Ziński, *Domniemanie konstytucyjności ustaw w Stanach Zjednoczonych Ameryki*, Warszawa 2016, *passim*.

42 The point is mainly whether this is the *ex tunc*, *ex nunc* or *pro futuro* effect. For more on this subject, see: B. Banaszak, *Porównawcze prawo konstytucyjne…*,. 595 ff.

43 Cf. L. Garlicki, *Sądownictwo konstytucyjne…*, p. 40.

44 Cf. H. Kelsen, *Istota i rozwój sądownictwa…*, pp. 55 ff.

but also because it puts the accent on just one aspect of the activity of European constitutional tribunals while ignoring the others. Therefore, legislators who introduce a constitutional court, or similar organ may grant it the status of the *sui generis* organ defined either by the power of guaranteeing (protecting) the constitution or simply the political organ (court) (*cour politique*), which Kelsen himself allowed, believing that the law-making activity was *nolens volens* a sign of political activity[45]. Finally, there are also those who wave aside the problem of the ontological identity of the organ of constitutional jurisprudence and simply classify it as a part of the judicial power, at the same time not granting it the status of the court proper (then the constitutional court or tribunal is a non-judicial organ of the judicial power).

The dispute about the political nature of the organ of constitutional jurisprudence also translates itself into the way such bodies are modeled. It provides the basis for making a division of the bodies settling the cases of incompatibility with the constitution into judicial and non-judicial organs (the latter sometimes directly called political organs)[46]. Sometimes, more typologies are identified, for instance, judicial organs, *quasi*-judicial organs and *sui generis* organs. Their intrinsic value is that these typologies depart from the fundamental division into the American (decentralized) and the European (centralized) models of organs adjudging in cases of incompatibility with the constitution. Their advantage is above all that they look at the issue of constitutional review in a slightly different manner, but unfortunately at the same time they are affected by the error of a one-dimensional, extremely subjective view. Hence, even though they are sometimes suggested, they cannot replace a textbook distinction into the American type review and the European type review. This distinction takes into consideration many more relevant criteria but at the same time different that they

45 On problems connected with the proper qualification of the organs of constitutional jurisprudence on the grounds of the European model, see: W. Sokolewicz, *Czy rak może być rybą a Trybunał sądem?*, [in:] *Państwo prawa, administracja, sądownictwo. Prace dedykowane prof. de. hab. Januszowi Łętowskiemu*, eds. A. Łopatka, A. Wróbel, S. Kiewlicz, Warszawa 1999, pp. 243 ff; J. Trzciński, *Czy Trybunał Konstytucyjny jest władzą sądowniczą?*, "Prawo i Życie" 1998, No. 1, pp. 12 ff.; B. Szmulik, *Trybunał Konstytucyjny a transformacja ustrojowa Polski*, [in:] *Kierunki ewolucji systemu politycznego Rzeczypospolitej Polskiej*, ed. M. Żmigrodzki, Lublin 1997, pp. 42 ff. Similar considerations regarding the political position of the constitutional court appeared, for example, in the Bulgarian doctrine. For more on this subject, see: M. Żmigrodzki, *Przeobrażenia polityczno-ustrojowe i Sąd Konstytucyjny w Bułgarii*, Lublin 1997, *passim*.

46 Cf. M. Cappelletti, *Judicial Review…*, p. 2.

reflect very well the specific character of both approaches to the problems of non-parliamentary constitutional review. Nevertheless, the substantive division, which starts with the specific character of the organ adjudging in matters of compatibility of law with the constitution is significant because it draws attention to the diversity of those organs and to the fact that they are far from homogeneous.

Apart from the universal feature, which is the existence of a separate organ of jurisdiction, the European model of review, exhibits diverse characteristics including, for example:

1) a few entities are able to initiate review proceedings;
2) complexity (universality) of protective activities means that in addition to having regard to the compatibility of norms entities can address other tasks more related to the observance of the constitutional order (*vide* settling constitutional disputes, or adjudging in matters regarding liability in tort); and
3) finality of decisions of the organ of constitutional jurisprudence means that no appellate measures are used towards them[47].

Of course, this latter solution might as well speak either in favour of the judicial character of the constitutional court or against it. The finality, protected – like in the case of all other courts – by the rule *res iudicata* supports the judicial character. What speaks against it is the impossibility of appealing from the unsatisfying settlement of the constitutional court to a higher jurisdiction, which violates the principle of right to appeal, which is after all the *sine qua non* condition of all court proceedings.

Emphasizing different elements identifying the so-called European (centralized) model must follow from the fact that despite appearances it is not uniform at all. A lack of uniformity mainly results from the fact that the model evolved, which means that the theoretical model developed by Kelsen looked different when it was applied in practice, and still more different with the explosion of constitutional courts after World War II. Hence, within the broad group of organs included in the European model, the so-called Kelsenian, or Austrian model, which was the original model is now practically absent (which is why is it sometimes also called the theoretical, or historical model), and the mutated, or contemporary model, which introduced into the classical model the solutions absent in the original, can be distinguished. The second model is also called a mixed or new model[48]. Now the European model of constitutional review is the

47 Cf. E. Zwierzchowski, *Europejskie trybunały konstytucyjne. Zarys rozwiązań konstytucyjnych*, Katowice 1989, pp. 27, 28.

48 Cf. M. Tushnet, *Advanced Introduction…*, p. 52.

mixed or new model and the Kelsenian historical model practically does not exist anywhere[49]. What changed this model to the greatest extent are:

1) introducing the preventive review (started before the questioned act of law comes into life[50]) besides the repressive review;
2) enabling different forms of concrete review besides the abstract review[51];
3) significantly broadening the circle of entities capable of initiating review proceedings[52];
4) extending the functions of the constitutional court (e.g. decreeing in constitutional conflicts, interpretation of the constitution and the laws, deciding on the legality of political parties, decreeing in election and referendum matters as well in cases concerning constitutional liability); and
5) enabling constitutional courts to adjudicate in reference to constitutional principles and values which, in Kelsen's opinion, should not be within the jurisdiction of the constitutional court since they refer to the political and axiological and not political matter[53].

The new or mixed version of the European model[54] compiles the elements once characteristic of the classical models of constitutional review, mainly through the adaptation of the elements of judicial review in European solutions[55].

---

49 Cf. R.R. Ludwikowski, *Prawo konstytucyjne porównawcze*, Toruń 2000, pp. 146 ff.

50 Which is sometimes considered to be a sign of politicization of constitutional review since, firstly, it is started in relation to a law which is not yet binding, so it takes place during the political process by definition, and – secondly – it considers arguments of more political than legal character. Cf. M. Cappelletti, *Judicial Review…*, pp. 2 ff.

51 Which is pointed out to blur the differences between the American and the European models of review. Cf. F. Hamon, C. Wiener, *La justice constitutionnelle…*, pp. 63, 64.

52 At the same time it is indicated that the development of constitutional courts in Central and Eastern Europe after 1989, when those courts (tribunals) were established and modified in relation to Kelsen's theoretical model. For more on this subject, see: A.M. Ludwikowska, *Sądownictwo konstytucyjne w Europie Środkowo-Wschodniej*, Toruń 2002, pp. 15 ff.

53 Kelsen opposed granting constitutional courts cognition in political or ideological matters. He claimed that constitutional courts should not express any opinion on such constitutional principles as "justice", "rightness", "equality", "freedom" or "morality" since these issues – as evidently political ones – remain within the field of political choice of the legislator, and not the juridical assessment of the constitutional court. Cf. H. Kelsen, *Istota i rozwój sądownictwa…*, p. 54.

54 Cf. L. Favoreu, *Constitutional Review in Europe…*, pp. 49 ff.

55 Cf. M. Tushnet, *Advanced Introduction…*, p. 52.

The modified version of Kelsen's model, which occurs most frequently now[56], does not, however, close the list of cases of arranging the non-parliamentary constitutional review of law. We can also encounter other ways of shaping the model, but are those other ways new models of constitutional review *per se*, or they are some extreme maximally mixed cases, without forming one methodological model or some separate pattern of review. Two such controversial cases are indicated. The first is France from the period of the Fifth Republic and its Constitutional Council as a surrogate of the constitutional court, and the second is the Scandinavian countries, which can by no measure be compared either to the American model or the European (classical or mixed) model. As for France, it is either another model of constitutional review[57] or it is an exception (*exception française*)[58]. However, recent constitutional changes that largely comprised the Constitutional Council are slowly blurring the differences of the French exception and make France similar to other mixed models of the non-parliamentary constitutional review of law[59]. Despite that, it is only France that has been for many years perceived as a completely different model of institutionalization of the constitutional review of law, standing in opposition both to the American and European models (the latter both in the classical version and the mixed or new one). The separate character of the French Constitutional Council comes down to the following features:

1) a distinct accent on the non-judicial nature of the Council (hence the name *conseil* and not *cour*);
2) the Council's activity pursued only according to the preventive procedure (which was clearly in opposition to the Kelsenian model, and at the same time made the Constitutional Council a political body);
3) treating the Council as an organ above all taking care of the separation of law-making competences divided between the government and the parliament, which corresponded more to the concept of an arbiter in institutional relations than the constitutional court proper; and

56 For example Germany, Spain and Italy and, indeed, all constitutional courts (tribunals) established after 1989 in Central and Eastern Europe.

57 R.R. Ludwikowski, *Prawo konstytucyjne porównawcze…*, p. 149.

58 F. Hamon, C. Wiener, *La justice constitutionnelle…*, p. 62.

59 Cf. M. Fromont, *La justice constitutionnelle en France ou l'exception française*, "La Revue Administrative" 1999, numero special 7, pp. 36 ff.

4) a clearly political character of the personal substrate of the Council, which was reflected both in the procedure of its appointment and the competences of the persons aspiring to be the Council members[60].

All those solutions stood in very sharp contrast to the model of review proposed by Kelsen and hence the Constitutional Council was for years treated as the *exception française*. However, it should be added that after the constitutional changes of 2008 this exception evidently lost its spectacular character, mainly because repressive (consecutive) review was made possible and concrete review was allowed and the Council was more strongly linked to common courts. Nevertheless, certain specific features of the Council still remain, which make it possible to continue regarding France as a solution that does not correspond to any of the other existing model solutions in the sphere of non-parliamentary constitutional review of law.

Referring to the Scandinavian case, it is also exceptional in a number of respects. Firstly, because they rejected the essence of the European model, which is centralization of control and appointing an organ, separate from courts, to realize it, which would have exclusive rights in matters concerning constitutional cognition. As a consequence, they established what can be called a cooperative model of constitutional review since it assumes the participation of a number of entities in assessing compatibility of law with the constitution without treating any of them as a priority. The features distinguishing this model include the following:

1) absence of a typical constitutional court or tribunal;
2) strong emphasis on parliamentary forms of the constitutional review of law;
3) participation of common and administrative courts in the review, which means strong reference to the de-concentrated form of reviewing the compatibility of law with the constitution[61];

60 In this respect the French Constitutional Council was certainly the most politicized organ of constitutional review. For more on this, see: A. Chmielarz-Grochal, *Francja*, [in:] *Powoływanie sędziów konstytucyjnych w wybranych państwach europejskich*, eds. A. Chmielarz-Grochal, A. Michalak, J. Sułkowski, Warszawa 2017, pp. 117 ff. It is directly said in the French literature that the Constitutional Council members (called members, and not judges) are "politicians", and the key to their selection (particularly the chairman of the Council) is above all political – cf. F. Hamon, C. Wiener, *La justice constitutionnelle...*, pp. 24, 25.

61 Cf. P. Mikuli, *Zdekoncentrowana sądowa kontrola...*, pp. 26 ff.

4) generally, a narrow view of review as formal assessment, that is, agreement in arriving at the effect of the examined act of law (e.g. Sweden); and
5) moderation of the courts in the review and, generally, adoption of interpretation favourable to the legislator (Iceland), with a simultaneous emphasis that the judicial constitutional review is dangerous from the point of view of respecting the rule of the separation of powers, which is why it should be applied very cautiously and in really exceptional cases (Norway)[62].

Clearly, the simple division of non-parliamentary forms of the constitutional review of law into the American (decentralized) and the European (centralized) models does not fully reflect the complex forms in which the constitutional review of law can occur. Many other proposed divisions are also controversial, especially the division into the review realized in the court procedure and the political control. It suggests that the review realized by courts (regardless of whether these are common courts or specially dedicated constitutional courts) has no political conditions and consequences. However, as the example of the American Supreme Court has shown, it is a political court to an increasingly greater extent, which is largely contributed to by judicial review[63]. The political context of the work of constitutional courts, or other organs of this character, is also shown by other cases. It seems that the political connotations of jurisprudence in constitutional matters (without treating them *a priori* as good or bad) are inevitable, and this is independent of the model within which the constitutional review is realized. This results from the very nature of the constitutional review of law. Apart from being a legal act, the constitution is a political act, producing political consequences and political discussions. Interpretation of the organs of constitutional jurisprudence concerning *droit politique*, as the constitution is frequently called, naturally must have its political repercussions. Obviously, this cannot justify the organs of constitutional jurisprudence entering the field of politics and hence the postulates for moderation of constitutional courts and passivism of constitutional judges[64]. These postulates seem increasingly louder since the

62 For more on this subject, see: S. Sagan, V. Serzhanova, *Kontrola konstytucyjności prawa w państwach nordyckich*, [in:] *Prawo w służbie państwu i społeczeństwu. Prace dedykowane Profesorowi Kazimierzowi Działosze z okazji osiemdziesiątych urodzin*, eds. B. Banaszak, M. Jabłoński, S. Jarosz-Żukowska, Wrocław 2012, pp. 179 ff.

63 Cf. P. Laidler, *Sąd Najwyższy Stanów Zjednoczonych Ameryki. Od prawa do polityki*, Kraków 2011, pp. 215 ff.

64 The phenomenon of judges' activism is observed both in the American and the European models. Cf. B. Banaszak, M. Bernaczyk, *Aktywizm sędziowski we współczesnym państwie demokratycznym*, Warszawa 2012, pp. 47 ff.

non-parliamentary constitutional review of law gives rise to more and more political, teleological and axiological tensions[65], which best proves its increasing importance in the scale of the whole world.

Post-Soviet States and the Model Solutions of the Review of Legal Norms

For many years the non-parliamentary constitutional review of law was the sole domain of the western political hemisphere. The countries of the so-called eastern block did not accept the establishment of any mechanisms that would verify compatibility of the law with the constitution outside the parliament. In common opinion, such mechanisms were regarded as inadvisable and purposeless, and above all undemocratic as they threatened the position of the parliament and, indirectly, the political status of the sovereign whose parliamentary deputation was the political representation reflected in the composition of the legislature. Therefore, the non-parliamentary constitutional review of law was opposed firstly for of juristic reasons (constitution), and only then for political reasons[66]. The former pointed to the incompatibility of such review with the paradigm of the unity of the state power, which was crowned by the parliament treated in all socialist countries as the "organ of the highest power". The consequence of such a view was the absence of constitutional regulation that would in any form institutionalize the non-parliamentary constitutional review of law (harmoniously perceived as a form of restricting the power of the parliament). Another reason of constitutional nature, referred to as a good justification of the impossibility of establishing constitutional review, was the very concept of the constitution. Judicial review, as a way of protecting the constitution, is after all possible only in those constitutional systems which approve of the principle of constitutionalism understood, for instance, as a command of direct binding of the constitution as the law of the highest order. In socialist countries, on the other hand, a completely different principle was binding for years, namely the indirect role of the act of law in transposing (introducing) the provisions of the constitution into legal transactions. As a result, the constitution without ordinary laws was an act deprived of legal

65 For more on this subject, see: P. Blachèr, *Contrôle de constitutionnalité et volonté générale*, Paris 2001, pp. 133 ff.

66 For more on this subject, see: H. Roussillon, *Le probléme du contrôle de la constitutionnelité des lois dans les pays socialistes*, "Revue du Droit Publiques et de la Science Politique en France et a l'Étranger" 1977, No. 1, pp. 62 ff.

effectiveness. It was treated as an obligation (of legal and political nature) of the parliament to establish laws that would specify the general provisions of the constitution. This meant that the possible non-establishment of the act which would specify constitutional provisions "froze" those regulations and made their application impossible in normal legal transactions. The constitution was then a specific plan of legislative work of the parliament and nothing more and this is what made it diametrically different from the western system. Its provisions, without the statutory decisions developing it, had no importance besides the declarative obligation of the parliament to specify them by way of ordinary legislation. This made constitutional review even more insubstantial and at the same time – in the opinion of the doctrine of constitutional law – gave it a thoroughly political status, since it ordered *de iure* to assess the way of realization of the constitution by the ordinary legislator, which was treated as a *par excellence* political activity. It is here where the political reasons for reluctance towards the non-parliamentary constitutional review of law became visible. The first was without doubt the origin of this kind of review, which meant it was perceived as completely occidental and so bourgeois, meaning thoroughly evil, backward and harmful. The second was treating constitutional review as a contradiction of the idea of democracy, which directly discredited it and labeled it undemocratic. The third reason was the assumption of incompatibility of constitutional review towards the role of the communist party, which in the political sense had control over the mechanism of political aggregation and articulation of interests. Finally, the fourth reason was the belief that the non-parliamentary form of constitutional review was a completely anachronistic solution and, in the conditions of the socialist state, completely useless. In the last case other mechanisms were at work that were believed to effectively eliminate the problem of the possible unconstitutionality of law. In the political aspect *stricte*, the latter was counteracted by the leading role of the communist party, which always behaved according to the will of the sovereign, while in the legal aspect it was secured by parliamentary controlling procedures that made it impossible to adopt a law contradicting the constitution. As a consequence, it was believed that the will of the parliament, reflected in the content of the act, could not be incompatible with the constitution since political mechanisms above all, and then legal ones as well, safeguarded it against such a possibility.

The socialist doctrine began to erode regarding the permissibility of the non-parliamentary constitutional review of law in the 1980's. The establishment of the first (apart from Yugoslavia) Constitutional Tribunal (in 1982) proved that the arrangement of constitutional judicature (in accordance with the European pattern) was also possible in the eastern block[67]. Although the solution *prima facie* undermining the sense of the constitutional review of law (which was insufficiency of judgments regarding unconstitutionality of the law which had to be confirmed by the parliament[68]) was included in the model then introduced in Poland, the above procedure was not so much falsification of the constitutional court but the enabling of its activity in the conditions of the socialist principle of the parliament's preponderance[69]. Soon afterwards the so-called block of socialist countries fell apart following the events named the "Autumn of Nations" from 1989, the final consequence of which was the collapse of the USSR and the establishment of independent states, in the past making up the entities of the federal state of the Soviet Union. The consequence of the events initiated in 1989 was that non-parliamentary organs of the constitutional review of laws began to be formed in the whole post-socialist region, including the area of Central-Eastern Europe and the former USSR (with the exception of Turkmenistan). It should be added that none of those sub-regions decided to appoint its own, new, endemic model of constitutional review[70]. Indisputably, there was a reaching for western solutions and only one – broadly understood – European model was taken into consideration, and the possible transplantation of the American institution of judicial review was rejected at the start. While on other levels of the formation of various constitutional constructions (*vide* the position of the parliament, the system of government, the status of the president, the system of individual rights and freedoms) many, frequently different, patterns were referred to, sometimes in the atmosphere of strong disputes, in the sphere of non-parliamentary review of laws there was no field for discussion. It was agreed that, firstly, a system of

---

67 Cf. L. Garlicki, *The Experience of the Polish Constitutional Court*, [in:] *Constitutional Justice. East and West. Democratic Legitimacy and Constitutional Courts in Post-Communist Europe in a Comparative Perspective*, eds. F. Laporta, A. Peczenik, F. Schauer, The Hague 2010, pp. 265 ff.

68 The insufficiency of the judgments of the Polish Constitutional Tribunal was not absolute. Firstly, because it concerned only negative decisions, that is those which found incompatibility of the examined norm with the constitution; secondly, because it referred only to the act. This means that affirmative judgments were not subjected to assessment by parliament in the same way as judgments addressed to the basic acts were not subjected to such assessment, even if they found their incompatibility with the constitution.

69 Hence, the above procedure became insubstantial after the collapse of the idea of the socialist state and that is why the new Polish constitution adopted in 1997 excluded it definitely.

70 For example, cf. A.M. Ludwikowska, *Sądownictwo konstytucyjne…*, pp. 31 ff.

constitutional review should be formed and, secondly, the so-called European model was the most suitable (without any thought devoted to the fact that the very definition of the European model is very broad and that the model contains various sub-models or smaller variants).

Actually, a non-conditional acceptance of the non-parliamentary constitutional review of law within the general European model (without going into details of the accepted final solutions) resulted from a few circumstances. The first was the wish to create political solutions standing in opposition to *ancien régime.* The second was the belief that the non-parliamentary constitutional review of law was a specific test of democracy of the newly established solutions and one of the conditions to effect real, and not only seeming political changes. The third was the common acceptance of the principle of the separation of powers, though without defining its concrete shape[71], one of the elements of which was believed to be constitutional judiciary. Finally, the fourth was recognizing the American model to be useless in the conditions of post-Soviet states, which followed both from the distance of that pattern and other cultural conditions (e.g. a lack of legal culture of the common law type)[72].

The European model (the mixed model, not the classical, Kelsenian form) was the only model really taken into consideration. Transposing the American model onto the post-Soviet ground was as inacceptable as adapting the original, classical model of the constitutional court in the shape developed by Kelsen. This was mostly due to the fact that on the threshold of the 1990's the classical model of the constitutional review of law was a purely theoretical solution, in practice strongly modified by a number of changes (e.g. the possibility of preventive review, the admissibility – to a greater or lesser degree – of concrete review, or other competences of the constitutional courts, not connected directly with the so-called judicial function[73]). Also, those states that actually formed their

---

71 For example, cf. J. Zaleśny, *Zasady podziału władzy w Rosji*, [in:] *Zasady podziału władzy we współczesnych państwach europejskich*, eds. S. Grabowska, R. Grabowski, Rzeszów 2016, vol. II, pp. 162 ff.

72 For more on this subject, see: W Sadurski, *Legitimacy and Reasons of Constitutional Review in Communism*, [in:] *Constitutional Justice. East and West…*, pp. 163 ff.

73 Understood as the function of adjudicating on the compatibility of legal norms with the law of higher order. Besides the judicial function, which was obligatory for each organ of the constitutional review of law, those organs were often equipped with so-called non-judicial functions, in some sense connected with a broadly viewed protection of the constitution but not referring to adjudicating on the constitutionality of legal norms, e.g. settling the validity of elections or reference, or decisions concerning the legality of the activity of political parties, etc.

political solutions in the 1990's based them, from the very beginning, largely based on the experiences of West Europe, which naturally made the solutions adopted there (with the modified original model by Kelsen) the reference point for the new constructions in the sphere of the protection of the constitution.

The German Federal Constitutional Court was especially attractive for a number of reasons. Firstly, the transformation of Germany after World War II was perceived as successful democratization of the state. Secondly, German was seen as a state of enormous political, legal and social effects, and so an appropriate model to follow. Thirdly, because the post-Soviet states became strongly linked economically to Germany, which only strengthened the role of Germany as a model. Finally, the judicial achievements of the German Constitutional Tribunal were a rich natural reference point for other countries. Obviously, the German pattern were not the only one. While building the organs of the constitutional judiciary in the post-Soviet states, the experiences of Spain, Italy and the countries of Central and Eastern Europe were also taken into consideration and the latter were especially analyzed since they were an example in the sense of both geographical and political experiences (and even more attractive because their effects could be observed as they arose).

The fact that the German Federal Constitutional Court was the principal model for post-Soviet states does not mean at all that the latter did not reach for others, if only occasionally. Two radically different examples are Kazakhstan and Estonia. In the Kazakhstan, the French model aroused particular interest. The second constitution of independent Kazakhstan (from 1995) made full use of the French model, which was reflected in the very name of the judicial organ, namely the Constitutional Council. The similarities went beyond the name of the organ, including the mechanism of appointing the members of the Kazakh Constitutional Council, its relation to the president (and the assumption that former presidents of Kazakhstan are members of the Council ex officio); introducing – as a principle – the preventive form of constitutional review (with a small exception for repressive review in a concrete procedure, resulting from a question of law); removing the Constitutional Council from the sphere of judicial power and ascertaining that it is not placed within any of the traditionally separated powers, which even more determined its non-judicial character. A strong reference to French models did not, however, mean simple acceptance. A few local solutions, at the same time characteristic of the majority of states of the post-Soviet region were also introduced into the organizational and functional arrangement of the Kazakh Constitutional Council. Those were, for example, a strong connection of the Council with the president, who sometimes plays the role of an entity controlling the Council (for instance, having the possibility of accelerating the proceedings in the Council). Another solution is the far-reaching restriction of the Council in realizing the judicial function through a significant narrowing of normative acts subjected to the cognition of the Constitutional Council[74].

In Estonia, on the other hand, interest was aroused by the solutions that are partly American, partly Scandinavian, and partly placed in a broad current of the European model. This referred not only to the concept of the constitutional review of law but also the whole constitutional mechanism of the state's activity. As a consequence, the mixed model was introduced in Estonia but it was done in a special way, namely combining the elements of concrete and decentralized review with the elements of abstract and centralized review. The constitutional review of law in Estonia was assigned to courts, assuming that the issue of compatibility of law with the constitution was the question subjected exclusively to the cognition of organs of the judicial type. At the same time it was decided that the competence in matters concerning the assessment of compatibility of law with the constitution belongs to all common courts (the model of decentralized review or the model of the American judicial review). If, however, those courts should come to the conclusion, during their proceedings, that the proceedings relate to a norm affected by constitutional defectiveness, then they are obliged to start proceedings the aim of which is to eliminate such a norm with the *erga omnes* effect. To this end, they initiate proceedings before the State Court (which is the highest judicial court in Estonia). It is only on a decision of the State Court (and the Chamber of Constitutional Review working within its structures) that a legal norm incompatible with the constitution may be removed from legal transactions. The proceedings started by common courts are of a concrete character, which corresponds to the model of judicial review. On the other hand, proceedings before the State Court can also be initiated in accordance with the abstract procedure by a very narrow group of entities, which is a solution typical of the European model of constitutional review[75]. Consequently, the Estonian system of the protection of the constitution is very specific. The literature points out that it is a compilation of elements of decentralized and centralized elements, simultaneously being concrete and abstract. At the same time, the fact that common courts have an obligation to turn to the State court in case of doubts concerning the constitutionality of the regulation, together with the fact that

74 For more on this subject, see: J. Szymanek, *Ustrój konstytucyjny Kazachstanu*, Warszawa 2013, pp. 189 ff.

75 Cf. S. Sagan, *Ustrój państwowy Republiki Estonii*, Rzeszów 2018, pp. 74, 75.

only the decision by the Constitutional Review Chamber of the State Council can achieve derogation of the unconstitutional regulation make the decentralized and concrete review of more theoretical than practical importance[76], since the abstract and centralized review predominates, especially in its effects.

The cases of Kazakhstan and Estonia are two extreme cases where model solutions other than the general European model of constitutional review were consciously reached for. In the other countries of the post-Soviet region the modernized, or mixed European model became the basis to create the mechanisms of non-parliamentary constitutional review of law. However, the new (mixed) European model was not transposed to these post-Soviet states without modification. Therefore, although we cannot say that a new model or sub-model of the constitutional review of law was created, we can say that it was equipped with certain endemic features characteristic of the post-Soviet political region. Those features included:

1) very strong inclusion of constitutional courts (usually, directly called so) into the structure of the judicial power;
2) usually, rather modest control of the system of the constitutional court on the level of the constitution, so that many matters regarding the competences of the constitutional court are included in the statutory regulation developing the constitution[77];
3) equipping constitutional courts with exceptionally numerous rights from the sphere of the so-called non-judicial functions;
4) introducing solutions which, in some measure, limit the activity of constitutional courts, which is assumed to counteract conflicts increasingly often evolved by the constitutional jurisprudence in reference to legitimacy and competences; and
5) despite the fact that constitutional courts are recognized as an integral component of the third power, they are rather paradoxically treated as a fully political power, actively participating in relations between the state's constitutional organs (but this, however, follows from practice, and not the regulations of law).

76 Cf. P. Mikuli, *Zdekoncentrowana sądowa kontrola…*, p. 78.

77 This undermined the sense of the judicial review of the constitutionality of law. Many authors consider the key competences of the constitutional court should be absolutely regulated on the level of the constitution, which is supposed to guarantee the stability of the position of the constitutional court. Cf. D. Kabat-Rudnicka, *Konstytucjonalizacja Unii Europejskiej a sądownictwo konstytucyjne*, Warszawa 2016, p. 119.

In a decisive majority of post-Soviet states the constitutional system consistently treats the constitutional court as an organ of judicial power. Contrary to Western or Central Eastern Europe, the significant problem of the ontology of the constitutional court was not raised here. A widespread and recognized problem in Europe is that the constitutional court remains outside the traditionally divided state power[78]; therefore, it is an organ of neither judicial power nor legislative power (even though it is its antonym in the form of Kelsenian negative legislator) nor, obviously, the executive. It is assumed then that, in the European model, the constitutional court (independently of its name) is a *sui generis* organ, which has the status of a separate, independent state organ placed across the classical tripartite division. In the post-Soviet states, on the other hand, a completely different assumption is made, according to which the constitutional court is an integral part of the judicial power (*vide* Armenia, Georgia, Latvia, Russia, Moldavia, Uzbekistan). This is confirmed both by the systematics of particular constitutions and the view of the doctrine that believes, for example, that the extension of the organs of judicial power with the constitutional court democratized this power, and especially strengthened it in relation to the other powers. At the same time, including the constitutional courts as an organ of more broadly treated judicial power is perceived as helping to guarantee that the constitutional court, as part of the judicature, is protected by the rules of independence and separateness.

Such strong inclusion of constitutional courts within the structure of the judicial power stands in contrast to the very broad extension of the functions of constitutional courts. Since the theoretical model proposed by Kelsen, the functions of organs adjudicating in constitutional matters have been systematically broadened. Nevertheless, the solutions applied in post-Soviet states go far beyond the usually modest non-judicial functions and from this point of view they are a distinctive feature of the versions of the constitutional review of law. Besides adjudicating on the compatibility of law with the constitution, the constitutional courts of post-Soviet states possess such competences as:

making commonly binding interpretations of the constitution and the laws (Azerbaijan, Kyrgyzstan, Moldavia, Russia, Ukraine);

1) settling constitutional disputes (Georgia, Russia, Tajikistan, Azerbaijan);
2) deciding on the constitutionality of the objectives and activity of political parties (Armenia, Moldavia), and sometimes also other civic associations (Georgia) and even religious organizations (Kyrgyzstan);

78 L. Favoreu, *Constitutional Review in Europe*..., p. 56.

3) deciding on the validity of elections and referendum procedures (Armenia, Kazakhstan, Kyrgyzstan, Moldavia);
4) deciding in matters of constitutional liability of the president, either definitely or at a certain stage of the proceedings (Armenia, Belarus, Lithuania, Kazakhstan, Kyrgyzstan, Russia), and at times also other high state and local officials (Armenia);
5) deciding on compatibility of the rulings of the Supreme Courts with the constitution and the laws (Azerbaijan, Tajikistan);
6) issuing opinions on the validity of the dissolution of the parliament (Moldavia);
7) deciding on systematic or serious violation of the constitution by the parliament (Belarus), or assessing all decisions by the parliament (Latvia);
8) issuing opinions on violations of the constitutions and laws by deputies in relation to whom procedures of penal liability were initiated (Lithuania);
9) issuing opinions in the sphere of changes to the constitution (Azerbaijan, Kyrgyzstan Moldavia);
10) legislative initiative (Belarus, Russia); and
11) making official interpretation of its own decisions (Belarus).

It can be seen, then, that the scope of competences of post-Soviet constitutional courts is exceptionally broad and is certainly a distinguishing feature of constitutional courts in this part of the world.

Limitations concerning the post-Soviet constitutional courts are of a different nature. They sometimes come down to a very clear demarcation of substantive borders of the cognition of the constitutional court, excluding certain legal acts. It is so for example in Kazakhstan, where the Constitutional Council assesses statutes and international agreements in accordance with abstract review only, excluding the acts of the basic rank (the resolutions of the parliament are the only exception). Alternatively, it could be the date for the constitutional court to take a position, with a simultaneous possibility of shortening this period, e.g. by the president, which can be applied in relation to all examined cases on the constitutionality of legal acts (Kazakhstan), or other competences (e.g. in Azerbaijan a strictly determined date is fixed for the constitutional court there to issue the commonly binding interpretation of laws). The preventive form of review can be place a form of restriction on the activity of an organ of constitutional jurisprudence (which is the case in Kazakhstan, the only exception being the concrete review evoked by a question of law of the common court). Only the preventive review of international agreements is provided for in Russia, where agreements recognized as incompatible with the constitution are not subject to enforcement and are not applicable. Still another kind of limitation of the activity of constitutional courts in post-Soviet states can be the competence of the constitutional court adopted in Belarus to revise their own decisions. Thus, the judgments by the Belarusian constitutional court are deprived of the attribute of immovability since this court can – should new circumstances be revealed – review the earlier issued decision[79]. Nevertheless, the most serious limitations in the sphere of the functioning of constitutional courts in post-Soviet states certainly result from distinct politicization of those organs and the fact that despite the stated principles of separateness and independence – additionally strengthened by including constitutional courts in a broad formula of the judicial power – they are treated as organs participating in the creation of the state's policy. As a consequence, the constitutional jurisprudence in at least some post-Soviet states has the status of a *stricte* formal institution, which materially does not fit the canon of the constitutional court[80]. What is more, despite the apolitical curtain behind it, it is often treated instrumentally and politically. It is, for example, pointed out that the Russian constitutional court, where attempts were made from the beginning to free it from political issues, does not practically realize this postulate although the federal law on the constitutional court includes a regulation clearly saying that "the constitutional court settles only issues of law", from which it should be *a contrario* concluded that it does not settle political issues[81]. Such assessment of the court certainly decreases its real importance. The Constitutional Council of Kazakhstan is an organ *de facto* deprived of any importance. It is mainly of advisory and opinion-forming character and it is most frequently treated as such.

However, the constitutional courts of post-Soviet states do not always and everywhere depart so materially from their high formal position. For example a high assessment of the Georgian constitutional court, whose role is even more significant since it addresses the lability of constitutional regulations and numerous interpretative doubts that the jurisprudence of the constitutional court tries to eliminate[82]. Also constitutional courts in post-Soviet states are well equipped with the competence to provide the official interpretation of the constitution and the laws and they frequently make use of this competence in practice,

---

79 Cf. J. Zaleśny, *System konstytucyjny Białorusi*, Warszawa 2011, p. 70.

80 Which is especially visible in cases submitted to its cognition, where constitutional and organizational issues predominate, while much less space is devoted to matters referring to individual rights and freedoms. The purpose of making the constitutional judiciary similar to courts (so-called judicialization) is served above all by shifting the accent of cases examined by constitutional courts and placing this accent on the protection of the legal situation of an individual. Cf. F. Hamon, C. Wiener, *La justice constitutionnelle…*, pp. 103 ff.

81 Cf. W. Sokolewicz, *Sąd Konstytucyjny Federacji Rosyjskiej*, [in:] *Sądy konstytucyjne w Europie*, ed. J. Trzciński, Warszawa 2000, vol. IV, p. 321.

82 Cf. G. Kuca, M. Grzybowski, *System konstytucyjny Gruzji*, Warszawa 2012, p. 62.

thus becoming an extremely important organ developing the provisions of the constitution and so complementing of its various shortcomings. In this respect, not only the Georgian constitution but also those of Ukraine[83] or, for instance, Russia[84], show activity, which must always make their assessment nuanced.

While analyzing the real position of constitutional courts in the post-Soviet states, one must address the division between strong constitutional and weak constitutional review. The criteria of this division are the real position of the court (its prestige and authority) and the relations that occur between them and the other organs of state power. If we slightly modify and generalize the models of strong and weak constitutional review[85], we can say that strong constitutional review:

1) determines the system and competences of the constitutional court in the constitution in as great a detail as possible, without providing for excessively developing laws that can, in practice, change the status of the constitutional court;
2) provides for a possibly broad catalogue of entities initiating the verifying procedure;
3) provides for a broad objective range of review (without excluding definite acts of law);
4) does not allow for a possibility to modify decisions of the constitutional court, e.g. by way of a sub-constitutional law or still another procedure; and
5) effectively amortizes the constitutional court against political influences and pressures, thus securing its full independence.

In the alternative model of weak constitutional review the aforementioned criteria are not fulfilled or they are realized in varying degrees.

While assessing the post-Soviet model of non-parliamentary constitutional review, it should be stated that with very few exceptions (Estonia, Georgia), they tend to fit the model of weak or close to weak review. This is so either because the constitutional regulation concerning the constitutional judiciary is very laconic (Latvia, Russia, Kyrgyzstan, Tajikistan, Uzbekistan) or because the list of entities capable of initiating constitutional review of law is very modest, or those entities are constructed in such a way that they *de facto* create an ideological and political monism (Belarus, Kazakhstan) or, finally, because it is only the formal criteria

83 Cf. J.-P. Massias, *Droit constitutionnel des États d'Europe de l'Est*, Paris 2008, pp. 673 ff.
84 *Ibidem*, pp. 623 ff.
85 Cf. A. Chen, M. Poiares Maduro, *The Judiciary and Constitutional Review…*, pp. 102, 103.

of the arrangement of the constitutional court in the political system of a given country which determine that it is not an authentically separate and independent organ (Russia, Belarus), and its activity is intrinsic in the political context, which, in case of constitutional courts, should be possibly most amortized.

Anahit Manasyan

Constitutional Justice in the Republic of Armenia

Abstract: The present text examines the characteristic features of the Armenian constitutional judiciary. It puts forward a thesis that in their assumptions they refer to the European model of reviewing the legal norms adapted to the domestic political needs.

Keywords: the European model of reviewing the legal norms, Constitutional Court, autonomy and independence, The Constitutional Court and other organs of state power, cognition of the Constitutional Court

Introduction

At the actual stage of the development of legal thought, enhancement of constitutionalism and constitutional system of the state are mostly determined by presence of an effective and efficient system of constitutional justice. Constitutional justice is an essential prerequisite and means of rooting the constitutional values in the social system, while legal acts of constitutional review bodies play an undisputable role in all spheres of public life.

However, despite this, theory and practice present many problematic issues with regard to the institute of constitutional justice, the resolution of which merit detailed discussion. Those issues include the place or role of the Constitutional Court of Armenia (CCA) in the public authority system, the place of decisions of the constitutional justice body in the hierarchy of legal acts, the establishment of a relevant system for exercising the decisions, clarifying the role of legal positions of the CCA, etc.

1 Motives for Introduction and Key Dilemmas of Establishing the Control Over Legal Norms

In one form or another, constitutional justice has existed throughout the whole human history. However, in the context of institutional approval and developing the institute of constitutional justice, the period starting from the 19th century is of particular importance, as the first document laying a legal foundation for resolving an issue of constitutionality of normative acts – US Supreme Court decision "William Marbury vs. Madison" – was adopted on February 24, 1803.

Conventionally, the professional literature distinguishes the following stages of transforming and developing constitutional review systems:

1) 1803–1920;
2) 1920–1940;
3) 1945–1990 and
4) after 1990[1].

The first stage coincides with the formation of the American model of constitutional justice, which is remarkable by its implementation by all ordinary courts. In contrast, the European model is characterized by the implementation of constitutional justice by a concrete specialized institution (Constitutional Court, Constitutional Council, etc.). The second stage of the development of systems of constitutional review coincides with the establishment of such institutions in Europe.

Clearly the fourth stage coincides with the wave of qualitatively new processes of democratization, i.e. with the period of establishment of numerous new independent states. The establishment of thorough systems of constitutional review became one of the first and main steps of state development for the young independent post-Soviet countries, taking the experience of the European states into account. The establishment of the institutes of judicial constitutional review was conditioned by the fact that the Constitution should be reliably protected, which in almost all the states was developed and adopted with concrete difficulties, as well as by the tasks, which determined the transition of the social development from crisis governance to dynamic development and ensuring social and state stability.

The Republic of Armenia was not an exception as well. Following the declaration of independence and the adoption of its Constitution, Armenia established a judicial body of constitutional review – the Constitutional Court.

The Constitution of the independent Republic of Armenia (RA) was adopted via referendum on July 5, 1995. This Constitution laid the foundation for the Constitutional Court of Armenia[2], which was established in 1996[3]. On November 27, 2005 and December 6, 2015, amendments were made to the Armenian

1 Հարությունյան Գ., Մանասյան Ա., Սահմանադրական վերահսկողություն. Լրամշակված վերահրատարակություն, Ուսումնական ձեռնարկ, Եր.: Իրավունք 2015, pp. 46–50.

2 Provisions on the Constitutional Court were included in the Constitution; Chapter 6 entitled "Judicial Power".

3 At this stage, Armenia actually borrowed the French model of constitutional justice.

Constitution, mostly affecting the status and powers of the CCA, while contributing to its further development.

Although in professional literature the fourth stage of constitutional review systems development includes the entire period after 1990, we believe that there are major differences in the process of establishment and development of constitutional justice system within this stage.

During the formation of constitutional justice bodies, the focus was not just on solving the issue related to the interests of a specific person, but also on social stability and dynamic development of society, by ensuring the constitutionality of the entire legislative system; so clarifying the role and place of constitutional justice bodies within the state power system was on the agenda as well.

Later on, the issue of clarifying the place of constitutional court decisions within the system of legal acts was raised, establishing balanced relations between the legislative, executive, and judicial powers, clarifying the mechanisms for exercising the acts of constitutional justice bodies, protecting the interests of a specific person via constitutional justice, resolving disputes between constitutional bodies on their constitutional powers, etc.

Presently, there is a new direction for developing the institute of constitutional justice, with the arising issue of introducing the integral system of permanent constitutional diagnostics/monitoring, as consistency and continuity of constitutional review are only possible under such conditions. As noted in the legal literature, deformation of constitutionalism is the main factor of destabilization and social cataclysms, especially in terms of social transformation. Dealing with this factor requires efficient and systematic constitutional monitoring, based on task-oriented and continuous constitutional diagnostics. This is both a history lesson and a challenge of time requiring urgent attention and adequate action. At that, we should keep in mind that, along with relevant state power institutions, certain constitutional and functional roles in implementing systematic constitutional monitoring also belong to civil society, as the necessary "nervous system" of the social organism[4].

2 Legislative Stability of Constitutional Review Body

As noted above, the Constitutional Court of the Republic of Armenia (CCA) was established in 1996, following the adoption of the RA Constitution in 1995. The National Assembly adopted the first RA law "On the Constitutional

4 G. Harutyunyan, *Constitutional monitoring. Monograph*, Yerevan, "Njar" 2016, pp. 297–298.

Court" on November 20, 1995. Then, on November 9, 1997, second law "On the Constitutional Court" was adopted. After amending the RA Constitution on November 27, 2005, the status and powers of the CCA were mostly changed, thus contributing to its further development. Provision for individual constitutional complaint was introduced into the RA legal system, and the range of objects/subjects of constitutional justice was extended. Given the above, new Law "On the Constitutional Court" was adopted on June 1, 2006.

On December 6, 2015, new amendments were made to the RA Constitution, resulting in major changes regarding the status, powers, and decisions of Armenia's Constitutional Court. Thus, institute of resolving disputes between constitutional bodies, which arise due to their constitutional powers; institute of defining the compliance of draft amendments to Constitution, as well as of draft legal acts submitted to referendum (prior to their adoption) to Constitution; institute of preliminary constitutional review of laws – based on application of President of the Republic were introduced into the legal system of the Republic of Armenia. From now on, termination of deputy's mandate, disciplinary penalties for judge of Constitutional Court, and termination of powers of judge of Constitutional Court are within the competence of Constitutional Court. It must be noted that constitutional reform also extended the range of objects / subjects of constitutional justice and modified a procedure of appointing the Constitutional Court judges. It is remarkable that, according to Article 103 of the RA Constitution (as amended on December 6, 2015), Law on the Constitutional Court is a constitutional law, which should be adopted by at least three fifths of votes of the total number of deputies. In this view, on January 17, 2018, Constitutional Law of RA "On Constitutional Court" was adopted for detailed regulation of the above issues.

The constitutional status of the CCA and the constitutional regulations regarding it contribute to the legislative stability of the Court. Thus, under Article 167 of the Constitution, while administering justice, the CCA is independent and subject only to the Constitution. Powers of Constitutional Court are determined by Constitution; procedure of its formation and activity – by Constitution and Law on Constitutional Court. The Constitution further enshrines the powers of the CCA, main issues with regard to application to the CCA, decisions and conclusions of the CCA. These constitutional regulations contribute to the stability of CCA activities.

Since its establishment, the CCA has continuously been implementing its activities. Moreover, constitutional and legislative changes regarding this body have not prevented, but, rather, widely contributed to the development of constitutional justice institute in the RA. All problematic issues, arising in the course of the CCA activities, were and are still finding solutions – both by changing the relevant law-enforcement practice and improving the legislation.

It should be noted that the constitutional provisions on the CCA were amended on a professional basis only. A professional commission established by the President of the Republic prepared the entire draft of the 2015 constitutional amendments.

3 Legislative Position of the Constitutional Court of the Republic of Armenia

Provisions regulating the activities of the Constitutional Court of Armenia are defined in Chapter 7 of the Constitution (as amended on December 6, 2015), entitled "Courts and Supreme Judicial Council", Article 163 of which states that Constitutional Court, Court of Cassation, Courts of appeal, first-instance courts of general jurisdiction, and an Administrative Court operate in the RA. According to Article 167 of the RA Constitution, constitutional justice is administered by the CCA, ensuring the supremacy of Constitution; according to Article 162, only courts administer justice in the Republic of Armenia – following the Constitution and laws.

The above indicates that the CCA is included in the system of judicial power. Provisions on the CCA were defined in the chapter on judicial power of all the wordings of the Constitution[5].

3.1 Constitutional Court and the President

Referring to the relationship between Constitutional Court of Armenia and the President, it should be noted that according to Article 166 of the Constitution (as amended on December 6, 2015), Constitutional Court judges are elected by the National Assembly – by at least three-fifths of votes of the total number of deputies, for a term of twelve years. The Constitutional Court consists of nine judges, three of whom are elected by nomination from the President of the Republic, three from the Government, and three from the General Assembly of Judges. Prior to the recent amendments to the RA Constitution, the CCA was composed of nine members, five of whom were appointed by the National Assembly and four by the President of the Republic. The President of the Republic can appeal to the CCA, while decrees and orders of the President are objects of constitutional justice. It is remarkable that, under Article 123 of the RA Constitution (as

5 http://concourt.am/russian/constitutions/index.htm (accessed: December 20, 2017).

amended on December 6, 2015), the President of the Republic observes the compliance with the Constitution. In terms of this function, the role of the President is important at the initiation of a preliminary constitutional review. Thus, Article 129 of the Constitution states that the President of the Republic shall sign and promulgate a law adopted by the National Assembly within twenty-one days or apply to the CCA within the same term – to determine the compliance of the law with the Constitution[6]. If the Constitutional Court holds that law is compliant with the Constitution, the President of the Republic shall sign and promulgate the law within five days.

3.2 Constitutional Court and the Government

Under Article 166 of the RA Constitution (as amended on December 6, 2015), the National Assembly on the proposal of the Government elects three of the CCA judges. Further, resolutions of the Government and the Prime Minister are objects of constitutional justice and the Government can appeal to the CCA[7]. Thus, the Government may appeal to the Constitutional Court to determine the constitutionality of relevant legal acts; resolve disputes between constitutional bodies that arise due to their constitutional powers[8]; determine the inability of the President to exercise powers; and suspend or prohibit the activities of a party.

The Government should exercise the CCA acts. According to the 2018 RA Constitutional Law on the CCA, the Government, no later than three months after publishing a CCA resolution, shall study and, if necessary, initiate the drafting of relevant legal acts and the submitting of them to the National Assembly. If the CCA resolution finds the normative legal act fully or partially incompliant with Constitution and sets a later date for termination of the legal force of the incompliant act or its part, the Government shall ensure the exercise of the resolution till the end of this period by submitting the relevant draft law or draft package.

---

6 This provision was prescribed in the constitutional reform in 2015; however, it just come into force and has not yet been applied.

7 The Government takes this opportunity extremely rarely. In 2011, the Government appealed to the CC, challenging the provisions of the RA Labor Code, which the CC found to be compliant with the Constitution.

8 This authority was granted to the CC in the constitutional reform of 2015. It has just come into force and has not yet been applied.

3.3 Constitutional Court and the Parliament

According to Article 166 of the Constitution (as amended on December 6, 2015), the National Assembly elects judges of Constitutional Court, by at least a three-fifths majority of votes of the total number of deputies, for a term of twelve years. Laws/resolutions of National Assembly are objects of constitutional justice; the National Assembly may appeal to the Constitutional Court. Other aspects of the relationship between the CCA and the Parliament are addressed elsewhere in this chapter – in particular, in discussion of the implementation of the acts of the Constitutional Court, its powers, subjects of control, legal status etc.

3.4 Constitutional Court and the Courts

Relations between the Constitutional Court and other courts, in particular, delimitation of their authorities, are especially important for studying the role of the constitutional justice body in the public authority system. As noted above, Constitutional Court of the Republic of Armenia is included in the system of bodies of judicial power. Under Article 163 Constitutional Court, Court of Cassation, courts of appeal, first-instance courts of general jurisdiction, and Administrative Court operate in the Republic of Armenia. Under Article 167 the CCA administers constitutional justice, ensuring the supremacy of the Constitution. From this it follows that:

1. the Constitutional Court is the only judicial body exercising constitutional justice in the Republic of Armenia;
2. no other judicial body may exercise constitutional justice in the Republic of Armenia; and
3. the Constitutional Court of Armenia is not the fourth instance in the system of bodies of judicial power.

Given the above, the most important issue here is to properly delimit authorities between the Constitutional Court and other judicial bodies in interpreting the laws, which are objects of constitutional justice.

According to Article 171 of RA Constitution, the highest court in the country, apart from constitutional justice issues, is the Court of Cassation, which, within the powers established by law and via the review of judicial acts:

1) ensures the uniform application of laws and other normative legal acts; and
2) eliminates fundamental violations of human rights and freedoms.

Under Article 167, the Constitutional Court administers constitutional justice, ensuring supremacy of Constitution. In this way the Constitution clarifies the mission of each judicial body, while granting the authority to ensure the uniform application of laws to Court of Cassation (as a body, administering justice) and the authority to administer constitutional justice to the Constitutional Court.

Thus, in terms of actual constitutional regulations, solution of the presented problem shall be such that any judicial body exercises its law-interpreting function within the scope of its jurisdiction – solely to ensure the fulfillment of its mission. In other words, the initial criterion, specifying the spherical boundary for scope of law interpretation by the above judicial instances, is the goal underlying the basis of their activities. That is, in one case, the Court of Cassation, interpreting the legal provisions, aims to ensure a uniform application of law; in other case, the Constitutional Court performs this function to ensure the administration of constitutional justice, which shall be the basis of self-restriction for activities of these judicial instances[9]. When considering the problem of law interpretation by the CCA from this point of view, we conclude that the Constitutional Court of Armenia may perform this function for disclosing the constitutional-legal content of the law or its relevant provisions and not with the aim of general interpretation of the law[10].

Although one of the tasks for the Court of Cassation is ensuring the uniform application of law, the presented constitutional regulations speak not about an arbitrary document titled as "law", but about a constitutional law. And law, which can be interpreted in several ways, may be considered as constitutional

9 In this context, the viewpoint expressed with regard to the case of Hungary should be noted, according to which these two interpretations ensure fundamentally different functions. The so-called "constitutional requirements" are set within the frames of control of legal norms, while decisions taken for uniform application of laws are aimed at eliminating the conflicting judicial practice (see The relations between the Constitutional Courts and the other national courts, including the interference in this area of the action of the European courts/Report of the Constitutional Court of Republic of Hungary prepared for the XII Congress of the Conference of European Constitutional Courts, http://www.confcoconsteu.org/reports/General%20report-EN.pdf (accessed: November 04, 2017).

10 This is an accepted and frequently used practice in the Federal Constitutional Court of Germany, which discloses the content of legislation just from the constitutional point of view. This interpretation becomes binding for other bodies and has the effect of law. See A. Rainer, *The decisions of the German Federal Constitutional Court and their binding force for ordinary courts*, www.constcourt.gov.az/en/download/.../9.../10.Rainer_Arnold_(eng).doc (accessed: November 04, 2017). The same is true for the Constitutional Court of the Russian Federation and bodies, administering constitutional justice, in many other countries.

only when perceived in the context of relevant constitutional requirements. This, in turn, implies that, in the above cases, interpretation of laws recognized as in compliance with the Constitution shall be used (in this case, the interpretation of the CCA), as it is the task of the body administering constitutional justice, to indicate the legal boundaries for understanding and applying the legal norm, and beyond the boundaries of which, the applied or interpreted norm will lead to unconstitutional results. Consequently, jurisdiction of the Constitutional Court of Armenia on interpreting laws is limited to the above framework and cannot be exercised beyond those boundaries[11].

Meanwhile, we should consider that the above applies to such interpretations, where one of them conflicts with constitutional requirements. However, when courts apply the interpretation of a norm compliant with the Constitution, from the viewpoint of differentiation of jurisdictions, it is ineffective to interpret it by the Constitutional Court differently. Given the above, if the interpretation of a legal norm given by other judicial instances complies with the Constitution, it is expedient for the CCA to apply this interpretation and disclose its constitutional-legal content another way only in the case of conflict between the accepted understanding of the norm and constitutional requirements[12].

---

11 Note the words of the judge of the European Court of Human Rights: "Interpretation of constitutional concepts is among the most important functions of the Constitutional Court, which is used to provide the criteria being important both regarding the constitutional text and constitutional interpretation of laws" (see L. Guerra, *Latent and Manifest Functions of Constitutional Courts*, [in:] Almanac "Constitutional Justice in New Millennium", Yerevan 2011, p. 54.

12 In the Republic of Slovenia, the Constitutional Court interprets the Constitution and general courts interpret the laws – apart from cases of abusing the Constitution. The Constitutional Court may interpret the laws if two different interpretations are possible – one conflicting with Constitution and another (provided in so-called "interpretative resolution" of the Constitutional Court) corresponding to the Constitution. Certainly, such interpretation becomes binding for courts. However, if several interpretations of legal provisions (none of which is unconstitutional) are possible, general courts will independently decide how to apply the norm (see The relations between the Constitutional Courts and the other national courts, including the interference in this area of the action of the European courts/Report of the Constitutional Court of the Republic of Slovenia prepared for the XII Congress of the Conference of European Constitutional Courts, http://www.confcoconsteu.org/reports/Slovenia-EN.pdf (accessed: November 04, 2017).

Thus, the main criteria with regard to the issue under discussion, which will also enable the effective distribution of jurisdictions between different judicial instances, can be summarized as follows:

- the initial criterion, specifying the spherical boundaries for the interpretation of laws by the Constitutional Court of Armenia and other judicial instances, is the purpose of their activities, which should form the basis for self-restriction of activities of the discussed bodies;
- the task of the Court of Cassation is ensuring the uniform application of constitutional law, and not an arbitrary document titled as "law", which assumes an interpretation of law that meets the constitutional requirements;
- the task of the body administering constitutional justice (the CCA) is to indicate, which interpretation of law complies with the Constitution and which does not – in other words, to indicate the legal boundaries for perceiving and applying the legal norm, beyond which the applied or interpreted norm will lead to unconstitutional consequences;
- the Constitutional Court of Armenia may perform this function for disclosing the constitutional-legal content of the law or its relevant provisions, and not with the purpose of general interpretation of the law;
- if a legal norm can be interpreted in several ways and interpretation given by courts is compliant with the Constitution, from the viewpoint of differentiation of jursidictions it is expedient that the Constitutional Court applies this interpretation;
- if a legal norm can be interpreted in several ways and there is a conflict between accepted perception of the norm and constitutional requirements, it is expedient that the body, administering constitutional justice, provides the interpretation consistent with the Constitution while disclosing constitutional-legal content of the norm; and
- taking into account the changes in the RA legislation on types of CCA decisons and bases for revision of judicial acts due to new circumstances and keeping in mind the need to ensure legal predictability, it is expedient to arrange a uniform practice of decision-making by the Constitutional Court in case of the probability of different interpretations of the norm, while applying the "principle of interpretation of law in compliance with the Constitution" and recognizing the legal norm conflicting with the Constitution only in cases, when it cannot be interpreted in the context of constitutional requirements[13].

---

13 See the details in A. Манасян, *Особенности толкования законов при осуществлении конституционного правосудия*, "Евразийский юридический журнал" 2012, № 12 (55), pp. 104–106.

According to Article 169 of the RA Constitution (as amended on December 6, 2015), courts apply to the Constitutional Court of Armenia regarding the constitutionality of a normative legal act applicable in a specific case before them, if they have reasonable doubts on its constitutionality and find that the adjudication of the case is possible only through the application of the regulatory legal act. A similar provision was prescribed in the previous wording of the Constitution and was often applied by courts. Thus, in 2017, Constitutional Court reviewed 4 cases based on appeals of courts. In all four cases, the norms in question were found to be compliant with the RA Constitution within the framework of legal positions reflected in the resolution[14].

Another important aspect of the review of relations between the Constitutional Court and other judicial bodies, is the execution of the decisions of the CCA by other courts and review of judicial acts, following the CCA decisions as a new circumstance, which is described below.

3.5 Constitutional Review Body and Other State Authorities

The relation between the Constitutional Court of Armenia and other state authorities is emphasized from the aspect of the mandatory force of Constitutional court's decisions and their execution. Thus, under Article 170 of the RA Constitution, decisions and opinions of the Constitutional Court are final and come into force upon their promulgation. In its turn, the RA Constitutional Law "On the Constitutional Court" states that the decisions of the Constitutional Court on the substance of the case are mandatory for all state and local self-government bodies and their officials as well as for the natural and legal persons in the whole territory of Armenia.

Also, under Article 169 of Armenia's Constitution, the Prosecutor General may apply to the Constitutional Court in respect of the constitutionality of provisions of regulatory legal acts related to specific proceedings administered by the Prosecutor's office, as well as in the case prescribed by paragraph 11 of Article 168 of the Constitution. This paragraph covers the issue of giving consent for initiating criminal prosecution against a judge of the Constitutional Court or depriving him or her of liberty with respect to the exercise of his or her powers.

Before the amendments, the Constitution stated that Prosecutor General might apply to the Constitutional Court of Armenia on the constitutionality

14 http://concourt.am/armenian/report/statistic/cc_decision_stat2017.pdf (accessed: January 10, 2018).

of provisions of normative acts regarding a specific case pending before the Prosecutor General. By the decision of Constitutional Court DCC-934 dated February 04, 2011, adopted on the basis of the appeal of the Prosecutor General of the RA, the CCA expressed legal positions of crucial importance for the implementation of this authority. In particular, while disclosing the constitutional-legal content of expression "specific case pending before the Prosecutor General", defined in Paragraph 7, Part 1, Article 101 of the RA Constitution, the Constitutional Court of Armenia found that, in the criminal-procedural sense, Armenia's legislation had no concretization of the concept "specific case pending before the Prosecutor General". Therefore, the latter cannot be interpreted on the basis of legal branch methodology, and this concept shall be interpreted within its constitutional meaning, in the framework of constitutional powers granted to the Prosecutor's Office. The Constitutional Court emphasized that the RA Constitution, while recognizing the Prosecutor General as a subject authorized to apply to the Constitutional Court, primarily considered the provision in Part 1, Article 103 of the RA Constitution, according to which, the Prosecutor's Office is a unified system headed by the Prosecutor General. So, in a constitutional-legal sense, the concept "proceeding before the Prosecutor General" is equivalent to the concept "proceeding before the RA Prosecutor's Office". As for the concept "his/her proceeding", the Constitutional Court of Armenia noted that, under the current legislation, pre-trial proceedings are performed by inquiry and preliminary investigation bodies, while Prosecutor's Office oversees the legality of the inquiry and preliminary investigation. During court examination, a court performs the proceedings, while the Prosecutor's Office supports the charge at the court. Based on the RA Law "On Amendments and Additions to the RA Criminal Procedure Code", of November 28, 2007, the Prosecutor General is no longer authorized to perform the preliminary investigation; thus, in this sense, he/she cannot take the case into or perform the proceedings. If the concept "specific case in his/her proceeding", defined by Paragraph 7, Part 1, Article 101 of the RA Constitution, is perceived just in its criminal-procedural sense, it turns out that the exercise of this authority by the Prosecutor General becomes impossible, as, in this view, the Prosecutor General must accept the specific case into his/her proceeding and act as a body, conducting the proceedings, which is beyond his/her authority. Following the above, the Constitutional Court of Armenia found that, when interpreting the concept "specific case in his/her proceeding" defined by Paragraph 7, Part 1, Article 101 of the RA Constitution, it is necessary to consider the constitutional-legal meaning of this concept – based on the content of constitutional authorities of the Prosecutor's Office prescribed by Article 103 of the RA Constitution. The Constitutional Court emphasized that broader interpretation of the concept "his/her proceeding" implies that the latter refers to all cases, where at a particular stage just this body is authorized to adopt the final legal act on the case. While recognizing the Prosecutor General as a subject authorized to appeal to the CCA within the frames of concrete control, the RA Constitution considers "specific case" (in its constitutional-legal sense) as the exercise of powers by Prosecutor's Office – in all cases, where this body is authorized for final decision within its constitutional functions[15].

Obviously, exactly those legal positions formed the basis for further development in the practice of appeals from the Prosecutor General to the CCA and amendments of the above constitutional provisions.

4 Structure of the Constitutional Review Body

4.1 The Legal Status of Constitutional Court Judges

Under Article 165 of the RA Constitution, a lawyer with higher education, having attained the age of forty, holding citizenship of only the Republic of Armenia, having the right of suffrage, with high professional qualities and at least fifteen years of professional work experience may be elected as a judge of the Constitutional Court. The Constitution also requires that candidates for judges must have command of the Armenian language. The Law on the Constitutional Court of Armenia may set additional requirements to candidates for judges. The Constitutional Law on the CCA has set such an additional requirement – namely, high moral qualities.

Under Article 164 of the Constitution, a judge, while administering justice, shall be independent, impartial, and shall act according to the Constitution and laws only. The judge cannot be held liable for an opinion expressed during the administration of justice or adopted judicial act – unless there is evidence of a crime or disciplinary offense.

An important change in the status of a judge of the Constitutional Court introduced in the 2015 amendments to the Constitution was functional immunity for a judge of the CCA[16], so that criminal prosecution against a judge of this institution, due to exercise of his/her powers, can be initiated only with consent of the Constitutional Court. A judge of the CCA may not be deprived of liberty, with respect to the exercise of his or her powers, without the consent of the

---

15 See http://concourt.am/russian/decisions/common/pdf/934.pdf (accessed: January 10, 2018).

16 This provision just came into force and has not been applied yet.

Constitutional Court, except where he or she has been caught at the time of or immediately after committing a criminal offense[17]. In this case, deprivation of liberty may not last more than seventy-two hours. The Chair of the Constitutional Court of Armenia shall be immediately notified of the deprivation of liberty of any of its judges.

A judge may not hold any position not related to his or her status in other state or local self-government bodies, any position in commercial organizations, or engage in entrepreneurial activities or perform other paid work, except for scientific, educational and creative work. The Law on the Constitutional Court of Armenia and the Judicial Code may prescribe additional incompatibility requirements. A judge may not engage in political activities.

According to the Constitution of Armenia[18], the powers of a judge shall discontinue upon expiry of the term of powers thereof, in cases of loss of citizenship of the Republic of Armenia or acquisition of citizenship of another State, entry into force of a criminal judgment of conviction rendered against him or her, termination of criminal prosecution on non-acquitting grounds, entry into force of a civil judgment on declaring him or her as having no active legal capacity, as missing or dead, or in the case of his or her resignation or death. In cases of violation of incompatibility requirements, engaging in political activities, impossibility of holding office for health reasons, in case of committing essential disciplinary violation the powers of a CCA judge shall be terminated upon the decision of the Constitutional Court[19].

The 2015 constitutional amendments introduced disciplinary liability for judges of the CCA – based on the appeal of at least three CCA judges[20].

As noted above, issues of terminating the powers of a Constitutional Court judge (based on appeal of the National Assembly) and giving consent to the initiation of criminal prosecution against a CCA judge or his/her deprivation of liberty due to exercise of his/her powers (based on appeal of the Prosecutor General) are also resolved by the CCA.

Article 164 of the RA Constitution provides that the remuneration of a judge shall be determined in compliance with his or her high status and responsibility. The amount of remuneration of a judge shall be prescribed by law.

17 No such case has yet been reviewed by the RA CC.
18 Article 164.
19 No such case has yet been reviewed by the RA CC.
20 This provision just came into force and has not been applied yet.

The Constitutional Law on the CCA establishes details regarding the status of judges of the Constitutional Court, providing that if the powers of a judge of the CCA discontinue due to the expiry of his/her term of office, or due to physical defect/illness (found after his/her appointment) preventing the further exercise of his/her powers as a judge, or the coming into force of a civil judgment declaring him or her as having no active legal capacity, the judge shall be granted a pension – in an amount and manner defined by the RA Law "On Social Guarantees of Persons Holding Public Offices".

4.2 Functions of the Constitutional Review Body

Under Article 167 of the RA Constitution, the powers of the Constitutional Court shall be prescribed by the Constitution, whereas the Constitution and the Law on the CCA shall prescribe the procedure for the formation and rules of operation of the CCA.

Under Article 168, the Constitutional Court of Armenia, as prescribed by the Constitutional Law on the CCA of the Republic of Armenia, shall:

(1) determine the compliance of laws, decisions of the National Assembly, decrees and executive orders of the President of the Republic, decisions of the Government and the Prime Minister, and secondary regulatory legal acts with the Constitution;
(2) prior to the adoption of draft amendments to the Constitution, as well as draft legal acts put to referendum, determine the compliance thereof with the Constitution;
(3) prior to the ratification of an international treaty, determine the compliance of the commitments enshrined therein with the Constitution;
(4) settle disputes arising between constitutional bodies with respect to the constitutional powers thereof;
(5) settle disputes related to decisions adopted upon the results of a referendum, those of the elections of the National Assembly and President of the Republic;
(6) render a decision on termination of the powers of a Deputy;
(7) render an opinion on the existence of grounds for removing the President of the Republic from office;
(8) render a decision on the impossibility of exercising the powers of the President of the Republic;
(9) decide on the issue of subjecting a judge of the Constitutional Court to disciplinary liability;
(10) decide on termination of the powers of a judge of the Constitutional Court;

(11) decide on giving consent for initiating criminal prosecution against a judge of the CCA or depriving him or her of liberty with respect to the exercise of his or her powers; and
(12) render a decision, in the cases prescribed by law, on suspending or prohibiting the activities of a political party.

Article 169 of RA Constitution determines who may appeal to the Constitutional Court of Armenia on the above issues. In particular, according to the Constitution:

1. The following may apply to the CCA:
   (1) the National Assembly — in the cases prescribed by point 12 of Article 168 of the Constitution, and in the case prescribed by point 7 of Article 168 of the Constitution upon the decision adopted by majority of votes of the total number of Deputies, whereas in the case prescribed by point 10 of Article 168 of the Constitution upon the decision adopted by at least three-fifths of votes of the total number of Deputies;
   (2) at least one-fifth of the total number of Deputies — in the cases prescribed by points 1, 4 and 6 of Article 168 of the Constitution[21];
   (3) a faction of the National Assembly — in respect of disputes related to decisions adopted upon the results of a referendum and those of the election of the President of the Republic[22];
   (4) the President of the Republic — in the cases prescribed by part 1 of Article 129, part 2 of Article 139, Article 150, as well as points 1 and 4 of Article 168 of the Constitution[23];
   (5) the Government — in the cases prescribed by points 1, 4, 8 and 12 of Article 168 of the Constitution;
   (6) the Supreme Judicial Council — in the cases prescribed by point 4 of Article 168 of the Constitution[24];

21 Compared to the National Assembly, which did not use this opportunity, in 2006–2017, one fifth of the total number of deputies applied to the Constitutional Court 11 times.

22 This provision was defined in the result of the constitutional reform of 2015, just came into force and has not yet been applied.

23 The President has applied to the Constitutional Court quite often. However, in most cases, his applications did not refer to the constitutionality of normative acts, but to determining the compliance of obligations enshrined in international treaties prior to ratification with the Constitution. As noted above, this authority is an expression of mandatory prior constitutional review.

24 This provision was defined in the result of the constitutional reform of 2015, just came into force and has not yet been applied.

(7) local self-government bodies — with regard to compliance with the Constitution of regulatory legal acts listed in point 1 of Article 168 of the Constitution, violating their constitutional rights, as well as in the cases prescribed by point 4 of Article 168 of the Constitution[25];
(8) everyone — under a specific case where the final act of court is available, all judicial remedies have been exhausted, and he or she challenges the constitutionality of the relevant provision of a regulatory legal act applied against him or her upon this act, which has led to the violation of his or her basic rights and freedoms enshrined in Chapter 2 of the Constitution, taking into account also the interpretation of the respective provision in law enforcement practice[26];
(9) the Prosecutor General — in respect of the constitutionality of provisions of regulatory legal acts related to specific proceedings administered by the Prosecutor's office, as well as in the case prescribed by point 11 of Article 168 of the Constitution;
(10) the Human Rights Defender — in respect of the compliance of the regulatory legal acts listed in point 1 of Article 168 of the Constitution with the provisions of Chapter 2 of the Constitution[27];
(11) political parties or alliances of political parties having participated in the elections to the National Assembly — in respect of disputes related to decisions adopted upon the results of elections to the National Assembly;
(12) candidates for the President of the Republic — in respect of disputes related to decisions adopted upon the results of election of the President of the Republic[28]; and

---

25 No local self-government body has so far applied to the CC.
26 Since the provision enabling individual complaints, most cases regarding the constitutionality of normative acts were reviewed on the basis of such applications.
27 In 2006–2017, the human rights defender applied to the RA CC 44 times. Based on these applications and relevant decisions of the CC, conditions for restoring the constitutional human rights were created.
28 Since its establishment, the RA CC has reviewed 44 electoral disputes. By its decisions, elections or decision of the relevant electoral commission made in the result of elections to the RA National Assembly by the majority system were recognized invalid 8 times. In other cases, decisions of the electoral commission remained in force. However, in decisions of reviewing decisions made by results of elections (President of Republic and National Assembly), legal positions expressed by the CC were crucial for development of constitutional culture and electoral law.

(13) at least three judges of the Constitutional Court — in the case prescribed by point 9 of Article 168 of the Constitution[29].

2. The National Assembly shall, in the cases prescribed by point 2 of Article 168 of the Constitution, apply to the Constitutional Court in respect of amendments to the Constitution, membership in supranational international organizations, or territorial changes. The authorized representative of a popular initiative shall apply to the Constitutional Court with regard to the issue of a draft law put to referendum upon popular initiative[30].
3. In the case prescribed by point 3 of Article 168 of the Constitution, the Government shall apply to the Constitutional Court[31].
4. Courts shall apply to the CCA in respect of the constitutionality of the regulatory legal act applicable in a specific case they are seized of, if they have reasonable doubts on the constitutionality thereof and find that the adjudication of the case is possible only through the application of the regulatory legal act.
5. In the case prescribed by point 6 of Article 168 of the Constitution, the Council of the National Assembly shall apply to the Constitutional Court[32].
6. The details related to the procedure for applying to the CCA shall be prescribed by the Law on the Constitutional Court.
7. The CCA shall examine a case only in case of availability of the relevant application.

Under the RA Constitutional Law on the CCA, appeal to the Constitutional Court is submitted in writing and signed by the authorized person. The appeal may also be submitted in electronic form. The appeal shall indicate: Constitutional Court of Armenia, as the body of appeal; name, address (legal address) of the applicant; required data of the applicant's representatives, if any; article of the Constitution authorizing the right of appeal to the CCA; request submitted to the Constitutional Court and justification of the applicant, with link to the relevant norms of the Constitution; in cases defined by Paragraphs 1, 5, Article 168 of the Constitution – the name of the state/local

29 This provision was defined in the result of the constitutional reform of 2015, just came into force and has not yet been applied.

30 This provision was defined in the result of the constitutional reform of 2015, just came into force and has not yet been applied.

31 As mentioned above, prior to constitutional reform, this authority belonged to the President of the Republic.

32 This provision was defined in the result of the constitutional reform of 2015, just came into force and has not yet been applied.

self-government body or their officials who adopted the disputable act; list of materials attached to appeal, if any.

4.3 Objects of Constitutional Review

The professional literature differentiates the concepts of comprehensive and limited constitutional review based on the objects of constitutional justice. In case of comprehensive review, all normative legal acts are covered by the judicial constitutional review. At limited review, their range is limited. As a rule, comprehensive review is typical for the American system of constitutional justice, and limited review for the European system.

According to the RA Constitution (as amended on December 6, 2015), judicial constitutional review covers laws; resolutions of the National Assembly; decrees and orders of the President of the Republic; resolutions of Government and Prime Minister; sub-legislative normative legal acts; draft amendments to the Constitution; draft legal acts submitted to referendum; obligations enshrined by international treaties subject to ratification by the RA; disputes between constitutional bodies arising from their constitutional powers; disputes on decisions adopted upon the results of a referendum, elections to the National Assembly, elections of the President of the Republic; issue of termination of the powers of a deputy; the issue of the existence of grounds for removing the President of the Republic from office; the issue of the impossibility for the President of the Republic to exercise his/her powers; the issue of subjecting a Constitutional Court judge to disciplinary liability; the issue of terminating the powers of a Constitutional Court judge; the issue of giving consent to initiation of criminal prosecution against a Constitutional Court judge or depriving him/her of liberty with respect to the exercise of his/her powers; and the issue of suspending or prohibiting the activities of a party.

In 2015, the range of objects of constitutional justice was significantly expanded. Thus, sub-legislative normative legal acts, draft amendments to the Constitution, draft legal acts submitted to referendum, disputes between constitutional bodies arising due to their constitutional powers, the issue of terminating the powers of a deputy, and the issue of subjecting a CCA judge to disciplinary liability became objects of constitutional justice, which will certainly lead to more effective system of administration of constitutional justice[33].

33 In 2015, at the initiative of the President of the Republic, extensive changes were made in the RA Constitution regarding all constitutional institutes. At that time, changes in the Constitution could be made only via referendum initiated by the President of the Republic or the National Assembly. The President established a Professional

Under the new constitutional regulations, citizens can appeal to the CCA under a specific case where the final act of court is available, all judicial remedies have been exhausted, where the appellant challenges the constitutionality of the relevant provision of a regulatory legal act applied against him or her upon this act, leading to the violation of his or her basic rights and freedoms enshrined in Chapter 2 of the Constitution, taking into account also the interpretation of the respective provision in law enforcement practice. The Prosecutor General can apply to the CCA in respect of the constitutionality of provisions of regulatory legal acts related to specific proceedings administered by the Prosecutor's office, as well as in the case prescribed by point 11 of Article 168 of the Constitution. The courts may apply to the CCA in respect of the constitutionality of the regulatory legal act applicable in a specific case before them, if they have reasonable doubts on its constitutionality and find that the adjudication of the case is possible only through the application of the regulatory legal act.

Following the constitutional reform of 2015, Article 205 of the RA Constitution prescribes that issues related to the accession by the RA to supranational international organizations, as well as those related with territorial changes of the RA shall be resolved through referenda, which means that the constitutionality of the mentioned drafts submitted to referendum will also be reviewed by the Constitutional Court. In this respect, Article 169 of the RA Constitution states that the National Assembly shall apply to the CCA on issues related to amendments to the Constitution, accession to supranational international organizations or territorial changes.

4.4 Preliminary and Posterior Review of Legal Norms

The preliminary and posterior reviews of legal acts are distinguished, based on the time factor. Preliminary review assumes that, prior to coming into force, the legal act becomes an object of constitutional justice, in order to prevent potential unconstitutional situations. In this case, two options are possible: 1. a draft legal act becomes an object of constitutional justice; or 2. an already adopted, but unsigned legal act, which has not come into force yet.

Commission for Constitutional Reforms that proposed all the above changes, and provided the relevant professional justification. The President approved the proposed constitutional reforms and draft changes, and they were adopted at a nationwide referendum.

Before the 2015 amendments to the RA Constitution there was just a preliminary review of obligations enshrined in international treaties subject to ratification by the RA.

This is an example of mandatory preliminary constitutional review. Thus, Article 116 of the RA Constitution defines that international treaties contradicting the Constitution may not be ratified. Therefore, prior to ratification of an international treaty, CCA shall review the mentioned issue and, only in case of positive decision, may the National Assembly ratify the treaty. Compared to previous constitutional regulations, according to which, the President of the Republic applied to the CCA on the noted issue, the 2015 wording of the Constitution established that the Government is subject of appeal to the CCA[34].

Following the 2015 constitutional reform, there is also provision for preliminary review for some other legal acts. Article 168 of the RA Constitution (as amended on December 6, 2015), defines that the Constitutional Court shall, prior to the adoption of draft amendments to the Constitution, as well as draft legal acts put to referendum, determine their compliance with the Constitution. Under Article 169 of the Constitution, the National Assembly applies to the Constitutional Court on issues related to amendments to the Constitution, accession to supranational international organizations, or territorial change. For a draft law submitted to referendum as a civil initiative, the authorized representative of civil initiative applies to the Constitutional Court.

Preliminary review is also expressed in Article 129 of the Constitution, according to which, the President of the Republic shall sign and promulgate a law adopted by the National Assembly within a period of twenty-one days, or shall apply within the same time period to the Constitutional Court for the purpose of determining the compliance of the law with the Constitution. If the CCA decides that the law complies with the Constitution, the President of the Republic shall sign and promulgate the law within a period of five days. If the President of the Republic fails to fulfill the requirements prescribed by this Article, the Chairperson of the National Assembly shall sign and promulgate the law within a period of five days.

Evidently, like in other constitutional systems, in Armenia, the posterior review of legal acts prevails. The purpose of posterior review is to ensure the constitutionality of legal acts during their application, primarily to ensure the constitutional harmony and stability of changing social relations.

---

34 Article 169, RA Constitution.

Posterior review also enables deep accounting for features of law enforcement practice. Thus, according to Article 169 of the RA Constitution, a citizen can apply to the Constitutional Court under a specific case where a final act of court is available, all other judicial remedies having been exhausted, where he or she challenges the constitutionality of the relevant provision of a regulatory legal act applied against him or her that has led to the violation of his or her basic rights and freedoms enshrined in Chapter 2 of the Constitution, taking into account also the interpretation of the respective provision in law enforcement practice. In its turn, Article 69 of the RA Constitutional Law on the CCA states that, where the Constitutional Court finds the provisions of the law applied against the applicant as null and contradicting the Constitution, or when the CCA recognizes its conformity with the Constitution but finds that the provision was applied to him/her in a different interpretation, the final judicial act made against the applicant is subject to review on the grounds of new circumstances in accordance with the procedure prescribed by law.

4.5 Legal Norm Control Procedure

The procedure of reviewing cases at the Constitutional Court of Armenia is set by the RA Constitutional Law on the CCA, and by the CCA Rules of Procedure. Under Article 169 of the RA Constitution, the Constitutional Court of Armenia reviews cases only after a relevant application.

According to the RA Constitutional Law on the CCA, an application submitted to the CCA must be registered. It is then submitted to the Chair of the CCA.

The case is admitted for review, unless there are legal grounds for rejection. By its decision to admit the case for review, the Constitutional Court also resolves the issues of involving the defendant party, starting the case review, appointing a rapporteur, the procedure of the case hearing, and other matters related to case preparation for review. Parties to proceeding are notified of the CCA's decision within three days.

The Constitutional Court of Armenia makes a procedural decision on a full or partial rejection to review the case:

1) if issues raised in the application are beyond its jurisdiction;
2) if the applicant is not authorized to appeal to the CCA on the case;
3) if the CCA's decision is available on the issue raised in any application submitted on cases indicated in Paragraphs 1–5, Article 168 of the Constitution;
4) if the case regarding the subject of application is reviewed at the Constitutional Court on the basis of another application;

5) if the legal act or its provision is no longer valid and has not been applied/not applicable; and
6) in other cases defined by Article 69 of the Law.

The appealing party may withdraw the appeal presented to the Constitutional Court before the beginning of the case review, except when the application is the obligation of the applicant. Withdrawal of application, on the basis of which the case was admitted for review, may be rejected by the Constitutional Court, if it finds that case review on the subject of application is in the interests of the society or state – except for cases defined by the Law, in which withdrawal of the application leads to termination of case review.

By the initiative of the applicant or the Constitutional Court itself, after the case is admitted, the CCA may suspend the application of the legal act, the constitutionality of which is challenged, if the absence of such a suspension can cause irretrievable or harmful consequences to one of the parties or the society.

The Constitutional Court shall review cases during its sessions. Each case is reviewed in a separate session of the Court. The CCA session is convened and chaired by the Chair.

The Chair and reporter(s) of the Constitutional Court define the circle of persons to be invited in the Court session. Copies of applications and other documents obtained during case preparation for review are sent to judges of the CCA, parties, and, if needed, to invited persons – as decided by the Chair.

At the Constitutional Court, cases are reviewed both under verbal and written procedure, in accordance with the law.

Before the start of the case review only cases referring to the same issue can be combined by a decision of the CCA.

The CCA and the rapporteur with regard to the case preparation for review and with the knowledge of the Chair of the CCA, are entitled to request the documents, data, and other materials from state/local self-government bodies and their officials, assign the expertise (except for expertise on legal issues), and request from individuals and legal entities the materials in their possession. The requirements shall be implemented within the period set by the CCA or rapporteur.

The evidences of the case are the data acquired by the procedure stipulated in the Law, based on which the Court determines the existence or absence of the facts that can be grounds for the requests and arguments of the parties of the trial. According to law, these data can be obtained via: 1) explanations of witnesses; 2) expert opinion; 3) written documents, materials, objects (written and material evidence), including formal certificates and other data obtained from state bodies or local self-government bodies; 4) explanations given by parties to the proceedings, as witnesses. The parties are not entitled to destroy/hide any evidence or otherwise prevent its study and evaluation, while making the collection/presenting of evidence impossible or difficult.

Parties may appear before the Court personally or through their representatives. As an *ex officio* representative of the party in the Constitutional Court there may be present the head of the applicant body, the head of the body that adopts the arguable act, a person appointed in the manner prescribed by RA Constitutional Law "Rules of National Assembly". The authorized person of a party can act as its representative in the CCA if he/she is an official of the party or is an advocate or has a higher legal education and whose authorities are confirmed by the order prescribed by Law. A party before the CCA shall have no more than three representatives.

When judges of the Constitutional Court enter the courtroom, present persons must rise; then the Chair invites them to take their seats. Deviation from this rule is only possible with permission of the Court. In due time, the Chair, having ascertained the presence of a quorum, opens the session and informs about the case to be reviewed. The Chair verifies the attendance of the parties to the proceedings and invited persons, checks the authorities of party representatives, and raises for discussion the question of whether the review of the case is possible. If the Court finds review of the case impossible, the Chair adjourns the proceedings and clarifies the rights and obligations of the parties present. Parties to the proceedings and invited persons must refer to the Court as "High Court", while standing during their explanations, clarifications or answers. Deviation from this rule is only possible with permission of the CCA.

The case review begins with the rapporteur's report. Judges of the Constitutional Court may ask questions to rapporteur. Following the rapporteur's report, the Court hears the opinions of the judges and proposals of the parties on the procedure of studying the case materials, while making a procedural decision with this regard. The Court can decide to change the procedure for studying the case materials. Proposals of judges on the procedure for studying the materials in the course of case review are discussed immediately.

The Constitutional Court of Armenia may suspend the case proceeding if:

1) an examination is assigned;
2) the CCA gives a judicial assignment;
3) necessary evidence shall be requested from other bodies or individuals;

4) any party of the trial requested the suspension of the case because of illness or any other valid reason; or
5) in other cases based on the justified procedural decision of the CCA.

All sessions of the CCA are recorded. The Presiding Member and the recording person shall sign the minutes of the session. The parties may get acquainted with the minutes and provide their comments, which are attached to the minute.

Constitutional Court issues its decision on the case or provides its opinion in closed Court session, which may be attended only by judges of CCA involved in the proceeding on the case. During this session, the attending judges may express their opinions on the issues under discussion or state their position on case resolution. There is no limit on the number and duration of session reports. The results of roll-call votes are not subject to disclosure. The session lasts until the Court adopts a decision or provides an opinion (excluding rest time and breaks). Till the CCA has adopted a decision at the CCA session, the judges must avoid disclosure of any data related to the decision.

The case proceedings are terminated by the Constitutional Court:

1) at any stage of case review, upon finding the legal grounds for rejection to review the case defined by Law;
2) if the legal act or its provision, the conformity of which to Constitution is disputed, was canceled or became invalid prior to or during the case review and was not applied;
3) in cases defined by Articles 75, 79, 80, 82–85 of the Law; and
4) in cases defined by Paragraph 5, Part 1, Article 56 of the Law, when grounds for suspension have not disappeared within a year since the decision to suspend the proceeding and the there are no prospects of resumption.

The principles of case review at the Constitutional Court include: clarification of case facts *ex officio*, collegiality, equality and publicity.

Constitutional proceedings are conducted in Armenian. Parties to the proceedings may speak at Court in their preferred language – upon provision of translation into Armenian. The Court provides free interpreter services for parties to the proceedings not speaking Armenian at the expense covered by the state budget, if they prove the lack of money for paid interpretation.

4.6 Individual Complaint as a Tool for Legal Norm Review

Under Article 3 of the RA Constitution, the human being is the highest value in the Republic of Armenia. The inalienable dignity of the human being constitutes the integral basis of his or her rights and freedoms. The public power has a duty to respect and protect the human and citizens' rights and freedoms. The public power is restricted by the basic rights and freedoms of the human being and the citizen as a directly applicable law.

Respect/protection of fundamental rights and freedoms are not limited just to their constitutional entrenchment. They depend on many other factors, including guarantees for protection of these rights. Protection via constitutional justice is one of the most important ways to protect fundamental rights and freedoms.

International practice notes two types of fundamental rights protection via constitutional justice – direct and indirect. In first case, citizens can apply to the Constitutional Court for protection of their fundamental rights and freedoms. In second case, protection of fundamental rights and freedoms is indirectly covered as part of exercising the other Constitutional Court powers – e.g., based on applications of courts, ombudsman, within the abstract normative control, etc.[35]

However, protection of human rights is nowadays among the key issues of constitutional justice, which can be successfully implemented primarily, *via* an individual complaint to the Constitutional Court.

Judicial constitutional review ensures the dual function – on the one hand, fundamental constitutional human rights and freedoms are protected; on the other hand, constitutionality of social relations is protected.

Initially, the RA Constitution (in its wording of July 5, 1995) was missing the institute of individual constitutional complaint: within the frames of constitutional justice fundamental constitutional human rights and freedoms could be protected only indirectly.

Following the constitutional reforms of 2005, the RA Constitution was amended so that any person could apply to the Constitutional Court on a particular case, when final judicial act is available, all other means of judicial protection are exhausted, and the constitutionality of a provision of a normative legal act is disputed. Later on, the RA Law on the CCA of 2006 made detailed regulations on case review on the basis of individual complaints.

The 2015 constitutional reform made significant changes to the constitutional regulations for individual constitutional complaints. Now, under Article 169, any person can appeal to the CCA on a particular case, when the final act of court is available, all other judicial remedies have been exhausted, and he or she challenges the constitutionality of the relevant provision of a regulatory legal

35 CDL-AD(2010)039rev//Study on Individual Access to Constitutional Justice, Adopted by the Venice Commission at its 85th Plenary Session (Venice, 17–18 December 2010), http://www.venice.coe.int/WebForms/documents/default.aspx?pdffile=CDL-AD(2010)039rev-e (accessed: December 20, 2017).

act applied against him or her upon this act, that has led to the violation of his or her basic rights and freedoms enshrined in Chapter 2 of the Constitution, taking into account also the interpretation of the respective provision in law enforcement practice.

The above proves that institute of individual constitutional complaint was substantially changed following the constitutional reform of 2015.

Individual complaint may be used as a basis for challenging the constitutionality of not just laws, but also other normative acts. This is one of the most important steps in reforming this institution, as constitutional human rights and freedoms are most commonly violated by sub-legislative legal acts, which the CCA has repeatedly noted.

The constitutionality of these acts may be disputed if their application has led to a violation of the fundamental rights and freedoms set in Chapter 2 of Constitution. The interpretation of the relevant provision given in law-enforcement practice is considered as well. Article 69 of the RA Constitutional Law on the CCA, in its turn, states that in the result of considering individual applications in the cases on recognizing the provisions of the law applied against the applicant as null and contradicting the Constitution, or when the CCA recognized it to be in conformity with the Constitution but found simultaneously that the provision was applied to the applicant in a different interpretation, the final judicial act made against the applicant is subject to review on the grounds of new circumstances in accordance with the procedure prescribed by law.

The introduction of individual constitutional complaint, following the constitutional reform of 2005, became one of the most important factors for effective development of the constitutional justice system and constitutionalization of social relations in the Republic of Armenia. Since then, most cases on constitutionality of relevant legal acts are reviewed in response to applications from citizens[36].

5 Legal Nature and Legal Force of Decisions of the Constitutional Review Body

Formal certainty is among the most important features of positive law. The essence of this is that legal norms are objectified, expressed, and contained in one form or another, which is the main prerequisite and means for their existance. Without this, legal norms become abstract, non-existent in reality, and unable to fulfill the mission of regulating social relations.

36 www.concourt.am (accessed: January 10, 2018).

In legal literature, sources of law (in formal/legal sense) are presented as official way for external expression of behavioral rules forming the content of law, which mostly contributes to achieving the goals of legal regulation and full implementation of law[37]. In other words, form of law is a way of internal organization and external expression of law[38].

The legal literature has no unambiguous opinion as to whether the decisions of Constitutional Court are the source of law in the formal sense (or in the form of which specific source they are expressed)[39].

Are decisions of Constitutional Court the result of a law-making activity? Do they form sources of law? Do CCA decisions create legal norms? In legal literature, law-making activity is characterized as the activity of competent bodies and organizations implemented on the basis of law and aimed at the development of normative-legal acts[40]. This covers not only the drafting of laws, but also any activity that meets those requirements.

The concept for the separation of powers prescribes that the body with the legislative power adopts laws[41], but this does not prohibit other bodies with the necessary powers exercising law-making functions[42]. So, although the adoption of laws rests with the body exercising legislative power, the adoption of laws and

---

37 Օհանյան Վ. Իրավունքի աղբյուրների հիմնախնդիրը ՀՀ-ում *(տեսագործնական վերլուծություն)*, Առենախոսություն, Երևան. 2009, p. 47.

38 See M. H. Марченко, *Источники права*, Moscow 2008, p. 40.

39 In this context the concept of the "Constitutional Court decision" is used for decisions on the substance of the case made as a result of the exercise of the authority defined in Paragraph 1, Article 168 of RA Constitution.

40 B. M. Лазарев (ed.), *Общая теория государства и права*, Moscow 2007, p. 200.

41 In the legal literature the separation of powers is absolutized, in particular, when the field of activity for legislative power is limited to "purely" law-making functions, respectively, for judicial power – to purely judicial functions. As shown by experience of other countries, successfully using the separation of powers for a long time, real life has no such strict, rigid, initially defined separation of activities and functions for various branches of government. It is so in theory, but not in practice, not in real life. See *M. H. Марченко, Источники права …*, p. 387 (about this, see also G. Danielian, *Modern problems of commenting the separation of powers,* "Constitutional Justice: Bulletin of Conference of Constitutional Review Bodies in Countries with Young Democracy" 2007, No. 4 (38), pp. 50–61.

42 See Г. Арутюнян, М. Баглай, *Конституционное право: Энциклопедический словарь*, Moscow 2006, pp. 184–185.

law making are not identical concepts, and the adoption of laws is just a type of law-making activity[43].

The activity of the CCA is actually a law making activity, being the function of a competent authority implemented on the basis of law and aimed at the development of legal acts.

On the question of whether the CCA creates legal norms via its decision-making, it should be noted that, under Part 1, Article 2 of the RA Law "On Normative Legal Acts", a normative legal act is a written legal act adopted by the people of the Republic of Armenia, as well as by bodies and officials defined by the Constitution, containing mandatory behavioral rules for an unspecified number of people. At the same time, Part 4, Article 61 of the RA Constitutional Law on the CCA prescribes that the decisions of the CCA on the substance of the case are mandatory for all state and local self-government bodies and their officials as well as for the natural and legal persons in the whole territory of the Republic of Armenia. So the Constitutional Court adopts normative decisions, thus creating legal norms; therefore, decisions of this body on the substance of the case are of normative nature. Moreover, it is obvious that these decisions adopted as a result of Court's activities are an official mode of expression of the law.

Considering the above, we conclude that the decisions of the Constitutional Court of Armenia are an official way for external expression of behavioral rules forming the content of law, which mostly contributes to achieving the goals of legal regulation and full implementation of law. In other words, this is a way for internal organization and external expression of law – i.e., a source of law in Armenia[44].

---

43 Types of law-making activity also include sub-legislative law making, law-making activities of local self-government bodies, judicial bodies, etc. (see, for example, В. М. Лазарева (ed.), *Общая теория государства и права* ..., pp. 200–201, А. Н. Головистикова, Ю. А. Дмитриев, *Проблемы теории государства и права*, Moscow 2005, pp. 458–461).

44 At the present stage of the development of constitutional law, this position is widespread (see G. Arutyunyan *Features of Constitutional Court functioning in terms of social transformation*, [in:] Report at International Scientific Conference in Dushanbe on November 04, 2010, http://concourt.am/russian/speeches/index.htm, (accessed November 04, 2017), N. Bondar, *Constitutional justice as universal institute for resolving the social conflicts of modern society*, "Constitutional Justice: Bulletin of Conference of Constitutional Review Bodies in Countries with Young Democracy" 2007, No 1 (35), pp. 13–14, B. Strashun, *RF Constitutional Court decisions as source of law*, "Constitutional Justice: Bulletin of Conference of Constitutional Review Bodies in Countries with Young Democracy" 2001, No 4 (14); 2001 – 2002, No 1 (15), p. 154).

In legal literature, the Constitutional Court is seen as a negative legislator[45] because legal acts adopted by the legislator lose their legal force following the CCA's decision. We do not share this opinion. The recognition of legal acts conflicting with the Constitution and therefore invalid is not the only type of decision made by the CCA. A practice is widespread when acts are recognized as compliant with the Constitution (including within the frames of legal positions of CCA) and keep exercising their function of regulation of social relations. So, in case of following the same logic the same could be said of the legislative power, as it not just adopts legal acts (being a "positive legislator"), but quite often amends them or recognizes invalid (being a "negative legislator").

Moreover, modern trends of the development of the theory and practice of constitutional justice show that, quite often, the CCA recognizes a legal act as compliant with the Constitution, while disclosing its constitutional-legal content (just within the frames of which the act may comply with Constitution, hence, it cannot be interpreted or applied otherwise, as that would conflict with legal positions expressed in the decision)[46], or, while recognizing the act compliant with Constitution, simultaneously expresses the legal position on expedience of concrete legal regulations in terms of constitutionality[47]. It is just such cases that

Moreover, the Constitutional Court of Lithuania's expressed legal position, according to which, acts of the Constitutional Court form the sources of law (see Ruling No. 21/2003 of Constitutional Court of Republic of Lithuania, 30 May 2003, http://www.lrkt.lt/dokumentai/2003/r030530.htm, application date: December 20, 2017).

45 See, for example, N. Chronowski, T. Drinóczi, T. Takács (eds.), *Governmental Systems of Central and Eastern European States*, Warszawa 2011, p. 801, I. Macejkova, *Influence of Constitutional Court of Slovak Republic on monism of Slovak Legal System*, "Constitutional Justice: Bulletin of Conference of Constitutional Review Bodies in Countries with Young Democracy" 2009. No. 1 (43), p. 77.

46 In the RA CC decision DCC-984 of July 15, 2011, Part 1, Article 426.9 of the RA Criminal Procedure Code and Article 204.38 of the RA Civil Procedure Code were found compliant with the Constitution, but within the constitutional-legal content, excluding the legal force of judicial act, which applied the norm recognized invalid and conflicting with the RA Constitution. Meanwhile, in operative part of the decision, the Constitutional Court stated that, in law-enforcement practice, Part 1, Article 426.9 of the RA Criminal Procedure Code and Article 204.38 of the RA Civil Procedure Code cannot be interpreted/applied in a different way, conflicting with their constitutional-legal content expressed in the above Decision (see http://concourt.am/russian/decisions/common/pdf/984.pdf (accessed: November 04, 2017).

47 In the RA CC decision DCC-984 of July 15, 2011 the CC emphasized "the need for deep reassessment of the entire methodology on judicial act revision on the basis of new circumstances, while finding that legal regulation of this institute shall be based

emphasize the essence of activity of the body, exercising constitutional justice, as, at the present stage of the development of the doctrine of constitutional law, the discussed decisions are no longer perceived just as documents, establishing the constitutionality or unconstitutionality of legal acts, but rather the main emphasis is on the fact that these decisions are important means of forming the uniform constitutional doctrine and development of Constitution[48]. So, given the above, to our mind, the claim that the CCA is unambiguously a negative legislator is unacceptable[49].

Now in which specific source of law do the decisions of the Constitutional Court appear? This mostly depends on the status and place of the CCA in the legal system of Armenia. The provisions on the Constitutional Court are defined in Chapter 7 of the Constitution (as amended on December 6, 2015) entitled "Courts and the Supreme Judicial Council", Article 167 of which states that the CCA administers constitutional justice, while ensuring the supremacy of the Constitution. Thus, the Court is in the system of judicial authorities, due to which, some legal experts come to the conclusion that the CCA's decisions (being a type of judicial acts) are expressed in the form of precedent as a source of law. However, in our opinion, this position cannot be unambiguous, as in order to

---

on obligation of the state to protect human fundamental rights and freedoms set by Article 3 of the RA Constitution – in accordance with principles and norms of international law. Constitutional Court finds that effective institute for review of judicial acts shall also be based on logic that the state shall ensure restoration of violated rights, as obligation to protect rights and freedoms of citizens implies that the state is responsible for restoring the rights violated by judicial acts. The Constitutional Court finds that, for further enhancement of guarantees on human rights protection, development of legislation in the Republic shall consider the above methodology". See http://concourt.am/russian/decisions/common/pdf/984.pdf (accessed: November 04, 2017).

48 On this issue, see *А. Манасян, Развитие Конституции Республики Армения как важнейшая предпосылка укрепления армянского конституционализма*, "Сравнительное конституционное обозрение" 2012, № 3 (88), pp. 141–146.

49 Modern legal thought is also developing towards justifying the viewpoint that, during its activities, Constitutional Court is not just a "negative", but also a "positive legislator", which indicates to legislators what shall not be done and what shall be done in a concrete situation – in other words, it sets positive regulations. See, for example, M. H. Марченко, *Источники права*, Moscow 2008, p. 401, Lo'ra'nt Csink, Bala'zs Schanda, Andra's ZS. Varga (eds.), *Basic Law of Hungary (First Commentary)*, Clarus Press, Dublin 2012, pp. 160, 163. A. Golovin, *Legal nature and legal force of acts issued by Constitutional Court of Ukraine*, [in:] *Almanac (Constitutional Justice in New Millennium)*, Yerevan 2011, p. 60.

be considered as a precedent, these acts must meet the requirements set for the discussed source of law and its specific features.

Although discussions on precedent in legal literature usually mention the Anglo-American doctrine of precedent, in some countries of the Romano-Germanic legal family, judicial practice is also a source of law and the *jurisprudence constante* doctrine is applied. Thus, we will analyze the specifics of the CCA decisions in the context of both the Anglo-American doctrine *stare decisis* and the doctrine *jurisprudence constante* applied in the Romano-Germanic legal systems.

Under the Anglo-American doctrine of precedent only the principle expressed in the reasoning part of the judicial act and justifying the judgment is binding[50]. However, this is not typical for CCA decisions, where legal positions are presented both in reasoning and operative parts of a decision. Moreover, these positions may refer both to a final conclusion on constitutionality of the act and also to the justifications underlying it. To this effect, the CCA has repeatedly stated that in order to guarantee the proper implementation of CCA decisions, it must be legislatively ensured that state bodies and officials guarantee the implementation of decisions in their integrity, with special attention to legal positions of the Court expressed not just in the operative, but also in the reasoning part of a decision, which, in their essence, are sources of constitutional law and official interpretation of constitutional provisions[51].

The next specific feature of the Anglo-American doctrine of precedent is the existence of mandatory and persuasive precedents[52]. Compared to the above, all decisions of the CCA on substance are mandatory. Part 4, Article 61 of the RA Constitutional Law on the CCA defines that decisions of the Court on the substance of the case are mandatory for all state and local self-government bodies and their officials as well as for all natural and legal persons in the whole territory of the Armenia.

According to this doctrine of precedent, in the course of law enforcement, all court decisions should be interpreted, taking into account the circumstances with regard to which they were adopted[53]. This feature is not specific to Constitutional Court decisions, as their binding nature and implementation are

---

50 See М. Н. Марченко, *Источники права* …, p. 628.

51 See Annual Reports of the RA CC on the implementation of decisions adopted in 2006–2016, http://concourt.am/armenian/report/index.htm (accessed: December 20, 2017).

52 М. Н. Марченко, *Источники права* …, p. 625.

53 Ibidem, p. 628.

not conditioned by the similarity of factual circumstances, and according Part 4, Article 61 of the RA Constitutional Law on the CCA, the discussed decisions are binding in any case.

As for the Romano-Germanic doctrine of precedent (*jurisprudence constante*), its main feature is: when any interpretation given by courts is supported for a long time, its approach is used as a basis for a uniform judicial practice on a certain issue, which actually becomes a source of law. Thus, it's not a concrete decision adopted before (as in the Anglo-American doctrine) considered as a source of law, but the stable judicial practice in other words, a set of decisions[54]. However, in the case of CCA decisions, such a set of acts is not required to become a source of law, one Court decision is enough.

In this context, there has been wide discussion in the legal literature that most modern continental legal systems are no longer "satisfied" with *jurisprudence constante* doctrine. According to these authors the mentioned legal systems actually formed a new, hybrid model of judicial precedent, which contains specific features of both *stare decisis* and *jurisprudence constante*. This model can be termed as "interpretation precedent"[55]. These authors draw a conclusion that from the viewpoint of the law-making role of courts, countries of continental and common law are converging, aiming to intersection in the point where there is a stable judicial practice based on law (interpretation precedent), and in this context, decisions of the Constitutional Court are considered as a manifestation of the above type of precedent[56]. However, we believe that, in the absolute sense, decisions of the Constitutional Court do not comply with features of this model of precedent either, as its essence is the presentation of casual interpretation (exemplary samples for interpretation of laws), which becomes an example for lower courts. Further application of this interpretation (in case of analogical incidents) pursues not so much a norm-making goal, but it is aimed at exercising the principle of equality before the law. However, CCA decisions, although being important means for ensuring of stability and development of the Constitution,

---

54 See Օհանյան Վ., Իրավունքի ..., pp. 67, 134.

55 See И. Богдановская, *Судебный прецедент и его эволюция*, „Законность" 2007, No. 3, p. 46, Օհանյան Վ., Իրավունքի ..., p. 66.

56 See, for example, Н. Ерошкин, *Понятие и юридическая природа правовых актов Конституционного Суда Российской Федерации*, https://studylib.ru/doc/1010027/eroshkin-n.---ponyatie-i-yuridicheskaya-priroda-pravovyh-aktov (accessed: November 04, 2013); Е. А. Ершова, *Правовая природа постановлений и определений Конституционного Суда Российской Федерации*, http://www.top-personal.ru/lawissue.html?1679 (accessed: November 04, 2017).

being of paramount importance for official interpretation of the Constitution and disclosing the constitutional-legal content of laws, at the same time, are perceived in the unity of their functions. From this point of view, the role of CCA decisions is emphasized both for ensuring the stability/development of the Constitution and for determining the compliance/conflict of legal acts with the Constitution, which forms an obligation for relevant subjects to follow all the above legal positions. Thus, apart from the above interpretations, the overall binding nature of these decisions also refers to other conclusions of the CCA regarding the constitutionality/unconstitutionality of legal acts.

The above indicates that decisions of the Constitutional Court, in terms of their features, significantly differ from the types of precedent available in the framework of all the presented doctrines. Although the model of precedent cannot be the same for all countries due to the features of their legal regulations on the issue and in light of developments at common and continental law countries, sometimes, there are such manifestations of the above source of law that cannot be characterized by one or another specific feature presented above. At the same time, there are some features, with which a specific source of law should comply, to be considered as a precedent. The most important of them is the secondary nature of precedent, compared to laws[57]. However, the above is not typical of CCA decisions, and the analysis of legislative regulations in the RA regarding the discussed issue shows that from the viewpoint of the hierarchy of legal acts, the legal force of relevant decisions is even higher than the legal force of laws. Another important aspect is that while precedent doctrine is actually based on the binding nature of a judicial act for other judicial bodies, in the case of CCA decisions, they are binding not just for courts, but also for all subjects mentioned in Part 4, Article 61 of the law[58]. So in terms of their features, decisions of the CCA, while significantly differing from types of precedent available within all the presented doctrines, are not expressed in the form of precedents.

Meanwhile, it is obvious that, while being of normative nature and being a normative legal act in that sense, decisions of the Constitutional Court are not

57 See M. H. Марченко, *Судебное правотворчество и судейское право*, Moscow 2008, pp. 339, 346.

58 See, for example, P. B. Шагиева (ed.), *Актуальные проблемы теории государства и права*, Moscow 2011, p. 282, H. Витрук, *Конституционное правосудие*, Moscow 2005, p. 128.

normative acts formed within the traditional classification of sources of law – given that, traditionally, judicial acts were not considered normative[59].

Summarizing the above, the special status of the Constitutional Court of Armenia, its powers and the issues it resolves, its decisions and their peculiarities, lead us to conclusion that, while being in the system of judicial power, the CCA is a special body, the activities and decisions of which significantly differ, by their nature, from the activities of other state bodies (including courts) and from acts adopted by them. Thus, in case of the discussed acts, we are dealing with a new legal phenomenon, which, while being a source of law, does not in its absolute sense correspond to any type of the sources of law available in the framework of the classical approach[60]. Meanwhile, it should be kept in mind that law is a dynamic phenomenon, and forms of its external expression and objectification cannot be static. In this view, some scholars rightfully note that, in theoretical textbooks, legal regulation sources are presented in a very simple scheme – listing the traditional sources of law and their hierarchy, which is not enough to form a complete picture of legal regulation. Simple listing of sources expresses the static form of legal regulation – instead of its dynamics and effect[61]. So, we believe that sources of law cannot be classified in a purely theoretical and abstract way, but that the classification must emphasize their practical role and meaning. This also applies to Constitutional Court decisions, as specifying their place among the sources of law is not an end in itself and is required to form a thorough system of their implementation, taking into account their specific features[62].

In this case, it should be noted that legal developments in the modern world have led to the formation of legal acts in the framework of the legal regulation mechanism, which, in an absolute sense, do not correspond to any source of law

---

59 See, for example, Р. В. Шагиева (ed.), *Актуальные проблемы* …, pp. 267–280, С. Дробышевский, Т. Данцева, *Формальные источники права*, Moscow 2011, p. 81.

60 As a rule, in the framework of the traditional approach, the following sources of law are distinguished: normative act, judicial precedent, authorized customs, agreement, legal doctrine and general principles of law (see В. Корельский, В. Перевалов (eds.), *Теория государства и права*, Moscow 1998, p. 287, В. М. Лазарева (ed.), *Общая теория государства и права* …, p. 173).

61 See Վաղարշյան Ա. Իրավունքի աղբյուրների ու իրավական կարգավորման միջոցների հարաբերակցությունը և հասարակական հարաբերությունների կարգավորման ստորակարգությունը//Պետություն և իրավունք, No. 2–3 (32–33), 2006, p. 5.

62 In the framework of the present article, we do not pretend to analyze all problems of classification of the sources of law available in theory. We review them only in the context of clarification of the place of RA CC decisions among the sources of law.

available in the context of the classical approach. Such legal acts also include Constitutional Court decisions, which, given the above approach, form special sources of law. Meanwhile, it is obvious that the discussed developments caused the need to form a common criterion for differentiating the legal acts and their classification on that basis. From this point of view, we consider it expedient to take normativity as a common criterion for the separation of legal acts, while classifying them in two main groups – normative acts and acts without normative nature[63]. At that, CCA decisions lie within the first group of sources of law.

In summary, decisions of the Constitutional Court of Armenia in an absolute sense do not correspond to any source of law in the framework of the classical approach, having certain features specific to those sources and, at the same time, a lot of differences. They form a special source of law in the framework of the classical approach, which, according to our classification, is in the system of normative legal acts[64].

Among the most important features of Armenia's Constitutional Court activities is the binding nature of legal positions expressed by the Court. Under Part 4, Article 61, the RA Constitutional Law on the CCA the decisions of the Court on the substance of the case are mandatory for all state and local self-government bodies and their officials as well as for all natural and legal persons in the whole territory of the RA. This implies that it concerns the whole decision of the CCA, hence, the legal positions, expressed both in the operative and in the reasoning parts of the decision. It is not accidental, as on the contemporary stage of the development of constitutional law decisions of the CCA are not perceived as a document just determining constitutionality or unconstitutionality of legal acts. Rather, more emphasis is given to the fact that they are a primary means for the formation of a uniform constitutional doctrine and development of the Constitution. This requires proper consideration not only of the conclusion on the issue of the constitutionality of the legal act, but also of other legal positions of the CCA. These last are a primary means for ensuring the stability and development of the Constitution and in this sense are no less important than conclusions on constitutionality. Moreover, from the aspect of legal consequences the legal positions are equivalent to them.

As was mentioned in CCA decision DCC-943 of 25 February 2011, the legal positions expressed in the Court decisions shall ensure more complete and

---

63 Some authors also present similar classification for sources of law (see, for example, В. Корельский, В. Перевалов (eds.), *Теория государства и права* ..., p. 288).

64 See the details in A. Manasyan, *Place of the Constitutional Court Decisions in the Legal System of the Republic of Armenia*, "Studia Politologiczne" 2014, No. 32, pp. 177–189.

uniform understanding of the RA Constitution and constitutional lawfulness in law enforcement practice, and shall purposefully direct the law enforcement practice to the understanding and application of the normative acts in accordance with their constitutional legal content. Declaring the challenged act as in conformity with the Constitution, the CCA often reveals the constitutional legal content of disputed legal norms through their interpretation and in the operative part of the decision, declares those norms as in conformity with the Constitution or as in conformity with the Constitution within the framework of certain legal positions or partially within the framework of certain legal regulation, thus indicating:

- the legal limits of understanding and application of the given norm;
- the legal limits beyond which the application or interpretation of the given norm shall lead to unconstitutional consequences; and
- the constitutional legal criteria, based on which competent authorities are obliged to provide additional legal regulations for the full application of the norm in question.

Therefore, it is not possible to fully implement the decision of the CCA without taking the above-mentioned legal positions into consideration, which, in its turn, presupposes that the legal positions expressed not only in the operative, but also in the reasoning part of the CCA decision are subject to mandatory implementation.

This is the reason that in pursuance of the Constitutional Court decision DCC-943 an amendment was made to Article 68, Part 8 of the RA Law on the CCA (dated on 1 June, 2006), according to which the Court can make decisions not only on finding the challenged act or its challenged provision in conformity with the Constitution or finding the challenged act fully or partially invalid and in non-conformity with the Constitution, but also on finding the challenged act or its challenged provision in conformity with the Constitution by the constitutional legal contents revealed by the decision of the CCA[65]. Moreover, Article 69, Part 12 of the RA Law on the CCA prescribed that in the cases defined by the mentioned Article if the provisions of the law applied against the applicant are recognized as invalid and contradicting the Constitution, as well as when the CCA, in the operative part of the decision, revealing the constitutional

65 Such regulation is also defined in the RA Constitutional Law on the CC, according to which, the CC also makes decisions recognizing the debated act/provision compliant with the Constitution in the interpretation of the CC.

legal content of the provision of the law, recognized it in conformity with the Constitution and simultaneously found that the provision was applied to the applicant in a different interpretation, the final judicial act made against the applicant is subject to review on the grounds of new circumstances in accordance with the procedure prescribed by law[66].

The systemic analysis of the legal regulations regarding the discussed issue leads us to a conclusion that they are aimed to the formation of a thorough system of the execution of the legal positions expressed in the reasoning part of the CCA decisions and serve as an evidence of their binding force[67].

Moreover, this issue is obviously essential from the viewpoint of relations between the Constitutional Court and other judicial bodies, as it assumes both mandatory implementation of CCA decisions and revision of judicial acts on the grounds of new circumstances among others, also in cases when CCA disclosed the constitutional-legal content of the provision, recognized it in compliance with the Constitution, and simultaneously found that this provision was applied to the applicant in different interpretation.

6 Constitutional Significance of the Constitutional Review Body

The enhancement of constitutionalism and the constitutional system of the state are mostly determined by the existence of an effective and efficient system of constitutional justice. Constitutional justice is an essential prerequisite and means of rooting the constitutional values in the social system, while acts of constitutional review body play an undisputable role in all spheres of public life.

Under Article 167 of the Constitution, while administering justice, the Constitutional Court is independent and subject only to the Constitution. The powers of the CCA are prescribed by the Constitution, whereas the procedure

---

66 As noted above, a similar regulation is also defined by the RA Constitutional Law on the CC adopted on January 17, 2018.

67 See the details in A. Манасян, *Обязательность правовых позиций Конституционного Суда Республики Армения: актуальные вопросы и тенденции развития*, (in:) *Конституция – Основной закон белорусского государства и общества (к 20-летию принятия), Материалы Международной научно-практической конференции (г. Минск, 11–12 марта 2014 года)*, Minsk 2014, pp. 372–374, A. Manasyan, *Development of Constitutional Doctrine and Stability of Legal Positions of Constitutional Courts*, Conference Proceedings, Seimas of Republic of Lithuania 2015, Lithuania 2015, pp. 116–127.

for its formation and its rules of operation are prescribed by the Constitution and the Law on the CCA. The Constitution further enshrines the powers of the CCA, main issues with regard to applications to CCA, decisions and opinions of the CCA. It should be noted that these constitutional regulations contribute to the stability and effectiveness of CCA activities.

Since its establishment, the Constitutional Court has been continuously implementing its activities. Moreover, constitutional and legislative changes affecting it did not prevent, but widely contributed to the development of the institute of constitutional justice in Armenia. All problematic issues arising in the course of CCA activities were and are still finding solutions both by changing the relevant law-enforcement practice and improving the legislation.

One thing is obvious – since its establishment the CCA has played an undisputable role in forming the new constitutional-legal thinking and rooting of constitutional values in the social system.

The CCA has passed a long way of evolvement and self-affirmation. Legal positions expressed in over a thousand cases reviewed by the Court have significantly contributed to the development of the law and strengthening constitutionalism in the RA. Thousands of people found protection of their rights at the Constitutional Court. This body formed a new quality of constitutional-legal thinking and a new school of constitutional science meeting the standards of a Rule-of-Law state. We can say without hesitation that, in the Republic of Armenia, the CCA turned into the driving force of constitutional-legal thought.

The active role of the Constitutional Court of Armenia has also been notable in the international arena. The Court was an active participant in the International Conference of Constitutional Control Organs of the Countries of Young Democracy, as well as the World Conference of Constitutional Courts. The Court had the honor of chairmanship in the first and the honor of presiding in the Bureau of the second. Finally, the Constitutional Court of Armenia is also represented at the Bureau of the Venice Commission, while being a member at the Conference of European Constitutional Courts[68].

Along with all that, perhaps its greatest achievement is the formation of new constitutional-legal thinking and the arrangement of reliable institutional guarantees for stable democratic development – an essential factor, indicating the undisputable constitutional significance of the Constitutional Court.

---

68 Г. Арутюнян, *Вступительное слово*, [in:] *Альманах (Конституционное правосудие в новом тысячелетии)*, Yerevan 2016, p. 6.

7 Valuation of the Constitutional Review Institute by Society

Social perception of control over legal norms is not an abstract phenomenon and directly depends on multiple social, political, legal and other factors. As a result, social perception of the constitutional justice institution becomes dependent on the level of constitutional and political culture of the society in general.

The institution of constitutional justice has continuously been improving since the establishment of the Constitutional Court of Armenia. Later on, exactly this system became the essential means for rooting constitutional values in the social system and began to play an undisputable role in all spheres of social life. Obviously, the stepwise formation and development of an effective and efficient system of constitutional justice in the RA greatly contributed to the enhancement of constitutionalism and the constitutional system of the state, which would necessarily influence the social perception of this institution. The CCA actually became one of the essential means for the protection of constitutional rights and constitutionalization of social relations in general, and it is still improving.

Conclusions

At the present stage of legal thought, enhancement of constitutionalism and the constitutional system of the state are mostly determined by the presence of an effective and efficient system of constitutional justice. Constitutional justice is an essential prerequisite and means for rooting the constitutional values in the social system, while acts of the constitutional review body play an undisputable role in all spheres of public life.

Provisions on the Constitutional Court are defined in Chapter 7 of the Constitution, entitled "Courts and the Supreme Judicial Council" (as amended on December 6, 2015), Article 167 of which states that this Court administers constitutional justice, ensuring the supremacy of the Constitution. Thus, the CCA is included in the system of judicial authorities, being the only body exercising constitutional justice in the Republic of Armenia.

The main criteria differencing the jurisdictions of the Constitutional Court of Armenia and other judicial bodies in the sphere of the interpretation of laws subject to constitutional justice, in our opinion, can be summarized as follows:

- initial criterion specifying the boundaries for the interpretation of laws by the Constitutional Court and other judicial bodies is the purpose of their activities, which should form the basis for self-restriction of activities of those bodies,

- the task of the Court of Cassation is ensuring the uniform application of constitutional law, and not an arbitrary document titled "law", which assumes the interpretation of law meeting the constitutional requirements,
- the task of the body administering constitutional justice is to indicate which interpretation of law complies with the Constitution and which does not – in other words, to indicate the legal boundaries for perceiving and applying the legal norm, beyond which the applied or interpreted norm will lead to unconstitutional consequences,
- the CCA may perform this function for disclosing the constitutional-legal content of the law or its relevant provisions, and not with the purpose of the general interpretation of the law,
- if a legal norm can be interpreted in several ways and the interpretation given by courts is compliant with the Constitution, from the viewpoint of differentiation of jursidictions it is expedient that the CCA applies this interpretation,
- if a legal norm can be interpreted in several ways and there is a conflict between the accepted perception of the norm and constitutional requirements, it is expedient that the body administering constitutional justice provides the interpretation consistent with the Constitution while disclosing constitutional-legal content of the norm,
- taking into account the changes in the RA legislation on types of CCA decisons and bases for revision of judicial acts due to new circumstances, and keeping in mind the need to ensure legal predictability, we consider it expedient to arrange a uniform practice of decision-making by the CCA given the probability of different interpretations of the norm, while applying the "principle of interpretation of law in compliance with the Constitution" and recognizing the legal norm conflicting with the Constitution only in cases when it cannot be interpreted in the context of constitutional requirements.

CCA decisions represent the official way for the external expression of behavioral rules, forming the content of the law, which mostly contributes to achieving the goals of legal regulation and full implementation of the law. In other words, this is a way for internal organization and external expression of the law – i.e., a source of law in the Republic of Armenia.

In terms of their features, CCA decisions differ significantly from types of precedent available in the framework of all the doctrines on the issue and are not expressed in the form of the noted source of the law. Meanwhile, it is obvious that, while being of a normative nature, and being a normative legal act in this sense, CCA decisions on the substance of the case do not fall under the perception of normative acts formed within the traditional classification for sources of law – given the fact that, traditionally, judicial acts were not considered in the context of the mentioned source. Therefore, we believe that, not corresponding in its absolute sense to any source of law available in the context of classical approach, having certain features specific to those sources and, at the same time, with a lot of differences, CCA decisions form a special source of law within the classical approach.

The binding nature of CCA legal positions is among their most important features. At that, legal positions expressed both in the operative and in the reasoning part of a decision are binding.

At the present stage of the development of the doctrine of constitutional law, CCA decisions are no longer perceived just as documents setting the constitutionality or unconstitutionality of legal acts, but are an important means for forming a uniform constitutional doctrine and development of the Constitution.

Following the constitutional reform of December 6, 2015, issues on status, powers, and decisions of the CCA were greatly changed to include resolving disputes between constitutional bodies; defining the compliance of draft amendments to the Constitution, as well as of draft legal acts submitted to referendum (prior to their adoption) with the Constitution; preliminary constitutional review of laws – based on the application from the President of the Republic. From now on, issues on the termination of deputy's powers, subjecting a CCA judge to disciplinary liability, and termination of powers of a CCA judge are within the competence of the CCA. That constitutional reform also extended the range of objects/subjects of constitutional justice and modified a procedure for appointing CCA judges.

The institution of constitutional justice has continuously been improving since the establishment of the CCA. Later on, exactly this system became the essential means for rooting the constitutional values in the social system and began to play an undisputable role in all the spheres of social life. Obviously, the stepwise formation and development of effective and efficient system of constitutional justice in the Republic of Armenia greatly contributed to enhancement of constitutionalism and constitutional system of the state, which clearly influenced the social perception of this institution. The CCA actually became one of the essential means for the protection of constitutional rights and constitutionalization of social relations in general, and it is still improving. The public perception of the role of the CCA is also changing and developing, which is one of the essential prerequisites for normal functioning of public authorities and rooting the relevant constitutional and political culture of the society.

The CCA has passed a long way of evolution and self-affirmation. Legal positions expressed in over a thousand cases reviewed by the Court have significantly contributed to the development of the law and strengthening constitutionalism in the RA. Thousands of people found protection of their rights at the CCA. The CCA formed a new quality of constitutional-legal thinking and a new school of constitutional science meeting the standards of the Rule-of-Law state. We can say without hesitation that, in the Republic of Armenia, the Constitutional Court turned into the driving force of constitutional-legal thought.

Kamal Makili-Aliyev

Constitutional Justice in the Republic of Azerbaijan

Abstract: The subject of the analysis is constitutional judiciary in Azerbaijan. A thesis is put forward that it played a significant role in preserving the divided power and realizing the constitutional rights and freedoms of an individual.

Keywords: the European model of reviewing the legal norms, Constitutional Court, autonomy and independence, The Constitutional Court and other organs of state power, cognition of the Constitutional Court

Introduction

Constitutional legal proceedings are among the most specific and interesting types of judiciary work in the Republic of Azerbaijan. As a method of constitutional control of the judiciary, constitutional legal proceedings and their development are among the fundamental state-making processes in the Republic of Azerbaijan.

It should be noted that despite Azerbaijan being a relatively young state, constitutional legal proceedings are already at a fairly advanced stage of development, with established jurisprudence and progressive legal provisions. One can argue that this state of affairs has been achieved thanks to a wide application of the rich constitutional legal experience of other countries, especially the European law[1].

At the same time, there is broad historical experience of constitutional law and law-making[2].

The Constitutional Court (CCAZ) exercises constitutional justice in the Republic of Azerbaijan (AR). This body of the judiciary is not only the supreme constitutional review body in Azerbaijan but it also plays an important role in the system of checks and balances on the part of the judiciary, which is very

---

1 XVI Congress of the Conference of European Constitutional Courts, *National report: Republic of Azerbaijan*, http://www.vfgh.gv.at/cms/vfgh-kongress/downloads/landesberichte/LB-Azerbaidjan-RU.pdf, (accessed: January 23, 2018).

2 Е.М. Ковешников, *Основы конституционного права зарубежных стран*, Moscow 2001, p. 131.

important for the development of a democratic country. The complex functions of this body of constitutional proceedings, its role in state-making as well as the constitutional justice it exercises will be examined further in this analysis.

1 The Reasons Why the Constitutional Court Was Established and Dilemmas in its Work

In 1995, the adoption of the new constitution by the AR following the collapse of the Soviet Union marked a new stage in the development of the legal system of this young independent state. In fact, Azerbaijan renounced the judicial system inherited from the USSR and embarked on a path towards judicial reform (learning from the generally accepted global standards), with the purpose of building an essentially new judicial system based on the idea of democratisation of the judicial system and judicial proceedings.

In order to implement constitutional innovations and the ideals of judicial reform, a number of new laws were adopted in Azerbaijan and new judiciary bodies were created, with an essentially new judicature being formed.

As part of the judicial reform, comprehensive measures were consistently adopted to reorganise the judicial system, establish new judiciary institutions, strengthen the foundations of independence and enhance the status of judges, decentralise management in the judiciary, establish new rules, procedures and proceedings in procedural legislation (including new appellate proceedings and essentially distinct cassation proceedings), abolish supervisory proceedings and restrict the functions of prosecutors in judicial proceedings, ensure better implementation of the right to qualified legal assistance, introduce judicial control over restrictions of such fundamental human rights as the right to liberty, the right to property, the right to personal inviolability, the right to inviolability of the home during the inquiry and preliminary investigation, and measures to apply many other innovations aimed at ensuring the exercise of justice under the law, within a reasonable time, without any preference, discrimination or predilection, on the basis of complete, objective and comprehensive court proceedings in compliance with the principles of equality and the adversarial nature of proceedings.

In this context, the establishment of the CCAZ in Azerbaijan in 1998 significantly expanded the possibilities for the judicial protection of human rights and freedoms. On the one hand, this is due to the broad powers of the Constitutional Court and wide opportunities to ensure the supremacy of the Constitution. However, on the other hand, as stressed by former CCAZ judge Eldar Mammadov, “The Constitutional Court is an institution of democratic transformation which exists in virtually all post-totalitarian states in order to protect new constitutional values, ensure stability of constitutions and planned constitutional development. These institutions are conducive to the correct interpretation and implementation of the universally recognised principles and norms of international law into the country's legal systems, thus creating the prerequisites for the rapprochement of the system with other systems, primarily with the European legal system"[3].

It is the rapprochement with the European legal system, the desire to approach the standards of justice established in European countries, as well as the implementation of international legal norms in the national legal system that motivated Azerbaijan to establish the institution of constitutional review and constitutional justice. This institution was founded according to the only option proposed by the government of Heydar Aliyev, as part of the new constitution, which brought it closer to its European counterparts. At the same time, the lack of appropriate historical and legal experience, the difficult economic and political situation in the 1990s, as well as pervasive and widespread corruption were the biggest obstacles to the effective execution of these plans.

Nevertheless, by implementing the experience of European countries, with the support of the European Union and, by its own efforts, Azerbaijan managed to overcome many of these challenges and made strong progress in the administration of constitutional justice.

2 Legislative Foundation and Stability of the Constitutional Court

The fact that the Constitutional Court is part of the judiciary system in the Azerbaijan Republic is referred to in Article 125 of the AR Constitution[4]. The second section of the same article lists the bodies that exercise judicial power in Azerbaijan, i.e. the CCAZ, the Supreme Court, the courts of appeal, as well as the general and specialised courts. Interestingly, the Constitutional Court is mentioned first, although the Supreme Court is the last cassation option in Azerbaijan. By doing this, the legislator highlighted the importance of the CCAZ as a special body of the judiciary.

---

3 Э. Мамедов, *Конституционный суд и суды общей юрисдикции в Азербайджане: теоретические и практические проблемы взаимоотношений*, "Кавказ и глобализация" 2007, № 3, p. 7.

4 Constitution of the Republic of Azerbaijan of 12 November 1995, http://ru.president.az/azerbaijan/constitution, (accessed: January 23, 2018).

At the same time, the third section of Article 125 establishes constitutional legal proceedings as a separate type, along with civil, criminal and other types of legal proceedings provided for by Azerbaijan laws. Thus, the Constitutional Court is part of the system of Azerbaijani courts and exercises judicial power through constitutional proceedings.

Interestingly, although the judicial system of the AR is regulated by the act "On courts and judges"[5], pursuant to Article 1 of that act there is a special act of law entitled "On the Constitutional Court" (the CCAZ Act) to regulate the CCAZ[6]. This raises the question: Does the Constitutional Court fall outside of the judiciary system and the judiciary power by virtue of this act? The legislative logic most likely was based on the fact that, in connection with the special nature and breadth of the powers of the CCAZ granted under the Constitution, the legislator specifically regulated the work of this body in a separate act of law for the convenience of normative regulations.

The Constitutional Court of Azerbaijan is an independent state body in accordance with Article 5 of the law "On the Constitutional Court" (the CCAZ Law) and does not depend, in organisational, financial or any other aspects, on legislative, executive or judicial authorities, local self-government bodies or legal entities and individuals. This must be taken into account when considering the fact that the CCAZ also plays a political role, which will be discussed further.

Nevertheless, the CCAZ cooperates bilaterally with courts of general jurisdiction. Any regulatory legal acts applied by the courts may be examined by the CCAZ. At the same time, in accordance with Article 33 of the CCAZ Law, courts of general jurisdiction can appeal to the CCAZ for the interpretation of the Constitution and the laws of the AR with regard to the exercise of human rights and freedoms.

As can be seen from the above, the Constitutional Court of Azerbaijan meets the established definitions of constitutional courts as political bodies that exercise constitutional review while being an integral part of the judiciary, which is confirmed by some scholars in the European doctrine[7].

---

5 The Act of the Republic of Azerbaijan "On courts and judges" of 10 June 1997, http://www.constcourt.gov.az/laws/42, (accessed: January 23, 2018).

6 The Act of the Republic of Azerbaijan "On the Constitutional Court" of 23 December 2003, http://www.constcourt.gov.az/laws/22, (accessed: January 23, 2018).

7 L. Favore, L. Philip, *Les grandes decisions du Conseil Constitutionel*, Paris 1984, p. 30; For an opinion that the Constitutional Court is both a court and a political body, see T. Koopmans, *Courts and political institutions: a comparative view*, Cambridge 2003, p. 322.

Since its inception in 1998, the legislative status of the Constitutional Court has been substantially modified only, once as a result of a referendum on amendments to the Constitution of Azerbaijan, held in the summer of 2002. As a result, a provision was added to the Constitution allowing private individuals to appeal to the Court directly. No significant legislative changes ensued after the adoption of the CCAZ Law in 2003. The minor changes made were of a technical nature and reflected general legal reforms in the country (for example, the names of executive bodies, labour legislation, targeting, etc.). Thus, since 2002, the CCAZ and its legislative underpinnings have been highly stable.

3 Legislative Position of the Constitutional Court

The Constitutional Court in Azerbaijan has no legislative powers or legislative initiative. However, given the special nature of the powers and the role of this institution in the governance system of Azerbaijan, the CCAZ should be regarded as one of the highest authorities in the country. This is also confirmed by the fact that the Constitution of Azerbaijan regulates the powers and legal status of the Constitutional Court along with the relevant provisions on the President, the Parliament (Milli Majlis) and the Government (Cabinet of Ministers) of Azerbaijan. Moreover, the CCAZ exerts a serious impact on the operation of most public bodies, which is confirmed by Article 130 of the Constitution, authorising the Constitutional Court to verify constitutionality of the laws of the AR, decrees and orders issued by the President, decisions of the Milli Majlis, decisions and orders of the Cabinet of Ministers, regulations of central executive bodies of Azerbaijan, as well as to check the same for compliance with higher-level normative acts. At the same time, the CCAZ has the authority to interpret the Constitution and laws of Azerbaijan.

Despite the breadth of its powers, the CCAZ as a state authority does not, whether in essence or by definition, stand above any other relevant bodies. Article 1.2 of the CCAZ Law clearly states that the main goals of the Constitutional Court are to ensure the supremacy of the AR Constitution and to protect the fundamental rights and freedoms of every person. Article 1.1 of the same act characterises the CCAZ as the supreme body of constitutional justice for issues falling within the competence of this Court in accordance with the AR Constitution.

At the same time, when pursuing constitutional legal proceedings and constitutional review, the CCAZ must conduct its activities in compliance with all procedural rules and norms only in the form of proceedings before the court[8].

---

8 Б.С. Эбзеев, *Конституция. Правовое государство. Конституционный Суд*, Moscow 1997, p. 129.

This is the form in which the Constitutional Court carries out its activities, even in those cases when it has to perform special functions. For example, such functions include the powers granted to the Constitutional Court under Article 130 section 4 of the Constitution which states that the CCAZ provides an interpretation of the Constitution and laws of the AR at the request of the President, the Milli Majlis, the Cabinet of Ministers, the Supreme Court, the Prosecutor's Office or the Ali Majlis of the Nakhchivan Autonomous Republic. The interpretation of laws and the Constitution is the competence of the Constitutional Court and no other body. This does not mean, of course, that other state bodies do not issue their own interpretations of these supreme state regulations but the official interpretation is issued only by the CCAZ, and such an interpretation is considered legally binding. The importance of the interpretation of the Constitution and laws for the development of a normal law-governed state is more than clear. After all, the provisions contained in those acts often need to be explained in more concrete terms, their content must be identified and elaborated upon, and gaps and conflicts must be eliminated.

Although there are reasons to believe that the breadth of powers and some activities of the Constitutional Court are positioned on the political plane, the CCAZ nevertheless is an institution of the justice system. In order to prevent its excessive politicisation the legislation contains a number of mechanisms, such as Article 1 of the CCAZ Act. In addition, Article 4 also states that the activity of the Constitutional Court is based on the supremacy of the Constitution of the AR, independence, collegiality and transparency, whereas Article 5 clearly defines responsibility in accordance with the legislation of the AR for imposing any restrictions on constitutional proceedings for any reason, whether directly or indirectly, for influencing the CCAZ, threatening it, interfering with its work, and disrespecting the CCAZ, and recognises such actions as inadmissible.

The exercise of constitutional justice (i.e. constitutional legal proceedings) and related procedures are enabled by special constitutional provisions[9]. The AR Constitution contains similar provisions in Article 130, devoted to the Constitutional Court. In particular, the Article 130 provides that the Constitutional Court is composed of nine judges appointed by the Milli Majlis upon a recommendation from the President. Thus, judges are appointed with the participation of the highest executive and legislative authorities, which is a

---

9 Т.Г. Морщакова, *Принципы и общие правила конституционного правосудия*, [in:] *Российское правосудие в контексте судебной реформы*, Moscow 2004, p. 66.

balancing element. Moreover, decisions of the CCAZ are binding on the entire territory of Azerbaijan and are subject to mandatory publication.

These provisions are explained in more detail in the CCAZ Act. Article 6 provides that the Court examines cases in the sessions of the chambers and the Plenum. It also states that all judges are members of the Plenum, and the sessions of the Court are convened, as a rule, by the Chair of the Constitutional Court (CCAZ Chair) and are conducted in the manner established by the relevant Internal Statute of the Constitutional Court. It is also noted that the sessions of the Plenum of the Court are chaired the CCAZ Chair or a substitute. The meeting of the Plenum is empowered to adopt decisions in the presence of at least six judges unless the law provides otherwise.

Unlike the Plenum, the composition of the chambers is determined by the CCAZ Chair whereas the rules of the organisation, convocation and meetings of the chambers are established by the Court's Internal Rules. The act notes that the sessions of the chambers have the competence to adopt decisions in the presence of at least three judges. In order to share administrative powers, it is decided that the CCAZ Chair and deputy cannot simultaneously be members of the same chamber. At the same time, the judges of the Constitutional Court preside at the sessions of the chambers in a rotational order, and the sequence of presiding is established during the sessions of the chambers.

The independence and impartiality of the court in exercising its powers also depends on the regulations that guarantee the independence of judges. Article 15 of the CCAZ Law sets out the mandatory independence of judges of the Constitutional Court and provides that they are only subordinated to the Constitution and laws of the AR. Article 14, in turn, establishes a fixed term of office for the judges of Constitutional Court, amounting to 15 years. At the same time, a CCAZ judge cannot be re-appointed. Moreover, despite the fact that there are posts of a chair and deputy chair of the Constitutional Court (mainly defined for the performance of administrative functions), the judges of this Court are equal when deciding on all matters within the competence of the Court, and the chair and deputy chair enjoy all the rights of a CCAZ judge and bear the same responsibilities. At the same time, judges of the Constitutional Court enjoy certain guarantees after the end of their term of office. For example, Article 24 of the CCAZ Law provides that a retired judge of the Constitutional Court cannot be held legally liable for any activities during the period when they exercised their powers, for voting and opinions expressed during that period, and they cannot be required to clarify such opinions or testify.

In addition to those powers of constitutional review and interaction with the highest authorities, the Constitutional Court of Azerbaijan also accepts citizens' appeals. A detailed analysis of citizens' complaints will be provided later, in section 4 of this paper.

Also Article 125 of the AR Constitution, entitled "Exercising the judiciary power" is fundamental. Section II of that article lists the judicial authorities: "The judiciary power is exercised by the Constitutional Court of the Republic of Azerbaijan, the Supreme Court of the Republic of Azerbaijan, the courts of appeal of the Republic of Azerbaijan, general and specialised courts of the Republic of Azerbaijan". Notably, the list of judicial bodies begins with the Constitutional Court. This highlights its special role in the justice system, even in comparison with the Supreme Court, which is the (cassation) court of last resort in the Azerbaijan justice. Section III of this article regulates constitutional proceedings.

Since the Constitution defines the links between the state authorities and the CCAZ, we can identify several groups in terms of their limited interaction. In accordance with the Constitution, direct interactions between the CCAZ and other authorities are very limited, which means that there are no specific features of practice in such interactions.

3.1 The Constitutional Court and the President

As state authorities, the Constitutional Court and the President of the AR engage in limited interactions, because of the principle of the separation of powers. The President of Azerbaijan has the right to submit a direct appeal to the Court to request an interpretation of the Constitution and the country's legislation, as well as verification of the compliance of subordinate regulatory legal acts with higher-standing acts. The President also submits candidacies for Constitutional Court judges to the Milli Majlis. Any presidential initiative to amend the Constitution is initially verified by the CCAZ, which issues a relevant conclusion afterwards.

The Constitutional Court plays a major role in relations with the President. It can extend the powers of the President in cases of martial law, announces the results of presidential elections and takes oath from the newly elected president. The President submits his statement to the Constitutional Court upon retirement, and the Court then decides whether the President has adopted this decision in person or not. It is also the Constitutional Court that decides whether the President has totally lost the ability to exercise his powers for health reasons and also initiates the removal of the President from office if the latter has committed a serious crime. The Court can also send a statement regarding the impeachment of the President to the Milli Majlis in accordance with Article 98 of the Constitution.

3.2 The Constitutional Court and the Government

The Government, represented by the Cabinet of Ministers, has the right to submit a direct appeal to the Constitutional Court to request an interpretation of the Constitution and the country's legislation, as well as verification of the compliance of subordinate regulatory legal acts with higher-standing acts. In other cases, no interaction between the Court and the Cabinet of Ministers is envisaged.

3.3 The Constitutional Court and the Parliament

The Milli Majlis and the Constitutional Court also engage in some interaction. The Milli Majlis has the right to submit a direct appeal to the Court to request an interpretation of the Constitution and the country's legislation, as well as verification of the compliance of subordinate regulatory legal acts with higher-standing acts. Moreover, the Milli Majlis appoints Constitutional Court judges to their posts. The Parliament also adopts decisions to dismiss Constitutional Court judges from office by a majority of at least 83 votes.

In the event that the martial law is introduced, the Constitutional Court may extend the term of office of the acting Milli Majlis, as well as verify and approve the results of the elections to the Milli Majlis. The Constitutional Court is also obliged to set the date of the first meeting of the new Milli Majlis after elections if the powers of at least 83 deputies out of 125 are not recognised in the period determined by law.

3.4 The Constitutional Court and the Courts

The Supreme Court, along with the highest bodies of other branches of power, has the right to submit a direct appeal to the Constitutional Court to request an interpretation of the Constitution and the country's legislation, as well as verification of the compliance of subordinate regulatory legal acts with higher-standing acts.

The remaining courts of Azerbaijan have the right to submit a direct appeal to the Constitutional Court only in cases when they need an interpretation of the Constitution and laws of Azerbaijan on issues related to the exercise of human rights and freedoms.

The Constitutional Court itself does not have any special powers to cooperate with the Supreme Court and other courts of Azerbaijan. At the same time, the decisions adopted by the Constitutional Court may partly or wholly overrule the decisions adopted by any other judicial body.

3.5 The Constitutional Court and Other State Authorities

The Prosecutor's Office and the Ali Majlis (Parliament) of the Nakhchivan Autonomous Republic also have the right to submit a direct appeal to the Constitutional Court to request an interpretation of the Constitution and the country's legislation, as well as verification of the compliance of subordinate regulatory legal acts with higher-standing acts. Municipalities do not have the right of direct appeal to the Court. They can only indirectly participate in cases submitted to the Constitutional Court if they are party to a case before the Supreme Court. However, the Court can verify acts adopted by municipalities for compliance with the laws and the Constitution of Azerbaijan.

4 The Organisation of the Constitutional Court as a Legal Review Body

4.1 The Legal Status of Constitutional Court Judges

The legal status of the Constitutional Court judges is set out in the Constitution, the third section of the Constitutional Court Law, as well as in certain provisions of the act "On courts and judges". Based on these normative acts, one can identify the main provisions and norms regulating the legal status of Constitutional Court judges.

In accordance with Article 126 section I of the Constitution, a Constitutional Court judge must be a citizen of the AR who is at least 30 years of age, has the right to participate in elections, a university degree in law and more than five years of experience of working in a legal profession. In accordance with Article 126 section II of the Constitution, Constitutional Court judges may not hold any other elective or appointed offices, may not engage in any entrepreneurial, commercial or other paid activities, except for academic, pedagogical or creative activities. Moreover, they may not engage in political activities or be members of any political parties, they may not receive any other income except for their salary other than remuneration for their academic, pedagogical and creative activities.

Pursuant to Article 130 section II of the Constitution, Constitutional Court judges are appointed by the Milli Majlis following the President's recommendation. After the appointment of at least seven judges, the CCAZ may proceed to exercise its powers.

The appointment of Constitutional Court judges is fairly depoliticised. As a rule, candidates for these posts have an extensive judicial experience. Most of them are judges of the Supreme Court or courts of appeal who enjoy high authority, or judges with considerable academic achievements in the field of constitutional law or constitutionalism. In any case, if the political component is present, it is levelled out through a compromise between the executive branch (the President) and the legislative branch (Milli Majlis).

In accordance with Article 14 of the Constitutional Court Law, judges of this body are appointed for a term of 15 years and cannot be re-appointed to their posts. Moreover, they can fulfil their duties only up to the age limit of 70 years. Upon reaching this age, the judge is no longer allowed to perform his or her duties. Pursuant to Article 15 of the said act, Constitutional Court judges are independent, subject only to the Constitution and laws of the AR. At the same time, their independence is protected through provisions related to their irremovability and immunity during their term of office, special order of appointment and prosecution, early termination of powers and removal from office, inadmissibility of disrespect for the CCAZ or interference in its activities. Judges of the Constitutional Court are provided with social and financial benefits and guarantees that correspond to the high status of judges.

The liability of Constitutional Court judges is also regulated by law. According to Article 128 sections I-III of the Constitution, the judges of the Constitutional Court enjoy inviolability. A judge of the Constitutional Court may not be held criminally liable, detained or arrested, or subjected to administrative measures in court. Further, judges of this Court may not be subjected to a search (incl. personal search) or brought to court by force. The inviolability of Constitutional Court judges also includes the inviolability of their home, flat, office, items, personal and office vehicles, communications equipment used, documents, as well as postal and telegraph correspondence. Judges of this Court may not be held liable before the law in connection with their activities, voting behaviour, or thoughts expressed in the CCAZ, and may not be required to provide explanations and testimonies in this connection.

If a Constitutional Court judge is detained as a suspect in a crime or administrative offense, he/she should be immediately released after identification. This event must be notified to the Court as well as the General Prosecutor, except where a Constitutional Court judge is detained at a crime scene. If there are signs of a criminal offense in the actions of a Constitutional Court judge, that judge may be removed from office in accordance with the procedure provided for in sections IV and V of Article 128 of the Constitution. Pursuant to those provisions, when a judge commits a crime, the President, following an opinion issued by the Supreme Court, may address the Milli Majlis with an initiative to remove the judge from office. A relevant opinion from the Supreme Court must be submitted to the President within 30 days after the request is made.

Moreover, the balance of powers is retained since the decision to dismiss a Constitutional Court judge is made not by the President but by the Milli Majlis by a majority of 83 votes out of 125. Article 16 of the Constitutional Court Act provides for the suspension of a judge's powers up until the entry into force of a court verdict related to that judge or until the final decision adopted by the prosecuting authority in the course of pre-trial proceedings, yet the judge is entitled to receive a salary until that time. After a Constitutional Court judge has been removed from office, upon the consent of the Court and on the basis of a resolution of the Prosecutor General the judge may be prosecuted and arrested in the manner prescribed by the AR criminal procedure legislation. The powers of the judge are restored if an acquittal comes into effect in his/her respect or if the case is terminated.

Judges of the Constitutional Court receive ample economic and social benefits. Upon the regular termination of their term of office, Constitutional Court judges have the status of retired CCAZ judges. Retired judges of the Constitutional Court may not be held liable for activities undertaken during the period when they exercised the powers of a CCAZ judge, for voting behaviour or opinions expressed in that period and they may not be requested to provide explanations or testimonies. Constitutional Court judges are granted 40 calendar days of annual leave. When a leave is granted to a judge, a one-off lump sum payment equal to two salaries is paid from the state budget. The life and health of judges are insured at the expense of the state budget of the AR for a sum equivalent to their five-year salary. If necessary, the security of judges is provided at the expense of the state budget. The damage caused as a result of destruction or damage to property belonging to a Constitutional Court judge or members of their family in connection with the judge's judicial activity is fully compensated to the judge or their family members. This damage is compensated from the state budget of the AR, and the perpetrators are required to reimburse those sums in accordance with the established procedure. A CCAZ judge who has no housing in the city of Baku is provided with a flat. To receive medical treatment, judges of the CCAZ judges are paid a one-time allowance equivalent to two salaries. After retirement, judges are also provided with benefits. Those having not reached the retirement age and retiring before reaching that age receive monthly financial support from the state budget in the amount of a monthly salary of an active CCAZ judge. Upon reaching the retirement age, the retired judge receives pension benefits in accordance with general rules.

It should be especially noted that in accordance with the act "On the Constitutional Court", judges employed in this Court are equal in adjudicating on all matters within the competence of the CCAZ, whereas the Chair and deputy enjoy all the rights granted to Constitutional Court judges and bear the same responsibilities.

In accordance with Article 17 of the Constitutional Court Law, judges of the Constitutional Court have the right to participate in court hearings, to express an opinion on the conduct of the meeting and to participate in the resolution of issues falling within the competence of the Court. When the CCAZ examines a case, judges have the right to ask questions to judge-rapporteur, parties to the case, stakeholders, witnesses and experts. Judges are also entitled to request the legislative, executive and judicial authorities, local self-government bodies, as well as legal entities and individuals to provide any document and other information on the matter being prepared for examination by the Court. They also have the right to hear explanations on the matter from officials and to examine petitions and materials presented at the court session. In their deliberations room, judges have the right to express an opinion on the matter being decided upon by the Court, to vote for or against the decision, to retain their own opinion in case they disagree with either the descriptive part or statement of reasons, or with the operative part of the judgement. Judges are also entitled to demand a CCAZ meeting within the time limits stipulated by the legislation of the AR and to exercise other rights stipulated by the legislation.

The obligations of judges are outlined in the subsequent article of the said law, which stipulates the principles to which Constitutional Court judges should adhere. They should follow the Constitution and the Constitutional Court Law. When examining cases at the Court, they should treat those cases impartially on the basis of acts (legislation) and the principle of justice. They should not miss court sessions without a good reason; they should take part in voting on issues examined by the Court (judges may not abstain from voting); they should not engage in actions or make utterances that discredit the high title of a CCAZ judge. Further, they should not violate the requirements provided for judges by the Constitution and they should not express an opinion on the substance of the case pending a decision.

4.2 Functions of the Constitutional Court

Within its powers, the Constitutional Court conducts constitutional proceedings in accordance with the provisions set forth in the Constitutional Court Law, chapter 6 of which is entirely devoted to constitutional proceedings and distinguishes two types in its initial Article 40:

1) constitutional court proceedings; and
2) special constitutional court proceedings.

As will be demonstrated later, these two types of proceedings are necessary under the act in order to separate the judicial function of constitutional review performed by the CCAZ from its functions in political life.

Article 40.2 develops the normative provisions of Article 40 and provides that the CCAZ exercises constitutional proceedings in two forms:

1) on cases related to requests or complaints submitted for resolving issues provided for in Article 130 section III points 1–7 as well as sections V and VII of the Constitution (i.e. verification of normative and legal acts for compliance with the Constitution and with higher-standing legal acts, as well as for any possible violations of human rights and freedoms therein), and
2) on cases related to requests in connection with disputes about the division of powers between the legislative, executive and judicial authorities. As can be seen, these types of constitutional proceedings organically fit into the judicial function of constitutional review performed by the CCAZ.

The political aspect of the Constitutional Court's activities is also related to its constitutional powers and, therefore, special constitutional proceedings are also divided into several types, as specified in Article 40.3 of the Constitutional Court Law. This article provides that special constitutional proceedings apply in cases relating to the following:

1) the extension of the term of office of the Milli Majlis during wartime;
2) the verification and confirmation of the results of the elections of the Milli Majlis deputies;
3) the timing of the first meeting of the newly elected Milli Majlis;
4) the extension of the term of office of the President;
5) the official announcement of the results of the elections of the President;
6) examining a resignation request filed by the President;
7) the appeal of the Milli Majlis to clarify information concerning the President's complete loss of the ability to perform his duties for health reasons;
8) the removal of the President from office;
9) requests and appeals requesting an interpretation of the AR Constitution and laws;
10) the issuance of the CCAZ's opinion on the proposals submitted by the Milli Majlis or the President regarding amendments to the text of the Constitution.

As can be seen from the above, the Constitutional Court of Azerbaijan has a very long list of powers of a political nature, and this determines its role in the system of governance. At the same time, as a judicial body that administers justice, the CCAZ represents an excellent link in the political participation of the judiciary in the system of checks and balances, with the separation of powers in the country. Moreover, according to some opinions in the Azerbaijani doctrine, the special characteristics of the CCAZ are associated with the fact that, although constitutional proceedings may be entrusted to a dedicated body, these proceedings also fall under the notions of legal proceedings and administration of justice, and the function of constitutional review (for example, interpretation of the Constitution) which often have serious political ramifications[10].

Nevertheless, the Constitutional Court of Azerbaijan has not used much of its political power to date. For example, no martial law has ever been introduced since the establishment of this Court, so it has never dealt with the prolongation of the term of office of either the President or the Milli Majlis. Further, the Constitutional Court has never had to consider the resignation of the President, his inability to perform his duties for health reasons or removal of the President from office. In accordance with the provisions of Article 88 of the Constitution, elections to the Milli Majlis of Azerbaijan have always resulted in recognition of the powers of more than 83 deputies and, therefore, this Court has never examined a case about setting the date of the first meeting for a Milli Majlis.

However, the Constitutional Court of Azerbaijan has regularly applied its powers in the sphere of verification and announcement of the results of the presidential elections and the Milli Majlis elections. For instance, the CCAZ passed decisions on the results of the Milli Majlis elections in 2000, 2005, 2010 and 2015. In 2000 and 2005, the Court overturned the results of elections in many districts due to mass violations and, as a result, repeated elections were held in 2001 and 2006, respectively. In 2010, the Court found no violations and approved the elections directly, whereas in 2015 the Court declared the elections invalid only in one district (Agdash), where a new vote was held. The Court also announced the results of presidential elections in 2003, 2008 and 2013, respectively, and never overturned their results.

The Constitutional Court also applied its powers to verify the proposals submitted by the Milli Majlis or the President to amend the text of the Constitution of Azerbaijan in the relevant referendums of 2002, 2009 and 2016. Section 6 of this chapter provides a vivid example of a decision issued by the Constitutional Court.

At the same time, the Court quite frequently deals with the interpretation of laws and the Constitution of Azerbaijan at the request of other judiciary bodies. For instance, a recent vivid example is the decision of the Constitutional Court

10 F.S. Abdullayev, *Azərbaycan Respublikasında Konstitusiya İcraatının Nəzəri və Praktiki Problemləri*, Bakı 2009, pp. 104–105.

dated 31 January 2017 concerning the interpretation of Article 54.3 of the Code of Administrative Offenses, following an appeal from the Sumgait Court of Appeal. The Constitutional Court needed to clarify the rights of the prosecutor (a public prosecutor) provided for in this article. The Court concluded that, in accordance with Article 54.3 of the Code of Administrative Offenses, the prosecutor participating in the examination of cases related to administrative misconduct has the right to file a protest against decisions or rulings passed by the court[11].

Furthermore, the judicial component of constitutional proceedings implies the application of all principles of justice regulated by the Constitution and international law. With regard to proceedings in the Constitutional Court, these principles as presented in the chapter 4 of the aforementioned act of law are:

1) impartiality and fairness;
2) equality of everyone before the law and the Constitutional Court of Azerbaijan;
3) transparency (except for cases involving state, professional and commercial secrets and the need to preserve the secrecy of citizens' personal life or family life);
4) equality of the parties and an adversarial procedure; and
5) proceedings conducted in the official language, with the provision of interpreter services, if necessary.

Constitutional legal proceedings naturally involve elements such as, for instance, the parties to the proceedings. Article 41 of the Constitutional Court Law provides that the parties to constitutional proceedings include the appellant(s) and defendant(s). Moreover, the state authorities specified in Article 130 sections III and VII of the Constitution may be involved in constitutional proceedings as appellants. This article also grants citizens the possibility to appeal to the CCAZ to protect their rights, and provides that the persons specified in Article 130 section V of the Constitution are referred to as "applicants" in constitutional proceedings. Further, the said article identifies the following parties as defendants:

1) the relevant state authority or a local government body that has adopted the contested regulatory legal, judicial or municipal act;
2) the official who signed the contested international agreement or an intergovernmental agreement that has not entered into force, or

11 The official website of the Constitutional Court of the Republic of Azerbaijan, http://www.constcourt.gov.az/decisions/375, (accessed: February 07, 2018).

3) the relevant state authority that committed the alleged violation in connection with the division of powers between the legislative, executive and judicial branches.

The article also states that applicants (persons submitting an appeal) as well as defendants may be represented by their representatives in constitutional proceedings.

Interestingly, no parties in special constitutional proceedings have been indicated. Instead, Article 42 of the act mentions entities that are interested in special constitutional proceedings. In accordance with that article, the participants in special constitutional proceedings include the bodies that have submitted a request or an appeal to the Constitutional Court in connection with circumstances that fall under the jurisdiction of special constitutional proceedings under the relevant articles of the Constitution, as well as bodies and persons whose interests are affected in connection with such requests or appeals. This form of proceedings also allows the possibility of legal representation.

This is because, in contrast with constitutional proceedings, there is no need for an adversarial component in special constitutional proceedings. Here, the main goal is to maintain the supremacy of constitutional provisions and to apply the principles of legality and justice.

4.3 The Subject Matter of the Review Performed by the Constitutional Court

The subject-matter of the review performed by the Constitutional Court in Azerbaijan is complex and comprises both regulatory review and political functions to ensure a normal separation of powers in the country. In principle, the content of constitutional review can be formal (to check compliance with procedural rules established for the adoption of laws and other regulatory acts) or substantive (to verify the content of laws and other regulatory acts from the perspective of their constitutionality), as well as abstract (on the initiative of any of the authorised bodies without a specific reason) or specific (carried out only in connection with a specific court case). The Constitutional Court carries out all these types of review.

Pursuant to Article 130 of the Constitution, the Constitutional Court, at the request of the President, the Milli Majlis, the Cabinet of Ministers, the Supreme Court, the Prosecutor's Office, or the Ali Majlis of the Nakhchivan Autonomous Republic, adjudicates the following issues in the hierarchical order of regulatory legal acts:

1) constitutionality of the laws of the AR, decrees and orders of the President, resolutions of the Milli Majlis, resolutions and orders of the Cabinet of Ministers, regulatory legal acts of the central executive bodies of the AR;
2) compliance of the decrees of the President, resolutions of the Cabinet of Ministers, and regulatory legal acts of the central executive authorities with the laws of the AR;
3) compliance of the resolutions of the Cabinet of Ministers as well as regulatory legal acts of central executive bodies with the decrees issued by the President;
4) constitutionality of decisions adopted by the Supreme Court and compliance of such decisions with the laws of the AR, in cases specified by law[12];
5) compliance of the acts adopted by municipalities with the Constitution, the laws of the AR, decrees of the President, resolutions of Cabinet of Ministers (in the Nakhchivan Autonomous Republic: also with the Constitution and laws of the Nakhchivan Autonomous Republic and with the resolutions of the Cabinet of Ministers of the Nakhchivan Autonomous Republic);
6) constitutionality of international treaties of the AR which have not entered into force; compliance of intergovernmental agreements of the AR with the Constitution and laws of the AR;
7) constitutionality of the Constitution and laws of the Nakhchivan Autonomous Republic, resolutions of the Ali Majlis of the Autonomous Republic of Nakhchivan, and resolutions of the Cabinet of Ministers of the Nakhchivan Autonomous Republic; compliance of the laws of the Nakhchivan Autonomous Republic, the resolutions of the Cabinet of Ministers of the Nakhchivan Autonomous Republic with the laws of the AR; compliance of the resolutions of the Cabinet of Ministers of the Nakhchivan Autonomous Republic with the decrees of the President of the AR and resolutions of the Cabinet of Ministers of the AR;
8) resolution of disputes related to the division of powers between the legislative, executive and judicial branches.

---

12 The Supreme Court does not consider the substantive content of cases. It merely checks whether or not there has been a violation. If its decision contains an interpretation that contradicts the Constitution and laws of the AR, then the CC may accept such a case for consideration. As a rule, if the case involves a court, citizens will appeal to the CC when they already have obtained a decision from the Supreme Court. The courts of 1st and 2nd instance examine the substantive content of cases and, therefore, the jurisdiction of the CC does not apply to their decisions.

This part of the subject-matter of constitutional review (except for the last paragraph) is a classic competence, also found in most judicial review bodies in European countries. In fact, it is the structure of the entire hierarchy of legal norms in the country that gets verified. Of course, constitutional provisions are at the top of this hierarchy. However, the need to ensure constitutionality of all legal provisions in the country predetermines the subject-matter of constitutional review for the Constitutional Court of the AR.

Interestingly, the state authorities of Azerbaijan, listed above, hardly ever use their right to appeal to the Constitutional Court for the verification of constitutionality and compliance with the law. The only bodies that have submitted a few appeals are the Supreme Court and the Prosecutor's Office. Moreover, the Supreme Court has used its competence only 15 times since 1999. On the last occasion, it appealed to the CCAZ in 2004 with a question on the constitutionality of the President's decree No. 392 of 5 January 1993 and resolution No. 267 adopted by the Cabinet of Ministers, dated 4 June 1993. The CCAZ then decided to recognise these acts as no longer in force[13]. The Prosecutor's Office has appealed to the Constitutional Court only four times, in 1999–2000. Its last appeal was filed in 2000 and was related to compliance of Article 54.1 of the Housing Code with Article 28.3, Articles 43 and 71.2 of the Constitution. The said article of the Housing Code was recognised by the Court as unconstitutional and was repealed[14]. However, the most interesting fact is that the Constitutional Court examined an appeal from a district executive body only once. In 2004, the CCAZ adopted a resolution stating that judicial acts were compliant with the Constitution and laws of the AR following a complaint submitted by the executive body of the Narimanov District of Baku. The Constitutional Court ruled in favour of the executive body of the Narimanov District and the relevant judicial acts were annulled[15].

The only case involving the settlement of disputes related to the division of powers between the legislative, executive and judicial authorities was examined by the Constitutional Court of Azerbaijan in 1999. The Court examined the dispute over the division of powers between different the authorities in connection with order No. 886 issued by the head of the executive body of Baku on 14 July 1995 "On repealing the resolution of the Executive Committee of the Baku City Council of People's Deputies No. 3/81 of 20 April 1990". This case was

---

13 The official website of the Constitutional Court of the Republic of Azerbaijan, http://www.constcourt.gov.az/decisions/96, (accessed: February 07, 2018).

14 Ibidem, http://www.constcourt.gov.az/decisions/28, (accessed: February 07, 2018).

15 Ibidem, http://www.constcourt.gov.az/decisions/79, (accessed: February 07, 2018).

examined on the basis of a request submitted by the Supreme Court. The CCAZ ruled that several provisions of the order issued by the head of the executive body of Baku were unconstitutional and repealed them[16]. This demonstrated that the executive branch of power had exceeded its scope of competences.

In addition to these state authorities, two more subjects also fall within the competence of the Constitutional Court of Azerbaijan. Pursuant to Article 130 section V of the Constitution, any person may appeal to the Constitutional Court asking it to examine regulatory acts issued by legislative and executive bodies, acts issued by municipalities or judicial decisions that violate the rights and freedoms of the person concerned, whereas the Constitutional Court undertakes to restore the human rights and freedoms that have been violated. Most cases examined by the Constitutional Court have been initiated upon appeals filed by private individuals[17]. Another entity that may file appeals is the Commissioner for Human Rights. Pursuant to Article 130 section VII of the Constitution:

> The Human Rights Commissioner of the Republic of Azerbaijan has the right to appeal to the Constitutional Court of the Republic of Azerbaijan, in accordance with the procedure established by law, in connection with regulatory acts adopted by legislative and executive bodies, acts adopted by municipalities and courts that violate human rights and freedoms, with a request that the Constitutional Court of the Republic of Azerbaijan rules on the issues specified in section III points 1–7 of this article[18].

One vivid example where the Ombudsman used his competence and the Constitutional Court adopted a relevant decision is described in section 7 of this chapter.

Thus, the Constitutional Court of Azerbaijan ensures the observance of human rights and freedoms as part of its review. This Court, located at the junction of the three branches of power, makes sure that the outcomes of activities undertaken by the authorities do not violate the rights and freedoms guaranteed by international law and the Constitution of Azerbaijan. This state of affairs is very logical if we consider Article 148 of the Constitution, which provides that international treaties to which the Republic of Azerbaijan is a party are an integral part of the legislation system in the Republic of Azerbaijan. Moreover, Article 151 of the Constitution states that when there is a conflict between regulatory

16 Ibidem, http://www.constcourt.gov.az/decisions/6, (accessed: February 07, 2018).

17 The civil complaint to the Constitutional Court will be considered in more detail further in this chapter.

18 Constitution of the Republic of Azerbaijan of 1995, http://ru.president.az/azerbaijan/constitution, (accessed: 23 January 2018), Article 130 (VII).

legal acts that are part of the legislation system in the Republic of Azerbaijan (excluding the Constitution of the Republic of Azerbaijan and acts adopted by referendum) and international treaties to which the Republic of Azerbaijan is a party, international treaties prevail. For this reason, constitutional norms concerning human rights and freedoms, as well as the norms of international human rights law arising from the treaties to which Azerbaijan is a party, are included separately in the constitutional review performed by the CCAZ. Incidentally, in its practice, the Constitutional Court faced this issue only once, in 1999, following a request submitted by the Supreme Court. In the request, the Supreme Court asked the Constitutional Court to verify the compliance of Article 60 of the Housing Code with Article 11(1) of the International Covenant on Economic, Social and Cultural Rights. In its decision, the Constitutional Court repealed a number of provisions of Article 60 of the Housing Code[19].

As regards the protection of human rights and freedoms, according to E. Mamedov, within the framework of certain conditions and limits, the Constitution grants the legislator the power to regulate human and civil rights and freedoms by adopting laws and corresponding regulatory acts regulating the conditions and rules under which human and civil rights and freedoms will be exercised, as well as guarantees for their protection and forms of liability for violation thereof.

> However, in most cases, the regulation of human rights and freedoms is accompanied by opposition of individual and public interests, as well as disparate rights and legitimate interests of various individuals. This delicate problem is often solved by the Constitutional Court, which verifies the constitutionality of acts adopted by the legislature. If the legislator or law enforcement agencies have failed to do this earlier for some reason, the main task of the Constitutional Court is precisely to draw such a distinction, to protect human rights and freedoms, to stop violations and prevent restrictions that are unreasonable from the point of view of the Constitution. The generally accepted limitations of human rights and freedoms are taken as criteria to determine the degree of freedom and protection of the individual. The Constitutional Court essentially establishes whether the restrictions imposed by various acts are compliant with the Constitution and laws, and when doing so it relies not only on the supremacy of the Constitution and the priority of human rights and freedoms, but also on other generally accepted norms of contemporary international law. They represent a coherent set of the Constitutional Court's activities. On this basis, the Constitutional Court has a mission of ensuring the unity of the judicial practice as a

---

19 The official website of the Constitutional Court of the Republic of Azerbaijan, http://www.constcourt.gov.az/decisions/9, (accessed: February 07, 2018).

> whole and the norm-setting activity of state authorities and municipalities that adopt various acts[20].

This opinion of an authoritative retired judge is certainly correct but only partially. Eldar Mamedov is mistaken when he claims that the Constitutional Court of Azerbaijan is called upon to ensure the unity of the judicial practice as a whole and the norm-setting activity of state authorities and municipalities. A work of this magnitude is beyond the capabilities of any single institution. Unity of all regulatory legal acts and judicial acts in a country can only be achieved thanks to higher professionalism of state bodies and judicial bodies and their effective mutual interaction in order to prevent situations where the results of their actions would go against the Constitution and international law. On the other hand, the role of the Constitutional Court consists precisely in controlling and thus solving certain problems that arise during the operation of state bodies and courts that endlessly strive for self-improvement.

There is also the political aspect of the activities of the Constitutional Court of Azerbaijan since such issues are also subject to review. It should be noted that the political aspect of such activities is the one that raises most questions about the role of this body in the political life at the interface of the three branches of power. On the one hand, pursuant to Article 86 of the Constitution, the Constitutional Court verifies and approves the results of the elections to the country's parliament (Milli Majlis). It also approves and announces the results of the presidential elections pursuant to Article 102, and subsequently takes the oath from the newly elected president. The Constitution of Azerbaijan also obliges the Constitutional Court to extend the term of office for the Milli Majlis deputies and the President in the case of martial law. This is how a balance between the different branches of power is ensured. All these competences exist in the context of the CCAZ's unequivocal power to resolve disputes between the legislative, executive and judicial branches.

Thus, the matters reviewed by the Constitutional Court of Azerbaijan are restricted in view of the separation of power in Azerbaijan, but also by the arbitration power vested in this quasi-judicial body. Moreover, not all constitutional norms are included in the competence of this Court. Article 154 of the Constitution establishes a clear restriction, namely that the CCAZ has no right to issue decisions amending the text of the Constitution adopted by referendum.

20 Э. Мамедов, *Конституционный суд и суды общей юрисдикции в Азербайджане: теоретические и практические проблемы взаимоотношений*, "Кавказ и глобализация" 2007, No. 3, p. 13.

Therefore, the will of the people of Azerbaijan, expressed directly in a referendum, restricts the CCAZ.

4.4 Preliminary Constitutional Review and Ex Post Constitutional Review

The powers of the Constitutional Court of Azerbaijan are heavily limited in matters of preliminary review of constitutional and other legal norms. Pursuant to Article 153 of the Constitution, "if amendments to the text of the Constitution of the Republic of Azerbaijan are proposed by the Milli Majlis of the Republic of Azerbaijan or by the President of the Republic of Azerbaijan, then an opinion of the Constitutional Court of the Republic of Azerbaijan on the proposed amendments must be obtained"[21]. This is how the separation of powers is ensured. If one of the two branches of government comes forward with a legislative initiative to amend the Constitution, then a preliminary opinion from a body representing both the judiciary and the constitutional review function is required. Moreover, the CCAZ has no legislative initiative and no law-making powers. Furthermore, if the initiative to amend the Constitution comes from Azerbaijan citizens (i.e. through direct democracy), then the opinion of the CCAZ is not required.

The second case when the Constitutional Court of Azerbaijan exercises preliminary review is connected with international agreements to which Azerbaijan is a party. As noted earlier, the President, the Government, the Parliament, the Prosecutor's Office, the Supreme Court or the Parliament of the Nakhichevan Autonomous Republic may ask the Constitutional Court to verify the constitutionality of international agreements signed by the government that have not entered into force or to verify the compliance of analogous intergovernmental agreements of the AR with the country's Constitution and laws. The fact that such agreements have not entered into force enables the CCAZ to exercise the preliminary review. However, in this case the CCAZ relies on the initiative of the aforementioned highest authorities from all branches of power and cannot initiate a review by itself.

In all other cases and within the limits of its powers, the Constitutional Court carries out *ex post* constitutional review of legal provisions, without having the right to initiate such review on its own. In fact, this is the most productive approach since, on the one hand, the CCAZ does not become a politically active

---

21 Constitution of the Republic of Azerbaijan of 12 November 1995, http://ru.president.az/azerbaijan/constitution, (accessed: 23 January 2018), Article 153.

body influencing various branches of power and, on the other hand, it is able to exercise effective constitutional review and arbitration between different branches of power, as well as protect human rights and freedoms.

4.5 The Legality Review Procedure Performed by the Constitutional Court

In accordance with Article 6 of the Constitutional Court Law, the Constitutional Court reviews cases during the sessions of its chambers and the Plenum. The Plenum of the Constitutional Court consists of all of its judges. Sessions of the Plenum of the Court are convened, as a rule, by the Constitutional Court Chair and are conducted in accordance with the procedure defined in the Constitutional Court Law and the Internal Rules of this Court (an internal document regulating its procedures of operation that are not regulated by law).

The Plenary sessions of the Constitutional Court are presided over by the Constitutional Court Chair or his/her substitute. The meeting of the Plenum is duly authorised to adopt decisions with at least six judges being present. The Court Chair, who has full discretion in the matter, determines the composition of the chambers. The Internal Rules establish the rules of organising the chambers, as well as convening and holding meetings. Moreover, the law provides that meetings of the chambers are duly authorised to adopt decisions with at least three judges being present, and the CCAZ Chair and his deputy may not both be part of the same chamber simultaneously. It should be noted that judges preside at the sessions of the chambers on a rotational basis. The order of presidency is established on a collegial basis during in the sessions of the chambers.

Article 7 of the Constitutional Court Law provides for the division of issues between the Chambers and the Plenum. In fact, the judicial aspect of constitutional review is exercised in such a way that the Chambers, in their sessions, decide on accepting inquiries, appeals or complaints regarding the issues provided for in Article 130 of the Constitution (as discussed earlier in this chapter). Cases accepted for review by the Chambers are examined as to their substance during the sessions of the Plenum with respect to the issues provided for in Article 130 of the Constitution. The political aspect of constitutional review, i.e. the issues stipulated in Article 84 section I, Article 86, Article 88 section I, Article 101 section V, Article 102, Article 104 sections II and III, Article 107 and Article 153 of the Constitution are examined directly during the meetings of the CCAZ Plenum, thus bypassing verification by the Chambers.

For the normal legality review procedure exercised by the Constitutional Court, the said act establishes the institution of an assembly of the Constitutional

Court judges. Article 8 of the act provides that meetings of the assembly of Constitutional Court judges are held in order to consider and decide on issues concerning the internal activities of the Constitutional Court and other issues, with the exception of issues resolved at CCAZ meetings. The Constitutional Court Chair convenes such assemblies of judges. Moreover, an assembly of judges may be convened at the request of any of the judges. The assembly of judges is duly authorised to adopt decisions with at least six Constitutional Court judges being present.

In accordance with the law, the Constitutional Court may resolve the following issues when convened as an assembly of judges:

1) adopt the Internal Rules of the Constitutional Court to organise its work;
2) approve the description of the official emblem and the seal of the CCAZ, the special clothing, the judiciary badge and a sample of the professional identity document for judges;
3) make proposals regarding the draft state budget of the AR aimed to support the Constitutional Court; and, in special cases,
4) make proposals regarding early termination of the powers of a Constitutional Court judge. The assembly of judges also resolves other organisational issues.

Moreover, the assembly of judges adopts, by majority of votes, all relevant decisions on issues examined at its meetings.

The legality review procedure performed by the Constitutional Court is based on rules stipulated by the law. Pursuant to the current legislation, judges examine cases independently, impartially and fairly during the proceedings carried out in the Court. Constitutional justice is exercised on the basis of equality before the law and before the Constitutional Court. Furthermore, the proceedings in the Constitutional Court are conducted openly. Pursuant to the law, a hearing in a closed session is permitted only if the court itself believes that open proceedings may entail the disclosure of state secrets, professional or commercial secrets, or when the court decides that there is a need to protect personal or family secrets. As a rule, Constitutional Court proceedings are conducted orally. If there is agreement between the parties or interested bodies, the Plenum of the Constitutional Court may examine the case using the written procedure, as established by the Constitutional Court Internal Rules. Under the law, notice of a meeting of the Plenum of the Constitutional Court must be published in an official state-owned newspaper no later than five days before the meeting. In urgent cases, when compliance with this procedure is not possible, the timing of the Constitutional Court session is announced on television and radio.

Article 28 of the Constitutional Court Law guarantees that constitutional judicial proceedings are carried out on the basis of equality and adversarial process. Moreover, it is interesting that during constitutional legal proceedings the Constitutional Court is not bound by the evidence and arguments presented by the parties: it should aim to fully investigate the issues under consideration. Thus, the powers of the Constitutional Court are broader than those of other courts. This is due to the fact that the main subject matter of its activity is to review the legality of constitutional and other legal norms, rather than exercise justice in the classic sense.

The Constitutional Court examines cases only collegially, in the official language of the AR. However, if participants in a case examined by the CCAZ do not speak the language of the proceedings, all the materials of the case will be translated into the language spoken by those individuals and interpreting will be provided at the CCAZ sessions so that those individuals can speak in their native language.

As noted earlier, the proceedings in the Constitutional Court are subdivided into (regular) constitutional proceedings and special constitutional proceedings. Features of each type are described in chapter 7 of the Constitutional Court Law. The most interesting differences stem from the separation of judicial and political functions of the Constitutional Court, which translates into different duration of constitutional proceedings.

For example, a request or a complaint submitted to the Constitutional Court in connection with issues provided for in Article 130 section III subparagraphs 1–7, sections V and VII of the AR Constitution is usually submitted to a session of a chamber within 30 days, and the chamber adopts a ruling on accepting or refusing to accept a request or a complaint for examination. Moreover, substantive examination of a request or a complaint at the Plenum of the CCAZ begins, as a rule, not later than 60 days after the date when they were accepted for examination.

On the other hand, a request regarding disputes related to the separation of powers between the legislative, executive and judiciary branch is usually submitted to a session of the Constitutional Court chambers within 15 days, and a ruling is adopted on whether to accept or refuse to accept the request for examination. Moreover, substantive examination of the request at the Plenum of the Constitutional Court begins, as a rule, not later than 30 days from the date when it was accepted for examination.

As can be seen in the latter case, the timing for having a case examined by the Constitutional Court has been cut by half. Thus, cases related to the separation of powers in the country enjoy a legislative priority. However, even more detailed legislative regulation exists for cases falling under special constitutional proceedings.

Special constitutional proceedings are regulated in Articles 53–1 to 61 of the Constitutional Court Law. Those articles lay down the details of the procedure whenever the Constitutional Court considers political aspects within the review it exercises. For example, issues related to the results of presidential elections in the AR are examined at the Plenum of the Constitutional Court. The law provides that the Constitutional Court examines documents submitted by the Central Electoral Commission regarding the results of the presidential elections in the AR, and must previously request appellate courts and the Supreme Court of the AR to provide information on cases related to the protection of electoral rights that have been examined. Moreover, if the electoral legislation has been violated, the Constitutional Court may declare the presidential elections invalid. The Constitutional Court is given 14 days to adopt a decision.

Another example concerns certain procedural peculiarities when the Constitutional Court is required to issue an opinion on amendments to the Constitution proposed by the parliament or the President. The key feature is that the Constitutional Court has no right to refuse to issue an opinion on amendments to the Constitution proposed by either the Milli Majlis or the President. However, the Constitutional Court may issue a decision stating that the proposed amendments do not comply with the requirements set out in Article 155 of the Constitution. This preserves the separation of powers.

The legality review exercised by the Constitutional Court and the arbitration in the separation of powers between state bodies always take into account the role of the CCAZ itself and its place in the separation of the legislative, executive and judicial branches.

4.6 A Civil Complaint in the Constitutional Court as a Means of Legality Review

The fifth section of Article 130 of the Constitution of AR states that:

> Everyone has the right to appeal to the Constitutional Court of the Republic of Azerbaijan to verify regulatory acts issued by legislative and executive bodies, acts of municipalities and courts that violate the rights and freedoms of that individual so that the Constitutional Court of the Republic of Azerbaijan can rule on issues specified in paragraphs 1–7 of section III of this article, with a view to restoring the violated human rights and freedoms[22].

22 Constitution of the Republic of Azerbaijan of 12 November 1995, http://ru.president.az/azerbaijan/constitution, (accessed: January 23, 2018), Article 130(V).

As can be seen from the text of the article, individuals can also appeal against any normative legal act that violates their rights due to its unconstitutionality or non-compliance with any other regulatory legal act of higher order. Moreover, a complaint to the Constitutional Court cannot be filed until the relevant decision adopted by the Supreme Court of Azerbaijan, which is the last instance of appeal for judicial acts, has come into force. For this reason, the Constitutional Court is considered to be the last instance of legal protection that must be approached before the case can be submitted to the European Court of Human Rights[23].

Thus, in order to resolve the issues specified in Article 130 section III paragraphs 1–7 of the Constitution of the AR, anyone can submit an appeal to the against regulatory legal acts adopted by legislative and executive authorities, or against municipal and judicial acts that violate that individual's rights and freedoms in order to restore the human rights and freedoms that have been violated.

Pursuant to the Constitutional Court Law, the Constitutional Court may examine complaints on issues provided for in Article 130 section III paragraph 4 of the Constitution of the AR in the following cases:

1) where a court has not applied the applicable regulatory legal act;
2) where a court has applied a regulatory legal act that was not applicable in the case; and
3) where a court misinterpreted a regulatory legal act.

In cases stipulated by Article 34.2 of the Constitutional Court Law, verification of the actual circumstances of the case that was considered by the Supreme Court is not allowed. Further, the said act provides that a complaint may be submitted to the CCAZ either:

1) within six months from the entry into force of the decision of the last judicial instance (decision of the Supreme Court of the AR) once the right to appeal against a judicial act has been fully exercised; or
2) within three months from the violation of the applicant's right of recourse to the courts.

23 XVI Congress of the Conference of European Constitutional Courts, National report: Republic of Azerbaijan, http://www.vfgh.gv.at/cms/vfgh-kongress/downloads/landesberichte/LB-Azerbaidjan-RU.pdf, (accessed: January 23, 2018), pp. 10–11.

Very importantly, a complaint can be submitted directly to the Constitutional Court if other courts could not prevent severe and irreparable damage to the applicant, inflicted as a result of a violation of rights and freedoms.

In Article 34, the Constitutional Court Law states that a complaint must specify the following: the name of the; the full name (with patronymic) and address of the individual lodging the complaint; the necessary information about the individual's representative and his/her powers; the name and address of the state authority or local government body that adopted the contested regulatory legal act or the contested judicial or municipal act; provisions of the Constitution of the AR and of the said act that entitle the applicant to appeal to the; the exact name of the contested act, the date of its adoption, its number, the source of publication and other relevant information; the individual's position on the matter and its legal rationale, with reference to the relevant provisions of the Constitution of the AR or other regulatory legal acts; a request addressed to the Constitutional Court in connection with the complaint; the list of all documents attached to the complaint. The absence of any of these data may entail a refusal to accept the complaint until the information specified by law has been provided.

Moreover, according to the law, the complaint must be grounded, i.e. the challenged regulatory legal act or a judicial or municipal act must have violated the applicant's rights and freedoms; the right to appeal against a judicial act must have been used fully, there is no possibility to apply to other courts in order to prevent a violation of the right to apply to a court or to prevent a serious and irreparable damage. It is the existence of these criteria that enables the CCAZ to apply its jurisdiction.

Article 35 of the Constitutional Court Law regulates appendices to civil complaints. According to the law, complaints submitted to the Constitutional Court must be accompanied by: explanations and documents deemed necessary to clarify the circumstances of the case by the person filing the request or appeal, or by the applicant; a power of attorney or another document confirming the attorney's powers, as well as copies of documents confirming the person's right to appear in the Constitutional Court as an attorney, except for cases when the representation is performed as part of the representative's duties; a copy of the contested regulatory legal act, judicial or municipal act, as well as a copy of the regulatory legal act whose interpretation was requested; Azerbaijani translations of all documents and other materials submitted in another language. The complaint should be also accompanied by documents confirming that the right of appeal against the judicial act has been fully used or that the right to refer to a court has been violated.

When summing up and analysing the legislative provisions regarding the individual complaint to the Constitutional Court, the legal doctrine in Azerbaijan expresses the opinion that,

> an individual complaint addressed to the Constitutional Court comprises the following three elements: 1) the concept and significance of a trial: the state acting as a legislative, executive or judicial body that has adopted a law or other act that violates constitutional rights and freedoms, and the applicant, 2) the subject-matter of the complaint: the person's request for their specific constitutional right to be protected, 3) the underlying basis of the application, consisting of two components: a) the legal basis, i.e. the uncertainty in the issue raised by the applicant as to whether the law or act is constitutional or not, and b) the factual justification: the application of the impugned law or act in respect of the applicant in a concrete case[24].

One can hardly disagree with this opinion as it basically captures the essence of the legal components of an individual complaint to the Constitutional Court. Nevertheless, one might also add the procedural element that arises from the aforementioned Article 34 of the Constitutional Court Law.

In conclusion, it should be noted that during 2016 the Constitutional Court adopted 113 decisions on the basis of individual civil complaints[25]. These decisions related to efforts to ensure the supremacy of the Constitution and the protection of human rights and freedoms[26].

5 The Legal Nature of the Constitutional Court's Decisions and Their Legal Force

The act adopted by the Constitutional Court is the main result of the CCAZ's activity in the process of constitutional legal proceedings. In fact, these acts are the basis for the regulatory influence and they represent the political contribution of the Constitutional Court to state-making in the AR. In the Russian doctrine, there is even a view that such acts should be classified as secondary

24 А. Рустамзаде, *Конституционный Суд Азербайджанской Республики*, Конституційне Та Адміністративне Право, "Юридичний вісник" 2012, No 4 (25), http://bit.ly/2CY2ass, p. 70, (accessed: January 23, 2018).

25 In fact, the number of complaints submitted to the Court is very high. Many of them are sent to the wrong addressee. The Court redirects them to the competent authorities. This is a normal practice of all state authorities in Azerbaijan.

26 The official website of the Constitutional Court of the Republic of Azerbaijan, http://www.constcourt.gov.az/news/436, (accessed: January 23, 2018).

sources of law, along with primary ones such as acts of law[27]. In fact, neither Russia nor Azerbaijan officially considers the decisions of the Constitutional Court to be secondary sources of law, and yet those decisions play a very important role in state-making.

Acts issued by the Constitutional Court are not classified into categories. They are considered to be equivalent regardless of the mode of proceedings, even if they are an outcome of special proceedings. Acts issued by the CCAZ are regulated in chapter 8 of the CCAZ Law. The act provides that the Court may adopt rulings in the sessions of its chambers, as well as decisions and rulings at the Plenum meetings. It is also noted that a decision adopted by the Plenum of the Constitutional Court reflects the conclusion reached by the Constitutional Court after examining the substance of a constitutional case and is a written document adopted at the CCAZ Plenum meetings. As a rule, such decisions are adopted by a majority of five votes cast by the judges, unless the Constitution or the law provides for other rules. Decisions adopted by the Constitutional Court Plenum are pronounced in the name of the AR and are final and, as such, may not be revoked, amended or officially interpreted by any authority or a person. The judge presiding over the meeting of the Plenum signs the decisions adopted by the Plenum and, as a rule, announces them in a session of the Constitutional Court within 15 days. As for legal definitions, it is noted that the chambers of the Constitutional Court pass resolutions on accepting a request, appeal or complaint for consideration, whereas the Plenum of the Constitutional Court passes rulings to resolve issues arising in plenary meetings and in other cases provided for by law. Rulings issued by the Plenum are adopted by a majority of at least five judges, while the rulings of the chambers are adopted by a simple majority of votes. The rulings adopted upon an examination of a constitutional case are entered in the minutes of the Constitutional Court session, and the presiding judge signs, respectively, the rulings of the chambers and of the Plenum of the Constitutional Court and, as a rule, announces them in the sessions of the Constitutional Court within five days.

Constitutional Court judges have the right to express a dissenting opinion. If a judge disagrees with the descriptive part and the rationale, or with the operative part of the CCAZ's decision, he/she may draw up a dissenting opinion in writing.

---

27 А.А. Белкин, *Вопросы юридической силы решений Конституционного Суда Российской Федерации*, "Вестник Конституционного Суда РФ" 1997, № 2, p. 20; А.А. Петров, *Решения Конституционного Суда Российской Федерации в механизме правового регулирования*, Irkutsk 2007, pp. 120–121.

The judge's dissenting opinion is published together with the decision adopted by the CCAZ.

So unlike the CCAZ's decisions, rulings are procedural acts aimed at administering the constitutional legal proceedings. Decisions of the Constitutional Court are the outcome of the activity of the Constitutional Court within the system of state bodies in Azerbaijan. For this very reason, Article 66 of the Constitutional Court Act confirms the constitutional provisions, stating that decisions of the CCAZ are binding on the territory of the AR and must be executed unconditionally after their entry into force. Moreover, officials who do not comply with the CCAZ's decisions bear liability in accordance with the law.

The legal consequences of the decisions adopted by the Constitutional Court are fairly far-reaching. Pursuant to Article 130 section X of the Constitution of the AR, laws and other acts or their separate provisions, intergovernmental treaties of the AR become invalid within the period established in the Constitutional Court's decision whereas international treaties of the AR do not enter into force. Moreover, judicial acts recognised as non-compliant with the Constitution and laws of the AR will not be enforced, whereas the relevant court cases will be reviewed in the appropriate procedural order. However, on the flip side, for example, if the Constitution of the AR underlying the Constitutional Court's decision is amended as a result of a referendum, the CCAZ recognises that decision as partially or completely invalid.

6 The Constitutional Significance of the Constitutional Court

As noted earlier, when referring to the special constitutional procedure, Article 40.3 of the Constitutional Court Act provides that the Constitutional Court also considers cases in connection with requests and appeals for an interpretation of the Constitution and laws of the AR. These powers of the Constitutional Court are important for development of the state and the constitution. Firstly, when using these powers, the Constitutional Court enables a more effective application of the provisions of the Constitution, and resolves problems with the understanding of the relevant constitutional provisions, as well as general provisions of the legislation. Its activity is also conducive to improvements in legislative practice as it detects errors in interpretation, thus offering a priceless service to the legislative branch. Secondly, and more importantly, the Constitutional Court accumulates invaluable experience in interpreting constitutional norms, since this quasi-judicial body is the main centre of expertise on issues of constitutional development in the country. Therefore, no other public authority has so much knowledge about the mutual relationships between the constitutional provisions, institutions and branches. Moreover, with its own interpretations, the Constitutional Court sets the direction of development for constitutional reforms and constitutionalism in general.

Nevertheless, the legislative and executive branches are much more likely than the Constitutional Court to come in contact with the changing social relations that entail the need to develop the legislation (including the Constitution as the Basic Law) and law enforcement (including direct applicability of constitutional provisions). Accordingly, it is these branches of government that are more sensitive to the need for constitutional reforms in order to develop the statehood and respect for human and civil rights and freedoms. Thus, it is the main bodies of these branches of power (Milli Majlis and the President) that have the right to propose amendments to the text of the Constitution in order to carry out constitutional reforms. Moreover, within the system of checks and balances, if amendments to the text of the Constitution are proposed by the Milli Majlis or the President, these proposals should be approved by the CCAZ in the form of a relevant opinion (Article 153 of the Constitution).

This state of affairs fits into the logic of the foregoing deliberations. The Constitutional Court, which has the most experience, is able to identify the strengths and weaknesses of the proposals submitted by the legislative and executive branches, and make its adjustments into the application of constitutional reforms. Thus, acting together, the three branches of government are able to achieve the best results. Moreover, the Constitutional Court has the ability to curb excessive ambitions of the other two branches of government in an attempt to preserve the integrity of the constitutional order in the country.

Based on the provisions of Article 152 of the Constitution, it seems obvious that any amendments to the text of the Constitution may be made exclusively through a national referendum (i.e. direct democracy). However, before putting any amendments proposed by the executive or legislative branch to a referendum, the Constitutional Court examines the amendments in special constitutional proceedings. As a result of such proceedings, the Constitutional Court issues a decision where it may propose additions to the amendments, correct them or recognise the proposed amendments as unjustified, thus *de facto* blocking them.

A relevant example from the current practice of the Constitutional Court is its resolution "Concerning an opinion on the draft Law of the Referendum of the Republic of Azerbaijan 'On amending the Constitution of the Republic of Azerbaijan'" of 25 July 2016. Within the framework of special constitutional proceedings, the Constitutional Court examined the amendments proposed by the President to the country's Constitution.

It follows from the text of the resolution that the Constitutional Court paid special attention to the verification of proposals for any contradictions with Article 155 of the Constitution. That article bans the organisation of a referendum regarding proposals to amend or abolish articles of the Constitution which concern the source of power, the sovereignty of the people, the inadmissibility of the usurpation of power, the foundations of the state, the head of state, the official language, the abolition of human and civil rights and freedoms enshrined in the Constitution, or limitation of such rights and freedoms to a degree higher than stipulated by international treaties to which the AR is a party. The CCAZ did not find any such contradictions in the resolution[28].

Moreover, having studied the structure of the proposed amendments and their consequences for the reform of the constitutional order in the country, the Constitutional Court proposed its own additions to the text of the amendments, and presented them in the final part of its resolution. In particular, the Constitutional Court proposed supplementing the article on the shortened term of office of members of the Milli Majlis elected in early elections with relevant provisions allowing further re-election of such members[29]. This proposal was taken on board and included in the 2016 referendum on amendments to the Constitution.

As can be seen from the foregoing, the Constitutional Court fully utilises its powers to participate in constitutional reforms and adjusts the direction of such reforms. It should be noted that all such resolutions were adopted by the Constitutional Court in 2009 and in 2002, i.e. before the relevant referendums were held. Each time, the Constitutional Court verified the proposed amendments for expediency, and also supplemented and corrected the text of the amendments to match their purpose, where such purpose was recognised by the Constitutional Court as expedient.

---

28 Resolution of the Constitutional Court of the Republic of Azerbaijan "Concerning an opinion on the draft Law of the Referendum of the Republic of Azerbaijan 'On amending the Constitution of the Republic of Azerbaijan'" dated 25 July 2016, http://www.constcourt.gov.az/decisions/359, (accessed: 23 January 2018).

29 Ibidem.

7 Social perception of the Constitutional Court as an institution

The public perception of the CCAZ's activities is mostly positive. To date, the Constitutional Court has maintained positive and established (albeit limited) relations with society at large.

In this vein, one should mention the annual school contest conducted by the Constitutional Court to celebrate the Constitution Day in Azerbaijan[30]. The topics of the annual school contest are always related to the constitution and the legislation of Azerbaijan and the contest is held in one of the municipal districts in Baku, the capital of Azerbaijan. The main purpose of the school contest organised by the Constitutional Court is to promote legal culture and knowledge among young people, and to encourage a more in-depth study of the fundamentals and essence of the Constitution. The Constitutional Court often publicly emphasises its interest in raising the level of legal education among young people, and in encouraging active participation in developing a law-governed state, as well as an in-depth study of the essence, principles and principles of constitutional review. In 2017, the school contest was held in the Sabunchinski district of Baku and was entitled "The fundamentals of a law-governed state"[31].

As regards the cooperation between the Constitutional Court and educational institutions, it is important to mention the participation of Constitutional Court judges in legal conferences held in Azerbaijan universities, including the Baku State University, the country's largest higher education institution[32].

The positive public perception of the Constitutional Court's activities also stems from the social focus of many of its decisions. For instance, in the last five years the Constitutional Court adopted a large number of decisions related to the restoration of rights and freedoms of applicants that had been violated. Moreover, the court formulated important legal positions from the perspective of law enforcement with regard to the judicial protection of rights and freedoms, the right to equality, property rights, the right to work, housing, rest and social security, as well as other issues of public concern. For example, in its decision adopted in 2016, following a request submitted by the AR Ombudsman, the Constitutional Court Plenum invoked the legal positions formulated in connection with the right to rest, enshrined in Article 37 of the Constitution, as well as

---

30 An official public holiday in the Republic of Azerbaijan, celebrated on 12 November.

31 See: The official website of the Constitutional Court of the Republic of Azerbaijan, http://www.constcourt.gov.az/news/471, (accessed: January 23, 2018).

32 Ibidem, http://www.constcourt.gov.az/news/413, (accessed: January 23, 2018).

international treaties to which Azerbaijan is a party, and noted that by exercising this right, an individual is released from the performance of duties under labour relations and may use such time at his/her discretion, primarily seeking mental and physical recovery, restoring the ability to work and improve one's health status. In addition, another important purpose of the right to rest is to develop and improve individual abilities and talents, and to enable participation in personal and public life. In another decision of 2016, adopted in connection with the appeal submitted by the Court of Appeal in Şirvan (Azerbaijan), the Plenum of the Constitutional Court invoked the legal positions formulated in previous resolutions and noted that the restriction of ownership rights must meet the requirement of legality, must be applied in order to protect the rights and freedoms of other persons, must be proportional, and must not change the essence of the constitutional right. The Constitutional Court noted that the decisions adopted in the sphere of the housing policy in a constitutional state may be used as a basis to restrict the right of ownership provided that the conditions enshrined in the Constitution are adhered to. In effect, the Constitutional Court constrained the role of the government in favour of citizens[33].

The social orientation of these decisions, of course, gives grounds for a positive perception of the Constitutional Court in the society. Notably, it is the Constitutional Court that receives the least criticism among the judiciary in Azerbaijan, both within the country and by international organisations.

Unfortunately, there have been no sociological surveys so there is no empirical evidence to assess the current public sentiment about the Constitutional Court. However, judging by the social focus of many decisions, the absence of any strong criticism in the mass media and the overall attitudes, one can assume that Azerbaijan citizens have sufficient confidence in the Constitutional Court.

Conclusions

Constitutional justice is one of the mechanisms that influence the process of state-making in the Republic of Azerbaijan. Any democratic country with a clear separation of powers needs an equilibrium of checks and balances between the three branches of power. In the course of its activities, each branch of government contributes to the development of the state and strengthens its democratic institutions, thus creating conducive conditions for a normal process of state-making and building an effective system of public administration.

33 Ibidem, http://www.constcourt.gov.az/news/436, (accessed: January 23, 2018).

In the judiciary branch in Azerbaijan, the Constitutional Court plays this role. The Constitutional Court in Azerbaijan conducts constitutional proceedings and, using the mechanism of constitutional review, verifies compliance of all regulatory legal acts adopted by state bodies with the constitution and higher-level acts. It also interprets those acts in order to eliminate conflicts of law. Moreover, in the political arena, the Constitutional Court has a broad array of competences that are necessary for effective participation of the judiciary in the country's system of checks and balances.

The Constitutional Court pays particular attention to constitutional reforms. Implementation of such reforms without the involvement of the Constitutional Court is impossible, both from the legislative perspective and from the point of view of expediency. After all, the Constitutional Court is the most "enlightened" state body when it comes to issues related to constitutional order and constitutionalism. As a result, the Constitutional Court plays a crucial role in the process of developing proposals for constitutional reforms to be put to national vote under a direct democratic process (referendum).

Thus, by carrying out two types of constitutional legal proceedings, the Constitutional Court constantly makes a significant contribution to the process of state-making in the Republic of Azerbaijan. By developing and specifying the legislative framework, by defending human rights, while also helping to ensure a political balance of power in the country, the Constitutional Court contributes to the democracy building and constitutional development in the country.

In principle, the role of the Constitutional Court of the Republic of Azerbaijan can be summarised as efforts to reinforce the supremacy of the constitution and respect for human rights and freedoms, also through the implementation of norms and standards of international law, in the relations between all state authorities, the society and each of its members. The Constitutional Court plays an important role in the formation of democratic institutions in the society and the rule of law, in ensuring democracy in its various forms, defending the constitutional principle of the separation of powers, developing the judiciary, and reinforcing universally recognised principles and norms of international law which can be seen as a concentrated legal expression of progress in the social development worldwide. As such, the Constitutional Court is an authoritative state body performing key functions in Azerbaijan.

At the same time, from the perspective of Azerbaijan's society and citizens, the Constitutional Court is an important instrument for the protection of rights and freedoms. According to Farhad Abdullayev, the acting Chair of the Constitutional Court:

The institution of constitutional complaint is an effective way to ensure the protection of human rights and freedoms, and the supremacy of the Constitution; it is very important for turning the Constitution into a document that does not simply consist of declarative provisions but, instead, contains directly applicable provisions[34].

34 Ibidem.

Alexander Vashkevich

Constitutional Justice in the Republic of Belarus

Abstract: The chapter examines the process of creation and evolution of the legal status and practice of the Constitutional Court of Belarus. A thesis is put forward that in the period 1994–1996, the Constitutional Court made an important contribution, ensuring the supremacy of the Constitution, protecting the fundamental rights and freedoms of the individual, and played an essential role in securing the separation of powers. However, after the November 1996 constitutional referendum, its legal status and practice has changed dramatically. At present the Constitutional Court does not play any significant role in the legal system of Belarus.

Keywords: the European model of constitutional review, Constitutional Court, autonomy and independence, The Constitutional Court and other organs of state power, competence of the Constitutional Court

Introduction

Back in the 1920s, Professor H. Kelsen developed the concept of centralised constitutional review carried out by the constitutional court[1]. However, in European countries, this idea became popular only after World War II. At present, the overwhelming majority of European countries have established constitutional courts or similar institutions that make a significant contribution to reinforcing constitutional legality and ensuring the inalienable rights and freedoms of the individual[2]. Therefore, starting with M. Cappelletti's fundamental research carried out in the 1970s[3], the interest of constitutional scholars and political scientists in problems related to the establishment and functioning of constitutional justice bodies continues to be strong.

This chapter offers a detailed analysis of the history of formation, legal basis and practice of operation of the Constitutional Court of the Republic of Belarus. To this end, a large number of sources were used. Some of the sources are not

---

1 Г. Кельзен, *Судебная гарантия Конституции (конституционная юстиция)*, "Право и политика" 2006, № 8, 9.

2 As of 1 January 2018, the Conference of European Constitutional Courts, established in Dubrovnik in 1972, brings together representatives of 41 European constitutional courts or equivalent bodies dealing with constitutional issues, https://www.cecc2017-2020.org/ (accessed: February 20, 2018).

3 M. Cappelletti, *Judicial Review in the Contemporary World*, Indianapolis 1971.

available outside Belarus, including documents and archival materials collected during the author's work as an expert of the Constitutional Commission of the Supreme Council of the Republic of Belarus, as an assistant to D. Bulakhov, the Chairman of the Legislation Commission of the Supreme Council of the Republic of Belarus of the first convocation, as a secretary of the Scientific Advisory Council of the Constitutional Court and as a judge of the Constitutional Court of the Republic of Belarus.

1 Reasons for the Introduction of Constitutional Review and the Key Dilemmas

One of the characteristic features of the Soviet form of governance was the absence of the constitutional court in the system of central authorities[4]. Therefore, until 1989, the Belarusian constitution did not contain any provisions that would regulate the status of a specialised body performing constitutional review or supervision. The ruling party (and, accordingly, the legislator) had a negative attitude towards the theory of the separation of powers. It was believed that the Councils (*Soviets*) should fulfil both legislative and executive functions simultaneously. It was argued that the supreme state authority was able to properly express the will and interests of all citizens and, consequently, no one could challenge the constitutionality of its acts[5]. The supreme body itself had to ensure constitutionality of the adopted laws. For this reason, the attempts undertaken in the period between 1924 and 1933, aimed at furnishing the Supreme Court of the USSR with the competence to review the constitutionality of the acts of the Soviet republics and the acts adopted by the USSR People's Commissariats, ended in failure[6]. In the late 1920s, one of the participants in a debate about the possibility of judicial protection of the constitution stated:

> …the nature of the Soviet power is that it is a living denial of the fiction of the theory of the separation of powers. Our class court is not 'independent' of the political power but, rather, it constitutes one of its functions. On a scale of the entire Soviet Union, it's not a supreme and constitutional court, independent of the government, that guarantees the

4 В.В. Маклаков (ред.), *Конституционное право. Словарь*, Moscow 2001, p. 461.

5 Д.А. Керимов, А.И. Экимов, *Конституционный надзор в СССР*, "Советское государство и право" 1990, № 9, p. 4.

6 For details, see: М.А. Митюков, *Судебный конституционный надзор 1924–1933 гг.: вопросы истории, теории и практики*, Moscow 2005.

> preservation of constitutional legality but, rather, this function is fulfilled by a supreme political body of the ruling class[7].

As noted by Professor M.A. Nudel in the 1960s, "the problem of constitutional review is very closely related to the position of the parliament. If its supremacy is recognised, then the possibility of establishing an extra-parliamentary body that exercises constitutional jurisdiction and, therefore, controls the activities of the parliament, must be ruled out"[8].

Therefore, all the proposals made by scholars who suggested that a special body for monitoring the constitutionality must be established were not supported by the legislator[9], and, according to Article 121 paragraph 4 of the Constitution of the USSR of 1977, the monitoring over the observance of the Constitution and constitutionality and legality of the constitutions and laws of the Soviet republics was vested in the Presidium of the Supreme Council of the USSR[10]. The 1978 Constitution of the Belarusian Soviet Socialist Republic (BSSR) did not provide for any mechanisms for monitoring the constitutionality of laws. As regards the constitutionality of government resolutions and decisions of the Minsk city council and regional councils of people's deputies, these acts could be repealed by the Presidium of the Supreme Council if they were found non-compliant[11].

It was not until the late 1980s, during the "*perestroika*" period, that these ideas were revised, and the fact that the parliament held self-review powers was recognised as ineffective. In 1988, an amendment was made to the USSR Constitution of 1977, which provided that a Constitutional Supervision Committee of the USSR should be established[12]. It was formed with the aim of

---

7 Б. Загорье, *Нужна ли нам судебная охрана конституции (в порядке обсуждения)*, "Вестник сов.юстиции", Kharkov 1928, № 17 (123), pp. 501–502.

8 М.А. Нудель, *Конституционный контроль в капиталистических странах*, Moscow 1968, p. 10.

9 Such suggestions were formulated by: Ю.П. Еременко (*Нормы советских конституций*: автореф. дис…канд. юрид. наук. Saratov 1968), М.А. Свистунова (*Проблемы конституционного контроля в СССР*: автореф. дисс. канд. юрид. наук, Moscow 1971), and certain other authors.

10 Б.Н. Пономарев (ed.), *Конституция СССР: Политико-правовой комментарий*, Moscow 1982, p. 311.

11 Article 108 paragraph 9 of the Constitution of the BSSR, http://pravo.by/pravovaya-informatsiya/pomniki-gistoryi-prava-belarusi/kanstytutsyynae-prava-belarusi/kanstytutsyi-belarusi/konstitutsiya-1978-goda/ (accessed: February 20, 2018).

12 «Ведомости Верховного Совета СССР» 1988, № 49, ст. 727.

creating a "socialist mechanism of checks and balances"[13]. However, the Act on the Constitutional Supervision Committee, adopted a year later, granted very limited competence to that body. In particular, the Committee only had the right to suspend, but not abolish, unconstitutional acts (with the exception of acts that violated fundamental human rights and freedoms)[14].

One characteristic feature of the constitutional development of the USSR was the presence of a considerable similarity, and, frequently, full uniformity of the texts of the USSR Constitution and the constitutions of the Soviet republics. For this reason, as early as on 27 October 1989, the Belarusian Constitution of 1978 was supplemented with a new article, devoted to the Constitutional Supervision Committee, which almost fully mirrored the analogous provision of the USSR Constitution, merely replacing the abbreviation "USSR" with "BSSR" and reducing the number of members from 27 to 11 persons:

> *The Constitutional Supervision Committee of the Belarusian SSR shall be elected by the Supreme Soviet of the Belarusian SSR for a period of ten years, from among experts in politics and law, and shall consist of the Chairman, the Deputy Chairman and nine members of the Committee.*
> *Persons elected to the Constitutional Supervision Committee of the Belarusian SSR may not simultaneously be members of bodies whose acts are supervised by the Committee.*
> *Persons elected to the Constitutional Supervision Committee of the Belarusian SSR shall be independent in the performance of their duties and subordinated solely to the Constitution of the Belarusian SSR.*
> *The Constitutional Supervision Committee of the Belarusian SSR:*
>
> 1) *on its own initiative, at the proposal of the Supreme Council of the Belarusian SSR, shall submit opinions to the Supreme Council of the Belarusian SSR regarding the compliance of draft acts of the Supreme Council of the Belarusian SSR with the Constitution of the Belarusian SSR;*
> 2) *shall supervise the compliance of resolutions and ordinances of the Supreme Council of the Belarusian SSR, as well as decisions of the regional and Minsk city councils and regional council of people's deputies with the Constitution of the Belarusian SSR and the laws of the Belarusian SSR.*
> 3) *shall, on its own initiative or following a proposal of the Supreme Council of the Belarusian SSR, the Presidium of the Supreme Council of the Belarusian SSR, the Chairman of the Supreme Council of the Belarusian SSR, or the permanent commissions of the Supreme Council of the Belarusian SSR, issue opinions on the*

---

13 Ж.И. Овсепян, *Правовая защита конституций. Судебный конституционный контроль в зарубежных странах*, Rostov-on-Don 1992, p. 9.

14 Act on the Constitutional Supervision Committee of the USSR, "Известия" (Izvestia) of 26 December 1989, No. 360.

> *compliance of acts issued by other state bodies and public organisations of the Republic with the Constitution of the Belarusian SSR and the laws of the Belarusian SSR.*
>
> *If any discrepancy is detected between an act or its individual provisions and the Constitution of the Belarusian SSR or the laws of the Belarusian SSR, the Constitutional Supervision Committee of the Belarusian SSR shall send its opinion to the body that issued the act concerned in order to eliminate the violation committed. The adoption of such an opinion by the Committee shall suspend the execution of the act or individual provisions of the act that contradicts the Constitution of the Belarusian SSR, or the law of the Belarusian SSR.*
> *The Constitutional Supervision Committee of the Belarusian SSR shall have the right to apply to the Supreme Council of the Belarusian SSR or the Council of Ministers of the Belarusian SSR with a request to repeal acts issued by their subordinated state bodies or officials which contradict the Constitution of the Belarusian SSR or the law of the Belarusian SSR.*
> *The organisation and the method of operation of the Constitutional Supervision Committee of the Belarusian SSR shall be defined by the Act on Constitutional Supervision in the USSR and the Act of the Belarusian SSR "On the Constitutional Supervision Committee of the Belarusian SSR*[15].

Thus, the Constitution provided for both preliminary and *ex post* review, ensured the opportunity to initiate a monitoring procedure on the Committee's own initiative, and also enshrined the Committee's right to suspend acts that contradicted the Constitution and the laws.

However, the Constitutional Supervision Committee of the BSSR shared the fate of the Constitutional Court of the Czechoslovak Soviet Socialist Republic, which was expected to be established under constitutional act No. 143 of the Czechoslovak Socialist Republic of 27 October 1968 "On the Czechoslovak Federation"[16], i.e. neither of those bodies was established, although for various reasons, and the aforementioned provisions represented merely a constitutional fiction.

As early as on 27 July 1990, the Supreme Council adopted the Declaration on State Sovereignty, which, for the first time in the history of the Belarusian state, proclaimed the goal of building a rule of law state and the separation of the legislative, executive and judicial powers was labelled as "the most important principle of the existence of the Belarusian state"[17]. The supremacy of the

---

15 Конституция (Основной Закон) Белорусской Советской Социалистической Республики, Minsk 1989, pp. 33–34.

16 Ústavní zákon o československé federaci, Sbírka zákonů ČR 1968, № 41.

17 Декларация Верховного Совета Белорусской Советской Социалистической Республики о государственном суверенитете Белорусской Советской Социалистической Республики, Minsk 1990.

Belarusian legislation on the territory of Belarus was proclaimed, and the need for a state authority that would review the constitutionality of the current legislation became even more pressing.

The Ministry of Justice drafted a law on the Constitutional Supervision Committee and Prof. V.G. Tikhinya, the then Minister of Justice, (who later became the chair of the Constitutional Court of Belarus) presented it for discussion at the first session of the Supreme Council of the 12th convocation, held in the second half of 1990. A major drawback of the draft project was that it almost duplicated the unfortunate provisions of the Act on the Constitutional Supervision Committee of the USSR. For example, according to Article 17 section 3 of the draft law, an opinion of the Constitutional Supervision Committee regarding unconstitutionality of an act adopted by the Supreme Council, or its individual provisions, could be overruled by a decision of the Supreme Council adopted by two-thirds of the total number of People's Deputies. It was expected that the Committee would include not only specialists in the field of law, but also "specialists in the field of politics", i.e. staff members of the Communist Party. Interestingly, the draft act provided for a preliminary review for all draft bills. The majority of deputies criticised the draft law and it was not adopted even in the first reading.

Moreover, during the same session of the Supreme Council, opinions were voiced about the need to establish a constitutional court with broad powers in Belarus rather than the Constitutional Supervision Committee with limited functions. Further development of the draft law on the constitutional review body was entrusted to the permanent commission on legislation of the Supreme Council. Due to the fact that work on drafting a new constitution of Belarus began at the end of 1990, the authors of the act on the constitutional court worked closely with the members and experts of the Constitutional Commission whose task was to create the new Basic Law for Belarus.

In November 1990, the author of this paper drafted an act on the constitutional court, and its main provisions were approved at a meeting of the parliamentary commission on legislation and incorporated into the relevant section of the Concept of Judicial and Legal Reform, approved by the Supreme Council on 23 April 1992[18]. Interestingly, the works of Polish constitutional scholars were used in the preparation of the draft law, in particular, the materials of the 27th All-Polish Congress of the Departments of Constitutional Law in Puławy[19],

18 Ведомости Верховного Совета Республики Беларусь 1992, № 16, ст. 270.

19 M. Granat, R. Mojak, J. Sobczak (eds.), *Kontrola konstytucyjności prawa*, Lublin 1987.

books by L. Garlicki[20] and Z. Czeszejko-Sochacki[21]. The concept envisaged that a constitutional court would be established as an independent body in the judicial system, designed to ensure compliance of laws and other regulatory legal acts with the Constitution and international legal obligations of the country, and it would also provide interpretations of the provisions of the Constitution. It was assumed that the right to file appeals with the Constitutional Court would be granted to the bodies entitled to have a legislative initiative as well as courts if, when considering a case, courts came to the conclusion that the normative act to be applied in the case was unconstitutional.

The draft act on the constitutional court was repeatedly submitted for consideration at Parliamentary sessions. It was included in the agenda of the sixth session of the Supreme Council[22], the extraordinary 11th session[23], and the 13th session (second reading)[24].

In parallel with the discussion in the Parliament, there was a discussion among legal scholars on the competence of the Constitutional Court, its place in the system of state bodies, and the legal status of members of the Court. In their academic publications on constitutional justice, Belarusian scholars analysed foreign experience and presented suggestions that a specialised body of constitutional review should be established in Belarus[25]. The rather long period of drafting the law was mainly due to the fact that work on a new constitution was

---

20 L. Garlicki, *Sądownictwo konstytucyjne w Europie Zachodniej*, Warszawa 1987.

21 Z. Czeszejko-Sochacki, *Trybunał Konstytucyjny PRL*, Warszawa 1987.

22 Ведомости Верховного Совета Республики Беларусь 1991, № 29, ст. 451.

23 Ведомости Верховного Совета Республики Беларусь 1993, № 14, ст. 141.

24 Ведомости Верховного Совета Республики Беларусь 1993, № 32, ст. 421.

25 See, for instance: Д. Булахов, М. Пастухов, *Конституционный суд: каким ему быть и зачем он нужен Республике Беларусь?*, "Народная газета" 15 октября 1991 г.; А. Вашкевич, *Конституционный Суд Республики Беларусь: место и роль в системе государственных органов de lege ferenda*, "Судовы веснік" 1992, № 3, pp. 53–55; *Конституция независимой Беларуси*, "Советская Белоруссия" 6 марта 1992; В.А. Кодавбович, *Вопросы Конституционного суда в проекте Конституции Республики Беларусь*, [in:] И.И. Басецкий (ed.), *Судебно-правовая реформа: концепция и пути ее реализации в Республике Беларусь*, Minsk 1992, pp. 185–187; А.А. Кебец, *Роль Конституционного суда в обеспечении качества закона,* [in:] И.И. Басецкий (ed.), *Судебно-правовая реформа: концепция и пути ее реализации в Республике Беларусь*, Minsk 1992, pp. 187–189; М.Ф. Чудаков, *Судебная власть: полномочия в сфере конституционного надзора,* [in:] И.И. Басецкий (ed.), *Судебно-правовая реформа: концепция и пути ее реализации в Республике Беларусь*, Minsk 1992, pp. 190–191.

being conducted in parallel, and one of the sections of the constitution was to be devoted to the constitutional court. There was no point in adopting the law before the adoption of the constitution, which was delayed for various reasons[26].

On 15 March 1994, the Supreme Council of the 12th convocation adopted the new Constitution, which, for the first time in the history of Belarusian constitutionalism, provided for the establishment a specialised constitutional review body in the country, namely the Constitutional Court. The Constitution included a dedicated chapter of eight articles entitled "The Constitutional Court of the Republic of Belarus". It regulated the procedure for the formation of the Constitutional Court, its competence and the legal status of judges. The said chapter was included in Section 6 of the Basic Law, entitled "State Control and Supervision", devoted to the legal regulation of the activities of the Constitutional Court, the Audit Chamber and the Prosecutor's Office.

On 30 March 1994, i.e. 15 days after the Constitution was adopted, the draft act on the Constitutional Court was submitted for consideration at the 87th meeting of the 13th session of the Supreme Council. D.P. Bulakhov, the Chairman of the Commission on Legislation, who spoke at the session, stated that the draft law presented to the deputies was the fifth version of the act[27]. Since the deputies were well acquainted with the content of the draft act, the Deputy Speaker of the Parliament, V.I. Shaladonov, suggested that it be passed in its entirety, rather than discussed article by article. Interestingly, a number of deputies made a proposal not to locate the Constitutional Court in Minsk (there was a proposal to erect a building of the Constitutional Court in Zaslavl – small town situated 30 kilometers near Minsk), explaining that there was no vacant space for, as one of the deputies put it, 'various kinds of offices'[28]. However, this proposal was not put to a vote. In general, 210 out of the 284 registered deputies voted in favour of the act on the Constitutional Court. No one voted against, two deputies abstained while 72 did not cast their votes[29]. Thus, the act on the Constitutional Court, consisting of 57 articles arranged into four chapters, was

26 For details on the adoption of the constitution, see: А.В. Курьянович, *Конституция независимой Беларуси: разработка, проекты, принятие. 2-е изд.*, Minsk 2011.

27 Трынаццатая сесія Вярхоўнага Савета Рэспублікі Беларусь дванаццатага склікання. Бюлетэнь № 87. Выданне Вярхоўнага Савета Рэспублікі Беларусь 1994, p. 22.

28 Ibidem, pp. 24–29.

29 Ibidem, p. 30.

adopted, quite symbolically, on the day when the new Basic Law entered into force, i.e. on 30 March 1994[30].

Since the text of the act is accessible to researchers, let us emphasise only one feature of the legal status of the Constitutional Court. According to Article 5 of the Act on the Constitutional Court, the Court had the right, at its own discretion, to consider compliance of normative acts issued by any state body and public association with the Constitution, laws and international legal acts ratified by the Republic of Belarus. The Constitutional Court, especially in the early days of its operation, quite frequently used the right to initiate cases on its own initiative (five times in 1994, twice in 1995, and six times in 1996)[31]. Interestingly, foreign experts (Prof. A. Blankenagel from Germany and Prof. G. Shaw from the USA), who reviewed the draft act on the Constitutional Court, pointed out that such a right could call into question the neutrality and political impartiality of the court. For instance, Prof. Blankenagel emphasised that the possibility for the Court to have its own initiative "predisposes the court to engage in judicial and legal activism and deprives the court of the opportunity to perform its original functions, while depriving the parties of the opportunity to treat this institution as a court"[32]. Nevertheless, the legislator did not heed those remarks and furnished the Constitutional Court with the right to initiate cases on its own initiative. The legislator's decision was influenced by at least three factors. Firstly, the experience of the Constitutional Supervision Committee of the USSR was taken into account, where the Committee had enjoyed such a right. Secondly, it was assumed that the Court would exercise this right with great caution, only at the first stage of its operation, using it solely in order to review acts that encroach on the constitutional rights and freedoms of citizens. Thirdly, the constitutional review body was a new phenomenon in the legal system of Belarus. Some parliamentarians believed that if such a right were not granted to the Court, it would be difficult to ensure that other entities authorised to appeal to the Constitutional Court would provide the Court with a sufficient number of cases to work on.

---

30 The Act of the Republic of Belarus on the Constitutional Court of the Republic of Belarus, Ведомости Верховного Совета Республики Беларусь 1994, № 15, ст. 220.

31 В.В. Подгруша, *Законодательство о конституционном контроле в Республике Беларусь: состояние и перспективы совершенствования*, [in:] *Правовое государство. Конституционный Суд. Материалы международных семинаров*, Minsk 2000, p. 20.

32 Author's personal archive.

Article 4 of the Law "On the procedure for the entry into force of the Constitution of the Republic of Belarus of 1994" provided that it was necessary *"to establish the Constitutional Court of the Republic of Belarus within one month from the entry into force of the Constitution in order to ensure unconditional compliance with the newly adopted Constitution of the Republic of Belarus"*[33].

To this end, a special extraordinary session of the Supreme Council was convened. On 28 April 1994, the issue of electing the members of the Constitutional Court was considered.

Different European countries have different approaches to the selection of candidates for the positions of constitutional court judges. Professor H. Steinberger described the appointment of judges as "the most delicate" issue. Even "the very question of who can nominate candidates for election or appointment is of key importance"[34]. In many European countries, the right to appoint constitutional court judges is held by several bodies or state officials representing different branches of government. Proposals to legislate such a procedure were also voiced when the Law on the Constitutional Court was being drafted[35]. However, the legislator chose a different path and set out in Article 126 of the Constitution that the Constitutional Court of the Republic of Belarus should be elected by the Supreme Council of the Republic of Belarus from among qualified experts in the field of law in the number of 11 judges. Developing this constitutional provision further, the Law on the Constitutional Court of 1994 stipulated that a judge of the Constitutional Court must be a citizen of the Republic of Belarus with a university degree in law, a high qualification in the field of law and high moral qualities[36]. Article 126 of the Constitution of 1994 set the maximum age limit for being a judge of the Constitutional Court at 60 (sixty) years.

The procedure for electing members of the Court was regulated in detail in Chapter 5 of the Provisional Rules of the Supreme Council[37]. In accordance with Article 71 of that Law, members of the Supreme Council would nominate candidates for the posts of Constitutional Court judges. Discussion and voting

33 Конституция Республики Беларусь, Minsk 1994, p. 29.

34 H. Steinberger, *Models of Constitutional Jurisdiction*, Strasbourg 1994, p. 30.

35 See, for instance: А. Вашкевич, *Конституционный Суд Республики Беларусь: место и роль в системе государственных органов*, [in:] И.И. Басецкий (ed.), *Судебно-правовая реформа: концепция и пути ее реализации в Республике Беларусь*, Minsk 1992, p. 181.

36 Article 14 of the Law on the Constitutional Court of the Republic of Belarus, Ведомости Верховного Совета Республики Беларусь 1994, № 15, ст. 220.

37 Ведомости Верховного Совета Республики Беларусь 1994, № 17, ст. 285.

was carried out on the basis of opinions on the candidates issued by two permanent parliamentary commissions, the legislation commission and the state system commission, as well as the Presidium of the Supreme Council, the membership of which included the speaker, the deputy speakers and the chairs of all permanent parliamentary commissions *ex officio*. In accordance with the adopted procedure, each candidate for the post of a judge was required to address the parliament with a short speech and answer questions asked by deputies. If the number of candidates exceeded the number of vacancies, a secret ballot was held and the candidates receiving the most votes were selected for the available vacancies. The rules prevented re-nomination within the same session if a candidate did not receive more than a half of the votes from the total number of deputies; also, it was not allowed to nominate the same candidate more than twice.

In April 1994, there were approximately 40 candidates for 11 vacant posts[38]. Following the discussion on candidates at a joint meeting of the permanent commissions, as well as at a meeting of the Presidium of the Supreme Council, it was decided that 11 candidates would be presented at the session. Of those, the deputies approved only eight candidates. Another candidate was nominated directly during the session. Thus, on 28 April 1994, in an extraordinary session of the Supreme Council, for the first time in the history of Belarusian constitutionalism, the first composition of the Constitutional Court was elected (in accordance with the requirements set out in Article 12 of the Law on the Constitutional Court, the set of members were competent to issue decisions and start work when it consisted of at least seven judges)[39]. (Two more judges were added from among eight candidates to fill the two remaining vacancies on 25 May 1996)[40].

Shortly after the Constitutional Court was established, a number of documents were developed and adopted by its members; the documents included the Rules of the Constitutional Court[41] and the Code of Honour of a Constitutional Court Judge of the Republic of Belarus[42]. On 23 September 1994, the Court issued its first opinion, marking the beginning of the first stage of its operation, which lasted until the end of 1996[43].

---

38 С. Мехов, *Громко молчащий орган*, "Фемида" 25 апреля 1994.

39 Звязда. 28 красавіка 1994 г.

40 Ведомости Верховного Совета Республики Беларусь 1996, № 18, ст. 338.

41 Ведомости Верховного Совета Республики Беларусь 1994, № 15, ст. 220.

42 Веснік Канстытуцыйнага Суду Рэспублікі Беларусь 1995, № 1, pp. 22–24.

43 Веснік Канстытуцыйнага Суду Рэспублікі Беларусь 1995, № 1, p. 25.

2 The Legislative Stability of the Legality Review Body

Throughout its existence, the legal status of the Constitutional Court of the Republic of Belarus (CCB) has not remained stable. One can distinguish three different stages in its activity when the legal framework surrounding the work of the Court changed significantly.

The first stage continued from the moment when the Constitutional Court was established on 28 April 1994 until December 1996. During that period, the legal status of the CCB was enshrined in a separate chapter of the 1994 Constitution, which consisted of eight articles, as well as in the Law on the Constitutional Court of the Republic of Belarus (CCB Act) adopted on 28 April 1994[44] and in the Rules of the Constitutional Court (CCB Rules), adopted on 27 May 1994[45]. In 1995, minor amendments were introduced in the CCB Law[46].

However, the status of the Constitutional Court underwent a deep transformation after amendments and additions were made to the Constitution in the referendum held on 24 November 1996. The CCB's opinion of 4 November 1996, stating that the mandatory referendum on proposed amendments and additions to the Constitution was unconstitutional, was not taken into account despite its binding nature[47].

The second stage of the Constitutional Court's activity took place from 1997 to 2008, under the new legal conditions. The main amendments to the status of the CCB boiled down to the following changes.

Firstly, only one article in the Constitution, namely Article 116, was devoted to the Court. It was included in Chapter 6 entitled "The Court" (before that, the constitutional review body was classified among review and supervisory bodies).

Secondly, the number of judges increased to 12, their maximum age while in office was increased from 60 to 70 years, and an additional requirement was formulated, i.e. that judges had to hold, "as a rule", an academic degree, i.e. a doctorate or a habilitation in law.

---

44 Ведомости Верховного Совета Республики Беларусь 1994, № 15, ст. 220.

45 Ведомости Верховного Совета Республики Беларусь 1994, № 15, ст. 220.

46 Law of 3 March 1995, No. 3634-XII, Ведомости Верховного Совета Республики Беларусь 1995, № 20, ст. 237.

47 Conclusion of the Constitutional Court of the Republic of Belarus of 4 November 1996 "On compliance of paragraphs 2.2, 2.5 and 3 of the resolution adopted by the Supreme Council of the Republic of Belarus on 6 September 1996 'On holding a Republican referendum in the Republic of Belarus and on measures to conduct it' with the Constitution and laws of the Republic of Belarus" No. 3–43/96, „Веснік Канстытуцыйнага Суда Рэспублікі Беларусь" 1996, № 4, pp. 32–35.

Thirdly, the list of bodies authorized to initiate constitutional proceedings was significantly limited. The parliament speaker, permanent parliamentary commissions, groups of deputies consisting of at least 70 people, and the General Prosecutor were excluded from the list (i.e. those who had used the right most actively between 1994 and 1996). In turn, the government was added to the list.

Fourthly, the Constitutional Court of Belarus lost the right to initiate cases on its own initiative.

Fifthly, the Constitutional Court lost the right to take part in the procedure for impeachment of the President. Previously, Article 104 section 2 of the Constitution had stipulated that after the CCB issued an opinion on the President's violation of the Constitution, the President could not perform his duties until the final decision on the case was adopted by the Supreme Council (see section 3.1 for more details). The new version of the Constitution contained a directly opposite competence of the Court. According to Article 116 section 6, following the President's proposal, the Constitutional Court would issue an opinion regarding systematic or gross violations of the Constitution by the chambers of the Parliament. In the event that such an opinion is issued, the powers of the Chamber of Representatives or of the Council of the Republic may be (but do not have to be) terminated early by the President and, in accordance with Article 93 section 3 of the Constitution, if the powers of one of the Parliament chambers are terminated, the President has the right to terminate the powers of the other chamber as well[48].

Sixthly, the material guarantees for the independence of judges were substantially reduced; in terms of legal and social guarantees, Constitutional Court judges were actually equated to judges of common courts[49].

Seventhly, a need arose to verify the constitutionality of the challenged normative acts for their compliance with the President's decrees and ordinances. These amendments were included in theLaw on the Constitutional Court[50].

---

48 http://pravo.by/pravovaya-informatsiya/normativnye-dokumenty/konstitutsiya-respubliki-belarus/ (accessed: February 20, 2018).

49 В.В. Подгруша, *Законодательство о конституционном контроле в Республике Беларусь:состояние и перспективы совершенствования*, [in:] *Правовое государство.Конституционный Суд. Материалы международных семинаров*, Minsk 2000, p. 19.

50 Law of 6 February 1997 No. 1–3, Ведомости Национального собрания Республики Беларусь 1997, № 7, ст. 162; Law of 7 June 1997 No. 51–3, Ведомости Национального собрания Республики Беларусь 1997, № 25–26, ст. 464.

The third stage of the changes the legal status of the CCB was initiated by the adoption of Presidential ordinance No. 14 of 26 June 2008 "On certain measures to improve the operations of the Constitutional Court of the Republic of Belarus"[51]. The ordinance was adopted due to the fact that the entities authorised to initiate constitutional proceedings, as defined in the Constitution, ceased to submit appeals to the CCB. The ordinance granted additional powers to the Constitutional Court, mainly the verification of the constitutionality of all laws adopted by the Chamber of Representatives and approved by the Council of the Republic but before they were signed by the President in accordance with the procedure of mandatory preliminary review (ordinance No. 14 paragraph 1 subparagraph 1.1). The ordinance provided for a number of other competences for the Constitutional Court, to be carried out on the President's initiative. Those competences will be analysed in section 3.1 below. A few years later, the provisions of the ordinance were fully incorporated into the code regulating the judicial system and the status of judges.

Since 2017, the legal status of the Court has not changed. Currently, this status is regulated by the following legal acts:

1) The Constitution[52]:
2) The Code on the Judicial System and the Status of Judges, approved in a new version in early 2017. The Code contains a large number of provisions regulating the activities of the Court; they are "scattered" throughout the entire text of the Code[53].
3) The Law on Constitutional Proceedings[54]. This act was developed over many years and the expediency of its adoption was discussed in a prolonged polemic with the Supreme Court. Following its adoption in 2014, the previous Law on the CCB, dated 1994, lost its legal force.
4) The Rules of the Constitutional Court[55]. According to Article 23 section 2 of the Code on the Judicial System and the Status of Judges, this act is approved

---

51 Нац. реестр правовых актов Республики Беларусь 2008, № 158, 1/9829.

52 http://pravo.by/pravovaya-informatsiya/normativnye-dokumenty/konstitutsiya-respubliki-belarus/ (accessed: February 20, 2018).

53 Национальный правовой Интернет-портал Республики Беларусь, 13.01.2017, 2/2451.

54 Национальный правовой Интернет-портал Республики Беларусь, 16.01.2014, 2/2122; 13.01.2017, 2/2451.

55 Approved by a decision adopted by the Constitutional Court of the Republic of Belarus of 8 April 2014 No. P-916/2014. Amended and supplemented by decision adopted by the Constitutional Court of the Republic of Belarus of 17 March 2017 No. P-1085/2017, http://www.kc.gov.by/print.aspx?guid=35213 (accessed: February 20, 2018).

by the Constitutional Court and regulates "the issues of organising, preparing and holding sessions of the Constitutional Court of the Republic of Belarus, ensuring conditions for the exercise of powers by the Constitutional Court of the Republic of Belarus and its judges, as well as other issues pertaining to the internal activity of the Constitutional Court of the Republic of Belarus, the procedure and forms of participation of the Secretariat of the Constitutional Court of the Republic of Belarus in preparing the cases for consideration in the court hearing, not regulated by this Code or other legislative acts"[56].

3 The Legislative Position of the Constitutional Court

3.1 The Constitutional Court and the President

Both these institutions were first enshrined at the constitutional level only when the 1994 Constitution was adopted, so they first emerged in 1994. However, the Constitutional Court had been established several months earlier[57], before the election of the first Head of State in the history of Belarus[58]. This circumstance seriously affected all the subsequent mutual relations between those authorities. According to the initial version of the Constitution, the Supreme Council elected CCB judges. The President could only nominate a candidate for the post of the chair of the CCB, who was elected to the post by the Parliament. The Constitutional Court also played a significant role in any ousting of the President from power under the impeachment procedure. Pursuant to Article 104 of the Constitution, if the President violated the Constitution, he could be removed from office by a decision of the Supreme Council, adopted by a majority of at least two thirds of the elected members of the Supreme Council, while an opinion regarding the violation of the Constitution by the President was issued by the CCB on the initiative of at least 70 members of Parliament. After the CCB issued its confirmation of a violation of the Constitution, the President could no longer perform his duties until the Supreme Council issued a relevant decision.

Between October 1994 and May 1996, a large number of acts issued by the President were declared unconstitutional. This caused serious discontent in the presidential administration. In March 1996, an article by A. Lukashenko was

56 Национальный правовой Интернет-портал Республики Беларусь, 13.01.2017, 2/2451.

57 The first 9 members of the Court were elected on 28 April 1994 at a session of the Supreme Council of the Republic of Belarus.

58 The first President of the Republic of Belarus (and the only one to date) was elected in the second round of presidential elections, held on 10 July 1994.

published in which he suggested that the legal status of the CCB be subjected to substantial reforms, and the procedure for electing judges be changed, giving the President the right to appoint a half of the judges[59]. On 24 May 1996, the pro-presidential parliamentary faction "Zgoda" filed a proposal to amend and supplement the CCB Act. According to the head of the faction V. Konoplev, because CCB judges were elected to their posts exclusively by the parliament, the Court was a "one-winged bird". To remedy this he proposed that the President should appoint half of the judges (five). The Supreme Council formally accepted the draft bill for consideration but refused to consider the document as a matter of priority, citing the previously approved six-month period for such a procedure. Moreover, on the same day, i.e. on 24 May 1996, the Supreme Council elected two additional judges of the CCB to fill the remaining vacancies[60].

In November 1996, the Constitutional Court of Belarus was involved in the procedure of impeachment of the President, initiated by 73 deputies. However, under pressure from the executive branch, ten deputies withdrew their signatures several days after the motion was submitted to the Court. Interestingly, the CCB approached some European constitutional courts asking them for an opinion on whether the CCB had the right to continue the proceedings in the case under the circumstances. A reply was received from the Chairman of the Constitutional Court of the Republic of Poland, A. Zoll, who stated that the consideration of the case was possible[61]. However, the Court ultimately decided to discontinue proceedings[62].

According to the new version of the Constitution, which came into force after the referendum (which was recognised as unconstitutional by the CCB), all previously existing highest state bodies, including the Constitutional Court, ceased to exist. The only exception was the President, who, according to Article 144, not only retained his powers, but also "reset" his term of office. This meant that the term of presidential powers was running from the moment the new Constitution came into force, while the period from 10 July 1994 to 26 November 1996 was not counted as part of the term, as if it had not occurred at all.

Under the new Constitution, the interactions between the President and the CCB take place in the following areas:

59 А. Лукашенко, *О послании Конституционного суда Республики Беларусь*, "Народная газета" 29 сакавіка 1996 г.

60 https://nn.by/?c=ar&i=160651&lang=ru (accessed: February 20, 2018).

61 Author's personal archive.

62 http://www.kc.gov.by/main.aspx?guid=11433 (accessed: February 20, 2018).

1) Election of Constitutional Court judges

According to Article 84 paragraphs 8, 10 and 11 of the Constitution, the President appoints six Constitutional Court judges; upon the consent of the Council (the upper chamber of the Parliament), he appoints and dismisses the CCB chair and judges. Since the chair of the Constitutional Court, appointed by the President, has the exclusive authority to nominate candidates for the posts of the other six judges for consideration by the upper chamber of the Parliament[63], the President has unlimited powers to determine the composition of the Court. Interestingly, the personnel Register of head of state[64] includes not only the chair of the Constitutional Court and six judges appointed by the President, but also the deputy chair of the Constitutional Court[65], who is elected by the judges of the CCB themselves (the chair of the CCB, appointed by the President, nominates a candidate for the post of the deputy chair). The presidential administration plays a key role in the selection of candidates for the positions of CCB judges[66]. According to some statements, the Chair of the Supreme Court must approve candidates for the position of a CCB judge.

2) Appeal to the Constitutional Court to initiate verification of constitutionality

Pursuant to Article 27 of the Law on the President,

> *the President has the right to address the Constitutional Court of the Republic of Belarus with a request that an ruling opinion be issued on the following:*
>
> - *compliance of law, presidential ordinances and decrees, international commitments of the Republic of Belarus under treaties, and other commitments with the Constitution of the Republic of Belarus and international legal instruments ratified by the Republic of Belarus;*

---

63 Article 21 section 2 of the Code on the Judicial System and the Status of Judges, http://www.kc.gov.by/main.aspx?guid=21725 (accessed: February 20, 2018).

64 Personnel Register of the head of state – this is a list of the key state offices which could be occupied only on the direct decision or approval of the President. It is similar to the former party "Nomenklatura".

65 Decree of the President of the Republic of Belarus No. 644 of 8 November 2001 "On approving the personnel register of the Head of State of the Republic of Belarus", with amendments and additions, http://pravo.by/document/?guid=3871&p0=P30100644 (accessed: February 20, 2018).

66 "On the optimisation of the Administration of the President of the Republic of Belarus", decree of the President of the Republic of Belarus No. 40 of 13 February 2017, http://www.pravo.by/document/?guid=12551&p0=P31700040&p1=1&p5=0 (accessed: February 20, 2018).

- *compliance of acts of interstate entities, to which the Republic of Belarus is a party member, and presidential decrees issued in execution of the law, with the Constitution of the Republic of Belarus, international legal acts ratified by the Republic of Belarus, laws and ordinances;*
- *compliance of resolutions adopted by the Council of Ministers of the Republic of Belarus, acts of the Supreme Court, the High Economic Court, and the General Prosecutor of the Republic of Belarus with the Constitution of the Republic of Belarus, international legal acts ratified by the Republic of Belarus, laws, decrees and ordinances;*
- *compliance of acts issued by any other state body with the Constitution of the Republic of Belarus, international legal acts ratified by the Republic of Belarus, laws, decrees and ordinances;*
- *presence of systematic or gross violations of the Constitution of the Republic of Belarus by the Chamber of Representatives and the Council of the Republic*[67].

In addition to the aforementioned powers, the Code on the Judicial System and the Status of Judges stipulates that following proposals made by the President:

(a) the Constitutional Court issues decisions on compliance with the Constitution of international treaties that have not yet entered into force;
(b) the Constitutional Court issues an official interpretation of ordinances and decrees issued by the President concerning the constitutional rights, freedoms and duties of citizens;
(c) the Constitutional Court reviews the constitutionality of guidelines for rule-making and law-enforcement practice of state bodies, including judicial and law-enforcement bodies; and
(d) following proposals made by the President, the Chamber of Representatives, the Council, or the Council of Ministers, the Constitutional Court expresses its position on whether documents adopted (issued) by other countries, international organisations and/or their bodies that affect the interests of the Republic of Belarus, comply with the universally recognised principles and norms of international law.

Despite this extensive list of powers, the President has only exercised the right to appeal to the Constitutional Court to recognise unconstitutionality of laws, and that just 14 times to date[68].

---

67 http://pravo.by/document/?guid=3871&p0=V19503602 (accessed: February 20, 2018).
68 И.И. Пляхимович, *Комментарий к Конституции Республики Беларусь, Т. 2*, Minsk 2015, pp. 582, 592.

3) Messages of the Constitutional Court to the President and chambers of Parliament

Pursuant to Article 22 section 3 of the Code on the Judicial System and the Status of Judges, the Constitutional Court "adopts annual messages to the President of the Republic of Belarus and the chambers of the National Assembly of the Republic of Belarus on the status of constitutional legality in the Republic of Belarus"[69]. The preparation of this document, as stipulated in Article 57 of the Rules of the CCB, "is based on the analysis of cases studied and examined by the Constitutional Court and other materials"[70]. The assessment of the institution of CCB messages in the doctrine is ambiguous. For example, when assessing the draft law on the Federal Constitutional Court of the Russian Federation, German Professor O. Luchterhandt pointed out that the proposed form of the court's activity has a very pronounced political character. He stressed that the court's decisions in specific cases should be the only messages given by the court[71].

According to former member of the Court, Prof. M. Pastukhov,

> the messages of the Constitutional Court are formalised reports on the work performed during the calendar year. They do not contain any critical assessments of the status of constitutional legality, and there are hardly any proposals to improve the legislation. In this regard, the messages on the status of constitutional legality in the country do not have any legal significance… [72].

At the same time, the former chairman of the CCB, Prof. G. Vasilevich points out that the messages:

> are sources of law: the message records legal ideas, which are a point of departure for the legislator and law enforcement agencies. In this regard, by virtue of its intellectual and legal nature, the message can also be characterised as legal doctrine based on scholarly research, which has been given statutory confirmation in a legal act issued by one of the highest authorities of the state, i.e. the Constitutional Court[73].

---

69 Национальный правовой Интернет-портал Республики Беларусь, 13.01.2017, 2/2451.

70 http://www.kc.gov.by/main.aspx?guid=21745 (accessed: February 20, 2018).

71 С.М. Омаров, *Основные проблемы реализации послания Конституционного Суда Российской Федерации*, "Право. Журнал Высшей школы экономики" 2011, № 4, p. 63.

72 М.И. Пастухов, *Когда слова равны молчанию. Белорусский опыт посланий Конституционного Суда о состоянии конституционной законности*, "Сравнительное конституционное обозрение" 2014, № 4, pp. 7–26.

73 Г.А. Василевич, *Послания Конституционного Суда Республики Беларусь о состоянии конституционной законности – реальный вклад в развитие правовой системы*, Minsk 2007, p. 37.

The court exercises its competence to adopt messages in practice. The first message on the status of constitutional legality was adopted on 27 January 1995[74], and the second one on 9 February 1996[75]. Interestingly enough, these two documents are not available from the Court's website for some unknown reason, although other decisions adopted in the same period have been posted. The year 1997 is the only one when no message was adopted[76]. All the messages adopted since 1998 are published on the Court's website[77]. Unfortunately, many proposals to improve the legislation expressed by the CCB in the texts of its messages have remained unimplemented. For instance, Belarus has not yet introduced the institution of the Commissioner for Human Rights (the proposal to introduce this institution has been periodically included in the text of the CCB messages since 1996)[78].

4) Disciplinary liability

According to a presidential decree, which has been in effect since 1999, all individuals whose posts are included in the President's personnel register (including the chair, the deputy chair and the CCB judges appointed by the President) must undergo "an annual in-depth medical examination at the state-owned 'Republican Clinical Medical Centre' managed by the Office of the President of the Republic of Belarus within the timeframe set by the President of the Republic of Belarus", whereas "those guilty of undergoing a medical check-up with delay are subject to disciplinary liability in accordance with established procedure"[79].

---

74 Веснік Канстытуцыйнага Суду Рэспублікі Беларусь 1995, № 2–3, pp. 14–23.

75 Веснік Канстытуцыйнага Суду Рэспублікі Беларусь 1996, № 1, pp. 4–12.

76 The message would have to provide an assessment of events related to the referendum held in Belarus, recognised by the Constitutional Court as unconstitutional.

77 http://www.kc.gov.by/main.aspx?guid=3371 (accessed: February 20, 2018).

78 See, for instance: Веснік Канстытуцыйнага Суду Рэспублікі Беларусь 1996, № 1, p. 21; Message on the status of constitutional legality in the Republic of Belarus in 2000, http://www.kc.gov.by/main.aspx?guid=19955 (accessed: February 20, 2018).

79 Decree of the President of the Republic of Belarus No. 32 of 18 January 1999 "On medical examination and certification of senior officials of state bodies whose positions are included in the personnel register of the Head of State of the Republic of Belarus" (amended and supplemented as of 18 January 2018), Консультант Плюс.

3.2 The Constitutional Court and the Government

The relations between the Constitutional Court and the country's government develop, among others, on the basis of Article 116 of the Constitution. On the one hand, government decisions can be considered by the Court for their compliance with international legal acts ratified by the Republic of Belarus, laws, ordinances and decrees. In practice, however, this happened infrequently. In 1995, the Court verified the constitutionality of three government decisions, all of which were recognised as constitutional[80]. Between 1997 and 2007, the government's decisions were subjected to verification six times, and unconstitutionality was ascertained in three cases[81]. After 2007, no decisions on the constitutionality of government decisions were issued.

On the other hand, the government is among the subjects authorised to appeal to the CCB with proposals to verify the constitutionality of normative legal acts. For the entire period of the Court's existence, however, this right has only been exercised three times[82].

In addition, the presidential decree of 2008 furnished the Council of Ministers with the competence to appeal to the CCB with a proposal that the CCB of the Republic of Belarus should outline its position on documents adopted (issued) by other countries, international organisations and/or their bodies and affecting the interests of the Republic of Belarus; verification should concern the compliance of these documents with the generally recognised principles and norms of international law. The Council of Ministers has not exercised this competence in practice.

The procedure of the government's appeal to the Constitutional Court is established in a regulation of the Council of Ministers, which, in 2017, was supplemented with rules regulating the procedure for examination of appeals

---

80 Decision of the Constitutional Court of the Republic of Belarus of 9 February 1996 No. (no number) "On the status of constitutional legality in the Republic of Belarus in 1995", http://www.kc.gov.by/main.aspx?guid=15843 (accessed: February 20, 2018).

81 И.И. Пляхимович, *Комментарий к Конституции Республики Беларусь. Т. 2*, Minsk 2015, p. 592.

82 П.П. Миклашевич, *Развитие форм конституционного контроля в современн ых условиях*, [in:] О.Г. Сергеева, В.В. Подгруша, С.П. Чигринов (eds.), *Развитие форм конституционного контроля в современных условиях: материалы Международного симпозиума, г. Минск, 30 июня 2016 г. Конституционный суд Республики Беларусь*, Minsk 2016, p. 35.

proactively submitted to the Council of Ministers by citizens and organisations (see section 4.6 for details)[83].

3.3 The Constitutional Court and the Parliament

The mutual relations between the Constitutional Court and the Parliament are regulated by the Constitution, as well as by the Rules of the Chamber of Representatives (lower chamber) and the Council of the Republic (upper chamber).

1) Formation of the Constitutional Court

According to Article 98 paragraphs 2 and 3 of the Constitution, the Council of the Republic elects six of the 12 Constitutional Court judges and gives consent to the President to appoint the Chair of the Court[84]. Decisions to give consent are formalised as resolutions of the Council, and in practice the presidential decree on appointment is issued first, and the relevant decision of the upper chamber is taken afterwards. As rightly noted by associate professor I. Plyakhimovich, "the role of the upper chamber of the Parliament is nominal. **There has not been a single case** (highlighted by the author) where the Council of the Republic would refuse to give consent to the President for the appointment of an official. The personnel decisions of both chambers of the Parliament are predetermined by the President"[85]. This is why, in practice,when the chair of the Constitutional Court proposes candidates for the position of judges to the Council of the Republic, the number of candidates corresponds with the number of vacancies. In other words, the selection of candidates and discussion on the candidates takes place outside the Parliament.

2) Regulation of the legal status of the Constitutional Court

At the constitutional level, the role of the Parliament is manifested not only in the formation of the Constitutional Court, but also in developing the legislative foundation for its activities. In accordance with the Constitution, the Parliament

---

83 Resolution of the Council of Ministers of the Republic of Belarus No. 526 of 14 July 2017 "On amendments to the Rules of the Council of Ministers of the Republic of Belarus", Национальный правовой Интернет-портал Республики Беларусь, 19.07.2017, 5/43954.

84 http://pravo.by/pravovaya-informatsiya/normativnye-dokumenty/konstitutsiya-respubliki-belarus/ (accessed: February 20, 2018).

85 И.И. Пляхимович, *Комментарий к Конституции Республики Беларусь. Т. 2*, Minsk 2015, p. 266.

adopts laws, including those relating to the competence, organisation and order of the activities of the CCB (for more details, see section 2)[86].

3) Participation in the financing of the Constitutional Court

According to Article 190 of the Code on the Judicial System and the Status of Judges, the courts of the Republic of Belarus are financed from the national budget and financing should be sufficient to ensure effective and independent administration of justice in accordance with legislative acts. Expenses for the maintenance of courts are provided in the national budget for the next financial year as separate items. The same approach has been adopted in the Budget Code.

The property necessary for the Constitutional Court to carry out its activities is the public property and is managed by the Court.

In accordance with the budget legislation, the CCB is both the administrator and the recipient of budgetary funds. As the administrator of budgetary funds, the CCB independently develops a draft budget estimate for the next financial year, which is then sent to the Ministry of Finance. In the annual act on the republican budget for the next fiscal year, the Parliament approves a separate specific amount for the upkeep of the CCB within the budget estimate. The Court manages the budget assignments and executes its budget[87].

3.4 The Constitutional Court and Other Courts

In many European countries, the right to approach the Constitutional Court directly is vested in the courts of general jurisdiction, and sometimes also in specialised courts, or the highest officials of these bodies (for example, the chair of the Supreme Administrative Court of the Republic of Poland or judges from Latvia's land registry department). In some countries, it is the courts that send the largest number of appeals to constitutional justice bodies[88]. In Belarus,

---

86 П.П. Миклашевич, *Конституционный Суд Республики Беларусь: функции и взаимодействие с другими органами государственной власти*, "Вестник Конституционного Суда Республики Беларусь" 2010, № 4, p. 136.

87 Constitutional justice: Functions and interaction with other public authorities (National paper of the Constitutional Court of the Republic of Belarus), the XV Congress of the Conference of the European Constitutional Courts., 23–25 May 2011, Bucharest, Romania, http://kc.gov.by/main.aspx?guid=21245 (accessed: February 20, 2018).

88 For details, see: А.Е. Вашкевич, *Доступ к конституционной юстиции: европейский опыт и законодательство Республики Беларусь*, [in:] *Актуальные проблемы международного публичного и международного частного права: сборник научных трудов. Выпуск 1*, Minsk 2009, pp. 45–50. For instance, in 2016, a total of 16 out of 21 appeals received by the Constitutional Court of Lithuania were submitted by

the right to appeal to the Constitutional Court is regulated in Article 112 of the Constitution, which has not changed since 1994. It reads: "Courts administer justice on the basis of the Constitution and other normative acts adopted in accordance with the Constitution. If, when examining a particular case, the court finds that a normative act is unconstitutional, it adopts a decision in accordance with the Constitution and sends the request for this normative act to be recognised as unconstitutional in the established order"[89].

The discussed provision did not appear in the text of the Constitution and the Act on the CCB by chance. Authors who drafted the text of the Constitution and the said act aimed to achieve direct application of constitutional provisions. As Prof. G. Vasilevich notes, "it was assumed that the courts would actively apply constitutional provisions, invoking them in their decisions, and whenever they detect contradictions between the Constitution and a subordinate legal act, they would appeal to the CCB. Such appeals were supposed to take the form of direct submissions by courts to the CCB without recourse to any intermediate instance (the Supreme Court or the High Economic Court)"[90].

In practice, however, this rule turned out to be defunct: during the 24 years of its existence, neither the regional courts nor district courts appealed to constitutional justice body even once. This situation can be explained by at least three reasons.

Firstly, since in Article 112 section 2 of the Constitution reads that courts apply to the CCB "in accordance with the established procedure", the Act on the Judicial System and the Status of Judges, adopted in 1995, enshrined such a procedure. However, the procedure proved to be very complicated and cumbersome. For instance, a district court judge who decided to appeal to the Constitutional Court first had to receive an approval from the president of the district court who, in turn, petitioned the Supreme Court to approach the CCB to verify the constitutionality of the normative act concerned[91]. Article 7 of the current Code on the Judicial System and the Status of Judges also provides that "if, when examining a specific case, the court of general jurisdiction concludes that a normative

---

courts, http://www.lrkt.lt/data/public/uploads/2018/01/annual-report-2016.pdf (accessed: February 20, 2018).

89 http://pravo.by/pravovaya-informatsiya/normativnye-dokumenty/konstitutsiya-respubliki-belarus/ (accessed: February 20, 2018).

90 Г.А. Василевич, *Конституционное правосудие,* Minsk 2012, p. 103.

91 Law of the Republic of Belarus No. 3514-XII of 13 January 1995 "On the judicial system and the status of judges", Ведомости Верховного Совета Республики Беларусь 1995, № 11, ст. 120.

legal act is inconsistent with the Constitution of the Republic of Belarus, the court shall adopt a decision in accordance with the Constitution of the Republic of Belarus and then request the Supreme Court of the Republic of Belarus to appeal to the Constitutional Court of the Republic of Belarus to recognise such a normative legal act as unconstitutional"[92].

Secondly, when Article 112 is applied, it is hypothetically possible that the Constitutional Court rules that the act applied by the court is not unconstitutional, but the lower-ranking court had already made a different decision, considering that the act in question was unconstitutional, and its decision had become effective. Such situations would, of course, undermine the legality in the country[93].

Thirdly, when a court of general jurisdiction considers a case, it is actually forced to exercise constitutional review, which, under Article 116 of the Constitution, falls within the competence of the CCB.

This kind of regulation has justly been and continues to be criticised in the doctrine. For instance, former judge of the CCB R.I. Filipchik pointed out that "the exercise of interim review of the proposals of lower courts by the Supreme Court and High Economic Court does not only hinder their initiative, but it can be regarded as interference in the administration of justice, and a violation of the independence of courts"[94]. Both the doctrine and the messages on the status of constitutional legality have repeatedly suggested that the courts should be granted the right to appeal to the CCB directly[95]. For instance, in its "Message on the status of constitutional legality in the Republic of Belarus in 2013", the CCB pointed out a problematic situation where "there is no proper legal mechanism

---

92 Национальный правовой Интернет-портал Республики Беларусь, 13.01.2017, 2/2451.

93 А.Н. Пугачев, *Судебный конституционной контроль: учеб.-метод. комплекс для магистрантов юрид. спец*, Новополоцк 2009, p. 366.

94 Р.И. Филипчик, *О роли Конституционного Суда в совершенствовании правового регулирования реализации гражданами конституционного права на судебную защиту*, "Весн. Канстытуцыйнага Суда Рэспублікі Беларусь" 2005, № 4.

95 See, for instance: А.Е. Вашкевич, *Конституционный контроль и судебная система. Отчет национального эксперта в области конституционного права А.Е. Вашкевича*, [in:] *Программа развития ООН в Республике Беларусь. Рекомендации по более широкому применению международных стандартов в области прав человека в процессе отправления правосудия в Республике Беларусь*, Minsk 2009, p. 203; Г.А. Василевич, *Конституционное правосудие: учебное пособие для студентов учреждений высшего образования по специальности "Правоведение"*, Minsk 2014, p. 161.

for initiating constitutional review of normative legal acts to be applied when examining specific cases in the courts of general jurisdiction. The current mechanism for the implementation of Article 112 of the Constitution, as set out in Article 7 section 2 of the Code on the Judicial System and the Status of Judges, does not properly regulate the possibility for a court of general jurisdiction to send a pre-judicial inquiry to the Constitutional Court regarding the constitutionality of a normative legal act to be applied in a particular case"[96]. However, this proposal has not been implemented to date.

Article 116 of the Constitution establishes the right of the Supreme Court and the High Economic Court to submit appeals for the verification of constitutionality of normative acts. Until now, the Supreme Court has exercised this right only five times while the High Economic Court has done so ten times[97].

It should also be noted that Presidential ordinance No. 6, adopted on 29 November 2013, abolished the High Economic Court as a constitutional body, and merged it with the Supreme Court[98]. According to point 1 of the Presidential decree, adopted on the same day as the ordinance, "in connection with the merger of the Supreme Court and the High Economic Court …: judges of the High Economic Court shall be considered as judges of the Supreme Court …"[99]. The mention of the High Economic Court was excluded from all presidential acts, but it remained in a number of articles in the Constitution. As V. Skobelev correctly noted, "the judicial reform is inconsistent with the Constitution of the Republic of Belarus, since the High Economic Court is repeatedly mentioned as one of the supreme bodies in the country in Chapter 4 of the Constitution entitled "President, Parliament, Government, Court", and this chapter can

96 Decision of the Constitutional Court of the Republic of Belarus No. P-915/2014 of 21 January 2014 "On the status of constitutional legality in the Republic of Belarus in 2013", http://kc.gov.by/main.aspx?guid=33763 (accessed: February 20, 2018).

97 П.П. Миклашевич, *Развитие форм конституционного контроля в современных условиях*, [in:] О.Г. Сергеева, В.В. Подгруша, С.П. Чигринов (eds.), *Развитие форм конституционного контроля в современных условиях: материалы Международного симпозиума, г. Минск, 30 июня 2016 г. Конституционный суд Республики Беларусь*, Minsk 2016, p. 35.

98 Ordinance of the President of the Republic of Belarus no. 6 of 29 November 2013 "On improving the judiciary system in the Republic of Belarus", Национальный правовой Интернет-портал Республики Беларусь, 30.11.2013, 1/14651.

99 Decree of the President of the Republic of Belarus No. 529 of 29 November 201329 November 2013 „On certain issues concerning the operation of courts in the Republic of Belarus" (extract), Национальный правовой Интернет-портал Республики Беларусь, 30.11.2013, 1/14649.

be changed only via a referendum. In this regard, the abolition of the High Economic Court by force of ordinance No. 6 is nothing more than an actual correction of the country's Basic Law in violation of the established procedure"[100]. Former Constitutional Court judge M. Pastukhov has supported this view: "there is a serious problem here, connected with the violation of the Constitution. On the one hand, the Code [the Code on the Judicial System and the Status of Judges – A.V.] was 'cleaned' and rid of the phrase 'economic courts', but, on the other hand, the Constitution retained a reference to economic courts (Articles 84, 98 and 116). It turns out that the new version of the Code contradicts the Constitution. Everyone sees and understands that but no one rushes to appeal to the Constitutional Court. A blatant violation of the Constitution was committed by judges themselves, as they involved parliamentarians in anti-constitutional activity"[101].

Also, Article 109 section 3 of the Constitution contains a direct indication that "the judicial system in the Republic of Belarus is defined by law", i.e. not by decrees and ordinances or similar acts. Moreover, Article 97 section 2 states that the Chamber of Representatives "considers draft laws, including … acts on the judicial system, judicial procedure and the status of judges"[102]. When commenting on this provision, G. Vasilevich pointed out: "Firstly, the competence of the Chamber of Representatives (and, therefore, the Parliament as a whole) includes the adoption of normative acts in the form of laws regulating the most important social relations; secondly, the fact that such a list has been formulated means that social relations in this sphere can be regulated only by an act of law (*zakon*). Therefore, one must speak here of the guarantees of the operation of a legislative body, and the inadmissibility of intrusions by other branches of government into this sphere of governance"[103].

Therefore, representatives of the doctrine are unanimous in saying that the publication of the above-mentioned ordinance was an illegal intrusion into the

---

100 В. Скобелев, *Белорусское судоустройство: свой курс, свои проблемы*, https://legal.report/author-16/belorusskoe-sudoustrojstvo-svoj-kurs-svoi-problemy (accessed: February 20, 2018).

101 М. Пастухов, *Де-юре. Как реформировать суды?*, http://naviny.by/article/20170724/1500875977-mihail-pastuhov-de-yure-kak-reformirovat-sudy (accessed: February 20, 2018).

102 http://pravo.by/pravovaya-informatsiya/normativnye-dokumenty/konstitutsiya-respubliki-belarus/ (accessed: February 20, 2018).

103 Г.А. Василевич, *Конституционное право Республики Беларусь: Учебник*, Minsk 2010, p. 631.

competence of the legislature and a violation of the Constitution. It is interesting to look at the reaction of the Constitutional Court, i.e. the body whose mission is to guard the Constitution. In its message on the status of constitutional legality for 2013, the Constitutional Court of Belarus merely noted that "following the adoption of legislative acts in accordance with Article 109 of the Constitution, aimed at establishing a unified system of courts of general jurisdiction, the merger of the Supreme Court and the High Economic Court into a single supreme judicial body, i.e. the Supreme Court, gave rise to the need to clarify certain provisions of the Constitution in order to remove legal uncertainty"[104].

3.5 The Constitutional Court and Other State Authorities

Among the other state authorities whose relations with the Constitutional Court are defined at the constitutional level, attention should be given to the Prosecutor General. As noted by G. Vasilevich, "the Constitutional Court and the prosecutor's offices have similar tasks, which they fulfil using specific methods within their respective competences. The tasks of the prosecutor's office include: ensuring the rule of law, legality, and legal order; protection of rights and legitimate interests of citizens and organisations, as well as public and state interests"[105]. According to Article 125 section 1 of the Constitution, "supervision over the exact and uniform execution of laws, ordinances, decrees and other normative acts by ministries and other bodies subordinate to the Council of Ministers, local representative and executive bodies, enterprises, organisations and institutions, public associations, officials and citizens is vested in the Prosecutor General of the Republic of Belarus and subordinated prosecutors"[106].

Until November 1996, the Prosecutor General's right to appeal to the CCB was enshrined in the Constitution. The Prosecutor General exercised that right on five occasions (in four cases, together with the Supreme Court and the Higher Economic Court)[107]. The current version of the Constitution does not provide for this right. In the doctrine, as well as in the annual messages of the Constitutional Court, the idea to restore this competence has been repeatedly proposed. For

104 Decision of the Constitutional Court of the Republic of Belarus No. P-915/2014 of 21 January 2014 "On the status of constitutional legality in the Republic of Belarus in 2013", http://kc.gov.by/main.aspx?guid=33763 (accessed: February 20, 2018).

105 Г.А. Василевич, *Конституционное правосудие* ..., p. 162.

106 http://pravo.by/pravovaya-informatsiya/normativnye-dokumenty/konstitutsiya-respubliki-belarus/ (accessed: February 20, 2018).

107 И.И. Пляхимович, *Комментарий к Конституции Республики Беларусь* ..., p. 581.

instance, the "Message on the status of constitutional legality in the Republic of Belarus in 2013" contains a proposal that the Prosecutor General should be granted the right to submit requests to the CCB regarding the verification of the constitutionality of normative legal acts[108]. Associate Professor A. Pugachev[109], Constitutional Court judge V. Podgrusha[110], the author of this paper[111], and other scholars have made similar proposals. However, the legislator has not yet taken them into account.

It should be noted that, according to Article 116 of the Constitution, the Constitutional Court of Belarus issues rulings"on the compliance of acts issued by the Prosecutor General with the Constitution, international legal acts ratified by the Republic of Belarus, acts of law, ordinances and decrees"[112]. In practice, however, they have never been examined by the Court.

As noted by the former chairman of the CCB, G. Vasilevich, the Constitutional Court and the General Prosecutor interact fairly often in cases where the CCB prepares to issue a decision on an issue under consideration and preliminarily analyses opinions of other instances[113]. For example, the opinion of the General Prosecutor's Office was sought when reviewing the constitutionality of capital punishment[114].

---

108 Decision of the Constitutional Court of the Republic of Belarus No. P-915/2014 of 21 January 2014 "On the status of constitutional legality in the Republic of Belarus in 2013", http://kc.gov.by/main.aspx?guid=33763 (accessed: February 20, 2018).

109 А.Н. Пугачев, *Судебный конституционной контроль: учеб.-метод. комплекс для магистрантов юрид. Спец.*, Novopolotsk 2009, p. 345.

110 В.И. Подгруша, *Некоторые проблемы инициирования конституционного производства,* [in:] *Конституционное правосудие в Республике Беларусь: пятилетний опыт, проблемы и перспективы. Сборник докладов и материалов*, Minsk 1999, p. 94.

111 А.Е. Вашкевич, *Конституционный контроль и судебная система. Отчет национального эксперта в области конституционного права Вашкевича А.Е.*, [in:] *Программа развития ООН в Республике Беларусь. Рекомендации по более широкому применению международных стандартов в области прав человека в процессе отправления правосудия в Республике Беларусь*, Minsk 2009, p. 203.

112 http://pravo.by/pravovaya-informatsiya/normativnye-dokumenty/konstitutsiya-respubliki-belarus/ (accessed: February 20, 2018).

113 Г.А. Василевич *Конституционное правосудие ...*, p. 164.

114 Decision of the Constitutional Court of the Republic of Belarus No. 3-171/2004 of 11 March 2004 "On compliance of the provisions of the Criminal Code of the Republic of Belarus providing for the application of capital punishment with the Constitution of the Republic of Belarus and international treaties of the Republic of Belarus", http://www.kc.gov.by/print.aspx?guid=10213 (accessed: February 20, 2018).

4 The Structure of the Constitutional Court

4.1 The Legal Status of Constitutional Court Judges

According to Article 66 of the Code on the Judicial System and the Status of Judges, "Judges of all courts in the Republic of Belarus have a unified status and differ in competences. A judge occupies a public position, is a civil servant, and is subject to the law of the Republic of Belarus of 14 June 2003 "On the civil service in the Republic of Belarus". The features of the status of a judge are defined in the Constitution of the Republic of Belarus, this Code and other legislative acts"[115]. The peculiarity of the legal status of a judge of the Constitutional Court involve special requirements for candidates, as well as a special order of appointment and dismissal.

The requirements for candidates for the position of a CCB judge are set out in Article 116 sections 2 and 3 of the Constitution: "The Constitutional Court of the Republic of Belarus consists of 12 judges from among highly qualified specialists in the field of law, who hold, as a rule, an scientific degree". "The age limit for Constitutional Court judges is 70 years"[116].

While the Constitution does not explicitly state the discipline of the scientific degree, a number of judges have held doctoral degree or habilitation only in law. In the first composition of the Constitutional Court, three out of 11 judges held a habilitation while four held a doctorate in law. In the current CCB, three out of 12 judges hold a habilitation in law while five hold a doctorate in law.

Article 73 of the Code on the Judicial System and the Status of Judges additionally requires that a judge must have Belarusian citizenship, a university degree in law, a command of two official languages: Belarusian and Russian, and must be characterised by a highly moral character.

The following individuals may not be appointed (elected) as judges of the CCB: a person in respect of whom a guilty verdict by a court has become effective; a person who is unable to perform the duties of a judge for health reasons, as evidenced by a medical certificate; a person recognised by a court as having a limited legal capacity or no legal capacity, where such a court decision has entered into force[117].

---

115 http://pravo.by/document/?guid=12551&p0=H11600013&p1=1&p5=0 (accessed: February 20, 2018).

116 http://pravo.by/pravovaya-informatsiya/normativnye-dokumenty/konstitutsiya-respubliki-belarus/ (accessed: February 20, 2018).

117 http://pravo.by/document/?guid=12551&p0=H11600013&p1=1&p5=0 (accessed: February 20, 2018).

Unfortunately, the legislation allows a re-election (re-appointment) of a judge, which, of course, reduces the guarantees of the independence of judges[118]. In the current Constitutional Court, two judges have held office since 1997. Several other judges were re-elected.

According to Article 114 of the Code on the Judicial System, "issues related to the salary of judges, availability of an official leave, guarantees associated with the liquidation of the court, a reduction of the number of judges or the number of staff, the provision of residential premises for commercial use, severance payments and other one-time allowances, pensions, medical services as well as other means of material and social security of judges are regulated by legislative acts"[119]. In the Belarusian law, "legislative acts" are understood as the Constitution of the Republic of Belarus, laws of the Republic of Belarus, as well as ordinances and decrees issued by the President of the Republic of Belarus[120]. In practice, the President most often regulates these issues[121].

Pursuant to Article 48 section 4 of the Law "On the civil service", the salary of the Deputy Chair and the judges of the Constitutional Court is set at, respectively, 90 and 85 % of the salary of the CCB Chair[122]. The original version of the Law on the Constitutional Court contained a provision whereby the salary of the Court Chair was equal to the salary of the Parliament Speaker, the salary of the Deputy Chair was equal to that of the Deputy Speaker, whereas the Constitutional Court judges had salaries at the level of those received by government ministers. Salaries for the aforementioned officials were established by the Parliament whose decisions were subject to publication. Since 1997, the President has set these salaries and the decisions are not published.

Much like other judges, CCB judges enjoy inviolability during their term of office. The inviolability of judges extends to their home, office space, transport

118 See, for instance: О. Люхьтерханд, *Роль и независимость Конституционного Суда в правовом государстве*, [in:] *Роль Конституционного Суда в реализации конституционных прав и свобод граждан: материалы международной конференции. Минск, 22 сентября 2009 года*, Minsk 2010, p. 34.

119 http://pravo.by/document/?guid=12551&p0=H11600013&p1=1&p5=0 (accessed: February 20, 2018).

120 http://pravo.by/document/?guid=3871&p0=h10000361 (accessed: February 20, 2018).

121 For details, see: A. Vashkevich, *Judicial Independence in the Republic of Belarus*, [in:] A. Seibert-Fohr (ed.), *Judicial independence in Transition*, Berlin, Heidelberg, New York: Springer 2012, pp. 1085–1088.

122 http://www.pravo.by/document/?guid=3871&p0=h10300204 (accessed: February 20, 2018).

and means of communications, correspondence, property and documents used by judges. The specific procedure for the instigation of criminal cases and the application of preventive measures in respect of CCB judges are set out in Articles 468–1, 468–2, 468–3 and 468–4 of the Code of Criminal Procedure. For instance, any decisions whereby a criminal case is instigated against a judge, where a judge is involved as a suspect or an accused in a criminal case brought against other persons, or in connection with a committed crime, are adopted by the Prosecutor General, the Chair of the Investigative Committee, the Chair of the State Security Committee or by persons acting in their capacity, with a prior consent of the President (in respect of the chair, deputy chair and judges appointed by the President, who are included in the President's personnel register) or of the Council of Republic (in respect of judges elected by the upper chamber). Constitutional Court judges may not be detained and otherwise deprived of personal freedom without the prior consent of the President, except for cases of high treason or detention at a crime scene. If a CCB judge has been detained, this fact is immediately communicated to the Chair or Deputy Chair of the Constitutional Court. In the event that no criminal case was instituted against the judge or if the judge was not brought in as a suspect or as an accused in a criminal case brought against other persons or in connection with a committed crime, the investigative actions carried out upon the approval of a prosecutor may be carried out only with the approval of the Prosecutor General or a person acting in that capacity. Personal searches of these individuals are not allowed, except for cases of detention at a crime scene[123].

Constitutional Court judges are subject to restrictions related to their civil service, as set out in Article 22 of the Law "On civil service". For instance, CCB judges have no right: to engage in entrepreneurial activity, whether personally or through other persons; to assist their spouse, close relatives or relatives-in-law in carrying out entrepreneurial activities, taking advantage of their official position; or to represent third parties on issues related to the activities of the state authority employing or controlling those judges; or to take part, whether personally or through proxies, in the management of a commercial organisation, except as set out in legislative acts. Judges may not serve as deputies in the Chamber of Representatives or the Council of Republic, or deputies of local Councils of Deputies. They may not be members of political parties or other public associations pursuing political goals; take part in strikes; perform other paid

123 http://etalonline.by/?type=text&regnum=HK9900295#load_text_none_1_ (accessed: February 20, 2018).

work, unrelated to the performance of their official duties at the primary place of employment, except teaching (carrying out educational programmes), scholarly, cultural, or creative activity and medical practice. Teaching activity (carrying out educational programmes), scientific, cultural and creative activity, and medical practice during working hours may be carried out with the agreement of the head of the state body where the civil servant holds a public office, or by a person authorised by the head of that state body. Civil servants are not allowed to accept property (gifts) or receive other benefits in the form of services in connection with their performance of official duties, with the exception of souvenirs handed over during official visits and other official events

Souvenirs with a value exceeding five basic units, received during official visits and other official events, must be given away to the state upon a decision adopted by a commission established by the head of the state body where the civil servant holds a public office. Civil servants may not hold accounts in foreign banks, except for cases where they perform official functions in other countries, and in other cases provided for by law. They are not allowed to receive state awards from foreign countries without the consent of the President; to receive documents from foreign countries, granting rights to privileges and benefits in connection with political, religious views or national identity, or take advantage of such privileges and benefits, unless otherwise provided by international treaties to which the Republic of Belarus is a party (one example of such a document is *Karta Polaka,* lit. a Polish person's card, regulated by the law adopted by the Polish parliament). These restrictions are not exhaustive[124].

A judge of the Constitutional Court has the right to demand convocation of a Court session, to propose issues for consideration by the CCB, to express a dissenting opinion on the rulings and decisions issued by the CCB. When working on all issues falling within the competence of the Constitutional Court, judges enjoy equal rights. They are entitled to attend open meetings (and, by invitation, also closed meetings) of any state bodies[125].

According to Article 108 of the Code on the Judicial System, the powers of a judge of the Constitutional Court of the Republic of Belarus can be terminated in the following cases: when the judge resigns; when the judge files an application for release from office at their own request; when the judge has reached the age limit set for the office of a Constitutional Court judge; when the judge's term of

124 http://www.pravo.by/document/?guid=3871&p0=h10300204 (accessed: February 20, 2018).

125 Article 71 of the Code on the Judicial System and the Status of Judges, http://pravo.by/document/?guid=3871&p0=hk0600139 (accessed: February 20, 2018).

office has expired; when the judge refuses to take the oath; when the judge's citizenship of the Republic of Belarus has terminated as a result of renouncement or loss of citizenship; when the judge has been appointed (elected) to another position or transferred to another job; when the judge has engaged in activities that are incompatible with the position of the judge, or failed to comply with the restrictions related to civil service; when the judge has committed a single gross violation of official duties recognised as such in accordance with legislative acts, committed an offence incompatible with the status of a civil servant; when a guilty verdict in respect of the judge has entered into force; when a court decision recognising the judge as having limited or no legal capacity has entered into force; when the judge has been recognised as unable to perform the duties of a judge for health reasons (as supported by a medical certificate); when the judge died, was declared to be deceased, or declared missing under a court decision which entered into legal force, without a special decision being adopted.

The powers of the chair and judges of the Constitutional Court are terminated by the President, also on the basis of the judge's personal written note of resignation or dismissal at his/her own request, upon request submitted by the CCB or by the Chair of the Court. The President notifies the Council of Republic on termination of the powers of a Constitutional Court judge[126]. In practice, in the vast majority of cases resignation was the reason for the termination of the powers of the chair or judges of the Court[127]. However, in one case judge M. Pastukhov, elected for 11 years in 1994, was removed from office due to "the expiration of the term of office"[128]. The UN Human Rights Committee recognised this fact as a violation of Article 25(c) of the International Covenant on Civil and Political Rights by the Republic of Belarus (whereunder every citizen has the right of access, on general terms of equality, to public service in their country) in

---

126 Ibidem.

127 See, for instance: Decree of the President of the Republic of Belarus No. 378 of 20 October 2016 "On dismissing V.P. Izotko", http://pravo.by/upload/docs/op/P31600378_1477083600.pdf (accessed: February 20, 2018); Decree of the President of the Republic of Belarus No. 120 of 12 March 2014 "On dismissing A.V. Maryskin", http://www.pravo.by/document/?guid=12551&p0=P31400120&p1=1&p5=0 (accessed: February 20, 2018); Decree of the President of the Republic of Belarus No. 18 of 11 January 2008 "On G.A. Vasilevich", http://laws.newsby.org/documents/ukazp/pos00/ukaz00430.htm (accessed: February 20, 2018).

128 Decree of the President of the Republic of Belarus No. 106 of 24 January 1997 "On dismissing M. I. Pastukhov", "Собрание декретов, указов Президента и постановлений Правительства Республики Беларусь" 1997 г., № 3, ст. 112.

conjunction with Article 14(1) of the Covenant, concerning the independence of the judiciary, as well as the provisions of Article 2 of the Covenant[129].

4.2 Functions of the Constitutional Court

Belarusian constitutional justice legislation does not contain the concept of a "function" or "functions" of the Constitutional Court. The legislator uses expressions such as "competence" or "powers" in the context of this body. Moreover, there is also no research on this issue in the Belarusian legal doctrine. Associate Professor A.N. Pugachev asserts that "the protection of the Constitution and the protection of rights and freedoms should be regarded as the dual function of the Constitutional Court"[130]. According to Article 6 section 1 of the Code on the Judicial System and the Status of Judges, "the Constitutional Court of the Republic of Belarus is called upon to defend the constitutional system of the Republic of Belarus, the human and civil rights and freedoms guaranteed by the Constitution of the Republic of Belarus, to ensure the supremacy of the Constitution of the Republic of Belarus and its direct application on the territory of the Republic of Belarus, constitutionality of normative legal acts issued by state bodies of the Republic of Belarus, confirm legality in rule-making and law enforcement, resolve other issues stipulated by the Constitution of the Republic of Belarus, the present Code and other legislative acts"[131].

4.3 The Subject-matter of the Review Performed by the Constitutional Court

At present, the CCB performs a review of normative acts as well as actions undertaken by state bodies.

4.3.1 Normative Acts as a Subject of Review

In the Republic of Belarus, a normative legal act is understood as "an official document in the established format, adopted (published) within the competence of the authorised state body (an official) or by referendum, in compliance with the procedure established in the legislation of the Republic of Belarus, containing

---

129 Comm. № 814/1998, Pastukhov v. Belarus (Communications adopted on 5 August 2003, the seventy-eight session), http://hrlibrary.umn.edu/russian/hrcommittee/Rview814sess78.html (accessed: February 20, 2018).

130 А.Н. Пугачев, *Судебный конституционной контроль* ..., p. 85.

131 http://pravo.by/document/?guid=3871&p0=hk0600139 (accessed: February 20, 2018).

generally binding rules of conduct intended for an indefinite circle of persons and repeated application"[132]. Thus, individual legal acts are not subject to review by the CCB though common courts may review them[133].

It should be noted that the normative acts that are the subject of review should, as a rule, be part of the existing legal system. According to Article 56 of the Law on Constitutional Proceedings, "The Constitutional Court shall terminate the proceedings in a case if: … the act, whose constitutionality is being verified, is amended and/or supplemented, thus excluding the grounds for the consideration of the case, or if such an act has been declared as no longer in force (invalid), or if participation of the Republic of Belarus in such an act has been terminated, except for cases when, as a result of this act, the constitutional rights and freedoms of citizens were violated, or when a new act regulating the same subject-matter has been adopted (issued), thus excluding the grounds for the consideration of the case"[134].

It is important to emphasise that review may be applied to acts adopted both after and before the entry into force of the 1994 Constitution, including acts that were adopted in the Soviet era[135].

Under Article 116 of the Constitution, the normative acts which are subject to an ex post review by the Constitutional Court include:

1) Laws

The Constitutional Court of Belarus has most frequently reviewed acts of this type (including codes). The Constitution refers to various types of laws (acts of law). They include laws introducing amendments and additions to the Constitution and laws on their enactment (Article 140 section 1), programme laws, which include laws on the main directions of domestic and foreign policy of the Republic of Belarus and laws on military doctrine (Article 104 section 4); laws on the interpretation of the Constitution (Article 97 section 1 of the Constitution). In accordance with Article 2 of the Law on Normative Legal Acts,

---

132 http://pravo.by/document/?guid=3871&p0=h10000361 (accessed: February 20, 2018).

133 See, for instance, Article 335 of the Code of Civil Procedure of the Republic of Belarus, http://etalonline.by/?type=text&regnum=HK9900238#load_text_none_1_ (accessed: February 20, 2018).

134 http://www.kc.gov.by/print.aspx?guid=35203 (accessed: February 20, 2018).

135 Law of the Republic of Belarus No. 261-3 of 28 May 1999 "On applying the USSR legislation on the territory of the Republic of Belarus"//Нац. реестр правовых актов Республики Беларусь 1999, № 42, 2/36.

acts of law also include codes, i.e. laws that ensure complete systemic regulation of a certain area of social relations. All of the aforementioned laws can be reviewed for compliance with the country's Constitution. Between 1994 and the present, a total of 37 laws have been subjected to an ex post review, and individual provisions contained in 27 laws have been declared unconstitutional[136].

2) Presidential ordinances and decrees

The right to issue ordinances was granted to the President under the new version of the Constitution, which entered into force in November 1996. According to Article 2 of the Law on Normative Legal Acts, "the ordinance of the President of the Republic of Belarus is a normative legal act issued by the Head of State, with the force of the law, issued in accordance with the Constitution of the Republic Belarus on the basis of legislative powers delegated to the President by the Parliament or in cases of particular necessity (a temporary ordinance), intended for the regulation of the most important social relations"[137]. Not a single presidential ordinance has been reviewed by the Constitutional Court.

In the period from 1994 to 1996, the Court examined a total of 16 presidential decrees, and found a violation of the Constitution in 14 cases[138]. Between 1997 and the present, only one decree has been reviewed by the CCB and it was recognised as constitutional[139].

It should be borne in mind that the President has the right to issue two more types of acts: directives (*директивы*) and orders (*распоряжения*). Orders are not listed among the acts subject to review by the Constitutional Court since those acts are not normative. However, according to Article 3 of the Law on Normative Legal Acts, the President's orders are non-normative only "unless otherwise stipulated by the President"[140]. It seems that a regulatory order should be subject to review by the Constitutional Court. A different approach would

---

136 A. Waszkiewicz, *Sąd Konstytucyjny Republiki Białoruś: przed i po referendum listopadowym 1996 roku*, [in:] J. Trzciński (ed.), *Sądy Konstytucyjne w Europie. Białoruś, Litwa, Łotwa, Rosja, t. IV*, Warszawa 2000. p. 32; И.И. Пляхимович, *Комментарий к Конституции Республики Беларусь* ..., p. 591.

137 http://pravo.by/document/?guid=3871&p0=h10000361 (accessed: February 20, 2018).

138 A. Waszkiewicz, *Sąd Konstytucyjny Republiki Białoruś* ..., p. 32.

139 И.И. Пляхимович, *Комментарий к Конституции Республики Беларусь* ..., p. 592.

140 http://pravo.by/document/?guid=3871&p0=h10000361 (accessed: February 20, 2018).

have undermined the very essence of the institution of constitutional review, since it would allow violations of the Constitution with impunity. An example is the case examined by the Constitutional Court on 29 April 1996 on the constitutionality of Presidential order No. 259 of 30 December 1995. Paragraph 1 of that order, addressed to state bodies, contained a requirement "to ensure unconditional compliance" with the provisions of eight Presidential decrees, which were recognised by the Constitutional Court as fully or partially unconstitutional throughout 1995. In paragraph 2 of the order, the Presidential administration was instructed to ensure the publication of a compilation of valid decrees issued by the President. Quite understandably, the Constitutional Court recognised that paragraph 1 of the order was non-compliant with the Constitution and laws of the Republic of Belarus in the section which ordered state bodies to ensure unconditional compliance with the provisions of decrees recognised as unconstitutional and having no legal force; the CCB recognised this part of the order as having no legal force after publication[141].

According to Article 2 of the Law on Normative Legal Acts, directives are a type of Presidential decrees. They are programming decrees issued by the head of state with a view to systematic regulation of issues that have a high political, social or economic importance[142]. Therefore, directives can be subject to constitutional review, but this has not yet happened in practice.

3) Decisions of the Council of Ministers (in the original version of the 1994 Constitution, the government was referred to as 'the Cabinet of Ministers') have been reviewed nine times between 1994 and 2008, with six decisions being recognised as fully or partially unconstitutional[143].
4) Acts of the Supreme Court, High Economic Court, and Prosecutor General.

Article 2 of the Law on Normative Legal Acts stipulates that not all acts issued by higher courts are normative legal acts: only resolutions of their plenums have this status[144]. Between 1994 and 2008, these acts were reviewed five times, with

141 http://www.kc.gov.by/main.aspx?guid=11533 (accessed: February 20, 2018).
142 http://pravo.by/document/?guid=3871&p0=h10000361 (accessed: February 20, 2018).
143 A. Waszkiewicz, *Sąd Konstytucyjny Republiki Białoruś* ..., p. 32; И.И. Пляхимович, *Комментарий к Конституции Республики Беларусь* ..., p. 581.
144 http://pravo.by/document/?guid=3871&p0=h10000361 (accessed: February 20, 2018).

four resolutions of the plenum of the Supreme Court being recognised as either fully or partially unconstitutional[145].

5) Acts issued by any other public authority.

It follows from Article 2 of the Law on Normative Legal Acts that such acts include resolutions of the Chambers of the Parliament, i.e. the National Assembly of the Republic of Belarus, resolutions and orders of the republican government bodies: ministries, state committees, other departments and the National Bank of the Republic of Belarus, decisions adopted by local Councils of Deputies, executive and administrative bodies, as well as other regulatory acts adopted by state bodies. The existence of such a broad list of national normative acts that fall under the review of the constitutional justice body stems, inter alia, from the absence of administrative justice in the judicial system of Belarus.

6) International treaties and acts of interstate entities, of which the Republic of Belarus is a member, are a special subject (and, at the same time, a model) of review.

In practice, the Constitutional Court of Belarus has never examined such cases, but since 2008, according to a Presidential decree, the CCB has been charged with the obligation, upon the President's request, to rule on the constitutionality of international treaties of the Republic of Belarus that have not entered into force.

4.3.2 Actions Taken by State Bodies as a Subject-matter of Review

The constitutional review may also cover actions taken by state bodies. For instance, the CCB may decide whether or not the chambers of the National Assembly have committed a systematic or a flagrant violation of the Constitution or whether or not the local Councils of Deputies have violated the law. In practice, however, these powers have not been exercised.

4.4 Preliminary and Ex Post Review of Legal Provisions

During the first stage (1994–1996) and the second stage (1997–2008) of the history of the Constitutional Court, only *ex post* review was applied. This review ends with the Court's ruling on the constitutionality (or non-constitutionality) of a reviewed act. However, after 2008, the authorised entities ceased to submit

---

145 A. Waszkiewicz, *Sąd Konstytucyjny Republiki Białoruś* …., p. 32; И.И. Пляхимович, *Комментарий к Конституции Республики Беларусь* …, p. 592.

appeals to the CCB. The last opinion (and the only one after 2008) was issued by the CCB in June 2014[146]. The CCB believes that the reason behind this passivity of the authorised state bodies lies in "the proper interaction among the bodies of all branches of power in the legislative process in order to achieve a balance of public and private interests, and stability in the society and state"[147], and also in the fact that "when drafting and adopting laws, state bodies at all levels find constructive solutions in order to regulate the social relations, with strict compliance with constitutional provisions"[148]. In the opinion of the Chairman of the CCB, P. Miklashevich, "in today's Belarus, the state mechanism is working clearly and smoothly, the branches of government interact in a constructive manner, with stability and harmony in society having been achieved"[149]. Associate Professor I. Plyakhimovich, with whom the author of this paper agrees, sees the main reason for the current situation in the fact that "unity of power has replaced the separation of powers, which, although in contradictory ways, existed until the adoption of the new version of the Constitution. In the context of the leading position of the President, who has a significant impact on the subjects of all branches of power, judicial mechanisms for resolving disputes between state bodies cannot develop to a large extent"[150].

The overall results of the activity of the Constitutional Court in application of this type of review are as follows: authorised entities appealed 67 times with requests to review the constitutionality of regulatory legal acts. In 50 opinions, the CCB recognised the provisions of acts of law and other acts as unconstitutional[151].

Given the total absence of appeals to the Constitutional Court from authorised entities, Presidential ordinance No. 14 of 26 June 2008 gave the CCB the competence to conduct preliminary review of all laws approved by the Parliament

146 http://kc.gov.by/main.aspx?guid=36613 (accessed: February 20, 2018).

147 Decision of the Constitutional Court of the Republic of Belarus No. P-1028/2016 of 20 January 2016 "On the status of constitutional legality in the Republic of Belarus in 2015", http://kc.gov.by/main.aspx?guid=42383 (accessed: February 20, 2018).

148 Decision of the Constitutional Court of the Republic of Belarus No. P-1084/2017 of 18 January 2017 "On the status of constitutional legality in the Republic of Belarus in 2016", http://kc.gov.by/main.aspx?guid=45433 (accessed: February 20, 2018).

149 П.П. Миклашевич, *Развитие форм конституционного контроля в современных условиях*, pp. 36–37.

150 И.И. Пляхимович, *Комментарий к Конституции Республики Беларусь ...*, p. 593.

151 П.П. Миклашевич, *Развитие форм конституционного контроля в современных условиях*, p. 34.

prior to their signing by the President, as well as some other competences "in order to improve the efficiency of work"[152]. (Subsequently, the text of the said act was fully incorporated into the Code on the Judicial System and the Status of Judges). The features of this competence are as follows: the obligation to conduct a review; an abstract character; implementation of the review after laws have been adopted by Parliament, but before they were signed by the President, which enables the Constitutional Court not to interfere in the powers of the legislature; a written procedure for examination, the absence of parties in the process, the absence of a dispute, a five-day period for the examination of the case by the Court. Theoretically, examination of an act of law under a preliminary review procedure does not deprive the authorised entities from the possibility of initiating a verification under an *ex post* review, considering the practice of its application. However, no such cases have taken place to date. According to O. Sergeevaa member of the CCB, when carrying out the mandatory preliminary review, the CCB is guided by three criteria of constitutionality: the first is

> compliance of the provisions of the law under review with the principles and provisions of the Constitution. Within mandatory preliminary review, the constitutionality of the act of law is checked outside the context of any particular case; compliance is verified not only in terms of the direct provision of the Constitution, but with its spirit and goals, as well as with the values enshrined in it. The review serves to verify both the content of the act (its provisions) and the correctness of its format and the way it was adopted. Thus, the review covers the compliance of the content of the act with the provisions of the Constitution, the compliance with the constitutional requirements for the issuance of the act (whether or not the publication of the act fell within the competence of the body concerned, whether procedural rules were observed, and whether the act was adopted in the appropriate format)[153].

The second criterion is

> the criterion of legal certainty, stemming from the principle of the rule of law, enshrined in Article 7 section 1 of the Constitution, referring to clarity, non-ambiguity of legal provisions, ensuring uniform application of provisions in practice.

The third criterion refers to the proportionality of restrictions on citizens' rights and freedoms, i.e. the review verifies whether or not the statutory norm entails an unreasonable restriction of rights and freedoms, and whether the interests specified in Article 23 section 1 of the Constitution were ensured when restrictions were introduced[154].

---

152 http://www.kc.gov.by/main.aspx?guid=7205 (accessed: February 20, 2018).
153 http://kc.gov.by/main.aspx?guid=21625 (accessed: February 20, 2018).
154 Ibidem.

When exercising this competence, the Constitutional Court of Belarus examined 102 laws in 2008,[155] 104 laws in 2009[156], 129 laws in 2010[157], 109 laws in 2011[158], and 113 laws in 2012[159]. In 2013, the constitutionality of 111 laws was verified[160], with 55 laws in 2014[161], 50 laws in 2015[162], and 53 laws in 2016[163]. In 2017, the CCB verified 31 laws passed by the Chamber of Representatives and approved by the Council of the Republic of the National Assembly, before being signed by the President[164]. Therefore, over a period of ten years, the Constitutional Court verified 857 acts of law under preliminary review. In a number of cases, the Court detected such shortcomings as uncertainty, inaccuracy, ambiguity of the content of certain provisions, absence of an implementation mechanism or gaps in legal regulations[165]. However, despite this, all laws were recognised as constitutional. As Associate Professor I. Plyakhimovich, author of the fundamental commentary to the Constitution, rightly notes, "the objectivity of mandatory preliminary review is hampered by the fact that the drafts of many laws are coordinated with the President before entering the Parliament. There were cases where the essence of the decision implied that the Constitutional Court considered certain provisions unconstitutional, but according to the wording of the decisions, such acts were nevertheless declared constitutional. As the

155 Message on the status of constitutional legality in the Republic of Belarus in 2008, http://www.kc.gov.by/main.aspx?guid=19875 (accessed: February 20, 2018).
156 Message on the status of constitutional legality in the Republic of Belarus in 2009, http://www.kc.gov.by/main.aspx?guid=19865 (accessed: February 20, 2018).
157 Message on the status of constitutional legality in the Republic of Belarus in 2010, http://www.kc.gov.by/main.aspx?guid=18495 (accessed: February 20, 2018).
158 Message on the status of constitutional legality in the Republic of Belarus in 2011, http://www.kc.gov.by/main.aspx?guid=18485 (accessed: February 20, 2018).
159 Message on the status of constitutional legality in the Republic of Belarus in 2012, http://www.kc.gov.by/main.aspx?guid=18475 (accessed: February 20, 2018).
160 Message on the status of constitutional legality in the Republic of Belarus in 2013, http://www.kc.gov.by/main.aspx?guid=20895 (accessed: February 20, 2018).
161 Message on the status of constitutional legality in the Republic of Belarus in 2014, http://www.kc.gov.by/main.aspx?guid=19095 (accessed: February 20, 2018).
162 Message on the status of constitutional legality in the Republic of Belarus in 2015, http://www.kc.gov.by/main.aspx?guid=25695 (accessed: February 20, 2018).
163 Message on the status of constitutional legality in the Republic of Belarus in 2016, http://www.kc.gov.by/main.aspx?guid=27975 (accessed: February 20, 2018).
164 Message of the Constitutional Court of the Republic of Belarus on the status of constitutional legality in the Republic of Belarus in 2017, http://www.kc.gov.by/main.aspx?guid=48223 (accessed: February 20, 2018).
165 http://kc.gov.by/main.aspx?guid=21625 (accessed: February 20, 2018).

Constitutional Court recognised all laws as constitutional… this cannot but suggest a prescribed position of the Court and a predetermined nature of its decisions"[166].

In his opinion, which one cannot disagree with, "the mandatory preliminary review conducted by the Constitutional Court of Belarus seems ineffective: it has a highly superficial, formal character"[167], especially considering that the analysis of an act of law must be conducted within five days after it was submitted to the Constitutional Court[168].

4.5 The Procedure for Reviewing Legal Provisions

The review procedure is detailed in the Law on Constitutional Proceedings and the Rules of Procedure of the Constitutional Court. The main principles of the activity of the Court are the legality, independence of judges of the Constitutional Court, collegiality, transparency, equality and adversarial process between the parties, as well as a comprehensive, complete and objective examination of the case materials. Article 13 of the Law on Constitutional Proceedings establishes the principle of presumption of constitutionality of the acts being reviewed.

The Constitutional Court is competent to hear cases in court, with at least eight of the 12 judges being present.

The cases are examined in a court session with the use of an oral form of constitutional proceedings, except for cases provided for in the Law on Constitutional Proceedings. The written form of proceedings is applied when examining a case concerning the verification of the constitutionality of a law adopted by the Parliament in the procedure of compulsory preliminary review, and in cases concerning systematic or gross violation of the legislation by a local Council of Deputies. This mode is also applied when giving an official interpretation of a presidential ordinance or a decree concerning the constitutional rights, freedoms and duties of citizens; when presenting the CCB's position on a document adopted (issued) by a foreign country, an international organisation and/or their bodies, where such a document affects the interests of the Republic of Belarus, when the Constitutional Court verifies such a document for compliance with generally recognised principles and

166 И.И. Пляхимович, *Комментарий к Конституции Республики Беларусь …*, p. 606.

167 Ibidem, p. 607.

168 Article 93 section 2 of the Act on Constitutional Proceedings, http://www.kc.gov.by/print.aspx?guid=35203 (accessed: February 20, 2018).

norms of international law, as well as in some other cases. Such examination of the case is based on written documents and other materials submitted to the CCB and/or requested by the CCB when preparing the case for consideration in the court session. As a rule, this takes place without summoning the parties or their representatives, witnesses, experts, specialists, or other persons to appear at a court hearing.

Examination of a case with the use of the oral form of constitutional proceedings is carried out by hearing the explanations given by the parties or their representatives, testimonies of witnesses, expert opinions, explanations of specialists, and other participants in the court session, and by reading out written documents and other case materials during a court sitting.

It is important to emphasise that when considering cases the CCB is not bound by arguments and considerations presented by the parties, with the exception of cases provided for in Article 53 section 2 of the Law on Constitutional Proceedings.

When verifying the constitutionality of a whole act or a certain part thereof, the Constitutional Court determines its compliance with the Constitution of the Republic of Belarus, international legal acts ratified by the Republic of Belarus and other normative legal acts specified in Article 116 section 4 of the Constitution of the Republic of Belarus. The following aspects are considered: a) the content of the provisions; b) their format; c) delineation of competence between state bodies, other state organisations, officials, as well as between the Republic of Belarus and interstate entities; d) the procedure applied to adopt (issue, sign or otherwise conclude) the act, as well as its official publication and entry into force (enactment).

The Constitutional Court of Belarus may also issue an opinion on acts based on a previously verified act or ones that reproduce separate provisions of such an act, even if they were not mentioned in the request to verify the constitutionality of that act.

When verifying the constitutionality of an act under an *ex post* review, the Constitutional Court considers both the literal meaning of legal provisions and the meaning attached to them through the practice of application. According to Article 93 of the Law on Constitutional Proceedings, "cases involving the verification of the constitutionality of acts under an *ex post* review shall be examined within no more than three months from the initiation of relevant proceedings in the CCB. The aforementioned period can be extended by the CCB Chair in view of the particular complexity or large volume of the case, but not by more than one month".

Cases involving the verification of constitutionality of laws adopted by the Parliament in the procedure of mandatory preliminary review are examined within no more than five days from the receipt of laws by the Constitutional Court.

Cases involving the verification of the constitutionality of international treaties which have been signed by the Republic of Belarus but have not entered into force, in the procedure of preliminary review are, as a rule, examined within no more than one month from the receipt of the relevant request from the President of the Republic of Belarus.

The periods of consideration of other categories of cases are defined by the CCB, but they must not exceed six months from the date when proceedings at the CCB were initiated[169].

4.6 Constitutional Complaint as a Means to Review Legal Provisions

Despite scholars' numerous suggestions that the institution of constitutional complaint should be introduced, this institution does not exist in Belarus at present. In this regard, there has been growing interest in the issue of the so-called indirect (mediated) access for citizens to the constitutional justice body and the procedure to improve this access. Article 22 section 4 of the Code on the Judicial System and the Status of Judges, as well as Chapter 5 of the Law on Constitutional Proceedings (Articles 26–29) establish a format called a proactive appeal of citizens, including individual entrepreneurs, as well as organisations (excluding government organisations) to entities that have the right to appeal to the Constitutional Court to verify constitutionality of a normative legal act that has been applied. Such an appeal is possible under two conditions. Firstly, citizens or organisations believe that their rights, freedoms and legitimate interests are violated by the application of a normative legal act and they doubt the constitutionality of that act. Secondly, no more than one year has passed since the effective date of the relevant decision of a state body or a court of general jurisdiction.

Proactive appeals are examined within no more than one month from the day following their registration with the authorised body. Following the analysis of the proactive appeal, the authorised body decides to either submit a request to the CCB to verify the constitutionality of the normative legal act or to refuse to submit such a request. A refusal to submit a request to verify the constitutionality of a normative legal act should be justified. The state body that considers the proactive appeal is not entitled to draw conclusions regarding the constitutionality

169 http://www.kc.gov.by/print.aspx?guid=35203 (accessed: February 20, 2018).

of the regulatory legal act concerned. An appeal to the CCB may be submitted if the authorised body has doubts as to the constitutionality of such an act.

The only example of the practical implementation of this mechanism was the request submitted to the Constitutional Court by the Chamber of Representatives of the National Assembly of the Republic of Belarus in June 2014 following an appeal by a citizen, Ms. T.I. Belyasova. In that appeal, she expressed disagreement with the termination of a preliminary investigation into a criminal case against her late son I.V. Belyasov and against him being found guilty of committing a traffic accident where he and a passenger were killed. She argued that the termination of the criminal case under unjustified grounds as well as the possible legal consequences significantly affected the honour and reputation of the deceased, as well as legitimate interests of his close relatives. As a result, the Constitutional Court recognised unconstitutionality of a number of provisions in the Code of Criminal Procedure in Article 25 section 1, as well as Articles 26, 28, and 60 to the extent that they allowed the authority conducting criminal proceedings to refuse to initiate a criminal case if the suspect or the accused was deceased, and to discontinue the proceedings without the consent of that person's close relatives[170]. However, this case has been the only example until now despite a significant number of proactive initiative appeals having been submitted by citizens and organisations to authorised entities. For example, in 2017, the Administration of the President, the Chamber of Representatives and the Council of the Republic, the Council of Ministers, and the Supreme Court received 72 proactive appeals but no authorised body submitted a single request to the Constitutional Court[171]. A similar picture was observed in 2016 (72 proactive appeals, 0 requests from authorised bodies)[172] and in 2015 (59 proactive appeals, 0 requests from authorised entities)[173]. Therefore, one cannot consider this form of indirect access as effective in any way.

Yet another channel through which citizens and organisations may influence the administration of constitutional review consists in appeals to the Constitutional Court submitted by state bodies, other organisations, as well as citizens, including individual entrepreneurs, where such appeals contain information on the existence of gaps, conflicts and legal uncertainty in regulatory legal acts. For example, in 2017, the CCB received 602 appeals from citizens and organisations, pointing out legal issues, and also requesting the CCB to verify

---

170 http://www.kc.gov.by/main.aspx?guid=36613 (accessed: February 20, 2018).
171 http://www.kc.gov.by/main.aspx?guid=30045 (accessed: February 20, 2018).
172 http://www.kc.gov.by/main.aspx?guid=27975 (accessed: February 20, 2018).
173 http://www.kc.gov.by/main.aspx?guid=25695 (accessed: February 20, 2018).

the constitutionality of normative legal acts, eliminate gaps and remove legal uncertainty[174]. The Court has the right (but not the obligation) to initiate proceedings in such a case and take a decision where the operative part would contain a conclusion about the existence of gaps, conflicts, or legal uncertainty in normative legal acts, as well as a proposal addressed to a specific state body or an official regarding the need to eliminate the gaps, conflicts and legal uncertainty in such acts, in accordance with the respective competence of such state bodies or officials[175]. In total, the Constitutional Court has adopted more than 200 decisions to eliminate constitutional and legal gaps[176]. For instance, in the decision of 21 June 2017 "On ensuring the right to unimpeded and timely legal assistance in criminal proceedings", the CCB noted that when drafting Articles 44 and 48 of the Code of Criminal Procedure, the legislator used the words "admit" and "admission" with reference to the initial moment when a lawyer offers assistance to a citizen with regard to materials and a criminal case. In the opinion of the CCB, when these words are interpreted literally, the law enforcement body might come to the conclusion that the provision of legal assistance by a lawyer is possible only after a relevant written or oral permission has been received to admit the lawyer to the materials or to a criminal case. In other words, this may lead to a conclusion that the legal assistance provided by an attorney depends on receiving permission. If legal assistance provided by lawyers depends on a permissive mechanism whereby lawyers need permission to be admitted to materials and criminal cases, this does not allow citizens to fully exercise their right to legal assistance from a lawyer at any time, and also creates obstacles for lawyers preventing them from fulfilling their professional role in a proper and prompt manner in order to provide qualified legal assistance, as established by the Constitution, the Law "On the bar and barristers' activity in the Republic of Belarus", the general provisions of the criminal procedure legislation and the norms of international law. This formulation of the rules of the criminal procedure law points to the legal uncertainty of the provisions of Article 44 section 4 and Article 48 section 1 point 5 of the Code of Criminal Procedure, providing for the admission of a defence lawyer to participate in proceedings based on materials and in criminal cases, since the implementation of these norms does not preclude arbitrary actions from the prosecution, whereby they may restrict

---

174 http://www.kc.gov.by/main.aspx?guid=30045 (accessed: February 20, 2018).

175 Articles 158–160 of the Act on Constitutional Proceedings, http://www.kc.gov.by/print.aspx?guid=35203 (accessed: February 20, 2018).

176 П.П. Миклашевич, *Развитие форм конституционного контроля в современных условиях*, p. 41.

the receipt of unimpeded and timely legal assistance in criminal proceedings. The Constitutional Court pointed out that the legal regulation where the possibility to use the assistance of a lawyer depends on the discretion of other persons does not ensure the complete exercise of the constitutional provision whereby everyone is entitled to receive legal assistance (Article 62 of the Constitution), does not allow interested persons to properly protect their rights and freedoms, does not contribute to the timely and effective restoration of violated rights and, therefore, the Code of Criminal Procedure should provide a mechanism of unobstructed and timely involvement of a lawyer in a criminal case at any stage (if the conditions stipulated in Article 44 section 4, and Article 87 section 1 points 1–6 of that Code are complied with, and if the lawyer possesses a lawyer's certificate and a warrant to participate in criminal proceedings), excluding the discretion of the prosecution authorities. Based on the provisions of the Article 7 sections 1 and 2, and Article 59 sections 1 and 2 of the Constitution, the Constitutional Court recognised the need to eliminate the uncertainty of the legal regulation of everyone's constitutional right to legal assistance in order to exercise and protect their rights and freedoms, including the right to use the help of lawyers at any time, stating that legal uncertainly affected the unimpeded and timely access of a lawyer to criminal proceedings at any stage. The legislators should eliminate the uncertainty by introducing relevant amendments and/or additions to the Code of Criminal Procedure[177].

Given that there have been absolutely no appeals to the Constitutional Court from authorised subjects, this form of activity allows the Court to stimulate progress in legislation and reinforce the protection of citizens' rights. However, it is noteworthy that none of the more than 200 decisions concerned any presidential act.

5 The Legal Nature and Legal Force of the Decisions Issued by the Constitutional Court

Article 2 of the Law on Normative Legal Acts classifies the acts issued by the Constitutional Court as normative legal acts[178]. The mandatory nature and legal force of the decisions of the Constitutional Court arises from Article 116 of the Constitution, which defines the status of the CCB as the only body performing constitutional review, and from the constitutional provisions regarding the

177 http://www.kc.gov.by/main.aspx?guid=47003 (accessed: February 20, 2018).

178 http://pravo.by/document/?guid=3871&p0=h10000361 (accessed: February 20, 2018).

supreme legal power of the Constitution (Articles 7 and 137 of the Constitution). More precisely, Article 7 section 3 of the Constitution reads: "Legal acts or their individual provisions recognised as unconstitutional in accordance with the procedure established by law shall have no legal force"[179].

Article 24 of the Code on the Judicial System and the Status of Judges provides that the conclusions and decisions of the Constitutional Court are final, not subject to appeal or protest; they apply directly and do not require confirmation by other state bodies, other organisations, or officials. Conclusions and decisions issued by the Constitutional Court come into force from the date of their adoption, unless otherwise specified in these acts[180]. The detailed regulation of the legal force of CCB's conclusions and decisions and their legal consequences is provided in the Law on Constitutional Proceedings. Article 85 of that act provides that normative legal acts recognised as unconstitutional in an ruling issued by the Constitutional Court have no legal force. Courts, other state bodies, other organisations, or officials cannot apply such normative legal acts. Unless otherwise specified by the CCB, court decisions based on such acts must be reviewed in due course, while legal acts adopted (issued) by other state bodies, other organisations, or officials must cease to be effective[181].

An essential shortcoming in the legal regulation of this issue is the lack of guidance in the legislation as to the period of implementation of the CCB's conclusions and decisions. As the Chair P. of the Constitutional Court Miklashevich noted in the National Report to the Fifteenth Congress of the Conference of European CCs, "the legislation of the Republic of Belarus does not define the time limits for amending regulatory legal acts recognised by the Constitutional Court as unconstitutional, whether in whole or in part, nor does it provide for a special procedure for making such amendments and additions"[182]. The Constitutional Court itself "does not establish any time limit for the execution of its decisions in most cases"[183].

179 http://pravo.by/pravovaya-informatsiya/normativnye-dokumenty/konstitutsiya-respubliki-belarus/ (accessed: February 20, 2018).

180 http://www.kc.gov.by/main.aspx?guid=21725 (accessed: February 20, 2018).

181 http://www.kc.gov.by/print.aspx?guid=35203 (accessed: February 20, 2018).

182 National paper at the XV Congress of the Conference of the European Constitutional Courts "Constitutional justice: Functions and interaction with other public authorities", https://www.ccr.ro/ccrold/congres/BELARUS%20ru.pdf (accessed: February 20, 2018).

183 http://www.kc.gov.by/main.aspx?guid=2931 (accessed: February 20, 2018).

This leads to a situation where the period for implementation of decisions can be very long. This can be illustrated by the following example. Under Article 57 section 2 of the Constitution "the procedure for undergoing military service, the grounds and conditions for exemption from military service, or the alternative military service shall be defined by law"[184]. However, conscripts who demanded that their military service be replaced with an alternative service due to their religious beliefs were denied the replacement based on the argument that the law did not regulate the relevant procedure. Criminal cases were initiated against the objectors, and a number of them were sentenced to imprisonment. On 26 May 2000, the Constitutional Court of Belarus examined this issue and recognised that it was necessary "to immediately adopt a law on alternative military service or to introduce the necessary changes and additions to the law 'On universal military duty and military service' with a view to determining the mechanism for exercising the right to alternative service".[185] Such a law was drafted and entered into force on 1 July 2016[186], i.e. it took 16 years for the CCB's decision (and a constitutional provision) to be implemented.

6 The Constitutional Significance of the Constitutional Court

At the first stage of its activity, from 1994 until the end of 1996, the Constitutional Court of Belarus made an important contribution, ensuring the supremacy of the Constitution, protecting the fundamental rights and freedoms of the individual, and played an essential role in securing the separation of powers. However, from 1997, the significance of the Constitutional Court as an authority ensuring the supremacy and direct applicability of the Constitution has gradually decreased. Under these circumstances, other aspects of the CCB's operations have come to the fore.

Firstly, one undisputed positive aspect in the operation of the CCB throughout its existence has been its reference to international legal acts setting out the fundamental rights and freedoms of the individual, as well as other international legal instruments. The CCB is virtually the only judicial body that regularly does this and relies on the provisions of international treaties in

---

184 http://pravo.by/pravovaya-informatsiya/normativnye-dokumenty/konstitutsiya-respubliki-belarus/ (accessed: February 20, 2018).

185 http://www.kc.gov.by/main.aspx?guid=10933 (accessed: February 20, 2018).

186 http://pravo.by/document/?guid=12551&p0=H11500276&p1=1&p5=0 (accessed: February 20, 2018).

its decisions[187]. In its decisions, the Court constantly refers to the provisions of the Universal Declaration of Human Rights, the International Covenant on Civil and Political Rights, the International Covenant on Economic, Social and Cultural Rights, the ILO Conventions and other international legal instruments[188]. Although Belarus is not a member of the Council of Europe and has not ratified the European Convention on Human Rights, the former Chair of the Constitutional Court G. Vasilevich repeatedly called on including the provisions of the Convention and the rulings of the European Court of Human Rights in judicial practice[189].

Secondly, despite the fact that it sometimes takes a long time for the CCB's decisions to be implemented and for the legal positions set out in them to be taken into account, they certainly have a positive effect on the protection of constitutional rights and freedoms of the individual. A number of the CCB's conclusions and decisions helped to strengthen the human rights guarantees, and to exclude acts violating the rights and freedoms of the individual from the legal system. The CCB contributed to the abolition of unconstitutional restrictions on freedom of movement, the right to apply to the courts to protect one's rights and freedoms, the right to legal assistance in order to implement and protect rights and freedoms, and in many other areas[190].

Thirdly, the very existence of a body of constitutional justice has stimulated progress in legal studies, inspired research related to the hierarchy of normative legal acts, a comparative analysis of constitutional review bodies as well as their formation and operation, as well as other issues related to this topic[191].

---

187 М. Чудаков, *Контроль Конституционного Суда за приведением законодательства Республики Беларусь в соответствие с ее международными обязательствами (1994–1998гг.),* [in:] Л.В. Павлова (ed.), *Имплементация норм международного права во внутригосударственное право,* Minsk 2001, pp. 132–148.

188 Г.А. Василевич, *Юридические документы ООН и Совета Европы в практике работы Конституционного Суда Республики Беларусь,* "Право Беларуси" 2005, № 8, pp. 41–43.

189 See, for instance: Г.А. Василевич, *Возможности реализации Европейской конвенции о защите прав человека и основных свобод практике Конституционного Суда Республики Беларусь и национальных судов,* "Белорусский журнал международного права и международных отношений" 2002, № 3, pp. 3–7.

190 For details, see: Г.А. Василевич, *Конституционное правосудие …,* pp. 172–277.

191 И.И. Пляхимович, *Комментарий к Конституции Республики Беларусь …,* p. 613.

7 Assessment of the Institution of Constitutional Review by the Public

As the operation of independent surveying companies is very complicated in Belarus, it is difficult to obtain objective data about attitudes towards various state institutions among the public. There are only fragmentary data on citizens' trust in courts. According to those data, "the citizens' trust in the Constitutional Court as a state authority" stood at 17.8 % in 1997[192], reaching 25.8 % in autumn 2003 and rising to 38.6 % in the autumn of 2008[193].

A nation-wide representative sociological survey conducted in 2012 found that 47.1 % of the respondents trusted the Constitutional Court of Belarus, with the figure among top managers being 50.9 %, with 53.9 % for law enforcement officers. For the sake of comparison, 40 % of the respondents expressed their trust in the government, and 38.1 % said they trusted the Parliament[194].

At the same time, many citizens spoke very negatively about the CCB in 2017 in comments posted on non-governmental websites, criticising it for not seeing any violations of the Constitution in Presidential decree No. 3 "On the prevention of social dependence"[195]. Under that act, Belarusian citizens, foreign citizens permanently residing in Belarus as well as stateless persons who did not participate in financing public expenditures or who participated in such financing for less than 183 calendar days in a year [that is, those who did not work – author's comment] were obliged to pay a fee of 20 base units. The act also imposed sanctions for non-payment of that fee in the form of a fine or administrative arrest of up to 15 days, with performance of public works.

According to Prof. M. Pastukhov, a former judge of the Constitutional Court, "the current Constitutional Court is given the mission to mislead the citizens, the society and the entire civilised world stating that everything is fine with law and human rights in Belarus and that we do not issue unconstitutional acts at all. As a result of the simulative work and the cheerful message on the status of constitutional legality, it seems that Belarus has a perfectly working legal sphere. In fact, this Constitutional Court should be subject to dissolution since it does not do anything useful for the good of the country and citizens"[196].

---

192 С. Королевич, *Куда ведет статистика*, "Белоруссия" 14–17 августа 1998.

193 *Хранитель конституционных ценностей*, "Советская Белоруссия" 30 апреля 2009.

194 Е.М. Бабосов, *Человек в социальных системах*, Minsk 2013, pp. 260–261.

195 See, for instance: https://people.onliner.by/2017/03/15/ks (accessed: February 20, 2018).

196 https://belaruspartisan.by/opinions/415778/ (accessed: February 20, 2018).

Conclusions

The constitutional status and the actual position of the Constitutional Court in the system of higher state bodies have undergone significant changes during the 25 years of its existence.

During the first stage of it operation, in the period 1994–1996, the Constitutional Court made an important contribution, ensuring the supremacy of the Constitution, protecting the fundamental rights and freedoms of the individual, and played an essential role in securing the separation of powers. Authorised subjects who had the right to initiate proceedings actively approached the Constitutional Court, and the Constitutional Court also regularly initiated cases on its own initiative. During that period, the Constitutional Court issued 35 opinions, where 17 acts of the legislature, 16 acts of the President, who headed the executive branch of government, were declared unconstitutional. However, the involvement in the conflict between the legislative and executive branches, which could not be avoided under the prevailing political circumstances, led to a significant change in the status of the Constitutional Court under the new version of the Constitution. The guarantees of its independence were weakened, and the Constitutional Court lost the right to initiate cases on its own initiative, and the group of subjects authorised to initiate constitutionality cases was considerably narrowed. Most of the judges from the first Constitutional Court resigned, or, like judge M. Pastukhov, were dismissed on the ground of "the expiration of the term of office".

During the second stage of activity (1997–2008), the Constitutional Court tried to find its place in the new legal reality. On 15 April 1997, at the President's request, the Court adopted a ruling on the revision of its own ruling dated 4 November 1996, which stated that a new mandatory referendum on the new version of the Constitution would be unconstitutional. In order to legitimise the referendum that had already been held, the Constitutional Court's conclusion of 4 November 1996 was revoked in violation of the then binding version of the Law on the Constitutional Court[197], and recognised as "having no legal force as of 4 November 1996"[198]. In the period 1997–2008, the Constitutional Court

197 И.И. Пляхимович, *Комментарий к Конституции Республики Беларусь ...*, p. 596.

198 Conclusion of the Constitutional Court of the Republic of Belarus No. 3-56/97 of 15 April 1997 "On revising the conclusion of the Constitutional Court of the Republic of Belarus of 4 November 1996 'On compliance of paragraphs 2.2, 2.5 and 3 of the resolution adopted by the Supreme Council of the Republic of Belarus on 6 September 1996 'On holding a Republican referendum in the Republic of Belarus

adopted 38 conclusions, but presidential acts were not brought to the attention of the Constitutional Court even though the constitutionality of many of those acts was dubious. During that period, only one Presidential decree was reviewed and was recognised as constitutional. Gradually, the number of appeals to the Constitutional Court from authorised subjects decreased. Between 2005 and 2007, the Constitutional Court issued only four conclusions.

The third stage of the Constitutional Court's activities began in 2008 and has continued until today. It is characterised by a complete absence of *ex post* constitutional review. The mandatory preliminary review of all laws, introduced by presidential decree No. 14 of 26 June 2008, turned out to be fairly ineffective: all laws without exception have been recognised as consistent with the Constitution. At this stage, the Court is attempting to "revive" indirect access of citizens and organisations to constitutional justice with the help of "proactive appeals", as well as appeals concerning gaps, conflicts and legal uncertainty in normative legal acts. However, regardless of the legal provisions in force, it can be argued that in the context of the super-presidential form of governance in Belarus, and a rigidly consolidated authoritarian regime, the absence of a Parliament elected in free elections and the absence of systemic opposition, it is impossible to establish an institution that would perform real review of the constitutionality of normative acts. Such an authority seems to have no place in the existing political and legal system, where one man makes all major decisions.

Therefore, one can agree with scholars' opinions that the Constitutional Court evolved from a body that ensured a review of constitutionality into an "expert-and-consultation body"[199], "an auxiliary expert unit of the government apparatus"[200], or "a decorative body that masks the absence of a real separation of powers"[201]

and on measures to conduct it' with the Constitution and laws of the Republic of Belarus'", http://www.kc.gov.by/main.aspx?guid=11333 (accessed: February 20, 2018).

199 И.И. Пляхимович, *Комментарий к Конституции Республики Беларусь ...*, p. 610.

200 А. Казакевич, *Институт судебной власти Беларуси: политологический анализ*, Kaunas 2009, p. 77.

201 A. Vashkevich, *The Republic of Belarus: The Road from the Past to the Past*, [in:] A. Sajó (ed.), *Out of and Into Authoritarian Law*, The Hague: New York 2003, p. 286.

Saule Koshkenovna Amandykova

Constitutional Justice in the Republic of Kazakhstan

Abstract: The present analysis is devoted to the characteristic features of controlling legal norms in Kazakhstan. Emphasis is placed on the evolution from the European model of constitutional courts to the model based on the French political solutions.

Keywords: the European model of constitutional court, the French model of constitutional council, autonomy and independence, Constitutional Council and other organs of state power, cognition of the Constitutional Council

Introduction

The institution of constitutional protection of the Constitution in the Republic of Kazakhstan was established in connection with the constitution-based formation of a law-governed state. One of the characteristics of a law-governed state is the unconditional supremacy of the Constitution over other normative acts. The rule of law, expressed in the subordination of the state and its agencies to the Constitution of the Republic of Kazakhstan, is another fundamental principle of law-governed state[1].

There are several reasons why constitutional review is needed. Firstly, constitutional provisions are of a constituent or primary nature. This is connected with the particular nature of the subject on whose behalf the Constitution is adopted. The preamble of the Constitution of the Republic of Kazakhstan states that the present Constitution is adopted by the people of Kazakhstan: "The people of the Republic of Kazakhstan, through a nation-wide referendum, hereby establish the present Constitution by universal suffrage". The main purpose of constitutional review is to verify the compliance of a contested act of law with the country's constitution[2]. This is done to ensure the legal supremacy of the constitution in the hierarchy of normative acts, and to protect the relations and connections in the society that represent the actual fabric of any country. These goals are

1 Further on, the acronym 'RK' is used in some cases instead of the full name of 'the Republic of Kazakhstan'.

2 Б.А. Страшун (ed.), *Конституционное (государственное) право зарубежных стран. Общая часть*, Mocscow 1996, p. 11.

achieved through the suppression of constitutional violations, restoration of violated rights of authorities, officials and citizens, and through measures aimed at preventing possible violations of constitutional legality.

In Article 1 of its Constitution, the Republic of Kazakhstan (RK) positions itself as a democratic and law-governed state, which entails, above all, the rule of law and supremacy of law. Therefore, the state is obliged to enforce compliance with the constitution through its agencies and to protect it from any violations. The institution of constitutional review, epitomised mainly by the Constitutional Council, considerably contributes to the development of the democratic foundations of the state.

1 Reasons for Introducing Legality Review and Key Dilemmas

The main reason behind the introduction of a review of legal provisions is the need to ensure a balanced legal system in the Republic of Kazakhstan. When defining its main goals, RK has focused on the formation of a law-governed state, giving priority to human and civil rights and freedoms and the formation of a democratic state. The main principle of the law-governed state is compliance with the Constitution, which is the main act of law in the country that regulates the most important social relations. The Constitution establishes the general rules that all state agencies, and their officials, must obey. Since the supremacy of the Constitution must be observed, this also presupposes the need to review constitutional provisions. In the hierarchy of legal provisions, the Constitution is the main law in the country, with the highest legal force. The supremacy of the Constitution means that all other acts adopted by public bodies provided for by the Constitution may not contradict the Constitution as an act of constituent power. Since the bodies established by the Constitution have an authority that is subordinate to the constituent power, any acts issued by those bodies must correspond to their constitutionally defined competences. The role of constitutional review has increased in the current situation where the Parliament is no longer the only legislative body of the Republic of Kazakhstan. The presence of other legislative bodies presupposes a hierarchy in the system of bodies endowed with the authority to create law and, as a consequence, it also presupposes a hierarchy of such legal acts. This increases the risk of inconsistency and unconstitutionality of such acts. In addition, the Constitution guarantees human and civil rights and freedoms, and one of the functions of constitutional review is to ensure the observance of those rights and freedoms in accordance with the Constitution.

The Constitution regulates only fundamental or foundational social relations. The Constitution cannot regulate all spheres of social life and, therefore, those legal gaps are filled by other legal acts. Obviously, such legal acts should not contradict the constitutional provisions.

The activities and organisation of public authorities must be in full compliance with the provisions of the current constitution.

In Kazakhstan, the need for constitutional review was articulated for the first time in the declaration "On the State Sovereignty of the Kazakh SSR" dated 25 October 1990. Point 8 of the declaration established the supremacy of the Constitution and laws of the Republic of Kazakhstan, which are to be observed and enforced by all state bodies, enterprises, institutions, organisations, citizens and stateless persons. The Republic of Kazakhstan has the right to suspend the laws and other acts adopted by the supreme bodies of the Soviet Union on its territory whenever they violate the sovereign rights and the Constitution of the Republic of Kazakhstan.

Article 10 of the Constitutional Law of RK "On the Independence of the Republic of Kazakhstan" dated 16 December 1991 unequivocally stated that the Constitutional Court of Kazakhstan was the supreme judicial body protecting the Constitution. The Constitutional Court in the Republic of Kazakhstan was established in 1992 and began its work in that year. The Constitutional Court worked until August 1995, i.e. until the adoption of the new Constitution. When the draft of the new constitution was discussed, opinions regarding the constitutional review body were divergent. Some academics suggested maintaining the Constitutional Court in some format as it had already accumulated some experience. At the same time, new forms of a constitutional justice body were actively discussed, for instance a constitutional council modelled on the Constitutional Council of France. As a result, the new Constitution adopted in 1995 provided for the Constitutional Council of RK as a quasi-judicial body.

2 Legislative Stability of the Legality Review Body

Constitutional review is understood as an activity undertaken by relevant public bodies in order to ensure the supremacy of the Constitution and constitutional legality. It is expressed through adjudicating on the constitutionality of acts and actions of public authorities and public associations in the light of the Constitution.

As Kazakhstan was searching for new legal forms, it chose to establish a dedicated constitutional review body after considering the idea of a constitutional court as the body to verify compliance with the Constitution. The Constitutional Court was established as the constitutional review body for the first time in the country's history. In accordance with the Constitutional Law of RK "On the

Independence of the Republic of Kazakhstan" dated 16 December 1991, the Constitutional Court was the supreme judicial body protecting the Constitution (Article 10)[3]. The introduction of constitutional review in the country was facilitated by the adoption of the following acts of law: "On the Constitutional Court of the Republic of Kazakhstan" of 5 June 1992[4] and "On Constitutional Legal Proceedings in the Republic of Kazakhstan" of 5 June 1992[5].

In accordance with the aforementioned acts and the 1993 Constitution of the Republic of Kazakhstan, the Constitutional Court examined claims regarding constitutionality of acts of law and other normative acts, as well as international treaties and commitments assumed by the Republic of Kazakhstan. The group of entities who had the right to appeal to the Constitutional Court was quite broad, as per Article 21 of the Law of RK "On Constitutional Legal Proceedings in the Republic of Kazakhstan". Citizens of RK were entitled to appeal to the Constitutional Court in case their constitutional rights were violated. In addition to citizens, the right to appeal to the Constitutional Court was granted to the Supreme Soviet of RK (at least one-fifth of its members) and its Plenum, the Chair and committees of the Supreme Soviet, the President, the Prime Minister, the Chair of the Supreme Court and its Plenum, the Chair of the Supreme Arbitration Court and its Plenum, and the Prosecutor General. Other entities that had the right to appeal to the Constitutional Court included country-level authorities of public associations, the Academy of Sciences, as well as regional representative and executive bodies. The aforementioned entities enjoyed the right to approach the Constitutional Court in connection with relevant issues specified in the legislation in accordance with Article 18 of the law "On Constitutional Legal Proceedings in the Republic of Kazakhstan".

Whenever laws or other normative acts were declared unconstitutional, their applicability on the territory of Kazakhstan was abolished.

---

3 Constitutional Law of the Republic of Kazakhstan "On the Independence of the Republic of Kazakhstan" dated 16 December 1991, Gazette of the Republic of Kazakhstan [Ведомости Республики Казахстан] 1991, No. 51, item 622.

4 Constitutional Law of the Republic of Kazakhstan "On the Constitutional Court of the Republic of Kazakhstan" dated 5 June 1992, Gazette of the Supreme Soviet of the Republic of Kazakhstan [Ведомости Верховного Совета Республики Казахстан] 1992, No. 10, item 266 (no longer in force).

5 Constitutional Law of the Republic of Kazakhstan "On Constitutional Legal Proceedings in the Republic of Kazakhstan" dated 5 June 1992, Gazette of the Supreme Soviet of the Republic of Kazakhstan [Ведомости Верховного Совета Республики Казахстан] 1992, No. 10, item 257 (no longer in force).

At present, in accordance with the 1995 Constitution and the Constitutional Law of RK "On the Constitutional Council of the Republic of Kazakhstan" dated 29 December 1995[6], the Constitutional Council is the constitutional review body in the country. Constitutional legislation defines the status of the Constitutional Council as a state body that ensures the supremacy of the Constitution of RK on its entire territory. Moreover, the Constitutional Council is defined by law as an autonomous body, independent of other state bodies, organisations, officials or citizens. When exercising its powers, the Constitutional Council (CCK) must only obey the Constitution. When examining issues within its competence, the Constitutional Council may not be guided by political or other motives.

The legislation that regulates the activity of the constitutional review body has been fairly stable. The constitutional status of the CCK is set out in chapter 6 of the Constitution and consists of four articles. In the course of twenty years of the Constitutional Council, only two amendments were made to the constitutional status of this body: in May 2007 and March 2017.

The amendments were related to the appointment of the Constitutional Council members. Previously, the Chair of the Senate had single-handedly appointed two members of the CCK whereas currently the Senate appoints them. However, the wording of this article reflects an imperfection in legal drafting: 'chosen' is likely to be more appropriate than 'appointed'. The aforementioned amendments also affected members of the Constitutional Council, who had been previously appointed by the Chair of the Majilis whereas at present they are appointed by the Majilis. Moreover, the powers of the Constitutional Council were supplemented in Article 72 of the Constitution. According to those amendments, the CCK is now empowered to review the constitutionality of resolutions adopted by the Parliament and its chambers.

Paragraph 2 of Article 74 of the Constitution was supplemented with only one word, i.e. 'unconstitutional'. In other words, this article officially enshrined the possibility of laws and other regulatory legal acts to be declared unconstitutional. This constitutional amendment raised the role of the Constitutional Council to an entirely new level since the recognition of unconstitutionality entails an abolition of regulatory legal acts and, accordingly, they cease to be applicable throughout the territory of the Republic of Kazakhstan.

---

6 Constitutional Law of the Republic of Kazakhstan "On the Constitutional Council of the Republic of Kazakhstan" dated 29 December 1995, https://online.zakon.kz/Document/?doc_id=1004022 (accessed: May 24, 2018).

The Constitutional Law of Kazakhstan "On the Constitutional Council of the Republic of Kazakhstan" (the CCK Act) was amended only five times in the twenty years of the operation of this body, i.e. on 24 November 2004, 17 June 2008, 3 October 2013, 4 July 2014, and 15 June 2017[7].

Initially, the legal status of the CCK was regulated by a normative legal act, i.e. a decree issued by the President that had the force of a constitutional law. The format and title of that act were changed in accordance with the CCK Law dated 24 November 2004. The said act omitted the preamble as unnecessary: the preamble had clarified the legal basis for adopting a decree with the force of a constitutional act.

Subsequent amendments were introduced via the RK Constitutional Law dated 17 June 2008, in accordance with the previously discussed amendments to the Constitution dated 21 May 2007. Article 3 para. 2 regulates the procedure for appointing Council's members. As already mentioned, the amendments concerned the members of the Constitutional Council, who are now appointed by the Majilis and the Senate respectively, upon a proposal from the Chairs of the respective chambers of the Parliament.

Article 15 para. 1 subpara. 2 of the act was also amended. It regulates the termination of powers of the Constitutional Council members who were appointed by the chambers of the Parliament. The Senate and the Majilis, respectively, can terminate the powers of those members.

Paragraph 10 of Article 15 was deleted. According to that deleted paragraph the powers of Constitutional Council members could be terminated upon their 60th birthday or, in exceptional cases, 65th birthday, with the exception of the ex-president of the Republic.

Article 17 para. 2 of the law was supplemented with subpara. 2 whereby the powers of the Constitutional Council were extended to enable it to examine the constitutionality of resolutions adopted by the Parliament and its chambers.

Amendments were made to Articles 12 and 14 of the act, strengthening the immunity of Constitutional Council members in accordance with the Constitutional Law of 4 July 2014 following the adoption of the new Criminal Code and the new Code of Criminal Procedure.

Article 20 of the act was amended to regulate the representation of participants in constitutional proceedings before the CCK. Previously, the powers of the

7 Constitutional Law of the Republic of Kazakhstan "On the Constitutional Council of the Republic of Kazakhstan" dated 29 December 1995, No. 2737, with amendments and additions, as of 15 June 2017, http://ksrk.gov.kz/rus/norpb/ocons (accessed: May 24, 2018).

participants in constitutional proceedings were assigned in accordance with the procedure specified in the Code of Civil Procedure, while the current version reads: "in accordance with the established procedure", which offers the possibility of participation for a larger number of participants in constitutional proceedings.

Article 22 of the law was supplemented with para. 3–1, which requires that the draft amendments and additions to the Constitution must be appended if the appeal raises the issue provided for in Article 91 para. 3 of the Constitution. On 10 March 2017, the Constitution was supplemented with Article 91 para. 3, which clearly states that amendments and additions to the Constitution must either be decided in a nation-wide referendum or by the Parliament, provided that the Constitutional Council has issued a previous decision regarding the compliance of such amendments with Article 91 para. 2 of the Constitution. This increases the doctrinal function of the CCK to include assessing the compliance of the proposed amendments and additions to the Constitution with the basic immutable values, i.e. the independence of the Constitution, unitarity and territorial integrity, the form of government in the Republic, and the fundamental principles of the Republic laid down by the First President of the Republic of Kazakhstan. The role of the Constitutional Council as a constitutional review body and a body responsible for constitutional legality and for suppression of any violations of constitutional values means that the CCK has the authority to shape the status of constitutionalism in Kazakhstan.

The Constitutional Council of Kazakhstan has played an increasing role in the protection of human and civil rights and freedoms, and in ensuring national security, sovereignty and the integrity of the state. The additions to the act of law are related precisely to these issues. First of all, in line with the extended presidential powers under Article 44 para. 10–1 of the Constitution, the President may approach the CCK, requesting it to examine the constitutionality of an act of law or another legal act that has already become effective. The President may do so in order to protect human and civil rights and freedoms, and to ensure national security, sovereignty and integrity of the state. In this case, the President may suspend effectiveness of a legal act, except for a constitutional act, a code or an act of law, until the CCK has reached a decision in accordance with Article 23 subpara. 4 of the Constitutional Act. These amendments strengthen the role of the CCK in ensuring stability and further democratisation.

Also, Article 34 of the Constitutional Law has been amended: at present, it regulates the timing of the Council's examination of appeals in more detail.

Another amendment to the Constitutional Law was made to Article 36 para. 2, which concerns the revision of decisions issued by the CCK. According to the amendment, revisions of the decisions issued by the Constitutional Council are initiated by the Elbasy – the First President of the RK, whenever the case involves the protection of human and civil rights and freedoms, or the national security, sovereignty and integrity of the state.

The conceptual nature of the amendments to Article 38 of the Constitutional Law must be noted here. These amendments are associated with the redistribution of power between the different branches, including the redistribution of power between the President and the Constitutional Council. In the past, the President used to have the right to object against final decisions issued by the CCK whereas after the amendments of 15 June 2017, these provisions were excluded from the Law. At present, the entire responsibility for the decisions is entrusted to the CCK as the body responsible for constitutional legality and the observance of constitutional values in the Republic of Kazakhstan. These amendments indicate the growing role of the Constitutional Council in the adoption of the most fundamental decisions concerning the life of the society and the state.

3 The Legislative Position of the Constitutional Council

3.1 The Constitutional Council versus the President

The main responsibility for the observance and protection of the Constitution is vested with public officials. In Kazakhstan, this is primarily the President who, according to the Constitution, is the guarantor of the Constitution (Article 40 para. 2). At the same time, the meaning of measures included in the concept of 'guarantor' of the Constitution remains unclear. Nevertheless, such duties have been imposed on, and voluntarily accepted by, the President, which means that he has the right and the duty to adopt independent decisions and to act in relevant circumstances.

First of all, the President actively participates in the formation of the constitutional review body. Pursuant to Article 71 of the Constitution, the President individually appoints and dismisses the Constitutional Council Chair and its two members.

It should be noted that the Chair and the members of the CCK, after being appointed at a solemn ceremony held at a joint meeting of both chambers of Parliament, are invited by the President to take an oath, as provided for in Article 6 of the Constitutional Law[8].

8 Further on, the Constitutional Law of the Republic of Kazakhstan "On the Constitutional Council of the Republic of Kazakhstan" will be referred to as 'the Constitutional Law' or 'the Constitutional Law', 'On the Constitutional Council'.

The President is one of the six entities that have the right to appeal to the Constitutional Council in all matters falling within the competence of the CCK. In the course of the history of the CCK, the President has made 22 appeals, mainly concerning a review of constitutionality of laws adopted by the Parliament.

According to Article 19 para. 6 of the said Constitutional Law, the Chair of the CCK, at the request of the President, provides the President with information on the status of constitutional legality in the country.

If the CCK receives appeals regarding the proper conduct of elections of the President of the Republic in accordance with Article 72 para. 1 subpara. 1 of the Constitution, the assumption of office by the President is suspended pursuant to Article 23 of the said Constitutional Law.

One of the most recent amendments to the constitutional legislation is the provision that strengthens the President's position in the protection of human and civil rights and freedoms, and in matters of national security, sovereignty and integrity of the state. According to the amendments to the Constitution dated 10 March 2017, when exercising his right laid down in Article 44 subpara. 10–1) of the Constitution, the President has the right to appeal to the CCK to review the constitutionality of an act of law or another legal act that has come into force. When the President appeals to the Constitutional Council in order to protect human and civil rights and freedoms, to ensure national security, sovereignty and integrity of the state, the President himself can suspend the effectiveness of such a legal act until the Council has ruled on the matter. It should be noted that the possibility to suspend the effectiveness of a legal act does not extend to constitutional acts, codes or acts of law of Kazakhstan. Therefore, this procedure may suspend the effectiveness of legal acts that are lower in hierarchy than the acts of law of RK.

The Constitutional Council of Kazakhstan plays a very important role in deciding on an early dismissal of the President from office. Moreover, this body is one of the key participants in launching the impeachment procedure with regard to the President pursuant to Article 47 of the Constitution.

According to Article 47 para. 1 of the RK Constitution, the President may be removed from office when he is permanently incapable of exercising his powers due to illness. In this case, the CCK issues a decision on launching the established constitutional procedures. In order to issue such a decision, the CCK, pursuant to Article 22 of the Constitutional Law, is authorised to ask for the list of members of the parliamentary committee and the decision adopted by that committee, and it is also authorised to ask for the content of acts related to the Parliament's consideration of early dismissal of the President due to illness.

According to Article 47 para. 2 of the Constitution, the President may be impeached from office and, in this case, the Constitutional Council of Kazakhstan issues a decision on launching the established constitutional procedures. In order to issue such a decision, the Council should receive information on the number of deputies of the Parliament who have initiated the impeachment procedure, information on the results of voting in the chambers of Parliament, and information on the Supreme Court's decision regarding the validity of the charges. The Constitutional Council has the right to issue an appropriate decision on the basis of the aforementioned documents.

According to Article 36 of the Constitutional Law, the President has the right to initiate a review of a decision issued by the Constitutional Council in cases involving amendments to the constitutional principles underlying the decision and if significant new circumstances related to the subject-matter of the appeal have emerged.

However, the President no longer has the right to object against the decisions of the Constitutional Council, as was the case previously. At present, decisions of the CCK are final and enter into force immediately after publication.

If the Constitutional Council of Kazakhstan recognises the elections of the President as unconstitutional, elections in the respective administrative territorial units and constituencies are declared invalid upon a decision of the Central Electoral Commission, in accordance with Article 39 of the Constitutional Law.

According to Article 71 of the Constitution, former Presidents of the Republic are, under the law, lifelong members of the CCK. This will certainly help to strengthen the position and authority of the CCK.

3.2 The Constitutional Council and the Government

The Constitutional Council and the Government have some minor points of contact. First of all, the Prime Minister is among the subjects entitled to appeal to the CCK in all matters falling within the competence of the Council. Pursuant to Article 18 of the Constitutional Law, the CCK has the right to request and receive documents, materials and other information from all official bodies, including the Government and its structural subdivisions. The CCK may invite experts whose work will be needed for this body to reach a decision.

When submitting an appeal to the Constitutional Council, the Prime Minister has the right to use his representatives, pursuant to Article 20 of the said act, and the powers of those representatives are defined in accordance with the procedure established by law.

The Constitutional Council also has an indirect influence on the Government since it is empowered to conduct preliminary constitutional review of laws initiated by the Government under its legislative initiative.

Since 1996, when the Constitutional Council was established, the Prime Minister has used his right of appeal to the CCK 27 times. The Prime Minister's appeals to the CCK mainly concerned the official interpretation of certain provisions of the Constitution, and the Prime Minister has also requested the CCK to examine the constitutionality of certain laws prior to their promulgation, i.e. before they were signed by the President. For instance, the Prime Minister appealed to the CCK requesting an official interpretation of Article 4 of the Constitution, asking whether the priority of international treaties ratified by the RK over the national laws and the direct application of such treaties also extended to decisions adopted by international organisations and their bodies formed in accordance with such treaties. Following the examination of the Prime Minister's appeal, the CCK adopted a regulatory decision dated 5 November 2009 No. 6 "On the official interpretation of the provisions of Article 4 of the Constitution with respect to the order of implementation of decisions adopted by international organisations and their bodies"[9].

In its decision, the CCK issued an interpretation of Article 4 of the Constitution with regard to subject of the Prime Minister's appeal: "The provisions of Article 4 of the Constitution of the Republic of Kazakhstan extend onto decisions adopted by international organisations and their bodies formed in accordance with international treaties signed by the Republic of Kazakhstan, with the ratified treaties enjoying a priority over the national laws and considering that such decisions are to be applied directly. At the same time, decisions made by international organisations and their bodies should not contradict the Constitution of the Republic of Kazakhstan. Moreover, the CCK noted that decisions made by international organisations and their bodies should not contradict the norms of the Constitution set out in its Article 4, paras 1 and 2. The position taken by the CCK is unambiguous in that decisions made by international organisations and their bodies that violate Article 2, para. 2, and Article 91, para. 2 of the Constitution may not be recognised as binding on Kazakhstan (the said articles of the Constitution provide that the sovereignty of the Republic extends over its entire territory, and any change to the unitarity and territorial integrity of the state

9 http://ksrk.gov.kz/rus/resheniya/?cid=11&rid=533 (accessed: May 24, 2018).

established by the Constitution, or to the form of government in the Republic, is inadmissible). In its decision, the CCK also pointed out that decisions made by international organisations and their bodies that infringe upon the constitutional rights and freedoms of individuals and citizens may not be applied directly and, accordingly, they may not have priority over the regulatory legal acts of the Republic of Kazakhstan".

The Prime Minister has repeatedly appealed to the Constitutional Council of Kazakhstan to examine the constitutionality of laws that were passed by the Parliament but not yet signed by the President. For instance, at the Prime Minister's request, the Council examined the RK act "On amendments and additions to certain legislative acts of the Republic of Kazakhstan on the bar", adopted by the Parliament on 30 November 2006 and submitted to the President for signature on 7 December 2006.

On 14 February 2007, the Constitutional Council of Kazakhstan adopted a decision "On the verification of the act of the Republic of Kazakhstan "On amendments and additions to certain legislative acts of the Republic of Kazakhstan on the bar"" for constitutionality and ruled that the said act was unconstitutional[10]. In its regulatory decision, the Council found that the said act restricted attorney practice, i.e. citizens who received a license to practice as attorneys had the possibility to be admitted to the bar only at their place of residence. In the opinion of the Constitutional Council, the legal provision establishing this restriction goes against Article 21 para. 1 of the Constitution which guarantees that everyone who lawfully remains in the territory of the Republic can enjoy the right of free movement within its territory and the right to freely choose a place of residence, and it also goes against Article 24 para. 1 of the Constitution, which establishes the freedom of labour that implies the freedom for everyone to make use of their abilities to work, regardless of their place of residence or tax registration.

The Prime Minister has actively participated in the work of the CCK related to the development of constitutional legality in RK.

3.3 The Constitutional Council versus the Parliament

The Parliament plays an important role in the formation, organisation and work of the Constitutional Council. Two members of the CCK are appointed by the Senate and Majilis each, upon a proposal by the Chair of the Majilis and the Chair of the Senate, respectively. It is the Parliament that takes the oath from

10 http://ksrk.gov.kz/rus/resheniya/?cid=10&rid=267 (accessed: May 24, 2018).

newly appointed members of the CCK in a solemn ceremony, at a joint meeting of both chambers.

Without the consent of the Parliament, neither the Chairman nor any member of the Constitutional Council may be brought to liability of any kind. In accordance with the procedure established by law, the Prosecutor General has the right to submit a proposal to the Parliament, asking for consent to prosecute the Chairman or a member of the CCK in criminal proceedings.

As a collective entity, Members of Parliament indirectly participate in constitutional proceedings since they have the right to submit an appeal. However, neither individual deputies nor collegial bodies such as the chambers of Parliament may appeal to the CCK. An appeal to the constitutional review body may be submitted by at least one-fifth of the total number of deputies, as stipulated in Article 72 of the Constitution. In fact, many such appeals to the Council have been submitted. The Chairs of the chambers of Parliament as well as deputies have submitted a total of 77 appeals to the CCK. The deputies have also initiated appeals to the CCK. On 7 June 2007, the Constitutional Council received an appeal signed by 47 deputies of the Majilis requesting an official interpretation of the provisions of the Constitution in connection with the adoption of the RK act of 21 May 2007 No. 254-III "On amendments and additions to the Constitution of the Republic of Kazakhstan" (hereinafter referred to as "the Law")[11]. The Council issued an interpretation of the constitutional provisions related to the introduction of new constitutional powers for the Parliament and its Chambers in accordance with Article 2 para. 1 of the RK Constitution Law.

Furthermore, on 17 April 2007, the Constitutional Council received an appeal from a group of deputies of the Parliament requesting an official interpretation of Article 26 para. 3 and Article 39 para. 1 of the Constitution. Following that appeal, the Council adopted a regulatory decision "On the official interpretation of Article 26 paragraph 3 and Article 39 paragraph 1 of the Constitution of the Republic of Kazakhstan" dated 28 May 2007, No. 5. Based on the deputies' request, the Council determined that the Constitution does not contain the concept of 'public needs', 'exceptional cases', or 'conditions for equal indemnity' and, therefore, these concepts cannot be the subject of official interpretation by the constitutional review body. However, at the same time, the CCK offered crucial guidelines on these concepts: "The nature of exceptional cases of compulsory alienation of property for public needs should be determined on the basis of the fundamental constitutional principles whereby the highest values of the

11 http://ksrk.gov.kz/rus/resheniya/?cid=11&rid=340 (accessed: May 24, 2018).

Republic of Kazakhstan include the human being, their life, rights and freedoms (Article 1 para. 1 of the Constitution); public property and private property are recognised and equally protected; ownership creates obligations: the use of property must simultaneously serve the public good (Article 6 para. 1 and 2 of the Constitution); citizens of the Republic of Kazakhstan may privately own any legally acquired property, and ownership is guaranteed by law (Article 26 para. 1 and 2 of the Constitution)"[12].

Moreover, deputies have the right to initiate the removal of the President from office or the early dismissal of the President from office pursuant to Article 47 of the Constitution. In these cases, the Constitutional Council is required to issue a decision on the constitutionality of compliance with all the established procedures under Article 47 para. 2 of the Constitution.

The Constitutional Council of Kazakhstan summarises the practice of constitutional proceedings and, on an annual basis, submits a report to the Parliament on the status of constitutional legality in the Republic (Article 53 subpara. 6 of the Constitution).

The Council performs both preliminary and *ex post* monitoring of laws adopted by the Parliament, following appeals submitted by authorised entities. The authority of this body is to review the constitutionality of decisions adopted by the Parliament and each chamber of the Parliament in accordance with Article 17 para. 2 of the CCK Law.

3.4 The Constitutional Council versus the Courts

The meaning of Article 78 of the Constitution implies that a court is entitled to appeal to the Constitutional Council in particular cases. The first case is when human and civil rights and freedoms enshrined in the Constitution (rather than any rights and freedoms) are violated. Secondly, the court holds this right only in connection with the proceedings in a particular case (whether criminal, civil or administrative). Thirdly, only the relevant court can appeal to the Constitutional Council, and the submission must be signed not by the judge (or judges) who are examining the case but by the president of the relevant court (Article 22 para. 3 of the CCK Law).

In cases when courts of Kazakhstan submit appeals to the CCK, monitoring over the constitutionality of legal acts becomes universal: it extends not only to acts of law, but also to all normative acts and government orders at all levels of the power structure.

12 http://ksrk.gov.kz/rus/resheniya/?cid=11&rid=300 (accessed: May 24, 2018).

When appeals submitted by courts are examined, constitutional review is deconcentrated (decentralised) since it is carried out from time to time, has a focused character and can be carried out by any court examining any case involving a legitimate interest of a citizen. The comprehensive nature of constitutional review is manifested through the fact that in each particular case the review pertains not only to the constitutionality of laws but also the constitutionality of any applicable regulatory legal act, which provides ample opportunities for the judiciary to implement constitutional legality as a whole.

However, at the same time, constitutionality review has a causal link. Such a review is possible only in a specific case involving a legal act that affects the constitutional human and civil rights and freedoms, e.g. when one party believes that the other party's demand is based on an unconstitutional rule. A court may only submit an appeal while the court's proceedings are in progress: this possibility ceases to exist once a procedural decision has been reached in the case.

In total, approximately 70 appeals from courts have been examined by the CCK to date[13].

3.5 The Constitutional Council versus Other Public Authorities

The activities of the Central Electoral Commission are monitored to a greater extent than the activities of any other public body. The Constitutional Council of Kazakhstan has the authority to review and resolve disputes on the proper conduct of the following:

1) elections of the President of the Republic of Kazakhstan;
2) elections of deputies of the Parliament;
3) nation-wide referendums.

Therefore, the activities of electoral bodies are under close scrutiny from entities entitled to submit appeals to the constitutional review body.

Throughout the history of the Constitutional Council in the Republic of Kazakhstan, a total of 17 decisions were adopted on issues related to electoral law and the electoral process. According to law professor M.A. Sarsembayev, a member of the Central Electoral Committee, they made a significant contribution to the development of electoral law in the Republic of Kazakhstan and improved Kazakhstan's electoral legislation[14]. We have already discussed the role

---

13 http://ksrk.gov.kz/rus/resheniya/?cid=9 (accessed: May 24, 2018).

14 И.И. Рогов, В.А. Малиновский (eds.), *Конституционный контроль в Казахстане: доктрина и практика утверждения конституционализма: Монография*, Almaty 2015, pp. 247–257.

of Prosecutor General in criminal prosecution. Pursuant to Article 12 of the said Constitutional Law, after registering the reason for initiating pre-trial investigation in the Unified Register of Pre-trial Investigations, a pre-trial investigation against the Chairman or a member of the CCK may be continued only upon the Prosecutor General's consent. The Prosecutor General turns to the Parliament with a request for a consent to prosecute the Chairman or a member of the CCK. In cases where the Chairman or members of the CCK have been detained at the scene of the crime, or have been found to prepare or attempt to commit a serious or a particularly serious crime, or if they have committed a serious or a particularly serious crime, pre-trial investigation against them may be continued before the Prosecutor General issues the relevant consent, but with mandatory notification within 24 hours. The Prosecutor General monitors legality during the investigation[15].

4 The Structure and Status of the Constitutional Council

4.1 The Legal Status of Constitutional Court Members

The legal status of members of the Constitutional Council is laid down in Article 71 of the RK Constitution and in the first and second chapter of the CCK Law. The Constitutional Council consists of seven members, including the Chair. Article 4 of the Constitutional Law lays down the requirements for members of the CCK. They should:

- hold citizenship of RK;
- be at least thirty years of age or older;
- hold a law degree;
- have at least five years of work experience in the legal profession;
- reside in the territory of RK.

The President and Parliament take part in the appointment of the members of the Constitutional Council: the Chair and two members of the CCK are appointed by the President, two members are appointed by the Majilis and two by the Senate. Memberships of the CCK are staggered so half are changed every three years but the term of all is 6 years.

Article 71 of the Constitution and Article 10 of the said Constitutional Law provide that the positions of the Chair and a member of the CCK cannot be

15 https://online.zakon.kz/Document/?doc_id=1004022&show_di=1 (accessed: May 24, 2018).

held in parallel with that of a member of Parliament, cannot be exercised in parallel with entrepreneurial activity, or with membership in a governing body or a supervisory board of a commercial organisation. Members of the CCK may engage in teaching, academic research and other creative activities.

The basic guarantees of independence and responsibility of the Chair and members of the Constitutional Council are laid down directly in the Constitution and are elaborated further in the CCK Act (in Article 4 on the requirements pertaining to candidates for Constitutional Council members, Article 5 on the term of office and the procedure for changing the composition of members, Article 6 on the oath of the Chair and members, Article 10 on the Chair and members as state officials, Article 11 on their independence, Article 12 on immunity, Article 13 on equal rights of the Chair and members, Articles 14 and 15 on the basis and procedure for suspension or termination of the term of office, and Article 16 on security and benefits).

Therefore, the main principles of work undertaken by the Constitutional Council members include independence, inviolability, irremovability and equal rights of the Chair and members of the CCK, as laid down in Articles 11–13 of the Constitutional Law. The independence of the Constitutional Council members is expressed in the fact that the CCK members are independent of anyone's will in the performance of their duties and are subject only to the RK Constitution and Constitutional Law, and no other acts are binding on them *a fortiori*. The law unequivocally prohibits any interference in their work, any pressure or any other influence on the members.

The work undertaken by the members of the Constitutional Council with regard to constitutional proceedings is not supervised by anyone. No one has the right to demand the Council's members to report on the exercise of their powers.

The work performed by the members of the Council is based on the principle of irremovability. Their powers cannot be terminated or suspended during their term of office.

The inviolability of the members of the Council is constitutionally enshrined (Article 71 para. 5 of the Constitution). The guarantees of the inviolability of the members of the Council have been strengthened. During their term of office, neither the Chair nor the members of the CCK may be detained, subjected to detention or house arrest, or subjected to administrative enforcement imposed by a court. The consent of the Parliament is required whenever the Chair or members are to be held liable for a crime or offence, except for cases of detention at the scene or the commission of serious and particularly serious crimes.

In addition, the Chair and members of the Constitutional Council are not subject to disciplinary action.

The equality of rights of the Chair and members of the Constitutional Council is provided for in Article 13 of the Constitutional Law and means that all members of the CCK enjoy equal rights when examining the constitutionality of various cases and when adopting decisions.

Article 14 of the Constitutional Law provides for the following grounds for the suspension of powers:

- more than three consecutive absences at a meeting of the CCK without a valid reason;
- being recognised as missing under a final court decision; or
- inability to perform one's duties for health reasons.

Article 15 of the Constitutional Law sets the following grounds for termination of the powers of the Constitutional Council members:

- terminated by the President;
- terminated by the state agencies and officials who appointed the member;
- upon the member's resignation;
- when held guilty by a court;
- when recognised as having no legal capacity under the law;
- upon death or when recognised as deceased;
- when a member has violated the oath or committed an act incompatible with his/her high status; and
- upon expiration of the term of office.

4.2 Functions of the Constitutional Council

Functions are understood as the main areas of activity of an official body, expressed in its powers (competences).

The main functions of constitutional review assigned to the Constitutional Council are, first of all, to ensure the efficiency and effectiveness of constitutional provisions by suppressing violations of constitutional legality and restoring the violated constitutional provisions. Naturally, the main function of the Constitutional Council is to prevent violations of the Constitution. According to A.A. Karaev, one of the functions of the CCK is to ensure the supremacy and direct applicability of the Constitution. This function is implemented through verification of the constitutionality of regulatory legal acts through formal interpretation of the Constitution[16]. Undoubtedly, the

16 A.A. Караев, *Конституционный контроль: Казахстан и зарубежный опыт: Учебное пособие*, Almaty 2002, p. 20.

main functions include the protection of constitutional rights and freedoms, which takes place through the examination of issues related to the proper conduct of the election process, as well as in the subsequent monitoring of regulatory legal acts.

This section will be devoted to the competence of the CCK enshrined in Article 72 of the Constitution and in Articles 17 and 18 of the Constitutional Law.

1. In the event of a dispute, the Constitutional Council determines the proper conduct of the following:
   a. presidential elections;
   b. parliamentary elections; and
   c. republic-wide referendums.
2. The Constitutional Council reviews constitutionality of the following:
   a. laws passed by the Parliament but not yet signed by the President;
   b. decisions of the Parliament and its Chambers; and
   c. international treaties, prior to their ratification.
3. The Constitutional Council issues official interpretations of the provisions of the Constitution. In the course of its history to date, the CCK has issued more than 80 official interpretations of the provisions of the Constitution[17].

Interpretation of constitutional provisions is another institution of Kazakhstan's constitutionalism. The text of the 1995 Constitution is the first text that regulates the procedure for the official interpretation of constitutional provisions. The official interpretation is provided by a dedicated body, entrusted with the duty to interpret normative acts. Acts containing official interpretations have a mandatory character for all law enforcement agents. The official interpretation of the constitutional law is provided by authorised state bodies and takes the form of special acts that are formally binding on those who execute the provisions in question. In other words, the interpretation serves as an official, universally binding directive on how to properly understand the relevant provisions[18].

The Kazakhstan scholar A.A. Matyukhin has defined the interpretation of constitutional provisions as an activity undertaken by law-making agents, law enforcement agents and constitutional supervision agents, holders of legal doctrines, etc. in order to establish the content and meaning of constitutional provisions, taking into account not only the objective letter of the law but also

---

17 http://ksrk.gov.kz/rus/resheniya/?cid=9&page=1 (accessed: May 24, 2018).

18 О.Е. Кутафин, *Предмет конституционного права*, Moscow 2001, p. 147.

clarifying the spirit of the official text[19]. Constitutional interpretation is a kind of law-explaining activity. The special nature of this activity arises from the subject-matter of the interpretation. The special features of constitutional interpretation are determined by its goals and objectives, the interpreting agents and the specific interpretation methodology. The process of interpretation carried out by the CCK differs significantly from other types of procedural activities.

By their nature, legal acts containing interpretations of constitutional provisions have the legal force of the constitutional provisions. Constitutional interpretation is important not only for the law-making process, but also for all types of law enforcement, including compliance, execution and implementation of legal regulations[20]. When we look at the acts containing official normative interpretations, acts containing constitutional interpretations must be singled out. According to the Constitution, the task of providing an official interpretation of constitutional provisions is vested in the CCK (Article 72 para. 4). The official nature of this abstract interpretation means that interpretations are issued by a body specifically authorised by the constitution to do so, they are expressed in special acts adopted by the CCK and are binding on all legal subjects. This makes the official interpretations normative since they become an inseparable part of the interpreted constitutional provisions. The Constitutional Council of Kazakhstan is the only body that provides interpretation of the provisions of the Constitution. The purpose of the interpretation is to determine, through a legal procedure, how to understand a specific provision of the Constitution, and whether or not its broad application is permissible.

The main purpose of constitutional interpretation is to overcome existing uncertainty as to the content of constitutional provisions: such generality stems, among others, from the generality of constitutional provisions. An interpretation provides an accurate and adequate understanding of constitutional provisions and what should be their proper implementation. In this regard, the preventive role of interpretation is important, and so is the focus on preventing a possible misinterpretation of constitutional provisions, also in judicial practice[21].

---

19 А.А. Матюхин, *Правопонимание по Конституции Республики Казахстан. (Юридико-герменевтическая техника понимания Идеи Права и толкование Конституции): Науч. тр.*, Almaty 1997, pp. 9–18.

20 Т.Я. Хабриева, *Толкование конституций (уставов) субъектов Российской Федерации: органы и процедура*, [in:] *Теоретические проблемы российского конституционализма*, Moscow 2000, p. 131.

21 Т.Я. Хабриева, Н.С. Волкова, *Особенности казуального толкования Конституции Российской Федерации*, [in:] *Теоретические проблемы российского конституционализма*, Moscow 2000, p. 39.

Official interpretation extends only to legal provisions. Legal and constitutional provisions represent obligatory rules of conduct and precepts. A specific term or a specific concept contained in the text of a normative act cannot be regarded as a norm of law. For example, the terms 'primordial Kazakh land' and 'Kazakhstan's patriotism' used in the Kazakhstan Constitution do not have the features of a legal norm. For this reason, they cannot be subject to official interpretation by the Constitutional Council. According to Article 22 para. 2 point 7 of the Constitutional Law, an appeal addressed to the judicial review body should specify the provisions of the Constitution that are to be subject to official interpretation. Failure to comply with this requirement means that the Constitutional Council will refuse to examine the appeal pursuant to Article 25 of the said act[22]. The authors of the commentary to the Constitution believe that the interpretation of the Constitution is a task vested in the Council with the aim to clarify the meaning and content of the constitutional legislator's intent, as expressed in the provisions of the Constitution[23]. Such an interpretation is official and mandatory for all state authorities, local governments, enterprises, organisations, citizens and their associations.

Consequently, the Constitutional Council is entrusted with the important task of developing a special school of constitutional interpretation based on the values of Kazakhstan's constitutionalism, i.e. the interests of humans as a supreme value in the society, the creation of favourable conditions for human life, and the extension of human rights and freedoms protected by the rule of law and supported by the law.

In order to carry out such an activity, the Constitutional Council must be independent of other state bodies and other organisations, officials and citizens, and it must also be free from political and other attachments. In order to make sure that the interpreting body obeys the Constitution only, it must rely on the deep foundation of objective law laid down in the text of the constitution, without adding its own 'additional content' to the constitutional provisions. In other words, the interpretation of constitutional provisions is not a law-making task but, instead, a legal and hermeneutical task, which means that the existing

22 Constitutional Law of the Republic of Kazakhstan "On the Constitutional Council of the Republic of Kazakhstan" dated 29 December 1995, Gazette of the Supreme Soviet of the Republic of Kazakhstan [Ведомости Верховного Совета Республики Казахстан] 1995, No. 24, item 173.

23 Г. Сапаргалиев (ed.), *Конституция Республики Казахстан. Комментарий,* Almaty 1998, pp. 28, 348.

constitutional provisions must not be changed, new ones cannot be created but, instead, the idea behind the legal act must be recognised.

Note that the Constitutional Council issues interpretations of constitutional provisions only upon an appeal submitted by certain legal subjects specified by law. This right is vested in the following state officials:

a) the President;
b) the Chair of the Senate;
c) the Chair of the Majilis; and
d) the Prime Minister.

In addition, the Constitutional Council may issue an official interpretation of the constitutional provisions upon an appeal submitted by the deputies of the Kazakhstan Parliament. In order for such an appeal to be submitted, at least one-fifth of the total number of deputies must vote to support it[24].

The regulatory decisions adopted by the Constitutional Council, which serve as official interpretations of constitutional provisions, are universally binding throughout the territory of Kazakhstan and constitute an integral part of the binding legislation in the Republic of Kazakhstan.

It seems that the activities of the Constitutional Council exert an increasingly significant impact on the development of constitutional theory. Between 1996 (the beginning of its work) and December 2017, the CCK reviewed more than eighty appeals concerning the interpretation of the Constitution[25]. In 1999, it clarified the provisions of Articles 4, 12, 53–57; Article 41 para. 2; Article 53 subpara. 1, Article 91 para. 1 and other provisions of the Constitution. During 2000, the Constitutional Council issued an official interpretation of the following articles of the Constitution: Article 6 para. 3; Article 26 para. 3; Article 88 para. 4; Article 92 para. 4; Article 61 para. 6; Article 55 subpara. 1; Article 82 para. 1; Article 23 para. 2; Article 83 para. 2; Article 84 para. 1 and others. Through its decisions, the CCK not only ensures the supremacy of the Constitution but also helps to improve Kazakhstan's legislation, bringing it in line with the Constitution[26]. In this regard, we agree with the opinion of E.B. Abdrasulov, a well-known scholar, who rightfully believes that the practice of interpreting the Constitution leads to certain theoretical conclusions, namely that the peculiar task of constitutional

24 Г. Сапаргалиев (ed.), *Конституция Республики Казахстан. Научно-правовой комментарий,* Almaty 2004, p. 560.

25 *Сборник нормативных постановлений Конституционного Совета РК (1996–2003 гг.) (по составлению на 1 декабря 2003 года),* Astana 2003.

26 Вестник Конституционного Совета РК. Вып. 2, Almaty 1999, p. 160.

review bodies is that they must not only apply the Constitution and the law but also 'identify' the law[27].

The Constitutional Council has explained that the definition of 'binding law' within the meaning of Article 4 para. 1 of the Constitution encompasses the system of norms contained in regulatory legal acts adopted in accordance with the established procedure, i.e. the Constitution and the relevant laws, presidential decrees, decisions adopted by the Parliament, its Chambers and the Government, other normative legal acts, international treaties, as well as normative decisions adopted by the CCK and the Supreme Court of the RK[28]. All these normative legal acts are considered to be part of the existing binding law if they have not been abolished at some time, and if international treaties have been ratified but not terminated. At the same time, the Constitutional Council has issued an interpretation of the notion of 'human rights and freedoms'. In the opinion of the CCK, they "should be understood as human rights and freedoms recognised and guaranteed by the state in accordance with the constitution. The recognition of rights and freedoms as being absolute means that they apply to every person on the territory of the Republic of Kazakhstan, regardless of whether such persons hold the citizenship of Kazakhstan or not. Inalienability of rights and freedoms means that a person cannot be deprived of rights and freedoms by anyone, also not by the state, except in cases stipulated by the Constitution and laws adopted on its basis"[29].

The Constitutional Council has actively participated in the development of the binding law in the Republic of Kazakhstan by clarifying the legislator's will embedded in specific constitutional provisions and by eliminating gaps and conflicts of constitutional provisions. In its official interpretation of Article 23 para. 2 of the Constitution, prohibiting judges from being members of political parties and trade unions, the CCK explained that this restriction does not extend to the right of judges to be members of other public associations and the right

---

27 Е.Б. Абдрасулов, *Толкование закона и норм конституции: теория, опыт, процедура: монография*, Almaty 2002, p. 400.

28 *Сборник Постановлений Конституционного Совета Республики Казахстан*, Almaty 1998, pp. 45, 46.

29 *Decision of the Constitutional Council of the Republic of Kazakhstan of 28 October 1996 No. 6 "On the official interpretation of Article 4 paragraph 1 and Article 12 paragraph 2"*, Collection of decisions adopted by the Constitutional Council of the Republic of Kazakhstan [*Сб. Постановлений Конституционного Совета Республики Казахстан*] Almaty 1998, p. 46.

to establish such associations for the exercise and protection of the common interests of the judicial community within the constitutional framework.

Analysis of the practice of Constitutional Council in providing official interpretations of the Constitution shows that an interpretation of constitutional provisions may be required for various reasons, e.g. internal contradictions and legal conflicts in the text of the Constitution, the existence of gaps, terminological ambiguities in certain constitutional provisions, and the need to develop new concepts in the field of constitutional law.

Continuing the list of competences of the judicial review body:

4. The Constitutional Council issues an opinion on compliance with the established constitutional procedures before the Parliament adopts the following decisions:
   a) regarding removal of the President from office;
   b) regarding early release of the President from office in case he is incapable of exercising his powers.
5. The Constitutional Council examines appeals submitted by the President of RK in accordance with Article 44 subpara. 10–1) of the Constitution. Pursuant to the new amendments to the Constitution dated 10 March 2017, the CCK, on the President's initiative, has the right to review the constitutionality of laws or other legal acts that came into force, in order to protect human and civil rights and freedoms, and to ensure national security, sovereignty and integrity of the state[30].
6. Moreover, pursuant to Article 91 of the Constitution, the CCK issues opinions on the constitutionality of amendments and additions to the Constitution before they have been considered by the Parliament in cases where it is the Parliament that adopts such amendments.
7. The Constitutional Council examines appeals filed by courts in cases provided for by Article 78 of the Constitution. Pursuant to Article 78, courts may not apply laws or other normative legal acts whenever such laws or acts infringe on human and civil rights and freedoms enshrined in the Constitution. In cases where the court finds that a law or a normative legal act to be applied infringes on human and civil rights and freedoms enshrined in

30 The Constitution of the Republic of Kazakhstan dated August 30, 1995, with amendments and additions, as of 10 March 2017, http://adilet.zan.kz/rus/docs/K950001000 (accessed: May 24, 2018).

the Constitution, the court is obliged to suspend the proceedings and turn to the CCK, requesting that such an act is declared unconstitutional.

In the course of just twenty years of its history, the CCK received more than 60 appeals from courts. This figure does not seem high.

8. The Constitutional Council prepares an address to the Parliament each year, reporting on the status of constitutional legality in the country.
9. Furthermore, in order to exercise its powers, the Constitutional Council fulfils organisational and administrative functions. According to Article 18 of the Act "On the Constitutional Council of the RK", they include the power to request and receive documents, materials and other information from all state bodies and organisations, as well as to invite experts to carry out specialised, scientific and advisory work in accordance with the established procedures[31].

The Constitutional Council is entitled to request that the powers of the Chair and members of the Council be suspended.

In order to exercise his powers, the Chair of the Constitutional Council is also equipped with organisational and administrative functions (Article 19 of the Constitutional Law). The Chair manages the preparation of cases for examination once they have been accepted by the Council for consideration, convenes the meetings of the Council and presides over them. The Chairman distributes duties among the members of the Council, organises the work of the CCK and its supporting services, identifies the measures to be applied to ensure that meetings are held, and delivers the address of the CCK in Parliament.

At the request of the President of the Republic of Kazakhstan, the Chairman presents information on the status of constitutional legality in the country. The Chairman signs decisions and minutes of the CCK.

The Chairman presents the rules of the Constitutional Council for approval, personally approves the "Regulation on the Support Services of the Constitutional Council", as well as the structure and staff list of the CCK's support services within the allocated budget. The Chairman decides on the appointment and dismissal of the staff of the CCK's support services.

The Chairman issues orders and ordinances in matters within his competence.

31 The Constitutional Law of the Republic of Kazakhstan dated 29 December 1995 No. 2737 "On the Constitutional Council of the Republic of Kazakhstan" with amendments and additions as of 15 June 2017, http://ksrk.gov.kz/rus/norpb/ocons (accessed: May 24, 2018).

4.3 Subject-matter of Reviews Conducted by the Constitutional Council

Constitutional review is a form of legal protection of the constitution along with constitutional supervision, constitutional liability, constitutional referendum and the right to veto, vested in the head of state. According to T.M. Pryakhina, the essence of legal protection is that this institution is called upon to ensure the existing balance of powers in society and the established legal relations in the country, as laid down in the constitution[32]. Since the institution of constitutional review is a form of legal protection, it has the same essence. However, this does not mean that these two concepts are completely identical. In fact, their coverages do not overlap in the following respects:

1) constitutional review is relatively independent within the system of legal protection;
2) in contrast to other elements of the legal protection mechanism, constitutional review is mandatory;
3) constitutional review is among the final stages of constitutional and legal protection whereas all other elements of this mechanism can only precede it; and
4) constitutional review is a defining element of this mechanism: if absent, one can argue that the legal protection system is inactive.

T.M. Pryakhina has defined the following functions of legal protection of the constitution:

1) ensuring the reality of constitutional provisions;
2) suppressing violations of constitutional legality;
3) restoring the violated constitutional provisions; and
4) preventing possible violations of the constitution.

Various studies with a similar focus are being conducted by Kazakhstan scholars, including A.A. Karaev, who understands the protection of the constitution as follows: "all the legal means applied to ensure the constitutional legality in the country and in society"[33].

---

32 Т.М. Пряхина, *Роль юридической охраны Конституции в обеспечении стабильного развития регионов*, [in:] *Правовая реформа и совершенствование управления регионами*, Saransk 1991, p. 82.

33 А.А. Караев, *К вопросу об эффективности конституционного контроля*, "Право и государство" 2000, № 3, pp. 22–26.

According to A.A. Karaev, the main purpose of constitutional review is to verify the constitutionality of the disputed act[34]. Furthermore, the legal supremacy of the constitution in the hierarchy of normative acts is ensured, while the relations and connections in society that represent the actual fabric of any country are protected. This is achieved through the suppression of constitutional violations, the restoration of violated rights of bodies, officials and citizens, and through measures aimed at preventing possible violations of constitutional legality.

The range of issues handled by the constitutional review body expands whenever there are contradictions in the legal system, when conflicts arise between the constitution and the actual social fabric, between the constitution and the current legislation, the domestic law and international law, etc[35].

The Constitutional Council handles a fairly broad range of issues, depending on the matters specified in the appeal. The Council examines the provisions of law and their compliance with the constitution of the Republic of Kazakhstan.

In accordance with its competence, the Constitutional Council determines the accuracy of the procedures followed during presidential elections in RK, elections of Parliamentary deputies and republic-wide referenda. In these cases, the Council checks the constitutionality of law enforcement activities undertaken by the participants in the electoral process during the organisation and conduct of the presidential and parliamentary elections, and by participants in the referendum process. The CCK has the right to check for violations of the provisions of material and procedural law, as laid down in, and regulated by, the country's constitution, the constitutional legislation of the RK whenever such violations may have been committed by subjects of electoral law. It should be noted that the Council may verify not only legal but also organisational aspects.

The Constitutional Council examines international treaties signed by RK before they have been ratified by the Parliament. At the initiative of the appealing agents, the Council has the right to verify international treaties for compliance with the Kazakhstan Constitution.

The CCK examines the laws adopted by the Parliament that have not yet been promulgated by the President, which means that laws can be subjected to verification for constitutionality before they are signed by the President.

In the case of appeals filed by a court, the Constitutional Council may examine the current laws and other normative legal acts if the court finds that they violate

---

34 А.А. Караев, *Конституционный контроль: Казахстан и зарубежный опыт. Учебное пособие*, Almaty 2002, p. 248.

35 А.А. Караев, *Правовая охрана Конституции: традиции демократического конституционализма и опыт Казахстана: Монография*, Almaty 2010, p. 44.

human and civil rights and freedoms enshrined in the constitution. However, these legal acts should be relevant for the specific criminal, civil or administrative case where the question about possible unconstitutionality of a regulatory legal act arose.

Moreover, the subject-matter of constitutional review has been expanded as a result of the amendments to the CCK Law, whereby, at the President's request, the Council may examine binding legal acts in order to protect human and civil rights and freedoms, and to ensure the national sovereignty and integrity of the state. At the same time, according to Article 23 para. 4 of the said act, the President may suspend the operation of any legal acts except for a constitutional act, a code or an act of law that have been submitted for review to the Council, until the CCK issues a decision. In these cases, the Constitutional Council examines laws and other legal acts that have come into force and has the right to review their constitutionality.

The Constitutional Council reviews decisions adopted by the Parliament, as well as decisions of the Majilis and the Senate i.e. decisions adopted by the two chambers of the Kazakhstan Parliament. The CCK has the right to review the constitutionality of all decisions adopted by the Parliament and its chambers, whether normative or individual.

In addition, the Constitutional Council may review the constitutional procedures for the removal of the President from office and the procedure for the early dismissal of the President from office in case the President is unable to perform his duties. In these cases, the CCK is obliged to examine the constitutionality of the relevant procedures regulated by the Constitution and carried out by the Parliament as a collegiate body, by the Supreme Court (when the President is being removed from office), as well as by the Parliamentary deputies and the relevant parliamentary commission in the case of the early dismissal of the President from office where the President is unable to perform his duties (Article 47 of the Kazakhstan Constitution).

4.4 Preliminary and Follow-up Review of Legal Provisions

The Constitutional Council exercises preliminary constitutional review, a review system designed to prevent an unconstitutional law from entering into force. The Kazakhstan model of constitutional review has much in common with the typical French model of preliminary review. According to Article 17 para. 2 subpara. 1 of the Constitutional Law, the CCK reviews the constitutionality of laws adopted by the Parliament before the President signs them. The CCK reviews the constitutionality of laws passed by both chambers of the Parliament before the promulgation of the law by the President, i.e. before the law enters into force.

The Constitutional Council carries out mostly a preliminary review of legal provisions. This stems from its competence. The subject of examination is the constitutionality of laws passed by the Parliament before they are signed by the President, i.e. in this case constitutionality review extends onto laws that have not yet entered into force. Pursuant to Article 42 of the Law of 6 April 2016 "On Legal Acts", laws enter into force and become effective in the territory of the Republic of Kazakhstan ten days after their first official publication[36]. Overall, the Constitutional Council has adopted 28 decisions following a preliminary review of legal provisions. Of these, amendments to the Constitution were reviewed twice for constitutionality. In 2011 and 2017, on the President's initiative, constitutionality of the law "On amendments and additions to the Constitution of the Republic of Kazakhstan" was reviewed. The aforementioned act, dated 14 January 2011, was considered unconstitutional under the regulatory decision of the CCK dated 31 January 2011, and was repealed, and, consequently, it was not signed by the President and did not enter into force[37]. In an open session, the Constitutional Council examined the appeal of President N.A. Nazarbayev regarding the constitutionality review of the act "On amendments and an addition to the Constitution of the Republic of Kazakhstan". The said act was adopted by the Parliament on 14 January 2011 and submitted to the President for signature on the same day. In accordance with Article 72 para. 1 subpara. 2 of the Constitution and Article 17 para. 2 subpara. 1 of the Constitutional Law[38], the President sent this act to the CCK for constitutionality review. Having analysed the materials submitted, the Constitutional Council found that the constitutional act "On elections in the Republic of Kazakhstan" (the Elections Law) defines the concept of universal active suffrage as follows: the right of citizens of the Republic to vote in elections after reaching the age of eighteen years, regardless of their parentage, social, official and property status, sex, race, nationality, language, attitude towards religion, beliefs, place residence or any other circumstances[39].

36 Law of the Republic of Kazakhstan "On Legal Acts" dated 6 April 2016, http://adilet.zan.kz/rus/docs/Z1600000480 (accessed: May 24, 2018).

37 http://ksrk.gov.kz/rus/resheniya/?cid=10&rid=644 (accessed: May 24, 2018).

38 Constitutional Law of the RK "On the Constitutional Council of the Republic of Kazakhstan" dated 29 December 1995, No. 2737, https://online.zakon.kz/document/?doc_id=1004022 (accessed: May 24, 2018).

39 Constitutional Law of the Republic of Kazakhstan dated 28 September 1995, No. 2464 'On Elections in the Republic of Kazakhstan' (with amendments and additions

Universal active suffrage is exercised both in the conduct of referenda and in the conduct of elections. By participating in elections, citizens exercise not only their active but also passive suffrage. Passive suffrage presupposes that citizens of Kazakhstan have the right to be elected to the respective elective offices. Pursuant to Article 4 of the Elections Law, citizens have the right to be elected as the President of RK, as well as a deputy of the Parliament of the RK or a deputy of a maslikhat, i.e. a local government body. Passive suffrage has certain limitations laid down in the Constitution and the Elections Law but, nonetheless, a significant number of Kazakhstan citizens have the passive right to be elected President of the Republic, and, in the event a referendum is held instead of elections, the rights of those citizens would be constrained.

Thus, the analysis of the Constitution and normative legal acts regulating both the referendum process and the election process led to the conclusion that if the procedure for extending the powers of the President is applied instead of regular elections, this would restrict the constitutional rights and freedoms of Kazakhstan citizens with regard to the exercise of their passive electoral rights.

While reviewing the constitutionality of the act "On amendments and an addition to the Constitution of the Republic of Kazakhstan" (the Amendments and Addition Law), and relying on the analysis of constitutional legislation, the CCK stated that point 1 of the said Law did not clearly specify how long presidential powers of the First President of RK may be extended. The Amendments and Addition Law does not determine whether such an extension will be a one-off event or a recurring one, or whether presidential elections will be completely abolished. In the opinion of the CCK, the vagueness of this constitutional provision can lead to an imbalance between the state bodies and public institutions enshrined in the Constitution. In addition, the CCK has repeatedly stressed that any law must comply with the principles of legal accuracy and predictable consequences, i.e. its provisions should be formulated with sufficient clarity, thereby excluding any possibility of arbitrary interpretation and application (regulatory decisions of the CCK dated 27 February 2008 No. 2[40], dated 11 February 2009 No.

as of 3 February 2011) online.zakon.kz/Document/?doc_id=1004029 (accessed: May 24, 2018).

40 'On the review of constitutionality of the first and fourth paragraph of Article 361 of the Criminal Code of the Republic of Kazakhstan' following an appeal submitted by the Kapshagai City Court in the Almaty region. Regulatory decision of the Constitutional Council of the Republic of Kazakhstan dated 27 February 2008, No. 2, http://www.constcouncil.kz/rus/resheniya/?cid=10&rid=476 (accessed: May 24, 2018).

1[41] and dated 20 August 2009 No. 5).

As a result of the examination of constitutional provisions and the constitutional legislation, and an analysis of expert opinions, the Constitutional Council decided that paragraph 1 of the Amendments and Addition Law adopted by the Parliament on 14 January 2011 and submitted to the President for signature did not comply with Article 2 para. 1 of the Constitution.

In its final decision of 31 January 2012 No. 2, the Constitutional Council recognised the said act, adopted by the Parliament on 14 January 2011 and submitted to the President for signature, to be non-compliant with the Constitution.

The preliminary review is carried out by the Constitutional Council when verifying laws once they have been adopted by the Parliament but not yet signed by the President. The CCK has examined 26 appeals regarding this issue. For example, the decision of the CCK of 21 April 2004 No. 4 "On the constitutionality review of the Law of the Republic of Kazakhstan 'On the Mass Media'", the said act "On the Mass Media", adopted by the Parliament on 18 March 2004 and submitted to the President for signature on 25 March 2004, was found to be non-compliant with the Constitution[42].

The system of constitutional review in Kazakhstan also seems to have some elements of *ex post* constitutional review. In our opinion, this is because the CCK examines appeals submitted by courts to recognise existing normative legal acts as unconstitutional. Any act of law or other normative legal act may be considered unconstitutional if, in the court's opinion, it infringes on human and civil rights and freedoms enshrined in the Constitution (Article 78 of the Constitution).

The Kazakhstan model has not fully embraced the idea of *ex post* constitutional review.

The application of an *ex post* review enables a correction of the legislator's errors and the law enforcement practice. However, this holds true only for certain elements of *ex post* constitutional review because courts have the right to appeal to the CCK only with regard to those laws and normative legal acts that they consider infringing on human and civil rights and freedoms enshrined in the

41 'On the review of constitutionality of the Law of the Republic of Kazakhstan 'On amendments and additions to certain legislative acts of the Republic of Kazakhstan related to religious freedom and the activities of religious associations.' A regulatory decision of the Constitutional Council of the Republic of Kazakhstan dated 11 February 2009, No. 1, http://www.constcouncil.kz/rus/resheniya/?cid=10&rid=476 (accessed: May 24, 2018).

42 http://www.ksrk.gov.kz/rus/resheniya?cid=10&rid=182 (accessed: May 24, 2018).

Constitution. Therefore, the jurisdiction of the CCK extends only to one group of acts of law and regulations that regulate a range of relations related to human and civil rights and freedoms laid down in the Constitution.

Based on Article 78, a court is entitled to appeal to the Constitutional Council only if human and civil rights and freedoms enshrined in the Constitution have been violated rather than any other human and civil rights and freedoms. Secondly, a court obtains this entitlement only in connection with a specific case it examines (whether criminal, civil, economic or administrative). Thirdly, only the relevant court can file an appeal to the Council, and the submission must be signed by the chair of the relevant court rather than the judge (or judges) who is (are) adjudicating in the case (Article 22 para. 3 of the CCK Law).

We believe that this combination of preliminary and *ex post* constitutional review is fully justified. Preliminary review is an essential safeguard against the adoption of non-constitutional provisions. At the same time, if this guarantee does not work, then an unconstitutional situation can be resolved by applying individual elements of the *ex post* constitutional review, as mentioned above.

To date, the Constitutional Council has examined more than 60 appeals from courts of the RK. In these cases, a particular provision of law that violates the constitutional human and civil rights and freedoms was subject to review.

In cases where a court has filed an appeal, the CCK may review the binding acts of law or other normative legal acts whenever the court finds that such acts violate the human and civil rights and freedoms enshrined in the constitution. However, these legal acts should be applicable in a specific criminal, civil or administrative case where the issue of unconstitutionality of the relevant regulatory legal act emerged.

Recently, the legislators have expanded the scope of *ex post* constitutional review, based on the amendments to the CCK Act whereby any legal act can be reviewed at the request of the President in order to protect human and civil rights and freedoms, and to ensure national security, sovereignty and the integrity of the state. According to Article 23 para. 4 of the said Act, the President can suspend the operation of any legal acts with the exception of a constitutional act, a code and an act of law of the Republic of Kazakhstan, in order to protect human and civil rights and freedoms, and to ensure sovereignty, integrity and national security. In these cases, the CCK examines acts of law or other legal acts that have come into force and that can be reviewed by the CCK for constitutionality.

The Constitutional Council may review decisions of the Parliament as well as decisions of both its chambers: the Majilis and the Senate. Such review is an example of *ex post* constitutional review in the Republic of Kazakhstan. The

CCK is entitled to review the constitutionality of all decisions adopted by the Parliament and its chambers, whether normative or individual.

4.5 The Procedure for Reviewing Legal Provisions

The Constitutional Council is a non-judicial body. The right to appeal to the Council is limited to a narrow group of entities. The CCK carries out its activities in accordance with the Rules adopted on 4 June 1996[43]. It should be noted that the procedure whereby the Constitutional Council examines appeals has been considerably simplified (compared with the Constitutional Court): there is one month instead of six months for the examination of cases; preparation of verbatim transcripts of hearings is not mandatory; the questioning (hearing) of participants in constitutional proceedings is also not mandatory; two days instead of ten days are allotted for presenting case materials to the CCK members before the meeting; there is a two-day period for the submission of copies of the decision to the relevant officials, etc.

The simplification of the working rules enables the CCK to examine appeals promptly. This reduces the possibility of politicisation of the Council and its involvement in various kinds of political games. Article 1 of the CCK Law unequivocally established a new provision whereby the CCK may not be guided by political motives when exercising its powers.

The one-month period for the adoption of the final decision may be reduced to ten days at the President's request. This may happen if the issue is urgent.

It should be noted that the legislation defines the basic principles of constitutional proceedings. The constitutional proceedings are understood as the procedure established by law for the acceptance and examination of an appeal, as well as the adoption of a procedural decision on the appeal in the form of a regulatory decision of the CCK.

The principles of constitutional proceedings are as follows:

- proceedings are subject only to the Constitution;
- these are stand-alone proceedings, independent of state bodies, organisations, officials and citizens;
- the proceedings are apolitical;
- members of the Constitutional Council are irremovable;
- members of the Constitutional Council and its chairman enjoy equal rights;

43 Rules of the Constitutional Council of the Republic of Kazakhstan dated 4 June 1996; Collection of decisions of the Constitutional Council of the Republic of Kazakhstan, Almaty 1998, pp. 24–36.

- decision-making is based on the collegiality principle; and
- voting is performed by secret ballot.

Pursuant to Article 1 of the Rules of the Constitutional Council, constitutional proceedings may be initiated upon an appeal filed by one of the entities listed in Article 72 of the Constitution. According to Article 22 of the Constitutional Act, appeals are submitted in writing. An appeal must be signed by the authorised entity.

The group of entities entitled to submit an appeal to the CCK is limited and includes the following: the President, the Chair of the Senate, the Chair of the Majilis, at least one fifth of the total number of Parliament deputies, the Prime Minister, and the courts of the Republic, all of whom are participants in constitutional proceedings. In addition, state bodies and officials whose acts are verified for constitutionality are also participants in constitutional proceedings.

We agree with AA. Karaev that such a limited number of participants in constitutional proceedings is a serious drawback, given that one of the most important tasks of constitutional justice bodies in an overwhelming majority of countries is to protect fundamental human rights and freedoms guaranteed by the constitution[44]. In this regard, in order to enhance the role of the CCK in protecting such fundamental rights and freedoms of individuals, citizens should be granted the right to file an appeal to the Council in case an act of law or another normative legal act applied by the authorities directly violates the citizens' constitutional rights and freedoms.

Participants in constitutional proceedings enjoy equal procedural rights. They have the right to get acquainted with the case materials, to present evidence, to express their arguments and ideas to the CCK, to make petitions and to provide both oral and written explanations.

Article 26 of the Constitutional Law establishes the procedure for preparing materials necessary for the examination of an appeal at a CCK meeting. The Chair issues an order to determine which member (or members) of the review body will prepare materials for the meeting.

The member of the Constitutional Council authorised by the Chair identifies participants in the constitutional proceedings, requests the necessary documents, invites academics and practitioners to act as specialists and experts, prepares the draft decision and, no later than two days in advance, hands in copies of materials to all members of the CCK.

---

44 А.А. Караев, *К вопросу об эффективности конституционного контроля*, "Право и государство" 2000, № 3, pp. 22–26.

After the completion of the preparatory activities, the chairman of the Constitutional Council sets the date of the Council meeting.

Article 27 of the Constitutional Law defines the procedure for holding a CCK meeting with the purpose to review an appeal that has been accepted for proceedings. The Chair presides at the CCK meeting.

The examination of each issue begins with a speech by a member of the Constitutional Council who has been appointed as the rapporteur. Members of the CCK can ask clarifying questions. The entities that have submitted the appeal as well as other participants in constitutional proceedings may participate in the CCK meeting where their appeal is being examined. If necessary, explanations and speeches of participants in constitutional proceedings can be heard.

Once the issue has been clarified, the Chair declares the sitting of the CCK open to arrive at the final decision.

As a mandatory requirement, minutes of the Constitutional Council meetings must be taken.

Constitutional proceedings can be terminated at any stage provided that the final decision has not been adopted.

Constitutional proceedings may be terminated:

- if the submitting entity has cancelled the appeal;
- if the act which is reviewed for constitutionality has been annulled or has lost its legal force; or
- if the appeal does not fall within the jurisdiction of the Constitutional Council.

The Constitutional Council adopts its rulings in the following forms:

- decisions, including regulatory decisions;
- opinions; and
- addresses.

Decisions are adopted by the Constitutional Council collectively, by a majority vote, either by open or secret ballot. It should be noted that regulatory decisions of the CCK are an integral part of the binding legislation of RK (Article 4 of the Constitution).

During the meeting, members of the review body are not allowed to abstain or refrain from voting. A member of the review body may express a dissenting opinion if they do not agree with the decision being adopted. A dissenting opinion is presented in writing.

The final decision of the Constitutional Council comes into force on the date of its adoption and cannot be appealed against. Such a decision is universally binding throughout the territory of the Republic of Kazakhstan. The final decisions of the Council entail significant legal consequences.

The Constitutional Council may take an additional decision if the participants in constitutional proceedings, state bodies or officials obliged to execute the decision request an interpretation of such a decision.

A decision adopted by the Constitutional Council can be reviewed pursuant to Article 36 of the Constitutional Law, either on the President's initiative or upon the Council's own initiative. There must be serious grounds for such a review, such as:

- if the provision of the Constitution underlying the decision of the CCK has been amended;
- if new circumstances have been discovered that are significant for the appealing entity; or
- to protect human and civil rights and freedoms, and to ensure national security, integrity and the sovereignty of the state.

4.6 Civil Complaints as a Means of Controlling Legal Provisions

In the Republic of Kazakhstan, the practice of the first constitutional court was that citizens could appeal directly to the court with a statement of claim. Under the institution of an individual complaint citizens had the right to initiate proceedings related to matters directly affecting their constitutional rights whenever:

- such matters did not fall under the jurisdiction of other courts; when other courts failed to apply the relevant provisions of the constitutional law;
- other courts applied the provisions of the Constitution that were not applicable in that particular case; or
- courts misinterpreted the provisions of the constitutional law.

Thus, citizens had the right to directly approach the Constitutional Court pursuant to Article 18 of the Law of the RK "On the constitutional legal proceedings of the Republic of Kazakhstan" of 5 June 1992. The Constitutional Court examined a civil complaint when citizens filed appeals in matters directly affecting their constitutional rights that did not fall under the jurisdiction of other courts. During the short period of its existence, the Constitutional Court examined a significant number of citizens' appeals, which had a great public and political resonance and helped to develop the principles and ideals of constitutional legality in the Republic of Kazakhstan. The Constitutional Court firmly and unshakably supported strict observance of constitutional provisions by all state authorities, including the supreme authorities in the country as well as the highest state officials. This approach was manifested in all decisions adopted by the CCK.

In our opinion, it should be possible to provide citizens with the opportunity to turn to the Council if their constitutional rights and freedoms have been violated.

5 The Legal Nature of the Decisions Adopted by the Constitutional Council and Their Legal Force

Pursuant to Article 4 of the 1995 Constitution, regulatory decisions of the Constitutional Council are part of the binding legislation. When developing the draft version of the current 1995 Constitution, its subject-matter was expanded to include, in Article 73, the legal consequences of appeals filed to the CCK by authorised entities.

The Constitutional Council issues its decisions within one month following the receipt of an appeal. At the request of the country's President, this period can be reduced to ten days if the matter cannot be delayed.

The Constitutional Council adopts its rulings in the following forms: decisions (including regulatory ones), opinions and addresses.

Decisions of this authoritative body are adopted collectively, by a majority vote, by open or secret ballot.

The final decision of the Constitutional Council comes into force on the date of its adoption and is not subject to appeal. These decisions are universally binding throughout the territory of the Republic of Kazakhstan and have significant legal consequences:

1. Laws and international treaties of RK recognised as non-compliant with the Constitution cannot be signed, ratified or put into effect.
2. Laws and other normative legal acts that have been found to infringe upon the constitutional human and civil rights and freedoms are, as such, recognised as unconstitutional. They become null and void and are not applicable. Decisions of courts and law enforcement bodies that are based on unconstitutional acts are not enforceable.
3. If the elections of the President are recognised as not compliant with the Constitution, then, following a decision by the Central Electoral Commission, they are recognised as null and void in the respective administrative territorial districts and constituencies. If the elections of members of the Senate and the Majilis are recognised as unconstitutional upon a decision of the Central Electoral Commission, they are recognised as null and void in the respective

administrative territorial districts and constituencies. If a country-wide referendum is recognised as unconstitutional upon a decision of the Central Referendum Commission, its results at the relevant polling stations are recognised as null and void.

An opinion regarding the non-observance of the established constitutional procedures before adopting a decision on the early dismissal of the President from office or removal of the President from office means that the examination of the aforementioned issues is terminated.

However, the following cases should be examined:

1) if acts of law are found constitutional, the periods for their signing are resumed;
2) if international treaties of RK are found constitutional, the process of their ratification is renewed;
3) if a presidential election is found constitutional, the elected President of the Republic is registered;
4) if elections of deputies of the Senate and Majilis are found constitutional, the elected deputies are registered;
5) if a republic-wide referendum is found constitutional, the results of the referendum are summed up anew;
6) if procedures related to the early dismissal of the President or the removal of the President from office in accordance with Article 47 para. 1 and 2 of the Constitution are found constitutional, the issue of early dismissal from office continues to be examined.

According to Article 40 of the Constitutional Act, the CCK may independently determine the procedure and deadlines for the execution of its decisions. If a decision adopted by the Council requires an increase in government spending or a reduction in revenues, the CCK determines the time frame for the execution of its decisions in consultation with the Government.

The final decisions of the Constitutional Council are published in the official language and in Russian in official nationwide print media.

Recommendations and suggestions on improving the legislation, contained in the CCK's decisions, are subject to mandatory review by authorised state bodies and officials and any decisions taken must be officially notified.

The final decisions of the Constitutional Council are mandatorily sent to the President, the Chambers of Parliament, the Supreme Court, the Prosecutor General, the Minister of Justice and, within two days after their adoption, they are forwarded to the entity that filed the appeal or to its representatives.

The Constitutional Council may adopt an additional decision in exceptional cases when: a) a decision of the Council is to be interpreted (at the request of the participants in constitutional proceedings, state bodies or officials obliged to execute the final decision), and b) certain editorial inaccuracies and errors in the final decision must be corrected (on the CCK's own initiative). An additional decision should not contradict the actual content, meaning and purpose of the final decision.

In very rare cases, decisions adopted by the constitutional review body may be subject to review on the President's initiative or the CCK's own initiative. This can be done only in two cases: a) if the provision of the Constitution underlying the decision has changed, and b) if new circumstances significant for the subject-matter of the appeal have been disclosed. Article 36 para. 2 includes one more reason: "In order to protect human and civil rights and freedoms, and to ensure national security, sovereignty and integrity of the state, a decision of the Constitutional Council can be revised by the Council on the initiative of the President of the Republic of Kazakhstan". The Constitutional Council adopts a resolution on a revision of its decision whereby it repeals the decision concerned.

6 Constitutional Significance of the Constitutional Council

The development of stable constitutionalism and the establishment of a lasting regime of constitutional legality is a strategic goal and an effective means for further reinforcement of RK as a modern, democratic and law-governed state. The practice of statehood in the form of a 'Soviet republic' and the experience of countries with stable and developing democracies have shown that it is virtually impossible to achieve this without an effective institution of constitutional review.

As early as in May 1990, almost immediately after the post of the President of the Kazakh Soviet Socialist Republic was established and N.A. Nazarbayev was elected to this highest post, a draft bill was prepared with the aim of establishing a constitutional review committee in the country, with very limited powers, modelled on the Constitutional Review Committee of the USSR. However, the Supreme Soviet never adopted the bill. Therefore, it is correct to say that constitutional review in Kazakhstan started with the Constitutional Act of RK of 16 December 1991 "On the Independence of the Republic of Kazakhstan". Article 10 of that historical act, marking the beginning of a new era of Kazakhstan, reads as follows: "The Constitutional Court of the Republic of Kazakhstan is the supreme judicial body that protects the Constitution". The constitutional acts adopted in 1992, regulating the work of the Constitutional Court, laid down the fundamental principles and details of constitutional proceedings to review claims filed by the relevant authorised entities. Thus, Kazakhstan's adherence to the principles of constitutionalism was declared and its values were embodied in the practice of constitution-making.

One element of the checks and balances mechanism was the declaration of laws as unconstitutional. Article 101 of the 1993 Constitution established, for the first time at such a high level, that the courts may not apply laws that contradict the country's constitution[45]. In cases where a court found that a law or another normative act to be applied was unconstitutional, the court was obliged to suspend proceedings in the case. As the next step, the court was required to appeal to the Constitutional Court requesting that the relevant law is recognised as unconstitutional. It seems that this constitutional amendment delineated important horizons for a strong judicial branch of power, which could thus act within the constitutional regulations and be significantly more authoritative.

Incidentally, this provision of the 1993 Constitution was also incorporated into the current 1995 Constitution. It ensures the protection of citizens' constitutional rights and freedoms by combining the competences of the judiciary and constitutional review.

Despite its fairly short period of existence (July 1992 to August 1995), the role of the Constitutional Court was very significant in developing constitutionalism in the country.

Overall, the Constitutional Court examined approximately fifteen cases on the merits, with a final decision. The cases concerned: the observance of ownership rights, labour rights and other constitutional rights of citizens; the separation of powers and new essential differences between the Supreme Soviet and local Soviets of People's Deputies; mandatory observance of constitutional procedures for passing laws; independence and accountability of courts and judges; as well as organisation and conduct of election campaigns. The Constitutional Council also dealt with other essential components of the emerging constitutionalism.

The decision adopted by the Constitutional Court in the so-called 'Kvyatkovskaya case' had a particular impact on the fate of Kazakhstan's constitutionalism and the emergence of a law-governed state. Following a meticulous preparation of the case, which took almost a year, the Constitutional Court agreed with the arguments presented by T.G. Kvyatkovskaya and stated, in its

---

45 Constitution of the Republic of Kazakhstan dated 28 January 1993, 'Gazette of the Supreme Council of the Republic of Kazakhstan' [*Ведомости Верховного Совета Республики Казахстан*] 1993, No. 3, Article 54 (no longer in force).

decision of 6 March 1995, that a number of acts issued by the Central Electoral Commission regarding the shrinking of electoral constituencies and determining the results of elections violated the principle of equal suffrage[46]. By two-thirds of the total number of judges, the Constitutional Court rejected the objections expressed by the President and the Chair of the Supreme Soviet.

The consequences of the decision turned out to be negative for the Supreme Soviet of the 13th convocation, i.e. the last 'communist parliament' in the country's history. In an additional resolution dated 11 March 1995, following President Nazarbayev's appeal, the Constitutional Court presented the following interpretation of the decision of 6 March 1995 to the President: "The legal consequence of the CCK's decision of 6 March 1995 is the unconstitutionality of the powers of the Supreme Soviet elected on 7 March 1994, and well as the powers of the deputies of the Supreme Soviet elected in supplementary elections on 22 January 1995… "[47]. It was also pointed out that the disproportion in the number of voters led to a violation of the principle of equal representation of citizens by deputies in the Supreme Soviet. At the same time, it was stressed once again that "the recognised violations of the Constitution of the Republic took place in the territory of the Republic of Kazakhstan and equally affected the constitutional rights of all citizens eligible to vote".

---

46 Decision of the Constitutional Court of the Republic of Kazakhstan on the case 'On verification of constitutionality of the resolution adopted by the Central Electoral Commission of the Republic of Kazakhstan' dated 17 December 1993 'On the formation of electoral districts for the elections of deputies of the Supreme Soviet of the Republic of Kazakhstan' regarding the establishment of the Abylaykhan electoral district No. 12 in Almaty: para. 1 of Appendix 1 to the Resolution of the Central Electoral Commission dated 11 January 1994, No. 17 'On the formation of polling stations to enable the voting for citizens of the Republic of Kazakhstan staying abroad'; Appendix 1 to the Resolution of the Central Electoral Commission dated 27 January 1994, No. 30 'On amending the forms of ballot papers for the elections of Deputies of the Supreme Soviet of the Republic of Kazakhstan,' adopted by the resolution of the Central Electoral Commission dated 1 February 1994; No. 37 of the letter from the Central Electoral Commission to the district and precinct electoral commissions 'On the organisation and procedure for voting, summarising the voting results in the elections of Deputies of the Supreme Soviet from the official list and the voting results in the elections of Deputies of the Supreme Soviet in the territorial electoral districts on 7 March 1994' regarding the vote counting procedure, dated 6 March 1995, The Councils of Kazakhstan [*Советы Казахстана*]. 18 March 1995.

47 An additional finding of the Constitutional Court of the Republic of Kazakhstan dated 11 March 1995, The Councils of Kazakhstan [*Советы Казахстана*], 18 March 1995.

The declared unconstitutionality of the Supreme Soviet and, accordingly, the cessation of its operation, could not but challenge the legitimacy of all branches of power. In accordance with the 1993 Constitution, the Supreme Soviet directly participated in the formation of various state bodies (it elected, appointed or approved such bodies). After the Constitutional Court's decision, all of them were formed anew. During the period from 19 April 1994 to 6 March 1995, the Parliament adopted a total of 314 acts, including 24 acts of law. Consequently, after a meticulous analysis of each of these acts, President Nazarbayev, by his decree of 23 March 1995 "On acts of the Supreme Soviet of the Republic of Kazakhstan", recognised 128 acts as binding and having legal force following their entry into effect.

Meanwhile, as rightly noted by another scholar from the Kazakhstan National Academy, S.Z. Zimanov, "it is hardly possible that the Constitutional Court intended to create a risk of paralysing all the political power in Kazakhstan"[48].

Politicians and scholars differ in their assessment of the aforementioned decision and the additional resolution adopted by the Constitutional Court. For instance, William Courtney, who was the U.S. ambassador to Kazakhstan in those days, wrote: "Kazakhstan is no longer a schoolboy but a teacher of democracy. All Kazakhstan people can be proud of this, and the United States has a reason to be proud of Kazakhstan"[49]. It was then that the Constitutional Court was awarded the honorary badge for courage by the OSCE Office for Democratic Institutions and Human Rights (OSCE/ODIHR). An opposite opinion was also expressed at that time: "Now, the sooner the President of the Republic separates himself from the current Constitutional Court, the better for democracy and the country, and also for the President"[50].

According to G. Sapargaliyev, a scholar from of the Kazakhstan National Academy of Sciences, the fate of the Constitutional Court turned out to be quite dramatic[51] since the Constitution, adopted at the republic-wide referendum on 30 August 1995, introduced a quasi-judicial review body (the CCK) to replace the Constitutional Court. At the same time, one must admit that the legislation

48 С.З. Зиманов, *Нужен ли такой Конституционный Суд?*, "Юридическая газета" 1996, 14 июля.

49 Панорама 1995, № 11, p. 9. [back-translated from Russian]

50 С.З. Зиманов, *Конституция и Парламент Республики Казахстан*, Almaty 1996, p. 220.

51 Г.С. Сапаргалиев, *Конституционное право Республики Казахстан: Академический курс*, Almaty 2002, p. 528.

regulating the organisation and work of the Constitutional Court was in line with the democratic transformations of Kazakhstan's socio-political system. By and large, hardly any country had an analogue of such a powerful constitutional review body.

The current Constitution of the Republic of Kazakhstan, adopted at the republic-wide referendum on 30 August 1995, changed the model of constitutional review, with the CCK vested with this role.

A distinctive feature of the current Constitutional Council of Kazakhstan, which ensures the supremacy of the Constitution throughout the country, is that its legal foundations are defined in more detail in the 1995 Constitution.

The Constitution contains a dedicated section VI entitled "The Constitutional Council", consisting of four articles. Article 71 defines the number of members in the CCK, the procedure for its establishment, incompatibility with other posts, and the immunity of the Council members. Article 72 is crucial as it defines the powers and the list of entities entitled to initiate constitutional proceedings. Article 73 stipulates the consequences of appeals filed with the CCK and the instrument of objection vested in the President. Article 74 defines the legal force and the consequences of the CCK's decisions. Particular attention should be paid to Article 78 in section VII "Courts and Justice" under which *ex post* constitutional review can only be initiated by courts.

Thus, the highest (i.e. constitutional) level of legal regulation is among the solid guarantees of the independence and stability of the CCK.

As a constitutional review body, the Constitutional Council performs its main function of protecting the country's constitution and observing the constitutional legality in the country. The Council is not part of any branch of power in the country and acts independently, being subordinated only to the Constitution.

Today, the regulatory decisions of the CCK are among the most important sources of law in Kazakhstan.

Overall, over the years of its operation, the Constitutional Council of Kazakhstan has reviewed more than 190 appeals and issued more than 140 regulatory decisions, which have gradually turned into incentives stimulating the development of constitutional doctrine and practice. Amendments and additions have been made to more than 65 acts of law.

A total of 76 appeals requesting an official interpretation of the constitutional provisions were examined, and 68 regulatory decisions were adopted on their basis, clarifying the protection of human and civil rights, the government system in the country, the principle of unity and separation of powers in the country, the status of state bodies and their officials, the judiciary system and legal proceedings, prosecutor's supervision and other important issues.

The majority of the appeals came from the chairs of the Parliament chambers and groups of deputies (approx. 77) as well as from the country's courts (66), the Prime Minister (27), with nine requests for a follow-up interpretation of the CCK's decisions[52].

On the President's initiative, the Council examined the following acts submitted to the President for signature: "On amendments and an addition to the Constitution of the Republic of Kazakhstan" (2011), the Constitutional Law "On the First President of the Republic of Kazakhstan" (2000), the ordinary acts "On amendments and additions to the act of the Kazakh SSR 'On pension provision of citizens in the Kazakh SSR'" (1996), "On languages in the Republic of Kazakhstan" (1997), "On political parties" (2002), the Land Code of the RK (2003), "On the mass media" (2004), "On the activities of international and foreign non-profit organisations in the Republic of Kazakhstan" and "On amendments and additions to certain legislative acts of the Republic of Kazakhstan related to non-profit organisations" (2004), "On amendments and additions to certain legislative acts related to religious freedom and the activities of religious associations" (2002) and "On amendments and additions to the legislative acts of the Republic of Kazakhstan on the freedom of religion and religious associations" (2009), and others. In some cases, the acts of law were found to be constitutional whereas others were found to be non-compliant with the constitution (the ones regarding amendments to the Constitution, the mass media, religious associations, international and foreign non-profit organisations, etc.).

The President requested an interpretation of the Constitution three times.

It should be noted that the President's active use of this power strengthens the constitutional legality and promotes harmonisation of relations between the head of state and the Parliament.

Overall, more than 26 acts of law and international treaties were declared either fully or partly unconstitutional, including the acts of law "On an amendment and an addition to the Constitution of the Republic of Kazakhstan", "On the activities of international and foreign non-profit organisations in the Republic of Kazakhstan", "On the mass media", "On amendments and additions to certain legislative acts of the Republic of Kazakhstan on the freedom of religion and religious associations" and others.

---

52 И.И. Рогов, В.А. Малиновский (eds.), *Конституционный контроль в Казахстане: доктрина и практика утверждения конституционализма: Монография,* Almaty 2015, p. 78.

In total, the provisions of 73 articles of the Constitution have been clarified either through an official interpretation or via constitutionality review of regulatory legal acts.

The legal positions expressed in the decisions, as well as recommendations included in the annual addresses of the Council entitled "On the status of constitutional legality in the country" open up space for accelerated implementation of constitutional reforms, promote further reinforcement of Kazakhstan as a democratic and law-governed state, and the development of the currently binding law system in line with the constitutional values, and also help to develop the doctrine of Kazakhstan's constitutionalism.

7 Society's Perception of Constitutional Review

The review of legal provisions was introduced as a result of constitutional practice, initially through the Constitutional Court, and was very positively received by the broad public, civil society institutions and citizens themselves. This is evidenced in the active work undertaken by the Constitutional Court.

Likewise, state bodies and officials currently perceive the work of the Constitutional Council as an indispensable element in the development of a law-governed state, contributing to the preservation of the constitutional foundations of the Republic of Kazakhstan, as well as the sovereignty and integrity of the state. In society at large, the CCK is perceived as a body that plays an essential role in resolving conflicts and contradictions between the highest authorities in the country, and acts as one of the most important tools in the system of checks and balances in the country's power system. In citizens' eyes, the CCK is a state body responsible for the observance and preservation of constitutional legality in the Republic of Kazakhstan. It should be noted that the Constitutional Council is one of those bodies that use civilised means to help ensure stability of society and its further democratisation as well as the development of constitutional legality in Kazakhstan.

Conclusions

At present, along with an overall positive assessment of the significant contribution made by the Constitutional Court of the RK to the reinforcement of constitutionalism, it would be useful to highlight some other 'lessons learnt' as well.

First, when the overall social order was changed in the country in parallel with the reforms of the state and power mechanisms, the status of the constitutional review body inevitably came into conflict with the functionally and institutionally imperfect government machinery, burdened by the legacy of the recent past.

Second, the situation was greatly complicated by the transitional status of the Constitution itself. Until 28 January 1993, it represented a motley mix of provisions and norms taken from the Constitution of the Kazakh Soviet Socialist Republic of 1978 (amended on multiple occasions), and the Constitutional Law "On the independence of the Republic of Kazakhstan", which stated that "the provisions of the Constitution and other legislative acts of the Republic of Kazakhstan are in force as they do not contradict this Law". Objectively speaking, the judges of the Constitutional Court had a very hard task selecting 'the original document' for comparisons. Moreover, the absence of the constitutionally established concept of 'binding law' and the official status of the main international human rights documents made it very difficult for the Constitutional Court to apply them directly when working on cases.

Third, the structure of a *de iure* powerful constitutional justice body was *de facto* grafted onto the imperfect and contradictory power system (according to the 1993 Constitution), including the judiciary and the institution of prosecutor's supervision, which at that time still had to undergo a substantive reform to shake off the negative 'Soviet relics'. In those circumstances, the Constitutional Court was granted the right to assess the constitutionality of law enforcement practices of those powerful bodies, as well as the regulatory legal acts issued by the Prosecutor General, the Supreme Court and the Supreme Arbitration Courts. To put it mildly, this solution was not very constructive on the quest for the supremacy and direct operation of the Constitution.

Fourth, the aspiration for unlimited 'democracy' at that time and the absence of the practice of effective yet highly balanced constitutional review (as of 1992) meant that the legislation on the Constitutional Court did not separate the constitutional (legal) sphere from the political sphere, and did not create any safeguards against the politicisation of judges[53].

Fifth, in 1992, the idea of having a purely judicial constitutional review in Kazakhstan led to the prevalence of the *ex post* constitutional review with all its consequences (traditional in terms of theory, but very dangerous for practice) such as the loss of legal effect for all decisions based on an act that was declared

---

53 С.К. Амандыкова, В.А. Малиновский, *Роль конституционного суда Республики Казахстан в становлении конституционной доктрины Казахстана,* "Евразийский научный журнал" 2012, № 10 (53), www.eurasialaw.ru/index.php?option=com_content&view=category&layout (accessed: May 24, 2018).

unconstitutional. The Supreme Soviet of the 13th convocation became hostage to this constitutional imperative.

The main outcome of the Constitutional Court's operations and, in particular, of its decision on the 'Kvyatkovskaya case', is that after the situation that emerged in 1995 the whole legal system was shifted onto the track of market reforms and a new government system thanks to the presidential decrees with the force of constitutional acts or 'ordinary' acts of law, even though the activities of the last Supreme Soviet in the country's history were terminated, and a temporary presidential 'monocracy' existed between March and December 1995. On 30 August, a new constitution of the RK was adopted in a nationwide referendum. With amendments and additions introduced by the acts of RK dated 7 October 1998, 21 May 2007, 11 February 2011 and 10 March 2017, the Constitution continues to operate successfully, ensuring stable progressive development of the society and the state.

The experience of the Constitutional Court is reflected in the provisions of the current Constitution and in the CCK Act.

Therefore, the competence of the Constitutional Council has been designed so as to:

- combine the maximum benefits of preliminary and *ex post* constitutional review, as well as abstract and specific types of constitutional review;
- take into account and consolidate the observance of the Constitution to ensure unity and separation of powers in the country, the operation of the highest state bodies and observance in the sphere of human and civil rights and freedoms;
- constructively autonomise the functions and operation of the Constitutional Council, courts and prosecutors while using the institution of constitutional review to strengthen the judiciary and vice versa;
- exclude, as much as possible, the politicisation of Constitutional Council members and the risk of misuse of powers;
- as the civil society and the state evolve, gradually enhance the capacity of the Constitutional Council by expanding its competences and ensuring access to the institution of constitutional review for a larger group of entities.

Ruslan Muratbekovich Myrzalimov

Constitutional Justice in the Kyrgyz Republic[1]

Abstract: While analyzing the specific features of constitutional judiciary in Kyrgyzstan, emphasis is placed on the transformations which took place in them. The European model of constitutional court adopted at the birth of independent Kyrgyzstan failed to work and was replaced by the review of legal norms passed to a chamber specially established in the Highest Court. The present text emphasizes that neither the creation of constitutional judiciary in Kyrgyzstan nor the process of establishing the political system of the country is a finished process.

Keywords: the European model of constitutional court, the South American model of constitutional judiciary, Constitutional Chamber of the Supreme Court, autonomy and independence, Constitutional Chamber of the Supreme Court and other organs of state power, cognition of the Constitutional Chamber of the Supreme Court

Introduction

Constitutional justice in Kyrgyzstan has operated for two decades – as a state-legal institute based on universal scientific-theoretical principles and law-enforcement practice. It has developed exclusive provisions to account for local terms and traditions. Its tasks include arrangement of conditions for supremacy and direct functioning of the Constitution, ensuring the rights and freedoms of person.

From an analysis of the constitutional justice body in Kyrgyzstan one must conclude that constitutional justice in Kyrgyzstan lacks some efficiency and effectiveness. Thus, it seems reasonable to assume that, at various stages during its formation and development, the constitutional justice body in Kyrgyzstan has discredited itself, taking essentially political, rather than constitutional-legal, position (as will be discussed in detail below). Let's provide a short list of the problems: as mentioned above, use of the specialized justice body as political

1 Our gratitude for help to Kubanychbek Daiyrbekovich Alybaev (Head of the Expert-Analytical Department, Constitutional Chamber at the Supreme Court of Kyrgyz Republic) and Zarina Tokonovna Esenaliyeva (Head of Department Analyzing the Administration of Decisions and Systematization of Laws at the Constitutional Chamber of the Supreme Court of Kyrgyz Republic).

tool; delay in exercising decisions requiring legislative or other regulation; the continued application of normative-legal acts after their recognition as unconstitutional; improper exercise or ignoring of constitutional justice decisions by public authorities, etc.

The institute of constitutional justice in Kyrgyzstan applies on a certain normative-regulatory basis. The development of constitutional legislation in Kyrgyzstan shares principles in common with other post-Soviet states. This is because Kyrgyzstan and the other Commonwealth of Independent States (CIS) countries formed after the collapse of the former USSR shared a common historical past, chose a similar model (constitutional structure in the form of constitutional courts), and a uniform type of object for constitutional regulation, promotion of state-political reforms, spread of international law (basics and innovations), and constitutional reforms.

However, depending on various historical, political, economic, and other factors, constitutional justice in Kyrgyzstan has individual features. This chapter examines the institute of constitutional review in the Kyrgyz Republic, the process of its formation and development, both in theory and practice.

The author is sure that constitutional will certainly continue to evolve – via a search for new forms, models, and standards of work, international experience of constitutional review accounting for specifics of national features. Accounting for the specifics of Kyrgyzstan and features of its current period (social and state-legal development) is really important here.

1 Motives for Introduction and Key Dilemmas of Establishing the Control Over Legal Norms

The genesis of the constitutional justice institute in Kyrgyzstan is inextricably linked with the history of the state. Each stage of state development revealed new features in public relations, the level of economy, the extent of state functions, powers and fields of work for state bodies. In its development, constitutional review underwent transformations similar to statehood as a whole.

In the development of the Kyrgyzstan Constitution, as well as the institute of constitutional review accompanying it in different periods, we can distinguish the following stages:

1918–1924, when Kyrgyzstan was part of Russia – i.e., from the first Constitution of the Russian Soviet Federative Socialist Republic (RSFSR) till the formation of the new state – the Union of Soviet Socialist Republics. In this period, parliamentary form of constitutional review was consolidated in terms of concentrating the absolute power, including constitutional review in the competence of the supreme public representative body;

1924–1929 – from the first Constitution of the Soviet Union till the formation of its own autonomy, where constitutional review was determined by the federative structure of the USSR;

1929–1937 – in this period Kyrgyz statehood existed with a form of autonomy; formation of its own bodies, which exercised constitutional review – among other functions. They acted within their competence – with parallel action of similar Russian, republican, and USSR bodies;

1937–1978 – qualitative transformation of Kyrgyz statehood and its further functioning in the format of the USSR republic; four decades of the USSR and a republican level of constitutional review;

1978–1993 – similar two-level constitutional review during the so-called developed socialism (common to all USSR republics); since 1980s – gradual progress along the new path of development, which can be characterized as gradual transition from parliamentary review to specialized constitutional review;

1993–until now – providing specialized constitutional review[2].

Let's omit the review of parliamentary control during the Soviet period and proceed directly to a study of specialized constitutional review. Regarding the history of establishing the constitutional bodies in post-Soviet states (including Kyrgyzstan), we have to mention the establishment of the USSR Committee for Constitutional Supervision (CCS) in 1989–1991. Amendments and addenda consolidating the establishment of this body were introduced by Article 125 of the USSR Law "On Amendments and Addenda to the USSR Constitution (Fundamental Law)", No. 9853-XI of December 1, 1988. CCS was elected by USSR Congress of People's Deputies – for a term of 10 years, from among the experts in the field of politics and law, including the Chair, Vice Chair, and 21 members (each USSR republic was delegating the representative). However, the CCS could not be elected. Legal scholars kept discussing options of the future law: some of them considered it necessary to maintain the *status quo* (i.e., keep the CCS); others championed an idea of establishing the Constitutional Court of the USSR; and some believed that functions of constitutional review could be exercised by the Supreme Court of the USSR only – despite the fact that this issue was on the agenda of the 1st Congress of People's Deputies of the USSR.

---

2 Р. М. Мырзалимов, *Вопросы конституционного правосудия в Кыргызстане*, Bishkek 2001, p. 125.

On December 21–23, 1989, the 2nd Congress of People's Deputies discussed and adopted Article 125 of the Constitution (new revision) and the USSR Law "On Constitutional Supervision in the USSR". In USSR Law No. 974-I of December 23, 1989 "On Amendments and Addenda to Article 125 of USSR Constitution (Fundamental Law)", CCS powers were slightly reduced. The new law came into effect from January 1, 1990. It contained a provision that CCS was not entitled to suspend the effect of constitutions in the USSR republics; laws adopted by the USSR Congress of People's Deputies, and some of their norms. The USSR Congress of People's Deputies was granted the right to reject CCS conclusions by two thirds of the votes. CCS staff was increased to 27 people, since 4 autonomies also claimed their rights for representation in the Committee. Casting of lots was assumed right after election of CCS members – to determine 13 Committee members, whose powers would expire in 5 years (in view of stepwise rotation). Members of the USSR Committee for Constitutional Supervision were elected by USSR Supreme Council resolution No. 1455-I of April 26, 1990. The members of the Committee were highly qualified, and included Doctors of Law (one Doctor of Historical Sciences, one PhD, and several Masters of Law were elected too). Well-known legal scholar R. Turgunbekov – Doctor of Law, Head of Department in Institute of Philosophy and Law at Academy of Sciences of Kyrgyz SSR, Corresponding Member of the National Academy of Sciences in the Kyrgyz Republic, was elected from Kyrgyzstan. The USSR CCS noted instances of noncompliance with the Constitution, international acts, and international obligations of the USSR for 18 acts under review, recognized 12 acts as invalid (for conflict with Constitution), suspended 2 acts, and twice obliged the prosecution bodies to protest against legal acts. Since the early "parade of sovereignties", acts and laws of the "transitional period" were issued at the USSR level; they stated that the Fundamental Law is valid only in part, which does not conflict with them – i.e., actually discredited the USSR Constitution.

On October 11, 1991, the USSR Committee for Constitutional Supervision announced that "the USSR, in its original state, actually ceased to exist". The Committee appealed to USSR republics with proposal to form, as soon as possible, local systems responsible for protection of the constitutional system. Let's note that the CCS was the only state body of the USSR that was not abolished till the end of 1991. It was eventually abolished in secret – without any statement of the fact of its dissolution and the resignation of its members in the "Bulletin of the Supreme Council of the USSR".

Kyrgyzstan also formed a structure similar to the USSR Committee for Constitutional Supervision. For the first time in the history of Kyrgyzstan, the Law "On Amendments and Addenda to Constitution (Fundamental Law) of

Kyrgyz SSR" dated September 23, 1989 established an institute of constitutional review. The operating procedure of the Kyrgyz Committee for Constitutional Supervision was specified by laws "On Amendments and Addenda to Constitution (Fundamental Law) of Kyrgyz SSR" dated April 12, 1990 and "On Constitutional Supervision in Kyrgyz SSR".

The main objectives of the Kyrgyz Committee for Constitutional Supervision were: ensuring compliance between acts of state bodies/public organizations and the Constitution of Kyrgyz SSR, protection of constitutional rights and personal freedoms, rights of peoples living in the territory of Kyrgyz SSR, and democratic grounds of Soviet society. The members of the CCS were elected by the Supreme Council of Kyrgyz SSR – for a term of 10 years, from among experts in the fields of politics and law, including the Chair, Vice Chair, and 7 Committee members. Item 3 of the above resolution from Supreme Council of Kyrgyz SSR assumed that, by terms of ensuring the activity and on issues of rights protection, persons elected to CCS were equated to people's deputies of Kyrgyz SSR. By another resolution "Formation of KSSR Committee for Constitutional Supervision", Muktar Tilekeyev, Honored Jurist of KSSR, was elected as CCS Chair. This non-judicial body exercised preliminary and subsequent constitutional supervision over legal acts of various levels. However, this body was not vested with great powers. Rather, it was a structure of mostly consultative-supervisory nature, which was evidenced by the powers of the Committee, its potential decisions, and the consequences of such decisions. Later on, while denying the principle of mandatory compliance between republican and USSR legislation or recognizing the rule of the latter, Kyrgyzstan was the first among the former USSR states to abolish the CCS and to establish the Constitutional Court. It happened during amending the Fundamental Law on December 14, 1990.

Under Article 111 of Kyrgyz SSR Constitution, the Constitutional Court (CCrt) had to be elected for 10 years, by the President's proposal to Jogorku Kenesh composed of: Chair, 2 Deputies, and 6 judges. To arrange the conditions and form the legal basis for work of the CCrt, the CCrt Chair (A.Sh. Sharshenaliyev) and Deputy (A.A. Lemeshenko) were elected in January 1991; however, till adoption of new local Constitution, this task was unfulfilled.

Since May 5, 1993, when the Constitution of the Kyrgyz Republic was adopted[3], a new stage of social-state development in Kyrgyzstan has started, as the Fundamental Law was of really great historical, political, and legal significance – it

3 Закон КР от 5 мая 1993 г. «О введении в действие Конституции Кыргызской Республики», Ведомости Жогорку Кенеша Кыргызской Республики. 1993. № 7, p. 85.

introduced significant changes (aimed at democratic transformations) in all spheres of society. The 1993 Constitution consolidated the key principles of an independent state with a democratic political-legal regime: formation of a law-bound state, aiming of the national state at revival and preserving the national gene pool, national culture, language, and traditions. These changes had a significant effect on the legal protection of the Constitution and the institute of constitutional review.

Establishment of new the CCrt, within the framework of state structure, was among the important features of 1993 Fundamental Law.

Jogorku Kenesh, on President's proposal, elected the Chair, Deputy, and 7 judges of the CCrt for 15 years. On May 8, 1993, based on the new Constitution, Jogorku Kenesh elected Ch.T. Bayekova as Chair of the CCrt in the Kyrgyz Republic (KR).

The structure, competence, and procedure of CCrt were assumed by Constitution, laws "On the Constitutional Court of Kyrgyz Republic" and "On Constitutional Proceedings of Kyrgyz Republic".

Constitutional reforms further implemented in the country had no practical effect on the CCrt (except for procedure of dismissing the judges from office). However, the fate of the CCrt was not easy or stable. The issue of its abolition – by combining the Supreme Court and the Supreme Arbitration Court, "in order to reduce the maintenance costs and ensure the effective judicial protection of population in republic"[4] – was raised more than once, but was not implemented. However, the CCrt was finally disbanded later, due to changes in socio-political and legal spheres of the country, which resulted in rearranging the system of state bodies – including the cessation of the CCrt's activities till there was a special governmental decision[5].

---

4 Ведомости Жогорку Кенеша Кыргызской Республики. 1995. № 11. Ст. 414, 424; 1996. № 2. Ст. 39.

5 Декрет Временного правительства Кыргызской Республики (ВП N 2 от 12 апреля 2010 года) «О расформировании Конституционного суда Кыргызской Республики»:

Throughout its activities, the Constitutional Court of Kyrgyz Republic (formed in 1993 to protect the Constitution of Kyrgyz Republic) did not meet the expectations and contributed to the concentration of power in one person – both under A.A. Akayev and K.S. Bakiyev.

Positive conclusions were provided for all amendments and addenda introduced to the Constitution of the Kyrgyz Republic by the referenda of 1996, 1998, 2003 which aimed to enhance the powers of the President of the Kyrgyz Republic. By its actions,

Let's emphasize that the institute of constitutional review was not abolished in this case – the Constitutional Chamber at the Supreme Court of KR was arranged instead.

The new Constitution of June 27, 2010 formed the Constitutional Chamber (CCh) at Supreme Court of Kyrgyz Republic.

The CCh is the supreme judicial body independently exercising constitutional review via constitutional proceedings and is the legal successor of the Constitutional Court in Kyrgyz Republic – under constitutional law "On Constitutional Chamber at Supreme Court of Kyrgyz Republic"[6]. The Constitutional Chamber is independent and subject to the Constitution, constitutional law "On Constitutional Chamber at Supreme Court of Kyrgyz Republic", and rules of Constitutional Chamber. CCh Judges are elected by Jogorku Kenesh,

---

the CCrt contributed to the destruction of checks and balances available in 1993 Constitution.

In 1998, in defiance of Constitution, the CCrt issued an opinion, which enabled the run of President A.A. Akayev for his third term.

After the 2005 revolution, the CCrt was subject to great expectations again. However, in a short period of time, the CCrt demonstrated its dependence again – by issuing an opinion on draft amendments and addenda to the Constitution (in September 2007). These amendments were adopted at a so-called "referendum", where K.S. Bakiyev, President of Kyrgyz Republic, legitimized the full usurpation of power.

In December 2009, K.S. Bakiyev submitted for review of Jogorku Kenesh a bill assuming the mechanism on transfer of President's powers via Presidential meeting, composition of which was not indicated in draft amendments. Despite the fact that this mechanism on the temporary transfer of the President's powers actually meant the transfer of power to close relatives of K.S. Bakiyev, with subsequent legal registration, the CCrt provided its positive opinion again, while "asking" to replace the Presidential meeting with State Council.

Thus, the CCrt actually failed the entrusted functions on protection of Constitution and turned into a body assisting the enhancement of power for one person.

Actions of the CCrt, which enhanced the power of one person, led to events of April 6–7, 2010 and fall of anti-national regime of K.S. Bakiyev.

To prevent the use of the CCrt for destabilizing the situation, the Provisional Government of Kyrgyz Republic, under Decree No. 1 of April 7, 2010, adopted the following Decree:

Disband the Constitutional Court of Kyrgyz Republic – till special resolution of Provisional Government of Kyrgyz Republic". R. Otunbayeva, Chairperson of Provisional Government in Kyrgyz Republic.

6 Конституционный закон Кыргызской Республики «О Конституционной палате Верховного суда Кыргызской Республики» от 13 июня 2011 года N 37.

on President's proposal, based on the proposal of a Council for Selection of Judges, with account for gender representation (first time – for 7 years, then – till age of 70). The CCh consists of 11 judges: Chair, Vice Chair, and 9 judges. From among its members, the CCh elects the Chair, Vice Chair, and Judge Secretary – for a term of 3 years. Mukambet Shadykanovich Kasymaliev was elected the first Chair.

After its establishment in 2010 the Constitutional Chamber did not immediately start operating because no staff had been appointed. The CCh did not start operating until July 2013. Even today, only 10 of the 11 judges have been elected. At the moment, one place in the CCh is vacant. I.e., the Chamber is not completely formed yet, which was mentioned, among other issues, at a recent meeting between newly elected President S. Jeenbekov and the CCh Chair[7]. The selection process for electing the last (11th) judge to this important constitutional body is ongoing during drafting of this material.

In June 2016, according to the Constitution and the constitutional law "On the Constitutional Chamber at the Supreme Court of the Kyrgyz Republic", the Chair, Vice Chair, and Judge Secretary were re-elected. Erkinbek Tobokelovich Mamyrov was elected as the new Chair (previously, he used to be the Vice Chair).

The fundamental goal of the CCh is protection of constitutional system, rights and freedoms of person and citizen.

The basic principles of the CCh activities include independence, collegiality, publicity, competitiveness, and equality of the parties.

Thus, in almost 30 years, the following transformation of specialized constitutional justice bodies took place in Kyrgyzstan:

1. Committee for Constitutional Supervision of Kyrgyz SSR: September 23, 1989 – December 14, 1990;
2. Constitutional Court of Kyrgyz SSR and Constitutional Court of Kyrgyz Republic: December 14, 1990 – April 12, 2010;
3. CCh at the Supreme Court of KR: June 27, 2010 – until now.

In history of Kyrgyzstan, the first chairs of the specialized constitutional justice bodies were:

1990 – Chair of Committee for Constitutional Supervision in Kyrgyz SSR – Muktar Tilekeyev;
1991 – Chair of Constitutional Court – Asanbek Sharshenalievich Sharshenaliev;

---

7 http://www.president.kg/ru/news/11208_prezident_sooronbay_jeenbekov_prinyal_predsedatelya_konstitutsionnoy_palatyi_verhovnogo_suda_erkinbeka_mamyirova (accessed: March 20, 2018).

1993 – Chair of Constitutional Court – Cholpon Tursunovna Bayekova;
2008 – Chair of Constitutional Court – Svetlana Kaldarbekovna Sydykova;
2013 – Chair of Constitutional Chamber of Supreme Court of Kyrgyz Republic – Mukambet Shadykanovich Kasymaliyev;
2016 – Chair of Constitutional Chamber of the Supreme Court of the Kyrgyz Republic – Erkinbek Tobokelovich Mamyrov.
2019 – Chair of Constitutional Chamber of the Supreme Court of the Kyrgyz Republic – Duisheev Karybek Arstanbekovich.

Now, the CCh is the central link in the protection of the Fundamental Law, as the constitutional review body with exclusive competence on verifying the constitutionality of normative legal acts. Although today, the CCh also has other important tasks: systemic ensuring of the rule of law, constitutionalization of society, and the ensuring and protection of human and civil rights and freedoms.

2 Legislative Stability of Legal Norm Controlling Body

The constitutional legislation of Kyrgyzstan has many common features with CIS countries. In general, this is due to the following features:

a. common historical heritage of CIS member states;
b. common chosen model of constitutional system;
c. similar object of constitutional regulation;
d. dynamics of state-political reforms;
e. effect of international constitutional process, international law, and common CIS law on constitutional transformations;
f. special mechanism of protecting the constitutional legislation[8].

The National constitution is the basic foundation of the local legal system. All CIS countries passed 2 stages of constitutional reforms. The first one was an evolutionary stage that reflected the initial transformation of totalitarian party-state socialism into liberal-democratic post-industrial society of Western type; the second was the revolutionary stage, characterized by the adoption of new constitutions and the dynamism of the constitutional process.

The Constitution Law "On the Constitutional Court of the Kyrgyz Republic", and the Law "On Constitutional Proceedings of the Kyrgyz Republic", simultaneously adopted on December 18, 1993[9], initially defined the position, functions,

---

8 И. В. Гордеев, *Конституционная юстиция в государствах-членах СНГ*, дисс. на соиск. уч. степ.канд. юрид. наук, Moscow 2007.

9 Ведомости Жогорку Кенеша Кыргызской Республики. 1994. № 2. Ст. 46; Ст. 48.

formation rules, and activity of the CCrt. According to Article 3 of Law "On the Constitutional Court of the Kyrgyz Republic", the above laws and rules of the CCrt were adopted as the basis of the regulatory framework, structure, competence, and activities of the CCrt. At that time, norms on the CCrt were included in Chapter 6, "Courts and Justice" of the KR Fundamental Law, articles of which regulated the activities of various courts. Besides, norms on the CCrt were also included in chapters of Constitution, which approved the status of such institutes as "President" and "Jogorku Kenesh", and in chapter "Procedure of amending and supplementing the Constitution". Requirements to candidates for judges of the CCrt, procedure of appointing the judges, and such definitions as competence, legislative specification of status for the CCrt, exercise of judicial power via constitutional and other proceedings, were included in chapter "Courts and Justice" (Articles 79–82, 86, 87 and 82, 83, 84, respectively). Thus, affiliation of the CCrt with the judicial branch of state power was established by Fundamental Law.

Fundamental postulates of its activity – legality, collegiality, publicity, independence, and subordination to the Constitution only – are defined in Article 2 of the Law "On Constitutional Court of Kyrgyz Republic". Also, 5 chapters and 21 articles of the law provide detailed description and development of constitutional norms – on staff and structure of the court, its competence, status of constitutional judges, and protection of their activities.

In most post-Soviet states, the special law on the constitutional court looks like a codified act of material and procedural norms. And Kyrgyzstan, until recently, had a special law clarifying the process of constitutional justice. Sixty articles of law "On Constitutional Proceedings of Kyrgyz Republic"[10], collected in 3 chapters, extensively regulated the principles of constitutional legal proceedings and scope of case resolution by the CCrt, while characterizing the subjects of appeal to this court and parties to constitutional legal proceedings, rules of initiating the legal proceedings, preparing the case reviews, and acts of the CCrt. At that, law "On Constitutional Court of Kyrgyz Republic" was constitutional, and law "On Constitutional Proceedings of Kyrgyz Republic" did not have this status; therefore, they differed in legal position. According to law on normative-legal acts of KR[11], constitutional laws were adopted and amended in special

---

10 Ведомости Жогорку Кенеша Кыргызской Республики. 1994. № 2. Ст. 48.

11 Закон Кыргызской Республики «О нормативных правовых актах Кыргызской Республики» (Ведомости Жогорку Кенеша Кыргызской Республики, 1996 г., № 7, ст. 101). Later on, its wording was changed twice: Законом от 20 июля 2009 года № 241 и Законом от 13 мая 2011 года № 23.

manner[12]; in this view, regulation of status for specialized constitutional review body emphasized the importance of this body in mechanism of state power and formed the additional guarantee of its independence and stability. In constitutional practice of post-Soviet states, term "constitutional law" turned into new noteworthy phenomenon. Such laws are adopted only on issues assumed by Constitution; so, this structure plays a special role in forming the constitutional foundation.

Significant role in establishing the norms of constitutional legal proceeding in Kyrgyzstan was played by the CCrt Rules[13]. Its meaning was not just in the fact of being an act of power delegated by the legislator to the CCrt, but also in the fact of providing the CCrt with the right to regulate the "internal issues of its activity, not regulated by law" (Article 3 of Law "On Constitutional Court of Kyrgyz Republic"). By constitutional law, the CCrt was delegated with power to adopt the rules, which confirmed its legal nature. Rules (adopted on the basis of Constitution and Law on the CCrt) were supposed to detail and develop the provisions of this law on constitutional legal proceedings, arrangement of work for the CCrt and its system. Besides, it referred to internal activity of the CCrt only, as the law defined the subject of regulation determined by legislation, which served as natural restriction. Rules controlling the operating procedures of the CCrt (i.e., its Regulations) formed a normative legal act, provisions of which were mandatory for all parties to the process participating/attending the sessions of the CCrt, for all departments and members of its staff, and constitutional judges – first of all, of course, assuming the representatives, witnesses, experts, and translators (similar to the parties). Rules of the CCrt in Kyrgyz Republic contained the norms on powers and rules of judge's actions on arranging a CCrt session.

Some issues of organizational nature related to Constitutional Court were settled by resolutions of Jogorku Kenesh (Parliament) – in particular, approving a description and sample of the robe for a judge of Constitutional Court and issues on binding the judges by oath[14]. Apart from special legislation on constitutional justice, some of its aspects were governed by norms of acts regulating

12 Constitutional laws are adopted in three readings at least, by no less than two-thirds of the total Jogorku Kenesh deputies. While ordinary laws and decisions of Jogorku Kenesh are adopted by majority of present deputies, but not less than 50 votes of Jogorku Kenesh deputies (can be adopted in the first reading).

13 Adopted by Resolution of Constitutional Court in Kyrgyz Republic of August 4, 1995.

14 Ведомости Жогорку Кенеша Кыргызской Республики 1995. № 6. Ст. 157; Ст. 176.

the other state institutions. For example, the pre-existing Arbitration Procedure Code of the Kyrgyz Republic[15] assumed that, in case of raising an issue on non-compliance of a law or other official act with the Constitution (during the review process), the arbitration court shall request the CCrt and follow its decision in the future[16]. Hence, it follows that CCrt powers could be established only by the Constitution and constitutional laws. However, issues related to the CCrt and its judges were resolved in other official acts – ordinary laws, resolutions of Jogorku Kenesh chambers. Even special laws on the CCrt of Kyrgyz Republic included the articles containing references to such acts. These acts were of auxiliary nature and were adopted in order to develop and detail some provisions of the law on the CCrt – without conflict or amendments to it. If conflict occurred, the constitutional law on the CCrt had to be followed, even if the available conflict was actually addressed. The law on the CCrt contained references to laws, which regulated the liability for interfering with CCrt activities, ignoring its decisions and requirements, providing the CCrt with knowingly false information (Part 1, Article 7 of KR Law "On the Constitutional Court of the Kyrgyz Republic" and Part 2, Article 14, Part 7, Article 16, Article 19 of KR Law "On Constitutional Proceedings in the Kyrgyz Republic").

After disbanding the CCrt of Kyrgyzstan, the Constitutional Chamber at the KR Supreme Court was established; its powers were approved by KR Constitutional Law "On Constitutional Chamber at Supreme Court of Kyrgyz Republic", No. 37 of June 13, 2011[17]. The first article of this law contains the following definition of the new constitutional review body: "Constitutional Chamber at Supreme Court of Kyrgyz Republic (hereinafter, Constitutional Chamber) is the supreme judicial body independently exercising constitutional review by means of constitutional legal proceedings". This definition extends and is more detailed than in the text of the local Constitution: "Constitutional Chamber at Supreme Court is the body exercising constitutional review" (Article 97). We consider the difference between the normative regulation of the Constitutional Chamber definition in the local Fundamental Law and in the law directly regulating it not quite successful and even fraught with certain risks. While for us, as professionals, such an approach is somewhat explicable, for most ordinary people, such variant reading (that's how it will be interpreted) is unclear at best.

---

15 Upon abolition of arbitration court system, KR Arbitration Procedure Code was canceled and became invalid.

16 Ведомости Жогорку Кенеша Кыргызской Республики 1996. № 5. Ст. 71.

17 Later on, wording of this constitutional law was amended and supplemented three times: 1) No. 66 of May 26, 2012; 2) No. 105 of June 26, 2013; 3) No. 136 of July 20, 2017.

Then, the KR Constitutional Law "On the Constitutional Chamber at the Supreme Court of the Kyrgyz Republic" contains 4 sections, 8 chapters, and 62 articles. This law (signed at the moment by R. Otunbayeva, President of Kyrgyz Republic for the transitional period) officially canceled the effect of two previous laws regulating the status and activities of the KR CCrt[18].

Legislators and the new leadership of the country combined substantive and procedural norms in the new law on the CCh. In our opinion, the name of the Constitutional Law "On the Constitutional Chamber at the Supreme Court of the Kyrgyz Republic" could be added as follows: "and constitutional legal proceedings in the Kyrgyz Republic". Then, the full name would read: "On the Constitutional Chamber at the Supreme Court of the Kyrgyz Republic and constitutional legal proceedings in the Kyrgyz Republic". Since the content of the law includes two major sections, such innovation would correspond to its text. Nevertheless, there are strong convictions that only separate legislative acts shall regulate the norms of a substantive and procedural nature. Besides, deep-rooted delimitation of law into procedural and formal is one of features specific to our legal system; therefore, we believe that it should not be neglected.

Among other things, it is proposed to give legislative interpretation of the concept "constitutional review", which is found both in the Constitution and in the law, but never explained.

Establishment of the CCh required relevant amendments to Law No. 153 of July 18, 2003 "On the Supreme Court of the Kyrgyz Republic and local courts". Currently, Article 12 in Section II on the Supreme Court (KR Law No. 39, as amended on June 13, 2011) reads as follows:

> 1. The Supreme Court is the supreme judicial body on civil, criminal, economic, administrative, and other cases.
> *The Constitutional Chamber operates as part of the Supreme Court* (italicized by author).
> Judges of the Constitutional Chamber are not included in plenum of Supreme Court.
> Powers, composition, and procedure of forming the Constitutional Chamber, election and dismissal of the Chair/Vice Chair, and procedure of constitutional legal proceedings are determined by constitutional law.

18 Article 62 of this law states: To declare invalid: Law of Kyrgyz Republic "On Constitutional Court of Kyrgyz Republic" (Ведомости Жогорку Кенеша Кыргызской Республики, 1994 г., № 2, ст. 46); Law of Kyrgyz Republic "On Constitutional Proceedings of Kyrgyz Republic" (Ведомости Жогорку Кенеша Кыргызской Республики, 2009 г., № 7, ст. 745).

The KR Law "On the Supreme Court of the Kyrgyz Republic and local courts", adopted in 2003 and signed by the first President, consists of 5 sections. The law underwent many amendments and addenda, but has not lost its effect. Thus, by decision of the former KR CCrt dated April 29, 2008, sub-Item 4, Item 1, Article 41 of the law was recognized as unconstitutional and contrary to Item 4, Article 15 and Item 1, Article 18 of the KR Constitution. In due time, the decision of the Plenum of the KR Supreme Court, No. 12 of August 2, 2003, was adopted to apply Article 41 of the law. The wording of the law was amended three times – in 2004, 2006, and 2007. It was again amended in 2008 and, as mentioned above, in June 2011 (the latest amendments due to a change in the status of the judicial constitutional review body).

We should also mention the Constitutional Law of Kyrgyz Republic "On Status of Judges in Kyrgyz Republic", No. 141 of July 9, 2008. The latest addenda to this law were introduced due to an arrangement of the CCh. It will be reviewed in detail in separate section on status of the judges.

So, it is absolutely clear that work on establishing the constitutional-legal basis of the KR judicial system has been done already – mostly, via the development and adoption of fundamental legislative acts. The basis consists of:

- the Constitution of Kyrgyz Republic. Adopted by referendum (national vote) on June 27, 2010;
- the Constitutional Law of Kyrgyz Republic "On the Constitutional Chamber at the Supreme Court of the Kyrgyz Republic", No. 37 dated June 13, 2011;
- the Constitutional Law of Kyrgyz Republic "On the Status of Judges in the Kyrgyz Republic", No. 141 dated July 9, 2008;
- the Law of Kyrgyz Republic "On the Supreme Court of the Kyrgyz Republic and local courts", No. 153 dated July 18, 2003;
- the Law of Kyrgyz Republic "On Judicial Self-Government Bodies", No. 35 dated March 20, 2008; and
- the Law of Kyrgyz Republic "On the Council for the Selection of Judges in the Kyrgyz Republic", No. 40 dated June 13, 2011.

However, let's keep in mind that, in our opinion, normative consolidation of KR SC CCh status is insufficient. This problem must be solved to ensure the successful development of the judicial system in Kyrgyzstan, ensure its independence, and guarantee its stability. It must be done to avoid potential negative risks, which may occur in relations with the Supreme Court and/or its structural divisions, and interaction with other public authorities. In our opinion, this aspect is of undoubted interest for scholars and practitioners.

3 Legislative Position of the Constitutional Chamber at the Supreme Court

3.1 The Constitutional Chamber at Supreme Court and President

An important role in legal protection of the Constitution is assigned to the head of state – the President. In the laws of most countries, the President's powers in this area are mostly supervisory by nature. The President's main types of response include suspensive veto, submission of particularly important bills to referendum, use of conciliation procedures for resolving the disputable situations.

Previous wordings of the KR Constitution[19] clearly stated: "the President is guarantor of Constitution". In the current wording, this legal provision is missing. It was a response from politicians and people – by the results of two revolutions, where Presidents ruling the country since 1991 were recognized as guilty. Upon a loss of faith in the presidential form of government, the constitutional reform of 2010 switched Kyrgyzstan to a "parliamentary track of development". As a result, presidential powers were reduced and parliamentary powers were increased, respectively. In addition, let's note that, previously, the Chair and Deputy of the former KR CCrt were elected by Jogorku Kenesh (Parliament), by proposal from President of the country – only the Secretary of the CCrt was elected from among the judges. Today, the situation has changed (the details will be provided further, in section "Legal status of judge at legal norm controlling body").

According to the current Constitution[20], the President has, among others, the following powers:

1) signing and promulgation of laws; return of laws to Jogorku Kenesh, with objections (sub-Item 1, Item 2, Article 64);
2) presenting candidates to Jogorku Kenesh – for election as judges of the Supreme Court and CCh, by proposal of the Council for Selection of Judges (sub-Item 1, Item 3, Article 64);
3) presenting the candidates to Jogorku Kenesh – for relief from duty of judges at the Supreme Court and the CCh, by proposal from Council of Judges or

19 Wordings of Constitution since 1993 till 2010.

20 Adopted by referendum (national vote) on June 27, 2010 (put into effect by KR Law of June 27, 2010). In wording of KR Law No. 218 dated December 28, 2016 (official text, with account for changes made by referendum (national vote) on December 11, 2016 and addressing of conflict between texts in state and official language).

Disciplinary Committee at Council of Judges, in cases assumed by the current Constitution and constitutional law (sub-Item 2, Item 3, Article 64);

According to the Constitution, only the President of the country and the Constitutional Chamber have so-called *counter-majoritarian difficulty*.

Only the President and CCh can legally resist the will of the majority and adjust the decisions adopted by the law-making body, if these decisions violate the constitutional rights and freedoms of person and citizen.

The President performs this function by imposing a veto on laws adopted by Jogorku Kenesh while the CCh does it by exercising constitutional review, i.e., recognizing the normative legal acts or their provisions as unconstitutional and annulling their effect in Kyrgyzstan.

Let's note that the President actively uses this power; as an example, we can show the following statistics of veto imposed by the President on laws adopted by the Parliament:

- September 2016–June 2017 – 10 veto;
- September 2017–until now – 9 veto.

Under Article 20 of the constitutional law on the CCh, the President may appeal to the CCh. However, since start of its operation, the President has never appealed to the CCh[21].

3.2 The Constitutional Chamber at Supreme Court and the Government

In addition to the legal protection of the KR Constitution by the CCh it is also a specific function of the KR Government – to ensure the supremacy of the Constitution in the system of normative acts and its direct effect on activity of subjects in public relations.

The Constitution is subject to special legal protection – to ensure its supremacy and stability, real effect and strict observance by state and municipal authorities, individuals and legal entities, to prevent violation of its norms and establish the constitutional law/order in state and society. The legal protection of Constitution is ensured by almost any state and municipal authority in the course of their law-making/law-enforcement activities and the exercise of their powers.

---

21 Previously, the President used this power and appealed to Constitutional Court of Kyrgyz Republic, although infrequently.

Under Article 83 of KR Constitution, Government, subordinate ministries, state committees, administrative departments, and local state administrations exercise executive power in KR. The Government is the supreme executive body of KR. The Government is headed by the Prime Minister and consists of Vice Prime Ministers, ministers, and Chairs of state committees.

Under Article 88 of the Constitution, the Government ensures the implementation of the Constitution and laws by all executive bodies, signs governmental decrees/orders and ensures their implementation; takes measures to ensure the rule of law, rights and freedoms of citizens, protection of public order and crime prevention; ensures measures are taken to protect state sovereignty, territorial integrity, protection of the constitutional system, and measures on enhancing the defense, national security, and rule of law. Article 90 of the KR Constitution assumes direct participation of the Government in ensuring the implementation of the local Constitution. Thus, on the basis of and pursuant to the Constitution/laws, the Government issues decrees and orders, which are binding on the entire KR territory; and it may also cancel the acts of ministries, state committees, and administrative departments.

Under Article 20 of constitutional law on the CCh, the Prime Minister may appeal to the CCh – with a proposal to recognize laws or other normative legal acts unconstitutional and to give an opinion on constitutionality of international treaties, which have not come into force for KR. To date, the Government has never used this power. In fact, there is a practice of appeal to the CCh by executive bodies (e.g., ministers or ministries) drafting international treaties, while Article 25 of the law states that appeal to the CCh shall be in writing and signed by an authorized person (among executive bodies – the Government and Prime Minister only). The previous practice of appeal to the CCh by ministries was due to the fact that another law ("On Regulations of Jogorku Kenesh in Kyrgyz Republic")[22] stated that the Government must submit a draft law on ratification or denunciation of an international treaty to Jogorku Kenesh in the prescribed manner, with the following documents:

1) the text of the international treaty;
2) the opinion of the Government on compliance of the treaty with KR legislation and an assessment of the possible financial, economic, and other consequences of its ratification;
3) information on progress of preparing and signing the international treaty; and

---

22 Закон Кыргызской Республики «О Регламенте Жогорку Кенеша Кыргызской Республики» от 14 октября 2011 г.

4) the opinion of the CCh on the constitutionality of the international treaty[23].

Therefore, responsible ministries preparing a package of mandatory documents for the Parliament appealed to the CCh for its opinion. However, due to the fact that ministers and ministries are not authorized persons, the CCh refused to accept and register such appeals.

Another explanation for absent practice of appeal by the Government or Prime Minister with such proposals is in Article 24[24], which provides the reasons and grounds for a case review in the CCh. The reason for a case review is revealed uncertainty as to whether the law, normative legal act, international treaty that has not come into force for KR, or draft law on amendments to the Constitution is compliant with the Constitution; where there is no uncertainty, there is no reason to appeal to the CCh. Otherwise, the CCh would be overwhelmed with such appeals on all drafts of international treaties (many of them are concluded every year)[25].

In case of appeal to the CCh on issues of competence, bodies and officials may provide submissions only to extent related to their competence. The Government may also appeal seeking a conclusion regarding the draft law on amendments to the Constitution. As in the previous case, there is no practice of providing a conclusion regarding the draft law on amendments to the Constitution.

Decisions and conclusions of the CCh are sent to parties, state and local self-government bodies, and officials, whose normative legal acts formed the subject of review; they are posted in official publications of state/local self-government bodies, in the "Bulletin of the Constitutional Chamber at the Supreme Court of the Kyrgyz Republic", on the CCh's official website, and in other publications, if necessary.

---

23 "Procedure for ratifying international treaties" – Article 68 of the law.

24 Конституционный закон «О Конституционной палате Верховного суда Кыргызской Республики» от 13 июня 2011 года № 37.

25 Article 3 of KR Law "On International Treaties of Kyrgyz Republic" defines the names and types of international treaties concluded by KR. An international treaty concluded by KR may be referred to as a treaty, agreement, convention, protocol, or may have other names. International treaties are concluded by KR with foreign states, international organizations, and other subjects of international law, on behalf of:

1) KR – inter-state international treaties;

2) Jogorku Kenesh of KR – inter-parliamentary international treaties;

3) Government of KR – inter-governmental international treaties;

4) ministries, state committees and administrative departments of KR, and other relevant state bodies – inter-departmental international treaties.

If the CCh finds the constitutional law, code or law to be in conflict with the Constitution (in whole/in part) or implies the need to fill the gap in legal regulation, the Government, within 4 months after publishing the CCh decision on its official website, shall provide the Jogorku Kenesh with a draft constitutional law or draft law arising from the above decision[26]. The above bills are subject to review by the Jogorku Kenesh, in extraordinary session.

3.3 The Constitutional Chamber at Supreme Court and Parliament

Separation of state power into 3 branches of government is one of the fundamental grounds for the modern constitutional system. It's a pre-requisite against the concentration and abuse of power, which forms a guarantee of human and civil rights and freedoms, law-bound state and democracy.

The constitutional review body performs an important function – keeping the balance between the branches of government and resolving conflicts arising between them – based on the principle for separation of powers consolidated in Article 6 of Declaration on State Sovereignty of the Kyrgyz Republic dated December 15, 1990, which declared that state power in the Republic is exercised via its separation into legislative, executive, and judicial power.

The primary role of the CCh (enhancing a system of checks and balances) assumes strict adherence to constitutional principles. Implementation and strict adherence to these principles allows complete achievement of the true goal of this system of checks and balances. However, upon abuse of power in one of the branches and excess of powers assumed by the Constitution, the constitutional review body shall demand compliance with the provisions of the Constitution and non-exceedance of the limits of competence – via available constitutional powers and legal mechanisms.

The CCh ensures complete constitutional review and so restrains the political forces entitled to adopt normative legal acts from exceeding their competence established by the Constitution and laws. For example, in 2014 the CCh reviewed a case with the Government as plaintiff and the Parliament as the defendant. In this case, the Government disputed the provision of the Law "On the Republican Budget of the Kyrgyz Republic", according to which, the relevant committee of Parliament had to consent to approval of the *development budget*, which was revised after adoption of the law – i.e., at stage of exercising

26 As is known, at present, within new legal guidelines, the Government is developing a bill on amending the law about advocacy; soon, it shall be submitted to supreme legislative body of the country.

the law on the republican budget. Having reviewed the case, the CCh came to the conclusion that the legislator's procedure on coordinating the planning of capital investments (from the republican budget) with the relevant committee of Jogorku Kenesh cannot be exercised during the implementation of the law on the republican budget. Providing the relevant committee with a power assumed by debated legal provisions (at this stage of the budget process) is interference in Government activities on exercising the republican budget, which conflicts with Part 3, Article 5 of the Constitution and violates the principle of separating state powers.

Besides, the CCh noted in this decision that "...parliamentary control – one of the primary functions of the Parliament following the legislative function – shall be exercised upon excluding the interference in direct executive-administrative activities of executive bodies".

Let's note that constitutional court decisions have enormous influence on the activity of rule-making bodies. The very nature of constitutional justice predetermines the legal nature of constitutional court decisions. They contain the legal result of constitutional-jurisdictional activity, which, in turn, affects the entire legal system of the state.

Another aspect of interaction between Constitutional Chamber and the Parliament can be determined as follows: a draft law arising from a CCh decision may be initiated by deputies of the Jogorku Kenesh. In presence of governmental conclusion, such bill shall be reviewed by Jogorku Kenesh in extraordinary session.

Under Article 74 of Constitution, the Jogorku Kenesh elects the judges of the Supreme Court and the CCh – by proposal of the President; also, under the Constitution and constitutional law, the Jogorku Kenesh may dismiss them from office – by proposal of the President. Also, the Jogorku Kenesh approves the composition of the Council for Selection of Judges (in the manner prescribed by law); later, this Council participates in the process of selecting CCh judges.

The Jogorku Kenesh, as a collegiate body, and a faction (or factions) of the Jogorku Kenesh, are entitled to submit appeals in the form of proposals to the CCh.

This right is not directly granted to the Toraga (Speaker of Parliament) – like, for example, to the President or Prime Minister. Despite the parliamentary form of government proclaimed in KR and the high status of the Speaker, he/she is actually ranked second in the state. Apart from heading the supreme representative body, which exercises the legislative power and control functions, under Article 68 of Constitution, he/she performs the duties of the President in the event of the early termination of presidential powers (for reasons defined in Constitution), till the election of a new President.

This right is not granted to members of the Parliament, although they used to be entitled to group/individual appeal to KR CCh. Nor is it granted to committees of the Jogorku Kenesh, although the status and competence of parliamentary committees are at the highest level now. Let's just note the fact that the consent of the Jogorku Kenesh to an election, an appointment, and a dismissal from public office is given only in presence of an opinion from the relevant Jogorku Kenesh committees[27].

3.4 The Constitutional Chamber of Supreme Court and Courts

Since the last third of the 20th century, based on a wide range of objectively conditioned and historically determined reasons, the tendency to full or partial refusal from constitutional review and the constitutional justice system, which was mostly exercised by courts of general jurisdiction, is getting more and more apparent. In such cases, the records are kept only for modifications directly/indirectly associated with a change in views on the classical doctrine of separating the powers, which is rooted in many countries of the continent.

The main principle of administering justice is the independence of the judicial power. Judicial independence assumes the independence of the judging institute and the independence of the individual judges. In turn, the individual independence of judges includes 2 elements: substantive independence (subordination to law only) and personal independence (guarantees against arbitrariness due to the judge's position). From an institutional point of view, judicial independence is part of the constitutional system (checks and balances) and the main factor guaranteeing the impartiality of judges. To ensure the independence of judges, international experience has the following legislative and administrative procedures: constitutional separation of powers; meritocracy in appointing of judges; fixed term (age) of retirement; guarantees against arbitrary removal; guarantees of terms for independent work; immunity from prosecution under civil suit (the immunity does not apply to cases in which judges are convicted of corruption or crimes); and institutionalized respect for judges, in the form of political conventions establishing the requirements to methods and tone of criticism against judging. Issues of judicial accountability and compatibility between the principles of independent judicial power and its social responsibility are not new, They have been evident for many years and were discussed in special literature of

27 Article 76 in Constitution of Kyrgyz Republic.

different states (both by practitioners and representatives of jurisprudential science). In our context, they cause especially heated debates. However, international practice has reached general consensus in terms of the requirement for accountability of judges. It is covered by the postulate that people with great power on behalf of the state shall be responsible to society. Is there a conflict between the principle of independent judicial power and the principle of its accountability? Is it possible to combine these principles or is it inevitable that preference will be given to one principle over the other? The correct answer is keeping the balance between the two principles. In developed democracies, the judicial branch is really independent – enhancing the responsibility of judicial (non-elected) manpower is quite a problem there. In developing countries, judicial power is not fully independent – the problem is that achieving judicial independence and accountability to society are the synchronous tasks of judicial reform, while civilian control is aimed at elimination of corruption in the judicial system.

Article 93, Part 3 of KR Constitution states: "the Constitutional Chamber operates within the Supreme Court". The law "On the Constitutional Chamber at KR Supreme Court" states that the CCh is the supreme judicial body, independently exercising constitutional review via constitutional legal proceedings (Article 1 of the law). No courts are directly subordinate to the CCh, although its decisions are essential for all other courts of Kyrgyzstan, thus affecting judicial practice.

Previously (under KR Constitution of 1993), KR CCrt and KR Supreme Arbitration Court were established in the KR judicial system, along with the Supreme Court. After that, all courts could be structured into 3 sub-systems (blocks). The first included the CCrt, the second the Supreme Court and courts of general jurisdiction, and the third the Supreme Arbitration Court and system of arbitration courts.

Part 3, Article 61 of Law on the CCh states: "the Constitutional Chamber is the legal successor to the KR Constitutional Court. Material guarantees of CCrt independence established prior to coming of this constitutional law into force (including the individual building previously occupied by the KR Constitutional Court) are reserved to the Constitutional Chamber…"[28].

Now, courts of general jurisdiction in KR are only entitled to file requests to the specialized body of constitutional justice to define constitutionality. Published information contains the following statistics:

---

28 Конституционный закон Кыргызской Республики «О Конституционной палате Верховного суда Кыргызской Республики» № 37 от 13 июня 2011 года.

- 2013 – 17 (12.14 % of the total appeals);
- 2014 – 4 (3.7 % of the total appeals);
- 2015 – 3 requests (4 % of the total appeals);
- 2016 – 1 request (1.51 % of the total appeals);
- 2017 – 0 requests (0 % of the total appeals).

To summarize, for independence and stability, judicial power must be funded at a decent level. Within the implementation of the State Target Program "Development of Judicial System in Kyrgyz Republic for 2014–2017"[29] and based on Article 98 of the KR Constitution, the state ensures funding and adequate terms for functioning of courts and activity of judges. Funding of courts is conducted at the expense of the republican budget and must ensure the possibility for the full and independent administration of justice.

3.5 The Constitutional Chamber of Supreme Court and Other Public Authorities

Under Article 20 of the CCh constitutional law, apart from the above bodies, right of appeal to the CCh is granted to the following subjects:

1. Local self-government bodies;
2. the Attorney General; and
3. the Akyikatchy (Ombudsman).

In case of appeal to the CCh on issues of competence, authorities and officials may submit proposals only to the extent related to their competence.
Statistics of appeals from three subjects under review is as follows:

No.	**Subject of appeal**	**2013**	**2014**	**2015**	**2016**	**2017**
1.	Local self-government bodies	0	0	1	6	2
2.	Attorney General	1	2	0	0	0
3.	Akyikatchy (Ombudsman)	1	2	0	2	1

29 Государственная целевая программа «Развитие судебной системы Кыргызской Республики на 2014–2017 годы» http://cbd.minjust.gov.kg/act/view/ru-ru/96404 (accessed: March 20, 2018).

Statistical data are given since first year of Constitutional Chamber activities (2013) till 2017. Results of statistics on appeals in 2018 have not been published yet.

4 Structure of the Constitutional Chamber of Supreme Court

4.1 The Legal Status Judges of Constitutional Chamber of Supreme Court

In KR, the judges elect the CCh Chair. In this case, we should give credit to the ideologists and legislators of Kyrgyzstan for creating an effective system ensuring the unity and equality of the legal status for judges, impartiality and independence of the judges and the constitutional review body on the whole. The fact is that administration of the CCh in Kyrgyzstan is not just democratically elected ("best among equals"), but rotated as well (Chair and Vice Chair are replaced every 3 years). In Article 6, the procedure for electing the Chair, Vice Chair, and Judge Secretary of the CCh adopts the following algorithm:

1. A meeting of the Constitutional Chamber judges elects the Chair, Vice Chair, and Judge Secretary from among its members, for a term of 3 years. A judge cannot be elected as Chair or Vice Chair of Constitutional Chamber for two consecutive terms.
2. The meeting of the CCh judges shall be deemed duly constituted when attended by at least two thirds of the total CCh judges. The oldest judge of Constitutional Chamber chairs the meeting of CCh judges on election of Chair, Vice Chair, and Judge Secretary. Applicants for Chair, Vice Chair, and Judge Secretary of CCh may be nominated by CCh judges or be self-nominated.
3. The Chair, Vice Chair, and Judge Secretary of the Constitutional Chamber are elected by secret ballot. The election procedure is determined by CCh regulations. The Chair, Vice Chair, and Judge Secretary are deemed elected if a majority of CCh judges voted for them.

Back in 2001, in my monograph "Issues of constitutional justice in Kyrgyzstan", I mentioned the need to introduce in KR the institute of electing the administration for the constitutional review body – based on rotation principles, to improve the independence of the CCrt and its administration (in particular, of government institutions, which appoint them), while supporting my position with the following conclusions:

> If the Chair is considered a representative of the Constitutional Court (as collective body) and conductor of its internal life, while in all other aspects he/she is equal to the other judges, the procedure of his/her election by the judges will be the most

> appropriate. If the Chair of the Constitutional Court and other officials are elected (appointed) by an outside competent body, it gives reason to believe that they stand apart within the Constitutional Court, acquire a status different from other members and, thus, can have certain effects on the other judges, while focusing on the political body, which elected (appointed) them – moreover, if law assumes the chance for their re-election[30].

Current legislation sets high requirements for the Constitutional Chamber judges, while using in their election the principle of "three keys", i.e.: (1) it is based on a proposal from the Council for the Selection of Judges, (2) the nationally elected President of Kyrgyz Republic presents the candidate, (3) submission of the candidate to Jogorku Kenesh (Parliament) for election. As a result the process of forming the Constitutional Chamber was delayed (see above). However, these mechanisms (assumed by legislation) ensure the high status and independence of the judges, as none of the appointing bodies can independently (individually) decide their fate in the future.

The status of a judge is determined by increased requirements for its acquisition and termination, setting of high requirements for the personality, qualifications, and behavior of the holder, increased responsibility for the improper exercise of judicial powers, providing financial and social security, and other guarantees corresponding to the high status.

Thus, under Part 2, Article 97 of Constitution, any citizen of KR, between 40 and 70 years old, with a law degree and least 15 years work experience in the legal profession may be appointed as a CCh judge.

Unfortunately, civil society notes that, sometimes, election of certain people as the Constitutional Chamber judges is affected by political circumstances instead of high legal qualifications and the professional merits of the candidates. The fact of involving the parliamentary factions in the selection of candidates and their nomination to the CCh is also important.

The status of a judge is acquired by a person upon taking the office of judge at the relevant court and ceases upon the issue of a document dismissing the judge and terminating the judge's powers, according to requirements of current legislation. The judge takes office after taking the oath.

The exercise of powers by elected or appointed judges in KR begins upon taking the oath. The oath of CCh judges is taken at the meeting of the Jogorku Kenesh on the date of their election.

---

30 Р. М. Мырзалимов, *Вопросы конституционного правосудия в Кыргызстане. Монография*, Bishkek 2001, p. 99.

The judge must:

1) strictly follow the Constitution and laws of KR, be loyal to oath of the judge;
2) comply with requirements in Code of Honor for KR Judges and avoid anything potentially discrediting the authority and dignity of the judge;
3) resist any attempts of unlawful interference in the administration of justice;
4) respect the confidentiality of meetings of judges;
5) declare his/her property, income, and expenses – according to KR legislation;
6) respect the rules of labor regulation.

The judge may not:

1) be a representative (except for legal representation) on cases of individuals or legal entities – in courts and other state bodies;
2) make public statements on an issue that is the subject of a court hearing – prior to the relevant judicial act coming into force;
3) disclose/use data (legally referred to classified/proprietary information), obtained by the exercise of the judge's powers – for purposes not related to exercise of the judge's powers;
4) use gifts received at protocol events and other official events. Such gifts are considered state property and must be handed over under the protocol to the court, where the judge holds office, except for cases assumed by law. Upon handover of the gift, the judge may buy it back in the manner set by normative legal acts of KR;
5) accept any honorary or special title, award, and other insignia of foreign states and political parties (apart from science and sports) without permission from the KR Council of Judges;
6) go on a business trip beyond KR (at the expense of individuals and legal entities) except for business trips conducted under KR legislation or international treaties or by mutual arrangements between the CCh and relevant courts of foreign states or international and foreign organizations;
7) be a member of any governing bodies, boards of trustees/supervisory boards, other bodies of foreign, non-profit, non-governmental organizations/their structural subdivisions operating in KR – unless otherwise assumed by KR laws, international treaties or mutual arrangements of the CCh and relevant courts of foreign states or international and foreign organizations;
8) participate in strikes and rallies;

9) be involved in business or combine the position of judge with deputy activities, activities in government/local self-government bodies or other paid work apart from:
   - pedagogical, scientific, expert, and creative activities (additionally paid from sources not prohibited by law, as agreed by the Chair of the relevant court). Such activity shall not affect the scope and quality of activities at the judge's place of work;
   - participation in activities of judicial self-government bodies, the KR Council for Selection of Judges, the Council of Judges Disciplinary Committee.

Besides, judges cannot be members of parties, speak in support of or against any political party.

Meanwhile, the judge is entitled to:

- transfer (rotation) to another court;
- election as Court Chair/Vice Chair, to the judicial self-government bodies, the Council for Selection of Judges and the Council of Judges Disciplinary Committee;
- resignation;
- demanding the refutation or recognizing as unjustified of any charges against him/her regarding the possible violation of requirements for irreproachable conduct of the judge;
- assistance from state and judicial self-government bodies in implementation of his/her legitimate interests; and
- ensuring the guarantees established by KR legislation.

According to KR law, a judge takes office and retains authority as long as his/her conduct is irreproachable. These requirements would be violated where there is essential or systematic commission of a disciplinary offense (misconduct) incompatible with high status of the judge.

The independence of the judge is ensured by:

1) administration of justice in accordance with the law only;
2) prohibition of interference with the judge's activities from any side – under threat of penalty;
3) irremovability of the judge;
4) immunity (limited, see below) of the judge from arrest or detention;
5) mandatory provision for the financial/social security of the judge corresponding to his/her high status – at the expense of the state;
6) functioning of judicial self-government bodies; and
7) the right to resign. This guarantees the judge's independence, assumed by Constitution, cannot be canceled or reduced under any circumstances.

So, current legislation prohibits any interference in the administration of justice. Persons guilty of interfering in a judge's administration of justice are liable under the law. Besides, the judge does not have to provide any explanation on the essence of reviewed cases or cases under review or provide the cases to anyone for familiarization – except as provided by law.

A judge has the right of immunity and cannot be detained, arrested, subjected to a search or body search – unless caught at a crime scene. A judge detained on suspicion of committing a crime, or on other grounds, or forcibly delivered to any law-enforcement body (if the identity of the judge is unknown at the moment of detention) shall be immediately released after the judge's identity is established. The body search of the judge is not allowed – except as provided for by law, to ensure the safety of other people.

On December 27, 2013, the Constitutional Chamber reviewed in open session a case verifying the constitutionality of Part 1, Article 30 in constitutional law "On the Status of Judges in KR" – due to appeals of citizens. According to amendments to the above law, "apart from the Attorney General, the right to initiate the criminal proceedings against a judge was also granted to authorized attorneys (in status not lower than regional attorneys, attorneys of Bishkek and Osh cities)".

In its decision, CCh has noted that the initiation of criminal proceedings against a judge – according to current laws, at reasonable suspicion of committing a crime – is not considered as interference in activities and independence of the judge. The special status of the judge consolidated in the Constitution and constitutional law "On the Status of Judges in KR" was ensured by the rule that only the Attorney General can initiate the criminal proceedings against a judge. Granting such power to Attorney General only was due to the need to limit the range of persons entitled to legal assessment on the presence/absence of grounds for initiating criminal proceedings against a judge. At that, the responsibility for justified initiation of criminal proceedings against a judge was assigned to the Attorney General only. This CCh decision once again confirmed the high status and independence of judges – only the Attorney General may initiate criminal proceedings against them.

4.2 Functions of the Constitutional Chamber of Supreme Court

The Constitutional Chamber at the Supreme Court is guarantor with decisive effect on systems of government. Its activities are related to democratic reforms in KR. This body protects constitutional review and belief in the law and legality. Experience shows that the constitutional review body plays an important role in the separation of powers and in the effective functioning of checks and balances between the branches of state power and personal interests. As history shows, usurping state power causes irreparable damage to democratic values and goal of building a law-bound state.

The main goal of the Constitutional Chamber is protection of the constitutional system, rights and freedoms of person and citizen.

For effective arrangement of its activities, CCh adopts its rules, approves the provision on staff to the CCh, its structure and staffing within the budget estimate.

In our opinion, the unique mission of the constitutional review body is that it is the only public authority in any state directly obliged to subordinate politics to the law and political actions/decisions to constitutional-legal requirements and forms. CCh is designed to prevent the usurpation of state power, while constantly maintaining a state of legally limited power only. Perhaps, this is the main mission of the constitutional review body, as guardian of democracy and pluralism in a democratic society. Strict observance of democratic norms and principles assumed by the fundamental law of the state is the key to a stable political situation in the country.

The CCh Constitutional law vested the CCh with the function of constitutional review administration *via* constitutional legal proceedings.

In this view, we can distinguish several aspects of value for constitutional review. First, constitutional review directly protects the foundations of the constitutional system in KR. Second, constitutional review guarantees and protects the rights and freedoms of persons and citizens in KR. Third, constitutional review ensures supremacy and direct effect of the KR Constitution in KR territory.

To sum up, we can say that constitutional review ensures the function of "constitutional protection" in a legal sense, while also contributing to addressing constitutional-legal conflicts and competition between legal norms.

As for the other powers inherent in such body, for example, the power to confirm election results was previously granted to CCrt; however, due to accusations of political bias, as one of the methods to extend the terms for Presidents A. Akayev and K. Bakiyev, this authority was not included in the competence of the new CCh.

Constitutional Chamber does not review disputes of state bodies regarding their competence.

Also, it does not accept conclusions in the case of high treason committed by the President of Republic (*impeachment*)[31].

---

31 According to Article 67 of KR Constitution, the President may be subject to criminal proceedings upon removal from office.

2. The President may be removed from office only following the Jogorku Kenesh accusation of committing a crime, as confirmed by the Attorney General's conclusion on signs of crime in the President's actions.

4.3 Subject of Review by Constitutional Chamber of Supreme Court

The legal supremacy of the Constitution assumes control of its observance. The subject of constitutional review in KR includes laws, sub-legislative normative legal acts, international agreements (with KR as a party) that have not come into force, and draft laws on amendments to the Constitution.

While verifying the constitutionality of a debated normative legal act, Constitutional Chamber establishes its compliance with the Constitution:

1) by the content of the norms;
2) by the form of the normative legal act; and
3) by the procedure of adoption, signing, publication, and coming into force.

To enhance cooperation with foreign states, KR also signs various international treaties and agreements – as part of the international community and a member of some international organizations. Such activity may also create conflicts, which require the harmonization of international and national legislation.

By giving an opinion on a draft law about amendments to the Constitution, CCh establishes the law's compliance with:

1) the fundamental rights and freedoms of persons and citizens, and the admissibility of their limitations;
2) the principles of the democratic, law-bound, secular state; and
3) the procedure for amendments to it.

Article 97 of the Constitution lists the CCh's powers as:

1) recognizing the unconstitutionality of laws and other normative legal acts that are in conflict with the Constitution;
2) providing opinions on the constitutionality of international agreements (to which KR is a party) that are yet to come into force; and
3) providing opinions on draft laws about amendments to the Constitution.

---

3. A Jogorku Kenesh decision to press charges against the President (for removal from office) must be adopted by majority of Jogorku Kenesh deputies, on the initiative of at least one-third of the deputies, and only in the presence of a conclusion from a special commission formed by Jogorku Kenesh.
4. A Jogorku Kenesh decision to remove the President from office must be adopted by majority of at least two-thirds of the total Jogorku Kenesh deputies – no later than three months after pressing charges against the President. If the Jogorku Kenesh decision is not adopted within this period, the pressed charges are considered to be rejected.

Article 4 of the constitutional law on the CCh lists the CCh's powers as:

1) recognizing laws and other normative legal acts that are in conflict with Constitution as unconstitutional;
2) giving opinions on the constitutionality of international treaties that are yet to come into force for KR;
3) giving opinions on draft laws about amendments to the Constitution.

Note that this statement of the second power for the CCh is slightly different from the wording of the Constitution. Is that just a mistake or a deliberate correction of the wording? It is unknown. One thing is clear having these two differently worded provisions is wrong.

As noted in the previous sections, the CCh actively uses only the first of the three available powers. There were no appeals on the other two powers; so, national practice on them has not been formed yet.

4.4 Preliminary and Subsequent Review of Legal Norms

Constitutional review is ensured to verify the compliance between Constitution and current laws/other normative legal acts, which assumes subsequent review. Prior to their coming into force, only preliminary constitutional review may be conducted.

The KR Constitution prescribes that the CCh is to conduct a preliminary review only with respect to KR international treaties that have not come into force, which prevents conflicts between the norms of national/international law and provides an opinion on draft law about amendments to Constitution. Other legal protection objects of KR Constitution are subject to subsequent review only.

Only the Jogorku Kenesh, Jogorku Kenesh factions, President, Government, and Prime Minister have the right to apply for an opinion on constitutionality of international treaties that have not come into force for Kyrgyz Republic. However, as noted above, practice in this field has not been formed yet.

The Jogorku Kenesh, Jogorku Kenesh factions, President, Government, and Akyikatchy (Ombudsman) have the right to apply for an opinion on a draft law about amendments to Constitution. In 2016, using its powers on ensuring constitutional legality, the CCh provided an opinion on draft amendments to the KR Constitution regarding compliance with the fundamental rights and freedoms of persons and citizens, admissibility of their limitation, principles of the democratic, law-bound, secular state, and principles of separating the branches of government.

The advantage of preliminary review is that it can prevent the adoption of an unconstitutional legal act or violation of constitutional legality. It also contributes to maintaining the stability of the national legislation system, while addressing the very problem of annulling normative legal acts adopted on the basis of laws that were recognized as unconstitutional in the prescribed manner.

The main advantage of subsequent constitutional review is that it enables strict compliance with the separation of powers and verifying the constitutionality of any normative legal act, with account for its practical application by courts and executive bodies – without interfering in legislative activity of the Parliament.

The right to apply for the recognition of laws or other normative legal acts as unconstitutional is granted to individuals or legal entities, if they believe that the laws or other normative legal acts violate their rights and freedoms recognized by Constitution; as well as to the Jogorku Kenesh; Jogorku Kenesh factions; President; Government; Prime Minister; judge (judges) of KR; local self-government bodies; the Attorney General; and the Akyikatchy (Ombudsman). Revealed uncertainty on the issue of compliance between law/other normative legal act and the Constitution forms the reason for this case review.

Subsequent constitutional review also finds its practical expression in verifying the constitutionality of a strictly defined normative legal act – due to a trial on a particular civil, criminal or administrative case. If the review of the specific case results in a court opinion that the norm to be used is not compliant with Constitution, the court must suspend the process and submit a request on its constitutionality to CCh. This is done on initiative of the court or by request from one of parties to the process.

4.5 Legal Norm Controlling Procedure

As noted above, Article 20 of the CCh constitutional law defines a clear range of subjects entitled to appeal to the CCh. According to this list, the right is granted to:

1) individuals or legal entities, if they believe that laws and other normative legal acts violate their rights and freedoms recognized by the Constitution;
2) the Jogorku Kenesh (Parliament);
3) Jogorku Kenesh factions;
4) the President;
5) the Government;
6) the Prime Minister;
7) judges of KR;
8) local self-government bodies;

9) the Attorney General; and
10) the Akyikatchy (Ombudsman).

Depending on the subject, the appeals may be submitted as:

- a petition;
- a proposal; or
- a request.

Thus, according to the provisions of the above constitutional law, individuals/ legal entities apply to the Constitutional Chamber with a petition, if they believe that laws and other normative legal acts violate their rights/freedoms recognized by Constitution.

Jogorku Kenesh (Parliament), Jogorku Kenesh factions, President, Government, Prime Minister, local self-government bodies, Attorney General, and Akyikatchy apply to Constitutional Chamber with a proposal.

Proposals on giving an opinion about the constitutionality of international treaties that have not come into force for Kyrgyz Republic can be submitted by:

- the Jogorku Kenesh;
- the Jogorku Kenesh factions;
- the President;
- the Government; or
- the Prime Minister.

Proposal on giving an opinion about draft law on amendments to the Constitution can be submitted by:

- the Jogorku Kenesh;
- Jogorku Kenesh factions;
- the President;
- the Government; or
- the Akyikatchy (Ombudsman).

Judges appeal with a request.

Article 25 of the above constitutional law sets out the general requirements for a proposal. According to these requirements, an appeal to CCh shall be submitted in writing and signed by an authorized person(s).

The proposal shall include:

1) the name of the CCh;
2) the name, address, and other necessary data of the applicant;
3) the name, address, and other data about the representative of the applicant and his/her powers – except for representation by virtue of position;

4) the name and address of the state body or official, who signed or issued the normative legal act, the constitutionality of which is subject to verification;
5) the norms of the Constitution and constitutional law "On Constitutional Chamber at Supreme Court of Kyrgyz Republic", which authorize the appeal to the CCh;
6) the circumstances forming the basis of the claim and evidence confirming the facts stated by the party;
7) the exact name, number, date of adoption, publication sources, and other details of the debated normative act;
8) the specific reasons for the review of appeal indicated in constitutional law "On Constitutional Chamber at Supreme Court of Kyrgyz Republic";
9) the applicant's position and legal justification of the raised issue – with reference to relevant provisions of the Constitution;
10) the claim related to the proposal, petition, request to the CCh; and
11) a list of attached documents.

The following shall be attached to the appeal:

1) a copy of the text from the normative legal act, the constitutionality of which is debated (in whole or in part) by the appealing party; and
2) a power of attorney or other document confirming the authority of the representative – except where representation is ensured by virtue of position.

Appeals may be sent by mail or delivered directly to CCh Office.

An appeal received by the CCh and compliant with the above requirements forms a reason for a case review and is subject to a resolution on accepting the appeal for proceeding, while arranging a panel of 3 CCh judges. The verified appeal and attached documents are assigned to one of the panel judges, whose review is used by the panel for decision-making (in 30 business days from the day the appeal was accepted or refused acceptance).

Grounds for refusal to accept an appeal for proceeding are clearly defined by provisions of Part 3, Article 28 of the CCh constitutional law under which the panel of CCh judges refuses to accept the appeal for proceeding:

1) if the form and content of the appeal do not meet the requirements of the above constitutional law;
2) if the appeal is submitted by an inappropriate body or person (subject);
3) if the appeal is submitted by a representative of the party, who has no authority for proceeding at the CCh, or a representative is a person not assumed by this constitutional law;

4) if the claim stated in the appeal is beyond the jurisdiction of the CCh;
5) if the constitutionality of the issue in the appeal was previously verified by the CCh (with presence of a valid certificate).

Also, annulment/invalidation of the certificate with debated constitutionality results in refusal to accept the appeal for proceeding by the CCh.

Let's note that legislator assumed for parties an opportunity to appeal the ruling from panel of judges (on accepting/refusal to accept the appeal for proceeding). By results of reviewing the issue, Constitutional Chamber adopts an individual resolution.

The CCh reviews the appeal accepted for proceeding within 5 months – according to the general requirements of constitutional proceedings defined by the above constitutional law, with the issue of a final certificate. The CCh Chair may extend this term for another month.

4.6 Civil Complaint as a Means of Controlling the Legal Norms

Under 2003 amendments to the KR Constitution, citizens lost the right for individual appeal to Constitutional Court – with statements on constitutionality of official certificates.

The present period of development is characterized by a new stage of constitutional justice in the KR legal system – with improved mechanisms ensuring the protection of human and civil rights and freedoms. So, the Constitution enables abstract constitutional review, according to which, anyone may dispute the constitutionality of a law or other normative legal act, while believing that it violates the rights and freedoms recognized by the Constitution. Undoubtedly, such type of review provided more citizens of the country with the opportunity to protect their rights via constitutional justice.

Powers of the SC Constitutional Chamber on the protection of human rights and freedoms are based on principles established in the KR legal system and consistent with fundamental ideas of a civil society. They include: recognition of human/civil rights and freedoms (as natural, inalienable values), their priority in the system of local and international law; consolidating a principle (at the level of Constitution and international pacts) meaning that human rights oblige the government to ensure their implementation, security, and protection.

Constitutional complaint is the appeal of a citizen or other person to constitutional justice bodies – regarding the violation of his/her constitutional rights. Unlike the other complaints/statements of claim, a resolution on constitutional complaint is not individual, but universal – i.e., applicable to all persons, whose rights may be violated by an unconstitutional act. On the one hand, constitutional complaint is an important procedural guarantee of rights and freedoms for individuals; on the other hand, it also serves as a means of protecting the public interests and maintaining constitutional order in the state as a whole.

Let's note that citizens/legal entities apply for the protection of their constitutional rights directly to the CCh – without any preliminary procedures.

But, in general, Kyrgyzstan has no direct institution of constitutional complaint.

5 Legal Nature and Legal Force of Constitutional Chamber Resolutions

The CCh adopts the acts in the form of decisions, conclusions, resolutions, and rulings.

Following the review of appeals, the Constitutional Chamber adopts a decision (on powers assumed by Item 1, Part 6, Article 97 of Constitution) or conclusion (under Items 2–3, Part 6 of the article).

The decision and conclusion of the CCh must be made in the name of KR and signed by the Chair/judge of the CCh.

Other acts of the CCh are adopted in the form of a resolution, individual or protocol ruling.

Acts of the Constitutional Chamber are adopted *via* open ballot, by roll call of judges in the jury room. In the course of advisement, judges may freely state their position on the issue under review and ask the other judges to clarify their positions. The number and duration of speeches cannot be limited. Only the CCh judges reviewing the case attend the advisement. The presence of unauthorized persons is not allowed. A judge may not abstain or avoid voting. In any case, the Chair votes last.

The record of advisement must reflect the issues put to the vote and the results of the vote. The record is kept by the Judge Secretary, signed by all present judges, and must not be disclosed. The judges present at the advisement are not entitled to disclose the content of discussions and results of the vote.

The case is considered essentially resolved, when the Constitutional Chamber satisfies (in whole/in part) or rejects the claims stated in the appeal. If a majority of the judges present at the advisement vote for an act of the CCh, it is considered adopted. If no proposal collects the majority of votes, the Chair must put the two proposals collecting the most votes to second vote. If votes are equally divided between the two proposals, the decision/conclusion is adopted with a focus on the constitutionality of the debated act. If the adoption of other acts resulted in a tied vote, the act supported by Chair is considered adopted.

The act of the Constitutional Chamber shall be justified and motivated. The decision/conclusion of the CCh is announced in full scope – in open session of the CCh, right after signing. As an exception, for particularly hard cases, a compilation of the statement part in the decision/conclusion may be delayed (up to 10 days), but the operative part is announced in the session. On announcement of the act, the CCh may correct any inaccuracies in names and definitions, clerical errors, and clear editorial/technical errors.

The CCh's decision (act) on the issue under review must indicate:

1) the name, date, and place of the issuing the act;
2) the CCh secretary, or staff adopting the decision/conclusion;
3) the parties and their representatives;
4) the subject of the claim, the reasons and grounds for review;
5) the norms of the Constitution and constitutional law "On Constitutional Chamber at Supreme Court of Kyrgyz Republic", which establish the right of the CCh to review the issue;
6) the reasons of the parties;
7) the actual and other circumstances revealed by the CCh;
8) the exact name of the normative legal act, the constitutionality of which was reviewed – with reference to its source of its publication or receipt;
9) the normative legal act, draft law on amending the Constitution or international treaty that has not come into force for Kyrgyz Republic, constitutionality of which was reviewed;
10) the reasons in favor of the act adopted by CCh (including, if necessary, reasons refuting the claims of the parties);
11) the norms of the Constitution and constitutional law "On Constitutional Chamber at Supreme Court of Kyrgyz Republic" followed by the CCh upon adopting the act;
12) the court findings on the essence of reviewed case;
13) a reference to the final and mandatory nature of the act;
14) the procedure of coming the act into force, procedure, terms, and features of its exercising and publication.

A Constitutional Chamber judge who disagrees with the adopted decision/opinion on the essence of issue, but is in minority, may state the dissenting opinion in writing. This dissenting opinion is attached to the case file and published together with the CCh decision/opinion.

Acts of the Constitutional Chamber are final and cannot be appealed – except for ruling on accepting the appeal for proceeding or refusing to accept it. Decisions/conclusions of the CCh come into force upon announcement; other acts upon signing[32]. The legal force of a decision on recognizing the normative legal act (or part) unconstitutional cannot be overruled by re-adopting the same normative legal act (or part) with the same content.

International treaties that have not come into force, and were found by the CCh to be unconstitutional must not be enacted or applied.

According to requirements of the above constitutional law, Constitutional Chamber acts are obligatory for all state bodies, local self-government bodies, officials, public associations, legal entities, and individuals and must be implemented throughout the country. The unconstitutionality of laws, other normative legal acts, or their provisions (as found by the CCh) obliges the relevant state bodies and officials to coordinate the normative legal acts with Constitution and acts of the CCh – except for judicial acts. Till their coordination/annulment, the Constitution and CCh decisions must be directly applied. Judicial acts based on legal norms/other normative acts, which were recognized unconstitutional, must be reviewed by the court adopting this act – in each specific case, by complaints of citizens, whose rights and freedoms were affected.

Decisions/conclusions of the Constitutional Chamber are sent to parties, state bodies, local self-government bodies, and officials, whose normative legal acts were reviewed and published in official sources of state authorities, local authorities, in the "Bulletin of the Constitutional Chamber at the Supreme Court of the Kyrgyz Republic", on the CCh official website, and, if necessary, in other sources.

If the Constitutional Chamber decision finds constitutional law, code or law conflicting with the Constitution (in whole/in part) or implies the need to fill the gap in legal regulation, the Government must submit to the Jogorku Kenesh a draft law/constitutional law arising from this decision no later than 4 months after publishing the CCh decision on its official website. The Jogorku Kenesh must review the above draft laws in an extraordinary session.

Jogorku Kenesh deputies may also initiate a draft law based on the CCh decision. The Jogorku Kenesh only reviews this draft at presence of conclusion from the Government, in extraordinary session

Sub-legislative normative legal acts must be coordinated with the Constitution and the CCh decision within 3 months – by the law-making body, the act of which was subject to constitutional review. In this case, state authorities and local self-government bodies (with law-making power granted by law) cancel

32 Статья 51. Юридическая сила актов Конституционной палаты. Конституционный закон «О Конституционной палате Верховного суда Кыргызской Республики» от 13 июня 2011 года № 37.

their normative legal acts, adopt new normative legal acts, or amend the normative legal act(s) recognized as unconstitutional.

Non-fulfillment, improper exercise, obstruction to exercising of CCh acts, and interference in CCh activities entail the liability assumed by law[33].

State authorities and local self-government bodies (with law-making power granted by law) cancel their normative legal acts, adopt new normative legal acts, or amend the normative legal act recognized unconstitutional in its individual part – within 3 months of publication of the CCh decision on the official website.

If the CCh finds laws, other normative legal acts, or their provisions unconstitutional the relevant state bodies and officials are obliged to coordinate the normative legal acts with Constitution and acts of CCh – except for judicial acts. Till their coordination/annulment, the Constitution and CCh decisions must be directly applied.

Judicial acts based on legal norms/other normative acts, which were recognized as unconstitutional, must be reviewed by the court adopting the act – in each specific case, by the complaints of citizens whose rights and freedoms were affected.

The laws on exercising CCh decisions have recently been amended.

CCh decisions are subject to unconditional exercising. However, as practice shows, the high rank of CCh decisions is not a guarantee for the universal establishment of a proper attitude to them. The need to improve the efficiency of CCh decisions and their impact on legal reality led to changes in the legislation. So on June 22, 2017, the Jogorku Kenesh adopted the constitutional law "On Amendments to the Constitutional Law of the Kyrgyz Republic "On Constitutional Chamber at Supreme Court of Kyrgyz Republic"", which was signed by the President on July 20, 2017.

According to the amendments, the KR Government is defined as the body responsible for the development of proper bills, if the CCh decision finds the constitutional law, code or law conflicting with the Constitution (in whole/in part) or implies the need to fill the gap in legal regulation. In this case, the Government, no later than 4 months after the CCh decision is published on the official website, must provide the Jogorku Kenesh with the draft constitutional law or draft law arising from the above decision. The above bills are subject to review by Jogorku Kenesh of Kyrgyz Republic, in extraordinary session.

33 Статья 52. Исполнение актов Конституционной палаты. Конституционный закон «О Конституционной палате Верховного суда Кыргызской Республики» от 13 июня 2011 года, № 37.

To implement the above norm of constitutional law, the Government adopted resolution No. 588 of September 18, 2017, in which the Ministry of Justice is defined as the executive body responsible for the development of normative legal acts pursuant to CCh decisions.

Thus, regarding the implementation of CCh decisions, the legislation provides the following:

1. The development of bills is assigned to the Ministry of Justice;
2. Specific deadlines (4 months) are set for submission of such bills for review by the Jogorku Kenesh;
3. The Jogorku Kenesh reviews the bills in extraordinary session; and
4. The CCh decisions must be published on the official website.

Prior to these amendments in the above constitutional law, the procedure for implementing CCh decisions was not regulated by law; therefore, assignments contained in CCh decisions were addressed to the law-making body (Jogorku Kenesh), which, in turn, charged the Government (via specialized committees) with developing the relevant bill and submitting it to the Jogorku Kenesh for review. Thus, CCh decisions were implemented quite arbitrarily and erratically, and as a result 9 of the CCh decisions from that time are still unfulfilled (see the list in Section 2 of present work).

Constitutional Chamber decisions must be implemented taking into account the legal positions stated in its final acts. The timely implementation of CCh decisions is aimed at addressing the defects in legal regulation revealed during the CCh review.

Obviously, recognizing a norm as unconstitutional inevitably leads to legal gaps, which violate the stability of law. So, when normative provisions are found to be unconstitutional, the legislator must promptly respond and introduce the relevant legislative amendments – to fill the formed legal gap. Under Part 3, Article 51 of the CCh Constitutional Law, the Constitution and CCh decisions are applied so as to bring the normative legal acts into compliance with the Constitution. Meanwhile, as noted above, CCh decisions formulate the legal positions, which set the benchmarks for relevant legislative changes.

Thus, the coordinated work of the Jogorku Kenesh and the Government is required to ensure constitutional legality – for the development and adoption of relevant bills to give effect to CCh decisions and on issues of applying the CCh decisions by law-enforcement agencies[34].

---

34 Annual report of Constitutional Chamber at Supreme Court of Kyrgyz Republic for 2017.

So, in summary, CCh decisions are characterized by special legal properties, including their generally binding and final nature, their call for immediate action, and their irreducibility, which finally testifies to their normativity and applicability to other subjects of law (apart from the applicants). In this view, any CCh decision must be viewed by law-making and other rule-making bodies *via* its operative part (with final conclusions on compliance or noncompliance of verified legal norms with the Constitution) and through the prism of legal positions stated to justify the conclusions. In this sense, the purpose of CCh decisions is to prevent deviation from the requirements of the Constitution – both in legislative activities and in law enforcement.

6 Constitutional Value of the Constitutional Chamber of the Supreme Court

Recognizing the supremacy of the Constitution and its direct action throughout the country is among the main principles of a law-bound state. It justifies the constitutional provision, according to which, laws and other legal acts adopted in Kyrgyz Republic shall not conflict with the Constitution. The legal supremacy of the Constitution assumes control of its observance. In the history of foreign countries and the local state, we can see many examples where published normative-legal acts and laws conflicted with the fundamental law of the country, causing various controversial situations (quite often, with negative consequences). The solution of this problem in KR is assigned to constitutional review bodies – in particular, to the CCh. Exactly this judicial public authority is vested with powers in the field of verifying the laws and acts for constitutionality.

Idea of abolishing the CCrt (to expand the prerogatives of legislative power), which was repeatedly expressed in various projects of constitutional reform in Kyrgyzstan (e.g., in 2007), was criticized by the Venice Commission back then – for its noncompliance with separation of powers and practice of democratic states[35]. Nevertheless, it was consistently implemented during the last revolution.

35 "…the decision of the country to abolish the actually functioning Constitutional Court may be considered as a step backwards. This decision shall be revised". п. 59. Заключение № 582/2010 по проекту Конституции Кыргызской Республики (edited May 21, 2010): Adopted by the Venice Commission at the 83rd plenary meeting (Venice, June 4, 2010) Based on comments by A. Endzinsha (Latvia), N. Eshanu (Moldova), A. Nussberger (Germany), A. Vogelklu (Sweden)/Unofficial lane with English implemented in the framework of the European Union and UNDP Project to support constitutional and parliamentary reform. Strasbourg June 8, 2010, 13 p. CDL-AD(2010)015 (Items 57–59, 69 provide assessment of abolishing the Constitutional Court).

Right after coming to power, the Provisional Government issued Decree No. 2 of April 12, 2010 "On Disbanding the Constitutional Court". In KR Law "On Enactment of Constitution in Kyrgyz Republic" (Item 10, Article 1), this act was confirmed – with the adoption of a provision to "consider the powers of Constitutional Court judges terminated since issue of Decree".

Later on, the new Constitution proposed an extremely disputable structure of judicial power. The status of constitutional justice was losing its priority position, while the constitutional review body was, in a sense, "reduced" to the structure of the Supreme Court. There is a certain problem when control of constitutionality is assigned to the CCh acting as part of the Supreme Court. The initial draft of the Constitution did not contemplate the CCh at all – it was about the Supreme Court acting within the constitutional legal proceedings. Only later, under pressure of civil society activists and recommendations of the Venice Commission[36], the wording of the new Constitution, which was later adopted in a referendum, inserted "Constitutional Chamber operates within the Supreme Court" (Item 3, Article 93). To a certain extent, it was a compromise between the urge to completely get rid of the CCrt distorted by politics and requirements to keep constitutional review, as an important democratic and legal institution.

Analogues of this system can be hardly found in world practice. According to Russian scholars[37], the constitutional justice model adopted in Kyrgyzstan differs from the European (Kelsen) model, where the Constitutional Court is guarantor of Constitution. However, this structure also differs from American model of Supreme Court, as it relies on continental principles of passing judgment (law instead of precedent)[38].

---

36 "The Venice Commission also believes that the abolition of the Constitutional Court, as an individual entity, is not the best solution. It expressed hope that this issue would be revised and a constitutional review system selected by Kyrgyzstan will, nevertheless, be implemented so as to ensure the full protection of constitutional rights and freedoms, while contributing to formation of stable political and legal culture in the country". Item 69. Ibid.

37 See: А. Н. Медушевский, *Революция в Киргизии: итоги и перспективы конституционных преобразований*, "Сравнительное конституционное обозрение" 2011, № 1 (80), pp. 13–32.

38 The closest analogue is the Supreme Court of Japan, which was patterned after the USA, but included features of the continental model. Its formation also depends on the Parliament or, rather, on the dominant party and the Government formed by it (judges are appointed by the Cabinet, and the Chief Justice by the Emperor, upon the recommendation of the Cabinet) (Article 79 of Japanese Constitution). This model,

If prerogatives of the Constitutional Court had to be limited in favor of the Parliament, instead of granting the latter a disputable right to elect/remove judges, this could have been done, for example, by forming a Constitutional Council (following the French model or its Kazakh interpretation). Or, as a last resort, by granting the Parliament a right to final review of Constitutional Court decisions, as is the case with the Romanian Constitution (Article 145, Romanian Constitution of 1991).

According to Professor A.N. Medushevsky[39], constitutional justice in Kyrgyzstan will face an unsolvable dilemma – either the politicization of constitutional justice or the legalization of politics – but, in either case, decisions will hardly be accepted by society (and parliamentarians) as legitimate ones. Resolution of complex constitutional review problems is ultimately delegated to the Parliament – actually, to the unstable and changing parliamentary majority, which conflicts with separation of powers and may cause the erosion of constitutionalism. Thus, judicial power in Kyrgyzstan can hardly be a full-fledged arbiter in deciding constitutionality issues for laws and disputes between the branches of government.

Of course, the CCh has a special place in the system of state bodies, including the courts. The legal nature of constitutional justice bodies and their position in the mechanism of power can be judged by the constitutional-legislative consolidation of their status/functions, although the legal result of their actual jurisdictional activity is the best illustration.

A brief overview of CCh activity (prepared by the CCh office) shows the following picture on ensuring the supremacy of the Constitution, its direct effect

---

however, is subject to sharp criticism in several fields: first, due to noncompliance with the separation of powers and dependence of the Supreme Court on the executive power (an overwhelming majority of decisions is made in favor of the state, not citizens); second, due to the Court's avoidance from solving the fundamental issues and transfer of this right to the Parliament (some reproduction of American doctrine with "political decisions"); third, due to legal inconsistency of these decisions (the Court still has not resolved a fundamental issue on the balance between the precedent of interpretation and precedent of decision). This hybrid structure of judicial power (mix of continental and Anglo-Saxon principles) is subject to criticism for politicizing of Court decisions on the most fundamental problems, which generally correspond to preferences of the dominant (liberal-democratic) party. It caused various reformation proposals, including strictly opposite ideas – a gradual transition to the US or German model.

39 А. Н. Медушевский, *Революция в Киргизии: итоги и перспективы конституционных преобразований*, "Сравнительное конституционное обозрение" 2011, № 1 (80), pp. 13–32.

in the country, which largely depends on the quality of implementation of CCh decisions. On the one hand, effective implementation of CCh decisions is part of effective judicial constitutional review; on the other hand it is a measure of its performance.

Implementation of CCh decisions is monitored to assess the effectiveness of implemented constitutional review; for that, CCh constantly reviews the implementing of its decisions by law-making bodies.

Thus, since of its formation on December 31, 2016, one conclusion and 65 decisions were made, of which:

- there were 49 decisions on recognizing normative legal acts not conflicting with the Constitution, 15 of which revealed the need for relevant amendments/addenda to the legislation by the Jogorku Kenesh;
- there were 16 decisions on recognizing the debated normative legal acts conflicting or partially conflicting with the Constitution, 13 of which revealed the need for relevant amendments/addenda to the KR legislation.

Analysis of data provided by rule-making bodies (acts of which are subject to review by CCh) shows that, as of December 31, 2016, of 28 tasks arising from CCh decisions, 18 have been implemented and 10 are being implemented.

Results for the latest reporting year show an improvement in implementing the decisions of the CCh. Thus, 64 % of decisions were implemented; 36 % of CCh decisions are being implemented[40].

An analysis of the implementation of CCh decisions shows a tendency towards improvement. However, this issue remains relevant – both for the CCh and other rule-making bodies. There were some proposals to establish a supervisory body for control of implementing CCh decisions[41].

Only the active position of the CCh will ensure the real implementation for supremacy of the Constitution. Ensuring this principle is fundamental for the CCh.

The main criterion for evaluating the activities of the constitutional justice body is the real effect of its activity on social processes, keeping the constitutional balance of social equilibrium, sustainable development and deepening of democratic processes in society. There is no doubt that enhancing constitutional

40 Annual report of Constitutional Chamber at Supreme Court of Kyrgyz Republic for 2016.

41 Proposals for improving the activity of the CCh of the KR. «Граждане о деятельности Конституционной Палаты» (результаты социологического исследования). Бишкек, 2015 г., p. 86.

legality in the country requires the interest of all public authorities. The CCh proposal on the need to involve people and non-governmental organizations in monitoring the implementation of CCh decisions is also true. "*To change the situation, people need to know more about CCh. Citizens shall be aware of basis for CCh decisions and how they are made. They shall be told that decisions are collectively discussed on the basis of the Constitution. Everyone should know that conflict of interests or pressure is not present within the CCh –this is an objective body providing objective solutions*"[42].

The CCh is an essential institution of state power designed to ensure the supremacy of the Constitution, protect the foundations of the constitutional system, human and civil rights and freedoms, and observe the separation of powers. While ensuring these functions, the CCh stays out of politics.

The Constitutional Chamber is independent, subordinate to the Constitution only, and exercising constitutional legal proceedings according to the requirements of the above constitutional law and Regulations of the CCh. Constitutional Chamber decisions are based on the Constitution and express the unbiased legal position of the judges. Constitutional Chamber judges adopt the acts in terms excluding the outside influence on freedom of their will. Any interference in CCh activity is not tolerated and will lead to prosecution under the law.

The CCh is not entitled to make a decision or reach a conclusion on the case without direct review – according to the procedure assumed by constitutional law. CCh Judges are personally involved in the case review from the opening till the closure of the session. No judge is entitled to evade the case review – apart from the aspects preventing the participation of judge in the session.

The parties enjoy equal rights and opportunities to uphold their position (on a competitive basis) in the session of the CCh. The Chamber sets and solves problems of law only, while deciding on the subject reflected in the appeal – only in that part of the normative legal act, the constitutionality of which is being questioned. The CCh is not bound by the reasons and considerations stated in the appeal.

The fundamental goal of the Constitutional Chamber is to protect the constitutional system, and the rights and freedoms of persons and citizens.

The institution of constitutional review has become an inalienable attribute of the democratic law-bound state and the main element in legal the protection of the Constitution.

---

42 From study materials, ibidem.

We are sure that the CCh will take an active part in building a democratic and legal state, while making a worthy contribution to ensuring the supremacy of the Constitution and protecting the rights and freedoms of persons and citizens[43].

7 Social Perception of Legal Control

At the first meeting with the Constitutional Chamber judges, former President A.Sh. Atambayev (the CCh was formed under his rule) expressed the hope that the CCh would honestly and faithfully serve the Constitution of the Kyrgyz Republic, while defending the constitutional rights and freedoms of citizens and effectively protecting the legitimate interests of the state and society.

In his speech, he noted the following:

> Dear judges of the Constitutional Chamber! People say: "He who forgets the past has no future".

The Constitutional Court, established in 1993 to protect the Constitution of the Kyrgyz Republic, failed to ensure the assigned functions on protection of Constitution. On the contrary, it turned into a body allowing the violation of Fundamental Law and aiding the enhancement of a family government system.

One of the main tasks faced by the judicial system today is restoring the trust of people and society. Today, unfortunately, it is hard to say that citizens respect the law.

The Constitution gives people an opportunity to defend their rights and restore them in case of violation. However, people are still unaware of this defense by legal means. The more actively/persistently people appeal to the CCh for protection of their constitutional rights, the less temptation there will be for state and local self-government bodies to violate those rights. For that, the people need to know their rights and understand that these rights are protected by laws and the Constitution.

Meanwhile, let's recognize that, at some point, the essential provisions of our Constitution (in particular, on human rights) may be seen as kind of declarative.

The Constitutional Chamber has an effective mechanism for influencing the law-making activity of state bodies – by verifying the constitutionality of normative legal acts, the CCh interprets the content of legal norms, thus playing

---

43 Appeal of Constitutional Chamber at Supreme Court of Kyrgyz Republic. Annual report for 2017. This report was approved at annual evaluation meeting of the Chamber, which took place on January 17, 2018, http://constpalata.kg/wp-content/uploads/2018/03/Godovoj-doklad-2017-web.pdf (accessed: March 20, 2018).

a specific role of controller of the law-making body. This right of interpreting permits the CCh to clearly distinguish the areas of activity for the legislative and executive branches of government.

The Constitutional Chamber shall become one of the essential state instruments for enhancing inter-ethnic harmony, civil peace, and the unity of the people of Kyrgyzstan. All citizens of the country are equal under the Constitution – regardless of their nationality, color of skin and eyes[44].

When discussing the proposals of the last constitutional reform, some representatives of civil society stated that the proposed amendments to Constitution denied the opportunity of citizens to defend their rights[45].

According to Rita Karasartova, the proposed changes in the fundamental law of the country (initiated by Jogorku Kenesh deputies Omurbek Tekebayev, Felix Kulov, Chynybay Tursunbekov) "do not reform the judicial system, but deny the opportunity of citizens to defend their rights".

Rita Karasartova explained that, upon detailed review of the changes, it appeared that, according to them, the CCh would be removed from the section "Judicial System". She noted that, at the moment, it was "the only body, where citizens could seek the implementation of court decisions". "And our deputies want to rob us of this last platform", she stated. Ms. Karasartova noted that over 90 % of cases reviewed by CCh judges are civil cases.

In turn, one of the initiators (Felix Kulov, leader of the "Ar-Namys" parliamentary faction) explained why he proposed to separate the Constitutional Chamber and the Supreme Court. He noted that the CCh is a state body, which has to review a document prior to it becoming law – to avoid the situation, when a law works incorrectly for some time. "If the Constitutional Chamber could make a decision prior to adopting a law, it would be OK. So, it is desirable to remove the CCh from within the Supreme Court", he said. He provided an example of setting the date for parliamentary elections (this fall), which causes questions and different interpretation today. Let's remember that the committee determined October 4 as the date of the election.

"The election was on October 10, 2010; they believe that powers will expire on October 10 and elections shall be held on first Sunday of the month – i.e., October 4. But there is another interpretation. On October 10, people voted for many

44 http://www.president.kg/ru/news/2387_prezident_almazbek_atambaev_vstretilsya_s_vnov_izbrannyim_sostavom_konstitutsionnoy_palatyi_verhovnogo_suda_kyirgyizskoy_respubliki (accessed: March 20, 2018).

45 Stated by Rita Karasartova, Director of Public Association "Institute of Public Analysis", at press conference in Bishkek, on June 1, 2016.

parties (5 of them passed to the Parliament). The mandates were announced and given on November 10. Central Election Commission (CEC) was delaying for a month and only gave mandates on November 10. What if it would take another 2–3 months? Constitution states that Parliament consists of 120 deputies elected for 5 years. If we were elected for 5 years (November 10 to November 10), the first Sunday is November 1. There's a conflict", said Mr. Kulov, while adding that such issues shall be reviewed by the CCh.

The country conducted various studies on access to justice, etc. However, one specialized sociological study on constitutional justice in Kyrgyz Republic should be highlighted – namely, "Citizens on the activity of the Constitutional Chamber" (results of sociological study). In 2015, it was held for the first time and, unfortunately, has not yet been repeated. The need for the study arose after the well-known revolutionary events of 2005 and 2010. In 2010, the provisional powers of Kyrgyzstan disbanded the former Constitutional Court due to politicization of its activities and accumulated public discontent with its work. Previous activities of the Constitutional Court affected its image and really undermined the public's confidence in it.

The renewed CCh seeks to establish a new tradition of constitutional justice in Kyrgyzstan, to build a more effective organization meeting international standards. It seeks to improve the CCh's efficiency, professionalism, transparency, and independence, while raising public awareness of its role and functions and improving its communication with society. That's the CCh needed by the people of Kyrgyzstan. It seeks to implement its mission in favor of people – *via* purposeful work on protecting the fundamental rights of people guaranteed by the Constitution, including the right to equality before the law, the right to freedom of expression and the right to a decent life. It aims to be closer to the people, gain the trust of the people, and contribute to enhancing the rule of law. Any citizen can file an appeal for the protection of constitutional rights and freedoms. The staff of the CCh assist the applicants (especially, poor and handicapped citizens) in preparing the required documents, while providing free advice on appeals to the CCh. Unfortunately, this path has objective problems that the CCh must overcome, including the difficulties inherent both to the political system and the low level of legal culture in authorities, legal nihilism at the level of the population, general weakness of the rule of law and legality, and the prevalence of non-legal ways for resolving various disputes in the still-fragile post-conflict environment.

Poor awareness of the CCh's activities, role, and functions is among the essential bottlenecks of constitutional justice. There is a problem of poor feedback between the CCh and the population. Only a narrow range of expert community and specialists of government bodies directly related to this work are aware of and know about the CCh's activities. Recent discussions in the country (on amendments to the Constitution) showed the level of nihilism, low legal awareness, and remoteness of people from constitutional justice (and, accordingly, from the role of the Constitution in their daily life).

Proposals on improving the activity of the Constitutional Chamber were made within the 2015 sociological study. Let's note that 60 % of the surveyed population could not say what was the ideal SC CCh. When answering the question on the ideal CCh, the remaining 40 % used the following words (by frequency of referencing):

- Honest, transparent, not corrupt;
- Open and fair;
- Professional;
- Independent of the state and officials;
- Informing people of their rights (via mass media and TV, education at schools and universities);
- Enjoying the confidence of people (informing about judges, their life and family, career, honesty, merits, and the reasons why they work at the CCh).

70 % of surveyed population was not aware of what measures should be taken, so the CCh could improve its efficiency, professionalism, transparency, and independence. Every third person believed (by frequency of referencing):

- They must be honest, prevent corruption;
- Professionalism and education of staff should be improved;
- They must be accessible to the public;
- A report on performed work should be provided to the mass media;
- SC CCh judges should be elected by the people;
- Young professionals should be recruited – they would not be afraid to change the country for the better;
- Enhanced control by the President;
- Open sessions with website publications;
- Introduction of advanced international experience;
- Keeping the Constitution unchanged;
- Closer work with government bodies on implementing their decisions;
- Teaching the youth about their constitutional rights – at universities and schools;
- Working on improved public confidence;
- Eradication of tribalism and clannishness in their work;
- Improving the legal knowledge and honesty of deputies;

- Frequent verification of judges – via certifications and exams.

63 % of the surveyed population could not answer the question: "What would you advise to improve the communication between CCh and society?" The rest of respondents believed that (by frequency of referencing):

- Informing people about the CCh: distribution of brochures, personal meetings;
- Accessibility for common people: hotline, public helpline, mass media publications, work with social networks and website – feedback;
- Constitution should be explained in the mass media, work with social networks;
- Code of ethics for CCh staff: honest work for people, without corruption;
- Establishment of a public relations department, introduction of regional representatives;
- Professional work – establishing quality indicators;
- Public report on CCh activities;
- Open processes;
- Eradication of tribalism;
- Work with government, local self-government, patriarch courts.

47 % of surveyed people found it difficult to advise anything to increase confidence among the population in the CCh. Other respondents believed: to increase public confidence in the CCh, it is necessary:

First, that "its work should be good, effective, honest, transparent, clear, legal, fair, professional, responsible, and mobile" (26.4 %).
Second, that communication with the people should be enhanced (10.8 %).
Third, that permanent mechanisms of reporting to the public should be created – e.g., periodic "Annual Reports on Performed Work" (4.5 %).

"Other" recommendations included: "informing the people on the CCh", "improving the professionalism of judges", "introducing a mechanism for election of CCh judges". There were some extreme statements: "I don't believe anything will change, no sense – thus, no advice", "Dismiss the entire CCh staff, re-elect the judges, recruit young people".

So, public demand for justice is very high. Besides, there is a major dissatisfaction with the way judicial power is handling its functions as a neutral arbiter in legal disputes. According to A. Musabayeva[46], this negative perception of

46 A. Musabayeva, *On current state of justice system in Kyrgyzstan*, February 14, 2012, http://ipp.kg/ru%3E/news/2239 (accessed: March 20, 2018).

the justice system, accumulated over the previous years, is expressed now as over-emotional and aggressive forms of demand for justice. Such accumulated discontent cannot be neutralized or relieved quickly and painlessly. The edge of public dissatisfaction is aimed at the judicial system and law-enforcement bodies, which makes reforming of these areas inevitable. It happens against the backdrop of a general crisis in state-governmental institutions, and a loss of confidence in them. Establishment of the justice system requires meeting the principles of judicial integrity (independence, impartiality, transparency, and accountability) by judicial power.

According to A. Musabayeva, it's no exaggeration to say that the future of Kyrgyzstan largely depends on establishing the justice system. The fate of reforms in the justice system will directly affect our society in coping with a number of objective system challenges – they are not mentioned by politicians in their speeches, but do not disappear anyway. These challenges include: processes of state-building, political institutional-building, ability/inability of formal legal institutions to play a socially-binding role in society. More and more often, we are convinced that the problem of reforming the judicial system in Kyrgyzstan is the key factor in forming the changes in the social, political, and economic sphere. It is exactly due to these problems that the public calls for "cleansing" and reforming the judicial power are so acute now. It is exactly due to the loss of public confidence in the courts (as institutions of justice), that the tasks of arranging civil control over the judicial system are so urgent. At that, the very subject of civil control over the justice system raises many discussions in society. On the one hand, there is a position, arguments of which are based on allegations that our judicial power never was an institution of justice, but served those in power, that corruption in courts and law-enforcement bodies has led to an almost complete loss of public confidence, and that unjust decisions of courts have formed the craving for permanent changes in the Constitution and permanent revolutions. As a rule, supporters of this position follow the idea of civil control in the judicial system, while accounting for differences in approach (with regards to ways and methods of implementation). The approaches include a wide range of decisions against corruption in judicial system – from radical measures on purge of judges and full replacement of staff in courts to more or less rational ways, in the form of monitoring court activities, education of citizens to raise the level of legal understanding, gradual increasing of transparency in courts, etc. On the other hand, according to one analyst, there is a position, arguments of which are based on the statement that all troubles in the judicial system are due to a lack of independence in the judicial branch of government (from the other branches). There is an opinion that the provision of independence to the courts will solve all the problems. Supporters of this position share an opinion that the judicial system should not be subject to any control (including civil control). According to A. Musabayeva, there are some judgments of a “defensive nature”, which try to focus the public’s attention on the fact that the judicial branch of government is part of society and that the situation of legal “lawlessness” was not formed by the judicial powers alone. Besides, we have attempts to explain the rejection of the judicial system by ordinary people due to the inherent properties of court disputes (with winners and losers), which can form a distorted perception of the legality or illegality of court decisions. Finally, many people refer to under-funding of courts and judicial infrastructure, problems of education and training. Using the mass media, representatives of judicial power began to provide their statistics on the percentage of appealed court decisions. They say that 80–85 % of decisions are not appealed; this fact is presented as an indication that the majority of people recognize the legality of decisions made by the courts. According to the same expert, the reform was one of powerful factors forming the conditions, where people found themselves on “different sides of barricades”, while contributing to negative manifestations (irrationalism, unconstructiveness, aggression) in approaches to reforming the justice system[47].

If we treat these positions as impartially as possible, of course, we cannot admit that both positions are flawless in their argumentation. However, to do justice, let’s note that judicial power in Kyrgyzstan is experiencing a serious crisis of confidence, which is mostly based on a rejection of the legitimacy of courts by a significant number of citizens. Explaining this only by the exceptionally low level of legal understanding of people or the inherent properties of the judicial system is simply wrong. Many people understand that. What are the causes of the legal crisis in the country and why is the problem of reforming the courts and civil control in the justice system is so acute? The key problem of the judicial system is a lack of public confidence in the courts. It must be reviewed in the context of a general crisis for state-governmental institutions in the country, a crisis of values, and a crisis of law. Long-term inefficiency of state institutions generated such massive discontent in society that the very essence of the legal system (which, among other social norms, should play the most essential socially-binding role) is being questioned. Legal norms are the rules, which can and should unite society – via their voluntary recognition by all members of society, without exception, which means following and adherence

---

47 A. Musabayeva, *On current state of justice system in Kyrgyzstan*, February 14, 2012, http://ipp.kg/ru%3E/news/2239 (accessed: March 20, 2018).

to them. However, by common consent, the country is currently in a situation of legal crisis – legal culture is characterized by nihilism and judicial power (by different definitions) is in collapse, deadlock, and destruction. After 1991, all attempts of Kyrgyzstan to reform the judicial system were conducted in an unformed institutional environment. As in all transit countries of the post-socialist world, the environment included "old" institutions (inherited from the Soviet and pre-Soviet stage of history) and "new" institutions (imported from the developed world). This applied to all spheres of society, including the sphere of law.

Participants of discussions within the sociological survey, who had experience of contact with the CCh, made the following proposals on improving the situation:

- recruit up to 11 judges, as prescribed by law. Probably, number of the judges could be increased – to accelerate their response to applications;
- analyze the workload of judges – to determine the number of full-time judges;
- make decisions by the whole staff of judges – not by 3 judges only;
- CCh staff should personally call the applicant and inform him/her on reviewing the application;
- establish a reception for visitors, where application procedures will be explained;
- in the reception, arrange the work of the judge on duty, who could give consultations more reasonably, and assist in filing more competent and justified applications (instead of advices from general department and security);
- hold the meeting of judges in presence of the applicant or his/her representative/lawyer, which would contribute to greater confidence in the CCh;
- provide the applicant with a detailed explanation on the reasons and grounds for the refusal or negative decision on the application;
- for greater independence of the CCh – separate the Constitutional Chamber from Supreme Court;
- reduce the time for review of applications;
- Constitutional Chamber should work on improving the legal knowledge of the population;
- conduct personal field meetings with population, NGOs, and mass media – for people to know the judges better and begin to trust them;
- improve the informing of the public (population, youth, schoolchildren/students, lawyers, judges, police) on the CCh's functions and activities – via mass media (TV and radio), round tables and seminars, distribution of thematic materials, bulletins.

As for the civil servants, they made the following interesting proposals: issue a digest of official comments to each article of decision. The digest shall provide explanations on applying/exercising the SC decisions and have a certain conceptual set. This material shall be used for practical training at legal universities. Introduce the mechanism of CCh involvement at the legislative stage.

The survey included CCh staff, who shared their opinion and made a number of proposals:

- Prepare more professional lawyers at universities;
- Form a register of journalists, who can properly/professionally cover CCh activities;
- Make legal and humane decisions;
- Conduct the online broadcast of court sessions;
- CCh should become a public structure – frequent seminars and lectures for people and civil servants, with the involvement of various experts;
- Increase the staff in departments working with the general public;
- Conduct a set of training for CCh staff – to improve their professional and communication skills, master the world experience, dealing with conflict situations;
- Develop a CCh communication strategy aimed at working with the population, civil servants, and deputies;
- Conduct a study on public opinion about the CCh;
- Simplify the form of public appeals to the CCh – enabling the filing of applications without visit to the CCh building;
- Improve interaction with other government agencies;
- Form a supervisory body monitoring the implementation of CCh decisions;
- Arrange a system for permanently informing the population;
- Allocate the individual CCh structure – for work with the mass media;
- Involve population/NGOs in monitoring the implementation of CCh decisions;
- Comment the annual report of the CCh;
- Improve the awareness of judges of CCh decisions – via round tables and training seminars.

In this view, the Constitutional Chamber is actively involved in openly informing people and society about its performed work. The CCh annual report is one such information document. Annual reports are discussed on an annual basis and approved at annual meetings of the Chamber, which summarize the activities. They are published in state (Kyrgyz) language and in official (Russian) language;

the electronic version is posted at the official website: http://constpalata.kg/ru/zhy-ldy-k-doklad/.

Besides this, to improve the social perception of constitutional review, the CCh implements the following activities:

- A Bulletin of the CCh is published;
- The Official website is created and maintained;
- Republican competitions are held;
- Guest lectures by CCh judges are held for students of universities;
- Open days are held at the CCh;
- Game (educational) trials are held on constitutional legal proceedings: "Moot court"[48] - "Adilet[49]-2017";
- Schools of constitutionalism are held at CCh.

The purpose of the above activities is to improve the communication of the CCh with various layers of society, establish strong feedback between them, define the bottlenecks in actual information flows, and promote the better coverage of CCh activities. We believe that transparency/openness of CCh activities and building its strategic communication with society will improve confidence in the institution of constitutional justice.

Conclusions

This chapter provides theoretical analysis for historical-legal aspects of the emergence, formation, and genesis of the institution of constitutional justice in Kyrgyzstan, as well as the study of practical activities at the national body of constitutional review.

The constitutional development of Kyrgyzstan is unique – this country is constantly experimenting with its constitutional system, while challenging the political stagnation and authoritarianism in the region. During the brief post-Soviet period, the country implemented 9 different constitutional reforms. Adoption of a new Constitution in the referendum on June 27, 2010 was the most radical attempt to change the political-legal regime in Kyrgyzstan (and in the territory

---

48 "Moot court" is one of the most common and successful methods on practical training of lawyers abroad, which includes reproduction of judicial process with elements of debate.

49 In Kyrgyz, word "Adilet" is really capacious and can be translated as "justice", "legality", "jurisprudence".

of post-Soviet space as a whole), which marked a transition to a parliamentary vector of development in the country.

Of course, it makes careful analysis of the constitutional system in Kyrgyzstan, and the role and place of constitutional justice in the country relevant and necessary.

It was determined that functioning of the constitutional justice body (at stage of forming, exercising its powers, and implementing its decisions) is due to a complex interrelation of politics and law. In terms of constitutional instability, the value of judicial power is increased but at the same time there is a threat of its politicization and dependence. This phenomenon occurred in Kyrgyzstan, where adoption of the European (Kelsen) model of abstract constitutional review faced the problem of court dependence on executive power. Indeed, the Constitutional Court in Kyrgyzstan (like in many other countries of the region) sided with the current government too often, while extending the powers of the current President or (in case of his overthrow) taking the side of the victorious leader and legitimizing his power by the doctrine of "revolutionary needs". It caused the loss of legitimacy of constitutional justice and the proposal of an oppositional idea – to cancel the Constitutional Court and expand the prerogatives of legislative power. Based on an analysis of acquired national and foreign experience, the feasibility of revising the status and form of constitutional justice body in Kyrgyzstan is analyzed – to enhance its role as guarantor of balance between the branches of government, i.e., the proposal is to return to status of Constitutional Court.

The following provisions are suggested as conclusions throughout the chapter:

1. The historical development of constitutionalism in the country served to establish constitutional justice in Kyrgyzstan. According to relevant scientific sources, based on their scrupulous analysis, the following periods were distinguished in the history of forming and developing constitutional review in Kyrgyzstan:

   1918–1924 – from the first Constitution of the RSFSR (Kyrgyzstan was part of Russia) till the formation of the new state (USSR); consolidating the parliamentary form of constitutional review with the underlying principle of concentrating absolute power (including constitutional review) in hands of the supreme public representative body.

   1924–1929 – from the first Constitution of the USSR till the forming of Kyrgystan's own autonomy, where constitutional review was determined by the federative structure of the USSR.

   1929–1937 – during which Kyrgyz statehood existed in the form of autonomy; formation of its own public bodies exercising constitutional review (among other functions) and acting within their jurisdiction. In addition to them, similar Russian, republican, and USSR bodies were acting, so there was a 3-level system of constitutional review.

1937–1978 – this period saw the transformation of Kyrgyz statehood and its functioning in the format of the USSR republic; it was a period of 2-level constitutional review system (USSR and republican, with prevalence of the first).

1978–1993 – in this period there was constitutional review during the so-called developed socialism; since the 1980s – there was a gradual transition to a new democratic path of development (from parliamentary to specialized review).

1993-present day – formation and functioning of specialized constitutional review.

2. The hasty reception of the Kelsen model for constitutional justice in Kyrgyzstan happened with insufficient democratization in society, which was then just taking its first steps. At that, the available mixed form of government (the result of political compromise in the transitional period) is usually unstable and does not always guarantee stability of the state system.
3. The development and functioning of constitutional justice in Kyrgyzstan has been mostly accompanied by the complex interrelation of politics and law, which is explained by: a) the political procedure of forming the constitutional justice body in terms of state bodies appointing and removing judges, which enables government bodies which nominated them to have non-legal influence on judges; b) the possible threat of politicization in the Constitutional Chamber (during the exercise of its powers), as interpretation/clarification of various aspects on the functioning of all branches of government (in acts of the constitutional justice body) may cause significant aggravation in the course of its activity, if politics and law are opposed to each other; c) dependence between the level of capacity/compulsory exercising of decisions made by the constitutional justice body and the political situation in the country, the authority of this body, and the level of legal culture in society.
4. We can talk about the need to correlate the legal nature of the constitutional justice body (the Constitutional Chamber at the Supreme Court of the Kyrgyz Republic) by bringing its status and role in line with the requirements of a modern law-bound state. This body should work with status of an independent court (Constitutional Court), but with newly elected staff and following the new law with revised competence.

Special attention should be paid to the fact that the establishment of the legal nature for the institute of constitutional justice and its place in the mechanism of separation of powers can use several approaches, namely: a) identifying the institute of constitutional justice with the judicial branch of government; b) considering the Constitutional Court as a type of control authority; c) recognizing the Constitutional Court as some superstructure in the system of separation of powers, which does not belong to any branch of government; d) definition of the constitutional justice institute should be comprehensive, accounting for a combination of judicial and control features. Modern constitutionalism develops the classical theory with the separation of powers; based on that, the Constitutional Court should be reviewed in complex, as a state institute comprising the features of judicial power and simultaneously exercising the supreme control function of state activity. Such an approach will allow both *de jure* and *de facto* consolidation of legal status for the Constitutional Court as an independent body, while emphasizing its independence in the system of separation of powers and contributing to its effective role in the mechanism of checks and balances.

5. Constitutional justice is a reliable link in ensuring the mechanism of checks and balances, however, the search for opportunities for effective enhancement of its role in establishing balanced relations between the legislative, executive, and judicial branches of government remains an actual theoretical and practical problem of legal science, the solution of which will ensure further development of the modern democratic state. The role of constitutional justice (growing in the 21st century) necessitates further scientific studies in countries of young democracy (on the functioning and genesis of a constitutional justice institute), as philosophical and theoretical approaches to its solution are constantly changing, while currently being at the stage of active research and improvement.
6. The establishment of a judicial constitutional review body in Kyrgyzstan is based on an objective need, has sufficient legal basis, and should be an important step towards enhancing the regime of constitutional legality and ensuring the legal mechanism for exercising the fundamental law of the specified state.
7. The establishment of constitutional justice bodies in countries of Central Asia led to the formation of a relatively independent group of constitutional-legal norms, which can be combined into a legal institute of constitutional justice. The need to study this relatively new institute of constitutional law is obvious.
8. It is really necessary to develop a special mechanism for the constitutional-legal liability of state bodies and officials – to address the non-implementation, improper implementation or obstruction to implementation of the

Constitutional Court's decisions. To this end, it is necessary to assume the norms with strict consolidation for types of liability and the procedure of constitutional-executive proceedings.

To some extent, this study can serve both theoretical and practical goals. One of the goals is to try and find the optimal constitutional formulations for regulating modern public relations in the field of constitutional justice – in Kyrgyzstan and other post-Soviet states.

Igor Yuryevich Ostapovich

Constitutional Justice in the Russian Federation

Abstract: In the text is analyzed constitutional judiciary in the Russian Federation. Its placement in the system of the organs of state power, the realized functions, effectiveness and the political status of judges of the Constitutional Court are studied. A thesis is put forward that the Constitutional Court in the Russian Federation is the key measure of protecting human constitutional rights and freedoms.

Keywords: the European model of reviewing the legal norms, Constitutional Court, autonomy and independence, The Constitutional Court and other organs of state power, cognition of the Constitutional Court

Introduction

In a law-bound state, the rule of law is not just some general social value, but a vector used to build the activity of government bodies and administration. Constitutional review is the instrument which ensures the rule of law. It is reported that the modern institute of constitutional review is known in more than 164 countries of the world, and this contributes to its considerable variability[1].

The purpose of establishing the Constitutional Court of the Russian Federation (hereinafter referred to as CCRF) is to protect the RF Constitution, ensure its supremacy and direct action. CCRF has the tasks of ensuring and protecting the foundations of the constitutional system and human rights.

The place of constitutional review bodies in the system of RF public authorities is determined with account for constitutional principles on separation of powers and federalism (M.V. Baglay[2], S.V. Bobotov[3], O.V. Brezhnev[4], N.V.

1 See: А. А. Клишас, *Конституционный контроль и конституционное правосудие в зарубежных странах:* дис. … докт. юрид. наук: 12.00.02, Moscow 2007, p. 14.

2 See: М. В. Баглай, *Конституционное право Российской Федерации*, Moscow 2007, pp. 665–686.

3 See: С. В. Боботов, *Конституционная юстиция*, Moscow 1994, p. 71.

4 See: О. В. Брежнев, Судебный конституционный контроль в России: проблемы методологии, теории и практики: дис. … докт. юрид. наук: 12.00.02, Moscow 2006, p. 14.

Vitruk[5], G.A. Gadzhiev[6], V.D. Zorkin[7], S.D. Knyazev[8], A.N. Kokotov[9], V.A. Kryazhkov[10], S.I. Nesmeyanova[11], Zh.I. Ovsepyan[12], O.V. Oprya[13], M.S. Salikov[14], V.A. Tumanov[15], V.E. Chirkin[16], B.S. Ebzeyev[17]). By virtue of provisions in Article 1, of the Federal Constitutional Law "On the Constitutional Court of the Russian Federation", No. 1-ФКЗ of July 21, 1994 (as amended December 26, 2016) (hereinafter referred to as FCL CC), the Constitutional Court of RF is a judicial body of constitutional review. Thus, it is vested with exclusive competence, which determines its independence from the legislative and executive bodies. The Russian system of judicial constitutional review bodies is not formed by the Federal Constitutional Court only. Thus, Constitutional (statutory) courts for RF subjects began to function at the end of the 20th century, and this was supposed to improve the efficient mechanism of judicial protection for constitutional rights and freedoms of person and citizen.

---

5 See: Н. В. Витрук, *Конституционное правосудие. Судебное конституционное право и процесс*, Moscow 2011, p. 59.

6 See: Г. А. Гаджиев, В. А. Кряжков, *Конституционная юстиция в Российской Федерации: становление и проблемы*, "Государство и право" 1993, № 7, pp. 3–11.

7 See: В. Д. Зорькин, *Россия и Конституция в XXI веке*, Moscow 2008, p. 6.

8 See: С. Д. Князев, *Конституционный Суд в правовой системе Российской Федерации*, "Журнал российского права" 2013, № 12, pp. 5–12.

9 See: А. Н. Кокотов, *Право конституции в российском праве*, "Актуальные проблемы российского права" 2014, № 10, pp. 2161–2168.

10 See: В. А. Кряжков, *Толкование Конституции Российской Федерации Конституционным Судом Российской Федерации*, "Вестник Конституционного Суда РФ" 1997, № 3, pp. 2–10.

11 See: С. И. Несмеянова, *Конституционный судебный контроль в Российской Федерации: проблемы теории и практики*, Yekaterinburg 2004, pp. 7–13.

12 See: Ж. И. Овсепян, *Судебный конституционный контроль в механизме «разделения властей». Ч. 1*, "Правоведение" 1993, № 4, pp. 80–87.

13 See: О. В. Опря, *Конституционные Суды в постсоциалистических государствах Восточной Европы (на примере Конституционного Суда Республики Болгария)*: дис. … канд. юрид. наук: 12.00.02, Moscow 2002, pp. 55–71.

14 See: М. С. Саликов, *Конституционный судебный процесс*, Moscow 2003, p. 45.

15 See: В. А. Туманов, *Судебный конституционный контроль за конституционностью нормативных правовых актов*, "Советское государство и право" 1988, № 3, pp. 10–19.

16 See: В. Е. Чиркин, *Конституционное право*, Moscow 2015, pp. 451–454.

17 See: Б. С. Эбзеев, *Конституция, власть и свобода в России. Опыт синтетического исследования*, Moscow 2014, p. 331.

At the present stage of federal relations, a study of the reasons causing the slowdown in the formation of constitutional (statutory) courts for RF subjects is still relevant. Summarized experience of the constitutional (statutory) courts enables recommendations aimed at improving the legal regulation of their activities and optimizing the entire system of judicial constitutional review bodies in the Russian Federation. Here we have some topical scientific problems, the resolution of which can enhance the theory of constitutionalism – based on understanding its essence and the nature of judicial constitutional review at the actual stage of the Russian state.

As a result, the place of constitutional review bodies in the system of RF public authorities can be determined regarding the binding nature of their decisions for law enforcers of any level, legislative and executive bodies. In Russia, a decision of the Constitutional Court is final, and not subject to appeal, coming into force right after its announcement/adoption, acting directly, and not requiring confirmation by other bodies or officials. "These provisions are expressly stated in Article 79 of the FCL CC"[18]. Thus, the legal nature of an act issued by the constitutional review body gains multi-aspect consolidation.

At the present historical stage, conversions in the field of justice and improving the mechanism on implementation of judicial power form an integral part of reforms in the Russian Federation. Compliance with the RF Constitution (hereafter 'the Constitution') and state laws became the most important term for the functioning of the political, social, and economic systems, their stability and sustainability. All subjects of law must follow the state constitution; so the issue of judicial constitutional review holds a prominent place in jurisprudence.

1 Motives for Introduction and Key Dilemmas of Establishing Control Over Legal Norms

Introducing the institute of constitutional review (in its actual form) was among the achievements of the state-legal reforms, which occurred during establishment of the Russian Federation. This type of specialized constitutional review body was not specific to the pre-revolutionary or Soviet period of development.

The call for the rule of law (independent of political trends prevailing in country) was first made long ago[19]. Thus, in 1912, eight years before the establishment of the first-ever Constitutional Court of Austria, the Russian scholar

18 О Конституционном Суде Российской Федерации: Федер. конст. закон от 21.07.1994 № 1-ФКЗ [принят Гос. Думой 24.06.1994] (по сост. на 08.06.2015), "Рос.газ." 1994. 23 июля. *Hereinafter – ФКЗ «О Конституционном Суде РФ»*.

19 Б. А. Кистяковский, *Социальные науки и право*, Moscow 1916, p. 654.

A. Yashchenko pointed to the potential establishment of a constitutional review body – Constitutional Court (Tribunal)[20].

Later, during the formation of the new state (Union of Soviet Socialist Republics) in the territory of former Russian Empire, it was necessary to discuss and resolve an issue on mechanism of ensuring the "supervision of legality in terms of the Constitution and all-union legislation"[21]. The pre-history of local constitutional justice is characterized by a period when the Supreme Court of the USSR ensured verification of constitutionality for acts of central public authorities of the USSR and union republics (1924–1933)[22].

Meanwhile, in Soviet legal literature, there were two views on constitutional review (supervision). According to one approach, it acts as a guarantee for the operation of legal norms, while interaction between Parliament and the Constitutional Court serves as a basis for the protection of human rights[23]. According to the other approach, judicial constitutional review is of an expressly political nature and is a bourgeois element of the constitution, which contributes to weakening the independence of the Parliament[24].

Then, in December 1988, USSR Constitution was amended to establish the USSR Committee for Constitutional Review (elected by the USSR Congress of People's Deputies for a term of 10 years). On December 23, 1989, the Law "On Constitutional Supervision in the USSR" was adopted[25]; and in 1990, the 27-member Constitutional Supervision Committee was elected. According to

---

20 А. Ященко, *Теория федерализма. Опыт синтетической теории права и государства*, Yuriev 1912, pp. 352–353.

21 П. Стучка, *СССР и РСФСР. Советская Конституция в вопросах и ответах. 4-е перераб. И доп издание*, Moscow 1924, p. 58.

22 See more details in: М. А. Митюков, *Судебный конституционный надзор 1924–1933 гг.: вопросы истории, теории и практики*, Moscow 2005, p. 208.

23 Л. Я. Дадиани, *К вопросу о сущности, формах и оценке института конституционного надзора*, "Труды Университета дружбы народов им. П. Лумумбы. Т. XX. Экономика и право" 1967, Вып. 2, pp. 39–64; И.А. Ледях, *Буржуазные конституции в период общего кризиса капитализма*, Moscow 1966, pp. 282–333.

24 Р. Х. Вильданов, *Конституции в политической системе буржуазного общества*, Moscow 1968, pp. 125–140; И. Д. Левин, *Крах буржуазной демократии и современное государственное право капиталистических стран. Вып. 1. США*, Moscow 1951, p. 61.

25 О конституционном надзоре в СССР: закон СССР от 23 декабря 1989 г. № 974–1, Ведомости Съезда народных депутатов СССР и Верховного Совета СССР. - 1989. - № 29. - Ст. 574.

the law, the Constitutional Supervision Committee was authorized to check draft laws and valid acts adopted by the Congress of People's Deputies, the Supreme Council and its chambers, acts of the USSR Attorney General and Chief State Arbiter, and acts of other state bodies/public organizations for compliance with the USSR Constitution. The Committee had legislative initiative and special rights regarding initiating the removal of the USSR President, reviewed disputes between the USSR and union republics, as well as between the republics and national-state entities. However, it had limited competence – the right to suspend (but not to annul) legal acts it recognized as unconstitutional – apart from those acts violating fundamental human rights and freedoms.

On December 15, 1990, provisions on establishment of a Constitutional Court, as a specialized body of judicial constitutional review, were included in the Constitution of the RSFSR (Rossiyskoy Sovetskoy Federativnoy Sotsialisticheskoy Respubliki).

The procedure of its formation and competence were regulated by the RF Law "On the Constitutional Court" of July 12, 1991. On October 30, 1991, the 5th (Extraordinary) Congress of People's Deputies of the RSFSR elected 13 judges. The establishment of the RF Constitutional Court in 1991 was an important milestone in the legal development of Russia[26]. The Court made a number of essential decisions. In particular, decisions on the constitutionality of acts related to CPSU (Communist Party of the Soviet Union) activities, on the constitutionality of law-enforcement practice related to indexing the income and savings of the population, etc.

After the events of October 3–4, 1993, during disagreements between the Chairperson of the Supreme Council and the RF President, Constitutional Court activity was suspended.

Article 125 of the RF Constitution of 1993 established new provisions regulating the structure and basis of Constitutional Court powers. In July 1994, FCL "On Constitutional Court of the Russian Federation" (FCL CC) was adopted. The powers, formation procedure, and activity of the Constitutional Court are determined by Article 125 of the Constitution and FCL CC (Article 3). This law is still valid. Amendments to it will be discussed in detail below.

Regarding its internal activities, the Constitutional Court has adopted CCRF Regulations[27]. The CCRF consists of 19 judges appointed to office by the

---

26 В. Д. Зорькин, *Конституционный Суд России: доктрина и практика: монография*, Moscow 2017, p. 5.

27 Регламент Конституционного Суда РФ (принят решением Конституционного Суда РФ от 1 марта 1995 г. № 2–1/6) (в редакции от 24 января 2011 г.) (изменениями и дополнениями), СПС «КонсультантПлюс» (accessed: February 20, 2018).

Federation Council (FC), under the proposal of the President (Article 4, FCL CC), with a right to operate if at least 2/3 of the judges are present.

The basic principles of Constitutional Court activities are independence, collegiality, publicity, competitiveness, and equality of the parties.

Constitutional Court judges are independent; when exercising their powers, they follow the Constitution and FCL CC only.

In their activities, RF Constitutional Court judges act in a personal capacity and do not represent any state or public bodies, political parties or movements, state, public or other enterprises, institutions, and organizations, officials, state and territorial entities, nations, and social groups.

Decisions and other acts of the CCRF express the legal position of the judges – in line with the Constitution and free from political bias.

RF Constitutional Court judges make decisions in terms excluding outside influence on freedom of their will. They are not entitled to request/receive instructions from anyone – on matters admitted for preliminary study or reviewed by the CCRF. Any interference in CCRF activity is not allowed and entails legal liability.

2 Legislative Stability of the Constitutional Court

Since its adoption in 1994, the Federal Law on the Constitutional Court has been amended and revised 15 times (as of January 27, 2018). One of the latest adjustments referred to legislative consolidation for the purpose of "clarifying" decisions ("introduced" on December 28, 2016).

Let's review these changes in more detail. In February 2001, the term of office for a CCRF judge was increased by 3 years, to 15 years. The provision on age limit for tenure (70 years) was excluded. The rule on a new term of office applies to all current CCRF judges appointed by the FC[28].

Then, in December 2001, amendments referred to clarification in the change of competence for the CCRF. It was noted that its competence could be modified only by amending the Federal Constitutional Law. The age limit for tenure of a Constitutional Court judge was set at 70 years. For a disciplinary offense, a CCRF judge may be subject to a disciplinary penalty – by decision of the Constitutional Court. The procedure for implementing CCRF decisions was

28 Федеральный конституционный закон от 8 февраля 2001 г. № 1-ФКЗ «О внесении изменений и дополнения в Федеральный конституционный закон "О Конституционном Суде Российской Федерации"», СПС «КонсультантПлюс» (accessed: February 20, 2018).

changed. Provisions requiring state bodies and officials to bring the laws and other normative acts in line with the Constitution (under decision of the CCRF) were adjusted.

According to the provided amendments, if the CCRF recognizes a federal law, normative act of President/Government, or normative act of an RF subject noncompliant with Constitution this forms the grounds for annulling the provisions of other normative acts, which are based on the normative act recognized as unconstitutional or reproduce any of its provisions recognized as unconstitutional. Provisions of such normative acts cannot be applied by courts, other bodies, and officials[29].

In 2004, norms regarding the procedure on reimbursement of court expenses for citizens and their associations (if CCRF recognized the federal law, law of RF subject or their individual provisions noncompliant with the Constitution) were clarified. At the expense of the federal budget or the budget of the relevant RF subject, these persons are reimbursed for paid state duties, expenses of representatives, travel and accommodation of applicants and their representatives due to court attendance, postal expenses due to case review, and compensation for actual loss of time[30].

In 2005, according to amendments made, the powers of CCRF judges are not limited to a specific term (previously – 15 years). The age limit for tenure of a CCRF judge was maintained at 70 years. A judge, who reaches the age limit for tenure, continues fulfilling the duties – until the final decision on the case initiated with his/her attendance or until the appointment of a new judge[31].

The following changes were made in 2007 – due to relocation of the CCRF from Moscow to St. Petersburg. Thus, Federal Constitutional Law was provided with the following norms. Instead of Moscow (Russia), St. Petersburg (Russia) became the city for permanent location of the Constitutional Court. At that, to

29 Федеральный конституционный закон от 15 декабря 2001 г. № 4-ФКЗ «О внесении изменений и дополнений в Федеральный конституционный закон "О Конституционном Суде Российской Федерации"», СПС ГАРАНТ (accessed: February 20, 2018).

30 Федеральный конституционный закон от 7 июня 2004 г. № 3-ФКЗ «О внесении изменения в статью 100 Федерального конституционного закона "О Конституционном Суде Российской Федерации"», СПС ГАРАНТ (accessed: February 20, 2018).

31 Федеральный конституционный закон от 5 апреля 2005 г. № 2-ФКЗ «О внесении изменений в Федеральный конституционный закон "О Конституционном Суде Российской Федерации"», СПС ГАРАНТ (accessed: February 20, 2018).

ensure the access of citizens and their associations to constitutional justice, a permanent connection of the CCRF with other RF public authorities, and RF subjects established in Moscow through the CCRF representative office[32].

In 2009, the procedure for empowering the Constitutional Court Chair and his/her deputies was changed. Thus, the Constitutional Court Chair and deputies are appointed to office by the FC, under the proposal of the President, from among the judges of the CCRF. Previously, the Chair, deputy, and Judge-Secretary were elected by CCRF judges (secret ballot). The term of office for the Chair and deputies was extended from 3 to 6 years. The post of Judge-Secretary was abolished; post of Vice-Chair was established. The Chair's powers on managing CCRF structure were clarified[33]. The current Chair and deputy will be able to exercise their powers until expiration of their current term.

In 2010, the amendments were aimed at improving Constitutional Court activities. It was clarified that citizens could file complaints regarding the laws applied in a specific case, while courts could file requests regarding the laws to be applied. Cases on their constitutionality can now be resolved without hearing. This also applies to the verification of normative acts from Federal Assembly chambers, the President and Government, and some others. However, on the motion of applicant, a hearing is mandatory.

From now on, all cases are reviewed by a full panel of judges (19 people), instead of chamber sessions. Thus, the chance for contradictions in legal positions of the chambers has been addressed.

Rulings (certain form of court decisions) have been canceled, as they entailed the review of resolutions issued by courts of general jurisdiction and arbitration courts.

As before, the age limit for tenure of Constitutional Court judges is 70 years. However, it does not apply to the Chair.

Upon the Chair's proposal, the President provides a CCRF judge with the highest qualification class – within 6 months of appointment to the relevant position.

The procedure on the early termination of powers of the Chair and deputies (upon improper performance of duties) has been changed. This decision is made

---

32 Федеральный конституционный закон от 5 февраля 2007 г. № 2-ФКЗ «О внесении изменений в Федеральный конституционный закон "О Конституционном Суде Российской Федерации"», СПС ГАРАНТ (accessed: February 20, 2018).

33 Федеральный конституционный закон от 2 июня 2009 г. № 2-ФКЗ «О внесении изменений в Федеральный конституционный закон "О Конституционном Суде Российской Федерации"», СПС ГАРАНТ (accessed: February 20, 2018).

by the FC – not by the Constitutional Court itself, as it was before. The trigger is a representation from the President – based on at least 2/3 votes of the total judges.

Norms on the amount of state duty (upon application to the CCRF) are excluded. This issue is regulated by the RF Tax Code[34].

In December 2010, amendments were made due to the establishment of the RF Investigative Committee. Under these amendments, within 2 weeks of signing, resolutions and conclusions of the CCRF must be sent, for example, not only to the Attorney General only, but also to the Chair of the Investigative Committee[35].

Then, in 2012, the FCLs on the CCRF, the judicial system, and military courts were adjusted. Instead of norms on the salary of judges, provisions on monthly remuneration and quarterly cash incentives were introduced. Retired CCRF judges (with work experience as judge at least 15 years) are now provided with a pension or non-taxable, monthly, life-long maintenance. It is specified that maintenance is paid in the amount of the monthly remuneration for a working CCRF judge (previously – 80 % of remuneration)[36].

In 2013, amendments were made regarding the procedure for bringing the legislation in line with court decisions. Thus, the period during which the Government submits a bill (developed in view of a CCRF decision) to the State Duma of the Federal Assembly of the Russian Federation (SD), has been extended. Now, this period is 6 months (instead of 3). However, the CCRF decision may specify a different period. The list of persons authorized to submit the relevant bills for SD review has been clarified. These are: the President, the FC, parliamentarians of the country, regional legislative (representative) bodies, the Supreme Court, and RF SAC (Supreme Arbitration Court of the Russian Federation) – on matters in their competence. If the Government provided a positive conclusion (comment) to bill developed by the above subjects, it may

34 Федеральный конституционный закон от 3 ноября 2010 г. № 7-ФКЗ2 „О внесении изменений в Федеральный конституционный закон «О Конституционном Суде Российской Федерации»“, СПС ГАРАНТ (accessed: February 20, 2018).

35 Федеральный конституционный закон от 28 декабря 2010 г. № 8-ФКЗ «О внесении изменений в отдельные федеральные конституционные законы в связи с совершенствованием деятельности органов предварительного следствия», СПС ГАРАНТ (accessed: February 20, 2018).

36 Федеральный конституционный закон от 25 декабря 2012 г. № 5-ФКЗ «внесении изменений в отдельные законодательные акты Российской Федерации в части совершенствования системы оплаты труда судей Российской Федерации», СПС ГАРАНТ (accessed: February 20, 2018).

postpone the introduction of its own bill. The norm on extraordinary review of these bills by SD has been excluded[37].

On March 12, 2014, individual FCLs were adjusted – due to adoption of the Law on Amendment to the Constitution "On RF SC and Prosecutor's Office"[38]. And amendments of June 4, 2014 were aimed at improving the arrangement of CCRF activities and procedures of hearing cases. Thus, the CCRF quorum (enabling its activities) was reduced from 3/4 to 2/3 of the total judges (19 people). The procedure for filling vacancies of CCRF judges was clarified. The general rule on retaining office (upon reaching the age limit, until the appointment of a new judge) was excluded.

It was assumed that, for some organizational issues and in sessions, a decision is made by a majority of votes – not from the total number, but from among the active judges.

Verification of compliance between an issue submitted to an all-Russian referendum and the Constitution is directly consolidated among CCRF powers.

In terms of specific compliance assessment, the deadline for filing a complaint to the CCRF was set as 1 year after case review in court. The number of document copies submitted by applicants to the CCRF was reduced to 1. Loss of legal force by debated act, as reason for refusal to accept the appeal for review, is regulated more clearly. It is clarified that the CCRF refuses to accept the appeal for review, if the act with debated constitutionality was canceled or became invalid. The exception is the case when this act is still applied in legal relations formed during the period of its validity.

Opportunities for case resolution without hearing were expanded. Thus, in a case of abstract compliance assessment, restrictions on applying this procedure to federal laws or constitutions (charters) of RF subjects were lifted.

---

37 Федеральный конституционный закон от 5 апреля 2013 г. № 1-ФКЗ «О внесении изменения в статью 80 Федерального конституционного закона "О Конституционном Суде Российской Федерации"», СПС ГАРАНТ (accessed: February 20, 2018).

38 Федеральный конституционный закон от 12 марта 2014 г. № 5-ФКЗ «О внесении изменений в отдельные федеральные конституционные законы в связи с принятием Закона Российской Федерации о поправке к Конституции Российской Федерации "О Верховном Суде Российской Федерации и прокуратуре Российской Федерации" и признании утратившим силу Федерального конституционного закона "О Дисциплинарном судебном присутствии"», СПС ГАРАНТ (accessed: February 20, 2018).

The situation where a decision of the European Court of Human Rights actually becomes an obstacle to applying the norms of Russian legislation was adjusted. The opportunity to request the CCRF to confirm the constitutionality of such norms, was provided[39].

The following changes were made in 2015. The amendments referred to electronic appeals to CCRF and Internet broadcasts of CCRF sessions. The amendments provided the opportunity of filing the electronic appeals to the CCRF – by filling a special form on the CCRF website or submitting the electronic document (provided with enhanced, qualified electronic signature). In this case, correspondence with the applicant can also be kept in electronic form. When filing the electronic appeal, the attached documents and other materials may be in electronic form as well. Hard copies of appeals, documents, and other materials are not required.

According to law, announcements on the date and time of CCRF sessions must be posted on its official website. Issues on Internet broadcasts of CCRF sessions were adjusted as well. Internet broadcasts of sessions are possible on the initiative of the CCRF or, with its permission, by request of parties to the case present at the session. The procedure of Internet broadcast is to be prescribed in CCRF regulations. Only open CCRF sessions may be broadcast over the Internet. At closed session, filming and photographing, video recording, live radio and TV broadcast, as well as Internet broadcast, are prohibited[40].

Since December 2015, the CCRF may resolve an issue on the potential implementation of an interstate body decision aimed to protect human rights and freedoms (e.g., European Court of Human Rights – ECtHR) and made by complaint against Russia – based on international treaty. The implementation of such decisions may be recognized as impossible, if it conflicts with the Fundamental Law of the country. Besides, the decisions shall not conflict with the CCRF's interpretation of the Constitution.

The Constitutional Court can resolve such cases in 2 ways. First, the federal executive body (FEB), vested with competence to protect the interests of Russia, may submit a request on verifying the constitutionality of legislative norms, found by international court to have flaws. The FEB gives an opinion

39 Федеральный конституционный закон от 4 июня 2014 г. № 9-ФКЗ «О внесении изменений в Федеральный конституционный закон "О Конституционном Суде Российской Федерации"», СПС ГАРАНТ (accessed: February 20, 2018).

40 Федеральный конституционный закон от 8 июня 2015 г. № 5-ФКЗ «О внесении изменений в Федеральный конституционный закон "О Конституционном Суде Российской Федерации"», СПС ГАРАНТ (accessed: February 20, 2018).

on the impossibility of implementing the decision – due to its conflict with the Constitution. Such cases may be reviewed without hearing, if problem can be resolved on the basis of decisions previously made by the Constitutional Court. Second, the President or the Government may submit a request on reviewing the conflict found between provisions of an international treaty (interpreted by an interstate body) and the provisions of the Constitution – regarding the potential implementation of the decision made by the relevant interstate body.

If the court adopts a resolution on impossibility to implement a decision of an interstate body, no actions (acts) aimed at implementing this decision can be adopted[41]. As of February 9, 2018, 2 resolutions of CCRF were adopted[42].

Culminating amendments were made in December 2016. The law on additional guarantees for proper implementation of CCRF decisions was adopted.

A new type of resolution (adopted by the CCRF following the review of case on verifying the constitutionality of a normative act from a state body or an agreement between state authorities) was introduced – namely, a resolution on recognizing such an act, agreement or their individual provisions as compliant with RF Constitution (as interpreted by CCRF).

In the presence of this resolution, any other interpretation of the relevant act/agreement is excluded. This rule also applies to final decisions on complaints of conflict between law and constitutional rights/freedoms of citizens. A principle on the inadmissible application of a normative act or its individual provisions

41 Федеральный конституционный закон от 14 декабря 2015 г. № 7-ФКЗ «О внесении изменений в Федеральный конституционный закон "О Конституционном Суде Российской Федерации"», СПС ГАРАНТ (accessed: February 20, 2018).

42 Постановление Конституционного Суда РФ от 19 апреля 2016 года № 12-П «по делу о разрешении вопроса о возможности исполнения в соответствии с Конституцией Российской Федерации постановления Европейского Суда по правам человека от 4 июля 2013 года по делу «Анчугов и Гладков против России» в связи с запросом Министерства юстиции Российской Федерации», СПС ГАРАНТ (accessed: February 20, 2018).

Постановление Конституционного Суда РФ от 19 января 2017 года № 1-П «по делу о разрешении вопроса о возможности исполнения в соответствии с Конституцией Российской Федерации постановления Европейского Суда по правам человека от 31 июля 2014 года по делу «ОАО «Нефтяная компания «ЮКОС» против России» в связи с запросом Министерства юстиции Российской Федерации», СПС ГАРАНТ (accessed: February 20, 2018).

in interpretation different from that given in CCRF resolution was directly consolidated[43].

Thus, amendments to FCL CC have enabled the self-sufficiency and independence of the CCRF in the Russian legal system – with activities aimed at protecting the foundations of the constitutional system, human and civil rights and freedoms.

3 Legislative Position of the Constitutional Court

As noted in the Russian legal doctrine, the special position of the Constitutional Court, as the constitutional public authority, puts it on the same level with other federal public authorities – the President, the Federal Assembly, and the Government[44]. At that, since the Constitutional Court may recognize normative legal acts adopted by them as incompliant with the Constitution (see B.S. Ebzeyev), in some cases, it becomes superior to those federal authorities. Meanwhile, the proposal is to differentiate constitutional features of the CCRF – from its institutional and functional position. From its institutional position, the CCRF acts as one of the federal public authorities, which independently and self-sufficiently exercise state power along with other supreme federal bodies; from a functional position, it acts as a judicial body implementing its activities via constitutional proceedings[45].

3.1 The Constitutional Court and the President

First of all, interaction between the Constitutional Court and head of state assumes his/her participation in the appointment and dismissal of CCRF judges, which reflects the President's degree of influence and interest in forming the membership of constitutional justice body. As is known, the current method of staffing the CCRF authorizes a wide range of subjects to propose their candidates

---

43 Федеральный конституционный закон от 28 декабря 2016 г. № 11-ФКЗ «О внесении изменений в Федеральный конституционный закон "О Конституционном Суде Российской Федерации"», СПС ГАРАНТ (accessed: February 20, 2018).

44 А. В. Безруков, *Конституционные основы деятельности судебных органов и прокуратуры в механизме обеспечения правопорядка*, "Конституционное и муниципальное право" 2016, № 4, p. 14.

45 Л. И. Гадельшина, А. Р Гарифуллина, *Правовые основы взаимодействия Конституционного Суда Российской Федерации с органами государственной власти Российской Федерации*, "Российский Судья" 2017, № 5.

to the President; however, only the head of state has the right to submit a proposal for the appointment of a Constitutional Court judge to the FC.

The leading role of President in forming the Constitutional Court is especially manifested at appointment of the Chair and deputies, who can be repeatedly re-assigned by the FC – on proposal from the head of state. The specific nature of the CCRF determines the special form of its interaction with the President – participation in taking the oath by newly elected head of state, which is expressed in verifying the President's actions on following his/her duty of protecting the Constitution from violations – in presence of the CCRF judges, as the main keepers of constitutional principles and values (Part 2, Article 82 of RF Constitution).

There is a need for further extension of Constitutional Court powers in the field of expert-advisory activities – with the inclusion of Constitutional Court judges in various consultative and advisory bodies established by the President for preparing recommendations and proposals on complex constitutional and legal issues – this can be considered the next area of cooperation between the CCRF and the President. The current practice of holding the regular meetings between the Constitutional Court Chair and the President – to discuss the most pressing issues of constitutional and legal policy, enhancing and development of constitutionalism in the Russian Federation – also deserves attention. The same purpose is served by annual meetings of the President with the entire CCRF staff (held on RF Constitution Day).

Another important form of interaction between the Constitutional Court and the President is the arrangement of implementing the CCRF's final decisions which, in some cases, necessarily implies the use of special legal mechanisms for the forced implementation of court resolutions in the activities of RF public authorities and subjects.

Another interesting aspect is the CCRF's authority to review cases on providing a conclusion about meeting the established procedure for accusing the RF President of high treason or committing other serious crimes. Article 107 of FCL CC states that FC can request such a review. Article 108 lists a number of requirements for the admissibility of this request: the charge must be brought by SD, with Supreme Court conclusion on the evidence of alleged crime in President's actions. According to Part 1, Article 109 of FCL CC, the request for review must be submitted to the CCRF no later than in 1 month after the adoption of the SD decision on bringing the charges. Then, within 10 days, the CCRF must provide its conclusion – on compliance or noncompliance with established procedure of bringing the charges. This is the limit of its competence on the issue.

Interaction between the Constitutional Court and the President can also be found in the authorities of the court. By request of the President, the CCRF resolves cases on compliance with the Constitution for: a) federal laws, normative acts of the President, FC, SD, and Government; b) republican constitutions, charters, laws, and other normative acts of RF subjects issued on matters within the jurisdiction of RF public authorities and joint jurisdiction of RF public authorities and public authorities of RF subjects; c) agreements between RF public authorities and public authorities of RF subjects, agreements between public authorities of RF subjects; d) international treaties of the Russian Federation, which have not come into force.

By request of the President, the CCRF provides interpretation of the Constitution.

3.2 Constitutional Court and the Government

Interaction between the Constitutional Court and the Government, as the executive body of RF state power (Part 1, Article 110 of RF Constitution), forms an independent activity of the CCRF within the separation of powers. First, it is expressed by the indirect nature of the cooperation – in particular, by providing additional material and social guarantees to ensure the self-sufficient and independent status of CCRF judges, and the unobstructed exercise of their powers on the administration of constitutional justice (Article 13, 19 of FCL CC). Second, it assumes participation of the Government in case hearings (during court proceedings). Third, it assumes cooperation in expert-analytical activities of the Ministry of Justice – on legal monitoring and relevant notification of the CCRF Secretariat[46].

Besides, abstract compliance assessment of governmental acts by the CCRF was consolidated on a legislative level.

At that, the possibility of specific compliance assessment for normative governmental acts was derived by the Constitutional Court itself. Thus, in Resolution No. 1-П of January 27, 2004, the CCRF justified a conclusion that

---

46 О мониторинге правоприменения в Российской Федерации: указ Президента РФ от 20 мая 2011 г. № 657, СЗ РФ. 2011. № 21. Ст. 2930; О мониторинге и анализе результатов рассмотрения обращений граждан и организаций: указ Президента РФ от 17 апр. 2017 года № 171, СЗ РФ. 2017. № 17. Ст. 2545 (данный документ направлен на эффективность реализации Федерального закона от 2 мая 2006 года № 59-ФЗ (ред. от 03 ноября 2015 г.) «О порядке рассмотрения обращений граждан Российской Федерации», СЗ РФ. 2006. № 19. Ст. 2060.) и др.

such assessment is possible in case of direct regulatory connection between a resolution of the Government and federal law – if these acts are applied or to be applied in a particular case, as indissoluble unity. In Resolution No. 8-П of May 14, 2009, on the case of verifying the constitutionality of a Government decision, the CCRF verified the constitutionality of decision, when the law (being in normative unity with it) was not applied[47]. At that, if relations regulated by debated provisions of a governmental resolution have already received substantive regulation in any federal law, the verification of such provisions is not within the competence of the CCRF[48].

Apart from defining the constitutionality of verified normative acts, the CCRF also adjusts the rule-making limits of executive authorities and other executive bodies. While reviewing the regulatory acts of specified bodies, the CCRF applies their broad interpretation, thus helping to protect the constitutional rights of citizens.

3.3 Constitutional Court and the Parliament

The interaction of the CCRF with Parliament is of equal importance – within the separation of powers, aimed at constitutionalization of Russian laws and assistance in legislative activities.

Besides, there are some debatable legal provisions, which were not properly implemented in practice (in the field of interaction between the CCRF and the Federal Assembly), namely:

1. The issue of the Constitutional Court exercising the right of legislative initiative in SD (Part 1, Article 104 of the Constitution). Unfortunately, the CCRF does not use this authority in practice – except for participation in developing the first revision of the FCL CC. According to M.A. Mityukov, unlike the first law on Constitutional Court of 1991, the specific feature of preparing this draft was its development by the CCRF – rather than by the legislative body. Then, M.A. Mityukov notes that, without due attention of the CCRF,

47 Постановление Конституционного Суда РФ от 14 мая 2009 г. № 8-П [Электронный ресурс], Конституционный Суд РФ. Режим доступа: URL: http://www.ksrf.ru (accessed: February 20, 2018).

48 See, for example, Постановление Конституционного Суда РФ от 3 февр. 2010 года № 3-П [Электронный ресурс], Конституционный Суд РФ. Режим доступа: URL: http://www.ksrf.ru (accessed: February 20, 2018).

the constitutional authority on the CCRF right for legislative initiative fell into a category of so-called "sleeping powers"[49].

2. Submission of annual Constitutional Court reports to the Federal Assembly on the state of constitutional legality (Part 3, Article 100 of the Constitution). Unfortunately, during present period, this authority was implemented only once – namely, on March 5, 1993, when the CCRF submitted to the Federal Assembly its only report "On the State of Constitutional Legality in the Russian Federation", which consisted of five sections[50].

Russian legal science expressed diametrically opposed positions on joint hearing of Constitutional Court reports by chambers of the Federal Assembly. Most authors consider submission of reports on the state of constitutional legality as an obligation of the constitutional review body[51]. Proponents of a narrower approach consider this type of activity as a sort of "backup tool"[52]. Constitutional Court reports are given quite cautious assessment – due to risk of unjustified "politicization" of constitutional justice[53]. As part of another position, the thesis is maintained that submission of reports is a right of the constitutional review body[54], using this indirect means to convince the authorized body of an actual

49 М. А. Митюков, *Федеральный конституционный закон «О Конституционном Суде Российской Федерации»: правовые дискуссии при разработке и принятии (введение в тему)*, "Конституционное и муниципальное право" 2006, № 12, p. 27.

50 Вестник КС РФ. 1993. № 1.

51 Г. А. Гаджиев, *Роль конституционного права и Конституционного Суда должна быть более активна*, "Юридический мир" 2004, № 11, pp. 5–12; Л. М. Жаркова, *Содержание и применение юридической конструкции «Послание Конституционного Суда Российской Федерации Федеральному Собранию Российской Федерации»*, [in:] Т. Д. Зражевская (ed.), *Конституционные чтения. Выпуск 2. Понятийно-категориальный аппарат для решения научных задач в конституционно-правовой науке*, Voronezh 2003, pp. 264–267; Т. Г. Морщакова, *Кризис правосудия?*, [in:] Т. Г. Морщакова (ed.), *Открытые глаза российской Фемиды*, Moscow 2007, pp. 4–19; Ю. А. Тихомиров, А. Я. Сухарев, И.Ф. Демидов, *Законность в Российской Федерации*, Moscow 1998, pp. 13–26.

52 В. Д. Зорькин, *Кризис доверия и государство*, "Рос. газ." 2004. 4 окт.; М. А. Митюков, *Методология исследования проблемы послания Конституционного Суда РФ*, "Конституционное и муниципальное право" 2010, № 12, pp. 27–33.

53 М. А. Митюков, *Послание Конституционного Суда: к истории вопроса и некоторые проблемы*, [in:] *Конституционное развитие России: межвуз. сб. науч. ст.*, Saratov 2011, Вып. 12, pp. 45–58.

54 С. А. Авакьян, *Конституционное право России: уч. курс. 2-е изд., перераб. и доп.: в 2 т.*, Moscow 2006, Т. 2, p. 641; Н. В. Витрук, *Конституционное правосудие в России (1990–2001 годы): очерки теории и практики*, Moscow 2001, p. 115.

problem, the resolution of which may require, along with other measures, an appeal to the CCRF[55]. The CCRF can also take such indirect action on the President, the Federal Assembly chamber, and other authorized bodies via its reports. The report format is convenient for highlighting systemic problems of Russian legislation and law enforcement (based on an analysis of constitutional-judicial practice), the addressing of which, apart from legislative changes, may also involve constitutional and judicial means – e.g., clarifying the content of constitutional provisions during the official interpretation of the Constitution[56]. However, a detailed legal mechanism was not established in this view, which was already mentioned in legal science[57]. In fact, submission of reports could become an important area of legislative activity, while simultaneously being an element of planning the legislative activity.

Improving the regulation of Constitutional Court reports formed the subject of legislative activity for the federal legislator. In September 2013, a bill "On Amendments to Federal Constitutional Law "On Constitutional Court of the Russian Federation"" was introduced to SD; a procedure of preparing such reports was suggested for development on its basis. The bill assumes two types of reports for submission. First, to SD of a new convocation (drafted every 5 years) – based on an analysis/summary of constitutional-judicial practice and systemic problems revealed in legislation and law enforcement. Second, topical reports to SD of the current convocation – on other actual issues of implementing CCRF decisions[58]. In the modern period, the CCRF pretty widely applies the

---

55 А.Н.Кокотов, *Насущные вопросы регулирования деятельности Конституционного Суда РФ*, "Российский юридический журнал. Екатеринбург: УрГЮА" 2012, № 2 (83), pp. 20–27.

56 See О посланиях Конституционного Суда, see: Е. Б. Абросимова, Э. Р. Уметбаева, *Ученый совет Института государства и права РАН обсуждает научный доклад Председателя Конституционного Суда РФ*, "Государство и право" 1992, № 5; Г. А. Гаджиев, *Федеральное Собрание и Конституционный Суд. Партнерство и контроль*, "Российская Федерация" 1994, № 8; С. Э. Несмеянова, *О возможном влиянии Конституционного Суда Российской Федерации на законодателя*, "Журнал конституционного правосудия" 2010, № 3, pp. 6–9.

57 С. М. Омаров, *Основные проблемы реализации послания Конституционного Суда РФ Федеральному собранию Российской Федерации*, "Право" 2011, № 4, pp. 61–70.

58 О внесении изменений в Федеральный конституционный закон «О Конституционном Суде Российской Федерации»: законопроект № 342513-6 [Электронный ресурс], Автоматизированная система обеспечения законодательной деятельности. Режим доступа: URL http://asozd2.duma.gov.ru/main.nsf/%28SpravkaNew%29?OpenAgent&RN=342513-6&02 (accessed: February 20, 2018).

compilation of information-analytical reports on content and implementation of its decisions (so-called "mini-messages"). From 2009 to 2017, nine of these mini-reports were prepared (whereas, CCRF exercised the right to submit reports to the Federal Assembly in 1993 only). Besides, the practice of interaction between the CCRF and SD included a pilot project adapting another form of "quasi-message"[59], where, in December 2014, V.D. Zorkin presented systemic problems of legal regulation (in the form of scientific report).

The status of the provided examples – preparation of various information documents and their legal value – enables their review regarding the actual rule-making activity in legislative process. It appears that, regarding the unification of available experience, legal regulation reflecting the preparation procedure and frequency of sending reports to the Federal Assembly (on the state of constitutional legality, as part of special proceeding) seems reasonable.

Then, Constitutional Court practice has certain effects on rule-making activity. For example, CCRF acts may create obligations for the federal legislator or formulate legal positions to be considered during adopting/improving the laws. While exploring some issues of CCRF powers in the field of law making, let's highlight two actual fields of CCRF activity in the law-making process: 1) recognition of current legal provisions incompliant with the Constitution; and 2) revealing the constitutional and legal meaning of certain legal provisions, if they are recognized as non-conflicting with the Fundamental Law.

In modern terms, constitutional courts drift away from their traditional characteristics as "negative" legislator. The CCRF is no exception. Its activity includes elements of the "negative" legislator (recognizing the laws compliant or incompliant with RF Constitution) and the "positive" legislator. When formulating new rules of social behavior, the CCRF implements the features of a "positive" legislator and determines the conceptual aspects of legal regulation (in its constitutional sense), which are further considered by the legislator.

3.4 Constitutional Court and Courts

In the Russian Federation, active participation in relations between constitutional review body and courts assumes interaction of the Supreme Court, courts of general and arbitration jurisdiction with the CCRF – to implement abstract and specific judicial constitutional review on cases of verifying the constitutionality

59 В. Д. Зорькин, *Конституция живет в законах [Электронный ресурс]*, "Российская газета" Режим доступа: URL https://rg.ru/2014/12/18/zorkin.html (accessed: February 20, 2018).

of the law to be applied in certain case, by request of the courts, at any stage of case review (Article 101 of FCL CC).

In its practice, the CCRF does not directly oblige the Supreme Court to bring the law-enforcement judicial practice in line with the CCRF's adopted decision – in contrast, for example, to prescription, which binds the legislator to bring the normative legal act in line with the CCRF decision. As a rule, the CCRF Secretariat interacts with the Supreme Court (to be exact – with the department of the Supreme Court Office).

A quite positive aspect of this constructive interaction is the Supreme Court practice of informing the courts on CCRF decisions having important legal value for case review by courts and compiling judicial practice reviews of the Supreme Court – with account for legal positions of the CCRF having precedential nature in the activity of courts (general/arbitration jurisdiction) during the review and resolution of similar case categories[60].

At present, the constitutional-legal meaning of a legal provision (revealed by Constitutional Court and recognized compliant/incompliant with the Constitution) is mandatory for use by courts. Unfortunately, CCRF decisions are not always properly implemented by Russian courts[61].

Besides, in practice, in response to appeals from the CCRF Secretariat, the Supreme Court Office submits information materials on individual measures taken with regards to civil complaints – in view of CCRF decisions adopted on their cases. The above contributes to the enhanced implementation of CCRF decisions.

3.5 Constitutional Court and Other Public Authorities

Apart from the above public authorities, the Constitutional Court actively interacts with the Attorney's Office. First, the Attorney's Office is authorized

---

60 О. Н. Кряжкова, *Правовые позиции Конституционного Суда Российской Федерации: теоретические основы и практика реализации судами России*, Moscow 2006, p. 144.

61 Об исполнении решений Конституционного Суда Российской Федерации, принятых в ходе осуществления конституционного судопроизводства в 2016 году: Информац.-аналитич. отчет (подготовлен Секретариатом Конституционного Суда Российской Федерации в соответствии с пунктом 2 § 67 Регламента Конституционного Суда Российской Федерации) [Электронный ресурс], Официальный сайт Конституционного Суда Российская Федерация. – Режим доступа: http://www.ksrf.ru/ru/Info/Maintenance/Informationks/Pages/default.aspx (accessed: February 20, 2018).

to appeal against illegal acts of supervised prosecution entities – including their conflict with the Constitution. In the case of a rejected protest (on non-compliance of provisions in constitutions and charters of RF subjects with the Constitution), the Attorney General has legal grounds to appeal to the CCRF. This authority was derived from the practice of the CCRF – e.g., see CCRF resolution No. 13- П dated July 18, 2003[62]. It was reflected in Part 6, Article 35 of Federal Law "On Attorney's Office of the Russian Federation".

Besides, the Attorney's Office actively cooperates with the Constitutional Court on most cases under review. Judges consider the professional opinion of the Attorney General's Office: on almost any public case, the conclusion in the process is given by the official representative of the Attorney General, which enables its use during forming the CCRF decision.

General methodological guidelines on protecting human and civil rights and freedoms in constitutional (statutory) legal proceedings are determined by the Attorney General's orders No. 155 of October 2, 2007 "On arrangement of prosecutor's supervision over legality of normative legal acts of public authorities, RF subjects, and local self-government bodies" and No. 195 of December 7, 2007 "On arrangement of prosecutor's supervision over exercising of laws, observance of human and civil rights and freedoms".

The commonality of tasks faced by prosecution authorities, the CCRF, and the constitutional (statutory) courts of RF subjects – protection and safeguarding of the Constitution, federal laws, constitutions and charters of RF subjects – specifies the need for ensuring the close cooperation of the prosecution authorities and indicated bodies. The basis for interaction between attorneys of RF subjects and constitutional (statutory) courts is authorizing the relevant attorneys (in some RF subjects) for request to those courts or attending of their meetings[63].

To improve interaction between constitutional (statutory) courts in RF subjects, relevant agreements are concluded. The purpose of these agreements is cooperation and interaction on joint protection of constitutional rights and freedoms – among others, via constitutional justice, data exchange on offenses in this area of legal relations, and measures taken in this view. Agreements define the forms of cooperation aimed at effective exercise of powers on control and supervision over fulfilling the constitutional obligations of the democratic

---

62 СЗРФ. 2003. № 30. Ст. 3101.

63 С. Г. Кехлерова, О. С. Капинус (eds.), *Настольная книга прокурора*, 2-е изд., перераб. и доп., Moscow 2013, p. 856.

law-bound state – recognition, respect, and the protection of human and civil rights and freedoms.

Unfortunately, prosecution bodies rarely use the power to make requests on compliance of normative legal acts, charters of municipal formations, and other normative legal acts of local self-government bodies with the Constitution (Charter) of RF subjects. This situation is not something extraordinary on national scale. Thus, analysis of A.M. Tsaliyev and O.Kh. Kachmazov shows that, throughout the operation of constitutional (statutory) courts, no resolution was made in view of appeal from attorney in North Ossetia-Alania, Mari El, Tatarstan, Tyva, Dagestan, Chechen Republic, St. Petersburg, Kaliningrad region. In other RF subjects, cases of appeal to constitutional justice bodies were isolated[64].

This problem has been recognized by scholars and practitioners. The Research Institute at the Academy of the Attorney General's Office prepared a manual on analyzing and assessing the state of legality at the regional level, which suggests the ways to estimate the effectiveness of attorneys at constitutional (statutory) courts of RF subjects[65]. At that, while being quite extensive, the jurisdiction of the CCRF and Attorney's Office is not universal; the powers of these bodies significantly differ (e.g., on the object of control and supervision, they mostly mismatch).

Apart from the above interaction with the Attorney's Office, the CCRF resolves disputes of competence between federal public authorities, between RF public authorities and public authorities of RF subjects, between the highest public authorities of RF subjects. Meeting the principle of constitutional legality assumes functionally different (in content), but common (in purpose) bodies of specialized constitutional review and non-specialized prosecutor's supervision, which forms the commonality of tasks faced by these state bodies – the protection of the Constitution, i.e., identifying and addressing the noncompliance between legal acts and Fundamental Law.

---

64 А. М. Цалиев, О. Х. Качмазов, *Правозащитная функция органов конституционной юстиции и прокуратуры*, "Законность" 2010, № 7, pp. 12–15.

65 О. С. Капинус (ed.), *Анализ состояния законности и правопорядка прокуратурами субъектов Российской Федерации: пособие*, Moscow 2012, 470 p.

4 Structure of the Constitutional Court

4.1 The Legal Status of Constitutional Court Judges

In general, the status of CCRF judges does not differ from the status of judges in other supreme courts of Russia. Article 128 of the Constitution also sets an identical procedure for appointing the judges of three supreme courts. Qualification differences are of an isolated nature.

An RF citizen, at least 40 years old on the date of appointment, with impeccable reputation, a degree in law, work experience in the legal field (at least 15 years), and a recognized qualification in law can be appointed as CCRF judge.

Powers of Constitutional Court judges are not limited to a specific term. The age limit for serving as a CCRF judge is 70 years. His/her authority is terminated on the last day of month, when he/she turns 70. A CCRF judge, whose term of office has expired, shall resign. A CCRF judge, who has reached the age limit keeps serving as a judge until the final decision on a case initiated with his/her attendance. Age restrictions do not apply to the Chair. Retired CCRF judges are usually involved in scientific and teaching activities.

Each Constitutional Court judge takes the following oath: "I swear to serve as a Constitutional Court judge honestly and in good faith, while obeying nothing and no one but the RF Constitution".

A Constitutional Court judge may not be a member (deputy) of the FC, SD or other representative bodies, hold/retain any other governmental or public position, have a private practice, be involved in business or other paid activities – except for teaching, scientific, and other creative activities, which must not interfere with duties of the CCRF judge and cannot serve as valid reason for absence at the session, unless agreed by the CCRF.

A Constitutional Court judge may not ensure protection or representation (except for legal representation in Court, Arbitration Court or other bodies) or patronize anyone in obtaining their rights and releasing them from duties.

While speaking in the press or other mass media, or before any audience, a CCRF judge may not publicly express his/her opinion on an issue that may be subject to review in the CCRF or studied/accepted for review by the CCRF – until after the matter has been decided.

A Constitutional Court judge may not belong to political parties/movements, support them financially, participate in political actions, conduct political propaganda or agitation, participate in campaigns on election to state and local self-government bodies, attend congresses and conferences of political parties/

movements, be engaged in other political activities. Besides, he/she cannot be a manager of a public association, even if it does not pursue any political goals.

The independence/immunity of Constitutional Court judges, as well as their guarantees, are determined by FCL CC and fully implemented in practice. Precedents of removing a CCRF judge due to disciplinary liability, as well as excluding the judge from the decision-making group are absent – due to the high qualification requirements, which, in turn, guarantees good faith of fulfilling legal obligations.

The economic and social rights of a CCRF judge – expressed in material guarantees of independence for the CCRF judge regarding the payment of his/her labor, provision of annual leave, social security, housing, social amenities, mandatory state insurance of judge's life and health, insurance of property belonging to him/her and members of his/her family – are set on the basis of relevant guarantees assumed by FCL CC and other normative legal acts of the Russian Federation[66]. To summarize this section, let's note that legal norms regulating the legal status of a CCRF judge are fully implemented in practice.

4.2 Functions of the Constitutional Court

As noted above, the Constitutional Court of the RF is a judicial body of constitutional review, which independently and self-sufficiently exercises judicial power – via constitutional legal proceedings. Its functions are determined by the content of certain powers.

Its main functions include:

1. Ensuring the sustainability and stability of the Constitution;
2. Official interpretation of the Constitution;
3. Participation in the legislative process. Potential expression of expert opinion on draft laws;
4. Protection of civil rights.
5. Participation in political process. This is not some primitive understanding of involvement in politics. We are talking about deeper aspects – in particular, resolution of issues of the separation of powers (in case of appeal from subjects). The political process is camouflaged via rules of law. Thus, in

66 Федеральный закон от 10 января 1996 г. № 6-ФЗ «О мерах по обеспечен ию материальных гарантий независимости Судей Конституционного Суда Российской Федерации»; Указ Президента РФ от 23 декабря 2007 г. № 1741; Указ Президента РФ от 7 февраля 2000 г. № 306; Указ Президента РФ от 14 сентября 1995 г. № 941, Справочная правовая система Консультант Плюс.

the resolution of January 18, 1996, harmonization of political wills (namely, determination of the balance between legislative and executive power) was established[67]. By resolving issues of law, the CCRF resolves political issues. CCRF is involved in balancing the political process.

General social functions performed by the CCRF and arising from its specific political-legal nature include:

1. Socio-political function: CCRF activities to ensure general political stability and sustainability of political system in Russian society and state – via special legal means on administration of constitutional justice. Implementation of this function is the most representative when the CCRF makes its final decisions on the protection of political rights and freedoms of persons and citizens, federalism, local self-government, and the proceedings on certain constitutional and legal disputes between RF public authorities and RF subjects.
2. Economic function: participation of the CCRF in ensuring the most important constitutional principles for economic activity of the Russian society and state. Protecting all forms of RF ownership, support of private initiative and business, fair competition, regulation of budget, financial, and tax legal relations.
3. Social function: CCRF activity in RF on protecting the social rights of persons and citizens, regulation of social relations in the field of social security, the pension system, and the control of labor relations between employees and employers.
4. Clerical-ideological function: active work of the CCRF on cultivating and establishing fundamental constitutional values in RF. Mostly, via formulation of legal positions on various constitutional-legal issues.
5. Theoretical-cognitive or ideological function: because of their content, CCRF decisions contribute to forming and developing the general theory of law. CCRF decisions have a generally important methodological effect on forming and development of constitutionalism in RF.
6. Educational function: the CCRF contributes to a high level of legal awareness among management of public and local self-government bodies – in terms

67 Постановление Конституционного Суда РФ от 18 января 1996 г. № 2-П/1996 «По делу о проверке конституционности ряда положений Устава (Основного Закона) Алтайского края», СПС «КонсультантПлюс» (accessed: February 20, 2018).

of respect/observing the most important constitutional values and ability to protect rights/interests by means of constitutional justice.
7. Organizational-administrative function: summarizing and spreading of practice, establishing and development of international relations with other equivalent bodies of foreign countries (as part of the Venice Commission) headed by the CCRF Chairs[68].

In the course of constitutional legal proceedings, the CCRF refrains from determining/investigating the actual circumstances of any case where these are within the competence of other courts or bodies. On issues of internal activity, the CCRF adopts the Regulation[69].

4.3 Subject of Review by Constitutional Court

When disclosing the subject of constitutional review, let's consider the provisions of Article 125 in Constitution, Article 3 of Law "On Constitutional Court of the Russian Federation", other federal constitutional laws, and legal positions contained in decisions of the CCRF.

Thus, Article 125 of RF Constitution defines 5 groups of CCRF powers, where the subject of constitutional review is determined. Under Part 2 of Article 125, the following is verified by request of listed subjects:

Group 1:

- verifying the constitutionality of federal laws, which includes FCL, FL, RF laws. Then, verifying the normative legal acts of the President, the FC, SD, and Government;
- verifying the normative legal acts of RF subjects. Here, we refer to sources accepted under Article 71, 72 of RF Constitution;
- verifying international agreements that have not come into legal force;

Group 2:

- resolving jurisdiction disputes between federal public authorities or between public authorities of RF and RF subjects;

Group 3:

- verifying normative legal acts upon civil complaints or request of courts;

68 Р. В. Енгибарян, Э. В. Тадевосян, *Конституционное право*, Moscow 2017, p. 144.
69 Е. И. Козлова, О. Е. Кутафин, *Конституционное право*, Moscow 2017, p. 121.

Group 4:

- official interpretation of the Constitution;

Group 5:

- at the request of the FC, providing an opinion on the issue of impeachment.

In the first group of powers, the subject and limits of constitutional review are important. The CCRF verifies the constitutionality of the following legal acts:

1. Acts at the federal level – federal laws, normative acts of the President, FC, SD, and Government. The term "federal laws" should be seen broadly, while understanding both federal constitutional laws (CCRF practice includes cases related to review of federal constitutional law provisions: No. 1-ФК3 of December 31, 1996 "On Judicial System of the Russian Federation"; No. 5-ФК3 of September 27, 2002 ""“On Amendments and Addenda to Federal Constitutional Law "On Referendum of the Russian Federation", etc.). The CCRF reviews normative acts of the President, Government, and Federal Assembly chambers only. Acts of a non-regulatory nature (individual legal acts) are not subject to constitutional review by the CCRF. Apart from the listed (namely, departmental) acts, other normative acts are not reviewed by the CCRF.
2. Acts at the regional level – constitutions, charters, laws, sub-legislative acts, and normative legal acts of RF subjects. Here, the point is that not all the above regional normative legal acts are subject to constitutional review by the CCRF – only those issued within the competence of the Russian Federation and joint competence of the Russian Federation and its subjects. Thus, the CCRF is not authorized to review acts issued by public authorities of RF subjects within their competence. Besides, despite the absence of direct prescription, let's keep in mind that the CCRF may control acts issued by supreme state authorities of RF subjects only.
3. Intra-federative treaties – i.e., treaties between federal and regional public authorities, as well as between the regional public authorities. Here, we include public-legal agreements primarily related to the separation of powers (e.g., disputes arising from property contracts).
4. International RF treaties, which have not come into force. Not all international RF treaties form the object of constitutional review – only those subject to ratification or other approval by federal public authorities (i.e., interstate treaties).

Summarizing the characteristics for the first group of CCRF powers, let's note that all the above acts are verified by the CCRF for compliance with the RF

Constitution only – verification of the acts for compliance with federal constitutional laws and federal laws falls under jurisdiction of general courts. The constitutionality of those acts can be verified within abstract constitutional control – i.e., without reference to the application of the debated act in a specific case[70].

Legal acts are verified by the CCRF as part of abstract constitutional review – based on request, which may be submitted by the President, the FC, the SD, 1/5 members of FC or deputies of SD; RF Government; RF Supreme Court; legislative and executive bodies of RF subjects. In resolution No. 13-П of July 18, 2003, in the case of verifying the constitutionality of certain provisions of the RF Civil Procedure Code and Federal Law "On the Attorney's Office of the Russian Federation", the CCRF came to a conclusion on the possibility of appeal to the CCRF with a request to verify compliance between charters/constitutions of RF subjects and the RF Constitution – as part of abstract normative control by the RF Attorney General.

Unlike abstract review, specific constitutional review is related to verification of the debated act by the CCRF only due to its application in a specific case (or if the debated act should be applied in a specific case, according to applicant). CCRF resolution No. 1-П of January 27, 2004, on the case of verifying the constitutionality of certain provisions of the Civil Procedure Code, states legal position, according to which, at direct normative link between RF Government resolution and federal law (if these acts are applied or to be applied in specific case in indissoluble unity), the CCRF may recognize admissible both a court request on a specific case under review and a civil complaint of infringed constitutional rights and freedoms, where the constitutionality of both the federal law and the normative act of the RF Government is challenged.

A constitutional complaint or court request may form the basis for a CCRF case review, as part of a specific constitutional review. The complaint may be individual or collective – i.e., filed by civil groups/associations (including legal entities – commercial or non-commercial organizations). Besides, a complaint to the CCRF may be filed by other bodies and persons, which were granted the right (by federal law) to appeal to the court in the interests of citizens – in particular, to prosecution authorities. The mandatory term for admissibility of a complaint is that the debated act shall affect the constitutional rights and freedoms – i.e., rights and freedoms assumed directly in RF Constitution. In this

70 Е.И. Козлова, О.Е. Кутафин, *Конституционное право России: Учебник. 3-е изд., перераб. и доп.*, Moscow 2015, p. 76.

respect, a court (judge) of any level may submit a request to the CCRF. At that, an appeal to the CCRF, with suspension of proceeding – in case of doubts on constitutionality of the law applied/to be applied in the specific case – is not the right, but the duty of the relevant court.

When disclosing the CCRF powers to resolve competence disputes, keep in mind the following. In this case, subjects of appeal to the CCRF include public authorities only: the Constitutional Court does not resolve disputes between citizens, between legal entities, between citizen and organization, between organization and state, etc. The right of appeal to the Constitutional Court (to resolve a competence dispute) is not granted to all authorities – only to state bodies at the federal and regional level. Local self-government bodies have no access to the CCRF. Competence disputes are possible both in "horizontal aspect", i.e., between state bodies of the same level – between federal state bodies (e.g., between the President and FC, between the Government and SD, etc.) or between supreme state bodies of RF subjects, including one RF subject (e.g., between mayor of Moscow and governor of Moscow region, between mayor of Moscow and Moscow City Duma, etc.), and in "vertical aspect" – between state bodies of different levels (e.g., between RF Government and Legislative Assembly of Krasnoyarsk territory, between RF President and governor of Sverdlovsk region, etc.). In such disputes, the only subject of appeal is the resolution of the conflict in positions of the parties – on the right (violation, non-exercising) of a certain state body to constitutional power.

The Constitutional Court does not resolve economic disputes between state bodies, disputes on jurisdiction of cases to courts, etc. The form of appeal to the CCRF (to resolve a competence dispute) is a petition from the relevant federal or regional public authority. Besides, the RF President may appeal to the CCRF with such a petition – to exercise the power (assumed by Part 1, Article 85 of the RF Constitution) of implementing the coordination procedures on resolving differences between relevant public authorities[71].

The Constitutional Court is the only RF body vested with authority on official interpretation of the RF Constitution. The right of appeal to the CCRF with a request for interpretation is held by: the RF President; FC; SD; RF Government; and legislative bodies of RF subjects. The interpretation of the RF Constitution given by the CCRF is binding on all state bodies, local self-government bodies, legal entities, and individuals. We mean interpreting the Constitution as the

71 Ю.В. Кудрявцев, *Конституционный Суд России: опыт и проблемы (Международный научный семинар)*, "Государство и право" 2016, № 1, pp. 135–137.

independent authority of the Constitutional Court, implemented on the basis of a special request for interpretation.

By participating in the procedure for the removal of the RF President from office (assumed by Article 93 of RF Constitution), the CCRF gives an opinion on meeting the established procedure of accusing the RF President of high treason or other serious crime. A request to the CCRF is submitted by the FC, when the SD has filed the relevant accusation and RF Supreme Court has given an opinion on the evidence of the relevant crime in the actions of the RF President.

Other powers of the CCRF include those assumed by federal constitutional laws and inter-federative treaties. As an example, we can mention the power of the CCRF on verifying the constitutionality of documents and materials submitted due to implementing the initiative of holding a federal referendum (assumed by Federal Constitutional Law No. 5 of June 28, 2004 "On Referendum of the Russian Federation"); the power to implement mandatory constitutional review of an RF international treaty with a foreign state – on the admission of a new subject to the Russian Federation (assumed by Federal Constitutional Law No. 6-ФКЗ of December 17, 2001 "On Procedure of Admission to the Russian Federation and Forming a New Subject of the Russian Federation").

When exercising any power, the Constitutional Court resolves legal issues only and refrains from defining and investigating the actual circumstances – in all cases when it falls within the competence of other courts or bodies[72].

The CCRF is not entitled to legal proceedings on its own initiative.

4.4 Preliminary and Subsequent Review of Legal Norms

Legislatively, preliminary constitutional review in Russia is allowed only with regard to verifying the constitutionality of international treaties – prior to their ratification. Thus, reviewing an issue on compliance of international treaties (prior to ratification) with the local constitution is conducted in Russia on the basis of Item "d", Part 2, Article 125 of the RF Constitution and Article 88 of FCL CC. Criteria on the admissibility of verifying the constitutionality of these normative legal acts has already formed the subject of scientific analysis[73].

Verification of constitutionality for international treaties illustrates the rule-making activity of constitutional review bodies. In this case, it allows the avoiding

72 Х. Шейнин, *Конституционный Суд Российской Федерации в системе органов Судебной власти*, "Российская юстиция" 2016, № 3, p. 27.

73 М.С. Саликов, *Международные договоры РФ как объекты конституционного контроля*, "Российский юридический журнал" 2014, № 6, pp. 21–26.

of potential problems – with application/implementation of international treaty rules. CCRF activity includes established practice on exercising the preliminary review of international treaties prior to their ratification.

Thus, on March 19, 2014, the Constitutional Court recognized the international agreement, which had not yet come into force (on admitting the Republic of Crimea to the Russian Federation and forming the new subjects within the Russian Federation), to be compliant with the RF Constitution, while indicating its nature as principal will be expressed by citizens of the subject[74].

Previously, in 2012, after verifying the constitutionality of Protocol on RF Accession to the Marrakesh Agreement on Establishing the World Trade Organization, the CCRF came to the following conclusions. In this case, the state would have an additional opportunity for legitimate access to international legal and economic space – with simultaneous access to the means of international legal protection guaranteed by WTO law. In particular, to most favored nation treatment and national treatment for goods and services, protection from discriminatory local taxes, excise taxes, and customs duties, free transit, protection from discriminatory use of technical, sanitary, and phytosanitary barriers. Besides, accession to the Marrakesh Agreement would create guarantees against arbitrary use of other trade and political means – including quotas, anti-dumping and countervailing measures[75]. In this case, the CCRF decision ensured the development of international economic cooperation, with the participation of Russian economic entities.

Subsequent constitutional review is always conducted for normative legal acts, which have been adopted and put into action, where their application has caused various practical consequences. In Russia, this form of review can be split into the following types:

- abstract constitutional review. Legal acts are verified by the Constitutional Court as part of abstract constitutional review – based on a request, which may be submitted by: the RF President; FC; SD; 1/5 members of FC or deputies of SD; the RF Government; the RF Supreme Court; and legislative and executive bodies of RF subjects. Besides, resolution No. 13-П of July 18, 2003, in the case of verifying the constitutionality of certain provisions of the RF Civil Procedure Code and Federal Law "On the Attorney's Office of the Russian

74 Постановление Конституционного Суда РФ от 19 марта 2014 года № 6-П, „Рос. газ." 2014. 20 марта.

75 Постановление Конституционного Суда РФ от 9 июля 2012 года № 17-П, „Рос. газ." 2012. 20 июля.

Federation", the CCRF came to a conclusion on possibility of appeal to the CCRF with a request to verify compliance between the charters/constitutions of RF subjects and the RF Constitution – as part of abstract normative control by the RF Attorney General.
- specific constitutional review. This form of review is conducted by civil complaints (in the field of infringed constitutional rights and freedoms) and by request of courts submitted to the CCRF.

Most appeals to the CCRF relate to subsequent specific constitutional review. Between 14,000 and 19,000 civil applications are received on annual basis[76]. This indicates the confidence of people in the CCRF.

4.5 Legal Control Procedure

Appeal to the Constitutional Court (in the form of a request, petition or complaint) forms the reason for a case review. The basis is uncertainty detected in a normative legal act.

The decision to review a case on accepting a complaint for review/refusal to accept a complaint for review must be made no later than three months after the registration of the complaint (Part 1, Article 42 of FCL CC)[77]. This term also includes the period required for preliminary study of the complaint by CCRF judges[78].

One of essential features in the constitutional legal proceeding is that the CCRF decision on the case (operative part) is not immediately adopted/announced. Actually, this is typical of the Western judicial system – e.g., for Dutch, English courts, etc. – but absolutely non-typical of Russia, where parties find out who "won" and who "lost" right in the end of court hearing[79].

When the parties receive the decision, the Constitutional Court can officially clarify it (at the request of the applicant) as prescribed by Article 83 of FCL CC.

---

76 Статистика по решениям Конституционного Суда Российской Федерации, Официальный сайт Конституционного Суда http://www.ksrf.ru/ru/Decision/Statisticses/Pages/default.aspx (accessed: February 20, 2018).

77 Федеральный конституционный закон от 21 июля 1994 г. № 1-ФКЗ «О Конституционном Суде Российской Федерации», Собрание законодательства Российской Федерации. 25 июля 1994. № 13 ст. 1447.

78 А.А. Петров, *Основания отказа в принятии обращения к рассмотрению Конституционным Судом РФ*, "Журнал российского права" 2016, № 12.

79 М.А. Митюков, *Как исполняются решения Конституционного Суда Российской Федерации и конституционных (уставных) судов субъектов Федерации*, "Журнал российского права" 2017, № 7.

However, based on practice, the Constitutional Court is not supposed to explain its decisions – on the one hand, because it has this right only in case of appeal from authorized subjects; and on the other hand, the decisions are absolutely justified, their content is clear, logical, and unambiguous. In fact, an applicant's request to clarify the decision is often explained by a wish to receive a new interpretation of the debated legal provisions from the CCRF.

Thus, in one response to a request for clarification of a decision, the Constitutional Court noted the following: "While formally demanding to clarify the above definition, the applicant actually raises an issue on clarifying the legal provisions by the CCRF, which does not refer to CCRF competence, as defined in Article 125 of RF Constitution and Article 3 of Federal Constitutional Law "On Constitutional Court of the Russian Federation" (definition No. 1056-O-P of May 29, 2012)"[80].

In another response: "While formally demanding to clarify the above definition, the applicant actually doubts its validity and raises an issue on clarifying the legal provisions by the CCRF, which does not refer to CCRF competence, as defined in Article 125 of RF Constitution and Article 3 of Federal Constitutional Law "On Constitutional Court of the Russian Federation" (definition No. 1057-O-P of May 29, 2012)"[81].

The Constitutional Court does not analyze a court decision (regarding the criminal or civil case). Specific grounds for rejecting the approval of a CCRF appeal verification are as follows: an appeal, which assumes another legal document (instead of the debated law) or court decision – executive order, acts of government bodies; appeal of claim, which is not related to the material case and does not contain an issue for review (on violation or possible violation of various rights and independence).

In fact, a theoretical statement is defined as a statement of a citizen on noncompliance of legislation with the RF Constitution; at that, there is no definition that this law is applied, thus resulting in violation of constitutional rights.

As an example of such a situation, we can refer to proceedings at the suit of citizen S. to the CCRF – on recognizing an article of the General Civil Procedure Act (filing a claim to carrier of a transport agency at the location of this agency only) noncompliant with the Constitution – in terms of violating the constitutional right to equality of citizens to courts and laws.

---

80 Официальный сайт КС РФ http://www.ksrf.ru (accessed: February 20, 2018).

81 Ibidem.

The applicant justified the claim by the fact that the Consumer Protection Law is a rule, according to which, the client of a service (including a transport agency service) is fully authorized to appeal to the court at his/her convenience: by place of residence or at the location of the transport agency. The CCRF Secretariat rejected complaint, due to which, the following clarification was provided:

> Your appeal actually raises an issue on compliance of laws in the appealed article on the protection of consumer rights, where various jurisdiction rules are constituted. Under Article 3, resolution of such issues does not refer to CCRF powers. Assuming the above, the CCRF considers the fact that concluding on issues about definition/modification of jurisdiction in various civil cases refers to powers of legislator and does not fall within the competence of the CCRF.

4.6 Civil Complaint as Means of Controlling the Legal Norm

Civil complaint, as means of controlling the legal norm, is a popular instrument for the protection of human rights and freedoms in the Russian Federation. As noted above, every year, the right to file a constitutional complaint is exercised by more than 10,000 applicants, who individually or collectively apply to the supreme body for constitutional justice in Russia. In this view, it seems relevant to review the legislative regulation of this institution, to identify some problems, and to determine the ways of their resolution.

The institution of constitutional complaint and the problems related to exercising the right of appeal to the constitutional justice body are widely discussed in the academic environment. It appears that the right to file a constitutional complaint is derived from the right to judicial protection (Article 46 of RF Constitution), since a special type of appeal is implemented to protect human and civil rights and freedoms by constitutional justice bodies.

The review of a constitutional complaint by the Constitutional Court is assumed in Part 4, Article 125 of Constitution: by complaints of infringed constitutional rights/freedoms of citizens and by request of courts, the CCRF verifies the constitutionality of the law applied or to be applied in a specific case, as prescribed by federal law. At that, the legislator has stated that the right of appeal to the CCRF (with individual/collective complaint of infringed constitutional rights and freedoms) is held by citizens, whose rights and freedoms are violated by the law applied in a specific case, as well as civil associations and other bodies/persons specified in the federal law. That is, for appeal to the Constitutional Court, a decision of a general/arbitration court (adopted at first instance) is enough. At that, options of parallel appeal (against a decision of an ordinary court, to a higher authority) are not ruled out. Practice in this field is implemented as follows. Citizens may file complaints regarding the laws applied in a specific case. Thus, there are no restrictions. In practice, I personally used this method – at appeal of an ordinary court decision to a higher court, while exercising the right of appeal to the CCRF[82].

Apart from the provisions of the FCL CC, constitutional legal proceedings on these case categories are regulated by other laws. As noted above, other laws include the RF Law "On the Attorney's Office of the Russian Federation" dated January 17, 1992. In particular, provisions of Article 35 provide the RF Attorney General with the right of appeal to the CCRF regarding the violation of constitutional rights and freedoms of citizens (by a law applied or to be applied in a specific case).

Criteria on the admissibility of a complaint are set by the FCL CC. Thus, the law shall affect the constitutional rights and freedoms of citizens; review of the specific case shall be completed or initiated in a court or other law-enforcement body; the law shall be applied/to be applied in the specific case. Thus, the subject of reviewing the complaint at the CCRF may only be formed by the norm applied in the specific case. The specific case is the case, where the court or other law-enforcement body resolves an issue (based on norms of the relevant law) affecting the rights and freedoms of the applicant – with definition and/or investigation of the actual circumstances[83].

An important aspect in the institution of a constitutional complaint is also formed by the limits of verifying the constitutionality of the debated act: the applicant may demand verification of constitutionality for a law – by its form, procedure of signing, adopting, publishing, and enforcing; by observing the separation of powers, by separation of competence between federal public authorities, authorities and powers between RF public authorities and RF subjects[84].

Exercising the right to appeal with a constitutional complaint and its review in the CCRF is greatly affected by the CCRF's practice: to settle some gaps in the legislation, a broad interpretation of the FCL CC (regarding the constitutional-legal sense of its norms) is provided. First of all, in its decisions, the CCRF broadly interprets the object of constitutional review (by constitutional complaint) and the range of appealing subjects. The literature suggests that, initially,

---

82 http://doc.ksrf.ru/decision/KSRFDecision209629.pdf (accessed: February 20, 2018).

83 С.А. Кажлаев, *Генезис правовых позиций Конституционного Суда Российской Федерации*, "Журнал российского права" 2007, № 3, p. 10.

84 И.А. Кравец, *Конституционная жалоба: традиции и новации в механизме гарантий прав и свобод личности*, "Журнал российского права" 2003, № 8, pp. 26–27.

the "law" was understood as federal constitutional laws, federal laws, as well as constitutions of the republics, charters of other RF subjects, and laws of RF subjects – due to their application in specific case (by applicant's complaint)[85]. As part of a constitutional complaint, laws of RF subjects adopted by jurisdiction of the RF subject can also form the subject matter, if they violate constitutional rights and freedoms.

At that, as noted by S.E. Nesmeyanova, constitutional rights and freedoms are often violated by sub-legislative acts[86]. To address this gap in the legislation, the CCRF applies a broad interpretation for the object of constitutional complaint and determines the normative acts of the RF President and Government as subject to verification[87] – in the case of a direct normative link between them, if those acts are applied/to be applied in a specific case, in indissoluble unity.

As for the acts of legislative bodies, in resolution No. 11-П, the CCRF has recognized admissible the verification of constitutionality (by complaints of citizens) for RF SD decisions on amnesty[88]. In another decision, the CCRF clarified the range of appealing subjects, as part of a specific compliance assessment[89].

---

85 О.Н. Кряжкова, *Рассмотрение жалоб граждан о защите прав в Конституционном Суде Российской Федерации*, "Вестник публичного права" 2004, № 5, pp. 4–5.

86 С.Э. Несмеянова, *Судебная практика Конституционного Суда Российской Федерации с комментариями*, Moscow 2007, p. 14.

87 See: Постановление Конституционного Суда РФ от 14 мая 2009 г. № 8-П "По делу о проверке конституционности положения подпункта "б" пункта 4 постановления Правительства Российской Федерации "Об утверждении Порядка определения платы и ее предельных размеров за загрязнение окружающей природной среды, размещение отходов, другие виды вредного воздействия" в связи с запросом Верховного Суда Республики Татарстан", Справочная правовая система Консул ьтант Плюс.

88 See: Постановление Конституционного Суда Российской Федерации от 5 июля 2001 г. № 11-П «По делу о проверке конституционности постановления Государственной думы от 28.06.2000 г. № 492-Ш ГД «О внесении изменения в постановление Государственной думы Федерального Собрания Российской Федерации "Об объявлении амнистии в связи с 55-летием Победы в Великой Отечественной войне 1941 — 1945 годов" в связи с запросом Советского районного Суда города Челябинска и жалобами ряда граждан», СЗ РФ. 2001. № 29. Ст. 3059.

89 Постановление Конституционного Суда Российской Федерации от 17 февраля 1998 г. № 6-П по делу о проверке конституционности положений части второй статьи 31 закона СССР от 24.06.1981 г. «О правовом положении иностранных граждан в СССР» в связи с жалобой Яхья Дашти Гафура, СЗ РФ. 1998. № 9. Ст. 1142.

Apart from individual applicants, civil associations may also apply to the CCRF. As noted by L.V. Lazarev, the CCRF broadly interprets the term "civil association", without restricting its range only to those public associations which were formed under Article 30 of RF Constitution[90]. Based on CCRF practice, the following are recognized as full appealing subjects: religious associations and associations established for joint exercise of such constitutional rights as a right to the free use of their abilities and property for business and other economic activities not prohibited by law – legal entities.

We tend to agree with M.A. Mityukov that CCRF practice (in the purely legal sphere) shows some new powers – mostly, due to tasks and objectives of constitutional legal proceedings[91].

Then, at Constitutional Court review of cases on constitutional complaints, there are certain features of exercising the principles of legal proceedings. In general, hearing in session is oral. However, due to the significant number of cases on constitutional complaints (since 2010), according to introduced amendments, the CCRF began to apply the written hearing of appeals (Article 47.1 of FCL on RF CC). Extension of written proceedings in the CCRF may be considered as means for optimizing the exercise of constitutional review. It seems logical – in two decades of CCRF operation, it formed a significant number of legal precedents, which can be used for the resolution of similar appeals. Within this type of proceeding, the rights of parties to the constitutional proceeding are not violated in any way (as follows from provisions in Item 1, Article 47.1 of FCL "On RF Constitutional Court"). Moreover, due to invariability of CCRF legal positions, the final decision is mostly obvious for applicants in this case.

The review of a constitutional complaint results in one of two decisions – a resolution or a ruling. The nature of CCRF decisions is a debatable issue in Russian science. Meanwhile, regarding CCRF decisions on constitutional complaints, we agree with opinion of V.D. Zorkin – on presence of precedents in them[92]. The CCRF acquires the functions of constitutional and control rule-making in its practice.

The review of a complaint may also result in a resolution (ruling) with positive content, where legal positions previously determined by the CCRF apply

---

90 Л.В. Лазарев, *Правовые позиции Конституционного Суда России*, Moscow 2003, pp. 32–33.

91 М.А. Митюков, *Полномочия Конституционного Суда РФ в его собственной интерпретации*, "Вестн. Том. гос. ун-та." 2004, № 283, pp. 5–9.

92 В.Д. Зорькин, *Конституцию надо менять лишь тогда, когда ее уже нельзя не менять*, "Закон" 2006, № 11, p. 9.

to a similar situation. The legal consequences of such rulings are similar to resolutions.

Constitutional Court decisions act directly and do not need confirmation by other bodies and officials. CCRF decisions are also characterized by finality; they are not subject to appeal. To protect civil and human rights and freedoms (within the institute of constitutional complaint), apart from a decision on the constitutionality/unconstitutionality of a law, its exercise is also important.

Summarizing the review on institution of constitutional complaint, let's note the following. The CCRF power to resolve constitutional complaints (within specific constitutional review) is the main field of CCRF activity on human rights protection. The CCRF resolves legal issues on the applicant's complaint and acts as a body for the protection of constitutional rights and freedoms from violation by unconstitutional laws.

While reviewing the constitutional complaints of applicants, the Constitutional Court verifies them for compliance with admissibility criteria and resolves cases within the limits set by the Constitution and relevant legislation. When deciding on constitutionality/unconstitutionality of law in a specific case, the CCRF restores the rights of the applicant, but also of other persons subject to application of the law, as a law conflicting with the RF Constitution loses its legal force and gets excluded from the legal system.

5 Legal Nature and Legal Force of Decisions Made by Legal Norm Controlling Body

In the modern period, some studies were conducted, where conceptual ideas on the place of Constitutional Court decisions in the system of Russian law sources (justified in 1990s) were further developed. Legal positions of the Constitutional Court are of an interdisciplinary nature; they modify the legal regulation of social relations, thus defining the area of their further development – for establishment and improvement of the law-bound state[93]. In Russian legal doctrine, 3 essential characteristics of decisions made by the constitutional review body were interpreted: state-power dictation, external orientation, and the binding

93 See: Е.В. Жучкова, *Правовые позиции Конституционного Суда Российской Федерации по вопросам уголовного права и уголовного процесса*: дис. … канд. юрид. наук: 12.00.02, Moscow 2009, p. 18; А.А. Хахинова, *Правовые позиции Конституционного Суда Российской Федерации в правовой системе Российской Федерации*: дис. … канд. юрид. наук: 12.00.02, Moscow 2010, p. 3.

nature for legal subjects[94]. The opinion that development of judicial law often goes ahead of legislative process has found its confirmation[95].

Knowledge of Constitutional Court legal positions is important during law-making and law-enforcement activities, when citizens protect their rights in courts and other bodies. Eventually, it contributes to the real embodiment of the principles and norms set by the RF Constitution in public relations[96]. Constitutional Court decisions are universally binding – in unity of their statement part (with legal positions) and operative part (of a normative nature). The following features are distinguished for acts of constitutional review bodies: their normative-interpreting nature, and their generalizing, generally binding nature[97]. Meanwhile, rule-making opportunities of CCRF activities are limited; the normativity principle is not formulated for final decisions of constitutional courts. However, it logically follows from peculiarities of their content, when they confirm or cancel normative acts, due to which, certain normativity is "transferred" from the verified act to the decision made within constitutional review[98]. For its enhancement, the proposal is to establish a procedure determining the annulment mechanism – apart from defining the compliance (noncompliance) of a verified provision[99].

In this context, it is appropriate to distinguish the formal consolidation and material content in legal positions of the constitutional review body. Thus, sources of law include both CCRF decisions and legal positions contained in them, while finally determining the latter as source of law[100]. General principles of law (revealed by the CCRF during exercising the constitutional legal proceeding) correspond to legal positions. They are embodied in constitutional principles of law,

---

94 Л.В. Козлов, *Роль правовых позиций Конституционного Суда Российской Федерации в обосновании конституционных принципов института собственности*: дис. … канд. юрид. наук: 12.00.02, Moscow 2011, p. 9.

95 Д.В. Петрова, *Правовые позиции Конституционного Суда Российской Федерации по вопросам его деятельности и конституционного судопроизводства*: дис. … канд. юрид. наук: 12.00.02, Moscow 2008, p. 19.

96 *Конституция Российской Федерации в решениях Конституционного Суда России*, Moscow 2005, pp. 7–10.

97 В.А. Кряжков, *Конституционное правосудие в субъектах Российской Федерации*, Moscow 1999, p. 106.

98 Ж.И. Овсепян, *Становление конституционных и уставных судов в субъектах Российской Федерации (1990–2000 гг.)*, Moscow 2001, p. 643.

99 А.А. Белкин, *Дело о полномочиях судов (Комментарий к Постановлению Конституционного Суда от 16 июня 1998 г.)*, "Уголовное право" 2000, № 1, p. 75.

100 Н.В. Витрук, *Конституционное правосудие*, Moscow 1998, p. 92.

while refracting to sectoral principles and norms. Legal positions formulating and justifying the constitutional principles (without textual expression in the RF Constitution, but complementing or revealing its spirit and letter and potentially doctrinal in nature) must be placed at the top of the hierarchical system[101]. This position seems to be somewhat abstract and complicated: it is not quite clear whether all legal positions of constitutional review body correspond to general principles of law. Besides, let's remember that legal uncertainty of the concept "generally accepted principles/norms of international law", consolidated in Article 15 of RF Constitution, was addressed only upon adoption of special resolution by Plenum of RF Supreme Court[102]. Drawing an analogy, we can assume that the CCRF can clarify those legal positions that are considered general. Unclear criteria of their classifying as general or particular (especially, without textual expression in RF Constitution) will create even greater legal uncertainty.

The legal literature has focused attention on the peculiarities of formulating the legal position by the CCRF – in the statement part of its resolutions[103] and in rulings with positive content[104]. In both cases, scholars pointed to a weak link with specific cases, i.e., the high degree of abstraction (a sign of universality specific to the source of law). As a result, legal positions of the CCRF acquire the features of final conclusions on a resolved case – based on the individually defined (or previously justified) system of arguments. Most authors define them as such[105]. Normativity of CCRF final

---

101 Г.А. Гаджиев, *Принципы конституционного права, общие принципы права и конституционные принципы*, [in:] Ю.А. Тихомиров, Т.Я. Хабриева (eds.), *Конституция и законодательство. По материалам международной научно-практической конференции. Москва, 29 октября 2003 г.*, Moscow 2003, pp. 37–44.

102 See: Постановление Пленума Верховного Суда РФ от 10 октября 2003 г. № 5 «О применении Судами общей юрисдикции общепризнанных принципов и норм международного права и международных договоров Российской Федерации» (в ред. от 05.03.2013), "Рос. газ." 2003. 2 дек.

103 Б.А. Страшун, *Решения Конституционного Суда Российской Федерации как источник права*, "Конституционное правосудие" 2002, № 4, p. 155.

104 К.Б. Калиновский, *Проблемы использования решений Конституционного Суда Российской Федерации в досудебном производстве по уголовным делам*, [in:] *Совершенствование деятельности правоохранительных органов по борьбе с преступностью в современных условиях*, Tyumen 2010, pp. 23–28.

105 See: Н.В. Витрук, *Актуальные проблемы модернизации конституционного правосудия в России*, "Журнал российского права" 2011, № 10, pp. 119–133; В.О. Лучин, О. Н. Доронина, *Жалобы граждан в Конституционный Суд РФ*, Moscow 1998, p. 140; Т.Я. Хабриева, Н.С. Волкова, *Особенности казуального толкования*

decisions (resolutions and rulings with positive content) is recognized by some scholars[106].

Undoubted interest is caused by the opinion of some constitutional scholars, who propose to use the detailed study of CCRF decisions for systematizing its legal positions in a hierarchical manner[107]. The traditional statement in Russian legal science is the assertion on immanent exercising of human rights function by constitutional review bodies[108]. Its optimization could be reviewed via a synthesis of legal positions of the constitutional review body. However, systematization of CCRF acts has formed a subject for a relatively small number of scientific studies[109]. With regards to CCRF acts, normativity is studied in two

---

Конституции Российской Федерации, [in:] *Теоретические проблемы российско го конституционализма*, Moscow 2000, p. 42.

106 See: В.В. Захаров, *Решения Конституционного Суда Российской Федерации, как источник конституционного права:* дис. … канд. юрид. наук: 12.00.02, Penza 2004, p. 54; Н.А. Марокко, *О правовой природе решений Конституционного Суда Российской Федерации*, «Российский Судья» 2006, № 6, pp. 3–5; М.А. Митюков, *Акты Конституционного Суда РФ и конституционных (уставных) судов субъектов РФ: общая характеристика и статистический анализ*, "Журнал российского права" 2001, № 6, p. 16.

107 Л.В. Козлов, *Роль правовых позиций Конституционного Суда Российской Федерации в обосновании конституционных принципов института собственности*: дис. … канд. юрид. наук: 12.00.02, Moscow 2011, p. 11; М.С. Саликов, *Правовые позиции Конституционного Суда Российской Федерации: понятие и система*, "Правоведение" 2003, № 5, pp. 43–49.

108 See: Л.В. Андриченко, *Современная модель и механизм разграничения полномочий между федеральными органами государственной власти и органами государственной власти субъектов Российской Федерации*, "Журнал зарубежного законодательства и сравнительного правоведения" 2014, № 2, pp. 172–187; М.У. Коркмазов, *Защита конституционных прав и свобод человека и гражданина органами судебного конституционного контроля в Российской Федерации и государствах Центральной и Восточной Европы*: автореф. дис. … канд. юрид. наук: 12.00.02, Moscow 2014, p. 9.

109 See: Б.А. Малинчев, *Процессуальные институты в деятельности Конституционного Суда Российской Федерации:* дис. … канд. юрид. наук: 12.00.02, Moscow 2010, p. 161; И.С. Парфейников, *Правовые позиции Конституционного Суда Российской Федерации в сфере осуществления правосудия по уголовным делам*: дис. … канд. юрид. наук: 12.00.02, Moscow 2014, pp. 15–38; В.А. Сивицкий, *Систематизация конституционно-правовых актов Российской Федерации*: дис. … канд. юрид. наук: 12.00.02, Moscow 1999, pp. 115–122.

polar planes: denial[110] and assertion[111]. This relatively compromised approach is based on an assumption about the special or unique nature of CCRF decisions[112]. Unification of scientific ideas in Russian legal doctrine is currently impossible – due to the absence of relevant legal regulation.

Thus, we can clearly note the absence of questions to the normativity of legal positions contained in the dissenting opinion of a CCRF judge or in his/her written disagreement. Strictly speaking, this is the doctrinal interpretation of the legal provision verified by the CCRF, which does not imply the disclosure of its constitutional and legal meaning. Article 76 of FCL CC assumes the possibility of a dissenting opinion of a judge during decision-making by the CCRF. However, it gets no legal force or legal consequences for the law enforcer or legislator, while being beyond the specific compliance assessment. In FCL CC, legal consequences of a dissenting opinion or written disagreement are not assumed. The dissenting opinion of a CCRF judge is recognized as an unofficial (doctrinal) interpretation[113] or as symbiosis of competent and doctrinal interpretation[114].

Analysis of the theoretical grounds for the legal nature and legal force of decisions made by legal norm controlling body allowed the following conclusions:

- identifying a problem of the relation between CCRF decisions and their legal positions;
- today, a CCRF decision does not form a normative legal act, although some of them have normative features. The law enforcer applies the formal source with its stated normativity – the resolution or ruling of the CCRF.

---

110 See: В.С. Нерсесянц, *Суд не законодательствует и не управляет, а применяет право*, [in:] *Судебная практика как источник права*, Moscow 1997, pp. 34–41.

111 See: Л.В. Лазарев, *Правовые позиции Конституционного Суда России*, Moscow 2003, p. 5.

112 В.Д. Зорькин, *Прецедентный характер решений Конституционного Суда Российской Федерации*, "Журнал российского права" 2004, № 12, pp. 3–9; А.А. Малюшин, *Вопросы совершенствования юридических форм и механизма реализации конституционно-судебного правотворчества в современных условиях*, "Российский Судья" 2012, № 11, pp. 4–7.

113 See: В.А. Кряжков, Л.В. Лазарев, *Конституционная юстиция в Российской Федерации*, Moscow 1998, p. 251.

114 See: Д.А. Басангов, *Юридическая природа особого мнения судьи Конституционного Суда Российской Федерации*, "Журнал российского права" 2006, № 2, p. 26; Л.А. Маршава, *Особое мнение судьи Конституционного Суда РФ, как вид неофициального толкования норм Основного закона*, "Вестник Челябинского гос. ун-та." 2012, № 27, pp. 27–29.

Thus, normativity of Constitutional Court decisions is characterized by the following legal consequences. First, courts of general jurisdiction/arbitration courts, when reviewing cases upon the coming into force of a CCRF resolution (including the cases with proceedings initiated prior to coming into force of this CCRF resolution), are not entitled to follow the normative act or its individual provisions that have been recognized by the CCRF resolution as noncompliant with the RF Constitution, or apply the normative act/its individual provisions in an interpretation different from the one given by the CCRF in its resolution. Second, legislative state bodies and officials must bring the laws and other normative acts in line with the RF Constitution – due to the CCRF resolution.

6 Constitutional Value of Legal Norm Controlling Body

Developing practice of constitutional review bodies affects the enhancing of constitutionalization in national legal systems. Constitutional review forms the value approach of legislative bodies to content of adopted laws. Perception of constitutional norms by current legislation forms an ideal result of its modernization process[115]. By its practice, CCRF makes a significant contribution to implementing the constitutional-legal ideas in normative legal acts. First of all, they include the concept of building a law-bound state, ensuring the rule of law and constitutional legality.

The constitutional principle of the law-bound state is disclosed in the legal positions of the CCRF[116]. The practice of constitutional review bodies plays an undeniable role in developing constitutionalism[117]. Constitutional review contributes to ensuring the rule of law[118], enhancing constitutional legality, and protection of human rights and freedoms. At that, a conclusion that there is a "crisis of identity for legal system"[119] does not appear justified. In this view, it

115 А.А. Уваров, *Вопросы адекватного отражения конституционных норм в действующем законодательстве*, "Конституционное и муниципальное право" 2015, № 12, pp. 15–18.

116 Постановление Конституционного Суда РФ от 25 апр. 2001 года № 6-П, "Рос. газ." 2001. 15 июня.

117 В.Д. Зорькин, *Аксиологические аспекты Конституции России*, "Сравнительное конституционное обозрение" 2008, № 4, pp. 7–20.

118 В.А. Кряжков, М. А. Митюков, *Конституционный Суд РФ: развитие конституционно-правового статуса*, "Государство и право" 2011, № 10, pp. 12–28.

119 В.Н. Синюков, *Российская правовая система: введение в общую теорию*, Moscow 2010, p. 7.

is necessary to study the influence of constitutional-control rule-making and development of constitutionalism in national legal systems.

The task of constitutional-control activity is the protection of constitutional values, where personal rights and freedoms form the highest one. Constitutionalization of the national legal system implies an exact reproduction of legal positions formed in sectoral legislation during constitutional-control practice.

The Constitutional Court became a symbol of establishing the democratic institutions of the constitutional system[120]. Due to constitutional-judicial control, the national legal system was subject to qualitative changes caused by implementation of modern constitutional principles[121]. While consistently following the rule-of-law direction, the Constitutional Court helped to bring the formal-legal content of constitutional norms in line with the objective needs of legal regulation. In terms of enhancing constitutionalization in the Russian legal system, identifying the goals of the legislator during law adoption (by constitutional review body) becomes essential. This practice, created by the CCRF, contributes to correct decision-making when assessing the compliance of a law with the constitutional provisions. Thus, this method was used by the CCRF for analyzing the legal provisions protecting the interests of minor children[122] and incapable citizens[123]. With regard to provisions of the RF Constitution, the constitutional review body used the term "legal logic", which helped to justify the constitutional idea on inadmissible opposition of legislative, executive, and judicial authorities[124]. Thus, the definition of target settings implemented in law adoption affects the constitutional-legal assessment of its content.

120 Р.Э. Арутюнян, *Конституционное правосудие, как фактор формирования судебного конституционализма*, "Вестник ПГЛУ" 2011, № 3, pp. 39–43.

121 Т.Я. Хабриева (ed.), *Конституция Российской Федерации: от образа будущего к реальности (к 20-летию Основного Закона России)*, Moscow 2014, pp. 41–46; И. Марино, *Конституционно-правовая школа Института законодательства и сравнительного правоведения при Правительстве Российской Федерации в теории и практике российского конституционализма*, "Журнал зарубежного законодательства и сравнительного правоведения" 2015, № 1, pp. 5–15.

122 Постановление Конституционного Суда РФ от 23 сент. 2014 года № 24-П, "Рос. газ." 2014. 3 окт.

123 Постановление Конституционного Суда РФ от 27 июня 2012 года № 15-П, "Рос. газ." 2012. 13 июля.

124 Постановление Конституционного Суда РФ от 11 дек. 1998 года № 28-П, "Рос. газ." 1998. 29 дек.

The legal position contained in the operative part of a Constitutional Court decision, in conjunction with the conclusions of the statement part, forms the basis for future legal regulation. It forms a reference point in the legislative process and in activities of all state and local self-government bodies[125].

This approach is perceived in the practice of constitutional legal proceedings of Russia. Thus, the dynamic-transforming function of constitutional justice[126] determines directions for the constitutionalization of national legislation. The CCRF consistently contributes to the development of "live" constitutionalism. It brings great results: from January 1, 1992 to January 1, 2018, the CCRF adopted 514 decisions (over 75 % were implemented)[127]. It was facilitated by detailed regulation of the process for implementing the CCRF decisions in federal constitutional law.

The Constitutional Court discloses the potential of constitutional norms – by setting limits for legal regulation of social relations. Thus, it came to the conclusion that regulatory norms, which directly consolidate certain rules of conduct, do not have to be contained in the same normative legal act with norms assuming legal liability for their violation[128]. It means that the legislator does not have to follow the "rule of conduct - liability" sequence, but may choose a different method of legal regulation. Thus, the constitutional review body actually improves the legal space and affects the modernization of the national legal system. The CCRF is an important public authority exercising constitutional review and protecting the constitutional rights of persons and citizens – in particular, by recognizing those laws that are compliant/incompliant with the RF Constitution, including the disclosure of their constitutional-legal meaning.

7 Social Perception of Legal Control

Unfortunately, the author does not have information on sociological studies regarding the confidence of citizens in the reviewed institute. Meanwhile, given

---

125 М.А. Мокосеева, А.С. Бакун, Ю.И. Ковалевская, *Конституционная юстиция Российской Федерации и Республики Беларусь: сравнительно-правовой анализ: м онография*, Yoshkar-Ola 2015, pp. 174–175.

126 Н.С. Бондарь, *Конституционное правосудие – преобразователь современного конституционализма (к вопросу о формировании судебного конституционализма)*, [Электронный ресурс], Конституционный Суд РФ. Режим доступа: URL: http://www.ksrf.ru (accessed: February 20, 2018).

127 http://www.ksrf.ru (accessed: February 20, 2018).

128 Постановление Конституционного Суда РФ от 16 июля 2015 года № 22-П, "Рос. газ." 2015. 29 июля.

the fact that the actual field of Constitutional Court activity is related to the review of complaints on the violation of constitutional rights and freedoms of citizens (annually, it receives 14,000–19,000 civil complaints), the CCRF really has a significant effect on protecting the constitutional rights of citizens and constitutionalization of the national legal system. This may indicate people's trust in the Constitutional Court of the Russian Federation.

Conclusions

Summarizing the present chapter, let's note that introducing the institution of constitutional review in its actual form – in particular, its exercise by the RF Constitutional Court – was among the achievements of state-legal reforms, which occurred during establishment of the Russian Federation.

Such a type of specialized constitutional review body was not specific to the pre-revolutionary or Soviet periods of development. At that, a statement on the rule of law (independent of the political trends prevailing in the country) was formed long ago[129]. Thus, in 1912, eight years prior to the establishment of the first-ever Constitutional Court of Austria, Russian scholar A. Yashchenko pointed to the potential establishment of a constitutional review body – Constitutional Court (Tribunal)[130]. Later, during the formation of the new state (Union of Soviet Socialist Republics) in the territory of the former Russian Empire, it was necessary to discuss and resolve an issue on a mechanism of ensuring the "supervision of legality in terms of the Constitution and all-union legislation"[131]. The pre-history of local constitutional justice is characterized by a period when the Supreme Court of the USSR ensured verification of constitutionality for acts of central public authorities of the USSR and union republics (1924–1933)[132].

In Soviet legal literature, the attitude to constitutional review (supervision) was of a dual nature. According to one approach, it acts as guarantee for the operation of legal norms, while interaction between the Parliament and the Constitutional Court serves as basis for the protection of human rights[133].

---

129 Б.А. Кистяковский, *Социальные науки и право*, Moscow 1916, p. 654.

130 А. Ященко, *Теория федерализма. Опыт синтетической теории права и государства*, Yuriev 1912, pp. 352–353.

131 П. Стучка, *СССР и РСФСР. Советская Конституция в вопросах и ответах. 4-е перераб. и доп издание*, Moscow 1924, p. 58.

132 See more details in: М.А. Митюков, *Судебный конституционный надзор 1924–1933 гг.: вопросы истории, теории и практики*, Moscow 2005, p. 208.

133 Л.Я. Дадиани, *К вопросу о сущности, формах и оценке института конституционного надзора*, "Труды Университета дружбы народов им. П.

According to another approach, judicial constitutional review is of an expressly political nature –a bourgeois element of the constitution that contributes to weakening the independence of the Parliament[134].

The main reason for forming a body for constitutional justice in the modern Russian Federation is a change of in the balance of society and state. The attitude to the RF Constitution, as the fundamental state law, has changed. Based on the meaning of the RF Constitution and role of modern the RF Constitutional Court in ensuring its full action, we can formulate the following basic functions: supreme public authority in Russia for protecting the constitutional system; supreme arbiter in constitutional disputes between sectors of the Russian government or between government and society, between government and citizens; supreme arbiter in conflicts of Russian legislation with international legal norms[135].

The modern RF Constitutional Court holds a special position. It corresponds to a specialized body of constitutional review formed by the state to ensure the correct application of the RF Constitution and laws determined by it, protecting the political, economic, social, and moral values of society. It forms an integral element of the state, due to which, it can be considered a law-bound state aiming to establish a strong socio-political system, a system of legality, protecting civil interests. The RF Constitutional Court is a judicial body of constitutional review, which independently and self-sufficiently exercises judicial power – via constitutional legal proceedings[136].

The main goals of the RF Constitutional Court include: protection of the constitutional system, protection of the fundamental rights and freedoms of citizens and ensuring the supremacy and direct effect of the Russian Constitution throughout Russian territory.

Лумумбы. Т. XX. Экономика и право" 1967, Вып. 2, pp. 39–64; И.А. Ледях, *Буржуазные конституции в период общего кризиса капитализма*, Moscow 1966, pp. 282–333.

134 Р.Х. Вильданов, *Конституции в политической системе буржуазного общества*, Moscow 1968, pp. 125–140; И.Д. Левин, *Крах буржуазной демократии и современное государственное право капиталистических стран. Вып. 1. США*, Moscow 1951, p. 61.

135 В.Д. Зорькин, *Право в условиях глобальных перемен*, Moscow 2013, p. 180.

136 О Конституционном Суде Российской Федерации: федер. конституц. закон от 21 июля 1994 г. № 1-ФКЗ (в ред. от 28.12.2016 г.), published on the Official Internet portal of legal information http://www.pravo.gov.ru (accessed: 20.01.2018).

Apart from independence and self-sufficiency, the basic principles of the Constitutional Court's activities include collegiality, publicity, competitiveness, and equality of the parties.

The RF Constitutional Court differs from other judicial bodies by its special legal position: only it has the right to exercise constitutional judicial review in Russia, determine the compliance of legislation with the Russian Constitution, resolve competence disputes between state bodies, etc.

Decisions of the RF Constitutional Court are binding throughout Russia – for all representative, executive, and judicial bodies of state power and local self-government, enterprises, organizations, institutions, as well as officials, citizens, and associations.

Thus, the RF Constitutional Court holds a special place in the Russian legal system, acts as means of restricting state power and guarantor of the balance of power, protects constitutional rights and freedoms of persons and citizens, and ensures the supremacy and top legal force of the Constitution.

Ion Guceac

Constitutional Justice in the Republic of Moldova

Abstract: A thesis is put forward in the analysis of constitutional judiciary in Moldova that it is based on the European model of judicial control of legal norms, and that the Constitutional Court plays a significant role in protecting the constitution and making it the actual basic law of the Republic of Moldova.

Keywords: the European model of reviewing the legal norms, Constitutional Court, autonomy and independence, The Constitutional Court and other organs of state power, cognition of the Constitutional Court

Introduction

Constitution is fundamental law, which has supremacy over other laws. This aspect is determined by the fact that the Constitution forms the mechanism of state structure and legal basis of the state, proclaims fundamental rights/freedoms of person and citizen, and ensures the legal guarantees of their implementation. Based on this undeniable reality, the Constitution of the Republic of Moldova proclaims the supremacy of law, while declaring the Constitution a supreme law of society and state. Any law or legal act conflicting with provisions of the Constitution is invalid (Article 7 of the Constitution of the Republic of Moldova).

To ensure that the supremacy of the Constitution shall not be just a constitutional principle, it requires an arrangement of conditions for the introduction of special guarantees, which would enable the manifest of the Constitution as law with supreme legal force. A system of penalties (in case of violating the constitutional norms by one of established powers) shall find its place within this system of guarantees.

It is widely recognized that monitoring the constitutionality of laws is the most reliable guarantee for the supremacy of the Constitution.

As a rule, the need to introduce the constitutional review is confirmed by the following arguments: the legislator is prone to mistakes, the Constitution contains gaps, and the absence of legal constitutional review forms conditions for legal instability, in addition to other arguments.

Upon the declaration of independence in the Republic of Moldova, the country put an end to the monopoly of the Communist Party, introduced various forms of property, and proclaimed the principles of national sovereignty, separation of powers, political pluralism, independence of judicial power, and other democratic freedoms. These changes took place in the context of applying the basic principles of European constitutionalism. Law-bound state, civil peace, democracy, human dignity, human rights and freedoms, free development of person, justice, and political pluralism were recognized as the highest values of the state. Thus, prerequisites for measures ensuring the supremacy of the Constitution (control over the constitutionality of laws) have appeared. In general, the introduction of control over constitutionality of laws can be defined as a necessary condition for building the law-bound state in the Republic of Moldova. Later on, the Constitutional Court of the Republic of Moldova played an important role in keeping the balance between main branches of government and ensuring the constitutionality of laws.

Given the recent events in our state and the ways that the Constitutional Court has used to fully or partially implement its mission, we believe that this institution (fundamental for any law-bound state) is subject to some changes, to ensure better definition of its role and avoid any doubts about authorities, training, and the morality of constitutional judges. The Constitutional Court cannot provide "magical" decisions all the time; by decision-making, the court cannot be turned into a panacea for all conflicts between public authorities. To avoid conflicts, which often prevent the uninterrupted functioning of public authorities, it would be better to base the reformation of the Constitutional Court upon prior negative experiences of this institution's activities.

1 Motives for Introduction and Key Dilemmas of Control over Legal Norms

Defining the concept of control over constitutionality and its regulation in Moldova's laws is a complex process, both in theory and in practice.

The state of affairs in this area is mostly determined by the specific development of national constitutionalism[1].

Constitutional control in Republic of Moldova was applied for the first time in 1918–1940, when the right-bank part of Moldova (Bessarabia) was part of the Romanian Principality. Thus, the Romanian Constitution of 1923 and 1938

1 I. Guceac, *Constituția la răscruce de mileniu, Ediția a II-a revăzută și adăugită*, București, Editura Academiei Române 2016.

authorized the Court of Cassation for verifying the constitutionality of laws, declaring the norms conflicting with the Constitution inapplicable.

Socialist constitutions, which were applied in the Republic of Moldova prior to the declaration of independence, granted the Supreme Council (Parliament) a status of the highest public authority with subordination of all other state bodies.

In this view, control over constitutionality of laws was within the competence of the Supreme Council. The very idea of establishing a special body exercising control over the constitutionality of laws adopted by a "supreme public authority" was missing. Thus, the Constitution of the Moldavian Soviet Socialist Republic of 1978 (Article 107, Part 4) referred the monitoring of compliance with the Constitution to powers of Presidium of Supreme Council of the Moldavian Soviet Socialist Republic (Moldavian SSR)[2].

Following the revision of the 1978 Constitution, the Constitutional Review Committee (elected by legislative body) was established, including a Chairperson, Vice Chairperson, and five Committee members. Experts "in the field of politics and law" could be candidates. Members of the Constitutional Review Committee were elected for 10 years. The Committee was entitled to a preliminary and subsequent review of laws and other normative acts on the initiative of Parliament, President of Republic, Chairperson of the Parliament, Parliamentary Committees, Government, Supreme Court, and Attorney of Moldova. However, during the validity of the 1978 Constitution, the Committee was not established, as the Supreme Council of MSSR had not approved this initiative, while analysing the draft law on constitutional review in the first reading.

The Declaration on Sovereignty of Moldova, adopted by the Parliament on June 23, 1990, established the full authority of the Republic on all issues of state and public life, as well as the supremacy of the Constitution and laws throughout the territory of Moldova. As a result, laws and other normative acts of the USSR were allowed for use only upon their ratification by the Parliament of the Republic. The effect of previously adopted acts, which conflicted with the sovereignty of Moldova, was suspended.

Equal legal opportunities on involvement in the administration of state and public affairs were guaranteed to all citizens, political parties, public organizations, mass movements, and religious organizations and operated according to provisions of the Constitution. The Declaration noted that the separation of

---

2 Constitution of Moldovan SSR of April 15, 1978, https://ru.wikipedia.org/wiki/Конституция_Молдавской_ССР_(1978) (accessed: March 20, 2018).

legislative, executive, and judicial power is a basic operating principle of Moldova as a democratic, law-bound state.

In the Declaration of Independence, adopted by the Parliament of the Republic of Moldova on August 27, 1991, Moldova was proclaimed a sovereign, independent, and democratic state, which could freely—without outside interference—resolve its present and future issues according to the ideals and sacred aspirations of people, in historical and ethnic spaces of national formation. The Parliament has also ruled to apply throughout the territory only the Constitution, laws, and other normative acts adopted by legally established bodies of Moldova.

In its essence, constitutional justice implies that institutionalization shall be ensured in the manner assumed directly by the Constitution, which states that basic rules for arrangement and functioning of constitutional courts shall be assumed by norms at the constitutional level.

Thus, the European model of constitutional review was taken as a basis for preparing a draft of a new constitution and consolidated in the Constitution of the Republic of Moldova, which was adopted on July 29, 1994[3].

The legal basis for the Constitutional Court of the Republic of Moldova is contained in provisions of the Constitution, Section 5 (Articles 134–140) and in some other articles of Fundamental Law. Thus, Article 62 of Constitution states that the Constitutional Court, by proposal of the Central Election Commission, decides on recognizing or not recognizing (in the case of election law violation) the deputies' mandates. Article 141 (assuming the right to initiate the revision of Constitution) states that drafts of constitutional laws shall be submitted to Parliament only with the opinion of the Constitutional Court adopted by at least four judges.

According to final and transitional provisions (Section 7, Article 5), the Constitutional Court had to be established within six months since the Constitution has come into force. However, the first staff of the Constitutional Court was formed on February 23, 1995 upon the adoption of the Law on Constitutional Court on December 13, 1994[4]. Judges of the Constitutional Court took office starting June 16, 1995, when the Code of Constitutional Jurisdiction was adopted[5].

---

3 Constitution of Moldova dated July 29, 1994. Monitorul Oficial No. 1 of August 12, 1994.

4 Law No. 317 of December 13, 1994 on Constitutional Court. Monitorul Oficial No. 008 of February 07, 1995.

5 Law No. 502 of June 16, 1995. Code of Constitutional Jurisdiction. Monitorul Oficial No. 053 of September 28, 1995.

2 Legislative Stability of Legal Norm Controlling Body

Even though it had no experience of exercising the constitutional review, the Republic of Moldova had to resort to a gradual revision of constitutional legislation. At that, the republic's "political atmosphere" played an important role, as did the resolutions and opinions of the Venice Commission, given the experience of foreign colleagues, recommendations of scientific-practical conferences, etc.

In a year, the Parliament of the Republic of Moldova made its first amendments to the Law on Constitutional Court (Article 25) and Code of Constitutional Jurisdiction (Part 1, Article 38)[6]. Due to these amendments, the list of subjects entitled to appeal to the Constitutional Court was added by the National Assembly of Gagauzia (Gagauz Yeri). The National Assembly of Gagauzia gained the right to appeal to the Constitutional Court upon verifying the constitutionality of laws, regulations, and resolutions of the Parliament; decrees of the President, decrees, ordinances, and orders of the Government; and international treaties involving the Republic of Moldova, which limited the powers of Gagauzia[7]. In 1998, the Parliament of the Republic of Moldova amended the Law on the Constitutional Court (Article 25) and Code of Constitutional Jurisdiction (Part 1, Article 38) again. At that, the right to appeal to the Constitutional Court was vested in the Parliamentary Lawyer[8].

After several years of Constitutional Court activity, issues of legitimacy regarding these acts arose. To clarify some issues related to Constitutional Court decisions, the Parliament stated that acts of the Constitutional Court were official documents, binding for all public authorities, legal entities, and individuals in the country. Normative acts (parts thereof) recognized unconstitutional shall be invalid and shall not be applied since the adoption of this Constitutional Court decision.

---

6 Law No. 917-XIII of July 11, 1996 on amendments to Law on Constitutional Court and Code of Constitutional Jurisdiction Monitorul Oficial al R.Moldova No. 54–55/513 of August 15, 1996.

7 Gagauzia (Gagauz Yeri) is autonomous territorial unit with special status, as form of Gagauz self-determination, forming an integral part of Moldova, which independently (within its competence) solves political, economic, and cultural issues on behalf of the entire population. Administration in Gagauzia is ensured on the basis of Moldovan Constitution, other laws of Moldova, which do not conflict with them, Code of Gagauzia, and normative acts of National Assembly (Halk Toplusu) of Gagauzia.

8 Law No. 18-XIV of May 14, 1998 on amendments and addenda to some legislative acts, Article XII. Monitorul Oficial al R.Moldova No. 60–61/411 of July 02, 1998.

The Law on the Constitutional Court was added with a new article (Article 28^1, mandatory exercising of Constitutional Court acts by public authorities), according to which, the Government, no later than three months after publishing the Constitutional Court resolution, had to provide the Parliament with a draft law on amendments/addenda to the normative act (part thereof) declared unconstitutional or recognizing it as invalid. The law obliged the President and the Government of the Republic of Moldova to provide amendments and addenda to the act (part thereof) declared unconstitutional or recognize it invalid (within two months since publishing the Constitutional Court resolution) and, if necessary, issue or adopt the new act[9].

In June 2002, the Parliament of the Republic of Moldova adopted an organic law expanding the powers of the Constitutional Court. Upon amending Part 1, Article 4 of the Law on the Constitutional Court, a constitutional jurisdiction body was able to confirm the results of the elections for Parliament and the President of Moldova, recognize the validity of mandates for deputies and the President of Moldova, and state the circumstances justifying the dissolution of Parliament, removal of President from office, temporary exercise of his/her duties, and the impossibility of exercising the President's duties for more than 60 days. The Constitutional Court was also entitled to state the circumstances resulting in annulment of the deputy's mandate, make decisions regarding the mandate's annulment, and declare the mandate vacant[10].

To avoid misunderstandings regarding decisions made by the Constitutional Court (at equally divided affirmative/negative votes of judges), the legislation on constitutional legal proceedings was amended. It was stated that in case of determining the results of an equally divided vote by judges (during the adoption of a resolution on the constitutionality of a normative act or international treaty), the normative act or international treaty would be considered constitutional and the case dismissed. In other cases (in the case of an equally divided vote by judges), it was assumed that the resolution, opinion, or decision was not made and review of relevant case postponed[11].

9 Law No. 1137-XV of June 14, 2002 on amendments and addenda to Law on Constitutional Court No. 317-XIII of December 13, 1994. Monitorul Oficial al R.Moldova No. 103–105/795 of July 18, 2002.

10 Law No. 1157-XV of June 21, 2002 on amendments and addenda to some legislative acts. Monitorul Oficial al R.Moldova No. 102/775 of July 16, 2002.

11 Law No. 1570-XV of December 20, 2002 on amendments to Article 27 of Law on Constitutional Court No. 317-XIII of December 13, 1994 and Article 66 in Code of Constitutional Jurisdiction No. 502-XIII of June 16, 1995. Monitorul Oficial al R.Moldova No. 1–2/4 of January 15, 2003.

The Moldovan legislation on constitutional proceeding was also amended regarding the subject of control. In 2010, the Parliament excluded certain resolutions of the Parliament, decrees of the President, and decisions of the Government in the category of subjects reviewed by the Constitutional Court. Relevant addenda were also made to Code of Constitutional Jurisdiction[12].

In 2016, Parliament expanded a list of subjects entitled to appeal to the Constitutional Court, while adding the councils of administrative units (1st, 2nd level) and the National Assembly of Gagauzia at verifying the constitutionality of laws, regulations, and resolutions of the Parliament; decrees of the President; decrees, ordinances, and orders of the Government; and international treaties involving the Republic of Moldova[13].

Amendments of the Parliament also affected the provisions of Law on the Constitutional Court (on early termination of judges' powers). Thus, the following was recognized as prerequisites for termination of the judge's powers by depriving of immunity: establishing the final act of transaction (directly or through a third party), making/participation in making a decision without resolving the actual conflict of interests (according to legislation on regulating the conflict of interests), and non-submission/refusal to submit a declaration on property and personal interests[14].

There were other legislative changes in constitutional jurisdiction, although some of these changes were cosmetic and affected the less important legal aspects on control over the constitutionality of laws. So, some innovations affected the circumstances resulting in annulment of the deputy's mandate[15], the remuneration of the Chairperson and judges of the Constitutional Court[16], some terms of pension benefits for judges of Constitutional Court[17], the status of the

---

12 Law No. 95 of May 21, 2010 on amendments and addenda to some legislative acts, Article I, Article II. Monitorul Oficial No. 98–99/295 of June 15, 2010.

13 Law No. 24 of March 4, 2016 on amendments and addenda to some legislative acts. Monitorul Oficial No. 100–105/192 of April 15, 2016.

14 Law No. 134 of June 17, 2016 on amendments and addenda to some legislative acts. Monitorul Oficial No. 245–246/515 of July 30, 2016.

15 Law No. 141-XV of March 21, 2003 on amendments to some legislative acts. Monitorul Oficial al R.Moldova No. 70–72/318 of April 15, 2003.

16 Law No. 447-XVI of December 28, 2006 on amendments and addenda to some legislative acts. Monitorul Oficial No. 51–53/239 of April 13, 2007.

17 Law No. 399-XVI of December 14, 2006 on amendments and addenda to some legislative acts. Monitorul Oficial No. 39–42/169 of March 23, 2007; Law No. 139-XVIII of December 29, 2009 on amendments to some legislative acts. Monitorul Oficial No. 197–200/674 of December 31, 2009; Law No. 264 of December 9, 2016 on amendments

Assistant Judge at the Constitutional Court[18], the status of staff at Secretariat of the Constitutional Court[19], etc.

The unfinished attempts to amend the legal status of the Constitutional Court in the Republic of Moldova could not be ignored. Thus, in 2009, the President of Moldova initiated an attempt to develop a new Constitution[20].

A commission on constitutional reform established a workgroup on constitutional study and analysis, which included prominent academic constitutionalists of Moldova, who drafted the new Constitution[21]. The draft assumed some changes in the arrangement and functioning of the Constitutional Court. Thus, to avoid political influence on judges of the Constitutional Court, a staff of nine judges (appointed for a nine-year term) was suggested, subject to proviso that one and the same person could not be elected to this position for more than one term. Powers of the court also included the exercise of constitutional review, upon request, for resolutions/ordinances of the Government as well as international treaties involving the Republic of Moldova prior to their ratification by the Parliament.

In 2016, the Ministry of Justice drafted a law to amend the Constitution of the Republic of Moldova, on arrangement and functioning of the Constitutional Court. Along with the deputies, representatives of the Parliament, the President's Office, the Ministry of Justice, and the Constitutional Court, the draft involved Evgeny Tankev (Deputy Chairperson of Venice Commission and former Chairperson of Constitutional Court in Bulgaria); Tudorel Toader (member of the Venice Commission, judge of the Constitutional Court in Romania, at the time); Miroslav Granat (a judge in Poland's Constitutional Court); Alexander Balthasar (Chairperson of the Institute on State System and Administrative Reform at the Austrian Federal Chancellery); Michael Grepper (former judge of

---

and addenda to Article 21 of Law on Constitutional Court No. 317-XIII of December 13, 1994. Monitorul Oficial No. 453–458/901 of December 23, 2016.

18 Law No. 1221-XIII of June 26, 1997 on amendments and addenda to Law on Constitutional Court and Code of Constitutional Jurisdiction. Monitorul Oficial al R.Moldova No. 51–52/457 of August 7, 1997.

19 Law No. 222 of September 17, 2010 on amendments and addenda to some legislative acts. Monitorul Oficial No. 210/696 of October 26, 2010.

20 Decretul privind constituirea Comisiei pentru reforma constituțională. În:Monitorul Oficial al Republicii Moldova No. 174–176/548, December 4, 2009.

21 I. Guceac, *Constituția la răscruce de milenii, Ediția a II-a revăzută și adăugită*, București, Editura Academiei Române 2016, pp. 316–324.

the Supreme Administrative Court in Germany); and Balazs Mazhtheny, Andras Pap, Gabor Sulek, and Balazs Vizi of the Hungarian Academy of Sciences.

The constitutional law draft proposed changes to subjects who entitled to appeal to the Constitutional Court and the number and term of office for constitutional judges.

As for the subjects with right to appeal to the Constitutional Court, Item g, Part 1, Article 135 of the Constitution (on powers of the Constitutional Court to resolve exceptional cases on unconstitutionality of legal acts submitted by the Supreme Court of Justice) proposed to replace the words "Supreme Court of Justice" with the words "judicial instances". Besides, it was proposed to increase the number of constitutional judges to 7:2 of them appointed by the Parliament, two by the Government, two by the Supreme Council of Magistracy, and one by the President of Moldova.

Regarding the term of office for the judge (and the number of these terms), it was proposed to elect one person—and the same person—for a nine-year term, without renewal. The Parliament could adopt a law amending the Constitution not sooner than six months after submission of the relevant proposal (Constitution of the Republic of Moldova, Article 143). The law is adopted by two-thirds of the deputies' votes. If, within a year after submitting a proposal to amend the Constitution, the Parliament does not adopt the relevant constitutional law, then the proposal is considered null and void.

At that, recognized experts in the field of constitutional review fear for the future of the Constitutional Court, believing that the destruction of mechanisms providing the final court decisions in disputes on constitutionality of normative acts (by Parliament) compromises the capabilities and potential of the Constitutional Court (as a body protecting the Constitution) and faith of society in its independence, impartiality, and objectivity[22].

3 Legislative Position of the Constitutional Court

3.1 The Constitutional Court and the President of Moldova

The legal nature, value, and functions of the President of Moldova require provision of presidential powers in the text of the Constitution. Thus, studying the relations between head of state and the Constitutional Court and defining their essence shall start with provisions of Article 77 in the Constitution of the

---

22 V. Puşcaşu, *Independenţa Curţii Constituţionale în oglinda strmbă a legislatiei*, Timpul, February 16, 2010.

Republic of Moldova, according to which, the President of Moldova represents the state and serves as guarantor of sovereignty, national independence, unity, and territorial integrity of the country.

Hence, it follows that presidential powers (regarding the only body of constitutional jurisdiction) shall be aimed at achieving the above goals. At that, the Constitutional Court of the Republic of Moldova believes that the President shall act as guarantor of sovereignty, national independence, unity, and territorial integrity of the country, while following constitutional norms, which consolidate the presidential powers and acts of supreme representative body in relevant areas[23].

According to legislation, the President of Moldova may appeal to the Constitutional Court to monitor the constitutionality of parliamentary laws/resolutions, decrees and ordinances of Government, interpretations of the Constitution, and a statement of circumstances justifying the dissolution of Parliament. Appeal to Constitutional Court is based on Law on the Constitutional Court and Code of Constitutional Jurisdiction.

To clarify the controversial issues on the constitutionality of some laws, 27 appeals were filed to the Constitutional Court on behalf of the President of Moldova from February 1995 to December 2005: three appeals in 1995, 1996, 1997, and 1998; six appeals in 1999; eight appeals in 2000; and one appeal in 2004[24]. In 2001, 2002, 2003, and 2005, the President did not appeal to the Constitutional Court[25]. In 2015, the President filed one appeal[26]; and in 2017, three appeals[27].

As for the powers of the Constitutional Court with regards to the head of state, it is agreed that they are designed to ensure the supremacy of the Constitution. Thus, the Constitutional Court ensures control of constitutionality (by request) for decrees of the President, confirms results of presidential elections, states the circumstances justifying the removal of the President from office or temporary

---

23 Resolution on control of constitutionality for Decree No. 376-V of June 24, 2010 declaring June 28, 1940 as Day of Soviet Occupation. Monitorul Oficial No. 126–128 of July 23, 2010.

24 Hotărîre pentru aprobarea Raportului cu privire la exercitarea jurisdicției constituționale în anul 2005. Monitorul Oficial al R.Moldova No. 9–12/1 of January 20, 2006.

25 Hotărîre pentru aprobarea Raportului cu privire la exercitarea jurisdicției constituționale în anul 2005. Monitorul Oficial al R.Moldova No. 9–12/1 of January 20, 2006.

26 Report on exercise of constitutional jurisdiction in 2015. lex.justice.md/UserFiles/File/2016/mo106.../raport_1.docx (application date: March 20, 2018).

27 Raportul privind exercitarea jurisdicției constituționale în anul 2017. Chișinău, Arc, 2018.

exercise of his/her duties, as well as the impossibility of exercising the President's duties for more than 60 days (Article 135 of Constitution).

Recently, appeals to the Constitutional Court (to clarify the circumstances on temporary fulfilment of duties by President of Moldova) have increased. Thus, on October 19, 2017, the Government of Moldova appealed to the Constitutional Court with a request to state the circumstances justifying the temporary fulfilment of duties by the President of Moldova, to ensure the constitutional duty on appointing and taking the office by candidate for Minister of Defence (nominated by the Prime Minister of the Republic of Moldova). Having reviewed this appeal, the Constitutional Court recognized the deliberate refusal of the President to fulfil his/her constitutional duty in the framework of the procedure on appointing the Minister of Defence (appointing the candidate repeatedly suggested by the Prime Minister) as a circumstance justifying the temporary fulfilment of duties by the President of Moldova, which, under Article 91 of the Constitution, indicates a temporary impossibility to fulfil this duty[28].

According to the Election Code (Article 112), resolution of the Constitutional Court confirms the results of elections and recognizes the election of certain candidates as valid[29]. In case violations of the Election Code (affecting the election results) are committed during elections/counting of votes, the Constitutional Court may invalidate the elections.

The Constitutional Court recognized that during the confirmation of results for elections of the President of Moldova, its main task is to assess the degree of compliance between election process, constitutional provisions, and other generally accepted principles of democratic elections[30]. The Court found that the 2016 election of the President of Moldova was arranged and held in terms of political, financial, and social crisis aggravated by distrust in state institutions. According to the Court, regulatory legislation ensuring the democratic election has certain gaps and ambiguities. This, in particular, refers to collecting/verifying the signatures in support of the candidates, funding/conducting the election campaign, actual results of election debates, introducing the provisions on mass media and provisions on holding the 2nd round of presidential elections, and

28 Conclusion on statement of circumstances justifying the temporary fulfilment of duties by President of Moldova—to fulfil the constitutional duty on appointing the Minister. Monitorul Oficial No. 18–26 of January 19, 2018.

29 Election Code, Monitorul Oficial No. 81 of December 08, 1997.

30 Resolution No. 34 of December 13, 2016 on confirming the election results and recognizing the validity of mandate for President of Moldova *(appeal No. 139e/2016)* Monitorul Oficial No. 2–8 of January 6, 2017.

the arrangement of voting at special and foreign polling stations (suspicion of using the methods similar to "election tourism"). In this view, the Constitutional Court emphasized the need to revise the entire electoral legislation related to the election of the President, Parliament, and local public authorities, while merging it into an amended Election Code, the general and special provisions of which shall ensure fair and transparent election under constitutional principles. To this end, the Constitutional Court sent six submissions to the Parliament.

A rather interesting practice was formed in the Republic of Moldova with stating the impossibility to fulfil presidential duties (by the Constitutional Court). Thus, the Constitutional Court believes (results of reviewing the only appeal are described below) that deliberate inaction of the President means a temporary inability to fulfil his/her duties for subjective reasons (reluctance), which justifies the statement on temporary fulfilment to ensure the exercise of these constitutional duties. Temporary fulfilment of duties (caused by a deliberate refusal to fulfil one or more constitutional duties) and circumstances justifying the temporary exercise of presidential duties are stated by the Constitutional Court in each specific case, according to powers provided by the Constitution[31]. In other cases, given the deliberate refusal of the President to fulfil the constitutional duty on appointing the candidates (repeatedly proposed by Prime Minister), the Constitutional Court noted that according to the Constitution, the President is temporarily unable to fulfil his/her duty, which justifies the statement on temporary fulfilment to ensure the exercise of this constitutional presidential duty. According to the Court, by deliberate refusal, the President removed himself/herself from exercising this constitutional duty[32].

3.2 The Constitutional Court and Government of the Republic of Moldova

The Constitution of the Republic of Moldova (Article 96, Part 1) states that the Government shall ensure the exercise of internal/external policy and general guidance of public administration. Thus, the fundamental role of the Government

31 Resolution No. 28 of October 17, 2017 on interpreting the provisions of Article 98, Part 6 in combination with Article 1, Article 56, Article 91, Article 135, and Article 140 in Constitution of Moldova (non-fulfilment of constitutional duties by President), Monitorul Oficial No. 18–26 of January 19, 2018.

32 Conclusion No. 1 of January 2, 2018 on statement of circumstances justifying the temporary fulfilment of duties by President of Moldova—to exercise the constitutional duty on appointing the certain members of Government. Monitorul Oficial No. 33–39 of February 2, 2018.

is to ensure the internal and external political line of the country. From a legal point of view, this aim is reflected in providing the Government with legal initiative (Article 73 of Constitution) and power to adopt resolutions, ordinances, and decrees for exercising the laws adopted by the Parliament. In the course of exercising its powers, the Constitutional Court may qualitatively affect the law-making activity of the Government. In one of its rulings, the Constitutional Court determined that normative acts adopted by the Government on the basis/in pursuance of laws cannot conflict with provisions of these laws or exceed their limits; in pursuance of its prerogatives, the Government shall strictly comply with constitutional and legislative provisions[33]. To ensure these principles, the Constitution (Article 135) entitles the Constitutional Court to exercise the constitutional review of governmental decrees and ordinances.

In turn, the Government participates in forming the constitutional review body. Thus, according to the Constitution (Article 136), it appoints two judges of the Constitutional Court. Later on, the Constitutional Court stated that in the course of appointing the judges, the Government shall act in the spirit of constitutional commitment to legality principle and appoint new judges within the period established by law[34].

3.3 The Constitutional Court and Parliament of the Republic of Moldova

In the Republic of Moldova, as in any state aiming to be law-bound, legislative power is exercised by a representative body, which is independent of other public authorities. According to the Constitution (Article 6), legislative, executive, and judicial authorities of Moldova are separated; in exercise of their prerogatives, they interact under provisions in the Fundamental Law of the country. Meanwhile, in the course of exercising the constitutional jurisdiction, Constitutional Court affects the activity of legislative body in one way or another. In turn, the Parliament has a certain effect on activities of the Constitutional Court. By general rules, the way the Constitutional Court is structured and

33 Decree on exceptional case of unconstitutionality for Item 18 in Regulation on Procurement of Medicines and Other Medical Products for Needs of Healthcare System, adopted by Governmental Decree No. 568 of September 10, 2009. Monitorul Oficial No. 258–261 of November 15, 2013.

34 Decree No. 12 of May 12, 2016 on interpreting the provisions of Article 116, Part 2, 4 and Article 136, Part 1 of Constitution (extending the term of office for judges till appointment of successors). Monitorul Oficial No. 416–422 of December 2, 2016.

functions are regulated by provisions adopted by the Parliament of Moldova. Under the Constitution of the Republic of Moldova (Article 72), the structure and activities of the Constitutional Court are regulated by organic law adopted by the Parliament. At that, the Parliament of the Republic of Moldova may amend the relevant organic law without consulting the Constitutional Court, i.e., there are no provisions obliging the legislative body to request its opinion, the rule following from general separation of powers.

Despite that, the Constitutional Court of the Republic of Moldova secured itself from an unreasonable restriction of independence by the Parliament. In this view, the Constitutional Court stated that Parliament was only allowed to "enhance and expand the functions and mechanisms of the constitutional jurisdiction body". According to the Court, if we interpret this constitutional norm to the effect that Parliament can limit, exclude, or reduce actual powers, this is equivalent to depriving it of its content, thus giving up the improvement of constitutional democracy (the aim pursued by the constitutional legislator when revising the Constitution), which is absolutely unacceptable. Any legal norm or legislative amendment adopted by the Parliament, which may result in any blocking of Constitutional Court activity, is primarily unconstitutional[35].

The Constitution of the Republic of Moldova (Article 62) provides the Constitutional Court with the power to recognize the mandates of deputies or reject them (at violation of electoral laws)[36]. According to the Court, its main goal in confirming the election results is to assess the degree of compliance between election process, provisions of national laws, and other generally accepted principles of democratic elections. At that, the Court cannot express its opinion on validity of evidence reviewed in court proceedings (regarding the legality of acts adopted by electoral bodies). According to the Court, it is competent to recognize the elections as invalid, in the case of violations that affect voting results[37].

According to the Constitution (Article 136), two judges of the Constitutional Court are appointed by Parliament. The Constitutional Court of the Republic of Moldova believes that by consolidating the relations between the authorities, the Constitution defines actions on their cooperation in decision-making

---

35 Decree on constitutional review, Part 4, Article 23, Law No. 317-XIII of December 13, 1994 on Constitutional Court. Monitorul Oficial No. 119–121 of May 31, 2013.

36 No such cases.

37 Decree No. 29 of December 9, 2014 on confirming the results of elections to Parliament of Moldova (held on November 30, 2014) and recognizing the validity for mandates of deputies elected to Parliament of Moldova. Monitorul Oficial No. 1–10 of January 16, 2015.

to establish balance and exclude arbitrary decisions/abuses. So, in the course of appointing judges, the Parliament shall follow the constitutional provisions and legal rules on interaction procedure[38].

By request, the Constitutional Court ensures constitutional review for laws/ resolutions of the Parliament (Article 135 of Constitution). The Court found that under Constitution, any law may be subject to constitutional review. Constitutional review of laws is an exclusive prerogative of Constitutional Court to ensure the separation of powers in the state[39].

Constitutional review of laws adopted by Parliament is not an obstacle to democracy, as it allows the parliamentary minority/citizens to oversee the compliance with provisions of Constitution, while being a counterbalance to parliamentary majority (in some cases, where it deviates from the spirit and letter of the Constitution)[40].

It's important to note that the Constitutional Court does recognize the actual risk of pressure from Parliament (during review of certain cases) and the fact that a potential responsibility to Parliament may indirectly affect the judge, who will try to avoid the decisions unacceptable to legislative power, or make decisions expected of them in order to earn "trust"[41].

3.4 The Constitutional Court and Courts of Moldova

Basic principles of a law-bound state include principle of legality, which follows from provisions in Part 3, Article 1 of Constitution, stating that the Republic of Moldova is democratic, law-bound state, and separation of state powers is the basis for the arrangement and functioning of a state institutional mechanism. According to the Constitutional Court, compliance with this principle is ensured

---

38 Decree No. 12 on interpreting the provisions of Article 116, Part 2, 4 and Article 136, Part 1 of Constitution (extending the term of office for judges till appointment of successors). Monitorul Oficial No. 416–422 of December 2, 2016.

39 Decree No. 15 on interpreting the Article 135, paragraph 1, Item g in Constitution of Moldova. Monitorul Oficial No. 033 of May 22, 1997.

40 Decree No. 2 on interpreting the Article 135, Part 1, Items a, g in Constitution of Moldova (exceptional case of unconstitutionality). Monitorul Oficial No. 55–58 of March 11, 2016.

41 Decree No. 18 of June 2, 2014 on constitutional review of Law No. 109 dated May 3, 2013 amending and supplementing some legislative acts (Law on Constitutional Court and Code of Constitutional Jurisdiction) (status of Constitutional Court judges, powers of Constitutional Court, and constitutional legal proceedings). Monitorul Oficial No. 256–260 of August 29, 2014.

only in case of meeting the other principles of a law-bound state—legality is a term for the existence and means of ensuring any constitutional principle. Thus, a practical separation of powers in the state is a primary condition for the establishment and functioning of a law-bound state[42]. The theory of separating the powers forms the very concept of *independent justice*. Being among three branches of government in a modern democratic state, justice assumes individual and institutional independence. In this view, "independence" defines the relations between judicial power, other branches of government, and bodies aiming to ensure real independence. The Constitutional Court of the Republic of Moldova determined that an exclusive right to administer justice in the name of law belongs to the judge (as the only holder of judicial power), who, according to the Constitution (Part 1, Article 116), is independent, impartial, and irremovable by law. Thus, judicial power is one of three state branches, which is independent, separated from legislative and executive branches, and has its powers exercised via court instances, according to principles and provisions assumed by Constitution, laws, and other normative acts[43].

According to laws, the Constitutional Court promotes the smooth functioning of public authorities, including judicial bodies, within the constitutional principle of separation and interaction. In turn, the state judicial system, along with Parliament and the Government, participates in forming the staff of the Constitutional Court. Thus, according to the Constitution (Article 136), two of six judges are appointed by the Supreme Council of Magistracy—an independent body established for the arrangement/functioning of the judicial system and serving as guarantor of independence for judicial power[44]. To fill the vacant position of the judge at the Constitutional Court of the Republic of Moldova, the Supreme Council of Magistracy holds a competition[45].

42 Decree No. 3 of February 9, 2012 on constitutional review for some provisions of Law No. 163 dated July 22, 2011 amending and supplementing some legislative acts. Monitorul Oficial No. 38–41 of February 24, 2012.

43 Decree No. 3 of February 9, 2012 on constitutional review for some provisions of Law No. 163 dated July 22, 2011 amending and supplementing some legislative acts. Monitorul Oficial No. 38–41 of February 24, 2012.

44 Law on Supreme Council of Magistracy. Monitorul Oficial No. 186–188 of August 22, 2003.

45 Who will take an office of Chairperson at Constitutional Court of Moldova? https://ru.sputnik.md/society/20180206/17136110/Kto-zajmet-mesto-predsedatelja-Konstitucionnogo-suda Moldovy.html (accessed: March 20, 2018).

Although the Superior Council of Magistracy is involved in nominating the judges, the fundamental difference between the Constitutional Court and courts of general jurisdiction is that under the Constitution, a body of constitutional jurisdiction is not a judicial body and cannot form the part of the judicial system or an integral part of judicial power[46].

According to Fundamental Law (Item g, Article 135), the Constitutional Court of the Republic of Moldova resolves the exceptional cases on unconstitutionality of legal acts (submitted by Supreme Court of Justice). Basic elements of exceptional cases of unconstitutionality are a need for constitutional review and triangular relation between party to proceeding (with rights and interests infringed by any unconstitutional norm), court instance (referred to in case of unconstitutionality), and the Constitutional Court (resolving the exceptional cases of unconstitutionality). The Constitutional Court of the Republic of Moldova came to the conclusion that syntagma (an exceptional case of unconstitutionality) may be interpreted as initiating the procedure (by courts of general jurisdiction, on initiative of the parties/own initiative) to verify the compliance of law or another normative act (in full or mostly in part) to constitutional norms[47] or procedural means of protection used to draw the attention of Constitutional Court to incompliance between Constitution and legal provisions applied by court in case review[48].

According to the Constitutional Court, requests on exceptional cases of unconstitutionality may be submitted by:

(1) court instance, on its own initiative, which, following the supremacy of the Constitution, has no right to apply controversial (from constitutional point of view) provisions;
(2) parties to proceeding (including their representatives) with rights/interests potentially infringed due to use of unconstitutional provisions in case resolution[49]. While resolving the exceptional cases of unconstitutionality,

46 Decree on constitutional review for provisions of Article 2, Part 2 and Article 52 in Law No. 216-XIV of December 12, 1998 "On budget for 1999". Monitorul Oficial No. 048 of May 13, 1999.

47 Decree on interpreting the Article 135, Part 1, Item g in Constitution of Moldova. Monitorul Oficial No. 033 of May 22, 1997.

48 Decree on interpreting the Article 135, Part 1, Items a and g in Constitution of Moldova (exceptional case of unconstitutionality). Monitorul Oficial No. 55–58 of March 11, 2016.

49 Decree on interpreting the Article 135, Part 1, Items a and g in Constitution of Moldova (exceptional case of unconstitutionality). Monitorul Oficial No. 55–58 of March 11, 2016.

Constitutional Court activities are intertwined with activities of court instances (general jurisdiction). Procedure on resolving the exceptional case of unconstitutionality assumes 2 stages:

- *judicial*—preliminary stage, which means filing a request on exceptional cases of unconstitutionality within the judicial proceeding (judge makes a decision, which may result in an appeal to the Constitutional Court);
- *constitutional review* for exceptional cases of unconstitutionality (exercised by the Constitutional Court only).

The Constitutional Court found that at the first stage, the decisive role was played by the judge of general jurisdiction, who ultimately decided on filing an appeal to the Constitutional Court. He may be considered *"the first constitutional judge"* defining unconstitutionality in the course of applying the law. Thus, when revealing the unconstitutionality of an applied act or receiving a request on unconstitutionality from the parties, the judge shall initiate a procedure of constitutional review.

Lately, exceptional cases of unconstitutionality have become quite important. Back in 1995, the Constitutional Court did not receive any appeal on exceptional cases of unconstitutionality; in 2016, 116 of 163 appeals were of such nature[50].

3.5 The Constitutional Court and Other Public Authorities

As a public political-legal body, the Constitutional Court does not belong to any state branch of government: legislative, executive, or judicial. Being independent, the Constitutional Court ensures its main function (constitutional review of normative acts, abolition of legal norms conflicting with Constitution) and interprets the Constitution, thus forming "a true support of state and democracy, which contributes to effective activity of public bodies within the constitutional principles of separation, balance, interaction, and mutual control of authorities in the state". Given the complexity/nature of powers and procedure of their exercise, the Constitutional Court concluded that it forms a public political-legal body[51].

Principles forming the basis of Constitutional Court activities include a principle of independence[52]. Due to special status and constitutional independence

---

50 Report on exercise of constitutional jurisdiction in 2016. Monitorul Oficial No. 73–77 of March 10, 2017.

51 Decree on constitutional review of Part 4, Article 23, Law No. 317-XIII of December 13, 1994 on Constitutional Court. Monitorul Oficial No. 119–121 of May 31, 2013.

52 Law No. 317 of December 13, 1994 on Constitutional Court. Monitorul Oficial No. 008 of February 7, 1995.

of other bodies, the Constitutional Court resolves organizational, financial, material-technical, informational, personnel, and other issues ensuring the conditions for its activities.

The Constitutional Court has its own budget (by proposal from Plenum of the Constitutional Court, it is approved by Parliament and included in the state budget—Part 1, Article 37 of Law on Constitutional Court). Thus, funds for ensuring its activities are assumed by the individual article of the state budget on an annual basis. The Constitutional Court independently determines the amount of expenses without any external interference[53].

To a certain extent, the procedure of applying to the Constitutional Court may be considered a cooperation mechanism. In institutional terms, several situations can be noted where the Constitutional Court interacts with other state bodies. One example covers state bodies involved in procedures conducted at the Constitutional Court. Thus, in the course of constitutional review, the Constitutional Court interacts with subjects of constitutional legal relations entitled to make a request. Apart from the President and the Government of the Republic of Moldova, this right is held by the Minister of Justice, the Supreme Court of Justice; the Attorney General, members of Parliament; the parliamentary faction, the People's Lawyer, the People's Lawyer protecting the rights of the child, councils of administrative-territorial units (1st, 2nd level), and the National Assembly of Gagauzia (Gagauz Yeri) in cases assumed by law.

The Law on the Constitutional Court (Article 9) states that within 15 days, public authorities and other legal entities, despite the type of ownership and organizational-legal form, shall provide data, documents, and other available materials requested by the Constitutional Court for the exercise of powers.

Constitutional Court activities are also in touch with activities of social insurance bodies, which assign/pay pensions and monthly life support to constitutional judges. At that, social insurance bodies are entitled to control the authenticity of documents confirming the seniority/insured income and issued by competent authorities (Article 21[1] of Law on the Constitutional Court).

According to the Constitution of the Republic of Moldova, the Attorney's Office is an independent public institution of judicial power, which contributes to the administration of justice and the protection of rights, freedoms, and the legitimate interests of individuals, society, and the state via criminal and

53 Decree on constitutional review for provisions of Article 2, Part 2 and Article 52 in Law No. 216-XIV of December 12, 1998 "On budget for 1999". Monitorul Oficial No. 048 of May 13, 1999.

other legal proceedings[54]. In the Republic of Moldova, the Attorney's Office is recognized as an autonomous public institution of the judicial system, which contributes (in criminal and other legal proceeding) to respecting the rule of law, administration of justice, and the protection of rights and legitimate interests of individuals and society[55]. The Attorney's Office is independent of legislative, executive, and judicial power; any political party; socio-political organization; and any other institutions, organizations, or individuals.

At that, the legal framework that defines the activities of the Attorney's Office (especially in terms of improvement) is becoming more attractive via certain resolutions of the Constitutional Court. Thus, the Court determined that the attorney's role in criminal proceedings is comprehensive and consists of protecting the rights and freedoms of individuals, society, and the state (from phenomenon of crime), in stating and disclosing all the committed crimes, in preventing the new crimes, etc. According to the Court, review of complaints by attorney (on appeal of the defendant, defence counsel, victim, and other persons, whose rights were, in their opinion, violated) is a special form of control to detect/prevent the violation of laws and mistakes made by prosecution authorities or bodies ensuring the operative-investigative activities[56].

The Constitutional Court also commented on the election and dismissal of the Attorney General. Thus, the Court noted that the procedure of appointing the Attorney General (consolidated in the Constitution) is a guarantee of his/her independence and impartial fulfilment of duties established by the Law on Attorney's Office. Regarding the position of Attorney General, the Constitutional Court noted that it corresponds to the highest rank in the system of prosecution bodies. The value of this position is determined by the functions of the Attorney's Office: representing the general interests of society; protecting the supremacy of law and rights/freedoms of citizens; managing/ensuring the criminal prosecution; and legal representation of prosecution at judicial instances[57].

---

54 Law on amending and supplementing the Constitution of Moldova. Monitorul Oficial No. 415 of November 29, 2016.

55 Law on Attorney's Office. Monitorul Oficial No. 69–77 of March 25, 2016.

56 Decree on constitutional review for some provisions of Articles 298, 300, and 313 in Criminal Procedure Code introduced by Law No. 264-XVI of July 28, 2006 "On Amending and Supplementing the Criminal Procedure Code of Moldova". Monitorul Oficial No. 175–177/23 of November 9, 2007.

57 Decree on constitutional review of some parliamentary decisions related to appointment and dismissal of Attorney General dated May 20, 2013. Monitorul Oficial No. 125–129/14 of June 14, 2013.

Among the subjects entitled to appeal to the Constitutional Court, the Law on the Constitutional Court also lists the Attorney General. Thus, the Law on Attorney's Office directly states that the Attorney General, who represents the Attorney's Office in relations with other public authorities (in country, abroad), is entitled to appeal to the Constitutional Court, according to the law. Statistical data serve as important indicators characterizing the effective use of this right. Thus, from February 1995 to December 2005, 25 appeals were sent to the Constitutional Court on behalf of the Attorney General (1 appeal in 1996 and 2005, 2 in 1998, 7 in 1999, 8 in 2000, and 6 in 2001)[58]. In 2011, the Attorney General filed 2 (5 % of the total) appeals—1 was returned, and 1 was rejected[59]. The same number of appeals was submitted to the Constitutional Court in 2017[60].

The Constitution of the Republic of Moldova (Article 59^1) consolidates the right of the People's Lawyer to ensure, promote, and protect basic human rights and freedoms[61]. Under current laws, the People's Lawyer (Ombudsman) ensures the observance of human rights and freedoms by public authorities, organizations, enterprises (despite the type of ownership and organizational-legal form), non-profit organizations, and officials of any level. He/she promotes the protection of human rights and freedoms by preventing their violation and monitoring/reporting the procedure on observing the human rights and fundamental freedoms at the national level (by improving the laws on the protection of human rights and freedoms, international cooperation in this field, and promoting the human rights, freedoms, and mechanisms of their protection via use of procedures regulated by law). The People's Lawyer, protecting the rights of the child, shall exercise the powers on ensuring the rights/freedoms of the child and national implementation of the UN Convention on Rights of the Child by central/local public authorities and officials of any level[62]. In one of its rulings, the Constitutional Court noted that the institute of the People's Lawyer is a guarantor

58 Hotărîre pentru aprobarea Raportului cu privire la exercitarea jurisdicției constituționale în anul 2005. Monitorul Oficial al R.Moldova No. 9–12/1 dated June 20, 2006.

59 Report on exercise of constitutional jurisdiction in 2011, submitted on the basis of Article 10 in Law on Constitutional Court No. 317-XIII of December 13, 1994 and Article 80 in Code of Constitutional Jurisdiction No. 502-XIII of June 16, 1995. http://www.constcourt.md/pageview.php?l=ru&idc=14&t=/obsie/godovoi-doklad

60 http://www.constcourt.md/tabview.php?l=ro&idc=13&t=/Prezentare-generala/Date-statistice& (accessed: March 20, 2018).

61 Law on supplementing the Section II in Constitution of Moldova. Monitorul Oficial No. 155–161 of May 19, 201.

62 Law on People's Lawyer (Ombudsman). Monitorul Oficial No. 110–114 of May 9, 2014.

of democratic development, which manifests itself as an intermediary between society and the state administration to ensure the dialogue between them and monitoring over observance of universal values (human rights and freedoms). According to the Court, the institute of the Ombudsman has a special legal nature, while being the only one overseeing the administration in its relations with citizens[63]. The Constitutional Court noted that the institute of the People's Lawyer plays an important role in the consolidation of democracy, the law-bound state, and human rights. It is a guarantor of democratic development and mediator in relations between society and the state, which ensures the dialogue and respect of universal values (human rights and freedoms). The Ombudsman's role also assumes increased administrative responsibility of authorities via an impartial and objective analysis of behaviour for public authorities, recommendations of *lex ferenda*, and filing the lawsuits to court instances. The Constitutional Court noted that by his/her activities, the Ombudsman in a democratic society shall fight for the improvement of mechanisms aimed at increasing the responsibility of all subjects involved in protecting fundamental rights, thus contributing to the establishment of proper administration in a law-bound state[64].

The Law on the Constitutional Court entitles the People's Lawyer and the People's Lawyer protecting the rights of the child to appeal to the Constitutional Court.

From February 1995 to December 2005, 49 appeals were sent to the Constitutional Court on behalf of the People's Lawyer: 2 in 2003 and 2005, 10 in 1999, 3 in 2000, 8 in 2001, 20 in 2002, and 4 in 2004[65]. In 2011, parliamentary lawyers submitted 8 appeals (22 % of the total). In the end, the Constitutional Court issued judgements on the merits of 5 appeals; 3 appeals were returned[66].

---

63 Decree No. 27 of November 13, 2014 on constitutional review of Article 21, Part 5, Item e in Law No. 52 of April 3, 2014 on People's Lawyer (Ombudsman) (non-admission of applications submitted by incapable persons). http://www.constcourt.md/ccdocview.php?tip=hotariri&docid=518&l=ru (accessed: March 20, 2018).

64 Decree on constitutional review of Parliamentary Decree No. 140 dated July 3, 2015 on appointment of People's Lawyer protecting the rights of the child. Monitorul Oficial No. 241–246 of August 28, 2015.

65 Hotărîre pentru aprobarea Raportului cu privire la exercitarea jurisdicției constituționale în anul 2005. Monitorul Oficial al R.Moldova No. 9–12/1 of January 20, 2006.

66 Report on exercise of constitutional jurisdiction in 2011, submitted on the basis of Article 10 in Law on Constitutional Court No. 317-XIII of December 13, 1994 and Article 80 in Code of Constitutional Jurisdiction No. 502-XIII of June 16, 1995 http://www.constcourt.md/pageview.php?l=ru&idc=14&t=/obsie/godovoi-doklad (accessed: March 20, 2018).

Of 163 appeals submitted to the Constitutional Court in 2016, only 3 were sent by the People's Lawyer[67].

While exercising the right to appeal to the Constitutional Court, the People's Lawyer has an undoubted effect on improving laws for the protection of human rights/freedoms and enhancing the law-bound state. The appeal of the People's Lawyer sent to the Constitutional Court in 2016 (on the constitutional review of some provisions in Law on Status of Military Staff) may serve as striking example. According to the author of the appeal, debated provisions (prohibition of multiple citizenship for contract servicemen, restriction of the right to work, free movement, and education) are discriminatory and conflicting with provisions of many articles in the Constitution. Following the review of the appeal, the Constitutional Court recognized Item e, Part 6, Article 28; Item g, Part 3, Article 35; and Part 2, Article 38 in Law on Status of Military Staff unconstitutional[68].

Another example is the appeal of the People's Lawyer on constitutional review of some provisions in the Labour Code, Railway Transport Code, and governmental decree approving the List of Enterprises, Areas, and Services, staff of which cannot participate in strike (according to the author, it conflicts with the Constitution)[69].

4 Structure of the Constitutional Court

4.1 The Legal Status of Constitutional Court Judges

The legal status of Constitutional Court judges (legal consolidation of powers for state bodies in the course of appointment, possibility of withdrawal by the same bodies, grounds for potential withdrawal, duration of mandate, and potential appointment of the same person for another term) are factors that determine the independence, forms, and allowed restrictions in the course of exercising the mandate.

---

67 Report on exercise of constitutional jurisdiction in 2016. http://www.constcourt.md/pageview.php?l=ru&idc=14&t=/obsie/godovoi-doklad (accessed: March 20, 2018).

68 Decree on constitutional review of some provisions in Law No. 162-XVI of July 22, 2005 on status of military staff (prohibition of multiple citizenship for contract servicemen). Monitorul Oficial No. 109–118 of April 7, 2017.

69 Decree on constitutional review of Article 369, Part 2, 3, 4 in Labor Code, Article 21, Part 2, 3 in Railway Transport Code, governmental decree No. 656 of June 11, 2004 on approving the List of Enterprises, Areas, and Services, staff of which cannot participate in strike *(limiting the right to strike for certain categories of staff)*. Monitorul Oficial No. 421–427 of December 1, 2017.

According to the Constitution of the Republic of Moldova (Article 136), the Constitutional Court consists of six judges appointed for six-year term.

The procedure of appointing Constitutional Court judges follows from separation of powers (consolidated in Article 6 of the Constitution) and exclusive material competence of the Court (aimed to ensure this principle). Thus, two judges are appointed by Parliament, two by the Government, and two by the Supreme Council of Magistracy. The Constitutional Court noted that during the establishment of the Court, the constitutional legislator laid the foundation for theoretical balance, while assuming the appointment of judges by three state bodies representing three classical branches of government: Parliament (legislative power), Government (executive power), and the Supreme Council of Magistracy (guarantor of independent judicial power)[70]. According to the Court, constitutional provisions consolidating the appointment of Constitutional Court judges form the guarantee of their independence and impartiality, for exercising the powers established by Supreme Law[71].

Requirements for the position of judge are defined in the Law on the Constitutional Court. According to this law (Article 11), the judge of the Constitutional Court shall be a citizen of Moldova residing in the country with higher legal education, high professional level, and have at least 15 years of experience working in the legal field (or in the field of higher legal education/science). The age limit for the appointment as a judge of the Constitutional Court is 70 years. In attending circumstances, the appointment is made only at prior written consent of the candidate. If the candidate holds a position incompliant with the position of judge at the Constitutional Court, or is a member of any party/other public political organization, his/her consent shall include an obligation to resign (on the day of taking the oath) and suspend membership in the party or other public political organization.

Terms of taking the office as judge of Constitutional Court include taking an oath before the Parliament, President of Moldova, and Supreme Council of Magistracy (the text is contained in Law on Constitutional Court, Article 12). On the day of taking the oath, the judge comes into office and his/her six-year mandate begins. The Constitution of the Republic of Moldova (Article 136) does

---

70 Decree on constitutional review of Part 4, Article 23 in Law No. 317-XIII of December 13, 1994 on Constitutional Court. Monitorul Oficial No. 119–121 of May 31, 2013.

71 Decree No. 12 of May 12, 2016 on interpreting the provisions of Article 116, Part 2, 4 and Article 136, Part 1 of Constitution. Monitorul Oficial No. 416–422 of December 2, 2016.

not establish the age limit for Constitutional Court judges; it just defines the six-year term of the mandate.

The Constitution of the Republic of Moldova (Article 139) states that the position of judge at the Constitutional Court is incompliant with any paid (public or private) position except for teaching and scientific activities.

According to the Law on the Constitutional Court, the powers of the judge at the Constitutional Court are terminated at the office term's expiration, resignation, revocation of authority, and death. The powers of the judge at the Constitutional Court are terminated by depriving of immunity, in case of a long-term (over four months in a row) inability to fulfil the duties for health reasons; a violation of the oath and official duties; conviction by court for a committed crime; incompliance of positions (established by a final ascertaining act); the committing of direct or third-party transactions (established by a final ascertaining act); deciding or participating in decision-making without resolving the actual conflict of interest (according to laws on regulating the conflict of interest); non-submission/refusal to submit the declaration on property and personal interests; and prescription to confiscate\unjustified property (via a court decision that came into force).

Besides these circumstances, a judge of the Constitutional Court may resign of his/her own volition.

In the case of terminating a judge's powers, the Chairperson of the Constitutional Court shall apply to the authorized body with a request to appoint a new judge within three days of the vacancy. The authorized body shall appoint a new judge within 15 days of the appeal from the Chairperson of the Constitutional Court.

The Constitutional Court noted that contrary to legal norms establishing the clear deadlines for the appointment of Constitutional Court judges, the experience shows that in case of a vacancy, the judge of the Constitutional Court is appointed with considerable delay[72]. According to the Court, the Constitution shall prevent discontinuity in exercising constitutional jurisdiction (due to the inaction of bodies appointing the Constitutional Court judges), and the late appointment of a new judge (at the expired mandate of the current Constitutional Court judge) damages the activities of this institute. To exclude potential obstacles in

72 Decree No. 12 of May 12, 2016 on interpreting the provisions of Article 116, Part 2, 4 and Article 136, Part 1 of Constitution. Monitorul Oficial No. 416–422 of December 2, 2016.

its activity, the Court stated that on expiry of the mandate, the judge shall keep fulfilling the duties until taking the oath by his/her successor.

At the office term expiration, the judge of the Constitutional Court is provided with a job (upon its liquidation, with an equivalent job at the same or another institution). If, at the office term expiration, the judge has reached the age and has the work experience necessary for retirement, he/she will retire. According to the Law on the Constitutional Court, a judge who reaches the age of 50 years and has at least 20 calendar years of work experience (including the experience as a judge of the Constitutional Court, for one full term of office) is entitled to long-service pension comprised of 55 % of the average salary plus 3 % for each full year of work over 20 years, but no more than 80 % of the average salary total, given the indexation of salary. A judge who retired upon reaching the age limit or because of a long-term (over four months in a row) inability to fulfil duties for health reasons is provided with severance pay in the amount of an annual salary.

Independence and the irremovability of Constitutional Court judges are guaranteed by the Constitution (Article 137), according to which the judges are irremovable during their term of office, independent, and are subject to the Constitution only. Along with the Constitution, the Law on the Constitutional Court and Code of Constitutional Jurisdiction also establish the guarantees of independence/neutrality for Constitutional Court judges, thus enabling the objective administration of justice.

The Constitutional Court stated that any attempt of authorized bodies to withdraw judges from office is excluded, as they are irremovable, which guarantees their independence in exercising powers. According to the Court, this principle protects the judges in the course of fulfilling duties (mostly from external influence). The main idea of the Constitutional Court is that during the exercise of powers, its judges are not subject to bodies that appointed them[73].

Immunity of Constitutional Court judges is among the essential guarantees of their independence. The Law on the Constitutional Court (Article 16) states that without prior consent of the Constitutional Court, the judges cannot be detained, arrested, searched (unless found at the crime scene), or brought to criminal or administrative liability. Judicial review of crimes/administrative offences committed by judges of the Constitutional Court is within the competence of the

73 Decree No. 18 of June 2, 2014 on constitutional review of Law No. 109 dated May 3, 2013 amending and supplementing some legislative acts (Law on Constitutional Court and Code of Constitutional Jurisdiction) (status of Constitutional Court judges, powers of Constitutional Court, and constitutional legal proceedings). Monitorul Oficial No. 256–260 of August 29, 2014.

Supreme Court of Justice; initiation of a criminal case and request for consent to bringing to justice is within the competence of the Attorney General[74].

The Constitutional Court also noted that material guarantees (as opposed to restrictions, prohibitions, and liability imposed by society) are among the basic elements guaranteeing the independence of constitutional judges[75].

At that, Constitutional Court judges must (Article 17, Law on Constitutional Court): impartially exercise the powers following the Constitution; respect the confidentiality of issues related to discussion and voting; avoid the public expression of opinion or consulting on issues within the competence of the Constitutional Court; vote "for" or "against" while adopting the acts of the Constitutional Court; inform the Chairperson of the Constitutional Court on their activities incompatible with exercised powers; avoid the use of their position for any propaganda; refrain from any actions contrary to status of the judge; and submit the declaration on property and personal interests (in the manner prescribed by the law).

4.2 Functions of the Constitutional Court in Moldova

Like most constitutional review bodies, the main function of the Constitutional Court in Moldova is the constitutional review of legal acts adopted by Parliament, the Government, and the President of Moldova. As noted above, the powers of the Constitutional Court of the Republic of Moldova are established by the Constitution (Article 135) according to which constitutional jurisdiction body shall: exercise (by request) the constitutional review of parliamentary laws/decrees, decrees of the President of Moldova, decrees and ordinances of the Government, and international treaties involving Moldova; interpret the Constitution; provide an opinion on proposals to revise the Constitution; confirm the results of republican referendums; confirm the results of elections for Parliament and the President of Moldova; state the circumstances justifying the dissolution of Parliament, removal of President from office, temporary exercise of his/her duties, and the impossibility of exercising the President's duties for more than 60 days; resolve the exceptional cases on unconstitutionality of legal acts submitted by the Supreme Court of Justice; and make decisions on matters related to the constitutionality of any party.

---

74 No such practice.

75 Decree No. 20 of June 23, 2015 on constitutional review of some provisions in Article 32, Part 1, Law No. 544-XIII of July 20, 1995 on status of judges (pensions of Constitutional Court judges). Monitorul Oficial No. 332–339 of December 11, 2015.

It should be noted that the Constitutional Court reviews the issues within its competence only; in case the review shows that issues are within the competence of other bodies, the Court shall resubmit the materials to them or inform the parties and concerned bodies, while providing the necessary clarifications.

Being independent of any state body and autonomous in arrangement of its activities, the Constitutional Court is vested with certain powers that ensure its functionality. The Code of Constitutional Jurisdiction (Article 5) sets the following functional duties of the Court: electing the Chairperson and deputy Chairperson of Constitutional Court; approving the Regulation for Secretariat of the Constitutional Court (structure and manning table), the Regulation of Scientific-Advisory Council at the Constitutional Court, regulations on the procedure of calculating the work experience for judges and staff at Secretariat of Constitutional Court; drafting the budget of the Constitutional Court and submitting it for approval to Parliament; setting the wages for the Chairperson and judges of the Constitutional Court; disciplinary responsibility of Constitutional Court judges; depriving the judges of their powers (in cases assumed by the Law on the Constitutional Court); review of complaints on penalties imposed by the Chairperson of the Constitutional Court and rulings held by judges of the Constitutional Court (on legal expenses); defining the main fields of relation with similar institutions of other states; providing the President of Moldova, Parliament, and the Supreme Council of Magistracy with an annual report on exercise of constitutional jurisdiction; and other issues assumed by the Law on the Constitutional Court and Code of Constitutional Jurisdiction.

It is recognized that exercise (by request) of constitutional review for parliamentary laws/decrees, decrees of the President of Moldova, decrees and ordinances of the Government, and international treaties involving Moldova are among the basic functions of the Constitutional Court.

The Constitutional Court of the Republic of Moldova expressed confidence that exercised constitutional review allows the parliamentary minority and citizens to oversee compliance with provisions of the Constitution, while being a counterbalance to the parliamentary majority (in cases where it deviates from the spirit and letter of the Constitution)[76]. According to the Constitutional Court, constitutional review of legal acts is not just a fundamental guarantee for

76 Decree No. 18 of June 2, 2014 on constitutional review of Law No. 109 dated May 3, 2013 amending and supplementing some legislative acts (Law on Constitutional Court and Code of Constitutional Jurisdiction) (status of Constitutional Court judges, powers of Constitutional Court, and constitutional legal proceedings). Monitorul Oficial No. 256–260 of August 29, 2014.

supremacy of the Constitution. It is a tool providing the Constitutional Court with authority on effective separation and balance of power in a democratic state[77].

A law-bound state is impossible without the guaranteed supremacy of the Constitution and legality (in the course of exercising the law). Interpretation of legal and constitutional norms is among the most important stages of exercising the law. In one of its decrees, the Constitutional Court of the Republic of Moldova noted that the authority to interpret the Constitution belongs to the constitutional jurisdiction body only and assumes defining the true will of the legislator, the exact and complete meaning of constitutional norms, and the correct application of the latter in space and time.

The prerogative of the Constitutional Court (under Article 135 of Constitution) assumes defining the actual and complete meaning of constitutional norms, which can be exercised via textual and functional interpretation, to the extent that it can be derived from the text of Constitution, given the general nature of the norm, specific situations that could not be foreseen by the legislator at the moment of developing the norm, subsequent provisions (related or even conflicting), complex situations of applying the norm, etc. As for the purpose of interpreting, the Constitutional Court believes that any interpretation shall ensure the unambiguous and correct understanding of content and the true meaning of constitutional norms. At that, the need for interpreting shall be confirmed by the essence of the legal issue arising from the ambiguous nature of constitutional norms. Based on the significance of interpreting constitutional norms, the Constitutional Court considers thorough review of such appeals as its task. According to the Court, they can be admitted for review only if the constitutional norm, the interpreting of which is requested, is unclear, ambiguous, or incomplete[78].

In general, the interpretation of constitutional norms is official and binding for all subjects of legal relations. As for the decree on interpreting constitutional norms, the Constitutional Court believes that it has the legal force and is binding

---

77 Decree on constitutional review, Part 4, Article 23, Law No. 317-XIII of December 13, 1994 on Constitutional Court. Monitorul Oficial No. 119–121 of May 31, 2013.

78 Ruling on refusal to admit for review the appeal No. 10a/2014 on constitutional review of some provisions in Law No. 96 of May 21, 2010 amending and supplementing the Article 4 of Parliamentary Regulation and interpreting the Part 2, Article 41 of Constitution (formation of parliamentary factions). Monitorul Oficial No. 127–133 of May 23, 2014.

for all constitutional bodies of Moldova by virtue of conclusions forming its basis[79].

The Court ensures the interpretation of the Constitution by request of subjects entitled to appeal to the constitutional jurisdiction body (Article 135 of Constitution). So far, the Constitutional Court of the Republic of Moldova has been reviewing the appeals from various subjects of this right.

Thus, of 66 appeals reviewed by the Constitutional Court in 2015, 18 appeals referred to the interpretation of the Constitution. Due to their review, the Court adopted 5 decrees on interpreting some provisions of the Constitution[80]. In 2016, 118 appeals were submitted to the Constitutional Court, 4 of which referred to the interpretation of the Constitution. In total, the Court reviewed 12 appeals on the interpretation of the Constitution this year (8 of them were appeals left since 2015). Of 35 decrees adopted by the Constitutional Court in 2016, only 3 decrees referred to the interpretation of some provisions of the Constitution (Article 135, Part 1, Item a, g in combination with Article 20, Article 115, Article 116 and 134; Article 106^1, Part 1; Article 93, Part 2; Article 116, Part 2, 4; Article 136, Part 1 of Constitution)[81].

The Constitutional Court's practice of adopting the decisions on issues, the subject of which is the constitutionality of some party, has been insignificant so far. As an example, we can cite only 1 appeal of deputy submitted in 2010, which required the constitutional review for the National-Liberal Party of Moldova. However, the Constitutional Court has not admitted this appeal of deputy for review, while referring to Article 38, Part 2, Item d, Code of Constitutional Jurisdiction according to which the deputy of Parliament is not a subject entitled to appeal to the Constitutional Court on the constitutionality of parties. Appeals on these issues are submitted by the President of Moldova, Chairperson of Parliament, and Government[82].

---

79 Decree on interpreting the Article 140 of Constitution. Monitorul Oficial of December 20, 2013.

80 Decree on approving the Report on Exercise of Constitutional Jurisdiction in 2015 http://www.constcourt.md/public/files/file/Actere%20Curtii%20rus/Raport_CC_2015_ru.pdf (accessed: March 20, 2018).

81 Report on Exercise of Constitutional Jurisdiction in 2016 http://www.constcourt.md/public/files/file/Actere%20Curtii%20rus/Raport_CCM_2016_rus.pdf (accessed: March 20, 2018).

82 Report on Exercise of Constitutional Jurisdiction in 2010. Monitorul Oficial No. 25–27/3 of February 11, 2011.

A report from the Chairperson of the Constitutional Court (presented at a ceremonial meeting devoted to the 15th anniversary of establishing the Court) noted that in 15 years of work, the constitutional jurisdiction body ensured the constitutional review of 365 normative acts, 178 of which were recognized as, in whole or in part, unconstitutional. Besides, the Constitutional Court issued 27 opinions on draft revisions of the Constitution and adopted 32 decrees on interpretation of 44 constitutional norms[83].

Although the legal status of the Constitutional Court is regulated by Section V of the Constitution, references to the Constitutional Court are also found in other articles of Fundamental Law. Thus, Article 62 of the Constitution (recognizing the deputies' mandates) states that the Constitutional Court, by proposal of the Central Election Commission, decides on recognizing or not recognizing (in case of violation of election laws) the deputies' mandates.

According to the Constitution (Part 2, Article 79), the Constitutional Court participates in the procedure of taking the oath by candidate for the President of Moldova, whose election is recognized as valid. The inauguration of the President includes an announcement of decree (by Chairperson of Constitutional Court) that recognizes the validity of election for the President of Moldova and the handling of the sign of the President of Moldova[84].

Besides, according to the Constitution (Article 89), in case of an initiation of the impeachment procedure, the President may provide the Constitutional Court with explanations on charges against him/her.

We cannot ignore another important function of Constitutional Court: the formation and development of constitutional law. According to the Court, the text of the Constitution shall not be changed without legal need, thus ensuring the inviolability of the Constitution and constitutional order[85].

---

83 D. Pulbere, *Alocuțiune rostită în cadrul ședinței festive consacrate aniversării a 15-a a Curții Constituționale a Republicii Moldova,* Conferința internațională „Asigurarea supremației Constituției, funcția de bază a Curții Constituționale". Chișinău 2010, p. 10.

84 Law on Inauguration of President of Moldova. Monitorul Oficial No. 3 of January 9, 1997.

85 Decree No. 7 of March 4, 2016 on constitutional review of some provisions in Law No. 1115-XIV of July 5, 2000 amending and supplementing the Constitution of Moldova (procedure of electing the President). Monitorul Oficial No. 59–67 of March 18, 2016.

4.3 Subject of Constitutional Review Exercised by the Constitutional Court

As noted above, the Constitutional Court of the Republic of Moldova ensures (by request) the constitutional review of parliamentary laws/decrees, decrees of the President of Moldova, decrees and ordinances of Government, and international treaties involving Moldova.

Final and transitional provisions of the Constitution (Section VII, Article II) assume that at the moment of their adoption, laws and other normative acts shall operate in part, not conflicting with its content. Within a year after the Constitution came into force, standing commissions of Parliament and the Government had to review the legislation for compliance with the Constitution and submit relevant proposals to the Parliament.

At first glance, the Constitution clearly identified the sources of law forming the subject of control exercised by the Constitutional Court. At that, for some time, the practice of the Court had certain ambiguities with access to the constitutional justice of state officials, who expressed special political or public interest.

The original version of Decree No. 16 of May 28, 1998, adopted by the Constitutional Court, noted that the "establishment of special procedures or constitutional jurisdiction for state officials expressing special political/public interest, appointed by parliamentary orders, decrees of President of Moldova, and governmental decrees (issued in pursuance of their powers and directly assumed by norms of Constitution or other laws), does not limit the access to justice. According to Article 135, Part 1, Item a of the Constitution, review of constitutionality for these normative acts falls within the competence of Constitutional Court"[86].

When Parliament adopted the Law on Administrative Court, which established the procedure of administrative jurisdiction, the Constitutional Court stated that constitutional review may cover acts that are normative in the essence (adopted or issued by public authority, with a compulsory, general, and binding nature). Administrative acts of individual nature—issued by public authority in pursuance of powers expressly assumed by constitutional/legislative norms, being the legal acts not containing the legal norms, being normative acts of personal nature with one-time legal consequences, applicable only once, and, thus, not compulsory for general public—may not be subject to constitutional review (by request of entitled entities), but may be subject to control of legality (by court

---

86 Hotărîre cu privire la interpretarea Article 20 din Constituția Republicii Moldova No. 16 of May 28, 1998 Monitorul Oficial al R.Moldova of June 25, 1998.

instance, according to the law). Thus, only acts of normative nature (listed in Article 135, Part 1, Item a of the Constitution) may be subject to constitutional review[87].

Later, the Constitutional Court revised its position on this view. Thus, in March 2010, Constitutional Court started reviewing the appeal on the constitutional review of Parliamentary Decree No. 30-XVIII of March 4, 2010 on dismissing the Chairperson of the Supreme Court of Justice. The Court noted that based on the Constitution of Moldova (Item a, Part 1, Article 135), it sees its authority in exercising the constitutional review for all acts adopted by the Parliament, despite their regulatory or individual nature[88]. The Constitutional Court recognized that at the beginning of its activities, it reviewed the appeals on debating the acts with regards to state officials[89].

By Law No. 726-XV of December 27, 2001, Parliament amended the Law on Administrative Court, while excluding from judicial administrative review acts against officials and positions, which were previously excluded by the Constitutional Court from constitutional review. As "purely political acts of Parliament, President of Moldova, and Government, as well as the individual administrative acts issued by Parliament, President of Moldova, and Government in exercise of powers directly assumed by constitutional/legislative norms regarding the election, appointment, and dismissal of public state officials expressing special political or public interests" appeared to be beyond

87 Decree on revising the Decree of Constitutional Court No. 16 of May 28, 1998 on interpreting the Article 20 in Constitution of Moldova. Monitorul Oficial No. 90–91/34 of August 2, 2001.

88 Decree on revising the Decree of Constitutional Court No. 16 of May 28, 1998 on interpreting the Article 20 in Constitution of Moldova, as amended by Decree No. 39 of July 9, 2001. Monitorul Oficial No. 58–60 of April 23, 2010.

89 Decree on constitutional review of Decree from President of Moldova No. 68 dated March 15, 1996 on administration of Ministry of Defense. Monitorul Oficial, 1996, No. 25; Decree on constitutional review of Decree from Parliament of Moldova No. 546-XIII of July 21, 1995 on early dismissal of some Chairpersons of standing parliamentary commissions. Monitorul Oficial, 1995, No. 53–54; Decree on constitutional review of Decree from Parliament of Moldova No. 545-XIII of July 21, 1995 on early dismissal of Deputy Chairperson of the Parliament. Monitorul Oficial, 1995, No. 53–54; Decree on constitutional review of Decree from President of Moldova No. 5 dated January 12, 1995 on dismissing the Court Chairperson. Monitorul Oficial, 1996, No. 25; Decree No. 4 of February 10, 1997 on constitutional review of Decree from Parliament of Moldova No. 912-XIII of July 5, 1996 on early dismissal of Chairperson in Commission on Control and Petitions. Monitorul Oficial, 1997, No. 13–14.

jurisdiction, the Court found it logical to revise its attitude regarding these acts. As a result, the Constitutional Court concluded the following:

- Individual administrative acts issued by Parliament, the President of Moldova, and Government—in exercise of powers assumed by constitutional or legislative norms regarding the election, appointment, and dismissal of public state officials expressing special political interest—cannot be subject to constitutional review by request of entitled entities;
- Acts issued by Parliament, the President of Moldova, and Government—with regards to state officials expressing special public interest, elected or appointed for a certain term of office—may be subject to constitutional review (by form and procedure of their adoption). Until approval of proper legislation by Parliament, the Constitutional Court will decide in each specific case on issues of public state officials with special public interest.

The constitutional review also covers the legal acts on appeals of the Supreme Court of Justice as exceptional cases of unconstitutionality. The Constitutional Court noted that Article 135, Part 1, Item g of the Constitution assumes the powers of the Constitutional Court in exercising the constitutional review of laws and other normative acts (to be applied when reviewing the case in courts of general jurisdiction). The procedure of constitutional review is initiated on an exceptional basis[90]. The Court believes that the Constitution of the Republic of Moldova includes decision-making on the constitutionality of laws and other normative acts of compulsory nature within the powers of the Constitutional Court—laws and acts that are general and mandatory in essence, are adopted by central public authorities, and have an impact on review of disputes by the court of general jurisdiction[91]. So-called administrative regulations (implementing, according to the Constitutional Court, the exercising of power granted by the Constitution to the President of Moldova, the Government, and Prime Minister) were categorized as "other normative acts". In this category of acts, the Court included decrees, resolutions, and orders,[92]

90 Decree No. 2 of February 9, 2016 on interpreting the Article 135, Part 1, Items a, g in Constitution of Moldova. Monitorul Oficial No. 55–58 of March 11, 2016.

91 Hotărîrea Curții Constituționale No. 15 of May 6, 1997 cu privire la interpretarea Article 135 alin. (1) lit. g) din Constituția Republicii Moldova (Monitorul Oficial No. 33–34/14, May 22, 1997).

92 Decree on constitutional review of some provisions in Law No. 548-XIII of July 21, 1995 on National Bank of Moldova. Monitorul Oficial No. 22 of March 4, 1999.

while stating that apart from laws, the exceptional case of unconstitutionality also covers other normative acts[93].

In reviewing the exceptional cases of unconstitutionality by the Constitutional Court, the laws of Moldova assign an important role to the Supreme Court of Justice. As the supreme judicial body ensuring the exact/uniform application of laws by all court instances and resolution of disputes arising during the application of laws, the Supreme Court of Justice, on its own initiative or by proposal of courts, submits to the Constitutional Court a request for the constitutional review of legal acts[94]. In 2012, given the new circumstances, the Civil Procedure Code of the Republic of Moldova (Article 12^1) was amended to address the exceptional cases of unconstitutionality. In this new revision, the law assumed that if a case review found that an applicable or applied legal norm conflicted with the Constitution of the Republic of Moldova, and constitutional review of the normative act fell within the competence of the Constitutional Court, the court instance should submit a request to the Constitutional Court via the Supreme Court of Justice[95].

The subject of constitutional review by the Constitutional Court also includes international treaties. According to the Court, the need to conclude the international treaties is assumed by the Declaration of Independence, where the Republic of Moldova declared its readiness to establish political, economic, cultural, and other relations with European states and all countries of the world, as well as the readiness to establish diplomatic relations, according to international law and current international practice in this field[96].

The Constitutional Court determined that "treaty" is a generic concept covering all kinds of international agreements: contracts, agreements, pacts, conventions, declarations, communiques, protocols, etc. Despite the name, treaties have similar legal force[97]. At the constitutional review of some provisions

93 Decree No. 2 of February 9, 2016 on interpreting the Article 135, Part 1, Items a, g in Constitution of Moldova. Monitorul Oficial No. 55–58 of March 11, 2016.

94 Law on Supreme Court of Justice. Monitorul Oficial No. 15–17 of January 22, 2013.

95 Law on amending and supplementing the Civil Procedure Code of Moldova. Monitorul Oficial No. 185 of August 31, 2012.

96 Decree No. 24 of October 9, 2014 on constitutional review of Association Agreement between Republic of Moldova, on the one hand, European Union, European Atomic Energy Community, and their member states, on the other hand, and Law No. 112 of July 2, 2014 on ratification of Association Agreement. Monitorul Oficial No. 333–338 of November 7, 2014.

97 Decree on interpreting some provisions in Article 4, Constitution of Moldova. Monitorul Oficial No. 118–119/64 of October 28, 1999.

in the Treaty between the Republic of Moldova and Ukraine (on state border) and additional protocols to this Treaty (signed in Kyiv on August 18, 1999), the Constitutional Court stated that its authority on the constitutional review of international treaties involving the Republic of Moldova (consolidated in Article 135, Part 1, Item a of the Constitution) shall be viewed through the prism of other constitutional provisions and in association with national and international norms in this field, as the above general constitutional norm does not specify the treaties subject to constitutional review and the stage of such review (before or after their coming into force). Referring to the principle of international law on fulfilling the international obligations by state, the Constitutional Court noted that constitutional review of this treaty would conflict with the international principle on faithful exercise of contracts, which could cast doubt on Moldova's credibility as a partner in relations stated by international treaties, as well as slow down or even block the development of inter-state and intergovernmental relations of this country[98].

The Court specified that under Article 135, Part 1, Item a in the Constitution, the constitutional review of international treaties may be implemented between expressing the consent of Moldova to binding international treaties and their coming into force (due to exercising the procedures assumed by law). The Constitutional Court noted that upon recognizing the unconstitutionality of an international treaty involving Moldova, state authorities cannot exercise procedures on implementing the treaty (assumed by law). According to Law No. 595-XIV of September 24, 1999 on international treaties of Moldova (Part 2, Article 22)[99], assuming that international treaties involving Moldova, recognized by the Constitutional Court incompliant with the Constitution of the Republic of Moldova, are not subject to coming into force and application[100]. Moreover, according to the Constitutional Court, meeting accepted

98 Decree No. 5, termination of proceedings on constitutional review of some provisions in Treaty between Moldova and Ukraine (on state border) and additional protocol to the Treaty (signed in Kyiv on August 18, 1999). Monitorul Oficial No. 137 of October 10, 2002.

99 Law on International Treaties of Moldova. Monitorul Oficial No. 24–26 of March 2, 2000.

100 Ruling No. 17 of November 7, 2013 on refusal to admit for review the appeal No. 35a/2013 on constitutional review of some acts regarding the Agreement between Government of Moldova and Government of Romania on cooperation in military field. Monitorul Oficial No. 312–314 of December 31, 2013.

international obligations is a legal tradition and constitutional principle, as an integral part of a law-bound state[101].

4.4 Preliminary and Subsequent Control of Legal Norms

Throughout its operation, the Constitutional Court of the Republic of Moldova could arrange the legal practice on application of Article 135, Part 1 of the Constitution, as a form of constitutional review limited to preliminary control of actual laws only.

Constitutional review covers only normative acts adopted after coming into force through the Constitution by July 29, 1994.

Still, in 2 cases, the Constitutional Court recognized the unconstitutionality of some normative acts adopted prior to the Constitution's coming into force. Thus, on October 2, 1996, the Court reviewed an appeal on the constitutional review of some provisions in the Law of February 10, 1995, Law of February 23, 1996, and the Decree of January 23, 1991 on exercising the right to utilize land. Among other things, the above acts regulated the exercising of rights to utilize owned land plots (via sale/purchase, donation, and exchange) from January 1, 2001 only. Authors of the appeal demanded the recognition of unconstitutionality for some provisions in these normative acts, since they conflict both with constitutional provisions on human rights/freedoms and the Universal Declaration of Human Rights, according to which anyone can enjoy the rights and freedoms proclaimed in it. As a result, the Constitutional Court recognized the unconstitutionality of some provisions in debated laws; regarding the Decree of Supreme Council of the Moldavian SSR "Procedure of Introducing the Law of the Moldavian SSR "On Property"" dated January 23, 1991, the case on constitutional jurisdiction was terminated[102].

The second case was in 1997, when the Constitutional Court reviewed in plenary session the appeal for the constitutional review of the Regulation on Drafting and Issuing the Identity Documents of the National Passport System (2nd

---

101 Decree No. 24 of October 9, 2014 on constitutional review of Association Agreement between Republic of Moldova, on the one hand, European Union, European Atomic Energy Community, and their member states, on the other hand, and Law No. 112 of July 2, 2014 on ratification of Association Agreement. Monitorul Oficial No. 333–338 of November 7, 2014.

102 Decree on constitutionality of some provisions in Law No. 369-XIII of February 10, 1995; Law No. 745-XIII of February 23, 1996; Decree No. 460-XII of January 23, 1991 on exercising the right to utilize the land. Monitorul Oficial No. 067 of October 17, 1996.

paragraph, Item 10), Annex No. 1 to the Decree of the Moldovan Government dated June 6, 1995 on additional measures for introducing the national passport system.

The author of the appeal debated the "registration" institute. The Court recognized the unconstitutionality of Item 10 in the Regulation on Drafting and Issuing the Identity Documents of the National Passport System, approved by the Governmental Decree of June 6, 1995 on additional measures for introducing the national passport system, and all orders containing words "residence" and "registration", as, according to Court, since the Constitution of the Republic of Moldova came into force, they had lost their legal force and could not be applied[103].

However, in scientific circles and elsewhere, the focus was always on issues about the form of the constitutional review exercised by the Constitutional Court. Moldovan researchers argue over preliminary (*a priori*) and subsequent (*a posteriori*) constitutional review and the direct application of these forms in the activity of the Constitutional Court. The prevailing view is that constitutional review in Moldova was introduced in legislation and exercised in the form of subsequent (*a posteriori*) control, i.e., after adopting and promulgating the law. It is assumed that society and state will get closer to democratic ideals if constitutional review is applied to draft laws and prior to their promulgation[104].

The Constitutional Court believes that the Constitution (Item a, Part 1, Article 135) assumes that the Court "exercises constitutional review of laws by request", without limiting the exercise of this power only to the control of laws that came into force. In this view, the Constitutional Court noted that under the Constitution, the constitutional review of the law is possible both before its promulgation and after its coming into force, by means of procedures. The Constitutional Court believes that any entity entitled to appeal to the Constitutional Court may debate a law not published in the Official Gazette of the Republic of Moldova, as well as the published law (under conditions assumed by legislation). Appeal on the constitutional review of law (prior to its publication) has no direct effect on the procedure of its promulgation by the President. In case of promulgating the debated law (prior to the issue of the Constitutional

103 Decree No. 16 of May 19, 1997 on verifying the constitutionality of prescriptions in Item 10 (paragraph 2), Regulation on Drafting and Issuing the Identity Documents of National Passport System. Monitorul Oficial No. 037 of June 5, 1997.

104 E. Aramă, *Controlul constituționalității legilor: istorie și actualitate,* Chișinău, Museum 2000. pp. 25–39.

Court decree), preliminary constitutional review of the law turns into subsequent constitutional review[105].

4.5 Legal Control Procedure

As mentioned above, the Constitutional Court is the only body of constitutional jurisdiction in Moldova. The Constitutional Court of the Republic of Moldova is vested with competence to make decisions on the constitutionality of provisions in normative acts within its jurisdiction established by law, only following the appeal of authorized entities. Thus, appeal is the initial phase of constitutional review for laws and other normative acts subject to such control. In this view, the Law on the Constitutional Court (Article 24) states that the Court exercises its jurisdiction on the initiative of entities defined by law and according to the Code of Constitutional Jurisdiction. According to legislation, the right to appeal to the Constitutional Court is held by the President of Moldova; the Government; the Minister of Justice; the Supreme Court of Justice; the Attorney General; members of Parliament; parliamentary factions; the People's Lawyer; the People's Lawyer protecting the rights of the child; councils of administrative-territorial units (1st, 2nd level), and the National Assembly of Gagauzia (Gagauz Yeri), in case of verifying the constitutionality of laws, regulations, and resolutions of Parliament; decrees of the President of Moldova; resolutions, ordinances, and orders of the Government, and international treaties involving Moldova.

Listed subjects may submit appeals on issues within their competence, apart from appeals: on revising the Constitution (submitted by subjects directly indicated in Article 141 of the Constitution); on the statement of circumstances justifying the dissolution of Parliament (submitted by the President of Moldova); on the statement of circumstances justifying the temporary removal of the President from office or temporary fulfilment of presidential duties (submitted by resolution of Parliament, signed by the Chairperson of the Parliament); on issues covering constitutionality of the party (submitted by the President of Moldova, the Chairperson of Parliament, the Government, and the Minister of Justice or Attorney General).

The Chairperson of Parliament may submit an appeal only on the basis of parliamentary decree; the Attorney General, following the decision from the Supreme Council of Attorneys; the Minister of Justice, following the decision from the Board of the Ministry of Justice.

---

105 Decree No. 9 of February 14, 2014 on interpreting the Article 135, Part 1, Item a in Constitution. Monitorul Oficial No. 78–79 of April 1, 2014.

Results of republican referendums, elections for Parliament, and the President of Moldova are approved after reviewing the report from the Republican Commission on Holding a Referendum or Central Election Commission; materials on recognizing the backup candidate as deputy of the Parliament are submitted by the Central Election Commission.

The Code of Constitutional Jurisdiction (Article 39) sets certain requirements to the form and content of an appeal. Thus, any appeal is submitted in writing (in Romanian). It must be justified and shall contain: the name of the Constitutional Court, as a body where the appeal is sent; the name and address of the applicant; the subject of the appeal; the statement of circumstances forming the basis for claims of the applicant; requirements of appeal; other information regarding the subject of the appeal; the list of documents attached to the appeal; and the signature, index, and stamp of the applicant.

Let's note that neither the Constitution nor other laws on activities of the Constitutional Court assume any dates of appeal to the court, after which the appeal is impossible. It follows that appeals on the constitutionality of certain normative acts may be submitted at any time after their coming into force, which is normal under the preliminary constitutional review of laws[106].

Upon admission by the Constitutional Court, the appeal may be withdrawn by the applicant at any stage of the case review.

This stage on the constitutional review of laws ends with a preliminary study of appeal. At this stage, judges study the opinion of various state bodies, scientific and educational institutions, non-governmental organizations, international organizations, laws of other states, and jurisprudence of other constitutional courts.

Upon submission of the conclusion on the preliminary study of appeal, the Chairperson of Constitutional Court provides materials for the session of the Constitutional Court. Preliminary review of the appeal, study of the appeal for admissibility, and preparation of case for review (in public session of Constitutional Court) are assumed in detail by the Provision on the Procedure of Reviewing the Appeals Submitted to the Constitutional Court[107].

Review of appeals in session. Two-thirds of the total judges shall be present for holding the plenary sessions of the Constitutional Court. Sessions of the

---

106 I. Guceac, *Curs elementar de drept cnstituţional*, Chişinău, Editura Reclama 2001, p. 180.

107 Ruling of Constitutional Court No. AG-3 of June 3, 2014 approving the Provision on Procedure of Reviewing the Appeals Submitted to Constitutional Court. Monitorul Oficial al Republicii Moldova No. 185–199 of July 18, 2014.

Constitutional Court are held in a solemn atmosphere, following the ethics of constitutional legal proceedings. The case review begins with a message of reporting to the judge the essence of the case, grounds for its review by the Constitutional Court, content of materials, and measures taken to prepare the case for hearing, after which, the presiding judge suggests that the parties state their positions. At that, the subject of appeal goes first, followed by the other party.

In Constitutional Court sessions, the proceedings are open except in cases where publicity may affect the state security and public order. At a case review in closed session, apart from parties to the process, other persons may be invited by decision of the Constitutional Court.

Consultation of judges. The closed consultation of Constitutional Court judges is held in a consultation room. Besides, judges of the Constitutional Court are not entitled to disclose the contents of the consultation. During consultation, judges can freely state their position on the issue under review. At the end of the consultation, the presiding judge puts draft acts of the Constitutional Court to the vote. The judge of the Constitutional Court is not entitled to abstain from voting. The presiding judge is the last to vote. At the stated equality of votes, the presiding judge may decide to resume the case for an additional study of circumstances essential for resolution. Decision to resume the case is possible in other cases, where judges come to conclusion on the need for additional case examination. At that, the presiding judge takes a recess in session or postpones the case review.

Decision-making. In the end, the decision on constitutionality/unconstitutionality of a reviewed normative act is made by the majority of Constitutional Court judges. A judge disagreeing to an adopted resolution or conclusion may state his/her dissenting opinion in writing.

4.6 Civil Complaint as Means of Legal Control

In some scientific works published in Moldova, authors speak in favour of establishing the constitutional complaint while considering this procedure necessary for our state[108]. When asked how necessary and justified granting a citizen with the right to access constitutional jurisdiction is, scholars in Moldova expressed an opinion that it depends on state structure and the place of

108 V. Zaporojan, *Premisele implementării instituției recursului constituțional în Republica Moldova*, "Justiția Constituțională în Republica Moldova" 2005, No. 3.

constitutional jurisdiction in a system of state bodies. It is believed that a modern state (positioned as law-bound, with an effective Constitutional Court) shall grant this right to citizens. In the presence of political will supported by public opinion, these initiatives will be materialized; it's just a matter of time[109].

Researchers of constitutional law believe that legislative consolidation for the right of citizens to appeal to the Constitutional Court is a serious step for the protection of human rights and freedoms[110]. According to other authors, the direct appeal of citizens of Moldova, foreign citizens, and stateless persons to the Constitutional Court shall take place only upon violation of constitutional material rights, not procedural ones. Only appeals on the violation of fundamental rights/freedoms of individuals by state bodies shall be admitted for review by the Constitutional Court. Besides, there is an opinion that legal entities could also apply to the Constitutional Court, in case some constitutional right is violated by a certain normative act, or this legal entity considers itself a victim of violating the fundamental rights/freedoms or guarantees of their ensuring[111].

In 2004, the Constitutional Court of the Republic of Moldova reviewed in plenary session a request of 35 deputies to provide an opinion of the Constitutional Court on the bill supplementing Article 135 and amending Article 136 in the Constitution of the Republic of Moldova. The bill assumed providing Article 135, Part 1 of the Constitution with the following paragraph: "expressed, when all proper means of protection were used, by complaints of persons positioning themselves as victims of violating the fundamental human rights and freedoms assumed by Section II or international treaties involving Moldova, arising from law, administrative act, court decision or omission of public authorities".

According to the bill, the procedure of constitutional complaint is constitutional and legal by means of subsidiary nature; the procedure is initiated only in case of the violation of the fundamental rights/freedoms of citizens or guarantees

---

109 V. Zaporojan, *Accesul direct al persoanei la justiția constituțională (Practica Germaniei)*, "Revista națională de drept." 2007, No. 4.

110 V. Mocrea, *Baza juridică și procedura de soluționare a recursurilor constituționale*, Materialele Conferinței "Rolul Curții Constituționale în sistemul protecției drepturilor omului și respectarea CEDO și jurisprudenței Curții Europene a Drepturilor Omului în jurisprudența și legislația națională". Chișinău, December 13–14, 2007, p. 38.

111 V. Zubco, *Probleme și soluții privind accesul direct al cetățenilor la Curtea Constituțională*, Materialele Conferinței "Rolul Curții Constituționale în sistemul protecției drepturilor omului și respectarea CEDO și jurisprudenței Curții Europene a Drepturilor Omului în jurisprudența și legislația națională". Chișinău, December 13–14, 2007, p. 134.

thereof; the procedure is initiated only in case of violating the constitutional right by law, administrative act, ruling or omission of public authorities; initiation of procedure is ensured by any person positioned as infringed in fundamental rights/freedoms or guarantees thereof.

Upon analysis of the bill, Constitutional Court noted that procedure of constitutional complaint introduced at national level will contribute to more effective protection of human rights and freedoms consolidated in Constitution of the Republic of Moldova and international treaties involving Moldova. According to draft constitutional law, it was assumed that by review of constitutional complaint, the Court will speak in first and last instance—on violation of rights and freedoms by public authorities and court instances. Under draft law, prior to submission to international court, constitutional complaints can be reviewed by Constitutional Court—the only body authorized to provide formal interpreting of constitutional norms. Constitutional Court stated that draft law does not violate the unity of constitutional matter and development/specification of procedure on review of constitutional complaint is within the competence of Parliament only[112].

In 2006, Minister of Justice requested the Constitutional Court to interpret Article 135 of Constitution, which states the powers of Constitutional Court. In appeal, the author believed that since Supreme Law does not prohibit the granting of other powers to Constitutional Court (apart from those assumed by Article 135, Part 1 of Constitution), Parliament may extend the competence of Constitutional Court by means of law. In author's opinion, Constitutional Court may be entitled to review the appeals of citizens considering themselves infringed (in any right guaranteed by Constitution or international treaties involving Moldova), without amending the Constitution. Court assessed the arguments and resulting conclusion of the author as unacceptable, while noting that hypothetical judgements (no matter how logical they seem) cannot form the basis for interpreting the Article 135 of Constitution. Due to inconsistency of the author's arguments, Constitutional Court recognized the appeal pointless and, thus, not subject to review in the essence[113].

Despite the efforts, today, civil complaint (as means of constitutional review) has no legal basis in Moldova. As Constitution does not assume the right of

112 Conclusion No. 1 of December 16, 2004 on draft law supplementing the Article 135 and amending the Article 136 in Constitution of Moldova. Monitorul Oficial No. 241 of December 27, 2004.

113 Ruling No. 16 of December 4, 2006 on appeal regarding the interpreting of Article 135 in Constitution of Moldova. Monitorul Oficial No. 189–192 of December 15, 2006.

citizens to appeal to Constitutional Court, the latter believes that due to exceptional case of unconstitutionality, individuals get the indirect access to constitutional jurisdiction, which fits a number of measures taken to guarantee the fair legal proceeding[114]. This indirect way, which grants the citizens an access to Constitutional Court, provides the Constitutional Court (guarantor of supremacy for Constitution) with ability to control the observance of human rights and fundamental freedoms by legislative power.

5 Legal Nature and Legal Force of Constitutional Court Decisions

According to current laws, the Constitutional Court of the Republic of Moldova adopts resolutions, issues rulings, and provides opinions.

The Constitutional Court adopts resolutions on the following issues: constitutionality of parliamentary laws, regulations, decrees, decrees of the President of Moldova, resolutions and orders of the Government, international treaties involving Moldova; interpretation of the Constitution; defining the results of republican referendums, the results of elections for Parliament and the President of Moldova; exceptional cases of unconstitutionality in legal acts from the Supreme Court of Justice, and other cases assumed by law.

The Constitutional Court provides opinions on proposals to revise the Constitution; circumstances justifying the dissolution of Parliament; circumstances justifying temporary removal of the President from office; circumstances justifying temporary fulfilment of presidential duties; and constitutionality of the party.

In cases assumed by the procedure of constitutional legal proceeding (except for cases requiring adoption of resolution and provision of opinion), the Constitutional Court issues the rulings.

Constitutional Court decisions (adopted by an analysis of appeals on constitutional review of certain legal acts) would be meaningless if they existed only on paper or were mentioned in scientific discussions. First of all, constitutional jurisprudence is not meant for interpretation by representatives of legal science, but for careful studying and use by Parliament, the Government, the President, and other state bodies or judicial instances of general jurisdiction to exclude unconstitutional laws and other normative-legal acts from the legal system of

---

114 Report on exercising the constitutional jurisdiction in 2016. Chisinau, January 19, 2017, http://www.constcourt.md/public/files/file/Actere%20Curtii%20rus/Raport_CCM_2016_rus.pdf (accessed: March 20, 2018).

the state. The Constitutional Court is authorized to recognize the debated law or other normative-legal act conflicting with the Constitution, thus excluding it from the national legal system. However, the Court has no competence to correct or cancel erroneous provisions. These measures are within the authority of the body adopting the unconstitutional law or other normative-legal act.

The Constitution of the Republic of Moldova states that laws and other normative acts (or parts thereof) become invalid since adopting the relevant decision by the Constitutional Court. Decisions of the Constitutional Court are final and not subject to appeal (Article 140). To develop these provisions, Law on the Constitutional Court (Article 28) assumes that acts of the Constitutional Court are official documents, binding on all public authorities, all legal entities, and individuals throughout the country.

The Constitution of the Republic of Moldova and Law on the Constitutional Court do not contain legal norms directly assuming the legal instruments that oblige competent bodies to ensure immediate practical implementation of Constitutional Court decisions, which could help avoid gaps in legislation or other undesirable effects resulting from the abolition of unconstitutional norms in the system of law. As compliance with Constitutional Court decisions is necessary and an important condition for proper functioning of state bodies and establishing a law-bound state, the Court noted to Parliament that its decisions (ensuring the supremacy of the Constitution) are indisputable and binding. *Erga omnes*, the binding nature of Constitutional Court decisions assumes constitutional obligation of all state bodies to ensure precise application of Constitutional Court decisions in specific situations, which fall within the norms recognized unconstitutional[115].

Based on the constitutional norm (Article 7) that states: "Constitution of the Republic of Moldova is its supreme law. No law or other legal act conflicting with Constitution is legally valid", the Constitutional Court noted that decisions of the constitutional jurisdiction body (ensuring the supremacy of Constitution) are final, indisputable, and binding.

The Court specified that as some legislative provisions or acts recognized unconstitutional may lead to a legislative vacuum, deficiency, and uncertainty in use of the law, measures addressing these negative consequences include provisions of the Law on the Constitutional Court (Article 28[1]), which assume that the Government, no later than three months after publishing the Constitutional

115 Decree No. 26 of November 11, 2014 on constitutional review of some provisions regarding the immunity of judges. Monitorul Oficial No. 39–45. February 20, 2015.

Court decision, shall provide the Parliament with a draft law amending/supplementing the normative act (or part thereof) recognized unconstitutional or recognizing it invalid. A relevant draft law shall be reviewed by Parliament as a matter of priority. At that, the Constitutional Court shall be informed within three months on results of reviewing the gaps found in legislation and related to the non-exercising of certain constitutional provisions indicated in the submission. In general, while revealing the content of constitutional norms and developing the rules derived from their interpretation, acts of Constitutional Court determine the direction in the development of the entire legislative system, as well as the process of interpreting and applying the law. Only such a position actually implements the supremacy of the Constitution. The Constitutional Court stated that despite the nature of its rulings (interpreting of Supreme Law or constitutional review of normative acts), based on the powers of the Constitutional Court, they result in consequences assumed by the Constitution and the law on authority exercised by the Court. Their legal force cannot be debated or confirmed by anyone. Therefore, Parliament or the Government (as the case may be) shall cancel or amend relevant normative acts, thus bringing them in compliance with the Constitution. At that, the Constitutional Court noted that legal (rather than political) factors shall be determining in response to Constitutional Court decisions, especially if they assume specific obligations of subjects. Another important statement of the Constitutional Court regarding its rulings is that they are applied to all legal relations unresolved before the date of adoption, respectively, to all situations where provisions recognized unconstitutional are further applied (via revision as well). In this case, the norm loses its legal force and ceases to exist in the absence of any activity from valid or authorized legislator[116].

The Constitutional Court of the Republic of Moldova believes that exercise of its rulings shall have a double legal effect: first, it must guarantee the protection of subjective right for every person; second, it must be a source of law for legislator and executive power, thus playing the lead role in the development of law[117].

The Republic of Moldova has no evidence of any obvious refusal to exercise the decisions of the Constitutional Court; however, in some cases, application of certain decisions may be delayed.

---

116 Decree on interpreting the Article 140 of Constitution. Monitorul Oficial of December 20, 2013.

117 Report on exercise of constitutional jurisdiction in 2016. Chisinau, January 19, 2017, http://www.constcourt.md/public/files/file/Actere%20Curtii%20rus/Raport_CCM_2016_rus.pdf (accessed: March 20, 2018).

Comparative analysis showed that all decisions of the Constitutional Court in 2011–2013 were exercised. Of Constitutional Court decisions adopted in 2014–2015, where at least one of the debated provisions was recognized as unconstitutional, 2 were not exercised. In 2016, 17 decisions (with at least 1 of the debated provisions recognized as unconstitutional) were adopted, which obliges Parliament and the Government to take corrective actions. Of those, 3 decisions were exercised at the moment of drafting the report, 4 were unfulfilled or in the course of exercising, and the deadline of 11 decisions has not yet expired[118]. In 2016, the Constitutional Court sent 17 submissions to Parliament. Given the information available to the Constitutional Court, on the date of drafting the report, 1 of 4 submissions was exercised. For comparison, of 5 submissions in 2015, 1 was exercised, 3 were at the stage of exercising, and 1 was unfulfilled. Of 8 submissions in 2014, only 3 were exercised. All submissions for 2012–2013 were exercised.

In general, via its decisions, the Constitutional Court of the Republic of Moldova contributes to the enhancement of constitutional legality, guarantees observance of constitutional norms, and ensures the unity of the legal system, protection of the constitutional system, and observance of human and civil rights/freedoms.

6 Constitutional Value of the Constitutional Court

Constitutional justice is a key element in the context of protecting/developing the basic values consolidated in the Constitution, which, in turn, represents the legal basis for activity of the Constitutional Court in Moldova, decisions of which have fundamental influence on the development of public relations. In this view, the Constitutional Court of Moldova stated that constitutional justice acts in place of protecting constitutional order and ensures the supremacy of fundamental law. The Constitutional Court also noted that the formation and development of official constitutional practice (e.g. new judicial interpretation of constitutional provisions and new interpretations due to certain changes in constitutional practice) assist with revealing the high potential of the Constitution without amending, allow its adaptation to social changes and ever-changing

118 Report on exercise of constitutional jurisdiction in 2016. Chisinau, January 19, 2017, http://www.constcourt.md/public/files/file/Actere%20Curtii%20rus/Raport_CCM_2016_rus.pdf (accessed: March 20, 2018).

conditions of society/state, and ensure the viability of the Constitution as a basis of society and state[119].

After the 1990s, the Republic of Moldova faced a number of constitutional problems. Right after the adoption of the Constitution (namely, during 1995), clashes between branches of power (even between the President and Prime Minister) have occurred as an inevitable result of ambiguity in some wordings of the Constitution. Unfortunately, even now, the Republic of Moldova has no true cooperation between institutional branches of state power; tensions between the President, Parliament, and the Government increase; and confrontation between the ruling and opposition parties grows.

Referring to the analysis of Constitutional Court activities, an opinion was expressed that this constitutional jurisdiction body made significant contribution to the establishment of a democratic legislative block in our country, while defining the functional limits of public authorities and insisting on independence of judicial power[120].

Unfortunately, in recent years, constitutionalism in Moldova notably has suffered from "persistent perseverance" of political party representatives on amending the text of Fundamental Law[121], "extensive" interpretation of the Constitution by the Constitutional Court (with significant effect on content of some features in the state political system, without any changes in Constitution), etc.

Under provisions of Fundamental Law, the Constitutional Court ensures constitutional review of normative acts and exercises its powers according to constitutional procedure. The Court is entrusted with the mission to protect the supremacy of the Constitution and its direct effect, while ensuring the compliance between normative acts of state bodies and the Constitution.

---

119 Decree No. 7 of March 4, 2016 on constitutional review of some provisions in Law No. 1115-XIV of July 5, 2000 amending and supplementing the Constitution of Moldova (procedure of electing the President). Monitorul Oficial No. 59–67 of March 18, 2016.

120 D. Pulbere, *Cuvânt de salut,* Materialele Conferinței "Rolul Curții Constituționale în sistemul protecției drepturilor omului și respectarea CEDO și jurisprudenței Curții Europene a Drepturilor Omului în jurisprudența și legislația națională". Chișinău, December 13–14, 2007, p. 7.

121 PDM propune modificarea Constituției prin introducerea referinței la integrarea europeană a Moldovei, https://www.publika.md › Știri › Politică, vizitat la 16.10.2017, Socialiștii caută semnături pentru proiectul de modificare a Constituției…, www.jurnal.md/.../socialistii-cauta-semnaturi-pentru-proiectul-de-modificare-a-constit..., vizitat la 16.10.2017, Deputații PLDM au elaborat un proiect de lege privind modificarea art. 13 din Constituție, vizitat la October 16, 2017.

To exercise the decisions of the Constitutional Court, Parliament (and if necessary, other state bodies) shall cancel the unconstitutional act and at best adopt the new normative act (or make relevant amendments, if this act was recognized unconstitutional only in certain parts).

A new law or amendments shall be adopted according to legal arguments and positions provided in the statement part of the Constitutional Court decision. Thus, via its decisions, the Constitutional Court contributes to the enhancement of constitutional legality and ensures constitutional norms, protection of the constitutional order, and respect for human and civil rights/freedoms.

7 Social Perception of the Constitutional Court

Any constitutional jurisdiction body, including the Constitutional Court of the Republic of Moldova, is subject to various (more or less critical) comments, as its decisions can never satisfy all interested parties involved in constitutional review.

In fact, the attitude toward Constitutional Court decisions indicates the level of political maturity for political forces and society as a whole. Indeed, everything can be criticized in a democratic society, including Constitutional Court decisions; however, critical comments on Constitutional Court decisions shall not result in the destruction of this institution[122].

According to former judges of the Constitutional Court, this body enjoys independence (special status) and authority (its decisions are final and binding), while occupying a special place in the system of state bodies (no involvement in forming state bodies, no interference in their powers, and no subordination to them—influence on their activities via its decisions only)[123].

Practices of the Constitutional Court were assessed positively by academic-teaching staff, who considered Court decisions as an example of "high principles

---

122 Al. Tănase, *Cuvânt de salut. „Rolul justiției constituționale în protecția valorilor statului de drept"*, Conferința Internațională „Rolul justiției constituționale în protecția valorilor statului de drept": 20 ani: Adoptarea Constituției Republicii Moldova, September 8–9, 2014, Chișinău. Arc, 2015, p. 11.

123 D. Pulbere, *Controlul constituționalității actelor juridice ale organelor centrale ale puterii de stat – o garanție a asigurării supremației Constituției*, Materialele Conferinței "Rolul Curții Constituționale în sistemul protecției drepturilor omului și respectarea CEDO și jurisprudenței Curții Europene a Drepturilor Omului în jurisprudența și legislația națională". Chișinău, December 13–14, 2007, p. 9.

and moral integrity"[124] and noted the "growing role of Constitutional Court in interpreting and ensuring the uniform application of international law"[125].

By proposal from Parliament and the Government of the Republic of Moldova, following the Strategy of Reform in Justice Sector for 2012–2016, EU experts drafted a report on the assessment of the Constitutional Court, which was published on May 27, 2016[126]. According to authors of the report, the Constitutional Court is functional and quite an organized and equipped institution that has the required human and material resources. Judges and staff of the Constitutional Court are adequately trained and fulfil their duties at a high professional level. The experts found that constitutional norms and legal provisions ensuring their practical implementation are generally compliant with European standards. Nevertheless, reality specifies the need to protect its independence from obstacles created by political persons. The experts noted that a list of subjects entitled to appeal to the constitutional jurisdiction body is quite extensive. Despite the fact that citizens cannot directly appeal to the Constitutional Court, *de jure*, they have some methods of indirect access via the People's Lawyer, attorney, and deputy of Parliament. In this view, experts do not recommend introducing a procedure for the direct appeal of citizens to the Constitutional Court of the Republic of Moldova, as such a procedure assumes complete change in the Court's structure and methods of work. They believe that entitling the lower court instances to appeal to the Constitutional Court will be expedient. As a result, authors of the report came to a conclusion on an absence of the need for substantial amendments to laws on Constitutional Court activities, as current provisions sufficiently guarantee independence of the Court and judges, while acts of the Constitutional Court comply with quality standards adopted in EU countries.

---

124 A. Smochină, *Tendințe actuale în evoluția jurisdicției constituționale moldovenești,* Materialele Conferinței "Rolul Curții Constituționale în sistemul protecției drepturilor omului și respectarea CEDO și jurisprudenței Curții Europene a Drepturilor Omului în jurisprudența și legislația națională". Chișinău, December 13–14, 2007, p. 157.

125 V. Gamurari, *Interpretarea tratatelor internaționale și a dreptului internațional de către Curtea Constituțională – o cale de implementare a acestora în ordinea juridică internă a statelor*, Materialele Conferinței "Rolul Curții Constituționale în sistemul protecției drepturilor omului și respectarea CEDO și jurisprudenței Curții Europene a Drepturilor Omului în jurisprudența și legislația națională". Chișinău, December 13–14, 2007, p. 166.

126 Raportul Uniunii Europene de evaluare a Curții Constituționale a Republicii Moldova. constcourt.md/.

Let's note that Constitutional Court activities are given less optimistic and even hostile assessments too. Thus, in 2002, on adoption of some Court decisions (disagreed on by some representatives of political power), it was proposed to revise the legislation so that Parliament could neglect the decisions of the Constitutional Court. A declaration from the leader of one party was quite alarming: "Constitutional Court judges are no gods descending to the Earth; they cannot make better decisions than 100 deputies"[127].

Kalman Mizsei, former special EU representative in the Republic of Moldova (2007–2011), expressed his attitude to the Constitutional Court decision of March 4, 2016 abolishing the deputies' right to elect the President of Moldova in Parliament. In his opinion, this strange decision is "just another one in the whole series of decisions motivated by short-term political considerations, rather than by wish to preserve the absolute rule of law, even if it does not fit at the moment"[128].

When asked to assess the Constitutional Court decision (the Declaration of Independence prevailing over the Constitution of the Republic of Moldova) of 6,411 respondents, a positive attitude was expressed by 17.2 % and a negative attitude by 59.0 %. Of these, 11.2 % believed that this decision was political; 9.0 % assessed it as hasty[129].

Conclusions

In the 21st century, the international community gained vast experience in forming a system of constitutionalism. Each state is different regarding its national, historical, political, ideological, cultural, and economic features, which determine its need and ability to form its own model of constitutionalism.

In practice, the constitutionalism of any country has individual features, which assumes the role of the Constitution as a fundamental law plus certain tools to ensure its observance.

The problem with a uniform application of the Fundamental Law can be solved in different ways, but the constitutional review of laws is one of the most reliable methods as it can address conflicts and gaps in legislation.

---

127 V. Puşcaşu, *Independenţa Curţii Constituţionale în oglinda strmbă a legislatiei*, Timpul, February 16, 2010.

128 K. Mizsei, *Principiul statului de drept este esenţial atât în Moldova, cât şi în Ucraina*, http://www.ipn.md/ro/integrare-europeana/75455.

129 All polls—NOI.md. https://www.noi.md/ru/polls (accessed: March 20, 2018).

When studying Constitutional Court activities, let's note the Court's aim to establish legal standards and universal constitutional values. Thus, the Constitutional Court can avoid arbitrariness and act so that applied motivational method becomes predictable. Based on that, provisions of the Constitution of the Republic of Moldova will be applied only in the way that they are provided in the Constitutional Court decisions used for their interpreting. As a result, constitutional jurisdiction becomes or may become the unifying factor for various elements forming the social whole.

As with interpreting certain norms in the Constitution, during constitutional review of laws and other normative acts, the Constitutional Court may perform a constructive role, while specifying or even expanding the meaning and value of constitutional norm, enriching and preserving the normative content of Fundamental Law (of course, based on actual constitutional norms only).

The state duty of ensuring human rights and freedoms is also exercised via activities of the Constitutional Court in Moldova, which, according to the Law on Constitutional Court (Article 1), guarantees the supremacy of the Constitution and responsibility of state to citizen and citizen to state.

These principles form the essence and purpose of the Constitutional Court, which acts under its constitutional status, thus exercising the protective function of law realized by the state.

According to the Constitutional Court, a law-bound state is a means for establishing the rule of law, which cannot recognize and exercise human rights in absolute and discretional form—only along with observing the rights of other persons and society as a whole[130].

Accordingly, the protection of human rights and freedoms by the Constitutional Court becomes an important guarantee for exercise of its inalienable powers.

The activity of this institute is closely related to the new role of the law, which shall be viewed as a normative expression of social justice—an imperative "obstacle" for attempts to reduce the content or guarantees of fundamental rights.

Of course, the ultimate goal of constitutional jurisdiction is to ensure and guarantee the supremacy of the Constitution of the Republic of Moldova throughout the country.

---

130 Decree on constitutional review of some provisions in Law No. 64-XII of May 31, 1990 on Government, as amended by Laws No. 107 and 110 of May 3, 2013, Presidential Decrees No. 634-VII and No. 635-VII of May 16, 2013, and Governmental Decree No. 295 of May 16, 2013. Monitorul Oficial No. 122–124/13 of June 7, 2013.

A competence of such nature, inherent to the Constitutional Court of the Republic of Moldova, ensures its turning into a unique institution with extremely high significance of the acts, which are final, excluding any means of appeal and making an integral part in formal sources of law.

However, this hypothesis is conditional; the Constitutional Court of the Republic of Moldova cannot replace the Parliament as a legislative body, while turning into a creator of new legal norms.

In conclusion, let's note that, today, unlike the period before 1994, Moldova has its Constitutional Court, which (although far from perfect) managed to lay the basis of national constitutionalism, an important element for building the law-bound state. Later on, the Constitutional Court shall become an example for discussion and thinking over relations between citizen and state (so necessary for Moldova), while acquiring the role of the actual creator in the public sphere of modern society. Without a strong and politically independent Constitutional Court, the Republic of Moldova can never become a democratic and law-bound state for the benefit of all our citizens.

Davlat Elnazarov

Constitutional Justice in the Republic of Tajikistan

Abstract: In Tajikistan, like in a predominant majority of the other post-Soviet states, constitutional court was built on the basis of the European model of reviewing the legal norms. It is aimed to protect the legal norms included in the constitution, hence protecting individual rights and freedoms. A thesis is put forward that in Tajikistan constitutional judiciary is not free from political conditions.

Keywords: the European model of reviewing the legal norms, Constitutional Court, autonomy and independence, The Constitutional Court and other organs of state power, cognition of the Constitutional Court

Introduction

For two decades, constitutional justice in Tajikistan functioned as a state-legal institute based on universal scientific-theoretical principles and law-enforcement practice; meanwhile, it developed exclusive provisions with account for local terms and traditions. Its tasks include the arrangement of conditions for supremacy and direct functioning of the Constitution to ensure individual freedoms and rights.

An analysis of constitutional justice bodies in Tajikistan leads to a conclusion that at the moment, constitutional justice in the Republic is not quite effective. Here is a brief list of problems: the use of specialized justice bodies as a political tool; delayed exercise of decisions requiring legal regulation; the use of normative-legal acts after recognizing them unconstitutional; and improper exercise/ignoring of constitutional justice decisions by public authorities.

The institute of constitutional justice in Tajikistan applies an extensive normative base. The formation of a modern democratic law-bound state with a republican government—which assumes major improvement in relations between people, society, and state, with reform of state bodies in Tajikistan—is a natural moment in the development of local constitutional legislation.

Now, constitutional justice is one of the inalienable elements of a modern democratic state, as the Constitutional Court is a state body exercising judicial protection of human and civil rights/freedoms. Constitutional review plays an important role in the democratization of public life and building the law-bound state in Tajikistan. In modern democratic foreign states, studying the mechanism behind the protection of human and civil rights and freedoms is incomplete without defining the role of constitutional courts as bodies that exercise judicial constitutional review.

Apart from adequate comprehension and timely legal regulation, recent changes in the economic, political, and social spheres of Tajikistan also require a scientific study of legal nature for such a conceptual phenomenon as the Constitutional Court of Tajikistan.

Such an approach assumes the detection of reasons for the establishment of special constitutional justice bodies, which apply models of judicial constitutional review (based on examples of modern civilized states) according to which constitutional justice bodies were formed to rethink the establishment of constitutional review bodies, detect the problems occurring during the exercise of powers by constitutional review bodies, and assess future prospects of functioning for constitutional review bodies in Tajikistan.

The study's relevance is also caused by the need to identify the details of the structure and activities of constitutional justice in Tajikistan as an element of a state body system and mechanism that protects human/civil rights and freedoms or develops the system approach to their legal regulation. The synthesis/analysis of legislation on constitutional courts, as well as the synthesis and analysis of experience on their functioning (by example of other states), is of particular interest to the science of local constitutional law to improve the institute of constitutional justice.

In this view, there is an objective need to review the legal nature and basis of constitutional justice in the context of Tajik legal reality, which helps determine its place in the mechanism of state power; identify its details and formation procedure; evaluate the legal status of constitutional review bodies; and analyze their powers related to ensuring the supremacy of the Tajik Constitution in the hierarchy of legal norms.

1 Motives for Introduction and Key Dilemmas of Establishing Legal Control

The practice of building a law-bound state and forming civil society under constitutional provisions in modern Tajikistan is only possible by improving the law-making, law-exercising, and effectiveness of law enforcement. The main problem with this process is ensuring the reality of constitutional provisions—more precisely, the reality of the ratio between constitutional regulations and relations in society.

On one hand, imperfections, gaps, and conflicts related to local laws, unconstitutionality of some legal prescriptions contained in the acts of various subjects, and the constitutional program of building a law-bound state all enhance the basis for the self-regulation of civil society. On the other hand, these require the formation of a mechanism that contributes to a pretty fast, adequate response of laws to changes in public practice and the detection of drawbacks in the current legislation. The basic principle of this mechanism is objectivity. Thus, a system of separating the powers vests relevant authorities in judicial bodies.

The emergence of a constitutional review institute in Tajikistan caused major changes in the development of local constitutional law (regulating the status of the Constitutional Court in Tajikistan, relations with other state bodies, constitutional proceedings, etc.). As rightly noted by D.D. Khoshimzoda: "Essence of constitutional review is that, by recognizing the norm unconstitutional, Constitutional Court ensures constitutional legality in the country, as well as stability and sustainability of national legal system, thus getting the legal possibility of indirect participation in rule-making process. In a sense, this body seeks and creates the law, while affecting the will of legislator and law enforcer"[1].

However, the problem with the interaction between specialized constitutional review bodies and the legal system of Tajikistan is not reduced to regulating the relations of constitutional justice and forming an independent sub-sector of constitutional procedural law (constitutional judicial procedural law). There is another (assumingly, more important) aspect of reviewing the problem: the impact of constitutional justice body activities on the national legal system (or, rather, the role and meaning of the decisions made by these bodies for law-making/exercising and the constitutional culture of Tajik society).

The role and meaning of decisions made by constitutional justice bodies (in the legal system of the state) is one of the most disputable issues of exercising the constitutional review in Tajikistan.

When forming an institute of specialized constitutional review, Tajikistan chose the European model of judicial constitutional review in the form of the independent Constitutional Court in Tajikistan.

---

1 Д.Д. Хошимзода, *Конституционная юстиция – гарантия законности в Таджикистане*, (in:) *Материалы международной конференции, посвященн ой 20-летию образования Конституционного суда Республики Таджикистан на тему: «Конституционное правосудие – гарант обеспечения верховенства Конституции»* (Dushanbe, September 17–18, 2015), pp. 78–83.

With the collapse of the USSR, independent post-Soviet states most often formed the institute of constitutional review as constitutional justice based on the establishment of specialized (i.e. constitutional) courts.

Due to the establishment of the Constitutional Supervision Committee of the USSR (in socialist republics including Tajikistan), the Decree of the Supreme Soviet of Tajik SSR dated August 23, 1990 formed a constitutional commission/workgroup, which prepared the first draft of the new Constitution of Tajik SSR, including 7 sections (some were divided into chapters) and 150 articles. Meanwhile, an amendment was made to Article 114 in the Constitution of Tajikistan[2] according to which the establishment of a constitutional review body (the Constitutional Supervision Committee of Tajikistan) was assumed in Tajikistan for the first time. Under this article, on April 23, 1990, the Supreme Council of Tajikistan adopted a decree on forming a new specialized body in a supreme power system: the Constitutional Supervision Committee of Tajikistan. The first Chairperson of the Constitutional Supervision Committee was elected at the 1st session, 12th convocation of the Supreme Council of Tajikistan. On August 27, 1990, the Law "On Constitutional Supervision" was adopted at the 2nd session of the Supreme Council of Tajikistan. The Deputy Chairperson and six members of Constitutional Supervision Committee were elected at the same session. Later, on December 8, 1990, another (7th) member of Constitutional Supervision Committee was elected at the 4th session of the Supreme Council.

A specialized constitutional review body was first established in Tajikistan in April 1990. It was known as the "Constitutional Supervision Committee". Under the laws of Tajikistan, the Committee was entitled to check the compliance of draft laws, valid acts (adopted by the Congress of People's Deputies of Tajik SSR, the Supreme Council of Tajik SSR, and its chambers), acts of the Attorney General of Tajik SSR, and normative acts of other state bodies and public organizations with the Constitution of the USSR. The Committee was entitled to supervise the legislative initiative. On introduction of the presidency in 1990, the Constitution stated that the removal of the President from office (in case

2 Постановление Правительства Республики Таджикистан от 23 апреля 1990 г. «Об образовании Комитета конституционного надзора Республики Таджикистан», „Ведомости Верховного Совета Республики Таджикистан“ 1990, № 32. Ст. 114; Закон Республики Таджикистан от 27 августа 1990 г. «О конституционном надзоре», "Ведомости Верховного Совета Республики Таджикистан" 1990, № 17. Ст. 291.

of violating the Constitution/laws) requires the opinion of the Constitutional Supervision Committee.

In any case, the Committee sent its conclusions to the issuer of the act, the initiator of reviewing the issue, and the Presidium of the Supreme Council of Tajik SSR.

The conclusion on incompliance of act (its parts) with the Constitution was suspending the act (its parts) until the incompliance was addressed. The suspension did not apply to acts adopted by the Congress of People's Deputies of Tajik SSR. The issuer of the act had to address the incompliance within 3 months. If the deadline expired and incompliance had not been addressed, the Committee could enter the Congress of People's Deputies, Supreme Council, or Council of Ministers with a proposal to annul an act (its individual provisions) incompliant with the Constitution.

In case the Supreme Council rejected the Committee's conclusion, the issue had to be submitted for review by the Congress of People's Deputies of Tajik SSR, the decision of which was final. The Congress of People's Deputies could reject the opinion of the Constitutional Supervision Committee by two-thirds of the total people's deputies of the Tajik SSR. If the proposal to revoke the opinion did not receive the required vote of the people's deputies at Congress, the act (its individual provisions) incompliant with Constitution became invalid.

Subjects entitled to initiate the review of issues at the Constitutional Supervision Committee of the Tajik SSR included: Congress, the Supreme Council or one-fifth of the people's deputies of the Tajik SSR, the President, supreme bodies of state power, and all-union bodies of public organizations.

On its own initiative, the Committee could review issues on compliance between acts of supreme state power/administration bodies (formed by the Congress of People's Deputies and Supreme Council of the Republic) and the Constitution/laws of the Tajik SSR. The issue could be submitted by the Chairperson, Deputy Chairperson, or Committee member, while being admitted for review by the majority vote of Committee members attending the session.

Defining the compliance between acts of supreme state power/administration bodies and the local Constitution was the main function of constitutional review exercised by the Constitutional Supervision Committee.

Let's note that for its short period of operation (until 1995), the Constitutional Supervision Committee of Tajikistan began its activities in strict compliance with the Constitution and adopted major conclusions that stated the unconstitutionality of state body acts, to confirm the need for such a body as the Constitutional Supervision Committee.

Example 1.
Opinion of the Constitutional Supervision Committee of Tajikistan. "Decision of Presidium of Cabinet of Ministers of Tajikistan dated July 9, 1991 Temporary Suspension (until 1995) of Buying-Out the Apartments in Houses Built by Facility Administration at Management Board of Council of Ministers of Tajikistan" (protocol No. 19, section XX).

On July 9, 1991, the Presidium of Cabinet of Ministers of Tajikistan adopted a decision: "Temporary Suspension (until 1995) of Buying-Out the Apartments in Houses Built by the Facility Administration at the Management Board of the Council of Ministers of Tajikistan", which prohibited the sale of apartments in houses built by the Facility Administration at the Management Board of Council of Ministers of Tajikistan (Article 2).

Having reviewed these norms on its own initiative, the Constitutional Supervision Committee of Tajikistan states:

Under Article 11 in the Constitution of Tajikistan, citizens may own houses, apartments, etc. Article 11 of the Law titled "On Property in Tajikistan" entitles the tenants of living quarters (at state/public housing stock) and members of their family to buy-out the relevant house or apartment from the owner. The Law "On Denationalization and Privatization of Property in Tajikistan" does not impose any actual restrictions on the privatization of housing. To recognize the supremacy of the Constitution and the laws of Tajikistan, based on inadmissible limiting of civil rights by subordinate acts and guided by Article 114 in the Constitution of Tajikistan and Articles 10, 11, 17, and 20 in the Law "On Constitutional Supervision in Tajikistan", the Constitutional Supervision Committee of Tajikistan came to the following conclusion. Article 2 in the decision of the Presidium of the Cabinet of Ministers of Tajikistan dated July 9, 1991: "Temporary Suspension (until 1995) of Buying-Out the Apartments in Houses Built by the Facility Administration at Management Board of Council of Ministers of Tajikistan" (protocol No. 19, section XX) does not comply with Constitution and laws of Tajikistan. This incompliance was subject to addressing within 2 months; until its addressing, the effects of Article 2 in the above decision of the Presidium of the Cabinet of Ministers of Tajikistan is suspended.

Example 2.
The Conclusion of the Constitutional Supervision Committee of Tajikistan. "On the Decision of the Presidium of the Cabinet of Ministers of Tajikistan about the Decision of the Council of People's Deputies in the Matchinsky District, No. 104 of December 21, 1991. "Approving the Provision on Public Order, Improvement, and Sanitation in the Matchinsky District"". By decision No. 104 of December 21, 1991, the Matchinsky District Council of the People's Deputies approved the Provision "On Public Order, Improvement, and Sanitation in the District". The provision sets a number of penalties (for violation of public order, improvement, and sanitation in the district) and forms an Improvement Fund (for transfer of fines and voluntary contributions from enterprises,

organizations, institutions, and citizens); at that, the Fund is exempt from any type of taxes to republican and regional budgets.

Based on the inadmissible limiting of civil rights by subordinate acts, considering the decision-making by state bodies within the powers provided by laws only, recognizing the addressing of offenses on the basis of legality only, and guided by Article 114 in the Constitution of Tajikistan and Articles 10, 17 in the Law "On Constitutional Supervision of Tajikistan", the Constitutional Supervision Committee of Tajikistan came to this conclusion: Items 5, 9, and a list of offenses/sanctions in the Provision on Public Order, Improvement, and Sanitation in the Matchinsky district, approved by the decision of the Council of People's Deputies in the Matchinsky district No. 104 of December 21, 1991, do not comply with the Constitution and laws of Tajikistan. Until the incompliance is addressed, the effect of these norms is suspended.

Example 3.
The Conclusion of the Constitutional Supervision Committee of Tajikistan on the Decree of the Supreme Council of Tajikistan, dated October 2, 1991. "Suspension of Activities for the Communist Party of Tajikistan, Its Successor, and Its Property".

On October 2, 1991, the Supreme Council of Tajikistan adopted a decree titled "Suspension of Activities for the Communist Party of Tajikistan, Its Successor, and Its Property", which suspended the activities of the Communist Party of Tajikistan and its successor until defining the extent of guilt in the events of August 1991; the Attorney's Office of Tajikistan, Ministry of Justice of Tajikistan, and Deputy Commission were instructed to check (within 2 months) the involvement of the Communist Party of Tajikistan in the attempt of a coup d'état by the State Emergency Committee; the Cabinet of Ministers of Tajikistan was proposed to ensure the protection of property owned by the Communist Party of Tajikistan, as well as the payment of salaries and benefits to the staff of party committees at the expense of the Communist Party of Tajikistan. Under Article 22 in the Law "Constitutional Supervision of Tajikistan", the Constitutional Supervision Committee of Tajikistan resolved to address the gaps in legislation by contacting the Supreme Council of Tajikistan with proposals to exercise the right of the Supreme Council to official compulsory interpreting of Supreme Council acts (by Item 18, Article 99, Constitution of Tajikistan) or amendments/addenda to the Law "On Public Associations in Tajikistan", which define the legal regime for suspending the activity of public associations.

There are many other examples, including the conclusion of the Republic of Tajikistan's Constitutional Supervision Committee on Article 2 in the Decree of the Republic of Tajikistan President dated August 23, 1991 "Terminating the Activity of Organizational Structures, Political Parties, and Mass Public Movements by Law-Enforcement Bodies and Office of Republic of Tajikistan President"[3]; the conclusion of Republic of Tajikistan's Constitutional Supervision Committee on the Decree of the Republic of the Tajikistan Supreme Council "Procedure of Voting in Electing the Chairperson of the RT Supreme Council", No. 13 of October 6, 1991[4]; the conclusion of the Republic of Tajikistan's Constitutional Supervision Committee on the Decree of the Republic of Tajikistan President dated July 23, 1991 "Forming a Committee for Control on Exercising the Laws/Acts of Republic of Tajikistan President, Cabinet of Ministers, and Coordination of Crime Prevention at Republic of Tajikistan President"[5]; the conclusion of the Republic of Tajikistan's Constitutional Supervision Committee on Part 4, Article 7 in the Republic of Tajikistan Law "On Freedom of Conscience and Religious Organizations"[6]; the conclusion of the Republic of Tajikistan's Constitutional Supervision Committee "On Part 1, Article 79 in the Regulation of the Republic of the Tajikistan Supreme Council"[7], etc.

By nature, it was a quasi-judicial body. Prior to establishing the Constitutional Supervision Committee, functions of the constitutional review were assigned to the Supreme Council, Presidium of Supreme Council, Government, Attorney's Office, etc.[8]

Let's note that the formation of a specialized constitutional review body in Tajikistan took place within the changes occurring throughout the former USSR. Thus, in some republics, the formation of constitutional courts was accompanied by dramatic events comparable to Russia. The Supreme Council of Ukraine started an election of CC judges in March 1993, but could elect the Chairperson only, who died in March 1995 (prior to the election of at least one more judge). The Constitutional Court of Ukraine was formed only in December 1996—after the adoption of a new Constitution. In 1995, by individual complaints on an uneven layout of election districts, the Constitutional Court of Kazakhstan recognized

3 Cf. Ведомости верховного совета РТ 1991 год № 23.

4 Cf. Ведомости верховного совета РТ 1992 год № 1.

5 Cf. Ведомости верховного совета РТ 1992 год № 1.

6 Cf. Ведомости верховного совета РТ 1992 года № 2.

7 Cf. Ведомости верховного совета РТ 1992 года № 3.

8 К.Н. Холиков, *Становление и развитие института конституционного надзора в Таджикистане*, Dushanbe 1998, p. 94.

the parliamentary election as illegal after which President N. Nazarbayev dissolved the Supreme Council and submitted to referendum the Constitution, which abolished the Constitutional Court. The Constitutional Court of Belarus (formed in 1994) was actively involved in opposition of the Supreme Council to President A. Lukashenko. In November 1996, under a procedure not recognized by the Constitutional Court, the Constitution was adopted and a new Parliament was formed without an election, after which judges were proposed to take an oath to the new Constitution or resign.

The first of the actual constitutional courts in post-Soviet republics was formed in 1993, in Lithuania. At about the same time, a constitutional review body appeared in Estonia—not an independent court, but the Chamber of Constitutional Review at the State Court.

In 1995, constitutional courts began to work in Georgia, Kyrgyzstan, and Moldova; in early 1996, in Tajikistan and Uzbekistan.

In February 1996, the Constitutional Court of Armenia was formed; in Kazakhstan (instead of previously operating Constitutional Court), the Constitutional Council was established under the Constitution of 1995. The end of the year was marked by a political crisis in Belarus, which resulted in the adoption of a new Constitution at referendum. It maintained such an institute as the Constitutional Court, but its members increased from 11 to 12 (6 judges are appointed by the President, and 6 others by the Council of the Republic, the upper chamber of the new Belarusian Parliament).

As noted by some scholars, the formation and development of constitutional justice in post-Soviet states were complex, involving several stages. Initially, back in Soviet republics, the reform of state bodies from 1988 to 1990 assumed the formation of specialized constitutional supervision bodies: so-called Constitutional Supervision Committees. In this view, Soviet republics made active changes to their legislation. However, although nearly all of them adopted relevant laws/amendments to the Constitution until 1991, most of the bodies exercising constitutional legal proceedings in the post-Soviet space actually began to operate in the mid-1990s[9].

With the adoption of the Constitution in 1994, the Constitutional Court (a specialized body of judicial constitutional review) was formed in Tajikistan.

---

9 И.В. Петрова, *Конституционный Суд – орган конституционного контроля в Российской Федерации, Дисс. на соиск. уч. степени. канд. юрид. наук*, Moscow 2004, p. 51; Д.В. Змиевский, *Осуществление конституционного судопроизводства на постсоветском пространстве*, "Пробелы в Российском законодательстве" 2008, № 2, p. 34.

2 Legislative Stability of the Constitutional Court

The adoption of some normative acts served as a legal/practical basis in the formation and development of a specialized constitutional review body in Tajikistan.

The Declaration of Sovereignty of Tajikistan, dated August 24, 1990, which proclaimed the separation of powers and supremacy of the Constitution/laws of the republic, was developed and adopted during the so-called parade of sovereignties in Soviet republics. So, it reflected a tendency toward sovereignty. Thus, the Declaration contained a provision on the supremacy of the Constitution/laws of republic over normative legal acts of the USSR, if they conflicted with interests of the republic. Literature of that time suggested that in case of conflict between acts of the USSR and interests of Tajikistan, the Supreme Council of Tajikistan could suspend the normative legal acts contrary to sovereign rights of Tajikistan.

The proclamation of state independence in Tajikistan complicated the political situation in the country; it resulted in civil war.

Unfortunately, the process of forming and developing the specialized judicial constitutional supervision in Tajikistan, along with the formation of new power structures, coincided with the political opposition and civil war in Tajikistan of 1992–1997. During this inter-Tajik conflict, the legal basis of public life was seriously shaken. In 1990–1994, the Tajik Constitution of 1978 was actually invalid, and a new Constitution had not been adopted yet. The 16th session of the Supreme Council convened in November 1992 in Khujand and adopted some important documents, which accelerated the political transformation. This session established a commission on drafting the new Constitution of Tajikistan.

The Constitution of Tajikistan, adopted by the national referendum of November 6, 1994, was another important act that established the specialized constitutional review. It assumes formation of some new institutes (democratic and still unknown to Tajik people): separation of powers, private property, political pluralism, etc.

Two institutes (still unknown in the statehood practice of Tajikistan) were formed in the field of constitutional legal proceedings:

1) Constitutional Court of Tajikistan;
2) Constitutional Legal Proceedings.

Thus, the Constitution of Tajikistan formed a legal basis for the new constitutional review body in the history of Tajikistan, but it was not enough for the forming and functioning of this body. The Constitution contained general provisions on the composition and powers of the Constitutional Court. The

Constitution did not clearly define the legal nature of the Constitutional Court, did not fully clarify the issues related to the legal status of this body, did not disclose the issues on arranging the activities of this body, etc.

In this view, the formation of the Constitutional Court in the republic required an adoption of special law. Based on that, the republic began the work on drafting the constitutional law "On Constitutional Courts of Tajikistan"[10].

Finally, the normative legal act that played a decisive role in forming the new institute was the constitutional law "On Constitutional Court of Tajikistan" of November 3, 1995. This constitutional law slightly corrected the provisions on the legal nature and status of the Constitutional Court contained in the draft. Now, the Constitutional Court is named as a body of "judicial power for protection of the Constitution in Tajikistan" (the Constitutional Supervision Committee was considered the body for exercising the specialized constitutional supervision).

Of course, the new law was discussed by national scholars—with the expression of quite a fair opinion that the Constitutional Court was not part of general jurisdiction courts (unlike them, it was established to resolve constitutional issues rather than ordinary disputes). The Constitutional Court was not supposed to play the role of a judicial body reviewing and resolving criminal, administrative, and civil cases.

Let's note that the formation of a specialized judicial constitutional review in Tajikistan was also aided with judicial reform conducted in those years. The Soviet judicial system applied in Tajikistan was subject to harsh criticism; a radical transformation of the judicial system and the development of its new legislative base began since 1992. In 1993, the laws of Tajikistan "On Judicial System", "On Status of Judges in Tajikistan", and "On Supreme Court of Tajikistan" were adopted. However, at that stage, judicial reform did not assume the formation of a judicial body in the field of constitutional review. The Constitutional Supervision Committee kept performing the function of constitutional supervision.

On July 20, 1994, the Law of Tajikistan No. 974 "On Constitutional Reform in Tajikistan, on Procedure of Adopting/Enacting the Constitution of Tajikistan"[11] was adopted, where the formation of the Constitutional Court (instead of the

10 Конституционный Закон Республики Таджикистан «О Конституционном суде» от 26 июля 2014 года. № 1084, "Ахбори Маджлиси Оли Республики Таджикистан", Душанбе 2014, № 7, ст. 380.

11 Закон Республики Таджикистан от 20 июля 1994 года, № 974 «О конституционной реформе в Республике Таджикистан, о порядке принятия и введения в действие Конституции Республики Таджикистан», "Ахбори Маджлиси Оли Республики Таджикистан", Душанбе 1994, № 13, ст. 194.

Constitutional Supervision Committee) was assumed. Thus, the formation of the Constitutional Court in Tajikistan was first assumed in the above law, rather than in the Constitution of 1994.

Thus, the institute of the Constitutional Court was introduced to Tajikistan in 1994. The formation of this new institute implements the concept on separation of powers and expresses the policy on establishing the law-bound state. Establishing the new form of judicial power (constitutional justice) in Tajikistan led to changes in the judicial system and in the legal proceedings of Tajikistan.

In modern terms, legislation has the most effect within interstate associations. Thus, similar Constitutions and other basic legal institutes are observed within the Commonwealth of Independent States (CIS) countries. Such interaction is due to common legal policy and similar legal sources in these countries.

One of the legal effects is the aim to borrow similar foreign laws. This happens while using the services of foreign consultants, who apply their legal experience and try to bring in the principles, norms, and institutes of their laws. Now, official channels of influence on the adoption/application of laws in foreign states are also used.

Beyond that, in terms of state cooperation (especially with interstate associations), there is a need for the mutual solving of common tasks related to adjusting, developing, and applying laws. This is achieved by the approximation/harmonization of laws in different states. During harmonization, the following tasks are solved: 1) forming the common policy of legal development; 2) measures taken to overcome legal differences; 3) measures taken with regards to the development of common, joint, and uniform legal rules[12].

The approximation and unification of laws pursue the following goals: 1) legal support for coordinated development of laws; 2) determination of common directions in the legal policy of states (namely in legislation); 3) the development of coordinated and joint (including model) legislative acts; 4) measures taken to overcome legal differences preventing the harmonization of laws; 5) formulation of common legal standards in developing and applying harmonized laws; and 6) forming the common concept for the development of national legislations.

The approximation of laws takes place on the basis of legal integration within various legal groups, namely interstate associations. Thus, the Inter-Parliamentary Assembly of CIS Member States—a consultative body aiding in

12 С.Б. Мирзоев, *Особенности конституционного нормоконтроля как гарантия нормализации национальных законодательств*, "Вестник ТНУ РТ" № 3/5 (166), pp. 69–73.

solution of common legal issues—plays an important role in the legal integration of CIS states. On September 16, 1992, the Inter-Parliamentary CIS Assembly adopted a resolution called "Main fields of approximation for national laws of CIS member states". To address conflicts between national laws, it is recommended to use the following types of work: advisory (model) legal acts; a mutual exchange of information on adopted (if necessary, prepared) legal acts; a joint discussion of legal issues; a review of legal approximation issues at the CIS coordination institutes; scientific conferences; and recommendations of scientists on ways and methods of legal approximation.

Attention shall be paid to joint efforts of CIS states, the Inter-Parliamentary Assembly, and the European Union. As part of their general and special programs, a great deal of advisory and methodological aid is provided, scientific-practical developments are funded, and international seminars and conferences are organized.

An important role is also played by the advisory legislative act called "On normative legal acts of CIS member states"[13], approved by the CIS Inter-Parliamentary Assembly, as well as the resolution of Inter-Parliamentary Assembly of May 18, 1994 "On development of model civil code for CIS member states"[14]. Draft model laws are also prepared by legal scholars. Thus, in 1992, specialists of Harvard University developed "Basic World Tax Code" within the framework of the international tax program.

Along with Parliaments and other government institutes, the Constitutional Court too plays a significant role in ensuring the harmonization of laws. Constitutional normative control is accompanied by comparative analysis for legal acts of state and international treaties concluded with the state. The Institute of Legislation and Comparative Law at the government of the Russian Federation developed "Guidelines on comparative analysis of laws for CIS member states"[15]. According to these guidelines, objects of comparative study include: the Constitutions of CIS states; memorandums of association; international treaties; laws and other acts of Parliaments; laws and other acts of supreme authorities of the former USSR; and normative-legal acts of Presidents and governments of CIS member states.

---

13 Межпарламентской Ассамблеей СНГ рекомендательный законодательный акт «О нормативных правовых актах государств-участников СНГ»//http://www.busel.org/texts/cat9ut/id5cwcyuc.htm (accessed: February 22, 2018).

14 Ibidem, p. 148.

15 Ю.А. Тихомиров, *Курс сравнительного правоведения*, Moscow 1996, p. 228.

3 The Legislative Position of the Constitutional Court

3.1 The Constitutional Court and the President

In a system of bodies exercising constitutional review of Tajikistan, one of the central places is occupied by the President of Tajikistan. Under Article 64 in the Constitution, as the head of state/executive power, the President is a guarantor of the Constitution, laws, human and civil rights/freedoms, national independence, unity, territorial integrity, continuity and durability of the state, the coordinated operation/interaction of state bodies, and compliance with international treaties of Tajikistan.

According to Yu. Tikhomirov, the Constitution "defines the President as its guarantor, characterizes the political role of this institute as protector of the entire state system"[16]. This norm of the Constitution has many aspects. It is expressed in fact that the President of Tajikistan ensures a strict observance of the Constitution by all state/local self-government bodies, organizations, citizens, and their associations. In this view, the Constitution of Tajikistan assumes some procedures and mechanisms vested in the President. First, under Article 62 of the Constitution of Tajikistan, the President vetoes the laws incompliant with the Constitution[17]. Second, under Article 69 of the Constitution, the President abolishes/suspends the acts of executive bodies (in case of conflict with the Constitution and laws); third, the President can personally act as guarantor of the Constitution, but also via applying to competent bodies (first of all, to courts).

---

16 Ю.А. Тихомиров (ed.), *Конституционное законодательство России*, Moscow 1999, p. 129.

17 For example: in 2006, President of Tajikistan, Emomali Rakhmonov, rejected and sent for revision three laws adopted by Tajik Parliament (for the first time). These are RT laws "On Hypothec", "On Amendments/Addenda to RT Tax Code", and "On Real Estate Mortgage". Let's note that Law of Tajikistan "On Hypothec" was adopted by deputies of Tajik Parliament during scheduled meeting of RT Majlisi Namoyandagon at Majlisi Oly (MN MO) on December 12, 2006. Then, Chairperson of RT Islamic Renaissance Party and Deputy Mukhiddin Kabiri noted that adoption of this law is premature and Tajik society is not ready for it yet. He also proposed to exclude Chapter 9 (land loan) from text of draft law. He expressed his doubts that preparation of the draft considered opinion of peasants. He was supported by Deputy Mirzobek Khodzhiyev, who noted that land is exclusive property of state and "its mortgage is contrary to logic and Constitution".

So under Article 40, the constitutional law "Constitutional Court of Tajikistan"[18], the President may appeal to the Republic of the Tajikistan Constitutional Court on the compliance between the Republic of Tajikistan's Constitution and amendments/addenda to the Republic of Tajikistan's Constitution, draft laws, and other issues submitted to national referendum, as well as on compliance between the Republic of Tajikistan's Constitution and laws, joint normative-legal acts of Majlisi Milli and Majlisi Namoyandagon at Majlisi Oly, normative-legal acts of Majlisi Milli at Majlisi Oly, Majlisi Namoyandagon at Majlisi Oly, the Republic of Tajikistan's President, the Republic of Tajikistan's government, international treaties of Tajikistan that have not come into force, and instructions of the Republic of Tajikistan plenums of the Supreme Court and Supreme Economic Court. By results of the study, the Republic of Tajikistan's President did not exercise the right to appeal to the Republic of Tajikistan's Constitutional Court regarding the compliance between the Constitution, local normative-legal acts, and international treaties.

Annual messages of the President to Majlisi Oly form another important type of presidential constitutional review. They define the main fields of action and exercising of constitutional provisions, determine the vector of legal reforms, and bring the entire array of legislation in line with the Constitution of Tajikistan. Let's note that in messages of the Republic of Tajikistan's President, issues on compliance between the Constitution, laws, and other normative-legal acts were not reflected.

Thus, specificity of presidential control is determined by the constitutional status of the President as head of state. Presidential control has a wide legal range of control powers. They apply to the entire executive vertical of state power and the government system. Objects of presidential control include all state executive bodies[19].

3.2 The Constitutional Court and Government

In Tajikistan, issues of constitutional review/supervision are included in functions of the President (head of government), Majlisi Oly (Parliament), the

18 Конституционный Закон Республики Таджикистан «О Конституционном суде» от 26 июля 2014 года. № 1084, "Ахбори Маджлиси Оли Республики Таджикистан" Душанбе 2014, № 7, ст. 380.

19 Е.В. Едалов, *Правовой статус президента Российской Федерации как гаранта Конституции России в сфере федерального вмешательства*, "Бизнес в законе" 2009, № 3, p. 23.

Attorney's Office, and specialized supervisory bodies (Ombudsman for Human Rights and National Legislation Center at the Republic of Tajikistan's President).

3.3 The Constitutional Court and Parliament

Parliament (Majlisi Oly of Tajikistan) plays a special role in exercising constitutional review.

According to N. Vitruk, "Parliament, as a democratic body expressing the national and state sovereignty, exercises preliminary review over the constitutionality of adopted laws—at any stage of their legislative activity. Parliament is entitled to amend and supplement the laws for their full compliance with provisions of the Constitution. To protect and defend the Constitution, Parliaments use various forms of parliamentary control"[20].

In Tajikistan, the exercise of constitutional review by the Parliament (Majlisi Oly) has a distinctive feature. It is expressed in the requirement of Article 61, the Constitution of Tajikistan, according to which interpretation of the Constitution is vested in Majlisi Oly and adopted in the form of constitutional law. Practice of Tajik Parliament has no facts of applying this authority.

National legal literature has expressed many proposals on this issue (the need to transfer the interpretation of the Constitution from Majlisi Oly to the Constitutional Court)[21]. Thus, K. Kholikov noted that the Constitutional Court had to be given powers to interpret the RT Constitution/laws. To justify his position, he noted that the interpretation of the Constitution is the object competence of the Constitutional Court[22].

Attention shall also be paid to the fact that Article 61 of the Constitution says the interpretation of the Constitution rests in the hands of Majlisi Oly only. In turn, the Constitutional Court has no right to interpret normative acts at all. And here we have a collision. And what body shall interpret constitutional and other laws? As right to interpret the Constitution is vested in Majlisi Oly, this body shall interpret the laws too. Yet, in our opinion, the exercise of interpreting by body developing/adopting the laws is incorrect. Therefore, the Constitution

---

20 Н.В. Витрук, *Конституционное правосудие. Судебно-конституционное право и процесс*, Moscow 2010, p. 49.

21 К.Н. Холиков, *Конституционный суд и конституционное судопроизводство в Таджикистане*, Dushanbe 2014, p. 117; А.М. Диноршоев, *Конституционные основы разделения властей в Республике Таджикистан*, Dushanbe 2007, p. 93.

22 А.М. Диноршоев, Д.С. Сафаров, *Процессуальные институты конституционного судопроизводства в Республике Таджикистан*, Dushanbe 2015, p. 13.

and laws shall be interpreted by an independent constitutional review body (the Constitutional Court). Such a practice exists in most countries of the world[23].

The Constitutional Court of Tajikistan has no power to interpret laws besides the acts adopted by the Constitutional Court itself. In Part 1, Article 63, the constitutional law "On Constitutional Court of Tajikistan" states that acts of the Republic of Tajikistan's Constitutional Court are interpreted in official form by the Constitutional Court of Tajikistan only[24].

Another important type of constitutional review (exercised by Majlisi Oly and one of its chambers, Majlisi Milli) is the procedure assumed by Article 21 of the Republic of Tajikistan's constitutional law, "On Majlisi Oly of Tajikistan", under which Majlisi Milli annuls decisions of people's deputies: Majlisi at Gorno-Badakhshan autonomous region, regions, Dushanbe city, cities, and districts that are incompliant with the Constitution, constitutional laws, and other laws of Tajikistan. Besides, Majlisi Milli may dissolve the people's deputies Majlisi at Gorno-Badakhshan autonomous region, regions, Dushanbe city, cities, and districts that are at systematic incompliance with the Constitution and laws of Tajikistan. This function enables the building of uniform vertical representative bodies and prevents the adoption of unlawful acts by local representative bodies.

Like the President of Tajikistan, Majlisi Oly exercises constitutional review with support of other government bodies. Thus, the power of Majlisi Namoyandagon to ratify/denounce international treaties is an important type of constitutional review. To exercise this power, Majlisi Namoyandagon may apply to the Constitutional Court of Tajikistan to determine the compliance of these international treaties with the Constitution of Tajikistan. Given that under Article 10 of the Constitution, international legal acts upon ratification form part of the local legal system, and this form of control is very important. Besides, Majlisi Oly also forms the subjects of appeal to the Constitutional Court on issues of compliance between the Constitution and amendments/addenda to the Constitution, draft laws, and other issues submitted to national referendum.

Under Part 1, Article 8, the constitutional law "On the Constitutional Court of Tajikistan", "Chairperson, Deputy Chairperson, and judges of Constitutional Court are elected by Majlisi Milli at Majlisi Oly of Tajikistan by proposal of the Republic of Tajikistan's President". So, two branches of state power are involved

23 А.М. Диноршоев, *Конституционные основы разделения властей в Республике Таджикистан*, Dushanbe 2007, p. 118.

24 Конституционный Закон Республики Таджикистан «О Конституционном суде» от 26 июля 2014года. № 1084, "Ахбори Маджлиси Оли Республики Таджикистан" Душанбе 2014, № 7, ст. 380.

in the formation of the composition of the Constitutional Court—legislative (Majlisi Milli) and executive (the Republic of Tajikistan's President). At that, let's note that the President is not directly involved in electing Constitutional Court judges—they just nominate the candidates. The Constitutional Court judge is elected directly by Majlisi Milli at Majlisi Oly. Parts 1–2, Article 89 of the Republic of Tajikistan's Constitution assumes that the Constitutional Court consists of 7 members (one of them is the representative of the Gorno-Badakhshan autonomous region). A person who is at least 30 years old, has Republic of Tajikistan citizenship only, has a higher legal education, and has at least 7 years of professional experience may be elected as judge of the Constitutional Court. The age limit for the Constitutional Court judge is set by constitutional law[25]. The person elected as Constitutional Court judge for the first time takes an oath at the session of Majlisi Milli[26].

3.4 The Constitutional Court and Courts

When forming the institute of specialized constitutional review, Tajikistan chose the European model of judicial constitutional review (functioning of independent RT Constitutional Court).

In Tajikistan, a specialized constitutional review body was first established in April 1990. It was known as the "Constitutional Supervision Committee". By nature it was a quasi-judicial body. Prior to establishing the Constitutional Supervision Committee, constitutional review functions were assigned to the Supreme Council, Presidium of Supreme Council, Government, Attorney's Office, etc.[27]

Let's note that the formation of a specialized constitutional review body in Tajikistan took place within the changes occurring in the entire former USSR. As noted by some scholars (including D. Zmievsky and I. Petrova), the forming/development of constitutional justice in post-Soviet states was complex, involving several stages. Initially (back in Soviet republics), the reform of state bodies from 1988 to 1990 assumed the formation of specialized constitutional supervision bodies: so-called Constitutional Supervision Committees. In this view, Soviet republics made active changes to their legislation.

25 As revised by referendum of May 22, 2016.

26 As revised by referendum of May 22, 2016.

27 К.Н. Холиков, *Становление и развитие института конституционного надзора в Таджикистане*, Dushanbe 1998, p. 52.

Thus, the Constitutional Court is a judicial body, the main goal of which is protection of the local Constitution. According to K. Kholikov, a specific feature of this norm is that without reference to the word "supreme," it defines the Constitutional Court as a judicial body protecting the Constitution of Tajikistan[28].

Also, based on Chapter 8 in the Constitution of Tajikistan, the Constitutional Court is a judicial body; therefore, it is included in the judicial system of Tajikistan. It forms an integral part in the structure of judicial power.

At that, the Constitutional Court of Tajikistan has significant differences from other courts within the judicial system of Tajikistan.

P. Blokhin and O. Kryazhkova list four key differences:

1) *Institutional* – In a system of state bodies, the Constitutional Court stands alone. It has no subordinate relations with the Supreme Court/Supreme Arbitration Court (as in an example of Tajikistan with the Supreme Economic Court); it does not form a superior/inferior body for them;
2) *Competence* – The Constitutional Court has special powers. It does not review cases subject to competence of general jurisdiction courts and arbitration courts;
3) *Organizational* – Constitutional Court performs activities in a special manner (constitutional proceedings);
4) *Structural* – The composition of the Constitutional Court, the procedure of filling the vacancy as judge of the Constitutional Court, which is subject to special requirements[29].

Based on this provision, we need to distinguish the following features of the Constitutional Court in Tajikistan: first, the Constitutional Court of Tajikistan has no subordinate judicial structures (in local administrative-territorial units); second, it is the only judicial body in the judicial system of Tajikistan with competence determined directly by norms of the Constitution (Part 3, Article 89); and third, due to granted competence (under the Constitution of 1994), it checks the constitutionality of legal acts from the Supreme Court and Supreme Economic Court of Tajikistan[30]. Within the scientific study, we have not found

---

28 К.Н. Холиков, *Конституционный суд и конституционное судопроизводство в Таджикистане,* Dushanbe 2014, p. 18.

29 П.Д. Блохин, О.Н. Кряжкова, *Как защитить свои права в Конституционном суде. Практическое руководство по обращению с жалобой в Конституционный суд России,* Moscow 2014, pp. 12–13.

30 К.Н. Холиков, *Конституционный суд и конституционное судопроизводство в Таджикистане,* Dushanbe 2014, p. 20.

that practice of the Constitutional Court involved a review of issues related to the above provisions.

Until the completion of a case review and relevant decision-making, the judge of the Constitutional Court may not give an opinion on the compliance/incompliance of a law, other normative act, instructions of plenums (the Republic of Tajikistan Supreme Court, Supreme Economic Court) with the Constitution or give opinion/advice on issues reviewed by the Republic of Tajikistan's Constitutional Court; besides, no one may demand such actions from a judge of the Constitutional Court (Part 3, Article 11, constitutional law "On Constitutional Court of Tajikistan").

3.5 Constitutional Court and Other Public Authorities

The Attorney's Office is one of the main public authorities supposed to ensure supervisory function, including constitutional supervision. According to A. Tarasov, "attorney's supervision covers practically any sphere of public relations (in part regulated by law). Attorney's Office has quite broad powers – for exercise of its specific activities"[31].

Under Article 93 of the Republic of Tajikistan's Constitution, supervision over exact and uniform exercise of laws in Tajikistan is ensured by the Attorney General and subordinate attorneys within their powers. Exercise of constitutional supervision by prosecution bodies is ensured in several ways.

Under the Republic of Tajikistan constitutional law "On Prosecution Bodies of Tajikistan"[32], the main one is supervision over exact observance and uniform exercise of laws by ministries, state committees, other departments, local self-government bodies, local self-government bodies, military authorities, control bodies, banks, enterprises, institutions, public/religious associations, political parties, other unions (despite subordination and ownership), and their officials, as well as over compliance of their legal acts with laws. This function is aimed at ensuring the uniform application of the Constitution/laws and prevention of the adoption of illegal acts.

Apart from the aforementioned powers on the exercise of supervisory activities, the Attorney's Office of Tajikistan performs a special supervisory function

31 А.М. Тарасов, *Проблемы законодательного обеспечения государственного контроля*, "Государство и право" 2004, № 10, p. 21.

32 Конституционный Закон Республики Таджикистан «Об органах прокуратуры Республики Таджикистан» от 25 июля 2005 года № 107, "Ахбори Маджлиси Оли Республики Таджикистан" № 7, ст. 398.

(participation of the attorney in Constitutional Court activity). So, the Attorney General attends sessions of the Constitutional Court. Besides, the Attorney General may apply to that Constitutional Court for compliance between the Republic of Tajikistan's Constitution and laws, joint normative-legal acts of Majlisi Milli and Majlisi Namoyandagon at Majlisi Oly, normative-legal acts of Majlisi Milli at Majlisi Oly, Majlisi Namoyandagon at Majlisi Oly, the Republic of Tajikistan's President, the Republic of Tajikistan's government, international treaties of Tajikistan that have not come into force, instructions of the Republic of Tajikistan plenums of the Supreme Court/Supreme Economic Court, normative-legal acts of ministries, state committees, other state bodies, and local self-government bodies. Regarding the above, let's note that such a practice was not used in activities of prosecution bodies.

Reviewing the issue of constitutional supervision by the Attorney's Office, let's focus on two aspects, which require clarification at, in our opinion, the legislative level. First, one of main functions of the Republic of Tajikistan Attorney's Office is supervision over observing the human/civil rights and freedoms by all structures and officials. This function, along with the function of supervision over the uniform application of laws, lets the Attorney's Office identify the incompliance between normative acts and the Constitution (in violation of human/civil rights and freedoms). In this view, it seems logical to ensure that the Attorney's Office, along with the Ombudsman for Human Rights, would be able to apply to the Constitutional Court on issues of compliance between the Republic of Tajikistan's Constitution and law, other normative-legal acts, and instructions of plenums (the Republic of Tajikistan Supreme Court/Supreme Economic Court) applied by relevant state/public bodies or judicial authorities regarding the citizens in a particular case (in violation of constitutional rights/freedoms of citizens). Second, under Article 34 in the Republic of Tajikistan's constitutional law "On Prosecution Bodies", attorneys (under procedural legislation of Tajikistan) participate in judicial review of cases, appeal, and file complaints/applications to orders, decisions, sentences, rulings, and resolutions conflicting with laws. Given that under Article 84 in the Republic of Tajikistan's Constitution, a judicial system is formed by the Constitutional Court, courts of general jurisdiction (headed by the Supreme Court), and economic courts (headed by the Supreme Economic Court), a logical conclusion from the above norm of constitutional law is that the Attorney's Office may also appeal against decisions of the Constitutional Court, which conflicts with provisions of Article 89 in the Constitution (finality of Constitutional Court decisions). In this view, we consider it necessary to clarify Article 34 in the Republic of Tajikistan's constitutional law "On Prosecution Bodies", by adding its content with the phrase "except for decisions of RT Constitutional Court". In such a revision, this norm will comply with provisions of the Republic of Tajikistan's Constitution.

In legal literature, specialized constitutional review bodies are divided into two types: judicial and non-judicial. According to K. N. Kholikov, constitutional review bodies are courts of general jurisdiction and specialized judicial bodies (constitutional courts). Along with judicial constitutional review bodies, national scientific doctrine also includes non-judicial (quasi-judicial) bodies[33].

The most effective means of protecting the Constitution is judicial constitutional review exercised by courts of general jurisdiction and specialized constitutional courts[34].

The Ombudsman for Human Rights was established to enhance the constitutional guarantees of state protection for human/civil rights and freedoms, promote their observance and respect by state and self-government bodies in villages (jamoats), their officials, and officials of entities, institutions, and organizations, despite the legal form.

In this view, the Ombudsman for Human Rights is vested with certain control functions to protect and restore violated rights. Thus, it has an opportunity to participate in the improvement of Republic of Tajikistan's legislation on human and civil rights/freedoms, not practiced yet. Along with that, the Ombudsman is entitled to appeal to the Constitutional Court on issues of compliance between the Republic of Tajikistan's Constitution and law, other normative-legal acts, instructions of plenums (the Republic of Tajikistan Supreme Court/ Supreme Economic Court) applied by relevant state, public, or judicial bodies regarding the citizens in a particular case, in presumed violation of their constitutional rights/freedoms. Such practice also was not used in the activity of the Ombudsman for Human Rights.

The National Legislation Center at the President of Tajikistan is another body. Its activities include exercise of constitutional supervision, along with other functions.

Under the Provision on the National Legislation Center at the President of Tajikistan, it is vested with the following functions: the development of concepts on improving the laws and concepts of draft laws, submitting them (in a prescribed manner) for review by the President and government of Tajikistan, development (by proposal of the Republic of Tajikistan President/government and on its own

---

33 К.Н. Холиков, *Конституционный суд и конституционное судопроизводство в Таджикистане*, Dushanbe 2014, p. 18.

34 Н.В. Витрук, *Конституционное правосудие. Судебно-конституционное право и процесс*, Moscow 2010, p. 51.

initiative) of draft laws, other normative-legal acts, and international legal acts, the development of proposals on bringing the normative-legal acts in line with the Republic of Tajikistan's Constitution, laws, acts of the Republic of Tajikistan's President, international legal acts recognized by Tajikistan, conducting (by proposal of the Republic of Tajikistan's President/government) the legal expertise of draft laws submitted for review by Majlisi Namoyandagon at Majlisi Oly, the clarification of main provisions in the current legislation of Tajikistan, etc.

So, this body is vested with tasks on monitoring the national legislation system, detection of conflicts in legislation, and systematizing the laws. While performing this activity, the National Legislation Center at the President of Tajikistan directly exercises the constitutional supervision.

4 Structure of Constitutional Court

4.1 The Legal Status of Constitutional Court Judges

The system of the Republic of Tajikistan's normative-legal acts on the Constitutional Court is a set of normative-legal acts directly dedicated to the Constitutional Court, the only specialized judicial body of constitutional review exercising supreme form of constitutional review and rules of constitutional legal proceedings in the country.

As a rule, the system of Republic of Tajikistan's normative-legal acts on the Constitutional Court is objectified in such normative-legal acts as the Constitution of Tajikistan (Akhbori Majlisi Oly of Tajikistan; Bulletin of the Republic of Tajikistan Government, the scientific-analytical journal "Legislation"—the official publication of the National Legislation Center at the Republic of Tajikistan's President; the Bulletin of the Republic of Tajikistan's Constitutional Court; the Bulletin of the Republic of Tajikistan's Attorney General's Office; the Ministry of Justice of Tajikistan; the Republic of Tajikistan's Central Information Bank "Adliya"; the Code of the Republic of Tajikistan Laws; the Unified Register of the Republic of Tajikistan Normative-Legal Acts; the theoretical and political-legal journal "Khayet va Konun"/Life and Law/); the constitutional law "On the Constitutional Court of Tajikistan", in other constitutional laws of Tajikistan and other acts of Majlisi Oly[35], Presidential

35 Конституционный закон Республики Таджикистан «О внесении изменений и дополнений в Конституционный закон Республики Таджикистан «О Конституционном суде Республики Таджикистан» от 18.03.2015 г. № 1175, принят Постановлением Маджлиси намояндагон Маджлиси Оли Республики

decrees[36], and the Republic of Tajikistan's government decrees[37]. They may also include individual acts adopted by the Constitutional Court (regulation, provision, instructions, etc.; local acts issued by the Constitutional Court are not included in other publications).

All listed documents regulate the status of the Constitutional Court, its structure, and procedure, as well as the rules of constitutional proceedings in Tajikistan. Normative-legal acts, which jointly form a system of the Republic of Tajikistan's normative-legal acts on the Constitutional Court, are different in legal force: only one of them has supreme legal force (the Constitution); the others have force of constitutional laws, laws, and subordinate acts.

In Tajikistan, the status of the Constitutional Court judge is determined by norms of the 1994 Constitution, the constitutional law "On the Constitutional Court of Tajikistan", and the constitutional law "On the Courts of Tajikistan"[38].

Thus, norms of the Republic of Tajikistan's Constitution defining the legal status of the Constitutional Court judge are consolidated in Chapter 8, "Court". Let's note that the norms of the Constitution regarding the status of the Constitutional Court judge are contained in Items 2–3, Article 56 (sets procedure of electing, recalling, and depriving the Constitutional Court judge of immunity), Part 3, Article 84 (defines the term of office for judges), Article 87 (sets the independence of judges and their subordination to the Constitution/law only), Part 1, Article 88 (judges review the cases collectively and individually)[39], Part 2, Article 89 (sets requirements for the candidate of Constitutional Court judge), Article 90 (prohibits other activities apart from judicial), and Article 91 (immunity of judges).

Specific features of norms in articles of the Republic of Tajikistan's 1994 Constitution: apart from the norm in Part 2, Article 89 (special), the others are general and also refer to judges at various levels of the Republic of Tajikistan's judicial bodies.

Таджикистан от 25.02.2015 г, № 1787, одобрен Постановлением Маджлиси милли Маджлиси Оли Республики Таджикистан от 05.03.2015 г. № 870.

36 Not applied in practice.

37 RT government decree signed by RT President determines the amount of salary, amount, and procedure of calculating the bonuses to RT Constitutional Court judges (for qualification classes and seniority).

38 Regulates the status of judge at any level of judicial power in Tajikistan.

39 Under Article 20 of constitutional law "On Constitutional Court of Tajikistan", cases at Constitutional Court are reviewed collectively—by at least two-thirds of the judges.

Among normative-legal acts regulating the status of the Constitutional Court judge, the Republic of Tajikistan's constitutional law "On the Constitutional Court of Tajikistan" is of paramount importance. In this law, the legal status of the judge is described in an individual chapter—namely, Chapter 3, "Status of the Constitutional Court Judge in Tajikistan" (norms of Articles 11–15). The independence of judges, immunity of judges, suspension of judges' powers, recall of judges, resignation of judges, protection of labor rights, and qualification classes of the Republic of Tajikistan's Constitutional Court judges are consolidated here.

Apart from Chapter 3 in the constitutional law, the legal status of the Constitutional Court judge is also regulated by Article 8 (defines composition/ requirements to candidates for judges), Article 9 (term of office for judges), Article 8 (procedure of electing the judges), Article 10 (text and procedure of the oath), Article 11 (independence of the judge in the course of constitutional proceeding), Article 12 (immunity of the judge in the course of constitutional proceeding), Article 4 (equality of judges), Article 24 (secrecy of judge's conference), and Article 49 (procedure of reviewing the cases).

The status of the Constitutional Court judge is also regulated by the Republic of Tajikistan's constitutional law "On Courts", but, unlike the previous one, this law defines the legal status of the judge in general norms.

General norms regulating the status of Constitutional Court judges are contained in such articles of the law: Article 8 (independence of judges), Part 3, Article 7 (inadmissible interference in a judge's activities), Article 10 (immunity of judges), Article 10 (ensuring the safety of judges), Article 12 (requirements of candidates for judges), Article 14 (requirements to judge), Article 15 (term of office), Article 16 (election and appointment), Article 13 (judges), Article 17 (oath), Article 18 (recalling and dismissal), and Article 19 (resignation).

Some aspects in the status of the Constitutional Court judge are also regulated by the Republic of Tajikistan's constitutional law "On Majlisi Oly of Tajikistan" (Article 19, Item 2 – "Election and Recalling of Constitutional Court Judge" and Item 3 – "Resolving an Issue on Depriving of Immunity")[40], the Regulation of Majlisi Milli at Majlisi Oly (Article 45–48)[41], the Resolution of Majlisi Oly "Establishment of Qualification Classes for Constitutional Court Judges, Grade Ranks for Constitutional Court Staff, Bonuses for Long Service, Salaries of Constitutional Court Judges and Staff of Constitutional Court"[42], Provision

40 Ахбори Маджлиси Оли Республики Таджикистан 2000, № 4, Ст. 108.

41 Свод законов Республики Таджикистан, Душанбе 2002, pp. 313–314.

42 Ведомости Маджлиси Оли Республики Таджикистан 1995, № 22, Ст. 283.

on qualification classes of judges, grade ranks of Constitutional Court staff, bonuses for long service to salaries of judges and the Republic of Tajikistan's Constitutional Court staff[43].

Let's note that the definition of the status for Constitutional Court judges shall distinguish the status of current Constitutional Court judges, status of a judge with suspended powers, and the status of a retired Constitutional Court judge. What caused such a distinction in the status of a Constitutional Court judge?

Need for such a distinction in the status of a Constitutional Court judge follows from the content of the legislation system on Constitutional Court. A legislator clearly defines the status of every judge (actual, with suspended powers, considered retired).

In the performance of duties and reviewing the cases, Constitutional Court judges are independent and only subject to the Republic of Tajikistan's Constitution, law on the Republic of Tajikistan's Constitutional Court, and other legislative acts of Tajikistan. They verify the evidence under inner conviction (Part 1, Article 11)[44]. Interference in activity of judges and any influence on them, in view of obstructing procedural activity, is not allowed (Part 2, Article 11). The deprivation of powers, restriction of powers, and recalling of the Republic of Tajikistan's Constitutional Court judge is prohibited, except in cases assumed by the Republic of Tajikistan's Constitution and law on the Constitutional Court (Part 5, Article 11). In activities on constitutional proceedings (hereinafter, proceedings), the Constitutional Court and its judges are not accountable to any person or body (Part 6, Article 11).

Membership of the Constitutional Court is regulated by Part 1, Article 89, the Republic of Tajikistan's Constitution and Part 1, Article 7 of constitutional law—i.e. the Republic of Tajikistan's Constitutional Court consists of 7 judges (1 is representative of the Gorno-Badakhshan autonomous region).

Principles/procedures for electing the Constitutional Court judges are listed in Article 8 of the constitutional law and assume the following:

1. Chairperson, Deputy Chairperson, and Constitutional Court judges are elected by Majlisi Milli at Majlisi Oly, by proposal of the Republic of Tajikistan's President (Part 1).

43 Ibidem.

44 Конституционный Закон Республики Таджикистан «О Конституционном суде» от 26 июля 2014года. № 1084, "Ахбори Маджлиси Оли Республики Таджикистан" Душанбе 2014, № 7, ст. 380.

2. Citizens of Tajikistan, with higher legal education, at least 30 and no more than 65 years old, and with professional experience over 10 years[45], may be elected as Republic of Tajikistan Constitutional Court judges (Part 2).
3. A Constitutional Court judge shall be fluent in the official language (Part 3).

Taking the oath by a Constitutional Court judge is listed in Article 10 of the Republic of Tajikistan's constitutional law and assumes the following: a person elected as Constitutional Court judge for the first time (upon election at a session of Majlisi Milli at Majlisi Oly) takes this oath: "I solemnly swear to fulfill the duty honestly and faithfully, observe and protect the Constitution, and follow its provisions only".

Immunity of the Republic of Tajikistan's Constitutional Court judge:

1. A Republic of Tajikistan Constitutional Court judge has the right of immunity.
2. Immunity of the Republic of Tajikistan Constitutional Court judge extends to his/her life, honor, and dignity, residential and office space, transport and communication means in his/her use, and to correspondence, belongings, documents.
3. Without consent of Majlisi Milli at Majlisi Oly, a Republic of Tajikistan Constitutional Court judge cannot be held criminally/administratively liable, arrested and placed under house arrest.
4. Criminal cases and cases on administrative offenses against Constitutional Court judges are initiated by the Republic of Tajikistan Attorney General only. Criminal cases and cases on administrative offenses against Constitutional Court judges are reviewed by the Supreme Court.
5. Compulsory procedural measures—arrest and house arrest of a Constitutional Court judge, temporary removal from office, home inspection, search of home/office, property arrest, tapping/record of phone or other conversations, arrest/seizure of correspondence, search and seizure of belongings, documents with information about deposits and bank accounts, and arrest of a judge's funds (stored on accounts/deposits, held by banks or credit institutions) are taken by request of an attorney/investigator, with consent of the Attorney General and a permit of the Supreme Court.
6. Detention, reconduction, personal search of a Constitutional Court judge, inspection of property, and transport/communication means in use are only allowed at his/her detention during committing a crime; in other cases, it is

45 В редакции КЗРТ от 18.03.2015 г. № 1175.

conducted under a procedure set by the Republic of Tajikistan legislation, only in view of criminal cases against a Constitutional Court judge.

7. A Constitutional Court judge may not be subject to any measures for expressed opinion (Article 12).

The non-party and apolitical nature of Constitutional Court judges were not mentioned in the practice of the Republic of Tajikistan's constitutional proceedings.

Information about incompatibility of duties and anti-corruption legal provisions is also missing.

There is no such practice for immunity/right of immunity for Constitutional Court judges.

Depriving the judge of the right to make decisions is admissible only by request of the judge (at own will) or due to satisfying the written statement of the Republic of Tajikistan's Constitutional Court judge on resignation.

A Constitutional Court judge is elected for 10 years. From a practical point of view, judges usually resign, retire, or find another job. If the term of office of a Constitutional Court judge expires during the review of his/her case, the powers shall remain until the end of the case review.

4.2 Functions of the Constitutional Court

As noted, a specialized constitutional review body of the Republic of Tajikistan was first established in April 1990[46]. It was known as the "Constitutional Supervision Committee". By nature, it was a quasi-judicial body. Prior to the establishment of the Constitutional Supervision Committee, functions of constitutional review were assigned to the Supreme Council, Presidium of Supreme Council, Government, Attorney's Office, etc.

With the adoption of the Constitution in 1994, the Constitutional Court (a specialized body of judicial constitutional review) was formed in Tajikistan. Legal status of Constitutional Court is consolidated in the Republic of Tajikistan's Constitution of 1994 (Chapter 8 "Court").

Let's note that in Constitutions of some CIS and Baltic countries (Lithuania, Kazakhstan, Moldova, Ukraine), the importance of a specialized constitutional review body is confirmed by an individual chapter (section) on the Constitutional Court (Constitutional Council). In Constitutions of other CIS states, including

46 К.Н. Холиков, *Становление и развитие института конституционного надзора в Таджикистане*, Dushanbe 1998, p. 20.

Tajikistan, the legal status of the Constitutional Court is consolidated in chapters "Judicial Power", "Court", and "Court and Justice".

First of all, the Constitutional Court is a judicial body; although, as noted before, Chapter 8 Constitution of 1994 does not define the Constitutional Court or disclose its purpose. Clear justification of the need to establish a Constitutional Court is given in Article 1 of the Republic of Tajikistan's constitutional law "On the Constitutional Court of Tajikistan"[47].

The Constitutional Court is an independent judicial body of constitutional supervision, established to ensure supremacy and direct action of norms in the Constitution of Tajikistan. A specific feature of this norm is that it defines the Constitutional Court as an independent judicial body for protection of the Constitution.

Based on Chapter 8 in the Republic of Tajikistan's Constitution[48] and Article 1 of the constitutional law "On Constitutional Court of Tajikistan"[49], we may state that the Constitutional Court is a specialized judicial body of constitutional review; therefore, it is included in the judicial system of Tajikistan. It forms an integral part in the structure of judicial power.

Under Article 3 in the Republic of Tajikistan's constitutional law "On Courts of Tajikistan"[50], the judicial system of Tajikistan is formed by the Constitutional Court, Supreme Court, Supreme Economic Court, Military Court, Court of Gorno-Badakhshan autonomous region, courts of regions, Dushanbe city, cities and districts, Economic Court of Gorno-Badakhshan autonomous region, and economic courts of regions and Dushanbe city.

When analyzing this norm of constitutional law, three independent, unrelated levels of judicial bodies are distinguished in judicial system: 1) the Constitutional Court; 2) the Supreme Court, with a system of lower, general jurisdiction courts (regional courts, court of Dushanbe city, city and district courts); and 3) the

---

47 Закон Республики Таджикистан «О Конституционном суде» от 26 июля 2014 г. № 1084, "Ахбори Маджлиси Оли Республики Таджикистан" Душанбе 2014, № 7, ст. 380.

48 Конституция Республики Таджикистан. Душанбе, «Ирфон» 2015, p. 14.

49 Конституционный Закон Республики Таджикистан «О Конституционном суде» от 26 июля 2014 г. № 1084, "Ахбори Маджлиси Оли Республики Таджикистан" Душанбе 2014, № 7, ст. 380.

50 Конституционный Закон Республики Таджикистан «О судах Республики Таджикистан» от 26 июля 2014 г. № 1084, "Ахбори Маджлиси Оли Республики Таджикистан» 2014, № 7, (Ч. 1), ст. 380.

Supreme Economic Court, with a system of lower economic courts (economic courts of regions and Dushanbe city).

From the context of constitutional norms and norms of constitutional law, four main functional areas of Constitutional Court activity can be distinguished: 1) ensuring the supremacy of the Constitution; 2) ensuring direct supremacy of the Constitution; 3) protection of the Constitution; and 4) protection of human/civil rights and freedoms.

Thus, the Constitutional Court is the only specialized body of judicial power, the main purpose of which is to ensure the supremacy (priority) of the Constitution in the system of the Republic of Tajikistan's normative-legal acts. The supremacy of the Constitution means that the Fundamental Law of the state has a supreme legal force and occupies a dominant position in the hierarchy of the legal system. For the first time, the norm establishing the supremacy of the Constitution in the legal system was defined by the Constitution of 1994 (Part 1, Article 10). It means that the Constitution forms the basis for the legal system. So, all legal acts of the country are only adopted on the basis and in compliance with the Constitution—otherwise, they lose their legal force.

In this case, the guarantor is the Constitutional Court, which analyzes the constitutionality of all legal acts in Tajikistan. At incompliance between the Constitution and a legal act, the Constitutional Court recognizes the latter unconstitutional, which results in its abolition.

Another key activity of the Constitutional Court is ensuring the direct effect of constitutional norms in Tajikistan. The Constitution of 1994 has a special norm regarding the direct effect of constitutional norms. Thus, under Part 1, Article 10 of the Constitution, "…its norms have direct effect". Let's note that in the Constitution, the direct effect of this norm is mentioned along with a thesis on supreme legal force of the Constitution.

The protection of the Constitution is the most important activity of the Constitutional Court. In this case, we are talking about judicial protection of the Constitution, which is ensured by a judicial constitutional review. As noted in legal literature, a judicial constitutional review is verification for compliance with the Constitution (in objects of such review) by judicial bodies (courts of general jurisdiction and specialized bodies)[51]. The Constitutional Court (referred to specialized bodies) exercises judicial constitutional review in Tajikistan. The latter is

---

51 Н.В. Витрук, *Конституционное правосудие. Судебное конституционное право и процесс*, Moscow 2010.

the main and basic purpose of the Constitutional Court. Judicial constitutional review is a control form of Constitutional Court activity to check the compliance of reviewed objects with the Constitution.

The protection of human/civil rights and freedoms is one of the main fields in Constitutional Court activity, which is consolidated in Part 2, Article 37 of the constitutional law "On Constitutional Court of Tajikistan".

Let's note that along with the Constitutional Court, other bodies of judicial power too protect constitutional rights and freedoms of persons/citizens. However, the protection of human/civil rights and freedoms by the Constitutional Court has its own specifics. First, this field of Constitutional Court activity can be referred to constitutional-judicial protection of human/civil rights and freedoms; second, under RT law, the Constitutional Court is entitled to verify the constitutionality of laws by civil complaints (on violation of constitutional rights and freedoms).

The above gives grounds to say that the Constitutional Court, as an independent and permanent body, holds a special place with special functional powers in the RT system of judicial bodies.

4.3 Subject of Review by the Constitutional Court

The subject of legal review by the Constitutional Court is closely related to its competence and powers.

When we talk about the subject of reviewing court cases, we mean referring certain cases or issues (disputes) to the jurisdiction of certain court types (subsystems)—civil (general) or military courts of general jurisdiction, arbitration courts or the Constitutional Court.

Thus, under the constitutional law "On Constitutional Court of Tajikistan", Chapter 7, Article 34 "Competences of RT Constitutional Court" assumes the following:

1. The Constitutional Court of Tajikistan has constitutional powers assumed by Article 89 in the Constitution and the law "On Constitutional Court of Tajikistan".
2. The Constitutional Court reviews cases in compliance with the Constitution of laws, joint resolutions of Majlisi Milli at Majlisi Oly and Majlisi Namoyandagon at Majlisi Oly, normative-legal acts of Majlisi Milli at Majlisi Oly, Majlisi Namoyandagon at Majlisi Oly, the Republic of Tajikistan's President, the Republic of Tajikistan's government, instructions of the Republic of Tajikistan plenums of the Supreme Court and Supreme Economic Court; international treaties of Tajikistan that have not come into legal force;

normative-legal acts of ministries, state committees, other state bodies; normative-legal acts of the people's deputy Majlisi at Gorno-Badakhshan autonomous region, regions, Dushanbe city and Chairpersons of Gorno-Badakhshan autonomous region, regions and Dushanbe city; normative-legal acts of people's deputy Majlisi in cities, districts and Chairpersons of cities, districts; and normative-legal acts of self-government bodies in settlements and villages.

3. The Constitutional Court also reviews draft amendments/addenda to the RT Constitution, draft laws, and other issues submitted to national referendum, and disputes between government bodies regarding their competence.

Let's remind that the Constitutional Court actually began its activity in 1996 (although it was formed in 1994). However, in more than 24 years of practice, more than half of case categories within the competence of the Constitutional Court were never reviewed in proceedings (international treaties of Tajikistan that have not come into legal force, legal acts of Supreme Court and Supreme Economic Court, treaties concluded by regions, districts, and cities, agreements between republican and local authorities, disputes on competence between state bodies, etc.); civil petition on compliance between the Republic of Tajikistan's Constitution and law, other normative-legal acts, and instructions of plenums (the Supreme Court, Supreme Economic Court) applied by state/public bodies or courts in particular case (in violation of constitutional rights and freedoms, in their opinion); exercises other powers defined by Republic of Tajikistan Constitution, law "On the Constitutional Court of Tajikistan", and other legislative acts of Tajikistan.

4. The Constitutional Court gives opinion, if the President commits high treason.

Other powers of the Constitutional Court:

1. In sessions, the Constitutional Court: adopts the Regulation of the Constitutional Court; discusses/adopts the text of the annual Message of the Constitutional Court on the state of constitutional legality[52]; elects the Secretary of the Constitutional Court; decides on the suspension of powers for a Constitutional Court judge (not practiced); decides on fines and other penalties against violators of judicial process (not practiced by the

52 Annually submits the Message of RT Constitutional Court to RT President, Majlisi Milli and Majlisi Namoyandagon at Majlisi Oly of Tajikistan—on state of constitutional legality in Tajikistan.

Constitutional Court); reviews activity of the Constitutional Court administration and adopts relevant decisions; decides on promotion and state awards for Constitutional Court judges and staff; approves the membership and Provision on the Scientific-Advisory Council at the Constitutional Court; and reviews other issues related to Constitutional Court activity.

While preparing the case for review in court session, the Constitutional Court may request and receive necessary information from all state bodies, enterprises, institutions, other organizations, public associations, scientific institutions, and involve specialists (in a prescribed manner) to expert and scientific-advisory work.

Besides, an analysis of case categories reviewed by the Constitutional Court and, accordingly, of its powers, enables a conclusion that in Tajikistan, unlike foreign countries (Russia, Kazakhstan, Belarus, Germany, Latvia, etc.), Constitutional Court powers are somewhat narrower. Thus, the Constitutional Court has no right to resolve issues on the constitutionality of elections/referendums or such an important power as official interpretation of the Constitution. Under the Republic of Tajikistan's legislation, an act is officially interpreted in a form similar to the form of the act (by the body which adopted it). The Constitution of Tajikistan was adopted by the people.

As, in this case, the legal norm on interpreting the acts is not applicable, and it would be logical to provide the right on official interpretation of the Constitution to the Constitutional Court (specialized constitutional review body formed to protect the Constitution); it also follows from its powers and activity, as, while exercising its powers and verifying some acts for compliance with the Constitution, the Constitutional Court interprets constitutional norms in the statement part of its final decisions. Regarding the above, we propose to refer official interpretation of the Constitution to powers of the Constitutional Court, while noting that local scholars with scientific activity related to constitutional legal proceeding (K. Kholikov, S. Safarov) adhere to the same position. Let's note that upon adding the legislation on constitutional legal proceeding with relevant norm (power of official interpreting), a form of exercising the power shall be considered in the norm—i.e. an implementation mechanism shall be assumed.

Another power (not vested in the Constitutional Court now) is legislative initiative. In our opinion, subjects of law enforcement (the most prominent representatives are courts and judges) shall have this right, as they face the use of legislation in their daily activities, while practically revealing the gaps and pitfalls of law, the addressing of which could be offered to the legislator, if they had the right to legislative initiative.

4.4 Preliminary and Subsequent Review of Legal Norms

Under legislation, control power of the Constitutional Court (check/resolution of case on compliance with Constitution) is the main function of specialized constitutional review body. At that, we shall consider these circumstances: first, in this field of judicial constitutional review, all types of normative-legal acts (with different level of legal force) fall under the jurisdiction of the Constitutional Court—parliamentary laws, presidential decrees, decrees of government, and even decisions of local authorities/their executive bodies; second, on ensuring the constitutional compliance of legal acts, standard of their constitutionality is the Constitution only; third, on verifying constitutional compliance, all types of legal acts fall under jurisdiction of the Constitutional Court—the list is defined by Article 6 of the Republic of Tajikistan's law "On normative-legal acts of Tajikistan"[53] (except for the Constitution itself, as it is given the first place in this list); fourth, in this field of power, the Constitutional Court uses two types of review—preliminary and subsequent.

Are constitutional laws subject to preliminary constitutional review? Of course, the answer shall be positive, as norms in Part 1, Article 10 of the Constitution state that laws and other legal acts conflicting with the Constitution have no legal force. As follows from this provision of the Constitution, the norm of Fundamental Law does not specify the types of law. Thus, this provision deals with all types of laws, including constitutional ones. A similar norm is contained in Item 1, Part 3, Article 89 of the Constitution, which defines the objects of constitutional review. This provision also states that the Constitutional Court defines compliance of laws (without indication of types) with the Constitution, although this problem is debatable[54]. Let's refer to practical activity of the Constitutional Court. Thus, the Constitutional Court admitted constitutional laws into proceeding (to verify their compliance with the Constitution) and issued relevant constitutional assessments on them[55]. However, due to the interpretation of Part 3, Article 89 (this provision of the Constitution refers to the competence of the Constitutional Court), December 12, 1997, Majlisi Oly adopted the following

53 Закон Республики Таджикистан «О нормативно-правовых актах» от 26 марта 2009 года. № 506, "Ахбори Маджлиси Оли Республики Таджикистан" 2009, № 3, ст. 506.

54 С.А. Авакьян, *Размышления конституционалиста: Избранные статьи*, Moscow 2010, p. 468.

55 Сборник нормативно-правовых актов и решений Конституционного суда Республики Таджикистан, Душанбе 2002, pp. 183–191.

resolution: "The Constitutional Court is not entitled and has no right to initiate, review, and decide on the Republic of Tajikistan's constitutional laws"[56]. Thus, the possibility of recognizing the constitutional law as an object of judicial constitutional review was restricted.

In this view, we consider it appropriate to use a preliminary constitutional review (verifying the constitutionality of presidential decrees prior to signing) for legal acts of the Republic of Tajikistan's President. Under legislation, preliminary (limited) constitutional review is only used for Republic of Tajikistan treaties that have not come into legal force.

Appeal or written petition, filed to the Constitutional Court under requirements of this constitutional law, forms the basis for case review by the Constitutional Court.

The following subjects are entitled to appeal to the Constitutional Court:

The Republic of Tajikistan's President, Majlisi Milli/Majlisi Namoyandagon at Majlisi Oly — on the Constitution, amendments/addenda to the Constitution, draft laws, and other issues submitted to national referendum;

The Republic of Tajikistan's President, joint session of Majlisi Milli and Majlisi Namoyandagon at Majlisi Oly, Majlisi Milli at Majlisi Oly and Majlisi Namoyandagon at Majlisi Oly, government, members of Majlisi Milli and deputy of Majlisi Namoyandagon at Majlisi Oly, the Supreme Court, the RT Supreme Economic Court, the Attorney General, the people's deputy Majlisi of Gorno-Badakhshan autonomous region, regions, Dushanbe city — on compliance of the Republic of Tajikistan's Constitution and laws, joint normative-legal acts of Majlisi Milli and Majlisi Namoyandagon at Majlisi Oly, normative-legal acts of Majlisi Milli at Majlisi Oly, Majlisi Namoyandagon at Majlisi Oly, the Republic of Tajikistan's President, the Republic of Tajikistan's government, international treaties that have not come into force, and instructions of plenums (Supreme Court, Supreme Economic Court);

The Attorney General, the people's deputy Majlisi of Gorno-Badakhshan autonomous region, regions, Dushanbe city and Chairpersons of Gorno-Badakhshan autonomous region, regions, and Dushanbe city — on compliance of the RT Constitution and normative-legal acts of ministries, state committees, other state bodies, and local state bodies;

The Republic of Tajikistan's government, ministries, other state bodies, people's deputy Majlisi of Gorno-Badakhshan autonomous region, regions, Dushanbe city, cities districts, Chairpersons of Gorno-Badakhshan autonomous region, regions, Dushanbe city, cities, and districts — on disputes between them regarding the competencies;

---

56 Постановление Маджлиси Оли Республики Таджикистан «О толковании ст.89 Конституции Республики Таджикистан» от 12 декабря 1997 года. № 510, "Ахбори Маджлиси Оли Республики Таджикистан" Душанбе 1997, № 23–24, ст. 343.

The Ombudsman for Human Rights in Tajikistan — on compliance of the Constitution and laws, other normative-legal acts, instructions of plenums (the Supreme Court, Supreme Economic Court) applied by relevant state/public bodies and judicial bodies to citizens in particular case (in violation of constitutional rights/freedoms, in their opinion); individuals — on compliance of the Constitution and laws, other normative-legal acts, instructions of plenums (the Supreme Court, Supreme Economic Court) applied by relevant state/public bodies and judicial bodies to them in particular cases (in violation of constitutional rights/freedoms, in their opinion);
Legal entities — on compliance of the Constitution and laws, other normative-legal acts, instructions of plenums (Supreme Court, Supreme Economic Court) applied by relevant state/public bodies and judicial bodies to them in particular cases (in violation of constitutional rights/interests, in their opinion);
Judges of the Supreme Court, Supreme Economic Court, and other courts (except the judges of the Constitutional Court) — on compliance of the Constitution and laws, other normative-legal acts, instructions of plenums (the Supreme Court, Supreme Economic Court) applied/to be applied by them to person/legal entity in certain cases.

Let's note that in its practice, the Constitutional Court never had to use preliminary constitutional review for the above case categories.

In the new revision of constitutional law, preliminary constitutional review was also set for draft amendments/addenda to the Constitution, draft laws, and other issues submitted to national referendum.

The use of preliminary constitutional review is relevant for legal acts of government, as they also fall under the jurisdiction of the Constitutional Court (in view of constitutionality). In this regard, let's note that under the RT Constitution, the Republic of Tajikistan President is the Head of the Republic of the Tajikistan Government. Under legislation, he/she issues decrees and orders. However, only normative acts of the Republic of Tajikistan's government are checked for constitutionality. Let's note that until now, the Constitutional Court has not had in its practice any cases on compliance between the Constitution and legal acts of government[57].

Legal acts of public bodies may also be subject to preliminary constitutional review. Let's note that in the post-Soviet space, Tajikistan is the only state whose legislation assumes the legal acts of public bodies as objects of judicial review. However, until now, the Constitutional Court has not had such case categories in its practice.

In this view, let's note that Article 7 of the Republic of Tajikistan's law "On Normative-Legal Acts", where the system of normative-legal acts is consolidated,

---

57 К.Н. Халиков, *Конституционный суд и конституционное производство в Таджикистане*, Dushanbe 2014, p. 203.

does not indicate the legal acts of public bodies. However, Chapter 2 of the law ("Types of normative-legal acts") refers to such acts as provisions (Article 26) and charters (Article 2)[58].

Specificity of the above proceedings in constitutional legal proceeding is manifested as follows: first, they refer to constitutional powers of the Constitutional Court and are directly set in norms of Item 1, Part 3, Article 89 of the Constitution of 1994; second, when reviewing/resolving these case categories, the Constitutional Court simultaneously applies two types of constitutional review: preliminary (for the latter type of proceeding) and subsequent.

On the one hand, mentioned case categories expanded preliminary constitutional review by the Constitutional Court; on the other hand, they ensure the prevention of potential anti-constitutional situations. Then, the expansion of preliminary review by the Constitutional Court resulted in new types of proceedings—namely, two independent case categories reviewed by the Constitutional Court. They include: 1) cases on verifying the constitutionality of draft amendments/addenda to the Constitution; 2) cases on verifying the constitutionality of draft laws and other issues submitted to national referendum.

Based on the above, let's note that the legislator was very rational by charging the Constitutional Court with preliminary review of the most important issues.

Let's note that by expanding the preliminary review of the Constitutional Court, the legislator enhanced its role/prestige in ensuring the superior position of the Constitution in the system of RT normative-legal acts.

When classifying the types of proceedings, constitutional proceeding also applies to the other criteria, the study of which is of real scientific interest. Thus, in our opinion, classifying the proceedings (in constitutional proceeding) on the basis of exercising a form of constitutional review is extremely important. In particular, by the time of exercise, this control is divided into preliminary (preventive) and subsequent (repressive) constitutional review. In the Constitutional Court, the classification of proceedings by this criterion is known as the proceeding of cases reviewed within preliminary and subsequent normative review.

Based on this criterion, the types of proceedings reviewed by the Constitutional Court within preliminary constitutional review include three case categories: 1) on compliance of international treaties, which have not come into force, with the Constitution; 2) on check of constitutionality for draft amendments/addenda to

---

58 Закон Республики Таджикистан «О нормативно-правовых актах» от 26 марта 2009 года. № 506, "Ахбори Маджлиси Оли Республики Таджикистан" 2009, № 3, ст. 506.

the Constitution; 3) on check of constitutionality for draft laws and other issues submitted to national referendum. Let's note that the Constitutional Court never had to use preliminary constitutional review of the above case categories in its practice.

Proceedings reviewed by the Constitutional Court within subsequent constitutional review include all actual laws and other normative-legal acts assumed in Item 1, Part 3, Article 89 of the Constitution (except for international treaties that have not come into force) and Article 34 of the constitutional law "On the Constitutional Court of Tajikistan".

In this view, let's note that in practice of the Constitutional Court, the most common form of constitutional review is subsequent constitutional review. Most case categories reviewed/resolved by the Constitutional Court throughout its operation were cases on the check of constitutionality for actual normative-legal acts of Tajikistan[59].

4.5 The Legal Norm Review Procedure

Most often, procedural rules are understood as an order of exercising any activity. In jurisprudence, they are normative in nature and consolidated in procedural norms.

Any appeal to the Constitutional Court is subject to mandatory registration. Submission/petition is provided by the Chairperson to judge of the Constitutional Court (for examination and verification). Having checked the submission/petition, the judge shall submit a proposal to the Constitutional Court within one month to initiate/reject the initiation of a constitutional proceeding. Having reviewed the judge's proposal, the Constitutional Court makes a decision to initiate a constitutional proceeding and instructs the judge to prepare the case for the Constitutional Court session or makes a decision to reject the initiation of a constitutional proceeding, while informing the applicant in writing[60]. A case review in the Constitutional Court session is subject to some procedural rules.

The constitutional law does not use the term "procedural rules of case review"; moreover, it does not use the other terms in this sense. In current law, the chapters are not united in sections at all. Upon analysis of constitutional law, laws of foreign countries, and legal literature, we may come to the conclusion that

59 Сборник решений Конституционного суда Республики Таджикистан (1996–2009 гг.), Dushanbe 2010, p. 348.

60 Ст. 43, Конституционного закона Республики Таджикистан «О Конституционном Суде Республики Таджикистан» 2014 г.

the concept of "rules of legal proceeding" is broader than the concept of "procedural rules of case review". In this view, the federal constitutional law "On the Constitutional Court", which contains in Section 2 "General rules of proceeding at the Constitutional Court", among other chapters, Chapter 7 "General procedural rules of case review at Constitutional Court"[61] seems more laconic to us.

In our opinion, procedural rules of case review apply to direct case reviews in court sessions, while proceeding, apart from all issues in the list of chapters of constitutional law, also includes the stage of court session; so, rules of legal proceeding assume a broader concept and apply to all stages of proceeding.

Thus, procedural rules of case review at the Constitutional Court include procedural norms, which regulate the relations, since calling the session until the judges' conference on the adoption of a final decision.

4.6 Civil Complaint as a Means of Reviewing Legal Norms

The Constitutional Court powers assumed in Article 34 of the constitutional law "On the Constitutional Court of Tajikistan" is the main goal and mission of the Constitutional Court, a main field of activity for this body[62].

As noted before, this power of the Constitutional Court refers to its legislative powers, as it is established within norms of constitutional law, rather than the RT Constitution. In this view, let's note that under constitutional law "On Amendments/Addenda to Republic of Tajikistan Constitutional Law on Republic of Tajikistan Constitutional Court", No. 368, approved by RT President on March 20, 2008, Constitutional Court powers on protecting the constitutional rights/freedoms of citizens have drastically changed toward expansion.

Judging by initial norms of the constitutional law "On the Republic of Tajikistan's Constitutional Court" (Part 3, Article 14, old revision), in response to complaints on the violation of constitutional rights/freedoms of citizens, as well as by requests of courts, the Constitutional Court checked the constitutionality of the law applied in certain cases (i.e. the subject of constitutional complaint was only seen in the law applied in certain cases). Established procedures

61 Федеральный Конституционный закон Российской Федерации «О Конституционном суде Российской Федерации» от 21 июля 1994 года (в ред. от 8.12.2016)//http://www.consultant.ru/document/ cons_doc_LAW_4172 (accessed: November 2, 2017).

62 К.Н. Холиков, *Основные направления деятельности Конституционного суда в условиях глобализации*, (in:) *Национальная правовая система стран СНГ в условиях глобализации и региональной интеграции, Матер. Междунар. конф.*, Dushanbe 2007, pp. 131–141.

narrowed the field of Constitutional Court activity on protecting the constitutional rights/freedoms of citizens. In this view, let's note that during operation, the Constitutional Court reviewed very few cases by constitutional complaints of citizens and court requests on constitutionality of law applied in certain cases. So, from 2003 to 2007, the Constitutional Court reviewed and made relevant decisions only in 25 cases by civil complaints/court requests on the constitutionality of law applied in certain cases.

A new rule, set in the constitutional law "On Amendments/Addenda to Constitutional Law "On Republic of Tajikistan Constitutional Court"", really expanded the field of Constitutional Court activity on appeals regarding the violation of constitutional rights and the freedoms of citizens.

The adoption of the new constitutional law "On Republic of Tajikistan Constitutional Court" assumes features on establishing a procedure of case review at the Constitutional Court by complaints on the violation of constitutional rights/freedoms of citizens. First, under the new rule, by complaints on the violation of constitutional rights/freedoms of citizens, the Constitutional Court checks the constitutionality of law (not just the one applied in certain cases, but also to be applied in certain legal relations). Second, under the new rule, the subject of constitutional complaint is not just the law, but other normative-legal acts too. Third, by the new procedure, the Constitutional Court defines the compliance of the Constitution and law, other legal acts, and instructions of plenums (the Supreme Court, Supreme Economic Court) applied by the court in certain cases, in a manner specified by the above constitutional law.

A new regulation in the revision of the new law, which sets the subjects of appeal to the Constitutional Court, defines three types of subjects entitled to apply to the Constitutional Court with request on constitutionality of law and other legal acts allegedly violating the constitutional rights/freedoms of citizens:

1) *Ombudsman for Human Rights in Tajikistan*—on compliance of the Constitution and laws, other normative-legal acts, and instructions of plenums (the Supreme Court, Supreme Economic Court) applied by relevant state/public bodies and judicial bodies to citizens in particular case (in violation of constitutional rights/freedoms, in their opinion) (Item 5, Article 40);
2) *Individuals*—on compliance of the Constitution and laws, other normative-legal acts, and instructions of plenums (the Supreme Court, Supreme Economic Court) applied by relevant state/public bodies and judicial bodies to them in particular cases (in violation of constitutional rights/freedoms, in their opinion) (Item 6, Article 40);

3) *Legal entities*—on compliance of the Constitution and laws, other normative-legal acts, and instructions of plenums (the Supreme Court, Supreme Economic Court) applied by relevant state/public bodies and judicial bodies to them in particular cases (in violation of constitutional rights/interests, in their opinion) (Item 7, Article 40).

Thus, completing the analysis for this part of Constitutional Court powers (the protection of constitutional rights/freedoms of citizens), let's note that in the future, this body will use its legislative powers for worthy contribution to the protection of human/civil rights and freedoms in Tajikistan.

At the first stage of constitutional proceeding, the most important role is played by the institute of appeal. Under law, the institute of appeal is recognized as an independent sub-stage. Above all, reason and basis for case review at the Constitutional Court is an appeal of relevant subjects entitled to apply to the Constitutional Court. An admission of appeal by the Constitutional Court triggers the mechanism of constitutional proceeding.

The form and content of appeal to the Constitutional Court are clearly set in norms of Article 41, the constitutional law "On the Republic of the Tajikistan Constitutional Court". Thus, appeal to the Constitutional Court is submitted in writing. Part 2 of the article clearly defines the cases where an appeal is made as submission or petition. Bodies/officials assumed by paragraphs 1–4, Article 40 of the constitutional law provide the Constitutional Court with submission; persons assumed by paragraphs 5–8 of the article provide the petition[63].

The next sub-stage of constitutional proceeding is known as "Preliminary study and check of appeals at the Constitutional Court". Under norms of the constitutional law "On the Republic of the Tajikistan Constitutional Court" (Article 43 "Review of submission/petition at Republic of Tajikistan Constitutional Court"), submission/petition is transferred by the Chairperson to the judge of the Constitutional Court for examination and verification.

Let's note that, previously, in case of refusal to initiate the constitutional proceeding, the Constitutional Court returned materials to the applicant, as stated in the ruling of the Constitutional Court[64]. At that, in some cases, the

63 Конституционный Закон Республики Таджикистан «О Конституционном суде» от 26 июля 2014 года. № 1084, "Ахбори Маджлиси Оли Республики Таджикистан" Душанбе 2014, № 7, ст. 380.

64 Сборник решений Конституционного суда Республики Таджикистан (1996–2009 гг.), Dushanbe 2010, pp. 206, 203, 198, 172.

return of materials to the applicant was not directly indicated in rulings of the Constitutional Court[65].

Now, under the new revision of the norm (Part 3, Article 43 of the constitutional law), the Court informs the applicant in writing. A copy of the ruling on initiation of legal proceeding is sent to the parties and applicant; a copy of the ruling on refusal to initiate the proceeding is sent to the applicant within 5 days[66].

In case of repeated appeal to the Constitutional Court (on matter with issued ruling of the Constitutional Court about refusal to initiate the proceeding), a copy of the ruling is sent to the applicant at simultaneous notifying on termination of further correspondence on the issue.

Thus, for the first reason (due to incompliance of form and content with requirements of Article 43 in the constitutional law), ruling of the Constitutional Court rejected the initiation of constitutional proceeding on some appeals and petitions admitted by the Constitutional Court. For example, such case categories include: a first petition from the Chairperson of the Customs Committee at the Government, R. Karimov "On suspension of Article 204 in Labor Code of Tajikistan"; a second petition from the Chairperson of the Presidium at the College of Advocates in the Leninabad region, H. Fayzulloev "On incompliance of Tax Code with constitutional law "On College of Advocates", by issue of collecting the state duty on income of advocates"; a third petition from G. Mirzoyev "On defining the compliance between Article 17, 27, 29, 30, 335 of Criminal Procedure Code; Article 10, Part 1 and 3; Article 14, Part 1; Article 17, Part 1; Article 19, Part 2; Article 88 with RT Constitution", etc.[67]

Exercise of second reason—refusal to initiate the constitutional proceeding, if submission/petition is provided by the body or person (subject) not entitled to appeal. In this view, let's note that the norm of the constitutional law (Article 40) clearly sets the range of subjects entitled to appeal to the Constitutional Court with submission, petition, or complaint. Despite that, bodies/persons not entitled to appeal sometimes appeal to the Constitutional Court, which results in refusal to initiate the constitutional proceeding. Thus, for this reason, ruling of the Constitutional Court refused to initiate constitutional proceeding in such

65 Ibidem, pp. 165, 178.

66 Конституционный Закон Республики Таджикистан «О Конституционном суде» от 26 июля 2014 года. № 1084, "Ахбори Маджлиси Оли Республики Таджикистан" Душанбе 2014, № 7, ст. 380.

67 Сборник решений Конституционного суда Республики Таджикистан (1996–2009 гг.), Dushanbe 2010, pp. 162–164; 199–201; 207–208.

cases: by petition of citizen N. Kirpo "Defining the compliance of Part 4, Article 249 in Criminal Code with Article 10, 17, 19, 20, 42 in Constitution and concept "foreign aid fund" specified in Article 12 of Constitution" (one of the reasons, according to which, she is not entitled to appeal to the Constitutional Court on this case, as her constitutional rights/freedoms were not directly violated; besides, the applicant did not have a power of attorney to represent her son at the Constitutional Court, i.e., P. Kirpo did not provide it to his mother); by petition from the Chairperson of the Tax Committee in the Leninabad region, Mr. Khudoynazarov "Interpreting Item "n", Article 3 in law "On State Duty"", No. 496 of January 6, 1992 (one of the reasons, under which, the Tax Committee is not entitled to appeal to the Constitutional Court); by petition from the Chairperson of Presidium at the College of Advocates in the Leninabad region, H. Fayzulloev "On incompliance of Tax Code with constitutional law 'On College of Advocates', by issue of collecting the state duty on the income of advocates" (one of the reasons was that the College of Advocates was not entitled to appeal to the Constitutional Court), etc.[68]

Submissions and petitions for the third reason (Part 3, Article 45 of the constitutional law, refusal to initiate the constitutional proceeding due to absence of the Constitutional Court jurisdiction on the case) are also available in practice of the Constitutional Court. Thus, initiation of constitutional proceeding was rejected (for the above reasons) on the following cases. For example, they include: a petition of the International Business Company "Irengen-LTD" "Defining the compliance of Supreme Economic Court decision of August 28, 2003 and Supreme Economic Court ruling of September 19, 2006 with Article 12 and 32 in Constitution"; a petition from the Chairperson of Khujand city, Sogdian region "Recognizing the decision of Economic Court in Sogdian region, dated September 3, 2002, invalid", etc.[69]

For the fourth reason, which also results in the refusal to initiate constitutional proceeding, Part 4, Article 45 of the constitutional law "On Republic of Tajikistan Constitutional Court" assumes that "constitutionality of issues in submission/petition previously reviewed by the Constitutional Court, with issue of decision"; let's note that such case categories were never met in practice of the Constitutional Court.

---

68 Ibidem, pp. 176–178; 197–198; 199–201.

69 Сборник решений Конституционного суда Республики Таджикистан (1996–2009 гг.), Dushanbe 2010, pp. 146–149, 162–164.

5 Legal Nature and Legal Force of Constitutional Court Decisions

Activity of constitutional jurisdiction bodies is related to the adoption of certain documents mediating the process of exercising powers, while also acting as a means of legal registration for results of such activity. The adoption of acts is one of the most important stages in constitutional proceeding. Acts of the Constitutional Court are a means of formalizing its will as the only state body of constitutional justice.

Acts of the Constitutional Court have the following features but are not limited to them. Thus, Article 56 of the constitutional law "On the Constitutional Court"[70], known as "Adopting the acts of the Constitutional Court", assumes a special procedural method of adopting its acts, as follows:

1. Acts of the Constitutional Court are adopted by open vote.
2. Judges are not entitled to abstain from or avoid voting.
3. In any case, the Chairperson votes after all judges.
4. Decision of the Constitutional Court is considered adopted, if most of the judges in court session voted for it.
5. At equal votes of judges, a decision is made on compliance of a debated law, other normative-legal acts, or instructions of plenums (the Supreme Court, Supreme Economic Court) with the RT Constitution.
6. After adoption, the rulings and conclusions of the Constitutional Court are announced immediately.

Another sign of Constitutional Court acts (perhaps its most peculiar feature, not specific to acts of any other body) is finality.

Noteworthy is the fact that this feature of Constitutional Court acts is consolidated in the RT constitutional law "On the Republic of Tajikistan Constitutional Court" (Part 2, Article 60) and in the Constitution (Part 4, Article 89).

The essence of the norm on the finality of Constitutional Court acts ("Constitutional Court acts are final") is disclosed in Parts 2–3, Article 60 of constitutional law, which states that "acts of Constitutional Court are final and not subject to appeal"; "exercise of Constitutional Court acts is mandatory for all state bodies, enterprises, institutions, other organizations, public

70 Конституционный Закон Республики Таджикистан «О Конституционном суде» от 26 июля 2014 года. № 1084, "Ахбори Маджлиси Оли Республики Таджикистан", Душанбе 2014, № 7, ст. 380.

associations (despite the form of ownership), officials and citizens, to whom they are addressed".

Upon analyzing the competence of the Constitutional Court, we may conclude that all of its powers are exercised via adoption of certain Constitutional Court acts. The same can be said about "other powers" of the Constitutional Court, consolidated in Article 35 of constitutional law, which assumes the other powers of the Constitutional Court:

1. At its sessions, the Constitutional Court adopts Regulation of the Constitutional Court; discusses/adopts the text of the annual Message of the Constitutional Court on the state of constitutional legality; elects the Secretary of the Constitutional Court; decides on the suspension of powers for a Constitutional Court judge; decides on fines and other penalties against violators of judicial process; reviews activity of the Constitutional Court administration and adopts relevant decisions; decides on the promotion and state awards for Constitutional Court judges and staff; approves the membership and Provision on the Scientific-Advisory Council at the Constitutional Court; and reviews other issues related to Constitutional Court activity.
2. While preparing the case for a review in a court session, the Constitutional Court may request and receive necessary information from all state bodies, enterprises, institutions, other organizations, public associations, and scientific institutions, and involve specialists (in a prescribed manner) to expert and scientific-advisory work.

Thus, we may assume that acts of the Constitutional Court form an individual type of legal act adopted by the Constitutional Court in a special procedural way (to exercise its powers); they are final and binding throughout the territory of Tajikistan.

Starting the issue on types of Constitutional Court acts, let's note that under Article 55 of the Republic of Tajikistan's constitutional law "On the Republic of Tajikistan Constitutional Court", this is a resolution, conclusion, and ruling.

Besides, there is another category of terminology: namely, acts of the Constitutional Court used in constitutional proceedings (regulation, message, appeal, statement). In our opinion, the problem here is in the use of terms. Thus, the constitutional law "On the Republic of the Tajikistan Constitutional Court" (title of Chapter 11) uses the term "acts" of the Constitutional Court, although the common name is "decision" of specialized constitutional review body.

Besides, the term "acts" is used in Chapter 11 only; articles of other chapters (e.g. Part 2, Article 18; Part 2, Article 19; Part 1, Article 20; Item 6, Part 1, Article 35; Part 9, Article 49, etc.) use "decision"; even Chapter 11 (Article 56 "Adoption of the

Republic of Tajikistan Constitutional Court acts", Part 4) consolidates: "Decision of RT Constitutional Court is considered adopted if…". The above examples enable a conclusion that a legislator makes no difference between an "act of the Constitutional Court" and a "decision of the Constitutional Court".

Regarding the legal nature of Constitutional Court decisions, let's note that they have different features. That was the reason why our study first reviewed the types of Constitutional Court decisions and then their legal nature. (In our opinion, each type of Constitutional Court decision shall be reviewed individually.)

Above, we reviewed the general concept of acts and the idea of legal acts. It turned out that acts of the Constitutional Court refer to legal acts and have their features. Now the question is, what type of legal acts they shall be referred to. By nature, are they normative or law-enforcing?

Summarizing the above arguments, we consider it necessary to consolidate the position of Constitutional Court decisions in the system of legal sources (the law "On normative-legal acts")—namely, to consolidate Constitutional Court decisions in the hierarchy of normative-legal acts, after the Constitution. The procedure of resuming the suspended proceeding is also regulated by the norms of the constitutional law "On the Constitutional Court" (Article 52), under which suspended proceeding is resumed, where it was suspended (i.e. case review is resumed, where it was suspended). The replacement of process parties is not an obstacle to resuming the proceeding, where it was suspended. In any case, if the composition of judges was changed, the suspended proceeding is resumed from the beginning of the trial. The suspended court session is resumed by initiative of the Constitutional Court on addressing the circumstances forming the basis for suspension (until expiry of the term established by the Constitutional Court).

1. Acts of the Constitutional Court consist of decisions, conclusions, and rulings.
2. Having reviewed the case, the Constitutional Court adopts a decision.
3. The Constitutional Court decision is adopted in the name of Tajikistan and signed by the Chairperson/Judge/Secretary of the Constitutional Court.
4. The Constitutional Court adopts a conclusion in cases assumed by the Constitution and constitutional law. The conclusion of the Constitutional Court is adopted and proclaimed in a manner determined for adoption of Constitutional Court decisions.
5. On other issues reviewed by the Constitutional Court, as well as in cases assumed by constitutional law, ruling is adopted.

6 Constitutional Value of the Constitutional Court

As noted above, the Constitutional Court occupies a central place in the system of judicial power. A legal basis of its formation, structure, and activity is defined by Article 89 of the Constitution. As a state authority, the Constitutional Court is a judicial body of constitutional review, which independently exercises judicial power via constitutional proceeding. The definition of its place and principles of interaction with judicial, legislative, and executive bodies is of real importance. This is confirmed by the fact that the Constitutional Court plays a decisive role in the system of checks and balances for all three branches of government.

According to N. Vitruk: "When evaluating the place and role of the Constitutional Court in the modern democratic world, we need to emphasize its arbitration function in resolving the political conflicts (peacekeeping, which determines Constitutional Court activity as guarantor of political peace). At that, pre-requisite lies in thesis that basis of any constitutional dispute is political issue"[71]. Almost the same situation.

When defining the role of the Constitutional Court in the separation of powers, I. Petrova says that the Constitutional Court is an important part in the mechanism of checks and balances, as its direct participation (as arbitrator) resolves legal collisions, conflicts between branches of state power, federation and its subjects, power, and personality. While resolving the conflicts/disputes between branches of state power, the Constitutional Court acts as a body of compromise, reconciliation, and guarantor of stability in society and the state[72].

Majlisi Oly and the President interact with the Constitutional Court within their competence (defined by the Constitution and other legislative acts of Tajikistan).

1. Thus, under the norm in Article 56 (Item 2) and Article 69 (Item 8) of the Constitution, the President submits to Majlisi Milli at Majlisi Oly the candidates for election and recalling the Chairperson, Deputy, and judges of the Constitutional Court. Let's note that staffing of the Constitutional Court is aided by two branches of government: legislative and executive.
2. Under Item 3, Article 56 in the Constitution, the issue on depriving the Chairperson, Deputy Chairperson, and Constitutional Court judges of immunity refers to the powers of Majlisi Milli.

---

71 В.Н. Витрук, *Конституционное правосудие. Учебное пособие*, Moscow 2012, p. 73.

72 И.В. Петрова, *Конституционный суд – орган конституционного контроля в Российской Федерации*, Moscow 2004. p. 92.

3. Under Part 3 (Item 1) in Article 89 of the Constitution, defining the compliance of laws, joint legal acts of Majlisi Milli and Majlisi Namoyandagon, legal acts of Majlisi Milli, Majlisi Namoyandagon, the President and Government refers to the competence of the Constitutional Court. This constitutional power lets the Constitutional Court verify the constitutionality of legal acts from legislative (Majlisi Oly, its Majlisi) and executive (the President and government) bodies, which means their direct interaction during the exercise of this power.
4. Interaction of the Constitutional Court with legislative/executive bodies is also observed during the exercise of Constitutional Court functions related to the resolution of competence disputes between government bodies, assumed by Part 3 (Item 2) of Article 89 in the Constitution: "Resolution of competence disputes between government bodies", etc.

Having reviewed the place of the Constitutional Court in the system of the supreme Republic of Tajikistan power, we can make the following conclusions:

1. The Constitutional Court is an independent body of state power. Its activity on issues of constitutional proceeding is not accountable to anyone.
2. The Constitutional Court ensures a supreme form of constitutional review, as its jurisdiction includes the verification of constitutionality for acts of legislative/executive bodies of state power, and as a result, its decisions (on the unconstitutionality of certain acts) may affect the activities of legislative and executive power.
3. The activity of the Constitutional Court (as a public body) is also aimed at ensuring compliance with separation of powers. The Constitutional Court is entitled to resolve competence disputes between legislative and executive bodies. Thus, we believe that the Constitutional Court is a guarantor of separating the powers.
4. Special status and competence ensure the position of the Constitutional Court in the system of supreme power bodies, along with Majlisi Oly and the President. It occupies a special place in the system of judicial bodies and state bodies as a whole and shall be a supreme judicial body.

To maintain constitutionality in Tajikistan, the Constitutional Court, first of all, ensures supremacy and a direct effect of constitutional norms.

The establishment of a new judicial body (the Constitutional Court) and forming a new and independent type of legal (constitutional) proceeding led to major changes in the system of judicial bodies and legal proceedings of Tajikistan. It resulted in some problems with the status, structure, and activities of the Constitutional Court, as well as the exercising of constitutional justice.

The establishment of the Constitutional Court is directly related to the adoption of the Constitution in 1994 and was dictated by time. Under Article 1 of the Constitution, Tajikistan is a law-bound state. The main feature of a law-bound state is a rule of law (first of all, supremacy of the Constitution). Supremacy of the Constitution and a direct effect of its norms in the Republic of Tajikistan territory must be ensured by the Constitutional Court. The Constitutional Court is the only specialized judicial body in the system of supreme power that is charged with exercise of judicial constitutional review.

Judicial constitutional review exercised by the Constitutional Court has specific features requiring in-depth scientific analysis. Identification of circumstances affecting Constitutional Court activity and exercise of constitutional legal proceeding is an extremely important scientific task. The question "may the Constitutional Court recognize the current law incompliant with the Constitution?" shall be answered that such cases were not reviewed in practice of the Constitutional Court yet.

Is the Constitutional Court really an important element of civil protection from adopting the laws incompliant with the Constitution? Of course, all legal foundations are laid under legal doctrine; many aspects of them are stated in the present report. However, in our opinion, practice is gained over time. At the moment, such cases have not been reviewed in practice of the Constitutional Court.

7 Social Perception of Legal Control

In this case, necessary materials are missing. It seems to us that sociological studies on this aspect have not been conducted.

Conclusions

Based on conducted scientific analysis, we assume that the main function of constitutional justice in Tajikistan is the exercise of constitutional judicial review in various forms. Constitutional judicial review is the "activity of specially authorized state bodies exercising judicial power – to ensure supremacy of the Constitution, prevent the issue of non-constitutional normative acts, the adoption of unconstitutional laws, other normative acts or actions, and, if necessary, applying the interpretation of the Constitution and laws".

Thus, a review is expressed in checking/assessing the constitutionality of laws, other normative acts and treaties that becoming invalid in case of being recognized as incompliant with the RT Constitution—an important aspect and activity of the Constitutional Court. However, judicial constitutional review is expressed both in the resolution of competence disputes and in the interpretation of the Constitution, which serve for the legal protection of the Constitution from misunderstanding/misapplication, and finally, for the protection of constitutional rights/freedoms of citizens.

The activity of state bodies, officials, public organizations, citizens, and normative acts shall clearly comply with the Constitution. A law-bound state cannot be formed without it. Such a situation can be achieved only in the presence of an effective constitutional review system, which ensures accurate, consistent exercise of the Constitution to enhance its role as Fundamental Law and serve as the main guarantor protecting the constitutional rights and freedoms of citizens. Finally, activity in the field of general legal review depends on its effectiveness.

The need for constitutional review is dictated by reality itself. International experience and the experience of our country suggest that acts incompliant with the Constitution/laws are adopted quite often, with the rise of disputes on the application of the Constitution and current laws. The resolution of such problems is in competence of constitutional review bodies, which must ensure effective and rational exercise of constitutional norms and principles within the national legislation.

Constitutional review (understood as verifying, identifying, stating, evaluating, and addressing incompliance with various acts of the Constitution and laws) is heterogeneous in nature and forms a combination of various options differing significantly from each other. The variety of constitutional review types is mostly associated with multiple powers exercised by constitutional review bodies and with multiple forms of structure/operation for these bodies.

Constitutional review includes control by public authorities (interdepartmental control; constitutional and other types of judicial control; prosecutor supervision; and social control).

In terms of forming a free civil society, real democracy, and law-bound state (with rule of law and the Constitution, as one of the essential features), constitutional justice is organically included in the state-legal reality of modern Tajik society.

The specific institute of ensuring/protecting the supremacy of the Constitution is constitutional review exercised by the constitutional justice body.

Thus, constitutional review is a specific function of competent public bodies to ensure supremacy of the Constitution in a system of normative acts, its direct action in activity of public relation subjects throughout Tajikistan. Constitutional review can act as a specialized mechanism for the protection of the Constitution, as a normative-legal act of a supreme legal force.

Public authorities exercising constitutional review in Tajikistan are the President and Majlisi Oly (Parliament). In Tajikistan, constitutional review falls within the functions of the President (head of government), Majlisi Oly (Parliament), Attorney's Office, and specialized control-supervisory bodies (Ombudsman for Human Rights and National Legislation Center at the President).

Constitutional justice is constitutional review exercised in the form of legal proceeding; as a result, we deal with independent types of state-power control activity within specialized judicial procedures. Exactly this form ensures objectivity and impartiality of constitutional review. Constitutional justice is a supreme form of constitutional review.

An analysis of forming/developing the specialized judicial constitutional review in Tajikistan shows that first, Tajikistan established the European model of judicial constitutional review; second, a specialized judicial constitutional review established in Tajikistan has its own features (due to the peculiarity of national legal system, procedure of arranging and exercising the judicial constitutional review); third, a specialized judicial constitutional review passed two stages of development, the first stage being the formation of a judicial constitutional review in terms of a contradictory transition period, and the second stage being its activation in terms of a stable political system.

Thus, the study enables some recommendations for improving the specialized judicial constitutional review in Tajikistan: a) the Constitutional Court shall be entitled to interpret the Constitution, which will really increase the effectiveness of judicial constitutional review; b) an analysis of Constitutional Court activity shows that it is less active in defining legal positions. So, the Constitutional Court shall intensify its activity in defining legal positions, as they have the power of legal source; c) an analysis of Constitutional Court decisions shows some drawbacks in their technical format. In this view: first, the Constitutional Court shall pay more attention to format of its final decisions, as they refer to an unlimited number of legal subjects; d) the Constitutional Court shall intensify its activity on interpreting the norms and provisions of the constitutional law "On the Constitutional Court", especially regarding the general binding nature of its final decisions; e) there is a need to consolidate the position of Constitutional Court decisions in the system of legal sources under the Law of Tajikistan "On normative legal acts".

Mykhailo Savchyn

Constitutional Justice in the Republic of Ukraine

Abstract: The analysis of constitutional judiciary in Ukraine cannot be carried out independently of constitutional changes or instability or unpredictability of constitutional Ukraine. They directly affect the functioning of the Constitutional Court and the way of behaviour of this Court's judges. A thesis is put forward that the activity of the Constitutional Court is affected by the dispute concerning the power distribution between the organs of the state and that this is a negative impact.

Keywords: the European model of reviewing the legal norms, Constitutional Court, autonomy and independence, The Constitutional Court and other organs of state power, cognition of the Constitutional Court

Introduction

Active research on constitutional justice in Ukraine actually began only after the adoption of the Constitution of Ukraine and the establishment of the Constitutional Court of Ukraine (CCU) in 1996. A number of dissertations on topics related to constitutional justice were defended only after the Constitutional Court was established[1]. Moreover, textbooks and academic course books on constitutional jurisdiction were published then[2]. Later on, authors began to analyse this subject from the perspective of judicial constitutionalism[3].

The first studies within dissertations and monographs devoted to constitutional justice were mostly in the spirit of statism and positivism, and studies

1 П.В. Волвенко, *Діяльність Конституційного Суду України щодо тлумачення Конституції України: теоретичний аспект*, Kyiv 2006; В.О. Гергелійник, *Правові проблеми становлення і функціонування конституційної юстиції в Україні*, Kyiv 1999; З.В. Лунь, *Правова охорона Конституції України*, Kyiv 2003; М.В. Савенко, *Правовий статус Конституційного Суду України*, Kyiv 2000; М.В. Савчин, *Конституційний Суд України як гарант конституційного ладу*, Kyiv 2004; Г.О. Христова, *Юридична природа актів Конституційного Суду України*, Kharkiv 2004.

2 Ю.Г. Барабаш, А.О. Селіванов (eds.), *Конституційна юрисдикція*, Харків 2012.

3 В.Д. Бринцев, *Судовий конституціоналізм в Україні: доктрина і практика формування*, Kharkiv 2013.

conducted in the last 10 years have leaned towards the anthropocentric and humanistic perspective. For example, in his doctoral theses A. Krusyan examines constitutional justice in terms of the condition of modern constitutionalism[4], whereas the author of this chapter does so from the perspective of the values related to constitutionalism, the implementation and interpretation of the constitution[5]. Studies devoted to constitutional justice have also been defended[6].

In the early days a judge ad hoc of European Court of Human Rights S. Shevchuk, a judge of the CCU, singled out the correlation between legal positivism and natural law as a legal justification for determining the effect of positive law, and the principle of fairness and due process in administering constitutional justice[7]. That author emphasises the importance of changing the legist paradigm of constitutional law, which prevails in Ukraine and has a decisive influence on the functioning of constitutional justice. At the same time, Shevchuk emphasises the features of constitutional norms which can be seen as a kind of "'open text' and 'empty vessels' which must be filled with concrete content during the application of the Constitution"[8]. The author views constitutional justice as one of the leading institutions for ensuring the supremacy of the constitution in the light of the rule of law and the protection of the fundamental principles of law, whether written or unwritten[9]. S. Shevchuk's work on judicial law-making is also considered considerably authoritative[10].

In his advanced doctoral dissertation, I. Slidenko cites arguments that constitutional review is the activity of state bodies aimed at implementing the principle

---

4 А.Р. Крусян, *Сучасний український конституціоналізм: теорія і практика*, Odessa 2010.

5 М.В. Савчин, *Конституціоналізм і природа конституції: теорія і практика реалізації*, Kyiv 2013.

6 О.І. Багрій, *Доктрина верховенства Конституції України (за матеріала ми практики Конституційного Суду України)*, Uzhhorod 2016; Т.О. Бринь, *Конституційний Суд України в механізмі захисту та забезпечення прав і свобод людини і громадянина*, Kharkiv 2010; О.О. Кравченко, *Захист прав і свобод людини та громадянина Конституційним Судом України: доктринальні, прикладні та компаративні аспекти*, Kyiv 2011; А.П. Ткачук, *Конституційний Суд у механізмі захисту основних прав і свобод людини: модельний підхід*, Kyiv 2012.

7 С. Шевчук, *Основи конституційної юриспруденції*, Kyiv 2001.

8 Ibidem, p. 9.

9 С. Шевчук, *Принцип верховенства права та найвища юридична сила Конституції України*, "Право України" 2011, № 5, pp. 21–24.

10 С. Шевчук, *Судова правотворчість: світовий досвід та перспективи в Україні*, Kyiv 2007.

of the supremacy of the constitution and supporting constitutional legality with the use of their specific methods[11]. V. Skomorokha, a retired Constitutional Court judge, stresses that "constitutional review of laws should be understood as an organised activity aimed at verifying the constitutionality of laws." As an institution, constitutional review "incorporates the rules pertaining to the authorities competent to carry out this review, and the procedure to be followed to implement this function"[12].

As regards the limits of interpreting the Constitution, a relatively common viewpoint is that "in the process of interpreting the constitutional provisions, the Constitutional Court can resort to the provisions of laws that make the constitutional provisions more concrete, and can determine the content of individual constitutional provisions with the help of those laws"[13]. A separate analysis of problems arising when the Constitution is interpreted can be found in the study by I. Slidenko, where the author examines the evolution, nature, types and ways of interpreting constitutional provisions and rules. The author emphasises that this ensures the implementation of the constitution, whereas "interpretation is an instrument that helps to observe the separation of powers, the system of checks and balances, and the priority of the protection of citizens' rights and freedoms, etc"[14]. In his academic works, Ukrainian scholar Yu. Todyka[15] adheres to the traditional point of view on the interpretation of the constitution.

Constitutional justice has been the subject of a number of academic and practical conferences, where discussion focused on the constitutional process[16], the protection of human rights by constitutional justice bodies (Kyiv, 16 September 2011)[17] and scholarly support of constitutional

---

11 І.Д.Сліденко, *Конституційний контроль в механізмі сучасної правової держави*, дисертація доктора юридичних наук, Kyiv 2010.

12 В.Є. Скомороха, *Конституційна юрисдикція в Україні: проблеми теорії, методології і практики*, Kyiv 2007, p. 53.

13 А. Єзеров. *Роль конституційної юстиції в розвитку сучасного українського конституціоналізму*, [in:] А.Р. Крусян (ed.), *Проблеми сучасної конституціоналістики. Вип. 3. Сучасний український конституціоналізм*, Odessa 2015, p. 472.

14 Сліденко І.Д., *Тлумачення конституції: питання теорії і практики в контексті світового досвіду*, Odessa 2003, p. 20.

15 Ю.М. Тодика, *Тлумачення Конституції і законів України: теорія і практика*, Kharkiv 2001.

16 Конституційний процес в Україні: здобутки та проблеми, Kharkiv 2009.

17 А.С. Головін (ed.), *Захист прав людини органами конституційної юстиції: можливості і проблеми індивідуального доступу*, Kyiv 2011; А.С. Головін

justice[18]. The author of this chapter also made his contribution to the development of the constitutional justice doctrine in Ukraine[19].

Taking into account the origins and the evolution of constitutional justice as an institution, this chapter will provide a description of the peculiarities surrounding the introduction of judicial constitutional review in the context of Ukraine's transitional democracy, the fundamental rules underlying the organisation of the CCU and the legal status of judges, as well as the grounds, the subject-matter and limits of powers exercised by the Constitutional Court, and the international and social context of the Constitutional Court's operation.

1 Legal Grounds and Motivations behind the Introduction of Judicial Constitutional Review

According to the Constitution of Ukraine, the country has been established as a "mixed republic". The prevailing opinion in the Ukrainian doctrine is that the power is more balanced under such a system. This decision was motivated by the view that authoritative presidential power is capable of implementing reforms effectively. This synergy enables to launch the constitutional mechanisms that prevent the concentration of power in one set of hands.

In turn, those who profess the doctrine of organic constitutionalism have always stressed the importance of judicial constitutional review as an important institution preventing the usurpation of power and an important instrument for

---

(ред.), *Питання захисту прав людини і громадянина органами конституційної юрисдикції у сучасних умовах*, Kyiv 2013.

18 Матеріали круглого столу «Науково-доктринальне забезпечення розвитку конституційної юстиції в Україні», "Вісник Конституційного Суду України" 2015, № 4, pp. 74–146.

19 М.В. Савчин, *Конституционалізм та природа конституції*, Uzhhorod 2009; М.В. Савчин, *Рішення і висновки Конституційного Суду України – специфічне джерело конституційного права* [in:] Ю.С. Шемшученко, О.І. Ющик (eds.), *Джерела конституційного права України*, Kyiv 2010, pp. 407–439; М.В. Савчин, *Права людини в Україні в контексті доктрини європейської та української юстиції* [in:] П.Ф. Мартиненко (ed.), *Права і свободи людини і громадянина в Україні (доктрина Європейського суду з прав людини і Конституційного Суду України)*, Kyiv 2013, pp. 123–144; W. Kampo, M. Sawczyn, *Legitymizacja orzeczeń sądów konstytucyjnych w kontekście panowania doktryny państwa prawa: aspekt komparatywny i prakseologiczny*, "Zagadnienia Sądownictwa Konstytucyjnego" 2012, No 2 (4), pp. 125–136; М.В. Савчин, *Конституційний Суд України та реалізація Конституції України*, "Публічне право" 2015, № 1, pp. 9–17.

the protection of human rights. However, the socio-political debate shows that there was considerable distrust towards the judiciary in this context, as followers of the statist post-Soviet approach believed that the judiciary, with its law-making competence, posed a threat to the legislature. The discourse about the legitimacy of the CCU also included opinions that showed a lack of understanding for the deterrent role of constitutional justice in the separation of powers, including checks and balances, and its role as a guarantor of human rights and freedoms.

1.1 Key Dilemmas Surrounding the Introduction of Judicial Constitutional Review

Modern systems of the separation of powers are characterised by the diffusion of power within the classic triad. As regards the functions performed by the parliament and the CCU, they are closely related to the implementation of power. Their functions are similar in nature since, under the existing codified constitution in Ukraine, both the parliament and the CCU engage in more concrete and detailed interpretations of constitutional provisions[20]. However, they exercise these prerogatives in different ways: the Verkhovna Rada (parliamentary assembly) formulates abstract provisions that regulate typical circumstances of life and are designed for an indefinite circle of persons and an indefinite number of cases. The Constitutional Court, guided by constitutional values and principles, adapts abstract constitutional provisions to specific circumstances, or evaluates abstract provisions of the law. Such an evaluation is carried out to analyse the legitimacy of interference in the autonomy of an individual in accordance with the three-part test, based on a systemic and teleological interpretation of Articles 3, 8, 22 and 64 of the Constitution. For example, when examining an appeal against decisions made in administrative proceedings, the CCU formulated the proportionality principle as follows (CCU decision No. 3/2015[21]): "... pursuant to the Constitution of Ukraine, the right to appeal and cassation appeal of a court

20 М.В. Савчин. *Конституційні інновації та вірність конституції*, "Віче" 2016, № 7–8, pp. 44–47.

21 Decisions of the CCU are available on its official website under the heading «Акти КСУ» ["Acts of the Constitutional Court"] (http://ccu.gov.ua/storinka/akty-ksu), where the sections relevant for the present paper are entitled «Рішення», «Висновки» & «Ухвали» ["Decisions", "Opinions" and "Resolutions"]. The site also contains judges' dissenting opinions special opinions of judges. The year of publication indicated in this text after the slash should be found in the corresponding section, and then the serial number of the decision given at the beginning. In this example, it is the third decision of the CC in 2015.

decision can be restricted (Article 129 section 3 paragraph 8), but such restriction may not be arbitrary or unfair. Such a restriction must be established solely by the Constitution and the laws of Ukraine; it must pursue a legitimate aim; it must be conditioned by a public need to achieve this aim, and must be proportional and justified. If the right to appeal against court decisions is restricted, the legislator is obliged to introduce such legal regulation that will enable the parties to achieve the legitimate aim in an optimal way, with minimal interference into the exercise of the right to judicial protection without violating the essential content of such a right." Therefore, both the parliament and the constitutional justice body engage in law-making but the latter creates the law in a different way, which consists of nothing else but the implementation of the Constitution.

The experience surrounding the introduction of constitutional justice in Ukraine demonstrates that the strong German model of the constitutional court was initially used as a point of reference. According to the 1992 version of the Law "On the Constitutional Court of Ukraine", it was envisaged that the constitutional justice body would be furnished with broad powers[22]. However, the CCU did not actually operate since the Verkhovna Rada merely appointed its Chair, Leonid Yuzkov, a well-known Ukrainian constitutionalist, but failed to appoint any other members of the CCU. That fact subsequently affected the formation of the CCU after its status act was adopted in October 1996 (first version). The conflict between the doctrines of constitutionalism and the supremacy of the parliament also played a role, which stemmed also from the distribution of political forces in the Parliament.

When the CCU was being formed, a parity principle was introduced whereby six judges were to be appointed by each of the following: the Verkhovna Rada, the President and the Congress of Judges. In the opinion of the authors of the Constitution, such a parity model was supposed to prevent obstruction during the formation of the Constitutional Court, since even if the procedure were to be blocked by any of the aforementioned institutions, the CCU would nevertheless retain its competence to resolve constitutional disputes. At the same time, the legislative regulation concerning the appointment of CCU judges, with a mandatory oath taken at the plenary session of the Verkhovna Rada, became a formal reason for blocking the rotation of CCU judges in 2005–2006, a situation that posed a serious threat to the constitutional foundations of statehood in Ukraine.

---

22 Закон України «Про Конституційний суд України» від 03.06.1992 р., "Відомості Верховної Ради України" 1992, N 33, ст. 471.

The main problems associated with the introduction of judicial constitutional review at the dawn of Ukraine's independence were as follows: 1) the dominant doctrine of legal positivism, whereby the constitution is regarded as a legal act adopted by the sovereign without any consideration of values[23]; 2) the prevailing view that the supremacy of the parliament is the basis of the constitutional system of the state, although this approach is criticised by representatives of constitutionalism[24]; 3) distrust towards the institution of a court whose decisions could substitute for the sovereignty of the people, represented by the national Parliament[25]. These problems affected the process of defining the competence of the CCU in the 1996 Constitution of Ukraine.

1.2 The Constitutional Court of Ukraine as a Constitutional Justice Authority

In the mechanism of public authorities, it is the Constitutional Court that holds primacy in ensuring the supremacy of the Constitution, and constitutional order, as well as fundamental rights and freedoms. Therefore, this body acts as a constitutional authority of special competence, and its functions are fully independent and play an important role in the constitutional system of checks and balances. Thus, the CCU is a constitutional body of specialised competence and the main

---

23 For example, this is manifested in the practice of the Constitutional Court, which formulated doctrines whereby it does not fill gaps in the law and does not resolve conflicts of law, although this legal regulation directly contradicts the foundations of legal certainty as a component of the rule of law, and it also contradicts the understanding of human rights as universals which the state, including the CCU, is obliged to protect. There is reason to believe that these approaches will be reviewed in connection with the competence to examine constitutional complaints, since such approaches are too restrictive from the perspective of human rights protection because the shortcomings of the current legislation cannot serve as a basis to refuse judicial protection of a constitutional right that has been violated.

24 А.О. Селіванов, А.А. Стрижак, *Питання теорії конституційного правосуддя в Україні: актуальні питання сучасного розвитку конституційного правосуддя*, Kyiv 2010, pp. 36–54.

25 During the post-Soviet period, the science of state law (constitutional law) considered courts to be a kind of antithesis to people's sovereignty, although sovereignty, if not interpreted in the democratic context as a procedure for decision-making by the majority while respecting the rights and interests of the minority, is a threat to constitutionalism as a system which restricts power and ensures human rights and freedoms.

authority in the system of legal protection of the Constitution of Ukraine (as the basic law for society and the state), protecting fundamental values and principles on the basis of the rule of law and due process.

Based on the foregoing, constitutional justice can be understood as a way of organisation and a special procedural order for resolving constitutional and legal disputes in order to ensure the supremacy of the Constitution, i.e. to restrict power, ensure the dignity of the individual as well as the supremacy of human and civil rights and freedoms, and to make sure that public authorities are bound by fundamental rights and freedoms. Constitutional justice is defined as a set of principles, rules and procedures that determine the following:

1) a system of legal means and mechanisms through which the rule of law constrains the activity of public authorities, and through which individuals and legal entities may seek the protection of their rights and freedoms;
2) depending on the type of organisation, it takes the form of: a) a single body of constitutional jurisdiction which has a monopoly in resolving constitutional disputes, or b) if a constitutional jurisdiction authority exists, some constitutional disputes are resolved on the basis of law by the administrative justice authorities, or c) a specialised chamber of constitutional justice in the structure of supreme courts, with less important constitutional disputes being resolved by common courts, or d) a system of common courts that have the right to resolve constitutional debates, however, the leading role in this system is given to the supreme courts due to the legal force of judicial precedent;
3) strict compliance with the requirements of due process, i.e. a special procedural format of constitutional proceedings, which differs significantly in the case of a specialised constitutional justice authority vis-à-vis the model of general judicial process;
4) constitutional law disputes are resolved through the interpretation of the Constitution and, as a result, legal acts may be recognised as unconstitutional, whether in whole or in part;
5) a special legal nature and a specific mechanism for the implementation of decisions adopted by constitutional justice authorities, based directly on the principles and values enshrined in the constitution; the purpose is to ensure the supremacy of the constitution, fundamental rights and freedoms, public peace and autonomy of various elements of the political system, in particular the separation of powers.

2 Legislative Stability of the Legality Review Body

According to the rule of law, the independence of courts is a key prerequisite for restricting power and ensuring respect for human rights, which is an integral part of organic constitutionalism. Based on the legal position of the CCU, the principle of legal certainty is manifested in the following: "The stability of the Constitution is among the most important conditions for the certainty of relations between the citizen and the state, and a guarantee of inviolability of human rights and freedoms enshrined in Article 21 of the Constitution of Ukraine; the stability of the Constitution is largely determined, among others, by the legal content of the Basic Law. If the Constitution of Ukraine contained provisions that would be too detailed, and concerned issues that should be regulated by regular acts of law, this could necessitate frequent amendments to the Constitution, thus affecting the stability of the Basic Law" (CCU opinion No. 2/99). Based on these assumptions, we will cast some light on the relationship between the CCU and the constituent power, and the construction of its legal status.

According to the principle of fidelity to the Constitution, constitutional provisions should be properly specified in the legislation and in law-enforcement practice. After the renewal of the Constitution[26] in version of 8 December 2004, taking into account CCU decision No. 11/2010, which allows independent deputies to be part of the parliamentary majority which establishes the government, the question of renewing Ukraine's democratic constitutional order came to the agenda. The problem was associated with constituent legitimacy and the need to overcome the consequences of the usurpation of power by Viktor Yanukovich, who was the president of Ukraine in 2010–2014, and whose term of office ended as a result of the so-called Revolution of Dignity (November 2013 to February 2014). What followed was an intensive public discussion about the need to adopt a new Constitution or to make major amendments to the existing one. As regards the legal status of the CCU, the main discussions focused on its formation guarantees for the independence of judges and the Court, the introduction of a constitutional complaint and the reorganisation of the structure of the CCU.

This motivated the newly elected President Petro Poroshenko to establish a constitutional commission in order to "develop and agree proposed amendments to the Constitution of Ukraine, involve representatives of different political forces, the public, national and international experts, and help to achieve a public and political consensus on improving the constitutional regulation of

26 Закон України «Про відновлення дії окремих положень Конституції України» від 21.02.2014 р. № 742-VII, Відомості Верховної Ради 2014, № 11, ст. 143.

societal relations in Ukraine"[27]. The main motivation behind the CCU reform, to be achieved through a constitutional reform, was to exclude a future possibility that constitutional justice could be used to usurp power, as was the case in the early days of Viktor Yanukovich's term in 2010.

The Constitution of Ukraine was amended in the sphere of justice, and the amendments came into force on 30 September 2016. Afterwards, a presidential commission consisting of leading scholars and lawyers[28] prepared a draft act on the Constitutional Court, which spelt out details of the new provisions of the Constitution. The following constitutional amendments regulating the status of the CCU can be named here:

- the amendments codified the rules of operation for the CCU, which had previously been included, in a fragmentary manner, in the previous version of the act on the CCU;
- the amendments introduced coherent criteria for the appointment of judges (high personal integrity and high authority as a lawyer), with a competitive procedure leading to appointment;
- the amendments strengthened the independence of CCU judges by establishing a clear list of grounds for their removal from office, and such removal was to be decided by the CCU itself, following the results of an independent internal investigation;
- the amendments modernised the structure of the CCU, which operates through meetings of the Grand Chamber and senates (the latter are established to examine constitutional complaints);
- the amendments introduced direct access for individuals and legal entities to the CCU through constitutional complaints regarding the violation of their rights and freedoms;
- following the amendments, the CCU may only interpret the Constitution of Ukraine, and its prerogatives in the interpretation of acts of law were passed on to the Supreme Court;

---

27 Указ Президента «Про Конституційну комісію» від 03.03.2015 р. № 119/2015, Офіційний вісник Президента України 2015, № 7, стор. 22, ст. 464.

28 In particular, it includes Prof. Sergiy Golovaty (representative of Ukraine in the Venice Commission), Prof. Vasily Lemak (Uzhgorod National University, corresponding member of the National Academy of Legal Sciences of Ukraine), Prof. Mykola Onishchuk (rector of the National School of Judges of Ukraine), Alexander Vodyannikov, PhD, LLM of the Eastern European University, Budapest (Head of the rule of law programmes at the OSCE Permanent Representative in Ukraine).

- following the amendments, a group of at least 45 deputies is entitled to approach the CCU with a request to determine the constitutionality of an international treaty; the aim behind this amendment was to prevent the adoption of laws that would undermine national security (as was the case with the ratification of the so-called 'Kharkiv accords').

These constitutional amendments were adopted in response to the previous, very controversial, decisions adopted by the Constitutional Court, in particular regarding the possibility for President Kuchma to stay in office for the third term in a row (since the introduction of presidency in Ukraine in 1991, a person may hold this office for maximum two terms in a row), thus violating the principles of legal succession and the continuity of state institutions (CCU decision No. 22/2003). This issue became especially relevant when the constitutional review body was actually used by Viktor Yanukovich as part of the power usurpation mechanism following a decision allowing non-party deputies to become part of the parliamentary majority and to form the government (CCU decision No. 11/2010), and then the Constitution of Ukraine was effectively revoked under Act No. 2222-IV of 8 December 2004 (CCU decision No. 20/2010). Therefore, it became crucial to ensure reliable and proper guarantees of the independence of the CCU, to prevent any forms of external pressure on the operation of the CCU, and to increase the requirements imposed on constitutional judges.

On the basis of these provisions, on 13 July 2017, the Verkhovna Rada adopted a new version of the act on the Constitutional Court. The draft bill specified the constitutional provisions relating to the organisation of the CCU, the examination of cases by the Grand Chamber and the senates, as well as the procedures for the CCU to examine cases and adopt decisions. The draft bill provided more details regarding the examination of cases involving verification of constitutionality of a nationwide referendum organised upon the people's initiative, cases regarding compliance with the investigation procedure where impeachment of the President is considered, as well as details of situations where the senate transfers cases for examination to the Grand Chamber. These elements will be analysed in more detail in subsequent chapters and paragraphs of this chapter.

2.1 The Constituent Power and the Constitutional Court of Ukraine

The nature of this relationship is rather complicated: like other public authorities (the Verkhovna Rada, the President, the Cabinet of Ministers, or the Supreme Court) the Constitutional Court is a constituted body, i.e. a secondary body which derives its legitimacy from the people of Ukraine. Today, the constitution is recognised as the basic law adopted in accordance with a special procedure (different from the legislative procedure). Therefore, the constitution is surrounded by special means of protection. The authority that establishes the constitution (the constituent assembly) may take various forms, depending on the specific historical features of the society concerned.

In its decision No. 3/2000 of 27 March 2000, the CCU noted that it verifies a draft bill amending the Constitution rather than a draft of the new Basic Law; in other words, the CCU ensures compliance with the constituent procedure and the requirements that make such procedure legitimate. The said decision also contained a requirement that the constituent power should be balanced: "When amendments are made to the Constitution of Ukraine, the Constitution provides for a balance between the actions of the President of Ukraine, the people's deputies of Ukraine, and the Verkhovna Rada of Ukraine when the same execute the will of the people as a bearer of sovereignty and the only source of power in Ukraine". *Mutatis mutandis*, these rules and requirements apply to the adoption of a new constitution of Ukraine.

In his dissenting opinion on the Constitutional Court decision of 27 March 2000, judge V. Shapoval noted that it is necessary to differentiate the adoption of a new constitution and amendments to the existing constitution. He also recognised the primacy of the constituent power with respect to the constituted authorities, i.e. the public authorities. Despite the fact that the current Constitution of Ukraine does not regulate the procedure for the adoption of a new basic law, it does not preclude such a possibility. In his dissenting opinion, the CCU judge N. Selivon stressed that the adoption of the new constitution "depends on the economic, social and political development of each country and is initiated by specific political forces". In his opinion, a new basic law may be adopted in two ways: through a referendum or by a specifically established body (a constituent assembly, etc.).

According to the established practice of the Constitutional Court, the people's power is recognised as "primary, unique and inalienable, and is implemented by the people through free expression of will in elections, a referendum, or other forms of direct democracy in accordance with the procedure established by the Constitution and laws of Ukraine, through state bodies and local self-government bodies established in accordance with the Constitution and laws of Ukraine The outcomes of people's will expressed via the forms of direct democracy defined by the Constitution and laws of Ukraine are mandatory". The constituent power of the people is realised "directly through a nation-wide referendum to determine the constitutional system in Ukraine, enshrined in the Constitution of Ukraine, and to change the constitutional system by amending the Constitution of Ukraine in accordance with the procedure established in its Chapter XIII". At the same time, the Court noted that the current Constitution of Ukraine merely defines the question of making amendments to its text (CCU decision No. 3/2000). In turn, CCU decision No. 6/2005 contained a reservation about the Verkhovna Rada being the only body that exercised this right by adopting the Constitution on 28 June 1996. In other words, the sovereign will of the people was specifically "mediated" by the relevant decision of the parliament.

In 2008, the CCU recognised that the constitution can be adopted at a nationwide referendum upon the people's initiative (CCU decision No. 6/2008). At the same time, it was noted that the procedure was not regulated by law when the case was being examined. Hence, it can be concluded that the possibility to adopt a new Constitution at a referendum upon the people's initiative (in accordance with the procedure provided for in Article 72) must be regulated by law since the absence of this possibility violates the principles of legal certainty. It should be noted that the decision of 16 April 2008 was made by the CCU shortly after President Viktor Yushchenko convened the National Constitutional Council, with the intention to adopt the new Constitution of Ukraine, heavily debated both in terms of its content and the manner of adoption.

One should also mention the practice of the *ex post* constitutional review over the constituent procedure in Ukraine. The *ex post* constitutional review over the constituent procedure is recognised in the constitutional doctrine and jurisprudence of India, Germany, Hungary and in other countries with parliament-based governance. According to the emerging state doctrine, the possibility of *ex post* constitutional review is recognised in Pakistan as a means of overcoming tribalism and Islamic fundamentalism (the Taliban). Such constitutional review is material in content, and it serves, in essence, to protect the fundamental constitutional values. The idea of *ex post* constitutional review of constitutional laws was first formulated in Constitutional Court decision No. 13-рп/2008 and implemented in decision No. 20/2010. However, in terms of its essence, it was a formal constitutional review because act No. 2222-IV was declared unconstitutional due to a procedural violation during its adoption. This decision was perceived ambiguously by constitutional experts since it did not focus on the constitutional values defined in Articles 3 and 157 of the Constitution. The Court did not take into account that when adopting Act No. 2222-IV, the parliament failed to recognise the CCU's opinions made when issuing an opinion on the constitutionality of Articles 157 and 158 in the context of constitutional bill No. 4180. For this reason, they were not examined by the CCU in decision No. 20/2010. Moreover, in the said decision the Constitutional Court did not distinguish between constitutional acts as acts adopted by the constituent power and, as such, enjoying supremacy, and ordinary acts of law, as set out in Article 85 paragraphs 1 and 3 and Chapter XIII of the Constitution. In the end, this CCU decision became a step in the usurpation of power by Viktor Yanukovich, who was not removed from office until the Revolution of Dignity.

2.2 The Legal Foundations of the Status of the Constitutional Court of Ukraine

Legal certainty is an important part of the rule of law, which was adopted as a fundamental principle underlying the national legal system in Article 8 section 1 of the Constitution of Ukraine. During the period of activity undertaken by the CCU after the adoption of its status act on 16 October 1996, the legal status of the CCU changed twice. The actual position of the review body in the constitutional system of checks, balances, and human rights guarantees is determined by the mechanisms which ensure its independence as well as the Court's ability to provide high-quality legal argumentation to support its decisions, this being an important source of the democratic legitimacy of the CCU.

Therefore, before discussing the doctrinal understanding of the status of the Constitutional Court in Ukraine, we should briefly compare the constitutional approaches towards defining the formal features of the legal status of the CCU.

The legal status of the CCU in the Constitution of Ukraine is defined differently in two versions of Article 147. In the initial wording of the Constitution of Ukraine, dated 28 June 1996, the status of the CCU was defined as the sole body of constitutional jurisdiction in Ukraine. In the current version, adopted on 2 June 2016 and effective from 30 September 2016, the legal status of the CCU is defined through its leading competences. Accordingly, the CCU "decides on the constitutionality of the laws of Ukraine and, in cases provided for by the Constitution, also other acts; it provides an official interpretation of the Constitution of Ukraine, and is vested with other competences in accordance with this Constitution".

In fact, these changes have not significantly affected the real legal status of the CCU. The legal certainty of the legal status of the CCU is crucially influenced by the following factors: 1) the system of checks and balances between the institutions of power; 2) the real readiness of the CCU to protect human rights and other constitutional values; 3) the legal style applied to justify its decisions, which is also the source of the Court's legitimacy; 4) the activities of the CCU in the international context, in particular in ensuring a minimum standard for the protection of human rights.

3 The Legal Status of the Constitutional Court

As regards the legal status of constitutional courts, post-Soviet scholars specialising in constitutional law (state law)[29] have characterised constitutional courts as: bodies established to protect the constitution[30], constitutional review bodies[31] and constitutional justice bodies[32]. Another group of scholars believes that the constitutional court, as a body of justice, "is, within its competence, superior to courts of general jurisdiction"[33]. According to A. Selivanov "constitutional jurisdiction should be understood as a set of powers of the CCU based on the Constitution and laws of Ukraine, where the CCU is a single body of judicial power competent in the resolution of constitutional and legal disputes (conflicts) and the official interpretation of the Constitution … of Ukraine, as well as competent in carrying out other activities in matters of constitutional importance"[34]. The CCU directly formulated the doctrine whereby it is a constitutional review body (CCU decision No. 8/97).

When resolving constitutional disputes, the CCU's mission is to ensure a balance of interests of the parties, based on the Constitution. As noted by Yu. Todyka, in such cases "it should be understood that a modern state is based on compromise, and the constitution is a compromise that reconciles the various claims and interests of the most influential social forces in the country"[35]. In the activity of constitutional justice bodies, the main focus is on resolving constitutional and legal disputes. Since the bodies of constitutional justice exercise the function of justice, the dispute resolution function is organic: it is part of organic

---

29 The post-Soviet science of state law mainly views the constitution as a social contract that expresses the sovereign will of the people and the balance of political forces. This interpretation has been known since the times of Ferdinand Lassalle, who apparently relied on the formalist doctrine of the rule of law, which prevailed in the Weimar Republic and Nazi Germany. A significant number, if not the majority, of Ukrainian scholars also adopt the same formalist positions. This author does not share this approach, as will be discussed below.

30 Р. Циппеліус, *Юридична методологія*, Kyiv 2004, p. 160.

31 Ю.Л. Шульженко, *Конституционный контроль в России*, Moscow 1995, p. 9.

32 С.В. Боботов, *Конституционная юстиция (сравнительный анализ)*, Moscow 1994; О.О. Мироненко, *Препозиційні витоки конституційної юстиції в Україні*, "Вісник Конституційного Суду України" 1998, № 4.

33 В. Скомороха, *Окремі питання поділу влад і юрисдикція Конституційного Суду України*, "Право України" 1998, № 5, p. 16.

34 Ю.Г. Барабаш, А.О. Селіванов (eds.), *Конституційна юрисдикція*, Kharkiv 2012, p. 7.

35 Ю.Н. Тодыка, *Основы конституционного строя Украины*, Kharkiv 1999, p. 280.

constitutionalism. Based on the following discussion, we will analyse the implementation of the CCU's status in the context of its interaction with other public authorities in Ukraine.

From the perspective of democratic legitimacy, the bodies of constitutional jurisdiction are bound by the rule of law and, in particular, by the requirements of due process as a guarantee that the rights of participants in constitutional proceedings will be observed as they present their legal position for public examination of the case. According to the principle of separation of powers, constitutional jurisdiction bodies may not interfere in the competence of the parliament. Acts adopted by the parliament may be recognised as unconstitutional if they disproportionately narrow or cancel the essential content of the law. Moreover, constitutional justice bodies should be cautious and aware that the parliament has a broad discretion, because it is the parliament (rather than the constitutional court) that has the right to determine the rules. However, the parliament is bound by the constitutional requirement that any encroachment on the very essence of the right is inadmissible with regard to human rights[36]. In this system of coordinates, constitutional justice puts the political process into a legal framework and protects the fundamental legal values and principles. This determines the nature of the interaction between the CCU and key participants in constitutional legal relations.

3.1 The Constitutional Court and the Verkhovna Rada

Modern systems of the separation of powers are characterised by the diffusion of power within the classic triad. As regards the functions performed by the parliament and the CCU, they are closely related to the implementation of power. Their functions are similar in nature since, under the existing codified constitution in Ukraine, both the parliament and the CCU engage in more concrete and detailed interpretations of the constitutional provisions[37]. However, they exercise these prerogatives in different ways: the Verkhovna Rada (parliamentary assembly) formulates abstract provisions that regulate typical circumstances of life and are designed for an indefinite circle of persons and an indefinite number of cases. The CCU, guided by constitutional values and principles, adapts abstract constitutional provisions to specific circumstances, or evaluates abstract provisions of

36 М.В. Савчин, *Конституціоналізм і природа конституції: теорія та практика реалізації, Дисертація доктора юридичних наук*, Kyiv 2013, pp. 377–378.

37 М.В. Савчин, *Конституційні інновації та вірність конституції*, "Віче" 2016, № 7–8, pp. 44–47.

the law. Such an evaluation is carried out to analyse the legitimacy of interference in the autonomy of an individual. This, based on the principle of proportionality, follows from the systemic and teleological interpretation of Articles 3, 8, 22 and 64 of the Constitution. Therefore, both the parliament and the constitutional justice body engage in law-making but the CCU creates the law in a different way, which consists of nothing else but the implementation of the constitution.

In the event of a conflict with the Constitutional Court, the Verkhovna Rada is inclined to adopt laws designed to "circumvent" the CCU's decision, i.e., it re-enacts a law that may contain provisions previously recognised as unconstitutional. However, the parliament has used its prerogatives regarding the CCU also in different ways, e.g. by dismissing the CCU judges. Therefore, during the Revolution of Dignity, the Verkhovna Rada dismissed five CCU judges it had elected, and also obliged the President and the Congress of Judges to dismiss two and five judges respectively. The Verkhovna Rada invoked the claim that the parliament has exclusive powers to amend the Constitution of Ukraine as an element of the constituent power and pointed out that a CCU decision may not repeal the Constitution Court by force of its decisions, while such decisions, in turn, were among the steps that enabled the usurpation of power by Viktor Yanukovich[38].

In relation to the Verkhovna Rada, the CCU can play a role of either a negative or a positive legislator. In the former case, the CCU may recognise a law or part of a law as unconstitutional, and in the latter case it may, by resorting to proper legal reasoning to justify its own decision, indicate to the Verkhovna Rada that the situation needs to be corrected. In other words, the CCU can point to the variant of the interpretation which is compatible with constitutional values and principles, and it may reject other variants and point out their inadmissibility as they may be regarded as a violation of the Constitution. In the event that a legislative omission is ascertained, the Court is obliged to formulate its decision so as to indicate to the Parliament the legal forms and means though which the omission may be eliminated or corrected. CCU decision No. 3/2012 is a negative example: contrary to the nature of the direct applicability of the Constitution of Ukraine, legality is interpreted as the government's ability to determine the scope and content of social rights by defining the amount of welfare payments in a government decree. This directly encroached on the essence of the content of

38 Постанова Верховної Ради України «*Про реагування на факти порушення присяги суддями Конституційного Суду України*» № 775-VII від 24.02.2014 р., "Відомості Верховної Ради України" 2014, № 12, ст. 201.

law and justified an arbitrary interference by the executive branch in the private autonomy of individuals who, in accordance with the Constitution, must receive social protection guarantees.

An unfortunate example of constitutional review is Constitutional Court decision No. 11/2010, which confirmed the constitutionality of non-factional deputies participating in a coalition of deputies' factions as a legitimate basis for government's investiture, although such a conclusion did not clearly follow from the analysis of section 3 of Article 83 of the Constitution existing at the time. To justify its position, the Court invoked the provisions of the Rules of the Verkhovna Rada, which contradicted Article 83 of the Constitution and its previous jurisprudence. Ultimately, one cannot interpret constitutional provisions through the lens of acts of law if the Constitution defines relevant fundamental principles and limits the discretion of the parliament, as was the case with Article 83 section 3 of the Constitution (Act No. 2222-IV, version of 8 December 2004).

The Constitutional Court admits that acts of law, being issued by the legislature which is a body enshrined in the constitution, must meet certain legal criteria and "be subordinated to the Constitution of Ukraine" (CCU decision No. 4/1997). Moreover, "the Constitution of Ukraine as the main source of the national legal system is… the foundation of the current legislation", which "specifies the provisions enshrined in the Basic Law" (CCU decision No. 3/2002). The Court also drew a conclusion that in "a state governed by the rule of law there exists a strict hierarchy of normative acts and, accordingly, resolutions and other decisions of executive bodies are of a subordinate nature and should not distort the essence and content of laws" (CCU decision No. 9/2001).

3.2 The Constitutional Court and the President

First of all, what plays a role in the system of these relations is the fact that the President appoints six judges of the CCU. In the Ukrainian doctrine, it is common to believe that the President does not belong to any branch of power[39], and, as the head of state, occupies a position above the legislative, executive and judicial

39 Prof. Yu. Tadyka believed that the powers of the President "in the sphere of ensuring constitutional legality, national security, stability of the constitutional system and its protection are central to its competence" (Ю.Н. Тодыка, *Основы конституционного строя Украины*, Харьков 1999, p. 202), although there have been cautious comments about the President leaning towards the executive branch (Ю.Н. Тодика, В.С. Журавський (eds.), *Конституційне право України*, Kyiv 2002, p. 394).

branches[40]. However, since the power in the state is based on the constitution, the exercise of arbitrary power by the President is subject to constitutional review. Essential elements of the constitutional status of the President of Ukraine is that the President, as head of state, is the guarantor of national sovereignty, territorial integrity of Ukraine, observance of the Constitution of Ukraine, and observance of human and civil rights and freedoms (Article 102).

Since Ukraine has a semi-presidential system, the President has certain levers with which to influence the selection of Constitutional Court judges, also through the parliament (Verkhovna Rada). The President's influence becomes particularly strengthened when a majority which is loyal to the president's political course exists in the Verkhovna Rada when the latter appoints a judge or judges. In that situation, the President may act as a moderator of the formation of the CCU and exercise significant influence through this instrument. During the period of the so-called co-existence, when a parliamentary majority opposes the president's political course, his ability to influence the appointment of CCU judges through the parliament is reduced only through factions that remain loyal to the president's political course.

The President can exert some influence on the Congress of Judges since, according to the Constitution of Ukraine, only the head of state may propose draft bills concerning the judiciary, after consulting the High Council of Justice. This factor considerably restricts the freedom of manoeuvre and the discretion of the Congress of Judges when appointing CCU judges.

It is difficult to understand why the Constitutional Court confirmed the constitutionality of the President's right to veto constitutional laws, referring to the fact that the procedure for their adoption is not different from the procedure for the adoption of ordinary acts of law (CCU decision No. 6/2003). The Constitution of Ukraine distinguishes the procedure for the adoption of ordinary acts of law and acts amending the Constitution, which are regulated, respectively, by Article 94 and Chapter XIII of the Constitution. Obviously, this legal position does not correspond with the nature of the Constitution as an act of the constituent power of the people. After all, a constituted authority (the President) cannot substitute the constituting authority by using its vetoing prerogatives.

---

40 Prof. V. Pogorilko defined the status of the President as follows: "as head of state, the President embodies national unity and the continuity of state authority, he is the guarantor of national independence and territorial integrity, and is sometimes also regarded as an arbitrator and a coordinator of the activities undertaken by state bodies, etc." (В.Ф. Погорілко (ed.), *Конституційне право України*, Kyiv 2000, p. 472).

Another instrument that can be used by the President to influence the CCU is his power to suspend acts issued by the Cabinet of Ministers as unconstitutional while simultaneously approaching the CCU for a decision on their constitutionality (Article 106 section 1 paragraph 15 of the Constitution)[41]. This directly contradicts the essentials of the rule of law, which prohibits a wide margin of discretion in the hands of the executive branch, as it may lead to abuses in practice. During the years 2006–2010, when this rule was in effect (it was revived in February 2014), there were periods when the President sent numerous constitutionality inquiries to the CCU, literally paralysing the Court's activities and, thus, this rule turned into an instrument of presidential obstruction of constitutional justice. In its version of 2 June 2016, the Constitution renewed these powers of the President; however, they have hardly been applied in practice. This is connected with the peculiarities of the constitutional form of governance in the country, which establishes dualism of executive power. Therefore, the period of "coexistence" is accompanied by conflicts within the Verkhovna Rada–the President–the Cabinet of Ministers triangle, leading to struggles aimed at recognising the legitimacy of acts issued by Yulia Tymoshenko's cabinet in 2008–2010. The cabinet was based on the parliamentary majority which opposed the political course taken by President Viktor Yushchenko. During the term of President Petro Poroshenko, the cabinets headed by Arseniy Yatsenyuk and Vladimir Groisman pursued a more loyalist political course. Furthermore, executive power was consolidated by the conflict between Ukraine and Russia.

Special relations between the Constitutional Court and the President evolved during the constitutional crisis of 2007. As a result of the 2006 parliamentary elections, the so-called government of national unity headed by Viktor Yanukovich was formed. Soon afterwards, Yanukovich began to concentrate power in his hands, ignoring the interests of the minority[42]. Following these developments, President Viktor Yushchenko, invoking his status as a guarantor of the supremacy of the Constitution and state sovereignty, considered it necessary to apply his prerogatives under Article 102 of the Constitution. The use of the arbitration prerogatives by the head of state was formalised through the adoption of Decree No. 264/2007, whereby the President announced an early

---

41 Конституція України (в редакции от 08.12.2004 г.) [Electronic source]. Access: http://zakon2.rada.gov.ua/laws/show/254%D0%BA/96-%D0%B2%D1%80/ed20060101 (accessed: February 20, 2018).

42 М.В. Савчин, *Становлення конституціоналізму та відповідальне парламентське правління в Україні: криза демократії чи „тиранія" парламентської більшості?*, "Держава і право" 2007, Вип. 36, pp. 148–156.

termination of the powers of the 5th convocation of the Verkhovna Rada due to the fact that deputies had violated the procedure for forming a coalition of majority parliamentary factions. In the President's opinion, the violation gave rise to a threat to national sovereignty, human and civil rights and freedoms, and also posed a potential threat of usurpation of power. On this basis, a decision on early termination of the powers of the parliament was adopted.

However, the implementation of Presidential Decree No. 264/2007 encountered significant problems, connected with the need to find a source to finance the elections, ensure organisational and methodological support of the elections by the Central Electoral Commission and the shortcomings in the existing regulations pertaining to early parliamentary elections. In view of the sharp confrontation between the parliament and the head of state, the president's available legal means were insufficient i.e. the decision-making evolved into a political process. On the other hand, Presidential Decree No. 264/2007 was appealed against the Artemovsky District Court of Lugansk. The court accepted the administrative action and initiated proceedings, which violated the principles of jurisdiction and competence for such cases. To secure the claim, the court suspended the validity of the decree on early termination of the powers of the parliament.

The legitimacy of the President's decision to dissolve the parliament was undermined by the subsequent series of decrees[43]. Decree No. 264/2007 was subjected to examination by the Constitutional Court. At the same time, the President continued political consultations, since the parliament blocked the financing of early elections by adopting relevant acts and changed the composition of the Central Electoral Commission.

The situation around the activities of the CCU and its expected decisions regarding the constitutionality of those presidential decrees was heavily publicised and became very important for the Ukrainian public in the period from May to July 2007. In addition, there was a long period of discussion about

43 Decrees of the President of Ukraine No. 476/2007 of 29 May 2007, No. 355/2007 of 26 April 2007, No. 497/2007 of 5 June 2007 and No. 675/2007 of 31 July 2007. In particular, Decree No. 355/2007 of 26 April 2007 stopped the validity of Article 2 of Decree No. 355/2007 for adoption of certain legislative acts. These acts included the acts of Ukraine No. 1114-V of 1 June 2007 and No. 1095-V of 29 May 2007, which amended the acts of law relating to certain issues related to early parliamentary elections and the replacement of people's deputies of Ukraine whose mandates were terminated early, as well as the activities of the Central Electoral Commission. Finally, Decree No. 675/2007 of 31 July 2007 also amended Decree No. 497/2007. Only then could early parliamentary elections take place on 30 September 2007.

the illegitimacy of the CCU. This was driven by some public announcements regarding possible signs of corruption in the activities of some judges, in parallel with presidential decrees dismissing a number of Constitutional Court judges for "a violation of the oath of a judge"[44]. In turn, the Verkhovna Rada also attempted to dismiss a number of judges. However, these legal acts were illegitimate since neither the parliament nor the head of state complied with the procedural requirements related to the investigation of the circumstances surrounding the "violation of the oath" by the CCU judges.

Therefore, in order to settle the political and constitutional crisis, at the end of May 2007 the President used political means, holding consultations with the Speaker of the Parliament, the leaders of parliamentary factions and the Prime Minister. Following the consultations, the President, the Chairman of the Verkhovna Rada and the Prime Minister issued a joint statement on the need to hold early parliamentary elections under Article 82 section 1 of the Constitution of Ukraine. These agreements were instrumental in resolving certain conflicts of law concerning the forthcoming electoral process and in unblocking the operation of the CCU.

After Presidential Election in April 2019, President of Ukraine Volodymyr Zelensky adopted Decree No. 303/2019 that terminated the powers of the Verkhovna Rada ahead of schedule and appointed an extraordinary election. This decree was appealed by 62 people's deputies to the Constitutional Court. The Constitutional Court declared constitutional decree number 303/2019, stating the following.

In the decision of the CCU stressed, that the Verkhovna Rada (VIII convocation), elected at the extraordinary elections on October 26, 2014, during the term of its authority did not restore in the Rules of Procedure of the Verkhovna Rada the legal regulation of the issue of termination of the activity of the coalition of parliamentary factions in the Parliament, with which the beginning of the course of a month's time for the formation of a new coalition of parliamentary factions and the constitutional prerogative of the President to terminate the powers of the Parliament ahead of time, if such a coalition deputies factions is not formed in

---

44 President Yushchenko initially dismissed CCU judges "for violating the oath of judges", but the wording was subsequently changed into dismissal "in connection with the filing for resignation". In particular, the following judges were dismissed: V. Ivashchenko (decree of 10 May 2007, No. 390, the underlying reason of dismissal was amended by Decree No. 529/2007 of 14 June 2007), V. Pshenichny (decree of 30 April 2007 No. 369, the underlying reason of dismissal was amended by Decree No. 528/2007 of 14 June 2007).

Parliament. Thus, the Constitutional Court expressed its reasoning in the spirit of the doctrine of a political question, that is, self-restraint of its own jurisdiction.

According to Article 5 section two of the Constitution, the people are the bearer of sovereignty and the only source of power in Ukraine. The Constitutional Court made it clear that the resolution of the constitutional conflict by the people through holding early elections to the Verkhovna Rada meets the requirements of Article 5 section two of the Constitution of Ukraine.

Consequently, there arose a constitutional conflict between the President of Ukraine and the Verkhovna Rada of Ukraine on grounds for early termination of powers, which is not a legal solution, since the Basic Law of Ukraine does not specify the order of termination of the activity of the coalition of parliamentary factions in the Verkhovna Rada of Ukraine.

Although the Constitutional Court pointed to the elements of the doctrine of a political issue, it did not consider the parliament's autonomy when forming a coalition of factions and government, as well as exercising parliamentary control over the government. It was also problematic in the presidential decree that there was no argument and guidance on the results of consultations between him and faction leaders and speaker of Parliament.

3.3 The Constitutional Court and the Cabinet of Ministers

When carrying out the constitutional review of acts issued by the government, the CCU ensures the constitutionality of activities undertaken by the executive branch. The CCU has not yet developed a clear point of view regarding the distinction between the legislative function of the parliament and the regulatory function of the government. However, an approach has already been developed in order to separate normative legal acts from individual legal acts. The CCU has merely outlined the characteristics of non-normative legal acts and stated that "… by their nature, non-normative legal acts, unlike normative ones, do not establish general rules of conduct but, instead, they establish specific instructions addressed to an individual or a legal entity, are applied only once and their effect ceases after implementation" (CCU decision No. 2/97).

The most intensive legal disputes about the validity of acts issued by the Cabinet of Ministers took place in the years 2008–2010, when there were disagreements between the head of state and the government. One example is the case of Vanco, where Ukraine was likely to face a claim of several billion US dollars for failure to fulfil its contractual obligations. A decision issued by the Ministry of Environmental Protection dated 25 April 2008, Vanco's special permit for subsoil use was cancelled. When adopting its decision the Ministry assumed that the procedure for the assignment of rights by the winning bidder in a tender does not entail an automatic assignment of the right to receive a special permit for subsoil use. On 8 May 2008, Vanco sent a written request to the government to conduct negotiations in accordance with the provisions of Article 49 of the Hydrocarbon Distribution Agreement.

The Cabinet of Ministers justified its decision to "terminate the participation of Ukraine" in the agreement by referring to the "protection of national interests", with a general reference to Vanco's "non-compliance with the legislation when the Agreement was drafted and signed".

On 18 June 2008, the President issued a decree whereby he stopped the Cabinet of Ministers' Order No. 740, and requested the CCU to assess the constitutionality of that order. After examining the President's constitutional petition, the CCU adopted a resolution on opening constitutional proceedings on 23 October 2008.

However, the President's constitutional petition was based on the argument that the Cabinet of Ministers' Order No. 740 undermined the foundations of "economic security of the state", and, as such, was not sufficiently substantiated. In fact, the CCU had to examine its constitutionality independently, without sufficient legal grounds. For these very reasons, the CCU later concluded that the case did not fall under its jurisdiction and discontinued the proceedings.

By its very nature, the Vanco case forced the CCU to resolve constitutional disputes in the context of conflicting constitutional values, and to develop the doctrine of self-restraint in terms of one's own jurisdiction, i.e. the doctrine of a political question. Even today there is an urgent need in the Ukrainian constitutional doctrine to study the notions of "public interest", "public economic order", "public social order" and others. This is related to the nature and purpose of constitutional legal proceedings, namely to ensure a balance of public and private interests.

In this context, it will be interesting to consider the subsequent practice of the CCU on the interpretation of government regulations in the light of the rule of law requirements, in particular legal certainty and proper concretisation of laws. For example, according to the European Court of Human Rights (ECHR) case law, "*In assessing whether the criterion of foreseeability is satisfied, account may be taken also of instructions or administrative practices which do not have the status of substantive law*" (Leander v. Sweden, 26 March 1987, 9 ECHR 433). That is, when examining constitutional complaints, the CCU will also have to consider acts issued by the public administration with respect to the principle of proportionality and sufficient concretisation in the light of constitutional values and principles.

3.4 The Constitutional Court and Courts of General Jurisdiction

Relations between the Constitutional Court and courts of general jurisdiction are manifested in three ways: 1) The Congress of Judges of Ukraine selects CCU judges in a competitive procedure from at least three candidates; 2) The Supreme Court may approach the CCU with a constitutional petition under the incidental review procedure if an act of law or its separate provisions are to be applied but there are grounds to believe that they are unconstitutional, which may significantly affect the essence of a judicial decision; and 3) Decisions adopted by the CCU may provide grounds for reviewing decisions adopted by common courts.

In the practice of the Constitutional Court, there have been periods when the judicial assistance bodies, in particular the Congress of Judges of Ukraine, have been used to put pressure on the exercise of constitutional justice[45]. For example, after the election of President Viktor Yanukovich, the pressure on the CCU was rather subtle and consisted in changing the configuration of the Court in two stages: first, one judge was substituted, and then four judges were replaced. This paved the way for influencing the composition of the CCU through the Congress of Judges, the most vulnerable institution that participates in the formation of the CCU[46].

---

45 In the early 2010, in the fight for the post of the President, Yulia Tymoshenko conceded to the representative of the pro-Russian Party of Regions Viktor Yanukovych. During the transitional stage, the CCU became the target of attacks carried out by representatives in the Verkhovna Rada and loyal judges at Congress of Judges.

46 The key step in strengthening authoritarianism was when the CCU adopted its decision No. 4-рп/2010 on the interpretation of Article 83 of the Constitution of Ukraine. Shortly after that decision, Yuri Nikitin, who served as judge-rapporteur in the case, resigned and his resignation was unusual (resignation is usually announced in disagreement with an objectionable decision on the eve of its adoption). Later, on 2 September 2010, judge Vyacheslav Dzhun resigned, and on 9 September 2010 resignations were submitted by judges Anatoly Didkovsky, Ivan Dombrovsky and Yaroslava Machuzhak. As stated by judge Yaroslava Machuzhak in her interview, the pressure on judges "was sophisticated" (Суддя КС, яка подала у відставку: до мене застосовували витончені методи, «Уніан.Інформаційне агенство» [Electronic resource]. Access: https://www.unian.ua/politics/401335-suddya-ks-yaka-podala-u-vidstavku-do-mene-zastosuvali-vitoncheni-metodi.html (last accessed on: 30 October 2017)) and consisted in amending the Rules of the Verkhovna Rada, whereby the judges of common courts, elected as constitutional court judges by the Congress of Judges of Ukraine and appointed to this position by transfer, were considered to have resigned from the position of judges of courts of general jurisdiction.

When the jurisdiction of the Constitutional Court is delineated from the jurisdiction of the common courts, the relationship between constitutional and administrative jurisdiction is of fundamental importance. According to R. Kuibida, V. Shishkin and others, there are three ways to determine the competence of administrative courts: a) general – through the notion of an administrative case (Article 3 paragraph 1 of the Code of Administrative Procedure, CAP); b) through a list of categories of cases falling under administrative jurisdiction (Article 17 paragraph 1 of the CAP); and c) through a list of categories of public law cases that do not fall under administrative jurisdiction (Article 17 paragraph 2 of the CAP)[47]. In turn, the CCU formulated a legal position (the CCU decision No. 8/2002) whereby the decision on the constitutionality of acts issued by the President of Ukraine does not preclude the possibility to appeal against presidential acts in the courts of general jurisdiction when such acts have an individual character and concern an appointment or a dismissal.

It should be emphasised that the decision of the Constitutional Court which recognises the unconstitutionality of an act of law applicable in a particular case may be used as a basis for reviewing the court decision. These provisions are contained in the procedural legislation and have been retained in the new version of the procedural legislation. For example, in the current version of the Code of Administrative Procedure, this basis for reviewing decisions adopted by administrative courts is set forth in Article 237. It should be noted that the CCU is not a super-judicial authority for common courts since it solves issues of constitutional law only.

3.5 The Constitutional Court and Other State Authorities

This section deals with bodies that are independent of the government but carry out their functions as public administration bodies. In the opinion of Y. Vashchenko, these authorities have a specific status: "In recent years, a group of new entities has emerged in Ukraine's system of public administration; they occupy a special place and have a special status. These are national commissions that carry out state regulation in certain spheres of the economy, in particular in the sphere of energy, utilities, communications and information, securities markets and financial services markets. These bodies have the status of collegial

---

47 Р.О. Куйбіда, В.І. Шишкін (eds.), *Основи адміністративного судочинства та адміністративного права*, Kyiv 2006, pp. 86–90.

authorities that do not belong to any of the branches of power"[48]. Their legal acts are subject to the jurisdiction of administrative courts but not to judicial constitutional review. However, there have been many cases where the CCU had to resolve cases on the inadmissibility of interventions by the President and the Cabinet of Ministers into the operation of the national commissions. The CCU pointed out that the legal regulation in the Constitution had been changed: according to the Constitution of 28 June 1996, the President had the possibility to take part in the formation of some public administration bodies, whereas according to the Constitution of 8 December 2004 (renewed by the Verkhovna Rada decision of 24 February 2014) the President no longer has such prerogatives (paragraph 3.2 of CCU decision No. 19/2008).

The CCU developed yet another line of activity to ensure constitutionality with reference to the acts adopted by the authorities of the Autonomous Republic of Crimea (ARC). The CCU was faced with the problem of delineating the competence of the ARC when resolving a case on time calculation (CCU decision No. 4/98). In that legal dispute, when the Verkhovna Rada of Ukraine adopted its resolutions No. 15-XII of 11 June 1990 "On amending the procedure for calculating time in the territory of the Ukrainian SSR" and No. 2176-XII of 6 March 1992 "On introducing summer time in Ukraine", the competent authorities of the ARC failed to take appropriate measures to implement these legal acts. The Constitutional Court recognised this inaction of the Verkhovna Rada of the ARC as unconstitutional, since such issues are resolved exclusively by laws of Ukraine (Article 92 section 2 paragraph 3 of the Constitution of Ukraine), and the responsibility for time calculation is vested exclusively with the Cabinet of Ministers of Ukraine. Moreover, Articles 137 and 138 of the Constitution of Ukraine do not provide such authority for the ARC. Notably, the results of this decision were very important for securing the unitary structure of the state: the CCU ruled that the Verkhovna Rada of the ARC did not have the powers to adopt normative legal acts in the form of an act of law since such actions would contradict the constitutional status of the Verkhovna Rada of Ukraine as the single legislative body of Ukraine (Article 75). The Court ruled that the use of the term "act of law" (*zakon*) with reference to the regulatory legal acts issued by the ARC was unconstitutional after the 1996 Constitution of Ukraine had been adopted.

---

48 Ю. Ващенко, *Незалежні регулятори в сфері охорони здоров'я: європейський досвід та перспективи розвитку в Україні*, "Право і громадянське суспільство" 2014, № 1, p. 215.

Furthermore, the Constitutional Court found that the Verkhovna Rada of the ARC exceeded its powers by adopting Rules which provided for the possibility of a draft normative legal act of an ARC body to be "put for public discussion" (Decision No. 1-rp/2001). Thus, the CCU ruled that the ARC was an integral part of Ukrainian society and its population was an integral part of the people of Ukraine in the meaning of Article 5 of the Constitution of Ukraine.

When examining the case of the ARC budget for 1998, the Court admitted that the ARC authorities should follow the single legal policy of the country in this sphere, primarily based on the laws on the taxation system, the budget system of Ukraine, and the act on the state budget for the current year. Since the Constitution of Ukraine provides that it is within the competence of the ARC to develop, approve and execute the budget of the autonomous republic on the basis of Ukraine's single taxation and budget policy, the Verkhovna Rada of the ARC may not introduce a procedure whereby the value added tax and excise tax would go to the republic's budget since, according to current Ukrainian legislation, this is the competence of the Verkhovna Rada of Ukraine (decision No. 7/98).

As regards the acts issued by the ARC bodies, the CCU issued a decision where it defined the hierarchy of legal acts issued by the ARC authorities as follows: "The Constitution of the Autonomous Republic of Crimea is the main normative legal act among all the legal acts adopted by the authorities of the Autonomous Republic of Crimea. The Constitution of the Autonomous Republic of Crimea is adopted by the Verkhovna Rada of the Autonomous Republic of Crimea and approved by the Verkhovna Rada of Ukraine. The legal acts issued by the authorities of the Autonomous Republic of Crimea may not contradict the Constitution of the Autonomous Republic of Crimea, or introduce provisions that impede the functions and powers of the Verkhovna Rada of the Autonomous Republic of Crimea, the Council of Ministers of the Autonomous Republic of Crimea, or other bodies of the Autonomous Republic of Crimea" (CCU decision No. 1/2001).

Further, in the same decision, the Constitutional Court delineated the powers of Ukraine and the ARC based on the delineation of the legislative and executive powers of the ARC authorities. In particular, this delineation manifests itself at least two levels: 1) regulatory legal acts of the Verkhovna Rada of the ARC and decisions of the Council of Ministers of the ARC are adopted in accordance with the Constitution and laws of Ukraine, acts issued by the President of Ukraine and the Cabinet of Ministers of Ukraine and in execution of such acts (Article 135 of the Constitution of Ukraine); 2) the powers, the procedure for the formation and activities of the Verkhovna Rada of the ARC and the Council of Ministers of the ARC are defined by the Constitution and laws of Ukraine, the normative legal acts of the Verkhovna Rada of the ARC relating to issues falling within its competence (Article 136 section 4). The number of decisions adopted by the CCU relating to the ARC was considerable, which indicated the subversive potential of the autonomy's authorities to act against the sovereignty and territorial integrity of Ukraine, and was confirmed during the annexation of the Crimea between 27 February and 15 March 2014.

3.6 The Constitutional Court and Local Self-government Bodies

When exercising constitutional review of legal acts, the Constitutional Court ensures the constitutional principle of the separation of powers between central and local government by virtue of the constitutional guarantees for local self-government (Article 7 of the Constitution). The jurisprudence of the Constitutional Court on this issue is quite relevant and noteworthy. According to CCU decision No. 2/99 of 2 March 1999, the Verkhovna Rada's interference in the competence of local self-government regarding utility prices and tariffs was unconstitutional. In particular, the CCU ruled that: "The pricing policy, i.e. the state strategy to establish and change prices, is among the constituent parts of the domestic economic and social policy of the state. The constitutional powers of the Verkhovna Rada of Ukraine to determine the foundations of the pricing policy have been exercised by the Verkhovna Rada, in particular, in the act 'On prices and pricing', which set out the basic principles for price and tariff setting and application, and the monitoring of their observance in the territory of Ukraine". Further, the CCU made a distinction between the pricing policy of the parliament, the regulatory acts adopted by the government and local self-government with respect to prices and tariffs. Since the regulatory functions should have a certain degree of flexibility and they depend on the characteristics of specific localities, the Verkhovna Rada made an unconstitutional intervention into the area of competence of the ARC and local self-government bodies guaranteed by Articles 137 and 143 of the Constitution of Ukraine. This approach was supported by the CCU in its decision No. 2/2000 of 2 February 2010, pointing out to the Verkhovna Rada that it was unconstitutional to "overrule" the decisions of the CCU by amending legal provisions that were recognised as unconstitutional. Thus, the CCU developed a legal framework to understand the vertical separation of powers and ensure guarantees for local government. According to the principle of subsidiarity, legislative regulations and the regulatory policy are distributed and must meet the criteria of flexibility and maximum accessibility for the public given that the state has a constitutional duty to ensure and guarantee human rights and freedoms (Article 3 of the Constitution of Ukraine).

The Constitutional Court adopted a decision on a case concerning the cancellation of acts issued by local self-government bodies. In that decision, the CCU ruled on the illegitimacy of repealing certain previously adopted individually applicable acts relating to human rights and freedoms, where such acts gave rise to certain legal relationships. In order to repeal such acts, local authorities must apply to a court of general jurisdiction requesting that such acts should be recognised as invalid.

In fact, the CCU reinforced its legal position regarding the legal certainty criteria applicable to acts issued by public authorities. By the way, the CCU judge V. Kampo, in his dissenting opinion on the decision dated 16 April 2009 in the case on repealment of acts issued by local government, noted that the practice of public authorities to repeal their acts of an individual character is a violation of the *nemo iudex idoneus in propria causa* principle (i.e. no one can be a good judge in their own case).

Prior to the entry of constitutional amendments into legal force on 30 September 2016, local self-government bodies had the right to defend the rights of local government by submitting a request to the CCU to provide an interpretation of the Constitution and laws of Ukraine. Today, this right has been modified somewhat: the CCU has the power to interpret only the Constitution of Ukraine.

In particular, it was proposed to introduce the institution of the prefect (instead of the existing heads of local administrations), appointed by the Cabinet of Ministers upon the President's proposal. The prefect would be vested with prerogatives to suspend the acts issued by local self-government bodies and to appeal against them to the administrative court (Article 118 and Article 144 section 2 of the draft bill). However, as a rule, acts issued by local self-government bodies are referred for suspension to administrative courts at the request of the plaintiff when such acts grossly violate human rights and freedoms, state sovereignty and/or territorial integrity.

As regards the powers of the CCU, the draft bill vested a similar power in the President, who already held that kind of power with regard to acts issued by the Cabinet of Ministers. In other words, according to the authors of the constitutional draft bill, the President could suspend acts issued by local self-government bodies while simultaneously requesting the CCU to rule on their constitutionality if such acts infringed upon human rights and freedoms, state sovereignty and/or territorial integrity of Ukraine. At the same time, the President would have the power to dissolve local self-government bodies and appoint a temporary public commissioner (Article 144 section 3 of the draft bill). Following a decision of the CCU stating that the local government body has violated the Constitution, the Verkhovna Rada could, upon the President's request, terminate the powers of a chairman of a community, a community council, a district council, or a regional council and could announce early elections in accordance with the procedure established by law (Article 144 section 6 of the draft law). Pursuant to the draft bill, the CCU should examine such a case without delay.

Recently, there has also been a lively discussion on the idea to introduce the institution of a complaint in the interests of local government. At present, there are disputes as to who can be the subject of such a complaint: local self-government bodies only or perhaps also residents of a community or a region.

3.7 The Constitutional Court and Other Participants in Legal Relations

When it comes to the protection of the rights and freedoms of individuals, the CCU differentiates its approaches depending on whether the case involves a natural person or a legal entity. In the case based on a submission by residents of the Zhovti Vody, the CCU recognised the universal nature of the constitutional human right to judicial protection (CCU decision No. 9/97), thus extending the jurisdiction to legal acts as well as actions/omissions of the prosecutor's office in criminal justice (CCU decision No. 6/2001). Further on, this constitutional jurisprudence influenced the principles of administrative proceedings and the procedure for appealing against legal acts, actions/omissions of staff involved in inquiry, pre-trial investigation and prosecutor's work in the field of criminal justice. However, following the constitutional amendments of 2 June 2016, the CCU will have to change its universalist approach since these amendments guarantee only appeals against judicial decisions at appellate courts, whereas cassation is allowed only in cases provided for by law (Article 126).

The approaches adopted by the CCU with regard to legal entities are ambiguous. The CCU recognises that in accordance with the rule of law, laws should be consistent with the principles of freedom, equality, and fairness (CCU opinion No. № 2/99, CCU decision No. 15/2004). From this point of view, the CCU ruled that restrictions of political parties' activities was constitutional (CCU decision No. 9/2007). At the same time, it should be noted that this approach has been applied by the CCU cautiously because, according to its legal position, this may encroach on the constitutional principle of the separation of powers (Article 6) and may be regarded as interference in the legislator's discretion. In its practice, the CCU also recognises that measures to fill gaps or overcome conflict in legislation violate the separation of powers, although such a view does not follow from the Constitution of Ukraine. This position of the CCU can be hardly defended from the perspective of protection of human rights and fundamental freedoms: a refusal to provide constitutional protection directly contradicts the rule of law. In particular, in its ruling No. 41-y of 10 July 1998, the CCU made the following observation in this regard: "… the nature of specific state-official relations, the elimination of contradictions and filling of the gaps in the current legislation does not fall within the competence of the Constitutional Court" (CCU ruling No. 2/2000). This approach is a denial of justice and an unconstitutional restriction of the right to judicial protection, where such right cannot be restricted even during martial law or in a state of emergency.

Formally speaking, despite not being parliamentary bodies, factions play an important role in the organisation of the legislature. In particular, factions ensure voting discipline and, in case of non-compliance, may impose disciplinary sanctions on deputies. According to Article 81 section 6 of the Constitution of Ukraine, a faction may remove a deputy, which entails the loss of the deputy's mandate (an element of an imperative mandate). However, a constitutionality question arises if a deputy loses his/her mandate after being excluded from the faction after voting against the position adopted by the faction. This should be answered in the negative, since it contradicts the basic right to freedom of speech (Article 34 of the Constitution) and such a sanction disproportionately narrows the essential content of this essential law (Article 22 sections 2 and 3). Factions are an important instrument of parliamentary control[49], since they can mobilise the necessary number of deputies to initiate a procedure of no-confidence vote (at least 1/3 of the constitutional composition of the parliament). As factions represent a variety of interests, free democratic discourse is important.

4 Ensuring the Supremacy of the Constitution of Ukraine and the Structure of the Constitutional Court

For an adequate discussion of this issue, it is necessary to draw attention to the composition of the CCU, the status of its judges, as well as the subject-matter and limits of authority.

---

49 Ю.Г. Барабаш, *Парламентський контроль в Україні (конституційно-правовий аспект)*, Kharkiv 2004; В. Шаповал, *Зарубіжний парламентаризм*, Kyiv 1993, pp. 130–137.

4.1 The Structure of the Constitutional Court

After the constitutional reform of justice, the composition of the CCU changed significantly. The act on the CCU dated 13 July 2017[50] provides that the CCU may work in the form of Grand Chamber meetings, where the Grand Chamber consists of all judges. Moreover, two senates are established within the CCU, and the examination of constitutional complaints must be distributed between those two senates. The CCU has retained the practice of working through boards of judges which decide on the admissibility of constitutional complaints and appeals. Each of the six boards (instead of three, as was the case earlier) must consist of three judges.

The work of the Grand Chamber is organised to ensure consistent practice of the CCU. The legislative amendments aim to introduce a function whereby the Grand Chamber distributes cases between the senates and boards of judges, and may change the jurisprudence of the CCU. In turn, senates may refer constitutional complaints to the Grand Chamber wherever such complaints may lead to a change in the CCU's jurisprudence or if the case is of fundamental importance and the senate is incapable of adopting a decision.

The structure of the CCU remains vulnerable because the Court is formed by three institutions of power: the Verkhovna Rada, the President and the Congress of Judges, each of them appointing six judges. When the Constitution was amended in the section concerning the justice system, this formation model was not changed, although many scholars emphasise that career judges often have difficulties in situations where they need to verify the legality of provisions contained in acts of law. This is due to their longstanding habits in the application of laws, which makes it difficult for career judges to overcome their professional habit of applying the law consistently. Neither the Constitutional Assembly nor the Constitutional Commission managed to overcome this controversial element in the formation of the CCU and retained the original formation model.

Practice has shown that this formation of the CCU may lead to its obstruction and, as a consequence, to a paralysis in the work of the CCU. For example, when the powers of many judges ended in October 2004, the remainder of the CCU proved to have no competence to examine cases (the CCU must have twelve judges to work in a valid way). This was because the Verkhovna Rada failed to appoint the judges within its quota, whereas judges appointed by the President and the Congress of Judges were not called to be sworn-in at Verkhovna Rada meetings. The CCU was able to resume its work only after judges were appointed

---

50 Закон України «Про Конституційний Суд України» від 13.07.2017 р. № 2136-VIII, *Відомості Верховної Ради України*, 2017, № 35, ст. 376.

by the parliament in June 2006. A similar situation was observed since the end of 2016: as at the end of 2017, there were five vacancies for CCU judges and the competitions were still open. Most probably, this is one of the main reasons why the CCU adopted its first decision for the year as late as at the end of November 2017.

4.2 The Legal Status of Constitutional Court Judges

CCU judges are appointed for nine years without the right to be re-appointed (Article 148 of the Constitution). Previously, the requirements for a CCU judge were more formal. In particular, the judge was required to have Ukrainian citizenship, a university degree in law, and 15 years of work experience in a legal profession. After the Constitution of Ukraine was amended on 2 June 2016, these requirements were retained and, in addition, constitutional judges were required to meet certain qualitative requirements such as, in particular, have high moral qualifications and be recognised as highly competent lawyers. This approach is criticised for being based on arbitrary criteria, which, as critics maintain, may lead to arbitrary appointments of judges. However, the appointments of constitutional judges are connected with socio-political debate, which means that the degree of citizens' control over this process plays a role, as well as the possibility to assess candidates in terms of their competence, ability to resist external pressure and ability to adopt complex decisions under conditions of legal uncertainty, while aiming to protect fundamental constitutional values and principles.

CCU judges must maintain political neutrality, and the position of the judge may not be combined with other spheres of activity. In particular, judges may not be members of political parties or trade unions, may not be involved in any political activity, have a representative mandate, hold any other paid positions and perform any other paid work, except for academic activity, teaching or creative work (Article 11 of the act).

Judges are appointed based on the results of a competitive procedure. The Legal Policy and Justice Committee at the Verkhovna Rada organises the competition. The selection committee, consisting of lawyers "with a recognised level of competence", is established at the office of the President whereas the judiciary is represented by the Council of Judges. The appointment of judges is finally determined at the plenary session of the Verkhovna Rada. In this case, Article 208^4 section 3 of the Verkhovna Rada Rules[51] does

51 Закон України Про Регламент Верховної Ради України від 10 лютого 2010 року N 1861-VI, "Відомості Верховної Ради України" 2010, № 14–15, № 16–17, ст.133 с последующими изменениями.

not correspond with Articles 3, 8 and 148 of the Constitution. According to the Verkhovna Rada Rules, candidates can only be proposed by parliamentary factions. However, parliamentary factions are not mentioned in Article 148 of the Constitution as subjects which may nominate candidates for CCU judges. Moreover, factions are not official bodies of the parliament but, instead, a form of association for the deputies. The selection committee refused to register four candidates by invoking exactly section 3 of Article 208^4 of the Verkhovna Rada Rules[52]. After interviews with the candidates and a special screening, the Verkhovna Rada elects the CCU judges at the plenary session, by an absolute majority.

The President appoints the judges of the Constitutional Court on the basis of the decision of the selection commission, taking into account the results of the interview, the special screening of candidates and analysis of their dossier. On the basis of the materials prepared by the Council of Judges, the Congress of Judges adopts a decision by a majority of votes at its meeting, thus electing its quota of judges. The process leading to the appointment of CCU judges should be carried out within three months following the announcement of a vacancy for the position of a CCU judge. The judge proceeds to exercise his/her powers from the day when he/she takes an oath at a special plenary session of the CCU.

A Constitutional Court judge may publicly express his/her opinion on the substance of cases only for cases where the CCU has already taken a decision or given an opinion. While being in office, a Constitutional Court judge may not receive state awards, distinctions, special titles granted in Ukraine, or any other awards, decorations, or diplomas, except for rewards for personal courage and heroism shown by risking his/her life.

The procedure of disciplinary liability applicable to Constitutional Court judges has been changed. Firstly, without the consent of the CCU, no judge may be detained or held in custody or detention until the court issues a guilty verdict, except for situations where the judge is detained while committing a grave or especially grave crime or immediately after such crime was committed (previously, this issue was decided by the Verkhovna Rada).

---

52 Рішення про конкурс на посади суддів Конституційного Суду України, Комітет Верховної Ради України з питань правової політики та правосуддя, [Electronic resource]. Access: http://kompravpol.rada.gov.ua/uploads/documents/31884.pdf (accessed: February 20, 2018).

Secondly, only the CCU may decide to hold a CCU judge liable (previously, such decisions were taken by the Verkhovna Rada, the President and the Congress of Judges, respectively, regarding the judges appointed by those bodies). The Constitutional Court can decide to dismiss a CCU judge from office by a two-thirds majority of its total number of judges (Article 149 of the Constitution). The Constitution also specifies the grounds for the dismissal of CCU judges, and those grounds are exhaustive:

1) if the judge is unable to fulfil his/her duties for health reasons;
2) if the judge has violated the requirements regarding incompatibility;
3) if the judge has committed a serious disciplinary offence, gross or systematic neglect of his/her duties, incompatible with the status of a CCU judge or incompatible with the position held;
4) if the judge has filed for resignation or dismissal upon his/her own request.

The act on the CCU regulates, for the first time, issues related to conflict of interest in the case of CCU judges. In particular, a CCU judge may not participate in the preparation, review or adoption of decisions, perform other powers in matters where there is a real or potential conflict of interest. If the judge has a real or potential conflict of interest, he/she must notify the CCU thereof in writing within one business day and withdraw from the case (Article 60 of the act).

The first precedent for the application of disciplinary sanctions was the dismissal of the Chairman of the Constitutional Court of Stanislav Shevchuk according to the court ruling of 14 May 2019 for committing „a serious disciplinary offence, gross or systematic neglect of his/her duties, incompatible with the status of a CCU judge or incompatible with the position held".

4.3 Functions and Competences of the Constitutional Court

The functions of the CCU are determined on the basis of its position in the state system as a key element of organic constitutionalism. The operation of constitutional courts reflects the dilemma of modern constitutionalism: "people's sovereignty or democracy, and their dependence on constitutional norms, i.e. on human rights and the separation of powers"[53].

Constitutional justice can influence the political process through legal means, with the art of legal argumentation to support decisions being the main one.

---

53 О. Гьофе, *Розум і право. Складові інтеркультурного правового дискурсу*, Kyiv 2003, p. 220.

In order to limit the influence of political circumstances on the operation of constitutional courts, the doctrine of the political question is used. The CCU formulated this doctrine in its own way as a doctrine "the question of political expediency", when examining the constitutionality of the 4 % threshold for political parties in parliamentary elections[54]. In its ruling of 5 March 1999, the CCU stressed that the resolution of political issues contradicted its mission as the only body of constitutional jurisdiction, since any political activity is incompatible with the activities of judges of common courts and judges of the CCU.

In addition, M. Teslenko proposes functions related to the resolution of competence disputes between various authorities[55]. In the opinion of N. Savenko, the functions of the constitutional jurisdiction body are aimed at implementing their competence and accomplishing the tasks assigned to it, primarily to ensure the rule of law and constitutional legality. The main functions of this body are as follows: administration of justice; constitutional review; official interpretation of the Constitution and laws of Ukraine; legal protection of the Constitution; and ensuring the observance of the separation of powers (arbitration function) and the protection of constitutional rights and freedoms[56].

Until recently, there was a widespread view that the CCU is not a judicial body. For example, the former deputy chairman of the CCU, V. Shapoval, believed that the CCU had no direct connection with the administration of justice[57]. According to N. Savenko, the notion of "justice" should be understood as encompassing the work of a competent court performed on behalf of the state in accordance with the procedure established by law. Such work involves the

54 In its decision No. 1-рп/98 of 26 February 1998, the CCU formulated a provision whereby "if the lists of parliamentary candidates proposed by political parties and/or electoral blocs of parties that have received less than four percent of votes are to be deprived of the right to participate in the distribution of deputy mandates, this is a matter of political expediency and, as such, should be resolved by the Verkhovna Rada of Ukraine." However, in this context, we can invoke the decision adopted by the Federal Constitutional Court of Germany regarding the protective threshold, based on a different concept and adopted in a very different context on 24 February 2014. According to that decision, the re-establishment of the 3 % cut-off threshold in European elections by the Bundestag was declared unconstitutional.

55 М. Тесленко, *Конституційна юрисдикція в Україні*, Автореф. канд. юр. наук, Kyiv 2000, p. 9.

56 М.В. Савенко, *Правовий статус Конституційного Суду України*, Автореф. канд. юр. наук, Kharkiv 2001, pp. 6–7.

57 В.М. Шаповал, *Проблеми розвитку конституційної юрисдикції в Україні*, "Вісник Конституційного Суду України" 1998, № 2, p. 45.

examination and resolution of conflicts or legal issues arising during the implementation of various norms of constitutional, civil, criminal, administrative or other law[58]. However, this opinion cannot be accepted since the CCU has all the features of a judicial body: independence and its guarantees; special status of CCU judges; the powers and procedure for dealing with cases is defined by law; the CCU takes decisions that are generally binding, final and do not require any additional approval by other authorities. The decisive factor is that the CCU can justify its decisions based on criteria such as the rule of law and respect for human dignity.

Taking these imperatives as a point of departure, the powers of the CCU were reformed in accordance with the law amending the Constitution of Ukraine with respect to justice, dated 2 June 2016. These amendments to the Constitution provide that the CCU may be approached to rule on the constitutionality of international treaties[59] and issues put on nation-wide referenda upon the people's initiative, and the institution of normative constitutional complaint was introduced with the condition that at least 45 deputies would endorse it. The area where the CCU may issue official interpretations was also reduced: the CCU is only competent in interpreting the provisions of the Constitution of Ukraine (formerly, the CCU could also interpret acts of law). Unfortunately, Article 8 section 3 of the act on the CCU also reinforces this problematic situation: the CCU may not consider the legality of decisions adopted by the Verkhovna Rada, acts issued by the President and the Cabinet of Ministers, although this competence is implicitly included in Article 8 section 2 of the Constitution of Ukraine, which establishes the hierarchy of legal acts: the Constitution – an act of law – a secondary legislative act. In fact, the main criterion should involve the proper

---

58 М.В. Савенко, *Правовий статус Конституційного Суду України,* Автореф. Диссертац. канд. юрид. наук, Kharkiv 2001, p. 7.

59 For example, when the Verkhovna Rada ratified the so-called 'Kharkiv accords' in violation of the constitutional procedure (І. Капсамун, *Як Харківські угоди підготували «Мінський котел»,* "День" 2017, 25 квітня [Electronic resource]. Access: https://day.kyiv.ua/uk/article/podrobyci/yak-harkivski-ugody-pidgotuvaly-minskyy-kotel (last accessed on: 29 October 2017)), which extended the lease of the city of Sevastopol by the Russian Federation until 2042 for the Black Sea Fleet, in violation of the constitutional ban on the deployment of military bases on the territory of Ukraine (Article 17), the opposition could not challenge this decision of the Parliament, since, until 2016, the competence to appeal to the Constitutional Court about the constitutionality of international treaties was vested only in the interested parties, i.e. the President and the Cabinet of Ministers.

concretisation of constitutional principles and values through legal acts (human dignity, freedom, equality and prohibition of discrimination, democracy, etc.).

4.4 Limits of Powers of the Constitutional Court and the Doctrine of Self-restraint of Constitutional Justice

In accordance with the doctrine of political expediency formulated by the CCU, the parliament independently determines the models of legal regulation of certain legislative spheres, as defined in Article 92 of the Constitution. In particular, when deciding on the constitutionality of the 4 % threshold for political parties (or groups of parties) in elections, the CCU acknowledged that this was a matter of political expediency. Moreover, the CCU recognised that the Verkhovna Rada operated exclusively within the limits of its constitutional powers when determining the mechanism of specific procedures during the electoral process. In particular, this doctrine was detailed in the ruling of 5 March 1999, where the CCU noted that the resolution of political issues contradicted its appointment as the sole constitutional jurisdiction body since any political activity is incompatible with the activities of judges of general jurisdiction as well as judges of the CCU.

The CCU has developed approaches whereby it refuses to consider issues of political expediency (CCU decision No. 1/98), the legality of legal acts (CCU ruling No. 5/99), conflicts of law (CCU rulings No. 20/2000 and No. 28/2005) and gaps in the current legislation (CCU ruling No. 9/2002), investigation of actual circumstances (CCU rulings No. 53/97 and No. 31/99) and political circumstances (CCU ruling No. 2/2000), as well as verification of constitutionality of legal acts that have become null and void (CCU ruling No. 62/97).

In particular, the CCU explains its refusal to examine conflicts and gaps in the current legislation by stating that filling in the gaps and resolving conflicts in the current legislation violates the separation of powers and interferes in the exercise of legislative power. This position stems from the view whereby resolution of conflicts and the filling of gaps in legislation is tantamount to the creation of legal norms. Article 57 of the Constitution of Ukraine obliges public authorities to ensure that the content of regulatory legal acts concerning the essence and scope of individuals' rights and duties is properly notified to the public, which means that gaps and conflicts in the current legislation are unconstitutional. This problem should be addressed exactly by the CCU, applying the analogy of the law or the analogy of rights.

As the basic law in society and the state, the constitution is a legal act that is applied in a particular social environment under specific historical circumstances and is a kind of "open text". Therefore, the constitution cannot be reduced solely to the analysis of its text. Instead, the constitution is a product of the evolution taking place in society; it reflects the legal awareness of the constituent power and the public consensus regarding social values protected by law – the established practice of applying legal norms and socially significant behaviour.

The concept of the constitution as an "open text" is based on the fact that the constitution cannot be reduced to a kind of "constitutional code", since the idea that "the constitution should cover all possible life situations and provide answers to all questions without any additional judicial interpretation is illusory and detrimental to the idea of legal regulation via a constitution"[60].

The realistic theory of constitutional interpretations[61] is filled with content during the exercise of powers to clarify the constitutional text (the semiotic aspect) in the context of the actual circumstances of a case (the sociological aspect, which includes the dilemma of effectiveness and the legal force of constitutional norms), based on the discretion of interpreting constitutional jurisdiction on the basis of the Constitution, the rule of law and due process of law.

4.5 The Subject-Matter of the Key Powers Vested in the Constitutional Court

Article 7 of the act on the CCU contains a systematic description of the powers vested in the constitutional justice body. These powers will be reviewed below in the light of current CCU practice and the amendments proposed in the course of the constitutional justice reform.

1) *Constitutional review of legal acts.* The CCU exercises limited constitutional review. It may verify the constitutionality of acts of law (*zakon*) and other legal acts issued by the Verkhovna Rada of Ukraine, the President of Ukraine, the Cabinet of Ministers of Ukraine, and the Verkhovna Rada of the ARC. This power is exercised by the CCU through *ex post* constitutional review, i.e. the constitutionality of these acts is the subject of verification. The constitutionality of legal acts in Ukraine depends on the grounds and limits of powers, the way they are exercised, the procedure for their adoption and enforcement: all of them must comply with the Constitution of Ukraine and properly specify its provisions in the light of fundamental principles of law (Article 19 section

---

60 С.В. Шевчук, *Загальнотеоретичні проблеми нормативності актів судової влади*, Дисертація доктора юридичних наук, Kharkiv 2008, p. 82.

61 М. Тропер, *Реалистическая теория толкования*, "Сравнительное конституционное обозрение" 2006, № 1.

2 and Article 152 of the Constitution). An important aspect in the *ex post* constitutional review is the question of how effectively the CCU protects the fundamental constitutional values.

The vision of the system of constitutional review of legal acts was formulated in the CCU's jurisprudence: "the first section of Article 92 of the Basic Law of Ukraine enshrines the principle of priority (supremacy) of acts of law in the system of other regulatory legal acts: acts of law are used to regulate the most important social relations. This norm stipulates the list of issues that should be regulated solely by acts of law of Ukraine and has an imperative character, which means that all those issues should be handled exclusively in the form of an act of law" (CCU decision No. 4/2008). Accordingly, when not directly exercised by the people of Ukraine, the right to enact laws is held exclusively by the Verkhovna Rada and cannot be transferred to other bodies or officials (CCU decision No. 15/2000). The constitution does not enable the parliament to delegate its legislative functions to any other authority (CCU decision No. 15/2009).

As regards the understanding of equality and procedural guarantees of human rights, the CCU has developed a fairly interesting practice. In particular, equality implicitly includes differentiation based on certain qualities of humans as social beings, which give rise to the need to ensure equitable distribution of social benefits in order to secure the needs and interests of the individual.

Following the practice of the ECHR[62] the CCU applies similar criteria when ensuring equality and non-discrimination but does not do it fully. One example is the case of A. Kozlov's constitutional appeal (CCU decision No. 7/2013). The CCU stated that there was a difference in the treatment of individuals as consumers on the one hand, and legal entities and individuals as entrepreneurs on the other hand. This difference in treatment is based on the fact that the penalties on loan agreements signed by legal entities may not exceed the double amount of the loan principal whereas no similar limitations for penalties are established in the law for individual borrowers. The CCU pointed out that the terms and conditions of consumer loans must be based on the idea that the consumer is the weak party to the contract and, as such, is subject to special legal protection, based on the principles of fairness, honesty and reasonableness. At the same time, the CCU confined itself to a warning and stated that if the state is to fulfil its constitutional duty to protect the rights of consumers, such protection must be specifically regulated by law.

---

62 *Запрещение дискриминации в рамках Европейской конвенции о правах человека (статья 14)*. Руководство для юристов, Interrights 2009.

Justice is a criterion through which one can understand the permissible limits of state interference into private life. This criterion determines the legal content of the activities undertaken by public authorities. Justice is viewed by the CCU as a humanitarian dimension of law (respect for human dignity)[63], which ensures equality and justifies difference (CCU decision No. 15/2004), and ensures the same application of laws and non-discrimination.

In particular, procedural fairness is manifested in the exercise of the right to judicial protection. In one of its decisions, the CCU noted the following in this context: "The right to judicial protection is among the basic inalienable rights and freedoms of humans and citizens. In particular, Article 64 section 2 of the Constitution does not allow restriction of the right to judicial protection even in conditions of martial law or a state of emergency" (CCU decision No. 6/2001).

In its decisions, the CCU indirectly admits that the function of the court, in terms of procedural fairness, is to ensure a balance of interests in society, ultimately protecting public interests. Accordingly, when administering justice, the court ensures the protection of human and civil rights and freedoms guaranteed by the Constitution and laws of Ukraine, as well as the protection of the rights of legal persons, and the interests of society and the state (CCU decisions No. 15/2004 and No. 1/2008).

From the perspective of procedural guarantees of human rights, it is important to consider CCU decision No. 1/2017 concerning judicial control over the application of a preventive measure of detention towards suspects. The Court stressed that the purpose of Article 29 section 2 of the Constitution is to prevent the arbitrary restriction (deprivation) of liberty, and there must be relevant periodic judicial monitoring of this issue, carried out at intervals defined by law.

Further, the CCU emphasised the arbitrariness of the second sentence of Article 15 section 3 of the Code of Criminal Procedure, which actually contains a kind of presumption of prolonged detention if none of the parties to the lawsuit requests otherwise. The CCU pointed out that judicial review is a prerequisite for an extension of detention or house arrest. At the same time, the investigator's conclusions regarding the circumstances and the essence of the suspicion that may substantiate the preventive measure at the stage of pre-trial investigation

63 In this context, attention should be drawn to the legal technique of substantiating decisions in constitutional jurisprudence on the basis of a combination of Article 3 section 2 and Article 22 section 3 of the Constitution of Ukraine, which, in essence, provide a systematic interpretation reflecting the doctrine of preservation of the essence of the fundamental right. See: CCU's decision No. 1/2001 and CCU's decision No. 5/2005.

are not prejudicial and, therefore, the CCU instructed the courts again to ascertain the validity of the continued detention as a preventive measure. If there is no proper justification of detention, the person in question must be immediately released.

In another case (CCU decision No. 12/2010), the CCU formulated the following conclusion: "As regards the constitutional understanding of evidence in a criminal case obtained as a result of operational search activities, the first sentence of Article 62 section 3 of the Constitution of Ukraine, which provides that an indictment may not be based on illegally obtained evidence, should be understood to mean that criminal charges may not be based on factual data obtained by an authorised person from operational search activity without observing the constitution, or on data obtained in violation of the procedure established by law; moreover, an indictment may not be based on evidence obtained through targeted actions aimed at the collection and recording of evidence using measures provided for in the act 'On operational investigative activities', if obtained by a non-authorised person".

This case concerned the constitutional procedural guarantees of human rights because Article 62 of the Constitution of Ukraine deals with the lawful procedure for the collection of evidence in order to prove the guilt of a specific person in the context of a crime, although it should be remembered that individuals are covered by the requirements of Articles 55 and 59 of the Constitution, which determine the structure of individual rights to protection and legal assistance.

2) *The official interpretation of the Constitution of Ukraine.* This is a rather unconventional way of formalising the powers of constitutional justice. The interpretation of the constitution is an inherent characteristic of constitutional justice and a necessary condition for the legitimacy of CCU decisions. The need to interpret the Constitution is due to the fact that the Basic Law establishes the limits of political activity. Therefore, there is a need to delineate credible and presumed legal limitations of political activity. Such reliability and predictability is achieved by the fact that the Court follows its own jurisprudence in similar cases where constitutional provisions are interpreted on the same grounds and under the same kinds of factual circumstances. The normative content of the Constitution means that disputes concerning the understanding of its provisions are shifted not towards the political plane, but towards the framework of a legal dispute.

However, the political process is bound by the rules of representative democracy, which should guarantee a free exchange of views, and a balance between the interests of the ruling majority and the opposition. Therefore, the following opinion is fair: "the purpose of interpretation is to translate the meaning of a legal provision into more accessible and understandable discourse, and to bring it closer to specific situations, so that there is no doubt that those situations are regulated by a relevant provision and that correct understanding and implementation can be ensured"[64]. When applying the law, one must take into account the reality and requirements of due process. The application of legal norms means that functions of the legislator and of justice must be separated. Thus, justice influences political activities and brings them into line with the rule of law. Therefore, the interpretation of the Constitution is the prerogative of the constitutional justice body and reflects the direct effect of constitutional provisions.

According to the amendments to the Constitution in the section referring to justice, introduced on 2 June 2016, the CCU has the power to interpret the Constitution of Ukraine, whereas the power to interpret the acts of law was passed to the Supreme Court as a court of cassation. Previously, the power of the CCU to interpret the Constitution and laws of Ukraine was of particular importance for the protection of constitutional rights and freedoms. Apparently, the power to interpret the Constitution has remained with the CCU in order to prevent a situation where it would be exercised by the Verkhovna Rada in violation of the fundamental principle of *nemo debet esse judex in propria causa*.

3) *Constitutional review of international treaties*. Such review is carried out at the request of the President or at least 45 people's deputies or the Cabinet of Ministers. The review consists in issuing an opinion on the constitutionality of valid international treaties or those international treaties that are submitted to the Verkhovna Rada for approval.

This power is exercised by the CCU through preventive constitutional review of the constitutionality of treaties. Approved international treaties are submitted to the Verkhovna Rada which consents to Ukraine being bound by those treaties. It is also exercised in the form of *ex post* constitutional review of existing international treaties. This form of review provides a legal mechanism ensuring that Ukraine fulfils international treaties in accordance with its own constitution.

When international treaties are incorporated into the national legal system, constitutional justice prevents cases where such binding treaties contradict the country's constitution. The idea of involving constitutional justice is to determine the constitutional mechanism for the implementation of such

64 М.В. Савенко, *Правовий статус Конституційного Суду України* ..., p. 7.

international treaties, since the country cannot refuse to fulfil those treaties on the grounds that they are contrary to national law (Article 27 of the Vienna Convention on the Law of Treaties). The invalidity of international treaties may only be resolved in accordance with the norms of international law (in particular, according to Articles 27, 46, 65, 66 et al. of the Vienna Convention on the Law of Treaties).

4) *Review of constitutionality of the subject-matter of a nation-wide referendum announced on the people's initiative.* Such a review is performed at the request of the President or at least 45 parliament deputies: the CCU issues opinions on the constitutionality of the issues proposed for a nation-wide referendum on the people's initiative. As a rule, the CCU verifies the constitutionality of issues or draft bills that are submitted for referendum. The results of a referendum are recognised as invalid only in cases where errors or irregularities in the course of campaigning and voting actually affected the outcome of the referendum.

This form of constitutional review was applied by the CCU directly when the President of Ukraine announced a popular referendum by force of decree No. 65/2000 of 15 January 2000. In that case, the CCU encountered legal uncertainty since the act "On nation-wide and local referendums" of 3 July 1991 No. 1286–12 did not directly regulate the exercise of the people's right of initiative to amend the Constitution in the context of the provisions of Chapter XIII of the Constitution. The CCU took the position that this form of direct democracy should be ensured and pointed out the possibility to carry out a referendum in accordance with the then current legislation of Ukraine. At the same time, the CCU's decision emphasised the possibility for the people of Ukraine to determine and change the constitutional system by combining direct and representative democracy. When the people's initiative is received by the competent public authorities, the President of Ukraine and the Central Electoral Commission have the discretion to determine the constitutionality of issues that are put to the vote and are obliged to carry out such preliminary verification. When amendments to the Constitution of Ukraine are to be made, the actions taken by the head of state, parliamentary deputies and the parliament as a whole are in collateral subordination, i.e. their balance and interaction are aimed at fulfilling the will of the people as the sole bearer of sovereign power (CCU decision No. 3/2000).

When considering the subject-matter of that referendum, the CCU ruled that certain questions were unconstitutional since they did not meet the requirements of legal certainty or the requirements related to the referendum format:

1) Article 2 paragraph 1 of the decree, which set out the following question: "Do you express your distrust towards the Verkhovna Rada of the 14th convocation and are you consequently in favour of making additions to the second section of Article 90 of the Constitution of Ukraine worded as follows: 'and also in case when distrust towards the Verkhovna Rada of Ukraine has been expressed in a nation-wide referendum, this gives grounds for the President of Ukraine to dissolve the Verkhovna Rada of Ukraine'?"; and
2) Article 2 paragraph 6 of the decree, which set out the following question: "Do you agree that the Constitution of Ukraine should be adopted by a nation-wide referendum?".

This referendum was notable due to the attempt made by the executive branch to manipulate public opinion and strengthen the concentration of power in the President's hands through the application of formally democratic procedures. In terms of legal force, this kind of referendum on amendments to the Constitution has only a recommendatory character since the procedures for amending the Constitution are regulated in its Chapter XIII.

5) *Review of the constitutionality of the impeachment procedure in relation to the President.* Following a request from the Verkhovna Rada, the CCU issues an opinion on adherence or non-adherence to the constitutional procedure which regulates the investigation and examination of a potential removal of the President from office through impeachment, as specified in Articles 111 and 151 of the Constitution. The consideration of cases on constitutional legal responsibility of officials is a traditional competence of constitutional justice bodies.

The act on the CCU of 3 June 1992 also furnished the CCU with the authority to examine impeachment cases also with regard to the Prime Minister and other members of the government, the chair of the Supreme Court, the chair of the Supreme Arbitration Court, the Prosecutor General of Ukraine, diplomats and other representatives of Ukraine.

The subject area of this competence of the CCU may have been reduced due to the sceptical attitude towards constitutional review versus the means of parliamentary control. The constitutional justice body assesses adherence to the due process of law, and this actually defines the limits of its competence in impeachment cases relating to the President. There is no existing CCU practice in such cases.

6) *Review of a draft bill amending the Constitution for compliance with fundamental values.* Following a request from the Verkhovna Rada, the CCU

issues an opinion on whether a draft bill amending the Constitution complies with the requirements of Articles 157 and 158. The subject-matter of constitutional review is the protection of fundamental constitutional values: human rights and freedoms, and the sovereignty and territorial integrity of Ukraine. Preliminary constitutional review is the main format applied here.

There is also some ambiguous experience of *ex post* constitutional review of acts amending the Constitution. For example, the CCU radically changed its jurisprudence when deciding on the compliance of Act No. 2222-IV with Articles 157 and 158 of the Constitution. Within two years its approach was changed versus the previous refusal to consider this issue within the framework of formal constitutional review for compliance with the requirements of the constituent process, as regulated by Chapter XIII of the Constitution.

7) *Providing, on the request of the Verkhovna Rada of Ukraine, a statement confirming that the Verkhovna Rada of the ARC violated the Constitution of Ukraine or laws of Ukraine.* This authority is exercised to establish the violation of the Constitution of Ukraine through an abstract review of acts issued by the Verkhovna Rada of the ARC. If the CCU issues an opinion stating that this body has violated the Constitution and laws of Ukraine, this will provide grounds for early dissolution of the Verkhovna Rada of the ARC and announcement of early elections to the legislature of the Crimea. However, there is no existing of the CCU practice in such cases.
8) *Reviewing, upon the President's request, in accordance with section two of Article 137 of the Constitution of Ukraine, the constitutionality and legality of normative legal acts issued by the Verkhovna Rada of the Autonomic Republic of Crimea.* The aim of this competence is to protect the sovereignty and territorial integrity of Ukraine. The CCU exercised this competence when considering cases related to the events surrounding the annexation of the ARC. The CCU promptly reacted to the violation of Ukraine's territorial integrity by recognising the unconstitutionality of the resolution "On holding a Crimea-wide referendum" adopted by the Verkhovna Rada of the ARC, since referendums are only announced by the Verkhovna Rada of Ukraine, and such a referendum should have been nationwide rather than regional. It should be noted that the CCU operated in difficult circumstances at that time, since a number of judges were dismissed for violating their oath, and new judges were appointed in their place in accordance with the Verkhovna Rada's resolution "On reactions to violations of oath by judges of the CCU of Ukraine" dated 24 February 2014.

The Constitutional Court stated that the Verkhovna Rada of the ARC exceeded its powers, and violated the territorial integrity of Ukraine (CCU decision No. 2/2014). There is an opinion that the CCU had no jurisdiction over that case, since the constitutional petition was made by the wrong subject, i.e. the acting President of Ukraine. According to dissenting opinions expressed by some judges, the Speaker of the Verkhovna Rada, Alexander Turchinov, was temporarily unable to exercise the powers of the President, since the dismissal of Viktor Yanukovich was carried out in a way not provided for by the Constitution, i.e. self-exclusion from the exercise of his constitutional powers. Indeed, the parliament adopted its resolution of 22 February 2014 on the removal of Viktor Yanukovich from fulfilling the powers of the head of state. By that date, the President should have fulfilled the "Agreement on overcoming the political crisis": under that agreement Viktor Yanukovich, as head of state, was expected to promulgate the act on restoring the Constitution of Ukraine in the version of 8 December 2004, taking into account the CCU's decision No. 11/2010 of 6 April 2010. At that time, a radical social confrontation took place, protesters in Institutska Street in Kyiv were shot dead (which was later known as the shooting of "Heavenly Hundreds"), and the authorities were incapacitated and failed to react to numerous cases of kidnapping and torture of participants in mass protests, while endorsing the activities of paramilitary structures (the latter actually acted as agents of the state). Thus, it was necessary to adopt essential measures to restore the legitimacy of authorities and a consensus in the society, expressed in the constitutional order. Under those circumstances, the Verkhovna Rada fulfilled the functions of the constituent power, filling vacancies for the positions of the President, Prime Minister, Foreign Minister, Minister of Internal Affairs, the head of the Security Service of Ukraine, etc. Therefore, as a defender of the Constitution, the CCU had to respond promptly to the encroachment on the territorial integrity of Ukraine.

In a dissenting opinion on the CCU's decision No. 2/2014, other judges pointed out that the CCU had no jurisdiction in the matter since the CCU was obliged to investigate the actual circumstances surrounding the adoption of the said decree by the Verkhovna Rada of the ARC, despite the decree having been formally promulgated. It should be noted that in this case the CCU exercised abstract constitutional review, rather than incidental or causal review of norms and, therefore, such arguments are simply unacceptable.

On the other hand, the CCU's decision did not indicate that the ARC was not a subject of international law. It only stated that the ARC adopted a resolution announcing that it was becoming part of the Russian Federation as a federal subject; it notified the President of the Russian Federation and the

Russian Federal Duma of the commencement of a procedure of joining the Russian Federation as a federal subject. The CCU's decision stated that by putting these questions to a referendum, the Verkhovna Rada of the ARC violated the territorial integrity of Ukraine and exceeded its competence. In turn, in its decision No. 3/2014 of 20 March 2014, the CCU pointed out that the ARC had no international legal personality or the authority to adopt a declaration on secession.

9) *Examination of constitutional complaints.* This power is exercised by reviewing the constitutionality of acts of law or individual provisions upon a complaint filed by a person who believes that the law applied in the final judicial decision in his/her case is unconstitutional.

After the act amending the Constitution in the sphere of justice and the act on the CCU, normative constitutional complaint has been enabled in Ukraine. At the time of writing this chapter, there has been no review of such complaints, although more than 1250 complaints had been registered by the CCU Secretariat, of which 500 are accepted for consideration. As of June 6, 2019, there were taken six decisions when Court considering constitutional complaints (1 – First Senate, 3 – Second Senate, and 2 – Grand Chamber). Therefore, the experience of foreign constitutional courts and similar jurisdictional institutions will be relevant. Moreover, the experience of the ECHR seems to be most effective, since the post-communist countries of Eastern Europe that are now EU members had followed the same path (the CCU was of the opinion that it could not consider constitutional complaints given the absence of relevant legislative regulations before the adoption of the new version of the act on the CCU on 13 July 2017; however, this opinion contradicted the fundamental principle of direct applicability of the Constitution and violated the essence of the right to seek defence at the CCU).

Today, the case in point is the application of universal principles of law and universal human rights in the examination of constitutional complaints. When it comes to implementing high standards of human rights protection in the practice of the CCU, one should also bear in mind the mutual correlation and conflicting jurisdictions in the light of the supremacy of the Constitution of Ukraine vis-a-vis international treaties.

Firstly, the CCU can attach a greater importance to the constitutional guarantees of human rights because they may prove to be wider than convention-based guarantees. This issue arises fairly frequently before constitutional jurisdictions or similar institutions in Germany, England, Sweden, etc.

Secondly, following the rule of adopting "a friendly attitude" towards international treaties, the CCU can interpret the provisions of the Constitution of

Ukraine in a way that conforms with international expectations. In particular, this kind of perspective should be adopted when interpreting the essence of the inviolability of the right to private property and the legal grounds for acquiring the right to property, i.e. in the light of convention-based guarantees for the unimpeded use of property.

Therefore, one should discuss acceptability criteria. In the context of Article 151^1 of the Constitution of Ukraine, and in the light of general principles of law (respect for human dignity, inexhaustibility of human rights, the state's duty of protection, etc.), these criteria include the following:

1) the essential nature of the right that has been violated and the threat that the harm to the rights and freedoms guaranteed by the Constitution of Ukraine may be irreversible;
2) the conventional legal remedies have been exhausted;
3) such legal remedies must be effective and efficient, ensuring effective restoration of rights and a fair compensation of damage;
4) the review focuses on verifying the constitutionality of the act of law and the practice of its application in the light of the essential content of human rights and fundamental freedoms;
5) ensuring the protection of human rights and freedoms guaranteed by the Constitution of Ukraine, at least at an internationally recognised level.

When the CCU protects human rights while examining constitutional complaints, it might be accused of excessive judicial activism. This may happen if the CCU applies interim measures, primarily by suspending the act of law concerned since the application of such an act may significantly breach constitutional rights and freedoms; such a step may also aim to prevent irreversible damage to a basic right, where such right might be difficult or impossible to restore in the future.

5 Constitutional Legal Proceedings

The act on the Constitutional Court does not regulate the detailed procedure for convening meetings of the Grand Chamber, senates and boards, leaving this issue to the discretion of the chair of the CCU. When the act on the CCU was being adopted, this problem was not addressed, i.e. the decision to open proceedings in a case following a request is not adopted at a meeting of a board of judges or the Grand Chamber.

The new version of the act on the Constitutional Court retained the role of the CCU chair in deciding on how cases are to be dealt with. However, in order to prevent any malpractice, this procedure should be determined by the Grand Chamber of the CCU. The best option would be to adopt a rule whereby the chair of the CCU, in accordance with the procedure established by the Grand Chamber, would instruct one of the judges to pre-examine the appeal, within no more than two months following the date of its registration with the Secretariat. The judge's conclusions from the preliminary examination of the appeal would be reported at the plenary session of the Grand Chamber. The new version of the act on the CCU provides for the following stages of constitutional proceedings.

5.1 Preliminary Examination of Appeals to the Constitutional Court and the Opening of Constitutional Proceedings

The act on the Constitutional Court defines the following forms of appeal to the CCU: a constitutional petition, a constitutional submission and a constitutional complaint. The constitutional petition is concerned with a decision on the constitutionality of a legal act and the interpretation of the Constitution of Ukraine (Article 51 of the law). Under the constitutional submission, the CCU is requested to issue an opinion regarding the constitutionality of a constitutional bill, the subject of a nationwide referendum on people's initiative, an international treaty or a violation of, or compliance with, the Constitution and laws of Ukraine in the actions taken by the Verkhovna Rada of the ARC (Article 53 of the law). A constitutional complaint is concerned with a violation of constitutional rights and freedoms in the course of the application of laws in a final court decision (Article 55 of the law).

The Constitutional Court Secretariat checks appeals for compliance with the formal requirements set out in the act. The act on the CCU contains an important provision whereby if an appeal is returned by the Secretariat due to formal grounds, this cannot prevent the filing of a new appeal (Article 57). To examine the appeal, a judge-rapporteur is appointed from among the board of judges to conduct a preliminary examination. The judge-rapporteur has a number of prerogatives, focused on preparing materials for examination (Article 59 of the law), in particular:

1) the judge examines the issues raised in the appeal and prepares materials to be examined by the board, the senate and the Chamber;
2) the judge requests subjects of law to provide documents, materials and other information related to the case;
3) the judge gives instructions to the relevant units of the Secretariat and sets the respective deadlines;
4) the judge invites specialists for consultations and document examination; and

5) the judge submits proposals to the senate and the Chamber in order to solicit expert opinions in the case, to invite specialists to take part in the constitutional proceedings, to summon officials, experts, specialists, witnesses and authorised persons; moreover, the judge exercises other powers provided for in the act on the CCU.

The decision about opening constitutional proceedings is finally made at a meeting of the boards, senates and the Grand Chamber. This means that if a refusal to open proceedings is to be issued, the decision will eventually be taken by the Grand Chamber. A refusal to open constitutional proceedings may be issued for the following reasons (Article 62 of the act on the CCU):

1) the appeal has been filed by an unauthorised entity;
2) the CCU has no competence to examine the issue raised in the appeal;
3) the appeal does not comply with the law;
4) a constitutional complaint is inadmissible;
5) the legal act which is to be reviewed for constitutionality has lost its legal force, except when this act continues to apply to continued legal relations and its application violates constitutional rights and freedoms; or
6) the issue raised in the appeal has already been resolved in an act issued by the CCU.

In some situations, the Constitutional Court may somewhat revise its approaches in determining the criteria for self-exclusion when examining appeals. For example, as of today, the Constitutional Court has taken a clear position regarding the examination of political issues. For instance, in its ruling No. 2-уп/2000 on the termination of constitutional proceedings in the case concerning a constitutional-legal dispute that arose as a result of the parliamentary crisis in January and February 2000, the CCU stated that the powers of the constitutional jurisdiction body do not include the resolution of political conflicts. The legal position taken by the CCU was based on the fact that the appeal arose from differences between parties/factions in the parliament, and had a procedural, political and moral significance, and thus the decisions adopted during that period were part of the political process.

5.2 The Hearing of a Case at the Constitutional Court

Article 64 of the act on the Constitutional Court establishes the written form as the main form for the examination of cases. In Ukraine, it is considered that constitutional justice does not involve an adversarial process and pleadings during oral hearings but, instead, the study of documents and expert conclusions written as *amicus curiae*. As was the case with the Rules of the CCU in the past, the current act on the CCU also determines the procedural status of the participants in the process but does not regulate the procedure to be followed during the court sitting (written or oral). This is a general drawback of Ukrainian laws, where procedures are often skipped and replaced with a definition of rights and duties, powers and responsibilities. This leads to conflicts in the case of high-profile cases and socially significant proceedings in court.

The general period for examining a case is set at six months, although in most cases the Constitutional Court does not adhere to this period. As an exception, one month is allotted for the examination of specific cases, i.e. where the CCU is approached to determine whether a draft law amending the Constitution complies with Articles 157 and 158, and whether acts issued by the Cabinet of Ministers are constitutional in a situation where the President has suspended such acts and simultaneously requested the CCU to review the constitutionality of such acts (Article 75 of the law on the CCU).

Practice has shown that during an oral hearing, the first persons to be heard are representatives of the entity which filed the appeal, followed by representatives of the authority that has issued an act whose constitutionality is being challenged. Subsequently, the CCU hears experts and specialists invited to ensure a full and comprehensive examination of the case. The hearing then moves on to the phase where participants deliver their closing speeches on the merits of the case. Depending on the specific nature of the case (e.g. when examining an issue involving the interpretation of the Constitution), the views of the representatives of the Supreme Court are heard in order to clarify the sources, causes and nature of the ambiguities in the application of the constitutional provisions by courts.

Separate attention is given to the procedure for the adoption of the CCU's acts: in the Grand Chamber, rulings are adopted by a majority of judges present at the meeting whereas decisions are adopted by at least 10 judges; in the Senate, rulings are adopted by the majority of judges present at the meeting (if the number of votes for and against the opening of constitutional proceedings is equal, the proceedings are considered to have been opened – the matter remains unresolved), whereas decisions are adopted by at least two-thirds of judges who examine the case in the senate (Article 66 of the law on the CCU). At Grand Chamber meetings, the quorum is not less than 12 judges, while the quorum at senate meetings consists of at least six judges.

5.3 Cases Referred by the Senate to the Grand Chamber for Examination

Since the composition of the Constitutional Court has changed, the procedure for referring a case for examination from a senate to the Grand Chamber has been introduced (Article 68 of the law on the CCU). This procedure was established in order to enable the harmonisation of legal positions between the senates and the Grand Chamber. Obviously, this tool will be used by the CCU to review its own jurisprudence. It should be emphasised that the senates have been established in order to examine constitutional complaints.

5.4 Adoption of Decisions by the Constitutional Court

According to Article 88 of the law on the Constitutional Court, this body makes a decision or issues a conclusion at the closed part of the plenary session of the senate and/or Chamber by a roll-call vote of the judges who examined the case. The decision is made by presenting a proposed draft decision or conclusion to the judges; and such decisions or conclusions are put to vote in the order in which they were received. When making a decision or issuing a conclusion, a judge has no right to abstain from voting. Decisions and conclusions of the Constitutional Court are signed separately by the judges who voted for and by the judges who voted against. The decision or conclusion of the CCU is final and may not be appealed against. Separate regulations apply to cases where judges write dissenting opinions (Article 83 of law act on the CCU). Article 67 of the act takes a restrictive position since a decision on a constitutional complaint may only be adopted by at least two-thirds of votes from the judges who examined the complaint in the senate. In other words, it is possible that a complaint is examined by a senate of seven judges and five must vote to adopt the decision, rather than four judges, as is customary in boards of judges (chambers, senates, etc.).

The Constitutional Court adopts decisions in the closed part of the plenary session, which begins immediately after the open part of the plenary session has ended. The closed part of the plenary session is where both the concept and the final version of the decision are prepared. In other words, the Constitutional Court takes a decision collectively. At the same time, a judge-rapporteur is appointed in each case, charged with preparing the case materials and, in particular, draft the CCU decision. Other judges participate in the development of the draft decision based on the principle of equality of CCU judges, although a judge may confine him/herself to writing a dissenting opinion if he/she does not agree with the legal argument and/or the operative part of the decision. Empirical experience has shown that this technique of decision-making at the CCU directly influences the degree of its validity and, consequently, legitimacy.

5.5 Implementation of Constitutional Court Decisions

In its decision or conclusion, the Constitutional Court may define the order and terms of implementation, and it may also oblige the relevant state bodies to ensure that the implementation of the decision and/or compliance with the conclusion are monitored. The Constitutional Court may also require the relevant authorities to provide a written confirmation that the decision has been implemented or the conclusion has been complied with (Article 97 of the law on the CCU). Also, amendments to the Code of Administrative Offenses have been made, introducing administrative liability for disrespecting the CCU and for non-compliance with the legal requirements formulated by a CCU judge.

6 The Nature and Legal Force of Decisions Adopted by the Constitutional Court

The act on the Constitutional Court provides that the Court issues acts such as decisions, conclusions, rulings and security orders. As regards internal issues, not related to the examination of disputes, the CCU adopts resolutions.

Most often, acts issued by constitutional courts are considered by Ukrainian scholars in the context of interpretative activity, which is an inherent feature of constitutional justice. In particular, P. Rabinovich considers them to be interpretative acts. Accordingly, decisions are taken with due consideration for the social context and, consequently, the Constitutional Court adopts decisions related to the protection of fundamental rights and freedoms, as well as in the resolution of competence disputes[65]. In S. Shevchuk's opinion, acts of constitutional justice are acts of constitutional jurisprudence[66], which ensures the solution of complex constitutional disputes related to political issues, as evidenced by the doctrines of the "political issue", "political expediency" and "the field of discretion of the

---

65 П. Рабінович, *Правотлумачення і герменевтика (за матеріалами практики Конституційного Суду України)*, "Вісник Академії правових наук України" 2006, № 4, p. 16.

66 С. Шевчук, *Основи конституційної юриспруденції*, Kharkiv 2002, pp. 99, 148–166.

state"[67]. The constitutional doctrine in Ukraine has gradually recognised acts issued by the CCU as a source of constitutional law. In particular, it is correctly asserted that "bodies of the judiciary fulfil not only a law-enforcement role but also a law-making function"[68].

Acts issued by the Constitutional Court specify and interpret the provisions of the Constitution of Ukraine. According to the rule of law (Article 8 section 1 of the Constitution), which includes the component of legal certainty, the CCU should follow the same approaches when dealing with similar constitutional law issues and provide proper legal argumentation for its decisions.

Based on the analysis of the activities of the Constitutional Court and the nature of its acts, all the acts issued by the Court, which provide unified approaches to the concretisation and interpretation of certain provisions of the Constitution of Ukraine, can be described as acts of constitutional jurisprudence. This means that the jurisprudence of the Constitutional Court consists of justifications for the legal provisions that constitute the essential core of its decisions. The jurisprudence of the CCU reflects its doctrinal approach to the understanding of complex and contradictory aspects of the Basic Law as well as its theoretical and practical aspects.

The algorithm for developing constitutional jurisprudence regarding specific aspects of constitutional disputes is as follows:

1) the Constitutional Court formulates its legal position in a particular case;
2) the Constitutional Court adheres to this legal position in a similar case, which is evidenced by the fact that this position is incorporated in the motivation and justification of the decision adopted in a new case, thus possibly formulating a principle of law;
3) the principle formulated by the Constitutional Court, which expresses its doctrine, is consistently applied; and
4) a set of decisions reflecting the jurisprudence of the CCU is formulated: in our example, this refers to the content and components of the principle of proportionality and its expansion in subsequent decisions.

---

67 С. Шевчук, *Концепція самообмеження суду: доктрина «політичного питання», «політичної діяльності» та «поля розсуду держави»*, "Вісник Академії правових наук України" 2006, № 3.

68 В.Ф. Погорілко (ed.), *Конституційне право України: Академічний курс*. У 2 т., Т. 1, Kyiv 2005, p. 343.

Proper justification of decisions is an important factor ensuring the legitimacy of the Constitutional Court's activities. In accordance with the rule of law, the following conditions should be met:

a) it should be predictable, clear and precise, i.e. it should meet the requirements of legal certainty of acts issued by the Constitutional Court; this means that the Court should adopt the same approach when dealing with similar cases;
b) it should be proportional, i.e. the means of settling a constitutional dispute should serve the purposes pursued by the authority concerned without setting excessive restrictions and prohibitions in the sphere of fundamental rights and freedoms; the conclusion that follows is that the Court, even if it finds a contradiction between the Constitution and an act of law, should interpret the latter in the light of the Constitution, and it should also determine the legal forms to implement the provisions of the law being reviewed in the practical activities undertaken by the participants in legal relations;
c) it should ensure a fair resolution of the dispute in keeping with the principles of justice and constitutional values, notably the rule of law, fundamental rights and freedoms, and democracy.

The act on the Constitutional Court provides for a new element, i.e. the so-called security order (Article 87 of the law), designed to prevent or ward off a risk of violations of constitutional rights and freedoms being considered in a constitutional complaint. Moreover, the act defines, for the first time ever, the legal position of the Constitutional Court, which indirectly entails that acts issued by the Constitutional Court should be properly motivated (Article 92 section 2 of the act on the Constitutional Court).

7 The Importance of the Constitutional Court in the International Context and the Supremacy of the Constitution

According to Article 9 of the Constitution of Ukraine, international treaties, which, according to the constitution, are to be approved by the Verkhovna Rada in order to be binding, are an integral part of Ukraine's legislation. On this basis, a specific type of interpretation of the constitution can be applied, known in the constitutional doctrine as the "international conformity interpretation". According to this interpretation, if the provisions of the current legislation do not correspond with the provisions of an international legal instrument, the latter is applied in the context of constitutional principles and provisions because the constitution enjoys supremacy in relation to international legal acts. At the same time, as constitutional provisions in the field of human rights have an open character (the constitutional "catalogue" of human rights and freedoms is inexhaustible), there is a dilemma regarding the mutual correlation between the constitution and international legal acts. Thus, the "international conformity interpretation" of the Constitution by constitutional courts can be seen as an element of a broader mechanism whereby a country conscientiously implements international treaties, i.e. it incorporates (transforms) universally recognised principles and norms of international law into the national constitutional system. Overall, the national constitutional courts respect ECHR case law but, at the same time, take note of their own national constitutional traditions and legal values. This raises questions about the understanding of certain provisions of national legislation, both in the light of the country's constitution and in the light of (international) conventions[69].

The Constitutional Court plays a decisive role in applying the international experience of human rights protection and the practice of foreign constitutional courts. The role of the Constitutional Court in the implementation of international standards has been discussed by a number of Ukrainian scholars and CCU judges[70]. A distinct area of research on constitutional justice is the research into friendly, international conformity-oriented interpretation of the Constitution of Ukraine, which is performed by comparing the practice of the CCU with that of ECHR[71].

When discussing the limits of the transfer of powers to supranational institutions, it is important to distinguish between supranational and

69 М.В. Савчин, *Конституційний захист прав людини та проблеми конкуренції юрисдикції*, "Український часопис міжнародного права" 2015, № 1, p. 56.

70 П. Мартиненко, *Місце і роль Конвенції про захист прав людини і основоположних свобод 1950 року в конституційно-правовому механізмі України*, "Вісник Конституційного Суду України" 2002, № 2; В.П. Паліюк, *Застосування судами України Конвенції про захист прав людини та основних свобод*, Kiev 2004. В. Скомороха, *Судовий конституціоналізм в аспекті співвідношення конституційної та конвенційної юрисдикції*, "Вісник Конституційного Суду України" 2015, № 1; С. Шевчук, *Європейська конвенція про захист прав людини та основних свобод: практика застосування та принципи тлумачення в контексті сучасного українського праворозуміння*, "Практика Європейського суду з прав людини. Рішення. Коментарі" 1999, № 2.

71 М. Савенко, *Роль практики Європейського суду з прав людини у конституційному судочинстві України*, "Вісник Конституційного Суду України" 2005, № 6; С.В. Шевчук, *Узгодженість практики Європейського суду з прав людини та Конституційного Суду України*, "Вісник Конституційного Суду України" 2011, № 4–5.

international institutions. For example, the Constitutional Court has indicated the International Criminal Court as an institution that complements the national criminal justice authorities. Unlike the jurisdiction of the ECHR, the jurisdiction of the CCU is based not only on the initiative of the state party, but also on its own initiative. This happens when the state which has jurisdiction over the person suspected of committing a crime under the Rome Statute "does not wish or is incapable of conducting an investigation or prosecuting properly" (CCU's opinion № 3/2001). Although the refusal to ratify the Statute has been noted in legal systems where, at the constitutional level, immunities of senior officials are associated with state sovereignty (France, Romania, Italy, etc.) or where an international treaty is considered to be an ordinary law that must undergo a special implementation procedure (USA).

When adopting a decision to ratify the European Charter for Regional or Minority Languages (CCU's decision No. 9/2000), the Constitutional Court had to assess the complex issues related to the limits of state sovereignty and compliance with the procedure whereby international treaties are ratified by the parliament. The practice of the Constitutional Court indicates that the transfer (delegation) of powers of individual authorities to supranational institutions must necessarily be accompanied by amendments to the Constitution of Ukraine.

These issues became especially relevant during the annexation of Crimea by the Russian Federation, in violation of the generally recognised principles of international law and the provisions of international treaties. The Constitutional Court promptly reacted to the violation of Ukraine's territorial integrity by recognising the unconstitutionality of the resolution "On holding a Crimea-wide referendum" adopted by the Verkhovna Rada of the ARC, since referenda are only announced by the Verkhovna Rada of Ukraine, and such a referendum should have been nationwide rather than regional (the CCU's decision No. 2/2014). Thus, the Constitutional Court stated that the Verkhovna Rada of the ARC exceeded its powers, violating the territorial integrity of Ukraine. Subsequently, the Constitutional Court decided to terminate the Memorandum on the Development of Cooperation with the Constitutional Court of the Russian Federation, which, in violation of international law, sought to confirm the constitutionality of the international treaty between the Russian Federation and the "Republic of Crimea", the admission of this entity to the Russian Federation and the establishment of new federal subjects within the Russian Federation (the CCU's decision 10/2014 of 17 April 2014).

The CCU, with the support of the constitutional courts of Lithuania, Georgia and Moldova, is presently obstructing the Constitutional Court of the Russian Federation, which, in violation of judicial practice (e.g., the case of Quebec, admitted by the Supreme Court of Canada, or the case of Åland Islands) and the generally recognised principles of international and constitutional law, legalised the criminal annexation of the Crimea. These efforts were manifested, among others, when the delegation from the Constitutional Court of the Russian Federation was not admitted to the 4th Congress of the World Conference on Constitutional Justice, held in September 2017 in Vilnius, Lithuania.

8 The Constitutional Significance of the Constitutional Court of Ukraine in the Social Context

According to a survey conducted by the Razumkov Centre, a reputable Ukrainian analytical think-tank, the Constitutional Court as an institution enjoys low trust in Ukrainian society. As there was no practice of reviewing constitutional complaints and no decisions were taken throughout 2017 up to the time of the survey, the public opinion was fairly critical of the CCU: 66.8 % of respondents expressed distrust (40.3 % admitted no trust at all, 26.5 % expressed some distrust) versus 14.9 % of those who trusted the CCU (12.3 % expressing some trust and 2.6 % admitting complete trust), with 18.4 % of the respondents being undecided (the overall balance of trust in the CCU is negative: -51.9 %)[72]. This means that full trust in the Constitutional Court is expressed by a number of respondents which is actually equal to the level of survey error. An even more negative balance of trust/distrust was found in the case of the government (-53.3 %), the Supreme Court of Ukraine (-58.9 %), the General Prosecutor's Office (-59.9 %), political parties (-62.1 %), local courts (-65.5 %), and the Verkhovna Rada (-66.9 %), with the judicial system as a whole having the most negative score (-71.6 %). A positive trust balance was observed for volunteer organisations (46.7 %), the church (41.9 %), the Armed Forces (24.0 %), non-governmental associations (11.0 %), and border guards (5.8 %). Trust of the patrolling police, with a negative indicator, is close to the level of survey error (-2.1 %) but performs better than other units of the National Police (-6.9 %).

---

72 Report on the results of a social survey «*Ставлення громадян України до судової системи*», Український Центр політичних та економічних досліджень імені Олександра Розумкова, Рада суддів України, Проект Ради Європи «Підтримка впровадження судової реформи в Україні», Kiev 2017, p. 25. This survey was conducted from 6 to 11 October 2017 in all regions of Ukraine except the ARC, the city of Sevastopol and the occupied territories of Donetsk and Luhansk regions, and included key socio-demographic indicators; the survey error should not exceed 2.3 %; a total of 2,019 respondents were surveyed.

According to the latest data from the sociological survey, the degree of trust in the CCU has increased from 14.9 % to 30 %[73].

Conclusions

Today, the CCU is at a crossroads: it needs to stop the obstruction and renew its authority after the problematic decisions adopted in 2010, related to the exercise of the constituent power of the people of Ukraine, which were used as an instrument leading to the usurpation of power by Viktor Yanukovich. Even though the anthropocentric stances in the academic publications of Ukrainian scholars have grown stronger, there are still many unexplored issues related to constitutional justice in Ukraine:

- resolving the dilemma of the supremacy of parliament and judicial constitutional review in the light of the values of constitutionalism;
- mutual relations between the legal positivism school and natural law, and their combination;
- the relationship between the practice of the CCU and that of the ECHR as human rights are only in their infancy;
- the main approaches and ways of interpreting the constitution, viewed within the framework of traditional interpretations;
- there is also a need to study the system of argumentation supporting the decisions adopted by the CCU in the light of ECHR practice and the arguments used by constitutional courts in other countries;
- as the institution of a constitutional complaint has been introduced at the CCU, there is a need for research into the organisation and procedure of handling cases at the Grand Chamber, the senates and boards of judges;
- the peculiarities of the case handling procedure at the CCU, the stages and procedural legal personality of its participants have not been fully studied;
- after constitutional complaint was introduced in Ukraine, a need arose to understand the nature of human rights and their protection through this institution.

73 Report on the results of a social survey of the sociological group Q&Q Research on June 2018. In: «*Проведено соціологічне дослідження: рівень довіри громадян до Конституційного Суду зростає*». URL: http://www.ccu.gov.ua/novyna/provedeno-sociologichne-doslidzhennya-riven-doviry-gromadyan-do-konstytuciynogo-sudu-ukrayiny (accessed: February 20, 2018).

These problems can be partially resolved if the Constitutional Court properly handles constitutional complaints, ensures high-quality protection of human rights, and distances itself from political issues. In the latter case, according to the rule of law, the Court must be cautious in exercising its own discretion, as it can only be justified if aimed to ensure robust and effective protection of human rights.

Omon Zakirovich Mukhamedzhanov

Constitutional Justice in the Republic of Uzbekistan

Abstract: Constitutional judiciary in the Republic of Uzbekistan was established with the aim of protecting the superior position of the constitution and protecting the citizens' rights and freedoms. A thesis is put forward that the scope of realization of goals established in this way is changeable in time and it depends on political changes taking place in the state.

Keywords: the European model of reviewing the legal norms, Constitutional Court, autonomy and independence, The Constitutional Court and other organs of state power, cognition of the Constitutional Court

Introduction

The most important condition of forming a law-bound state is ensuring the supremacy of the Constitution in the system of normative-legal acts, which assumes the need for its special legal protection. Thus, implementing the idea of a law-bound state directly depends on an effective protection mechanism for the Constitution. Constitutional review is the main defining element of this mechanism[1].

The successful development of an independent Uzbekistan is reasonably associated with the stability of a constitutional system and an expression of public value navigators in the Constitution. In fact, the Constitution integrates and raises to the highest normative-legal level of the main ideas, norms, and directions of democratic development in the society and the state.

---

1 Legal literature determined two main directions in studying the essence of constitutional review: 1) considering it as element in separation of powers; 2) considering it as organizational-legal form for legal protection mechanism of Constitution (см.: Т.Я. Насырова, *Конституционный контроль*, Kazan 1992, pp. 7, 8). V.E. Chirkin suggests the alternate approach to defining a place of constitutional review within the separation of powers. Thus, he mentions the modern-world tendency in separation of powers—namely, isolation of control power (см.: В.Е. Чиркин, *Контрольная власть*, "Государство и право" 1993, № 4, pp. 11, 12). French political scientist L. Favore takes a different view. The essence of it is that constitutional justice shall be beyond three branches of government, thus ensuring the observance of their powers (see: L. Favore, *Les cours constitutionnelles*, Paris 1992, p. 14).

When Uzbekistan gained independence in August 1991, there was need for a deep transformation in the state-legal sphere, adopting a set of laws ensuring the transfer from an old administrative-command system, where ideology dominated over the law, to a truly democratic, law-bound state and society, which ensures a priority of principles and norms prescribed by the local Constitution.

In a short period of time, significant steps were made in reforming the legal and judicial sphere, the legal start of which was initiated by the adoption of the Uzbek Constitution on December 8, 1992[2], which marked the formation of an independent judicial power, designed to ensure harmony in society and the protection of human rights and legitimate interests via the administration of justice.

First of all, the purpose of judicial-legal reforms was to ensure the constitutional rights and freedoms of person, harmony and stability in the society.

The need to ensure the supremacy of the Constitution assumes the exercise of control over its observance. There are various constitutional justice models in the world[3]. Thus, there are specialized and non-specialized bodies designed to prevent the adoption of laws and other normative-legal acts conflicting with the Constitution. In general, a specialized constitutional review is the most important and effective way to protect the supremacy of the Constitution by legal means.

Today, there is an actual need for a comparative-legal analysis of constitutional laws in Central Asian states, an analysis of the essence and tendencies in transforming the institute of the constitutional review, and a study of the features of constitutional review objects and specific activities of constitutional review subjects.

Over the years, constitutional review in Uzbekistan was in consistent development given the global trends of constitutional justice, but maintained the constitutional identity and specific development of the Uzbek statehood. The need to study the organizational-legal mechanism of constitutional review in Uzbekistan and the task of optimizing/stabilizing the institute of constitutional justice were also caused by the fact that the Law on the Constitutional Court was substantially updated in 2017[4].

---

2 Cf.: Конституция Республики Узбекистан, Tashkent 2017.

3 Cf.: В.Е. Чиркин (ed.), *Сравнительное конституционное право. Учебное пособие*, Moscow 2002, pp. 95–104.

4 Cf.: Конституционный закон Республики Узбекистан «О Конституционном суде», „Ведомости Олий Мажлиса Республики Узбекистан", Собрание законодательства Республики Узбекистан 2017, № 22, ст. 407.

1 Motives for Introduction and Key Dilemmas of Establishing the Regulatory Control

The formation of constitutional review in Uzbekistan began in March 1990, when the Constitutional Review Committee (elected by the Supreme Council) was established[5]. The Law of Uzbekistan "On Constitutional Review in Republic of Uzbekistan", adopted on June 20, 1990[6], was the first consolidation of a constitutional, quasi-judicial review in the history of the country. Although the law introduced constitutional review rather than justice, in many respects, the Constitutional Review Committee of Uzbekistan and Constitutional Review Committee of Karakalpakstan fulfilled the functions of judicial body. They ensured the compliance of acts issued by state bodies and public organizations with the Constitution of Uzbekistan and Constitution of Karakalpakstan, respectively: the protection of constitutional rights and personal freedoms, the rights of peoples in Uzbekistan and Karakalpakstan, and the democratic foundations of society.

The above law determined the basic principles of activity for constitutional review bodies' (legality, collegiality, publicity) procedure of their election (by Parliament, under proposal of the Chairperson, for 10 years, 50 % renewal of staff every 5 years), early termination of judges' powers, and authority and procedure of the Constitutional Review Committee in Uzbekistan.

The constitutional review system was changing within the ongoing (until now) justice reform. At the initial stage of judicial-legal reform, the national strategy for the fundamental reformation of the judicial-legal system was determined, and its constitutional-legal grounds were established. The task of forming an integral system of judicial power—aimed to transform the court from body that punishes and protects the interests of the state into a body ensuring the rule of law and protection of human rights—was set and solved.

Given the international experience of the country, the Constitutional Court was established instead of the Constitutional Supervision Committee. As in post-Soviet countries, the classical European (Kelsen) model of centralized constitutional review was used to establish the Constitutional Court of Uzbekistan. In our view, the selection of a European centralized model is caused by a number of reasons.

---

5 Cf.: Ведомости Верховного Совета Республики Узбекистан 1990, № 10–11, ст. 226.

6 Cf.: ibidem. 1990, № 16–18, ст. 289.

First, during transformations and reforms in the late 20th century, the role of all branches of government and the need to exercise the separation of powers was increasing.

Second, the formation of law-bound states in the former USSR required the concentration of efforts in forming the new statehood, ensuring the dynamism of social development, stability of political processes, and formation of national legal systems.

Third, the establishment of a special constitutional review body with constitutional powers (the Constitutional Court) determined its role as "guardian" of the Constitution.

The President of Uzbekistan adopted Decree No. УП-2612 of June 2, 2000 "On measures to implement the Program for Liberalization and Deepening the Reforms in Political, Economic, and Spiritual Sphere of Society, Ensuring the National Security"[7]. Among others, the Program assumed measures on improving constitutional justice.

Dated August 14, 2000, the Decree of the President of Uzbekistan "On Improving the Judicial System of Uzbekistan"[8] determined the tasks on reforming and further deepening the democratic foundations for a judicial system. The Law of Uzbekistan "On Courts"[9], adopted in a new revision on December 14, 2000 and providing the legislative reflection of basic and fundamentally different guarantees for the independence and effectiveness of judicial power, served as a logical completion for the initial stage of reforming the judicial-legal sphere.

The most important program task of the next stage was enhancing the independent judicial system and the protection of human rights and freedoms. Measures on further democratization and liberalization of the judicial-legal system, raising the authority of court, ensuring the exercise of court decisions, and obtaining the qualified legal assistance formed the specific features of this stage.

Further reform of the judicial-legal system is associated with adopting the Decree of the President of Uzbekistan "Strategy of Actions on Further Development of Uzbekistan", dated February 7, 2017, No. УП-4947[10]. In this document, priority areas for further reform in judicial-legal system are raising the status, level of material incentives, and social security for judges and court staff; enhancing the material-technical base of courts; effective measures preventing

7 Cf.: URL: http://lex.uz/pages/GetAct.aspx?lact_id=202004 (accessed: February 27, 2018).
8 Cf.: Ведомости Олий Мажлиса РУз 2000, № 7–8, ст. 246.
9 Cf.: Ibidem. 2001, № 1–2, ст. 10.
10 Cf.: Собрание законодательства Республики Узбекистан 2017, № 6, ст. 70.

the undue influence on judges; the complete exercise of court independence and impartiality, competitiveness and equality of parties to legal proceeding; and the introduction of modern information and communication technology in court activities.

In April 2017, the Law of Uzbekistan No. ZRU-426 "Amending and Supplementing the Constitution of Uzbekistan"[11], with fundamental provisions aiming to implement the tasks determined in Action Strategy on 5 Priority Areas of Uzbekistan Development in 2017–2021, came into force. The Fundamental Law was amended by the decrees of the President of Uzbekistan: No. UP-4850 of October 21, 2016 "Measures on further reform of judicial-legal system, improving the guarantees on reliable protection of civil rights and freedoms"[12] and No. UP-4966 of February 21, 2017 "Measures on fundamental improving of structure and increasing the efficiency of judicial system in Uzbekistan"[13].

According to the above amendments, the Supreme Economic Court and Supreme Court were combined into a supreme judicial body in the field of civil, criminal, administrative, and economic legal proceedings: the Supreme Court of Uzbekistan. A new institute—the Supreme Judicial Council of Uzbekistan, which replaced the former Supreme Qualification Commission for the Selection and Recommendation of Judges at the President of Uzbekistan—was introduced in the judicial-legal system. The Constitution provided the Supreme Judicial Council with broad powers. The Chairpersons/Deputy Chairpersons of regional courts and courts of Tashkent city, as well as the Chairperson of Military Court in Uzbekistan, are appointed by the President by proposal of the Supreme Judicial Council. At that, the Council, in consultation with the head of state, independently appoints and dismisses the judges of military courts, regional courts, and courts of Tashkent city, Chairpersons and judges of inter-district, district, and city courts. Let's note that previously, this category of judges was appointed by the President of Uzbekistan.

On May 31, 2017, the Law of Uzbekistan No. ZRU-430 "On Amendments to Some Articles in Constitution of Uzbekistan (Articles 80, 93, 108, 109)"[14] was adopted. This law is aimed at implementing the tasks on reforming the judicial-legal sphere; expanding the guarantees on the reliable protection of civil rights and freedoms; improving access to justice, efficiency, and quality of legal

11 Cf.: СЗ РУз. 2017, № 14, ст. 213.
12 Cf.: СЗ РУз. 2016, № 43, ст. 497.
13 Cf.: СЗ РУз. 2017, № 8, ст. 109.
14 Cf.: СЗ РУз. 2017, № 22, ст. 406.

proceedings; and further improving the system for selecting candidates and appointing judges.

To improve constitutional justice, the Law of Uzbekistan "On the Constitutional Court of Uzbekistan" was adopted in a new revision (within the ongoing judicial reform); it introduced the new election procedure for the Constitutional Court, clarifying and notably expanding its powers[15]. Improving the institute of constitutional review in Uzbekistan means further practical exercise for the separation of powers and implementing an effective mechanism for the protection of the Constitution.

Thus, we can talk about a trend of the increasing role of constitutional justice in modern Uzbekistan. This trend is reduced to the following:

- Increasing the authority of democratic constitutional values. Constitutional and legislative amendments are aimed at improving the guarantees and expanding the powers for the institute of constitutional justice;
- Clarifying and specifying the functional powers of a constitutional justice body, which aim to enhance the guarantees on direct action and protection of the Constitution;
- System support of Constitutional Court functions and powers;
- Enhancing the mechanism on the protection of the Constitution, ensuring the guarantees of constitutional stability;
- Expanding the opportunities for detection and assessment of violations against the supremacy of the Constitution;
- The democratization of staffing the Constitutional Court, with clarification of requirements to candidates for members of the above constitutional justice body.

2 Legislative Stability of the Legal Norm Controlling Body

The formation and development of constitutional review in Uzbekistan, including the evolution of legal basis for its activities, can be divided into several stages:

I. 1990–1992: A period of forming and establishing the constitutional review. This stage was characterized by determining the constitutional-legal status of the Constitutional Review Committee as a body with control and supervisory functions.

15 Cf.: СЗ РУз. 2017, № 22, ст. 406; СЗ РУз. 2017, № 22, ст. 407, № 37, ст. 978.

II. 1993–2016: Constitutional Court activity on the constitutionalizing of processes related to the active formation of a local constitutional justice system. Based on the Constitution of Uzbekistan, the Law "On the Constitutional Court of Uzbekistan"[16] was adopted, where the role and place of the Constitutional Court in a judicial power system was clarified with regard to the new constitutional and legal status.

During this period, a national legislation system was formed on the basis of developing constitutional provisions and generally accepted principles/norms of international law. The main efforts of the Constitutional Court were aimed at assessing the compliance between laws/law enforcement practice and constitutional provisions, their full and consistent implementation, and legislative development of mechanisms for implementing the constitutional rights and freedoms of citizens. The Constitutional Court also made decisions aimed at addressing the gaps and conflicts in legislation.

By legal positions, the Constitutional Court actively helped with constitutionalizing social relations, while orienting the legislator to the consistent, purposeful exercise of constitutional principles and norms in the legislation, development, and protection of constitutional values and goals.

III. 2017: The current stage of development; began with the adoption of the Decree of the President of Uzbekistan "Strategy of Actions on Further Development of Uzbekistan", February 7, 2017, No. UP-4947[17].

This stage of development in constitutional justice is aimed at expanding the powers of the Constitutional Court and enhancing its role in the life of the society and state. Such a formulation of tasks is caused by the need to ensure the direct action of the local Constitution and its supremacy. In terms of an established legal system, the achieved political and social stability in the country, and the close interaction of authorities in the legislative process, there is an emphasis on improving and detailing the legal proceeding in the Constitutional Court.

While recognizing pretty high social value in the stability of the Uzbek Constitution, we would like to note that keeping the continuity of Fundamental Law and its adaptation to varying social-legal conditions are equally justified and necessary. While "stiffness" and absolute immutability of the Constitution

---

16 Закон Республики Узбекистан «О Конституционном суде», "Ведомости Олий Мажлиса Республики Узбекистан" 1995, № 9, Ст. 178.

17 Cf.: СЗ РУз. 2017, № 6, ст. 70.

conflict with the socio-historical nature of local development, amendments to the Constitution are of objectively conditional nature.

It must be admitted that introducing the term "constitutional justice" into the scientific use of legal science, as well as the studying of essence, content, and features in this special branch of justice are long overdue. Being a judicial body, the Constitutional Court exercises justice.

To improve constitutional justice, the Law of Uzbekistan dated May 31, 2017, No. ZRU-430 "On Amendments to Some Articles in the Constitution of Uzbekistan (Articles 80, 93, 108, 109)"[18] and the Constitutional Law of Uzbekistan dated May 31, 2017, No. ZRU-431 "On the Constitutional Court of Uzbekistan"[19] were adopted in the framework of ongoing judicial reform.

These laws clarified and notably expanded the powers of the Constitutional Court in Uzbekistan. Thus, the following powers were consolidated:

- Defining the compliance between the Constitution, constitutional laws, and laws on ratifying the international treaties of Uzbekistan, prior to their signing by the President of Uzbekistan;
- Reviewing the appeals of the Supreme Court initiated by courts on compliance between the Constitution and normative-legal acts to be applied in a particular case;
- The annual presentation of data on constitutional legality in the country for chambers of Oliy Majlis and the President of Uzbekistan, by results of generalizing the practice of constitutional proceedings.

Besides, the procedure of electing the judges, their term of office, and requirements to candidates for judges were changed. Now, the Constitutional Court is elected by the Senate at Oliy Majlis, under proposal of the President, from among the persons recommended by the Supreme Judicial Council. The Judges of the Constitutional Court may not be elected more than twice, while maintaining the five-year term of office. The age limit for candidates for judges was changed from 30 to 35 years; the age limit of being a judge was consolidated at 70 years. Grounds for early termination of a judge's powers have been expanded.

The range of entities authorized to submit issues for review by the Constitutional Court was expanded (Cabinet of Ministers, Oliy Majlis

---

18 Cf.: СЗ РУз. 2017, № 22, ст. 406.

19 Cf.: СЗ РУз. 2017, № 22, ст. 407, № 37, ст. 978.

Ombudsman of Uzbekistan for Human Rights). The order of legal proceedings at the Constitutional Court has been detailed.

Thus, the Constitutional Court is the supreme constitutional body of specialized constitutional review, independently exercising judicial power in the form of constitutional proceedings to limit the public authority and ensure a balance between branches of government, the rule of natural law over positive law, the Constitution over law, and the principles of law over political/administrative discretion. Achieving these goals encompasses Constitutional Court activity, i.e. the implementation of constitutional justice.

3 The Legislative Position of the Constitutional Court

The Constitutional Court is constantly involved in studying adopted laws and normative acts, which reveals their compliance with the Constitution and the presence of legislative norms that conflict with each other.

An analysis of decisions made by the Constitutional Court of Uzbekistan shows that in most cases, they were aimed at ensuring the civil rights and freedoms guaranteed by the Constitution[20]. Thus, in the case on verifying the constitutionality of Item 17, Part 5, Provision on the Procedure of Assigning and Paying the State Social Insurance Benefits, the Constitutional Court came to the conclusion that the norm of this Provision, which restricts the right of staff (on regular or additional leave) to receive benefits for care after a sick family member, does not comply with the Constitution. As a result, the legislation was brought into compliance with the Constitution to ensure its supremacy.

By defining the compliance between local Fundamental Law and certain acts (its norm), the Constitutional Court protects civil rights and freedoms. Thus, Article 536 in the Criminal Procedure Code of Uzbekistan determined that an early release on parole and replacing the unserved part of a sentence with a milder penalty is applied by a judge under proposal from the administration of penal institution. This norm did not assume an opportunity for the direct appeal of convicted persons to court with request for early release on parole and replacing the unserved part of a sentence with a milder penalty. Having studied the issue, the Constitutional Court decided that such practice does not comply with Article 44 in the Constitution of Uzbekistan, according to which, the judicial protection of rights and freedoms is guaranteed for everyone. According to the resolution of the Constitutional Court, Oliy Majlis of Uzbekistan adopted a

---

20 Materials are prepared on the basis of data from website of Constitutional Court of Uzbekistan (www.ksu.uz), (accessed: January 21, 2018).

law on amending this article, which assumes the right of a convicted person to apply to court with request for early release on parole/replacing the unserved part of sentence with a milder penalty.

By exercising its authority on the interpretation of constitutional norms and laws, the Constitutional Court of Uzbekistan resolves ambiguities and removes incorrect/conflicting practices of applying these norms by officials and state bodies in all three branches of government. While using this authority in the review of the case on interpreting the Article 59 of the Tax Code (TC), the Constitutional Court decided that the benefits assumed in Article 59 of TC RUz also apply to income received on dividends/interest. Such an interpretation of a legal norm addressed its incorrect application.

As we can see, in the course of defining the essence and content of legislative norms, the Constitutional Court develops some of its legal positions. For proper law-enforcement practice, the Constitutional Court needs to understand the meaning of an act in question based on constitutional provisions and the spirit of Fundamental Law, thus giving the legal-technical assessment via its conclusion or interpretation. In an aspect under review, the opinions and interpretations of the Constitutional Court form an important source of law.

3.1 The Constitutional Court and the President

Under Article 25 in the Constitutional Law "On the Constitutional Court of Uzbekistan", the President of Uzbekistan is entitled to submit to the Constitutional Court the issues, the review of which is referred to its competence by the Constitution and laws; however, this power has not been used.

According to laws, the Constitutional Court and the President of Uzbekistan interact in two main fields. The first is on staffing issues. Under Article 5, the Constitutional Court is elected by the Senate at Oliy Majlis in Uzbekistan by proposal from the President of Uzbekistan, from among the persons recommended by the Supreme Judicial Council of Uzbekistan, including a representative from the Republic of Karakalpakstan. Every judge of the Constitutional Court is elected individually. The person that gains the majority vote from all members of the Senate at Oliy Majlis in Uzbekistan is considered elected.

Besides, the President is one of the subjects mentioned in Article 25 of the Law, with authority to submit issues to the Constitutional Court.

Under Article 76 in Regulations of the Constitutional Court of Uzbekistan, when deciding on consent to the President of Uzbekistan regarding the dissolution of the Legislative Chamber or Senate at Oliy Majlis of Uzbekistan, the Constitutional Court shall verify the presence/absence of the following:

- The formation of insurmountable differences in the Legislative Chamber or Senate at Oliy Majlis of Uzbekistan, which may affect their normal functioning;
- The repeated adoption of their decisions conflicting with the Constitution of Uzbekistan;
- The formation of insurmountable differences between the Legislative Chamber and Senate, which may affect the normal functioning of Oliy Majlis of Uzbekistan.

Following the case review, the Constitutional Court makes one of the following decisions:

- On consent to the President of Uzbekistan regarding the dissolution of the Legislative Chamber or the Senate at Oliy Majlis of Uzbekistan;
- On refusal to the President of Uzbekistan regarding the dissolution of Legislative Chamber or the Senate at Oliy Majlis of Uzbekistan.

3.2 The Constitutional Court and Government

An executive body system cannot actually avoid rule-making activities, although a rule-making function is kind of incompatible with the legal nature of executive power. As is known, the main task of this system is to ensure the control of law-enforcement processes. However, management process is impossible without a law-making function.

In its daily activity, the Cabinet of Ministers of Uzbekistan specifies the legal norms of laws, while giving them the operative tone. Thus, one of these issues was related to providing the disabled veterans of the Great Patriotic War and families receiving pensions for loss of their breadwinner (serviceman) with benefits on payment for housing/communal utilities. The Constitutional Court decision proposed the Cabinet of Ministers to bring the normative acts on this issue in compliance with a presidential decree.

Acts issued by the government in the management sphere are diverse; they form one of the most numerous arrays of normative-legal acts. And they need control.

In modern states, the interaction of the constitutional review body and the government is an institute and process of political and legal decision-making, with the Constitutional Court as the subject and law-making activity of government as the object. Such interaction ensures public exercise of critical effect—namely, control over implementation of law-making functions at the supreme body of executive power.

3.3 The Constitutional Court and Parliament

Interaction of the Constitutional Court with chambers of Parliament is determined by the Constitution with constitutional laws "On the Legislative Chamber at Oliy Majlis of Uzbekistan" and "On the Senate at Oliy Majlis of Uzbekistan"[21], constitutional law "On the Constitutional Court of Uzbekistan", among others.

Oliy Majlis of Uzbekistan determines the system/powers of judicial bodies in Uzbekistan, including the Constitutional Court. Let's note that the Constitutional Court of Uzbekistan is entitled to legislative initiative (Article 83 of Constitution), i.e. the right to submit draft laws to the Legislative Chamber of Oliy Majlis. The Constitutional Court used this right only a few times; however, draft laws reached the stage of coming into legal force every time. So, based on this right, the Constitutional Court submitted to the Legislative Chamber of Oliy Majlis a draft law on amendments and addenda to Article 74 in Law "On Joint Stock Companies and the Protection of Shareholders' Rights"[22]. As a result, the provision of the Law, which assumed the need to notarize the power of the attorney for voting at a general shareholder meeting (on behalf of a legal entity), was abolished.

According to Article 109 of the Constitution, the Constitutional Court determines the compliance of laws/resolutions issued by Oliy Majlis of Uzbekistan with the Constitution of Uzbekistan.

Election to the Constitutional Court of Uzbekistan is ensured by the Upper Chamber of Parliament: the Senate. Subjects of appeal to the Constitutional Court are chambers of the Parliament, the Speaker of the Legislative Chamber, and the Chairperson of the Senate at Oliy Majlis, group of deputies—at least one-fourth of the total deputies in Legislative Chamber, and group of senators—at least one-fourth of the total Senate members. More than once, the Constitutional Court used the right of legal initiative ensured by the Constitution. It made proposals to Oliy Majlis on improving the administrative, criminal, civil, labor, criminal-procedure, and criminal-executive legislation. Thus, having reviewed an issue "Submission of proposal on addressing the incompliance between Articles 53, 54, 257 in the Administrative Code of Uzbekistan to Oliy Majlis of Uzbekistan", the Constitutional Court recognized provisions of Articles 53, 54 incompliant with Part 2, Article 257 in the Administrative Code of Uzbekistan and, as part of

21 Ведомости Олий Мажлиса Республики Узбекистан 2002, № 12, Ст.ст. 213, 215.

22 Cf.: Ведомости Олий Мажлиса РУз. 1996, № 5–6, ст. 61.

legal initiative, provided the Parliament of our country (Uzbekistan) with proposal to address this incompliance[23].

Under Article 95 of the Constitution, the Legislative Chamber/Senate may be dissolved by the decision of the President of Uzbekistan made in agreement with the Constitutional Court at insurmountable differences in the Legislative Chamber and Senate, which may affect their normal functioning, or repeated adoption of decisions conflicting with the Constitution, as well as the insurmountable differences between the Legislative Chamber and Senate, which may affect the normal functioning of Oliy Majlis. In parliamentary practice, such a situation was not yet observed.

Meetings of the Legislative Chamber and Senate, as well as the meetings of their bodies, may be attended by the Chairperson of the Constitutional Court, which happens quite often at plenary sessions of the chambers and almost always at joint sessions of the chambers. Under Article 21 of the Law, the Speaker of Legislative Chamber, his/her deputies, the Chairperson of Senate, and his/her deputies may attend the meetings of the Constitutional Court. However, at that, representatives of legislative power shall not interfere in activities of the Constitutional Court. This is due to the constitutional provision that judges of the Constitutional Court are independent in their activities and subject to the Constitution only. The Chairperson of the Constitutional Court also attends the meetings of legislative bodies, without interfering in their activities.

Under Article 83 of the Constitution, the Constitutional Court of Uzbekistan is entitled to legislative initiative, i.e. the right to submit draft laws to the Legislative Chamber. In accordance with the Law, the bill shall be discussed at the meeting of the Constitutional Court (collegially) and a decision shall be made on submitting the bill to the Legislative Chamber. When a draft law is submitted to the Legislative Chamber at Oliy Majlis, this decision shall be provided by the Constitutional Court.

If a draft law submitted by the Constitutional Court does not comply with the Law "On procedure of preparing the draft laws and submitting them to the Legislative Chamber at Oliy Majlis of Uzbekistan"[24] and the Regulation of Legislative Chamber, Kengash of the Legislative Chamber may decide to return the draft law to the Constitutional Court. The Constitutional Court may re-submit the revised draft law to the Legislative Chamber, considering the

23 Cf.: С. Хакимова, *Становление и совершенствование конституционного правосудия в Республике Узбекистан РУз.*, "Вестник Конституционного суда РУз." 2005, Выпуск 12, p. 95.

24 СЗ РУз. 2006 г., № 41. ст. 406.

proposals of the Legislative Chamber. The Constitutional Court may withdraw the draft law submitted to the Legislative Chamber, prior to adoption in the first reading.

The Constitutional Court provides an official interpretation of constitutional norms and laws adopted by a legislative body. Interpretation of constitutional norms and laws is ensured in case of detecting the ambiguities, irregularities, or conflicting practices of application. In the course of interpretation, no amendments/addenda are allowed in norms used for interpretation. When the Constitutional Court reviews the case on interpreting laws and constitutional norms, a representative of the legislative body is invited to the Constitutional Court meeting, as a party.

3.4 The Constitutional Court and Other Courts

In April 2017, the Law of Uzbekistan No. ZRU-426 "Amendments and Addenda to Constitution of Uzbekistan"[25] came into force with fundamental provisions aimed at implementing the tasks defined in Action Strategy on 5 Priority Areas of Uzbekistan Development in 2017–2021. The Law provided amendments and addenda to Articles 80, 81, 83, 93, 107, 110, 111, and 112 in the Constitution of Uzbekistan. According to the above amendments, the Supreme Economic Court and Supreme Court were merged into a unique supreme judicial body in the field of civil, criminal, administrative, and economic legal proceedings: the Supreme Court of Uzbekistan.

Thus, judicial bodies in Uzbekistan can be divided in two groups: the Constitutional Court and courts of general jurisdiction, which include military courts and economic, administrative courts. All of them are independent, with individual fields of activity. Their relations are based on non-interference in each other's activities. The Constitution of Uzbekistan includes a provision assuming that the Constitutional Court reviews the cases on constitutionality of acts issued by legislative and executive power only[26].

---

25 Cf.: СЗ РУз. 2017, № 14, ст. 213.

26 In some CIS countries, Constitutional Court also reviews the cases on constitutionality of acts issued by judicial power. Thus, under Article 116 in Constitution of Belarus, Constitutional Court provides conclusions on compliance of acts issued by Supreme Court and Supreme Economic Court with Constitution, international legal acts ratified by Republic of Belarus, laws, decrees, and orders. And, under Article 130 in Constitution of Azerbaijan, Constitutional Court verifies compliance of Supreme Court decisions (in cases assumed by law) with Constitution and laws (см.: *Конституции государств-участников СНГ*, Moscow 2001).

The Constitutional Court of Uzbekistan, as well as the constitutional courts of other countries, is in a kind of privileged position among judicial bodies. This is due to the fact that powers of the Constitutional Court are established by the Constitution. Powers of other judicial bodies are established by laws instead of the Constitution.

Second, legal status of the Constitutional Court is determined individually by the constitutional law "On the Constitutional Court of Uzbekistan"; legal status of other courts is determined by the Law "On Courts".

Third, instead of the usual procedure established by procedural codes of Uzbekistan (used by other courts), the Constitutional Court reviews the cases according to the rules and norms of the constitutional legal proceeding consolidated in the Regulation of the Constitutional Court. This Regulation is approved by the Constitutional Court itself[27].

Fourth, the ethics of judges in other courts are regulated by the Rules of Ethical Conduct, approved by the Supreme Qualification Committee on the Selection and Recommendation to Posts of Judges at the President of Uzbekistan; ethics of Constitutional Court judges are regulated by the Code of Honor of the Constitutional Court Judge, approved by the Constitutional Court itself.

The issue of relations between the Constitutional Court and other courts is closely linked to the issue of their common and different features. Thus, the Constitutional Court reviews cases on the constitutionality of normative-legal acts. Previously, civil/economic courts were entitled to review the cases on the legality of normative-legal acts. Under Article 12 in the Civil Code of Uzbekistan[28], an act of state/local self-government body that does not comply with the law and violates civil rights or interests of a citizen/legal entity protected by law, may be recognized invalid by court.

Until 2002, the Law "On the Constitutional Court of Uzbekistan" assumed that a judge of the Constitutional Court cannot be held criminally liable, arrested, or subjected to administrative penalties, imposed by court, without the consent of Oliy Majlis (in a period between sessions, without the consent of Council [Kengash] at Oliy Majlis). Such a norm conflicted with the constitutional principle on the separation of powers. Besides, the Law "On Courts" assumed that a judge cannot be held criminally liable/detained without the consent of the Plenum of the Supreme Court or the Plenum of the Supreme Economic Court,

---

27 April 17, 2015, Constitutional Court decision approved the Regulation of Constitutional Court in Uzbekistan (cf.: Конституционный Суд Республики Узбекистан (Сборник документов), Tashkent 2015).

28 Cf.: *Кодексы Республики Узбекистан. Сборник*, Tashkent 2016, 1119 pp.

respectively. In this norm, the separation of powers was taken into account. So, the Law "On Constitutional Court of Uzbekistan" was amended, while assuming that a judge of the Constitutional Court cannot be held criminally/administratively liable or detained without consent of the Constitutional Court.

Under Article 83 of the Constitution, both the Constitutional Court and Supreme Court are entitled to legislative initiative and interact with each other during exercise of this right. Thus, under the Decree of the President of Uzbekistan "On Arrangement Measures for Further Improvement of Court Activities" dated November 30, 2012, the minimum age of judges (courts of general jurisdiction, economic courts) was set at 30 years. Now, the age limit for a candidate to judge has been increased from 30 to 35 years.

According to the decree, the Supreme Court prepared a bill assuming amendments and addenda to relevant laws. While discussing the bill in the Constitutional Court, it was proposed to apply this age to judges of the Constitutional Court too. The Supreme Court took into account the Constitutional Court's opinion on the issue and submitted this proposal to draft law. On the adoption of addenda to the Law "On the Constitutional Court of Uzbekistan", a citizen of Uzbekistan who is at least 30 years old may be elected as a judge of the Constitutional Court.

The Supreme Court of Uzbekistan (represented by the Chairperson) is among the subjects entitled to submit issues to the Constitutional Court (Article 83 of the Constitution). Until now, unfortunately, the Supreme Court of the country has not used this right in practice. However, by its status/nature of exercised functions, it refers to bodies interacting with the Constitutional Court very closely. On many issues admitted for review, the Constitutional Court requests an opinion or other position expressed by the Chairperson of Supreme Court. Under Article 4 in the Law of Uzbekistan "On the Constitutional Court of Uzbekistan", the Constitutional Court may review an appeal of the Supreme Court of Uzbekistan (initiated by courts) on compliance between the Constitution of Uzbekistan and normative-legal acts to be applied in a particular case.

The Plenum of the Supreme Court of Uzbekistan adopts resolutions of a normative nature, but they are beyond the constitutional review, which requires individual legal decision.

3.5 The Constitutional Court and Other Public Authorities

Along with judicial protection, extrajudicial protection of human rights is used in Uzbekistan (applied by the Ombudsman for Human Rights at Oliy Majlis of Uzbekistan and the National Center of Uzbekistan for Human Rights).

Their main task is the protection of civil rights/freedoms proclaimed by the Constitution and laws of Uzbekistan by legal means inherent to each of them.

Thus, the legal status of Ombudsman was defined in the Law "On Ombudsman for Human Rights at Oliy Majlis of Uzbekistan", adopted on April 24, 1997[29]. On August 27, 2004, the Law "On Ombudsman for Human Rights at Oliy Majlis of Uzbekistan" was adopted in a new revision; now, it regulates the powers and activities of the Ombudsman[30]. The legal status of the National Center of Uzbekistan for Human Rights is defined in the Decree of the President of Uzbekistan dated October 31, 1996 "On Establishment of National Center of Uzbekistan for Human Rights"[31] and a relevant provision approved by the Decree of the Cabinet of Ministers of Uzbekistan dated November 13, 1996[32].

The Ombudsman is a constitutional body assumed by the Constitution. It is defined in Item 16, Article 78, Constitution of Uzbekistan. According to laws, the Ombudsman is an official who is granted the powers to ensure parliamentary control over observing the laws on human rights and freedoms by state bodies, enterprises, institutions, organizations, and officials.

All this predetermined the need for cooperation of the Constitutional Court with the Ombudsman and the National Center for Human Rights. On December 2, 1998, the agreement "On Cooperation in Ensuring the Supremacy of the Constitution and Protecting the Human Rights and Freedoms" was signed between the Constitutional Court and the Ombudsman of Oliy Majlis for Human Rights. The basis for this agreement was formed by such principles as supremacy of the Constitution/laws, independence of these bodies, and coordination of their activities on ensuring civil rights and freedoms. Cooperation of the Constitutional Court with the Ombudsman and National Center for Human Rights is also based on independence and non-interference in each other's affairs, while taking the following forms:

1) The Administration of the Constitutional Court, the National Center for Human Rights, and the Ombudsman invite each other to events and meetings affecting human rights and freedoms. Thus, the Ombudsman and Head of National Center for Human Rights personally attend the meetings of the Constitutional Court, where particular cases are reviewed. However,

29 Ведомости Олий Мажлиса Республики Узбекистан 1997 г. №№ 4–5, Ст. 102.

30 Ведомости Олий Мажлиса Республики Узбекистан 2004 г. № 9 (1341), Ст. 170.

31 Ведомости Олий Мажлиса Республики Узбекистан 1996 г., № 10, Ст. 202.

32 Собрание постановлений Правительства Республики Узбекистан 1996 г., № 11, ст. 32.

they do not interfere in court activity. This is due to the constitutional provision that in their activity, judges of the Constitutional Court are independent and subject to the Constitution of Uzbekistan only. The Chairperson of the Constitutional Court attends the events of the Ombudsman and National Center for Human Rights without interfering in their activities as well.

2) Cooperation is also ensured in preparing the proposals on the improvement of laws. So, draft laws prepared by the Ombudsman are studied by experts of the Constitutional Court, with issue of specific proposals on them. Thus, the Constitutional Court approved the proposal of the Ombudsman to be included in a list of subjects entitled to submit issues for review at Constitutional Court meetings. Bills prepared by the Constitutional Court are sent to the Ombudsman for studying and preparing the proposals.
3) For scientific study of some legal issues in civil appeals and rendering the qualified aid to the Ombudsman, two volunteers of the Constitutional Court are included in expert council at the Ombudsman of Oliy Majlis for Human Rights.
4) Regular data exchange is ensured in the framework of cooperation between the Constitutional Court, the Ombudsman, and the National Center for Human Rights. Thus, the Constitutional Court submits materials of the Constitutional Court meeting, materials of normative-legal nature, as well as the periodical *Bulletin of Constitutional Court of Uzbekistan*. The Ombudsman provides the Constitutional Court with annual reports and other materials.
5) The Constitutional Court, Ombudsman, and National Center for Human Rights prepare and hold scientific-practical conferences and seminars with attendance of state bodies, non-governmental organizations, and citizens, on issues of protecting civil rights and freedoms.

The Practice of Uzbekistan shows that the Constitutional Court is also requested to interpret the legal norms by bodies, which have no right to do so (under the Constitution and the Law "On the Constitutional Court"). Thus, the Institute for Monitoring of Current Laws at the President of Uzbekistan appealed to the Constitutional Court on two issues:

1) The interpretation of Article 118 in the Labor Code, on the potential reduction of working time for certain categories of staff;
2) On verifying the constitutionality of norms regulating the granting and payment of benefits due to care of a sick family member. Both issues were recognized by Constitutional Court judges as worth reviewing in court session. Their correct resolution significantly expanded the rights of staff to reduced working hours and benefits due to care of a sick family member.

The charitable foundation Mahalla requested the court to interpret Article 105 of the Constitution on civil self-government bodies. The procedure of withdrawing the land and buildings used by legal entities and citizens, procedure of privatizing the apartments, indexing of deposits kept in people's bank, etc., were studied by copies of the khokimiyat (local government body) decisions received from citizens.

Under Article 25 of the constitutional law "On the Constitutional Court of Uzbekistan", the Attorney General is entitled to submit issues for review by the Constitutional Court. He/she may attend the court session and state his/her position on all issues under review.

4 The Structure of the Constitutional Court

The Constitutional Court is a permanent body elected for a term of five years. Under Article 5 in the law "On the Constitutional Court of Uzbekistan", the Constitutional Court is elected by the Senate at Oliy Majlis of Uzbekistan, by proposal of the President, from among persons recommended by the Supreme Judicial Council of Uzbekistan, including the representative of Karakalpakstan. Every judge of the Constitutional Court is elected individually. The term of office for judge of the Constitutional Court: five years. A person may not be elected as judge of the Constitutional Court more than twice. A person gaining a majority vote from all members of the Senate at Oliy Majlis of Uzbekistan is considered elected.

Article 9 of the law emphasizes that via resolutions, judges of the Constitutional Court express their legal position free from aspects of practical expediency, political inclinations, and other external influence. Under Article 19, judges of the Constitutional Court cannot be senators or deputies of state representative bodies. Judges of the Constitutional Court cannot be members of political parties and/or movements, or be involved in any other type of paid activities apart from scientific and educational ones.

The Constitutional Court consists of seven judges, including the Chairperson and his/her Deputy. The Chairperson and his/her Deputy are elected from among the judges, at the meeting of the Constitutional Court. According to the law, a citizen of Uzbekistan who is at least 35 years old and from among the experts in politics and law with high moral qualities and necessary qualifications can be elected as a judge of the Constitutional Court.

For organizational, scientific-expert, information-reference, and other support of Constitutional Court activities, the Court's structure is provided with an administration (Article 35 of the law). The provision on the Administration of the Constitutional Court in Uzbekistan was approved by the Constitutional Court of Uzbekistan on April 17, 2015. The main task of the administration is organizational-technical, scientific-analytical, information-reference, and financial-economic support of Constitutional Court activities.

4.1 The Legal Status of Constitutional Court Judges

The law assumes guarantees aimed at ensuring the independence of the Constitutional Court. Thus, judges of the Constitutional Court cannot be senators or deputies of state representative bodies. Judges of the Constitutional Court cannot be members of political parties and/or movements, or be involved in any other paid activities apart from scientific and educational ones.

The constitutional law "On the Constitutional Court of Uzbekistan" assumes that judges of the Constitutional Court are irremovable during the exercise of their powers. Irremovability of the judges means that their powers can be terminated ahead of time only in cases assumed by law by decision of the Senate at Oliy Majlis of Uzbekistan. The law assumes the following grounds for terminating the powers of Constitutional Court judges:

- Violation of a judge's oath;
- Filing the written application (1 judge);
- Reaching the age limit of judge;
- Entry of court judgment against him or her into legal force;
- Continuation of activities incompatible with the position of judge after warning or suspension of powers;
- Long-term failure to perform duties (for health reasons or other valid reasons);
- Loss of Uzbekistan citizenship;
- Recognizing the judge incapable or impaired (in a prescribed manner);
- Death or declaration of death (by court order).

Judges of the Constitutional Court were selected from among the judges of general jurisdiction and economic courts. Thus, judge Genjemurat Pirzhanov has judicial experience at courts of general jurisdiction and judge Fatima Husanova worked as a judge of the Tashkent Civil Court for many years. Mirza-Ulugbek Abdusalomov, former Chairperson of the Constitutional Court, used to be Head of Supreme Economic Court for a long time.

On May 1, 1998, Oliy Majlis dismissed the Deputy Chairperson O. Ernazarov (according to his application) and elected Bakhtier Mirboboev (Deputy Chairperson) and Yuldash Zhurayev (member of the court). Due to the fact that on December 5, 1999, Y. Zhurayev was elected as Deputy of Oliy Majlis, since 2000, the Constitutional Court was operated by five members only[33].

Judges of the Constitutional Court have immunity, cannot be held criminally and administratively liable, or detained without consent of the Constitutional Court. A criminal case against a judge of the Constitutional Court may be initiated by the Attorney General only. Taking into custody, detention, inspection of personal belongings, baggage, transport, or residential/office premises of a judge of the Constitutional Court are not allowed. Such practice is not applied.

Powers of the judge may be suspended (by decision of the Constitutional Court) in the following cases: criminal prosecution; involvement in activities incompatible with position of the judge; and recognizing him/her missing (by court decision). Suspension of powers (except for cases where judge was taken into custody, as a preventive measure) does not assume suspension of his/her salary or annulment of immunity. Powers of the judge shall be suspended until failure of grounds for their suspension.

Under Article 14, the Code of Honor of Judge of the Constitutional Court in Uzbekistan (approved by the Constitutional Court of Uzbekistan on January 30, 2004, amended on April 17, 2015), for commission of misconduct or other crime, a judge shall be liable in accordance with legislation.

For commission of an act discrediting the Constitutional Court, powers of a judge may be suspended or terminated ahead of time (in a prescribed manner).

Article 79 in Regulations of the Constitutional Court states that powers of a judge of the Constitutional Court shall be suspended by the decision of the Constitutional Court (adopted no later than one month after revealing the grounds for suspension). At criminal prosecution, powers of a judge of the Constitutional Court are suspended simultaneously with consent to his/her criminal prosecution.

The Constitutional Court shall suspend the powers of judge until failure of grounds for suspension. Restoration of powers is formalized by decision of the Constitutional Court.

Article 24, which refers to the guarantees of employment for a judge of the Constitutional Court (on expiry of powers), states that on expiry of powers, a judge of the Constitutional Court is given the previous job/position held before election as a judge of the Constitutional Court (in its absence, the equivalent job/position).

---

33 Cf.: Б. Мирбобоев, *Дальнейшая демократизация взаимоотношений Конституционного суда Республики Узбекистан с другими судами и национальными институтами по правам человека*, "Вестник Конституционного суда РУз." 2015, Выпуск 19; Б. Эшонов, *Становление и развитие Конституционного Суда Республики Узбекистан*, "Вестник Конституционного суда РУз." 2001, Выпуск 5.

4.2 Functions of the Constitutional Court

Competence and daily activity of the Constitutional Court embody the independence of judicial power from legislative and executive power, as one of the most important constitutional principles. Unlike other courts, the Constitutional Court reviews and resolves the cases on constitutionality of acts issued by legislative and executive power and gives opinions based on the Constitution of Uzbekistan. It ensures the supremacy of the Constitution by resolving issues submitted for its review.

The Constitutional Court reviews cases on constitutionality of acts issued by legislative and executive power, while making a relevant decision on the basis of review.

Main principles of Constitutional Court activity: supremacy of the Constitution of Uzbekistan, independence, collegiality, publicity, competitiveness, and equality of the parties (Article 7 of law on the Constitutional Court of RUz). While making decisions, judges express their legal position free from aspects of practical expediency, political inclinations, and other external influence.

Independence of the Constitutional Court is ensured by way of electing and dismissing judges (set by the Constitution), their immunity, the legal procedure of resolving cases and issues in the competence of the court, secrecy of a judge's conference at decision-making, liability for disrespect to the Constitutional Court or interference in its activity, the formation of required arrangement-technical conditions for Constitutional Court activity, as well as the material and social support of judges.

The function of the Constitutional Court is not formed by will of government institution, but directly vested in the Constitutional Court by supreme law: the Constitution.

The advantages of preliminary (preventive) control include the fact that this control:

1. Pre-clarifies the issue on constitutionality of a normative act, which ensures the reliability and stability of the legal system.
2. Contributes to the most productive work of the legislator and improves its credibility.
3. Prevents the difficulties that may arise if the law (applied for several years) or its individual provision is recognized as unconstitutional.
4. Prior to ratification of international agreements and adoption of international obligations by state, it ensures a final and authoritative decision on the constitutionality of these obligations.

4.3 The Subject of Control by the Constitutional Court

Constitutional justice is a powerful means of ensuring the stability of the legal system, state, and society by ensuring the consistency and legitimacy of their functioning. The latter is the most important criterion for the effectiveness of constitutional justice.

Subject of control by the Constitutional Court of Uzbekistan includes:

- Compliance between Constitution of Uzbekistan and:
  a) laws of Uzbekistan (constitutional laws, laws on ratifying the international treaties of Uzbekistan prior to signing by President of the country), and resolutions of Oliy Majlis chambers,
  b) decrees, resolutions, and orders of the President of Uzbekistan,
  c) governmental decrees,
  d) decisions of local public authorities,
  e) inter-state (contractual and other) obligations of Uzbekistan;
- compliance between the Constitution of Karakalpakstan and the Constitution of Uzbekistan, and the laws of Karakalpakstan and laws of Uzbekistan;
- the sense/essence of constitutional norms and laws of Uzbekistan (interpreting);
- appeals of the Supreme Court of Uzbekistan on compliance of the local Constitution and normative-legal acts to be applied in a particular case (no practice);
- the state of constitutional legality in the country.

Thus, the subject of control by the Constitutional Court covers the range of relations associated with ensuring the supremacy and direct effect of the Constitution, as well as the protection of basic constitutional principles and values proclaimed and guaranteed by Fundamental Law.

The subject of constitutional review includes ensuring the constitutionality of legal acts (as early as the development stage), which ensures a better quality of legislative work.

4.4 Preliminary and Subsequent Review of Legal Norms

The president of the country may apply to the Constitutional Court a proposal to verify the compliance between the local Constitution and any draft NLA (prior to signing a law or concluding an international treaty as well). The procedure is standard, like the review of any other appeal from properly authorized bodies and officials.

Although the legislation of Uzbekistan does not directly mention the preliminary constitutional review of norms, in fact, the Constitutional Court is entitled to participate in the law-making process, as it is included in a range of subjects with right to legislative initiative. On the other hand, in practice, all bills are actually sent to the Constitutional Court for opinion.

Besides, according to the competence of the Constitutional Court, it ensures a so-called subsequent constitutional review. Participation of the Constitutional Court in a normative review is mostly ensured by resolution of cases on the constitutionality of NLA and official interpretation of constitutional norms.

Thus, we can talk about two aspects of Constitutional Court activity:

- a review of issues on compliance of all NLA with the Constitution of RUz—i.e. implementing the function of a "negative" legislator;
- initiating the adoption of new laws—implementing the function of a "positive" legislator.

4.5 Legal Review Procedure

Being an independent procedural form for the functioning of the Constitutional Court of Uzbekistan, constitutional legal proceedings form a set of procedures and legal relations (regulated by procedural constitutional norms) between the Constitutional Court and other parties to constitutional legal proceedings, on review of constitutional-legal issues and competence disputes, for achieving the set goals and tasks. The establishment of proper legal procedures and rules for constitutional legal proceeding does contribute to ensuring the proper understanding and application of the prescriptions of substantive constitutional norms, protecting the rights, freedoms, and legitimate interests for subjects of constitutional legal proceeding, and to the final issue of a comprehensive and objective Constitutional Court decision by result of reviewing a particular case.

Constitutional legal proceeding is an individual and independent (along with civil, criminal, economic, and administrative) type of legal proceeding. The establishment of a special procedure for the Constitutional Court to exercise judicial power is due to differences between the constitutional-legal status of the Constitutional Court and legal status of other judicial bodies in terms of competence, organization, nature of cases under review and decisions taken, and their legal force/enforcement mechanism. Exercise of an exclusive Constitutional Court function (control over constitutionality of normative acts in the state) predetermines a special procedure for the exercise of judicial power: constitutional legal proceeding.

Court sessions represent the organizational form of exercising the constitutional legal proceeding. A special note shall be made that a session of the Constitutional Court of Uzbekistan is held under rules and procedures set by the Regulation. Constitutional Court sessions are convened by the Chairperson (in his/her absence, by the Deputy Chairperson; in the absence of Chairperson/Deputy or failure to fulfill their duties, by the oldest judge of the Constitutional Court). While resolving the cases, the Constitutional Court is guided by the Constitution of Uzbekistan only.

Under Article 18 in the Regulation of the Constitutional Court of Uzbekistan dated April 17, 2015, parties to constitutional legal proceedings include the state body/official who submitted an issue to the Constitutional Court; the state body/official who adopted or issued the normative legal act, the constitutionality of which is subject to verification; the state body, the competence of which includes issues contained in inter-state contractual or other obligations of Uzbekistan; the chambers of Oliy Majlis (on cases of interpreting the constitutional norms/laws of Uzbekistan or giving consent to the President of Uzbekistan regarding the decision to disband the Legislative Chamber, Senate at Oliy Majlis of Uzbekistan); Zhokargy Kenes of Karakalpakstan (on cases of giving opinions about compliance between the Constitutions of Karakalpakstan and Uzbekistan, and the laws of Karakalpakstan and Uzbekistan).

When submitting an issue for review by the Constitutional Court (on the initiative of Constitutional Court judges), the party is a state body or legal or natural person whose appeal was a reason for submitting the issue.

The party may have one or more representatives who represent its interests at the Constitutional Court. When submitting an issue for Constitutional Court review (by a group of deputies or senators), they must appoint one or several representatives.

Lawyers, experts, and other persons may act as representatives of the party based on a power of attorney issued by the party, with indication of their authority.

By virtue of office, heads of state bodies and legal entities (see first and second part of the article) may act as party representatives at the Constitutional Court. Party representatives (by virtue of office) represent party interests without a power of attorney.

Article 19, Regulation of the Constitutional Court of Uzbekistan, emphasizes that parties and their representatives may get acquainted with all materials of the case; state their position on the case; provide written feedback; submit petitions (including those on disqualifying a judge, appointing an expertise, summoning of witnesses, experts, specialists); nominate experts and specialists; and ask questions to parties of constitutional legal proceeding.

The Constitutional Court adopts decisions on specific issues under review (with questioned constitutionality). Upon verifying the constitutionality of a normative act, it may simultaneously adopt a decision on normative acts, which are based on a verified normative act, or reproduce its provisions, although they were not mentioned in the issue submitted for Constitutional Court review. A decision of the Constitutional Court is adopted by open vote. A decision is considered adopted if a majority of the judges present in session voted for it.

The Constitutional Court shall adopt a decision on issue under review no later than in three months from the receipt of relevant materials (Article 26 of the law). The Constitutional Court adopts decisions on specific issues under review only. At that, on verifying the constitutionality of a normative legal act, the Constitutional Court may simultaneously make a decision on other normative legal acts, which are based on a verified normative act, or reproduce its provisions, although they were not mentioned in the issue submitted for Constitutional Court review.

Constitutional Court decisions come into force at their publication. They are final, are not subject to appeal, act directly, and do not need confirmation by other bodies and officials. This procedure for entry of the Constitutional Court decision into force ensures an independent exercise of judicial power via constitutional legal proceedings.

4.6 Civil Complaint as Means of Legal Review

The right of citizens to appeal is one of the most important factors for ensuring the effective protection of human rights (assumed under Article 35 in the Constitution of Uzbekistan). In the laws of Uzbekistan, this issue has a special place with definition of principles for its exercise. In this area, the government ensures the stepwise reformation of current laws. At the moment, some laws are adopted, applied, and being improved.

One of such legal acts is the Law of Uzbekistan "On Appeals of Individuals and Legal Entities"[34], adopted in a new revision on September 11, 2017. This law improved the procedure of filing appeals to state bodies, as well as their review. Liability for violations in this field was assumed; procedure of appeal to state bodies and officials was specified.

This law defined such important provisions as: procedure of filing appeals by individuals/legal entities; procedure of reviewing appeals by state bodies; and

34 Собрание законодательства Республики Узбекистан 2014 г., № 49, ст. 578.

rights of individuals/legal entities and obligations of state bodies during review of appeals. The law defined forms, types of appeals, and requirements to them, while consolidating the guarantees for admission of individuals and representatives of legal entities. This legal act reflects the norms on the procedure and deadlines of appeal filing/reviewing, grounds for leaving appeals without review, rights of individuals/legal entities and obligations of state bodies during review of appeals, compensation for material/moral damage, and liability for violation of laws on appeals.

One of the basic changes (due to scientific-technical progress and IT technology) was the consolidation of the right to appeal in electronic form. Now, individuals and legal entities may apply in a prescribed manner to relevant departments/officials, while using information and communication technology.

Despite the fact that the constitutional law "On the Constitutional Court of Uzbekistan" does not assume the review of civil appeals on the unconstitutionality of law, as well as the appeals on interpretation of the Constitution, appeals of individuals/legal entities may form the grounds for review of issue at the Constitutional Court, if this issue is submitted for review on the initiative of at least three judges of the Constitutional Court.

A judge of the Constitutional Court who studies a civil appeal containing the issues within the competence of the Constitutional Court may:

- Summon the citizen who filed the appeal to clarify the issue under review and collect the additional materials;
- Analyze the practice of exercising a legislative act with questioned conformity to the Constitution;
- Invite representatives of an authorized organization, which ensures the exercise of a legislative act with questioned conformity to the Constitution;
- Demand additional information on the case under review from relevant bodies and officials.

A conclusion on a studied appeal is prepared by a judge of the Constitutional Court (for submission to session of the Constitutional Court) and presented to the Chairperson/Deputy of Constitutional Court.

Judges of the Constitutional Court (on their initiative, based on study of appeals and materials received by Court) may submit for Court review the issues on the protection of human rights and freedoms.

Under Article 44 in the Constitution of Uzbekistan, everyone is guaranteed judicial protection of rights and freedoms; illegal decisions and actions (or inaction) of state bodies, public associations, and officials may be appealed at court. In this mechanism of protecting the rights/freedoms of person and citizen, the

Constitutional Court holds a special place. Unlike courts of general jurisdiction and economic courts, it is assigned a decisive role in ensuring the supremacy of the Constitution and laws[35].

Article 4 of the constitutional law "On the Constitutional Court of Uzbekistan" contains a list of issues reviewed by this court only. Besides, it differs from courts of general jurisdiction, as the legislator limits the range of subjects entitled to submit issues for review of this court.

The Constitutional Court determines the compliance of laws and other legal acts with the Constitution of Uzbekistan, thus protecting the citizens from violation of their rights and freedoms by unconstitutional law, which was applied/subject to application.

The protection of civil rights/freedoms is also ensured, if the Constitutional Court (using the right of legal initiative) appeals to the legislative body with a proposal to amend the legal acts, and this initiative is supported.

From Article 4 in the constitutional law "On the Constitutional Court of Uzbekistan", it follows that citizens or stateless persons may initiate an appeal of a body/person entitled to apply to the Constitutional Court with relevant request, if they:

a) believe that their rights are violated by the law of Uzbekistan/another act adopted by Oliy Majlis, decree of the President, government or local government, international treaty or other obligations of Uzbekistan, which do not comply with its Constitution;
b) believe that the Constitution of Karakalpakstan or the law of Karakalpakstan does not comply with the Constitution of Uzbekistan or law of Uzbekistan;
c) ask for interpretation of the constitutional norms and laws of Uzbekistan[36].

---

35 См.: Н. Кариева, *Конституционный Суд и обращения граждан*, "Вестник Конституционного суда РУз." 2004, Выпуск 10, pp. 171–174.

36 So it was, for example, with cases on interpreting Paragraph 5, Part 1, Article 6 in Law of Uzbekistan "On Advocacy", initiated due to statement of lawyer Kh. Nurmukhamedov; on interpreting the Article 59 in Tax Code of Uzbekistan, initiated due to statement of citizen S. Muratkhojayev; on interpreting Part 4, Article 62 in Law of Uzbekistan "On Courts", reviewed after appeal of lawyer K. Muzaffarov to court, etc. Cf.: Н. Кариева, *Конституционный Суд и обращения граждан*, "Вестник Конституционного суда РУз." 2004, Выпуск 10, p. 173.

Thus, sole proprietor V. Frolov filed a complaint to Constitutional Court on unlawful depriving him of benefits assumed by Part 2, Article 16 in Law of Uzbekistan "On Guarantees of Freedom for Entrepreneurial Activity". It was about misunderstanding

Under Article 25 of the constitutional law "On the Constitutional Court of Uzbekistan", the right to submit issues for review of the Constitutional Court is vested in chambers of Oliy Majlis of Uzbekistan; the President of Uzbekistan; the Cabinet of Ministers of Uzbekistan; the Ombudsman for Human Rights at Oliy Majlis of Uzbekistan; Zhokargy Kenes of Karakalpakstan; a group of deputies—at least one-fourth of the total deputies in the Legislative Chamber at Oliy Majlis of Uzbekistan; a group of senators—at least one-fourth of the total members of Senate at Oliy Majlis of Uzbekistan; the Supreme Court of Uzbekistan; and the Attorney General of Uzbekistan.

Issues may also be submitted for review by the Constitutional Court of Uzbekistan on the initiative of at least three judges of the Constitutional Court. Thus, the norm of this article in law strictly limits the range of subjects entitled to submit to the Constitutional Court an issue falling within its competence. Therefore, civil appeals cannot directly initiate constitutional proceedings. In other words, civil appeals and the right to submit issues to the Constitutional Court are different concepts. Citizens are not authorized to submit issues for review by the Constitutional Court, which means that an appeal submitted by them will be reviewed in the manner assumed by the Law "On Appeals of Natural Persons and Legal Entities"—not within legal proceedings. That is, the review of civil appeals cannot directly entail the issue of the Constitutional Court decision (in a procedural manner).

In this regard, the Constitutional Court developed and adopted the "Regulation on the Procedure of Reviewing Civil Appeals to the Constitutional Court of Uzbekistan", which regulates the mechanisms allowing citizens to exercise the constitutional right to protection of their rights and legitimate interests.

A lot of applications, complaints, and proposals are submitted to the Constitutional Court. In 2010, it was about 428; in 2015, it was 497. As we can see, the number of appeals to the Constitutional Court (on violation of constitutional rights and freedoms) tends to increase. It means that more and more citizens of the country are mastering the legal system and are starting to use it actively.

---

and improper applying of legal norm by tax and financial bodies. Upon studying the case circumstances and relevant arguments from Ministry of Finance and State Tax Committee of Uzbekistan, three judges of Constitutional Court took the initiative of submitting this issue to the Court. Following the review, the Court came to conclusion on need for interpreting this norm, as the above bodies interpret it in their own way, which entails the occurrence of certain legal consequences—not just for V. Frolov, but for other small and private businesses. С. Хакимова, *Становление и совершенствование конституционного правосудия в Республике Узбекистан*, "Вестник Конституционного Суда РУз." 2005, Выпуск 12, p. 94.

5 The Legal Nature and Legal Force of Constitutional Court Decisions

Under Article 31 of the law "On Constitutional Court of Uzbekistan", the Constitutional Court makes decisions on specific issues under review only if their constitutionality is questioned. Upon verifying the constitutionality of a normative act, the Constitutional Court may simultaneously adopt a decision on normative acts, which are based on a verified act, or reproduce its provisions, although they were not mentioned in the issue submitted for Constitutional Court review.

A decision of the Constitutional Court is adopted by open vote. A judge of the Court may not abstain or skip voting. A decision of the Constitutional Court is deemed adopted if a majority of judges present in the session voted for it. In a case where votes are equally divided, the vote of the Chairperson shall be decisive.

A judge of the Constitutional Court who disagrees to the Constitutional Court decision may state his/her opinion in writing and attach it to the protocol of the Court session.

Article 32 of the law states that a Constitutional Court decision on the essence of a reviewed case (constitutionality of international treaty and normative act) is known as a decree. Decrees are passed by the Constitutional Court in the name of Uzbekistan. In other cases, a Constitutional Court decision is known as a conclusion or may be of another form.

The procedure of publishing Constitutional Court decisions and their entry into force is reflected in Article 33 of the law. Decrees, conclusions, and other decisions of the Constitutional Court are published in mass media and on the website of the Constitutional Court. Official sources of publishing the Constitutional Court decisions: Legislation Bulletin of Uzbekistan, newspapers *Hulk Suzi* and *Narodnoe Slovo*, *Bulletin of the Constitutional Court of Uzbekistan*, and the National Legislation Database of Uzbekistan. A Constitutional Court decision comes into force at its official publication. A decision of the Constitutional Court is final and not subject to appeal.

Constitutional Court decisions are pre-judicial in nature. Article 33 of the law assumes that a Constitutional Court decision may be revised on its own initiative:

- Given newly discovered circumstances unknown to the Constitutional Court during the passing of the decision;
- Upon change of a constitutional norm used as a basis for decision-making;
- If the Constitutional Court recognized the adoption of a decision in violation of established legal proceedings.

A Constitutional Court decision comes into force at its publishing. A decision of the Constitutional Court is final and not subject to appeal. Constitutional Court decisions are binding on all state bodies, public associations, enterprises, institutions, entities, officials, and citizens.

6 The Constitutional Value of the Constitutional Court

In a system of supreme state bodies, the place of the Constitutional Court is defined by the need to ensure the unity of the legislation system, address conflicts within it, and ensure the compliance of normative acts with the Constitution. The activity of a constitutional review body is an essential element of a state mechanism built on a separation of powers, as it allows the monitoring of compliance between each body and competence assigned to it.

The unique mission of the Constitutional Court is that it is the only body of state power directly responsible for the subordination of politics to law and political actions and decisions to constitutional-legal requirements. The function of the Constitutional Court is not formed by will of government institution, but directly vested in the Constitutional Court by supreme law: the Constitution. A constitutional justice system can function effectively and fully at certain necessary and sufficient prerequisites. They include: functional, institutional, organizational, material, and social independence of judicial constitutional review; consistency in constitutional exercise of separation of powers; adequacy/comparability of basic constitutional principles and relevant constitutional mechanisms of exercising state power; correct/reasonable choice of objects for constitutional review; defining an optimal range of subjects entitled to apply to the Constitutional Court; system approach in ensuring the functional integrity of judicial power; presence/ensuring of clear law-making policy; and required level of perceiving democratic values in society.

An analysis of the concepts "constitutional review" and "constitutional supervision": a review function is more active, as recognizing a normative act (its provision) not compliant with the Constitution entails the loss of its force. A supervisory function aims to focus the attention of bodies and officials on the unconstitutionality of adopted or issued normative acts, while triggering the relevant measures.

The constitutional law "On the Constitutional Court of Uzbekistan" contains a detailed list of powers; at that, two inter-related aspects can be distinguished in Constitutional Court activities.

The first aspect is that the Constitutional Court protects the Constitution via its inherent powers, including separation of powers, as grounds for democratic constitutional order. With that, in its decisions, the Constitutional Court develops relevant legal positions (including those related to exercising the separation of powers), interprets the principle, and thus determines its real content. Constitutional justice becomes a guarantee of keeping authorities within their competence, outlined by the Constitution on the basis of the separation of powers.

The second aspect is that the Constitutional Court, as a judicial body, is part of separating the powers itself. Constitutional Court activity is part of relations on the exercise of state power based on its division into legislative, executive, and judicial branches. Powers of the Constitutional Court determine the vector of activities on the protection of constitutional values, including the resolution of competence disputes regarding the separation of state power.

The Constitution, as a political-legal document, defines the grounds of the constitutional system and determines the conditions/principles that form the branches of government. The main role of the Constitutional Court in strengthening the system of checks and balances is the strict adherence to constitutional principles. Exercise and strict observance of these principles enable full achievement of the true goal for a system of checks and balances. However, at abuse in one of the branches or abuse of powers assumed by the Constitution, the task of a constitutional review body is to demand compliance with constitutional provisions without exceeding the limits of competence (via available constitutional powers and legal mechanisms).

As we can see, the Constitutional Court as a constitutional review body plays a key role in building an effective system for the separation of powers and ensures their coordinated functioning and business interaction in sustainable development of the country, given the independence for branches of government.

The peculiarity of human rights activity in the Constitutional Court is that while making decisions and resolving disputes, it indirectly affects the legal norms in a particular case (expressed in the assessment/interpretation of the norm during application). The Constitutional Court provides a legal description of a normative act in view of its compliance or incompliance with the Constitution. Acts of the Constitutional Court are final and not subject to appeal, binding on all state bodies, local self-government bodies, officials, public associations, legal entities, and individuals, while being subject to exercise throughout the country.

Constitutional review body exercises its powers for protecting the foundations of constitutional system, constitutional rights/freedoms of person and citizen, ensuring the supremacy and direct action of Constitution.

Let's note that role of Constitutional Court is insufficiently active yet. In this view, activation of judicial-legal reform, which moved to new stage since

2016–2017 (including issues on improving the legal basis and practical activities of Constitutional Court), ensures confidence.

7 Assessment of the Constitutional Review Institute by Society

Under the State Program on Implementing the Action Strategy on 5 Priority Areas of Uzbekistan Development in 2017–2021, the Public Opinion Research Center "Izhtimoiy Fikr" (Uzbek for "public opinion") conducted a sociological survey on the subject "Judicial and Legal Reform in Public Opinion"[37]. Although this survey was not directly related to Constitutional Court activity, it is relevant for the civil assessment of the judicial system in Uzbekistan. By results of this survey, most of the citizens in Uzbekistan (namely, 89.6 %) noted that measures on reforming the judicial-legal system, taken under leadership of the President, inspire great hopes to strengthening the rule of law, as a main guarantor for the protection of civil rights, freedoms, and legitimate interests and building a democratic, legal state. Along with that, the survey revealed that every third respondent is not fully aware of the main objectives of judicial-legal reform. In this view, issues on developing and putting into practice the effective measures aimed at improving the legal culture of population are of particular relevance.

A total 69.7 % of respondents noted that the positive effect of reform in a judicial-legal system covers many areas of society and state. During the survey, citizens indicated improvements related to ongoing judicial-legal reform: crime prevention, ensuring the rights and regulating the relations in the field of business development, protecting the interests of entrepreneurs, and improving the business climate.

Every third respondent stated they believe that an insufficient level of public awareness about stages of judicial-legal reform and an inappropriate level of legal culture/education are significant obstacles to successful reforms in this field.

The survey showed that 67.1 % of citizens are sure that they can protect their interests and achieve the restoration of violated rights in a legal manner. The monitoring revealed that from 2015 to 2017, the percentage of citizens sure of their ability to restore their legitimate rights and interests remains stable.

So, the results of public opinion research showed that Uzbeks realize the importance of reforms in the judicial-legal system and support the local policy on further democratization of the judicial system, reliable protection of human

37 http://uza.uz and http://pv.uz (accessed: January 21, 2018).

rights/interests, ensuring strict control over meeting constitutional norms on independence of judicial power, and improving the level of civil access to justice.

Effective constitutional justice is the most important criterion of "maturity" in the civil society of a modern state. It ensures necessary functioning of the constitutional system, exercise of relevant forms/methods of arranging the social relations, and priority and strict adherence to constitutional principles/norms. In turn, institutes of civil society promote constitutional justice, protect the Constitution from abuse and violations, and contribute to setting the supremacy of constitutional legality.

Today, in terms of implementing a strategy for the renewal of the country, democratic constitutional norms and values of civil society need relevant protection and development. Society is looking for ways ensuring direct action of each constitutional institute, principle, and norms of the Constitution.

The essence of a democratic state is determined by the degree of exercise for constitutional norms and guarantees of their real protection, which ensure the respect and trust of people to the institute of constitutional justice.

Conclusions

In the past, Uzbekistan formed legal mechanisms for the constitutional review of laws and other normative-legal acts to protect the rights and freedoms of people and citizens. An available constitutional-legal basis enables the further development of constitutional review, an active search for the optimal combination of constitutional review forms, and the improvement of the constitutional-legal proceeding and constitutional justice.

The Constitutional Court seeks to contribute to the development of a democratic social legal state, the formation of a constitutional doctrine, and the deepening and developing of ideas on the content of constitutional values, goals, principles, and norms. The activity of the Constitutional Court aims to exercise the supremacy of the Constitution and establish constitutional legality and constitutionalism.

An analysis of Constitutional Court activity in Uzbekistan shows that current laws, which regulate constitutional justice, need democratization and liberalization. Improving Constitutional Court activity on verifying the constitutionality of laws and subordinate acts adopted in the country is impossible without developing a clear legal mechanism and procedure of constitutional legal proceeding with substantial expansion of its powers. Thus, we consider it necessary:

- to develop/adopt the law of Uzbekistan "On Constitutional Legal Proceeding", which sets clear deadlines and a method of procedural actions for the Constitutional Court;

- to develop a detailed legal mechanism for the submission/review of individual and collective appeals to the Constitutional Court;
- to provide the Constitutional Court with additional powers on reviewing the cases of compliance between the Constitution and the activity of political parties/public movements and the resolution of issues on recognizing them unconstitutional.

Besides, it is necessary to provide the Constitutional Court with additional powers on confirming the results of election for the President of Uzbekistan, the Lower Chamber of Oliy Majlis, and referendum. A review of disputes related to constitutionality of election is referred to the competence of the Supreme Court, although Article 110 of the Constitution strictly refers it to areas of civil, criminal, and administrative proceeding.

Thus, an effective constitutional justice becomes one of the most important criteria for the "maturity" of civil society. It assumes an improvement of relevant forms and methods for the arrangement of legal proceeding.

Constitutional justice is a special form and type of exercising special state powers granted to a specialized body (the Constitutional Court) via constitutional legal proceeding. This is an authoritative court resolution on the issue of constitutionality of laws and other legal acts, exercised in procedural forms prescribed by law (via objective assessment of this issue), passing a binding decision in strict compliance with current legislation.

Jacek Zaleśny and Veniamin Evgenyevich Chirkin

Constitutional Justice in the Post-Soviet States. A Comparative Analysis

Abstract: The subject of the present analysis is a comparison of constitutional judiciary adopted in particular countries of the post-Soviet states. A thesis is put forward that post-Soviet states above all refer to the European model of reviewing legal norms. At the same time, they adapt the model European solutions to their own needs. In this group of countries, the political factor is a more important factor than in a considerable number of European countries (although disputes take place there against this background).

Keywords: constitutional courts in post-Soviet states, the models of legal norms review, autonomy and independence, constitutional courts and other organs of state power, cognition of the constitutional courts

Introduction

Constitutional courts are a standard in the post-Soviet states. Only Kazakhstan selected the Constitutional Council model, close to the French model. Turkmenistan is the only country where there is not a special organ of constitutional control. It has, instead, the rule of the primacy of the parliament, declared by the doctrine (with the actual political preponderance of the president) and the resulting rule of the prohibition of the non-parliamentary review of laws. Consequently, constitutional courts or any other form of constitutional control of the constitutionality of laws (and presidential legislative acts) were not established in Turkmenistan. In all the other states of the region, centralized constitutional courts specialized in controlling the constitutionality of law were established as organs separate from other courts[1]. But in the Constitution of Turkmenistan, there is no principle of the primacy of the parliament, it names only a legislative organ. In other post-Soviet states in their doctrines, the parliaments consider they have priority (also with the actual political preponderance of the president).

At the same time it should be noted that in none of the studied group of post-Soviet states was a decentralized model of controlling the constitutionality of

1 А.А. Клишас, *Конституционная юстиция в зарубежных странах*, Moscow 2004, p. 29.

law adopted where – within the frameworks of settling a concrete case – courts are competent not to apply the regulations of law recognized by itself as inconsistent with the constitution. This is the effect of the belief predominant in the doctrine of those countries, that court judges are appointed to settle individual disputes, while having no duty to affect the law-forming activity of the parliament[2]. This task is entrusted to constitutional courts (now the Constitution of the Russian Federation, 1993 provides for the possibility of direct application by courts of general jurisdiction, if such need arises, for example, as a result of the vagueness of legal norms, but the judge seeking to make direct application of the Constitution must contact Constitutional Court of the Russian Federation).

The idea of the constitutional court became very popular in the process of establishing the political basis of particular countries of the region, above all within the frameworks of adopting republican constitutions in the period of the collapse of the USSR. The constitutional court was expected to strengthen the constitutionality of law[3], and this goal is to a large extent successfully realized.

The political leaders in the post-Soviet republics aiming at independence were aware of the limited effectiveness of the existing Soviet political models. The historical process in the form of the collapse of the USSR and the dysfunctions occurring not only in the sphere of political but also economic or social relations, spoke to their disadvantage. The native, pre-Soviet models, on the other hand, were anachronistic and inadequate to the needs of the contemporary state. In this context, the West European political models associated with democracy and the values of the Council of Europe[4], which were aimed at by a considerable part of the region's countries, seemed attractive and applicable. The universal, scientific and theoretical rules and the practice of countries such as Austria, Germany or Italy, where constitutional courts had been established some ten years before were based on. At the same time, however, attention was drawn to local conditions to avoid establishing an institution inadequate to local needs as a result of a thoughtless replication, but rather to make constitutional

2 Likewise, see: W. Sadurski, *Prawo przed sądem. Studium sądownictwa konstytucyjnego w postkomunistycznych państwach Europy Środkowej i Wschodniej*, Warszawa 2008, pp. 75 ff.

3 Р.М. Мырзалимов, *Органы конституционной юстиции в странах Центральной Азии: проблемы теории и практики. Автореферат диссертации на соискание ученой степени доктора юридических наук*, Moscow 2013, p. 11.

4 For more on this subject, see: J. Jaskiernia, *Влияние Совета Европы на системные изменения в государствах бывшего Советского Союза*, "Studia Politologiczne" 2014, No. 32.

courts fit into the local conditions and as such fulfill the functions they were entrusted with.

Constitutional courts in the post-Soviet states were supposed to create proper conditions for the primacy of the constitution in the system of normative acts and its direct effect on legal relations taking place in the state. Besides, as it was emphasized, it was expected to guarantee the freedom and rights of an individual. The radiation of the constitution onto the whole of legal, political, economic or social relations occurring in the state promotes the stability of the state's political system, the protection of values important for the citizens, especially so because we speak about the citizens of states newly formed on the ruins of the USSR who were filled with fears about their future. To make it happen, proper political conditions were necessary and within them – the control of the new normative acts in the context of their compatibility with the laws of higher legal force, including above all the constitution.

1 Motifs and Key Dilemmas in Introducing the Review of Legal Norms

In the contemporary world, different models of protecting the primacy of the constitution are used, including two, namely the model of dispersed control (the so-called American model of constitutional review of law) and the model of control simultaneously concentrated in the constitutional court and carried out by courts *a casu ad casum* (the so-called European model of constitutional review of law[5]) are of particular relevance. As shown by political practice, they are a point of reference for countries introducing constitutional courts. They are referred to by states building their political system anew which use them as the basis to make the decision on the preferred model of proceedings.

A characteristic feature of the USSR and the republics was the lack of constitutional courts. This followed from the negative attitude of the communist party to the theory of the distribution of power. It was believed in the USSR that the councils of deputies should at the same time perform the functions of legislative and executive powers. The councils, as the only organs of state power (federal, republican and local respectively), were to express the will and interests of all citizens freely and, as a result, no organ could control their acts[6].

5 For more on this, see: Г.Х. Нуриев, *Европеская модель конституционного судопроизводства*, Moscow 2015.

6 Д.А. Керимов, А.И. Экимов, *Конституционный надзор в СССР*, “Советское государство и право” 1990, № 9, p. 4.

Controlling the councils' acts would mean questioning their dominating political role in the system of public power (here, we leave out the motif of relations between the organs of public power and the leading role of the communist party in determining the political system of the state) and thus undermining the rule of democracy. This would mean that there was an organ which was competent to question the legality of the council's activity and reject the expression of its will as the law. Therefore, *de facto* the organ which was not the emanation of the people would stand above the councils and would in itself really become the supreme organ of public power in the sphere of determining the constitutionality or non-constitutionality of laws passed by the councils of people's deputies. It was for these axiologically important reasons, inconsistent with the values and rules of the communist state, and this was why the latter rejected the idea of constitutional review. It was supposed that the parliament (the Supreme Soviet of the USSR) itself would evaluate the constitutionality of laws. In practice, the Presidium of the Supreme Soviet of the USSR (the body elected by the Supreme Soviet) tested the constitutionality of laws in the republics of the USSR. The same procedure applied in the Soviet republics.

Councils of deputies themselves as the highest representative of the citizens' will and interests were supposed to guard the compatibility of laws with the constitution. They were to keep their passed normative acts compatible with the constitution. It was for this reason that attempts undertaken in the years 1924–1933 to entrust the Supreme Court of the USSR with the constitutional review of normative acts in the federal republics and on the federal level were rejected[7]. In this context, differences in the constitutional development of Moldova should be mentioned. The constitutional review of law was for the first time introduced in the territory of Moldova in the years 1918–1949, when a part of Moldova (Bessarabia) was included within the Kingdom of Romania (Румынское княжество). The constitutions of Romania from 1923 to 1938 equipped the Cassation Court with the right to examine the constitutionality of laws and decide on the inapplicability of a norm that was incompatible with the constitution.

The constitution of the USSR from 1936 provided that the Presidium of the Supreme Soviet of the USSR repealed the government's ordinances and laws in the case where they were incompatible with the constitution. According to Art. 121 item 4 of the USSR constitution from 1977, control over adherence to

7 См. подробно: М.А. Митюков, *Судебный конституционный надзор 1924–1933 гг.: вопросы истории, теории и практики*, Moscow 2005.

the regulations of the constitution and coherence of the constitutions and laws of federal republics with the constitution and laws of the USSR were entrusted to the Presidium of the Supreme Soviet of the USSR. A similar mechanism referring to the protection of republican constitutions against republican laws incompatible with the former was provided in some federal republics (e.g. Moldovan).

Modifications in the sphere of securing the primacy of the constitution in the system of the sources of law took place on 1 December 1998. The amendments introduced to the USSR constitution from 1977 stipulated the establishment of the USSR Constitutional Review Committee[8]. In accordance with the law on the USSR Constitutional Review Committee passed in 1989, the effect of recognizing the unconstitutionality of the law was to be the suspension of its binding force, with an exception of legal acts violating fundamental human freedoms and rights[9]. The Constitutional Review Committee took several decisions only (one of which was the abolition of the so-called machinations -«прописка», which limited the choice of human residence permission by organs of executive power). The effect of a limited scope of the effects of the review of legal norms combined with an insufficient attachment to the principle of the rule of law was that the USSR Constitutional Review Committee did not play any significant political role. In particular, it did not become the ancestor of the constitutional court for post-Soviet states. In the process of establishing the constitutions of post-Soviet states and in their search for adequate political models, it did not exert any great influence[10].

At the end of the 1980s, following the model of the USSR, constitutional review committees were also introduced into the republican constitutions (e.g. September 1989 – the Kyrgyz SSR, the Kazakh SSR, October 1989 – the Belorussian SSR[11], March 1990 – Uzbekistan, April 1990 – Tajikistan). Their

---

8 Ведомости Верховного Совета СССР 1988, № 49, Ст. 727.

9 Закон о Комитете конституционного надзора СССР, “Известия”, № 360 от 26 декабря 1989 г.

10 In the latest literature on this subject, see: Б. Страшун, *Эволюция института конституционного контроля в России: от надзора к правосудию. Часть 1*, “Сравнительное конституционное обозрение” 2016, № 1. The activity of the USSR Constitutional Review Committee is assessed differently by О.С. Хромова, *Индивидуальная жалоба в конституционный суд Российской Федерации: диссертация на соискание ученой степени кандидата юридических наук*, Kemerovo 2006, p. 42.

11 In fact, in the Belorussian Soviet Socialist Republic, the Constitutional Review Committee was not created.

members were elected by the supreme republican councils. For the needs of the presidia of the supreme councils, the constitutional review committees were expected to conduct control of compatibility of drafts of laws (and sometimes drafts of other republican normative acts) with the republican constitutions. Hence, they were in fact of auxiliary character, above all in relation to the supreme councils in the process of decision-making. In addition, they protected the primacy of the acts of the supreme councils from their violation by other organs of republican power.

The establishment of a mechanism of protection of republican constitutions gained importance in 1990, when – together with the increasing decomposition of the USSR – particular republics began to create the frameworks of their own statehood and establish the desired system of the relations of power by themselves. During that process, the importance of the protection of the constitution and the need to introduce the system of separation of power and its protection began to be accepted. In that context, the constitutional review of law was supposed to play a significant role. The first of the republics of the former USSR which abolished the Constitutional Review Committee and established a Constitutional Court was Kyrgyzstan. This happened by way of amending the constitution from 14 December 1990. A day later, on 15 December 1990, similar amendments were introduced into the constitution of the Russian Socialist Federative Soviet Republic. The appointment of the Constitutional Court, as the highest organ of judicial protection of the constitution, was provided in Kazakhstan in the constitutional law «On State Independence of the Republic of Kazakhstan» from 16 December 1991. It functioned until 1995, i.e. when the new constitution came into life. A key question was the choice of the model of the constitutionality of law. Reference to another model, namely the French one, prevailed in the model of the constitutional court (modeled on Austrian solutions) which was in progress and, consequently, the constitution from 1995 stipulated the appointment of a Constitutional Council. Significantly, the political system of the Constitutional Council outlined in the regulations of the Constitution was not specified in the law but in the presidential decree on the Constitutional Council of the Republic of Kazakhstan, which had the force of constitutional law[12]. It was issued in a period when the parliament was dissolved. With its name as well as the performed political role, the organ was expected to refer to

12 Ведомости Верховного Совета Республики Казахстан 1995, № 24, Ст. 173.

the French Constitutional Council[13]. An important factor in favor of rejecting the Constitutional Court (for the benefit of the Constitutional Council) were its political entanglements and its inner divisions connected with the former and negatively affecting the effectiveness of the realization of the entrusted tasks[14].

After the events of 3–4 October 1993 in Russia which were connected with antagonistic relations between the Supreme Soviet and the President as well as the active influence of the Constitutional Court on political relations[15], the President suspended the activity of the Constitutional Court[16].

For the first time in this region, the newly passed constitutions of sovereign post-Soviet states provided for the establishment of constitutional courts as specialized organs of the constitutional review of law (Uzbekistan – 8 December 1992; Kyrgyzstan – 5 May 1993; Russia – 12 December 1993; Belarus – 15 March 1994; Moldova – 29 July 1994 r.; Tajikistan – 6 November 1994; Armenia – 5 July 1995; Kazakhstan – 30 August1995 r.; Azerbaijan – 12 November 1995; Ukraine – 28 June 1996). The necessity to form them did not give rise to any greater political controversies. The example of Belarus is characteristic in this respect. On 30 March 1994, during the voting in the Supreme Council on the draft of the law on the Constitutional Court not even one of the deputies voted against that project, and only two abstained.

Together with the strengthening of new, already post-Soviet political systems, the former Soviet republics saw constitutional courts as an important instrument to stabilize the state's political system and to cause a dynamic development of society through securing constitutionality and thus the inner coherence of all the system of law. At the same time, however, attention should be drawn to the main problems, characteristic of the region, which are related

---

13 J. Szymanek, *Ustrój konstytucyjny Kazachstanu*, Warszawa 2013, p. 189. А. Куртов, *Конституционное правосудие в Республике Казахстан и институт выборов*, "Сравнительное конституционное обозрение" 2003, № 2, pp. 171–174.

14 И.Ю. Остапович, *Конституционный Совет Республики Казахстан: вопросы теории и практики: диссертация на соискание ученой степени кандидата юридических наук*, Томск 2005, pp. 59–61.

15 T. Ginsburg, *Judicial Review in New Democracies. Constitutional Courts in Asian Cases*, Cambridge 2003, p. 101.

16 For more on this subject, see: Н.Дж. Браун, Д.Дж. Уоллер, *Конституционные суды и политическая неопределённость: разрыв конституционной преемственности и «правление судей». Часть 1.* "Сравнительное конституционное обозрение" 2017, № 4, pp. 38–39.

to the adaptive ability of constitutional courts. The first one is a typically communist way of viewing the constitution as above all a kind of declaration of political self-determination, a declaration seemingly composed of legal norms but in fact not applied directly and directly having no effect on the actual structure of legal, political or social relations. In communist states the longer the constitutions were in force, the deeper was the discrepancy between their content and political reality. Of course, in the Socialist constitutions there were very important existing provisions reflecting the realities (e.g., dominance of Socialist ownership in the economy or the leadership role of the Communist Party in the political system of totalitarian socialism) but largely they had the character of fictional and superficial constitutions which did not reflect the real system of legal relations. What is more, that was their assumption[17]. Firstly, the legal nihilism developing against this background became a significant part of the political practice in the states of East Europe and as such, it negatively affected the political practice of post-Soviet states. Secondly, the doctrine of communist states was dominated by the rule of the people's power, with the parliament as an organ of the superior power, standing above the other organs of public power. Although together with the collapse of the communist system the rule of the people's power itself lost its political significance, the belief that the parliament, as emanation of the nation, can freely shape legal relations and that in the dispute of law with politics the political will should be given priority did not prevail. This is directly connected with the third danger, namely a limited trust of courts and judges and a fear that courts could try to interfere with the nation's sovereignty articulated by the parliament. This limited social trust in courts and judges is a remainder of the communist relations of power and the courts' and judges' entanglement in it. Therefore, constitutional courts were established in post-communist legal and political relations which did not promote the building of lawful relations of power. That fact did not serve its full reception, but, at the same time, it did not determine the lack of influence of constitutional courts on the protection of the constitutionality of the state's political system. On the other hand, it did mean that the key role in the proper process of the constitutional review of law would be played by the participants of legal and political relations and that it would be a resultant of their decisions.

---

17 For more on this subject, see: J. Szymanek, *Tradycje konstytucyjne. Szkice o roli ustawy zasadniczej w społeczeństwie demokratycznym*, Warszawa 2006, pp. 197 ff.

2 Political Stability of Constitutional Courts

For the post-Soviet states, the constitutional basis of the constitutional courts had the value of stabilization. The decisions concerning the system of constitutional courts and its place in the system of the state's power (except Belarus and Kyrgyzstan) were not subject to change. This does not mean, however, that their status did not undergo any changes at all. It did not remain unchanged. The changes included supplementing the competences of constitutional courts and modifying the procedure of proceedings before them or the legal status of judges. In some countries, e.g. in Russia there were even several changes in the law on constitutional courts. Nevertheless, they were all based on the constitutionally determined model of the constitutional review of law. The first important and current in those changes was extending the competences of constitutional courts with the measures of concrete review of legal norms, i.e. the control taking place in the process of applying the regulations of law and treating an individual case where a constitutional problem appeared as the point of reference. These are the questions of law by courts and the constitutional complaints lodged by citizens or their associations (Azerbaijan). The second group of changes important from the point of view of constitutional courts affecting the state's political system referred to the efficacy of their decisions and their enforceability. It was for this reason that in some post-Soviet states (Armenia, Moldova, Russia) an obligation was placed on their governments to prepare and submit in the parliament the drafts of laws on changing or amending the laws recognized as unconstitutional or which had lost their legal force.

Of key importance for the political significance of the Constitutional Court in the Russian Federation were changes implemented in December 2015. They took place as a consequence of the far-reaching decisions of arbitration courts and the European Tribunal of Human Rights which were unfavorable towards the Russian Federation. Based on the changes from December 2015, the Constitutional Court was authorized to examine questions concerning the possibility of an international judicial organ making a decision against Russia on the basis of an international agreement. Consequently, the Constitutional Court has the power to decide that such decisions are not possible due to their incompatibility with the Constitution. In such a situation, any actions (acts) aimed at making this decision are unenforceable and unapplied. In Belarus, the constitutional referendum from 24 November 1996 proved to be of key importance for the change of the political role of the Constitutional Court. In the decision of 4 December 1996, the Constitutional Court decreed that the referendum on changing and amending the constitution had had no constitutional basis and as such could not be legally binding. The president did not agree with this decision and, by way of a decree, he repealed it and recognized the referendum as valid; the effect of this was that the bodies of state power (with the exception of the President), including the Constitutional Court, were dissolved and formed anew, subordinated to the President[18]. Earlier, in the years 1994–1996, the Constitutional Court had decreed the unconstitutionality of presidential acts many times. The new structure of power relations defined the role of the Constitutional Court in the system of organs of state power anew. The process of limiting the importance of the judicial control of legal norms began. The number of entities competent to initiate review proceedings before the Constitutional Court was reduced significantly. In 1997 the Chairman of the Parliament, permanent parliamentary committees, groups of deputies, the Attorney General, i.e. the entities which most actively turned to the Constitutional Court with a petition to have the compatibility of normative acts with the Constitution examined, were removed from that group. The Constitutional Court was deprived of the right, which it had made use of earlier, to instigate proceedings independently[19]. It also lost the right to participate in the process of holding the president constitutionally accountable (removing him from the office). On the other hand, it acquired the right to decide – on the President's motion – on systematic or significant violation of the Constitution by parliamentary chambers. On this basis, the President is competent to dissolve parliamentary chambers.

The effect of the changes was a radical reduction of the number of cases brought to the Constitutional Court, which resulted in its actual death. In 2008, the phenomenon gave rise to the president's reaction, which was aimed to increase the influence of the Constitutional Court on relations in the state and in society[20]. Unusually for European countries, the President extended the scope of the jurisdiction of the Constitutional Court with the decree (and not a law[21]) from 26 June 2008 «On certain measures aimed to improve the work of

18 The subject is broadly discussed by М.И. Пастухов, *Конституционная юстиция и судебная власть в Республике Беларусь: законодательство и практика*, "Сравнительное конституционное обозрение" 2011, № 4, pp. 124–125.

19 М.И. Пастухов, *Особенности судебного конституционного контроля в Республике Беларусь*, "Studia Politologiczne" 2018, No. 48, p. 34.

20 П.П. Миклашевич, *Развитие конституционного контроля в Беларуси: особенности доктрины и практики*, (in:) В.Д. Зоркин (ed.), *Конституционный контроль: доктрина и практика*, Moscow 2012, p. 253.

21 М.И. Пастухов, *Конституционная юстиция и судебная власть в Республике Беларусь:законодательство и практика*, "Сравнительное конституционное обозрение" 2011, № 4, p. 125.

the Constitutional Court of the Republic of Belarus»[22]. It was obliged to carry out preventive control of the constitutionality of laws passed by the parliament before they were signed by the President. On the President's motion, it is expected to have a preventive control of the constitutionality of international agreements. What is not typical of contemporary countries, on the President's motion the Constitutional Court is to present an official interpretation of presidential decrees and ordinances concerning the constitutional rights, freedoms and duties of the citizens. On the motion of the second chamber of the parliament, it decrees on systematic and significant violations of law by city councils (местные советы). On the motion of the President, parliamentary chambers, Council of Ministers, the Constitutional Court states its position on the documents adopted by other countries, international organizations or their organs and concerning the interests of Belarus, in the context of compatibility of these documents with the commonly binding rules and norms of international law[23].

Compared to the countries of the region, the dynamics of transformations including the Kyrgyz Constitutional Court is not typical[24]. By virtue of the decree by the Provisional Government of the Republic of Kyrgyzstan from 12 April 2010, it was dissolved as not satisfying the political hopes placed in it. This was reflected in not preventing the accumulation of political power in the office of the President. The Constitutional Court approved the constitutional referendum administered by the President which resulted in greater violation of the rule of separation and balance of powers, the consequence of which was intensification of political and social tensions and this, in turn, culminated in the so-called color revolutions taking place in Kyrgyzstan in 2005 and 2010. The dissolution of the Constitutional Court did not mean doing away with constitutional courts as such in Kyrgyzstan. The constitutional review of law was given to a specially formed new chamber of the Supreme Court, namely the Constitutional Chamber of the Supreme Court of the Republic of Kyrgyzstan. Its existence was stipulated

---

22 Нац. реестр правовых актов Респ. Беларусь 2008, № 158, 1/9829.

23 In accordance with this procedure, the Constitutional Court (on the motion of the first chamber of the parliament) decided on 7 April 2011 that the "Polish Card" passed by the Polish parliament violated the commonly binding human rights as far as the possibility of issuing it, rejecting it or annulling it in the territory of Belarus is connected with the decision taken in this respect by an organ of the Republic of Poland.

24 A comprehensive picture of its system is discussed by P.M. Мырзалимов, *Конституционный суд Кыргызской Республики (Конституционные основы организации и деятельности): диссертация на соискание ученой степени кандидата юридических наук*, Moscow 2000.

in the Constitution from 27 June 2010. Nevertheless, due to political problems connected with electing constitutional judges by the parliament, it was not until the middle of 2013 when the Constitutional Chamber was constituted (although still not in its full composition) and it started its judicial activity.

3 The Political Position of Constitutional Courts

Constitutional courts in the post-Soviet states are organs of state power whose political status is determined by the constitutional regulations and made more precise in the regulations in the rank of laws, including constitutional ones. Constitutional courts are constitutional organs separated from other organs of public authority. As constitutional courts of state power, they are placed on one level with other organs of state power such as the president, the parliament, the government and the courts. Within the constitutional separation of powers, they are classified as organs of judicial power (Armenia, Azerbaijan, the Russian Federation, Tajikistan, Uzbekistan), which is interpreted as judicial power also realized by the constitutional judiciary[25]. Exceptions are Kazakhstan[26] and Moldova, where – within the frameworks of the separation of powers – an organ of the constitutional review of law is included neither in the judicial nor any other power[27].

A phenomenon observed in the contemporary world are the conflicts between parliaments and constitutional courts concerning the law-making capacity of parliaments and the competences of constitutional courts to stop them[28]. Democratically elected parliaments, based on the rule of parliamentary majority, are not bound by the rules of rationality[29]. There is no political force

25 К. Макили-Алиев, *Конституционное судопроизводство в Азербайджанской Республике*, "Studia Politologiczne" 2014, No. 32, p. 191; Я. Залесны, *Конституционный суд в системе судебной власти Азербайджанской Республики*, "Studia Politologiczne" 2014, No. 32, p. 204.

26 А.А. Елеупова, *Осуществление конституционного контроля Конституционным Советом Республики Казахстан: диссертация на соискание ученой степени кандидата юридических наук*, Chelyabinsk 2006, p. 52.

27 А. Казаклиу, *Актуальные проблемы конституционной юрисдикции Республики Молдова*, "Сравнительное конституционное обозрение" 2001, № 4, p. 8.

28 In the Ukrainian doctrine, this conflict is drawn attention to by M. Савчин, *Сучасні тенденції конституціоналізму у контексті глобалізації та правового плюралізму*, Uzhgorod 2018, pp. 159–161.

29 Cf. А.А. Клишас, *Конституцинный контроль и конституционное правосудие зарубежных стран*, Moscow 2015, pp. 124–128.

which would make them act rationally and at the same time in agreement with the constitution. Parliaments treat law as an instrument of creating and steering the political, social or economic processes freely, and constitutional regulations are sometimes an obstacle in this. From the point of view of constitutional freedoms and individual rights, democratic governments are a permanent threat. They carry a constant risk of power abuse. It is for this reason, mainly due to the unpredictability of parliaments' power, that constitutional courts are appointed. They are expected to ensure that the laws and acts of lower order will be compatible with the constitution and if they are found incompatible, they will lose their binding force. In this way, the constitutional review of law is treated as a condition necessary for balanced governments to exist. In practice, however, constitutional courts, which were supposed to guarantee the existence of balanced governments based on the principle of separation and balance of powers, became themselves a threat to those values. This threat results from the arbitrariness of the power to judge, which is not bound by the commonly binding and shared techniques of legal interpretation. Based on different techniques of legal interpretation, constitutional courts can arrive at very different settlements, including those which interfere into the policy realized by parliaments. The multitude of competitive and contradictory concepts of the interpretation of the constitution undermines trust in interpretative decisions. Constitutional courts usurp the competences of a superior power, thus breaking the rule of the separation and balance of powers. The process in which constitutional courts interpret constitutional values actually becomes the process of establishing those constitutional values and enforcing them on other participants in political relations. Courts pursue their own policy, thus infringing the competences of parliaments, which gives rise to anti-judicial reactions of parliaments[30].

Expansionism has not been observed in the constitutional courts of the post-Soviet states (with an exception of the years 1992–1993 in the Russian Federation). Consequently, there has been none of the tension between parliaments and constitutional courts that might justify a claim by the participants in political relations that courts abuse their power and illegally interfere into the competences of parliaments (or other organs of state authority) with the aim of realizing their own policy. Certain differences are observed in this respect in Ukraine, where, if the Supreme Council does not approve of the decision of the Constitutional

30 I discuss this problems broadly in: Я. Залесны, *Защита доминирующей роли конституции и разделение власти – спор о методах создания права в современных государствах*, "Studia Politologiczne" 2018, No. 48.

Court, it may again pass a law similar in content to the law recognized by the Constitutional Court as incompatible with the constitution, thus trying to «bypass» the decision of the Court and deprive the latter of its actual importance. And in 2014 (during the revolutionary events) the Ukrainian Supreme Council terminated the appointment of five judges of the Constitutional Court and obliged the President and the Assembly of Judges (Съезд судей) to terminate the appointment of, respectively, two and five other judges. The fact of the Supreme Council terminating the appointment of constitutional judges was a specific kind of reaction to the activity of the President, whose pressure on constitutional judges in 2010 made five of them resign from their office. The Ukrainian, Russian and Belarusian experiences should be treated as a reflection of a lack of comprehensive guarantees of the independence and stability of constitutional courts in a period of political transformations, when the political foundations of an independent states were built. A significant and constitutionally provided effect of the constitutional court on important political process taking place in the state gave rise to processes which were destructive towards the constitutional court and its political limitation[31].

Presidents of Eastern European states are the key entities competent to initiate proceedings on the constitutionality of the review of law although they usually rarely use this right (Armenia, Azerbaijan, Belarus, Kyrgyzstan, Russia, Tajikistan, Uzbekistan). The presidents of Moldova and Kazakhstan submit a motion for the constitutional review of law more often (against the background of the region – typically, a few times a year). On the president's initiative, constitutional courts provide interpretation of constitutional provisions (Azerbaijan, Russia, Uzbekistan). In Kazakhstan and Azerbaijan, constitutional interpretation is also provided on the initiative of the prime minister (Kazakhstan), the government (Azerbaijan), the deputies (Kazakhstan), the parliament (Azerbaijan), courts (Azerbaijan), the Attorney General (Azerbaijan) or the parliament of the Nakhchivan Autonomous Republic. The interpretation provided by the Constitutional Court in Azerbaijan also comprises the laws (on the motion of the courts).

Constitutional courts participate in the procedure of holding the President constitutionally accountable (Azerbaijan, Kazakhstan, Moldova, Russia). They decree on the President's inability to perform his/her duties (Azerbaijan,

31 Cf. Г.Г. Арутюнян, *Конституционный Суд в системе государственной власти. Диссертация на соискание ученой степени доктора юридических наук*, Moscow 1999, p. 30.

Kazakhstan, Moldova) and in 2017 this competence was used by the Moldovan Constitutional Court.

Referring to the French solutions, the organs of the constitutional review of law sporadically decree on the validity of elections (Moldova, Kazakhstan).

4 The Creation of Constitutional Courts, Their Structure and the Legal Status of Constitutional Judges

Legitimation of constitutional judges[32] (like that of court judges) is based on the social trust that they will settle the case entrusted to them in an impartial way, independent of their own interests and the interests of the participants in the proceedings. Without this trust, judging loses its importance and becomes one of the many forms of the activity of the organs of public authority. The special status of constitutional judges is expected to enable them to perform their duties in a professional manner[33].

In the majority of states in the region the legal status of judges of constitutional courts is regulated in constitutional regulations and the laws. From this point of view, Belarus does not adopt typical solutions. There, the legal status of judges is also determined (and such is the practice) by way of presidential decrees and ordinances[34]. The political system of the Kazakh Constitutional Council, and within it, the legal status of the Constitutional Council members, was also specified by way of a presidential decree.

In principle, the legal status of constitutional judges of the post-Soviet states has been established according to the model of court judges. Its leading features follow from the very fact that like in courts, people appointed to judge sit in constitutional courts. Far-reaching consequences follow from this attribute. He who judges, i.e. settles conflicts independently of the background of those conflicts (in the process of law application as in case of court judges, or in the process of law establishment, as in case of constitutional courts) must provide guarantees of objective, impartial adjudgment. It is for this reason that the creation of the

---

32 In Kazakhstan (following the French model), the persons constituting the Constitutional Council are called «members», and not «judges».

33 В.А. Машкин, *Конституционный Суд как институт российского правового го сударства: становление и развитие: диссертация на соискание ученой степени кандидата юридических наук*, Eagle 2002, p. 80.

34 См. подробнее: A. Vashkevich, *Judicial Independence in the Republic of Belarus*, [in:] A. Seibert-Fohr (ed.), *Judicial independence in Transition*, Berlin, Heidelberg, New York: Springer. 2012. pp. 1085–1088.

composition of constitutional courts is conditioned by restrictive requirements set for the candidates for constitutional judges which are, above all, of formal character concerning their professional qualifications. High professional qualifications of constitutional judges are supposed to provide a specific kind of warranty that they will be competent to perform the tasks entrusted to them, on the one hand, and that they will be people of high personal authority radiating to their jurisdiction. The Belorusian code on the judiciary and the status of judges directly stipulates that judges of all kinds of courts have the same legal status and they differ from each other in their realized competences.

In the studied group of countries, the conditions to be fulfilled by candidates to be judges of constitutional courts are determined in a similar manner. In Belarus, constitutional judges are elected from the group of highly qualified specialists in the field of law, who – in principle – have a scientific degree, Belorusian citizenship and a university legal education. They must know both official languages, namely Belarusian and Russian, and have a flawless character (high moral values). They cannot have been sentenced with a valid sentence. They are expected to be of good health and have full public rights. In Belarus, a judge of the Constitutional Court cannot be more than 70 years old. In Uzbekistan, a candidate for a constitutional court must be at least 35 years of age, be a specialist in the field of politics and law and be characterized by high moral qualifications. In Kyrgyzstan, a citizen of at least 40 years of age (likewise: Armenia, Russia) and not more than 70 years of age (likewise: Azerbaijan, Moldova, Russia) with a university legal education who has pursued a legal profession for at least 15 years (likewise: Armenia, Moldova, Ukraine) can be a judge in Kyrgyzstan. In Tajikistan, a candidate for a judge of the Constitutional Court must be a person not younger than 30 years and not older than 65 years of age who has pursued a legal profession for a minimum of 10 years. One of the judges is expected to represent the Kuhistani Badakhshan Autonomous Region. A similar solution to that in Tajikistan or Uzbekistan was not adopted in the other post-Soviet states whose administrative system assumes the autonomy of certain components of the territorial division of the country. In Kazakhstan, a person chosen to be a member of the Constitutional Council must be at least 30 years of age and have an at least 5-year experience in the legal profession. Similar regulations are binding in Azerbaijan and the Russian Federation: in those countries, a candidate for a constitutional judge must have an experience of at least 15 years in a legal profession.

There are different numbers of constitutional judges: 6 (Moldova), 7 (Tajikistan, Uzbekistan), 9 (Armenia, Azerbaijan), 11 (Kyrgyzstan), 12 (Belarus), 18 (Ukraine), 19 (Russian Federation). The Kazakh Constitutional Council is composed of the chairperson and six members but, referring to the French solutions, by virtue of law all former presidents are also its members.

The key role in establishing the personal composition of constitutional courts in post-Soviet states is played by presidents. Even if they do not directly choose the judges, they present candidates for judges to the parliaments for approval. In Belarus, the President independently appoints six judges of the Constitutional Court, while the candidacies for the other six judges to the Council of the Republic (the second chamber of parliament) are presented by the Chair of the Constitutional Court who is appointed by the President with the agreement of the Council of the Republic (in practice, this agreement is given *post factum*). In this way, the President actually establishes the whole personal composition of the Constitutional Court. The President of Belarus relieves the chair and the judges of their offices.

In Russia, the right to present the Council of the Federation (the second chamber of parliament) with the candidates for constitutional judges belongs exclusively to the President. Unusually for the majority of post-Soviet states, during the presidency of B. Yeltsin the Council of the Federation turned down the candidates proposed by him for constitutional judges (this was connected with a political conflict between the President and the parliament). Since the first presidency of V. Putin, no conflicts have occurred on this ground between him and the second chamber of the Federal Assembly. The President of Azerbaijan also has an exclusive right to present candidates for judges to the parliament[35]. In Kazakhstan the President appoints the Chair of the Constitutional Council and its two members and he/she relieves them from office. In Ukraine the President chooses six constitutional judges.

In Kyrgyzstan, the President – on the motion of the Council for the Election of Judges – presents the parliament with candidates for judges of the Constitutional Chamber of the Supreme Court. A similar procedure is applied in Uzbekistan: constitutional judges are appointed by the Senate on the motion of the President from among the candidates recommended by the Supreme Judicial Council. In Tajikistan and Uzbekistan, the Chairman of the Constitutional Court, vice-chairman and judges of the Constitutional Court are chosen by the parliament on the motion of the President. In Kazakhstan, the President chooses the Chairman and two members of the Constitutional Council, while each of the parliamentary chambers chooses two members.

---

35 А.Ш. Будагова, *Конституционный суд Азербайджанской Республики*, [in:] В.В. Маклаков (ed.), *Конституционный контроль в зарубежных странах*, Moscow 2007, p. 598.

In Armenia, the judges are elected by the National Assembly with the majority of at least 3/5 of the statutory composition of deputies. Three judges are elected on the motion of the President, three on the motion of the Government and three on the motion of the General Assembly of Judges. In Azerbaijan, the judges are chosen (and relieved from office) by the parliament, in Uzbekistan – by the second chamber, i.e. the Senate. In Moldova and Ukraine, the appointment of constitutional judges is divided between different bodies of public power[36]. In Moldova, two judges are elected by the parliament, two by the government and two by the Supreme Judicial Council – an organ appointed to guard the independence of judicial power. In Ukraine, three judges are chosen by the highest Council, three by the President and three by the Council of Judges. Due to the factional divisions in the Highest Council, in practice there are problems with this organ electing constitutional judges, which has a negative effect on the ability of the Constitutional Court to effectively examine the cases[37]. In Kazakhstan, two members of the Constitutional Council are chosen on the motion of the chairs of parliamentary chambers by each parliamentary chamber (and the other two as well as the chair – by the president). In Kazakhstan (on the French model) the composition of the Constitutional Council includes former presidents.

In principle, constitutional judges are elected for a term of office[38] which is different from the term of office of the organ which chooses constitutional judges[39]. It lasts for 5 years (Uzbekistan); 6 years (Moldova, Kazakhstan[40]);

36 А.В. Нечкин, *Формы правления в странах Содружества Независимых Государств*, Moscow 2018, p. 166.

37 Cf. М.В. Савчин, *Современное состояние конституционной юстиции в Украине: вызовы и новые решения*, "Studia Politologiczne" 2018, No. 48, p. 18.

38 In Kazakhstan, the former presidents are exceptionally life-long members of the Constitutional Council and there is no practice in this respect.

39 In the Belorussian doctrine a postulate was formulated according to which constitutional judges should be elected by the parliament for the period of its term of office, with the right of reelection. Cf. М.И. Пастухов, *Конституционное правосудие в Республике Беларусь (1994–2014 гг.)*, "Studia Politologiczne" 2016, No. 39, p. 138.

40 In Kazakhstan, every three years, the composition of half of the members of the Constitutional council is renewed according to the principle that the term of office of each of the Council members lasts six years. However, that does not mean that new people are elected to the Constitutional Council. As decided by the Constitutional Council in 2011, the «renewal of the composition of the Constitutional Council» («о бновление состава Конституционого Совета») can be understood as the possibility of choosing new people into the composition of the Constitutional Council who

9 years (Ukraine); 10 years (Tajikistan); 11 years (Belarus), 12 years (Armenia) and 15 years (Azerbaijan). The doctrine emphasizes that changeability of the personal composition of constitutional courts in the countries of the region is supposed to guarantee the dynamics of their jurisdiction and protect against the situation in which the constitutional court would be dominated by the judges symbolizing the relics of the «pre-constitutional epoch»[41]. Against the background of the region, different legal regulations were adopted in Russia, where currently the judges of the Constitutional Court are elected for an indefinite period[42] and it is only the age of 70 which stops them from continuing as judges. A similar legal construction is applied in Kyrgyzstan, the difference being that constitutional court judges perform their function until they are 65 years of age. In Kazakhstan, on the other hand, members of the Constitutional Council can hold their office until the age of 60, and exceptionally 65, with an exception of the former presidents of Kazakhstan, who sit in the Constitutional Council for life.

In some countries of East Europe a repeated election into the composition of the Constitutional Court is allowed, which in the doctrine of law is recognized as weakening the judge's independence. In Azerbaijan, Moldova and Uzbekistan the function of a judge of the Constitutional Court can be held for two terms of office[43]. A repeated election is not forbidden in Belarus. In the Belarusian practice, one of the judges has held his office since 1994, i.e. since the establishment of the Constitutional Court in Belarus.

The period of holding an office has the nature of a guarantee. Apart from ensuring the rotation of the personal composition of the constitutional court, it

---

were not its members before as well as those who performed this function before. Постановление Конституционного Совета Республики Казахстан от 16 марта 2011 г. № 3 «Об официальном толковании нормы абзаца второго пункта 3 статьи 71 Конституци Республики Казахстан». http://ksrk.gov.kz/solutions/np-ks-rk-ot-16032011-g-no3-ob-oficialnom-tolkovanii-normy-abzaca-vtorogo-punkta-3-stati (accessed: January 23, 2018).

41 Н.С. Бондарь А.А. Джагарян, *Правосудие: ориентация на Конституцию*, Moscow 2018, p. 154.

42 Originally, they were elected for a 12-year term of office, with a reservation that a judge may hold his office maximally till the age of 70. In February 2010, a 15-year term of office was introduced without any limitations as to the age but in December of that year the age limitation of 70 at the most was restored. In 2005, the regulations that are now in force were introduced.

43 A similar regulation was included in a previously binding law on the Constitutional Court, according to which the judges of the Constitutional Court were elected for a 10-year term of office and after it ended they could be appointed once again.

makes the legal status of judges stable. It is a legal guarantee of the irremovability of a judge. As long as a judge performs the tasks reliably and in accordance with the regulations law, he/she has a guaranteed function as a judge. In situations established by law, it is allowed to terminate the function of a judge before the end of term. Such situations are enumerated in the regulations of law and these are listed (complete) enumerations. Typically, the powers of a constitutional judge expire when the judge violates the oath of appointment (Uzbekistan), resigns (Moldova, Uzbekistan, Armenia), reaches the maximal age (Kazakhstan, Kyrgyzstan, Russia, Uzbekistan), receives a final sentence against him in criminal proceedings (Armenia, Uzbekistan), undertakes an activity inconsistent with the function of a judge (Armenia, Uzbekistan), is of failing health (Uzbekistan), loses citizenship (Armenia, Uzbekistan), acquires the citizenship of another country (Armenia), is declared to have a limited capacity to act in law or no capacity to act in law (Armenia, Uzbekistan) or he dies (Armenia, Uzbekistan). In Kazakhstan, there is a possibility – apart from the typical reasons to terminate the function of a judge – to terminate the functions of a judge who has not participated in sittings of the Constitutional Council three times without valid reason. The decision on the expiry of the term of office is undertaken by the organ which elected the given member of the Constitutional Council, without applying to the Constitutional Council. In Uzbekistan, the decision is made by the Senate, without the agreement of the Constitutional Court. In Azerbaijan, the President does not need the consent of the Constitutional Court to terminate the function performed by a constitutional judge when the basis of the decision in this matter is the final court sentence on the judge who has committed a tort. In Tajikistan, on the other hand, the decision is made by the first chamber of parliament (Majlisi milli Маджлиси милли) on the initiative of the President.

The above procedure of an earlier end of the function of a constitutional judge should be separated from the legal solutions adopted in Armenia, Belarus and the Russian Federation. In this group of countries, the decision on an earlier end of the function of a constitutional judge is taken by the organ electing the judge, but it does so only on the motion of the Constitutional Court, which is supposed to make the procedure more objective and thus serve the independence of constitutional judges. In Kyrgyzstan, on the other hand, it is the decision of the Council for the selection of judges taken on the initiative of the President. In Ukraine, it is the decision of the Constitutional Court itself but on the condition that the basis is a sentence in a criminal case against the judge where the court declared that the judge committed a tort. In the case where a judge violated the judge's oath, the decision on closing the function of a constitutional judge is made by the Supreme Council. From the point of view of objective proceedings on the early removal of a constitutional judge, a different solution is applied in Moldova. There, the decision of an earlier expiry of the function of a judge is taken by the Constitutional Court itself[44].

An extended list of conditions for a judge to lose the function of a judge was provided by the Belarusian legislator. The function of a judge in Belarus can be ceased before the end of the term of office if the judge resigns, turns 70 years of age, loses Belarusian citizenship, undertakes another economic activity, undertakes an activity incompatible with the function of a judge, fails to observe the restrictions associated with the civil service, seriously violates his duties; a judgment of conviction comes into force, a sentence on declaring the judge to have a limited capacity to act in law or depriving him of the capacity to act comes into force, he loses his ability to hold the function of a judge due to health reasons, or he dies. In Belarus the expiry of the function of a judge is declared by the President on the initiative of the judge concerned, the Constitutional Court or its Chairperson. It happened in Belarus that the judge elected for an 11-year-long period in 1994 was removed from his office due to the «end of his term of office».

In Uzbekistan, the decision to end a judge's powers is taken by the Senate; in Ukraine by the Constitutional Court; and in Armenia by the Constitutional Court, on the initiative of the National Assembly.

Judges of constitutional courts are granted two process privileges: formal immunity and inviolability. In principle, this is a common standard for all judges. A formal immunity and the privilege of inviolability are the judges' special rights. They are supposed to enable them to perform the function of judging in a free way. In Belarus, Azerbaijan, Tajikistan and Uzbekistan a judge's inviolability extends to their accommodation, service space, transport, means of communication, correspondence, possessions and the documents used by them.

The decision on initiating criminal proceedings against a constitutional judge is taken by the Attorney General (Kyrgyzstan, Uzbekistan). In Belarus the decision on initiating criminal proceedings against a judge of the Constitutional Court of the Republic of Belarus is taken by the Attorney General, the Chair of the Investigative Committee of the Republic of Belarus, the Chair of the State Security Committee of the Republic of Belarus or by a person performing his duties after a previous consent of the President (referring to the Chair, Vice-Chair and the judges elected by that president) or after a previous consent of the

44 А.В. Нечкин, *Формы правления в странах Содружества Независимых Государств*, Moscow 2018, pp. 168–169.

Council of the Republic (referring to those judges elected by the Council of the Republic).

In Tajikistan, consent for criminal proceedings against a judge of the Constitutional Court is given by the parliament (like in Kazakhstan, but with the exception of arresting a judge at the scene of a crime or in case of serious or exceptionally serious crimes), and criminal proceedings are continued before the Supreme Court. In Ukraine, consent is given only by the Constitutional Court. In Azerbaijan, in the case where the court declares that a judge of the Constitutional Court committed a crime, the President, on a motion by the Supreme Court, can apply to the first chamber of the parliament to have the judge removed from office.

In principle, in the countries of the region judges cannot be arrested, detained or deprived of their freedom in any other way except when they are caught red-handed. In this respect, a wider range of freedom limitations is applied in Belarus, where the judges cannot be arrested, detained or deprived of freedom in any other way without the previous consent of the President (respectively, the Council of the Republic), with the exception of not only being caught red-handed but also in the case of committing high treason. The Chair of the Constitutional Court is immediately informed of the arrest of the judge.

In Belarus, the prosecution of judges on private accusation is not permissible except when the judge is caught red-handed.

The separation of constitutional courts from other entities and their independence towards the latter require not only functional and organizational separation but personal separation as well. A prohibition to combine the function of a judge with certain other positions and forms of activity is necessary. Judges cannot pursue economic activity personally or by means of others, nor can they help run such an activity. Whether directly or indirectly, they cannot participate in managing an entity pursuing economic activity. A judge of the Belarusian Constitutional Court cannot accept pecuniary benefits, except presents received in the situations provided for in the protocol and in other official events. In Kyrgyzstan, even such gifts have to be passed on to the Supreme Court, but the judge has priority in purchasing them.

Judges of constitutional courts are not allowed to belong to political parties or pursue any kind of political activity. The legislations of Belarus and Kyrgyzstan directly provide that judges cannot participate in strikes or any public gatherings (Kyrgyzstan).

Judges cannot pursue any other paid activity not related to their function as a judge, except for didactic, scientific or creative activity. In Belarus, cultural activity and medical practice are also exempted. Additional activity can be pursued by judges with the consent of the Chair of the Constitutional Court (Belarus) or with the consent of the Chair of the Constitutional Chamber of the Supreme Court – Kyrgyzstan.

A Belarusian judge cannot have an account in a foreign bank. Without the President's consent he cannot accept any national awards of other countries. In Kyrgyzstan, to accept such awards a judge needs the consent of the Council of Judges of the Kyrgyz Republic. In Ukraine, on the other hand, a judge cannot accept any Ukrainian awards or national distinctions except awards for personal bravery and heroism in conditions connected with a threat to life.

Guarantees of the judges' independence are accompanied by material guarantees in the form of adequate remuneration. In Belarus, emoluments of the Vice-Chair of the Constitutional Court and the judges of the Constitutional Court are, respectively, 90 % and 85 % of the emolument of the Chair of the Constitutional Court, while the emolument of the latter is established by the President and it is not published. This is not a typical solution in comparison with other countries of the region.

Of significance are also the material guarantees of a judge's independence which are applicable after the judge's function stops. After the term of office finishes, the judge has the right to return to a previously occupied post, and if this proves impossible – an equivalent one (Moldova, Tajikistan). A former judge of the Russian Constitutional Court receives 80 % of the emolument of the judge in office of the Constitutional Court. In Russia, a judge leaving an office that has been held for at least 15 years receives a pension of the monthly emolument of a Constitutional Court judge.

An important guarantee of a judge's independence is the possibility to present a dissenting opinion (*votum separatum*) towards the sentences and decisions of the constitutional court.

5 Functions of Constitutional Courts

Two distinct functions of constitutional courts predominate in the doctrine of post-Soviet states: 1) protection of the supremacy of the constitution in a hierarchical order of normative acts, and 2) protection of the constitutional freedoms and rights of an individual[45]. To this can be added the third function: support of the balance of powers, the Center and places authorities and local selfgoverment, but this still needs more research.

45 Cf. А.Н. Пугачев, *Судебный конституционной контроль: учеб.-метод. комплекс для магистрантов юрид. спец.*, Novopolotsk 2009, p. 85.

The hierarchical constitutional review of law is especially important in compound (federal) states, where – like in the Russian Federation – the constitutions of their components (such as the entities of the Russian Federation) and the laws of their components are binding, alongside the federal constitution and the federal laws. A similar importance is attached to the vertical control of the constitutionality of law in the countries where (like in Azerbaijan) certain regions enjoy autonomy and, within the latter, an autonomous system of the organs of public power and an autonomous system of the establishment of law for a given region, which law must at the same time be the state law and this is achieved by the constitutional judiciary, among other things.

In this respect, the most comprehensive definition of the functions of constitutional courts, which expresses the essence of their goals, was formulated in Belarus. According to the Belarusian code on the system of courts and the status of judges, the Constitutional Court is appointed to protect the constitutional system of Belarus, the constitutionally guaranteed rights and freedoms of persons and citizens, secure the supremacy of the Constitution and its direct application in the territory of Belarus, the compatibility of normative acts of state bodies with the Constitution, and ensure legality in law creation and application.

An additional feature typical of the countries of the region (rarely established for constitutional courts in the countries of Western Europe[46]), which serves the coherence of the constitutional system of the state, is interpretation of constitutional regulations. It is realized by constitutional courts in Azerbaijan, Moldova, Russia, Uzbekistan and Ukraine as well as by the Constitutional Council in Kazakhstan. For the latter, it is the key aspect of its activity. The Council has provided interpretation of constitutional regulations more than 80 times. In some states of the region, constitutional courts take part in the process of changing the constitution. For amendments to the constitution to be adopted by the parliament or submitted to a referendum, they are sometimes submitted to review by constitutional courts concerning the proper course of their adoption (Moldova). The constitutional courts of Azerbaijan and Moldova perform the function of securing compatibility of the most important political events taking place in the country with the constitution. Within this function, in some countries they declare the validity of the national referendum as well as the validity of presidential and parliamentary elections. They also state the existence of reasons to dissolve the parliament or remove the president from his office.

46 И.А. Кравец, *Конституционное правосудие: теория судебного конституционного права и практика судебного конституционного процесса*, Moscow 2017, p. 63.

6 The Subject of the Review by the Constitutional Court

The principal function of constitutional courts is to ensure the hierarchical order of normative acts, while in a narrower (supplementary) scope also the acts of law application – activities of the bodies of the state authority. Normative acts are submitted to control from the point of view of their compatibility with an act of law occupying a higher place in the hierarchy of the sources of law. The notion of a review of legal norms assumes indicating both the models of the review and the subject of the review. The major model of control and the point of reference in the process of verifying the constitutionality of law is the constitution itself. The criteria of control, on the other hand, are the content of the normative act, the competence to adopt it, as well as the procedure of adopting the normative act. These three criteria can be applied independently of each other, and the violation of any is a sufficient premise to find the normative act unconstitutional.

The subjects of control include above all the laws (in Kazakhstan, in principle only, before they are signed by the President), the executive acts under them (above all, ordinances - постановления) and the government's resolutions. In some countries, acts of executive power are checked by the supreme courts of these countries. In Belarus, these subjects of control include also laws on amendments and additions to the Constitution and laws imposing them in action, policy laws, which include laws on the main directions of domestic and foreign policy of the Republic of Belarus and laws on military doctrine as well as laws on the interpretation of the Constitution. Presidential decrees, which are of normative character and the force of laws (like in Russia), are also subject to control. Significantly, they have never been subject to court control of their compatibility with the Constitution. In Belarus, presidential directives, i.e. acts of law of program character issued by the president with the aim of systemically regulating issues of political, social or economic priority, are also subject to the competences of the Constitutional Court. Concerning these acts, there is no practice to control their compatibility with the Constitution. The Belarusian Constitutional Court is competent to declare the compatibility of the resolutions of the plenum, resolutions of the Supreme Court and the Highest Economic Court (like the Constitutional Court in Tajikistan) and the acts of the Attorney General with the Constitution. It can examine the constitutionality of acts passed by the parliamentary chambers, laws and recommendations of the organs of state authority – ministers, state committees and other offices, the central bank, resolutions of local councils of deputies, executive and administrative organs, as well as other normative acts passed by state bodies. A wide range of acts of law controlled by the Constitutional Court follows from the fact that in

Belarus a separate administrative judiciary was not distinguished and, therefore, the Constitutional Court is supposed to perform certain competences with the character of administrative courts.

Control over the constitutionality of international agreements and law-making acts of international organizations was included within the competences of constitutional courts (Belarus). In Kyrgyzstan, control is exercised over international agreements which have not come into effect (likewise in Azerbaijan, Moldova, Russia and Tajikistan), in Uzbekistan there is control over laws on the ratification of international agreements before they are signed by the President, while in Kazakhstan there is control over international agreements before their ratification by the parliament.

In Armenia, Kyrgyzstan and Tajikistan, there is control over the compatibility of draft amendments with the constitution. In Tajikistan draft projects of issues submitted to a referendum are subject to the control of compatibility with the Constitution. Presidential decrees are subject to the control of compatibility with the Constitution in Uzbekistan.

Some constitutional courts are competent to check the compatibility of acts of local law with the Constitution (Azerbaijan, Belarus, Tajikistan, Uzbekistan). The Constitutional Court in Ukraine, on the other hand, is competent to review the constitutionality not only of normative acts but individual acts of law[47] as well.

In Belarus, the subject of control also includes acts passed both before and after the Constitution from 1994 came into force, including those adopted in the Soviet period. In Moldova only those normative acts which were issued after the Constitution from 1994 came into life are subject to control.

On the substance, binding normative acts are included within control. The constitutional court discontinues proceedings if the reviewed normative act loses its binding force. There is an exception in Belarus, where proceedings are not discontinued if based on a given act, citizens' constitutional rights and freedoms are violated, or when a new act of law has been adopted on the same subject of regulation which excludes the possibility of examining the case. In such a situation, the Constitutional Court is competent to examine the meritum of the case and settle the constitutional dispute.

An important role in the mechanism of realizing the constitution is played by the proper interpretation of legal norms included in it. A legally binding

---

47 В. Шаповал, *Статус Конституционного Суда Украины в контексте принципа разделения властей,* (in:) *Конституционный Суд как гарант разделения властей. Сборник докладов,* Moscow 2004, p. 145.

interpretation of the constitution presented by the constitutional court enables its internally coherent application, proper fulfillment of constitutional assumptions, values and principles of which the constitution is the carrier. It aims to limit the risk that in the process of the application of the constitution interpretative dilemmas unsolvable in practice appear which would have a negative effect on the coherence of the state's system of law. This type of risk is minimized by case law, which is interpretative towards the constitution. It also minimizes the risk that the effect of the wrong interpretation of constitutional norms will be that law-making organs will issue normative acts incoherent with it[48]. The Russian Constitutional Court has competence to interpret the Constitution (as used in practice).

The subject of constitutional review, which is not typical of the states of the former USSR, is the control of the activity of the organs of public authorities. The Belarusian Constitutional Court can decide on systematic or significant violation of the Constitution by the chambers of the National Assembly and legal requirements by the local councils of deputies. There is no practice in this respect. All resolutions by the Parliament (both normative ones and those of individual character) are subject to control by the Constitutional Council of the Republic of Kazakhstan.

In Armenia, the Constitutional Court decides on the validity of a referendum (likewise in Kazakhstan, but only in the case of a dispute against this background), parliamentary and presidential elections (also in Kazakhstan, but only in the case of a dispute against this background), on the expiry of the mandate of a deputy, the basis to remove the President from office and the President's incapacity to fulfill his/her competences[49]. In Tajikistan the Constitutional Court takes a decision (принимает заключения) on the President committing high treason. In Russia and Kazakhstan, it decides on the correct nature of parliamentary proceedings on the impeachment of the President; in Ukraine on impeachment of the President, Prime Minister and the other members of the government, the Chair of the Supreme Court, the Chair of the Supreme Court of Arbitration, the Attorney General, as well as diplomatic and other representatives of Ukraine.

The Constitutional Court of Armenia decides on the suspension or prohibition of the activity of political parties. It examines conflicts of competence between

48 С.Э. Несмеянова, Т.Я. Хабриева, *Подведомственнось дел*, (in:) М. С. Саликов (ed.), *Конституционный судебный процесс*, Moscow 2004, p. 64.

49 Г.А. Шмавонян, *Конституционное правосудие Армении в системе разделения властей: диссертация на соискание ученой степени кандидата юридических наук*, Moscow 2000, pp. 146–148.

the constitutional organs which arose in connection with their constitutional competences. In Azerbaijan and Tajikistan, it settles conflicts of competences between state bodies. In the Russian Federation, these are conflicts of competences between the organs of state authorities and the organs of the entities of the Russian Federation.

In principle, and this is typical of the contemporary constitutional judiciary, the review of constitutional courts does not include individual acts of law. These are controlled by courts of general jurisdiction and specialized courts.

7 Prevention and Ex-post Control of Legal Norms

The countries of Eastern Europe adopt the European model of constitutional courts based on the *ex-post* (repressive) compatibility of laws with the Constitution. It is the predominant form of law review. It is assumed that it is only in the process of law application that the whole of effects associated with the application of a given regulation of law can be seen. Additionally, preventive control of legal norms is admissible. In Armenia, before a law is signed, the President is competent to submit a motion to the Constitutional Court to have its compatibility with the Constitution checked. Referring to the French model of the constitutional review of law, the Kazakh Constitutional Council is an organ focused on the preventive control of the compatibility of law with the Constitution and aimed to prevent constitutionally questionable laws from being introduced into the legal order. For this reason the Constitutional Council examines laws passed by the parliament before they are signed by the president. In principle, on the other hand, the *ex-post* control of the compatibility of laws with the Constitution is not allowed. It is only exceptional that the President is competent to apply to the Constitutional Council for an abstract examination of the compatibility of a law with the Constitution. The President can suspend the action of any act of law, except constitutional laws, the Code and law on the Constitutional Council, with the aim to protect the rights and freedoms of persons and citizens, secure sovereignty, territorial integrity of the state and national security. In these cases, the Constitutional Council examines the constitutionality of the binding legal acts.

Only the *ex-post* control of the compatibility of law with the Constitution was realized by the Constitutional Court in Belarus until 2008. As a consequence, it decided on the compatibility (incompatibility) of the reviewed act with the Constitution. Together with the political changes in the state, this control lost its importance and, with time, it disappeared. This resulted from the fact that the law-making process in the country was subordinated to the President as an organ which coordinates and harmonizes the activity of all organs of public authority and eliminates the discrepancies between them. The president became the single organ which defines the strategy of the state's development and sees to its realization, also in the sphere of legislative issues in practice. This meant that not even one motion for the constitutional review of law was submitted to the Court. This resulted from the fact that the President resolved any doubts concerning the constitutionality of the new law. Finding out the passivity of the *ex-post* constitutional review of law, in 2008 the President changed (significantly, by way of a decree) the scope of competences of the Constitutional Court and supplemented the *ex-post* control of laws with preventive (prior) control of laws. All laws, before they are signed by the president, are subject to constitutional review. The Constitutional Court has five days to perform this duty. Although *ex-post* review of the compatibility of laws with the Constitution has not been liquidated, in practice it does not exist. During the 10 years of the existence of the preventive constitutional review of laws, the Constitutional Court has submitted more than 850 laws to control and it recognized all of them as compatible with the Constitution.

The constitutional review of international agreements differs from the *ex-post* review of law predominating in the studied region. Due to their double force (in the national as well as the international law) attention is drawn to avoiding any risk associated with an agreement incompatible with the Constitution. Therefore, in this scope of cognition of constitutional courts, core importance is attached to the control of the compatibility of agreements with the Constitution. They are examined before they are implemented in the legal order of the state, i.e. at the stage preceding the moment when the state is bound by a given international agreement. This type of mechanism of preventing collisions between constitutional norms and those of international law was applied in Armenia, Azerbaijan, Kyrgyzstan, Russia, Tajikistan and Uzbekistan. In Armenia, it is obligatory. In Ukraine, on the other hand, both preventive and *ex-post* constitutional reviews of international agreements is provided for.

The mechanism of preventive constitutional review is applied in reference to draft laws on amending the constitution (Armenia, Azerbaijan, Kazakhstan, Kyrgyzstan, Tajikistan).

Independently of the model of abstract constitutional review of law (*ex-post* vs. preventive) adopted in a given country, the majority of states which were created as a result of the collapse of the USSR also apply concrete constitutional review of law, i.e. the control taking place in the process of the application of the regulations of law whose point of reference is a specific case and the constitutional issue occurring in it. In this type of case, if it refers to the applied regulations of law, this means that these are binding regulations. Therefore, this is *ex-post* constitutional review of law but having a narrow application – exclusively to the acts of law applied in a specific, and hence constitutionally problematic, case.

8 The Procedure of the Constitutional Review of Laws

The procedure of the constitutional review of law is a separated one, independent towards other court and administrative proceedings. All of it is conducted before the constitutional court. The proceedings on the constitutional review of law are sequential. It is composed of submitting a motion for an examination of the compatibility of a normative act with the constitution, preparation for the examination of the case, the main proceedings and the implementation of the decision.

To allow the constitutional court to affect the state's system of law, it is important to identify who has the right to initiate proceedings before it[50], how developed and differentiated the circle of subjects may be and how dependent it is on one decision-making body. Three basic courses of proceedings are distinguished. The first one includes the abstract constitutional review of law, and it is realized independently of the application of a constitutionally questionable regulation. The other two procedures of examining the compatibility of the regulations of law with the Constitution, on the other hand, refer to the specific constitutional review of a law. They adopt the constitutionally objectionable legal regulation applicable in a specific case as the point of reference. The queries of courts and the complaints of the citizens (or, possibly, also other entities of private law) are of a concrete nature.

The circle of entities competent to apply to the constitutional court with an abstract motion to have the compatibility of an act of law with the constitution examined is formed in different ways. In Kyrgyzstan, right of application is given to the parliament, fractions of deputies to the parliament, the President, the Government, the Prime Minister, the Attorney General, the Ombudsman, as well as local self-government bodies. A motion for preventive examination of compatibility with the Constitution can be lodged by the parliament, fractions of deputies to the parliament, the President, the Government and the Prime Minister. The initiative to apply for the examination of the constitutionality of a draft law on an amendment to the Constitution, on the other hand, is limited

50 В.В. Маклаков, *Конституционный контроль в зарубежных странах*, (in:) В. В. Маклаков (ed.), *Конституционный контроль в зарубежных странах*, Moscow 2007, p. 63.

to the parliament, fractions of deputies to the parliament, the President, the Government, and the Ombudsman.

In Moldova, the right to apply to the Constitutional Court for the constitutional review of legal regulations belongs to the President, the Government, the Minister of Justice, the Highest Judicial Chamber, the Attorney General, a deputy to the parliament, the parliamentary fraction, the People's Advocate, the People's Advocate for Children's Rights, local resolution-making organs and the People's Assembly of Gagauzia. Otherwise in other countries of the region, their legitimation to appeal from the normative act is materially limited. They can only appeal in cases concerning their competences. In Moldova, a special circle of entities possessing the right to appeal to the Constitutional Court is applied in relation to a draft amendment to the Constitution.

In Uzbekistan, the right to file a motion to the Constitutional Court to examine a case belongs to Oliy Majlis, the Senate (the first and second chambers of the parliament), at least one-fourth of the deputies, at least one-fourth of the senators, the President, the Cabinet of Ministers, the Authorized Person of the Olij Madżlisu for Human Rights, the Jokargi Kenes of the Republic of Karakalpakstan, the Supreme Court and the Attorney General. Unlike most of the post-Soviet states, at least three judges of the Constitutional Court also possess this right.

A wider circle of subjects is provided for in Kazakhstan. The President, the Chair of the Mazhilis (the first chamber of parliament), at least one-fifth of the statutory composition of deputies of the parliament and Prime Minister can file a motion to the Constitutional Council.

In Tajikistan and Uzbekistan, the Constitutional Court can examine a case on its own initiative.

In the states of Eastern Europe, courts are a subject legitimated to apply to a court. To this aim they use a question of law (constitutional question). Its subject is broader than the subject of control conducted within the constitutional complaint. It does not only include a suspected violation of constitutional freedoms or rights of the party in the proceedings but also a suspected violation of any other provision of the constitution[51]. A question of law has the character of a concrete measure to control the constitutionality of law. It can be posed only by that court before which the proceedings take place, within the framework

51 Н.А. Марокко, *Функция защиты основных прав и свобод человека и гражданина в контексте реализации полномочий Конституционного Суда Российской Федерации: диссертация на соискание ученой степени кандидата юридических наук*, Moscow 2009, p. 52.

of which a constitutional problem arose. A question of law in the Russian Federation can be posed by a court of any kind (of either general or special jurisdiction) and any instance, if the constitutionally questionable legal regulation has already been applied in the case under examination or if such a regulation is expected to be applied in the case[52]. For the period when the Constitutional Court is examining a question of law, it suspends all proceedings taking place. In this way, it limits the risk of making an unconstitutional regulation in the legal basis of the case settled by it. Due to the concrete character of the question of law, a premise for directing it to the constitutional court is that the questioning court must prove that the settlement of the case within which the constitutional question is formulated depends on the answer to the question. Therefore, there must be a relation between the question of law and the settlement of the case in front of the questioning court. The questioning court is obliged to prove this premise. If the constitutional court considers that the answer to the question is of no significance for the settlement of the case, the substance of the question is not examined.

In a narrow sense, the proceedings before the constitutional court can be initiated by physical persons and similar legal entities of private law. They have to prove their legal interest in settling the problem of the constitutionality of a normative act. Hence, in the post-Soviet states a general complaint is not applicable; it can be formulated by anybody who sees the incompatibility of a legal regulation with the constitution, independently of whether this regulation is applicable to it or not.

The rule is that constitutional courts are bound by the scope of the motion filed. The other wordings in the decision of a Constitutional Court are considered to be *obiter dictum*. They decree on the compatibility of those regulations which were questioned by the mover with the Constitution. In this aspect, Uzbekistan adopted solutions which are not typical of the countries of Eastern Europe. While addressing the constitutionality of a normative act, the Constitutional Court can also undertake to settle the normative acts based on the reviewed normative act or those copying its decisions despite the fact they were not mentioned in the motion submitted to the Constitutional Court.

The proceedings before constitutional courts in the countries established as a result of the collapse of the USSR were regulated according to the proceedings

52 О.В. Брежнев, *Судебный конституционный в России: проблемы методологии, теории и практики: диссертация на соискание ученой степени кандидата юридических наук*, Moscow 2006, p. 119.

before courts. They apply such principles of court proceedings as legality, judges' independence, collegiality of adjudication, public nature of the hearing, free assessment of evidence, secret nature of judicial deliberations and openness of the decisions. The presumed compatibility of the reviewed act of law with the constitution is applicable[53].

The issue of the term of recognition of the motion is solved differently. The Constitutional Council in Kazakhstan is expected to examine the case within a month of filing. On the President's request, this term can be made shorter to 10 days if the matter is urgent. In Belarus, within the preventive review of the constitutionality of laws, the Constitutional Court examines the case within five days of the law being submitted. Within the frameworks of *ex-post* control, on the other hand, this term cannot be longer than three months from the day the proceedings before the Court began. Due to the special complexity or the ample scope of the case, the Chair of the Constitutional Court can extend this term, but not by longer than one month. Cases concerning the preventive examination of the compatibility of an international agreement with the Constitution are recognized by the Court within a month of it being brought. The terms of examining other categories of cases are determined by the Constitutional Court but cannot be longer than six months after the beginning of the proceedings.

The Constitutional Court in Uzbekistan must make its decisions within three months of the case being brought. The Constitutional Chamber of the Supreme Court in Kyrgyzstan is required to examine the motion within five months. By the decision of the Chair of the Constitutional Chamber, this period can be extended by one month. In Ukraine the period is six months.

Decisions issued by the constitutional court are final and without appeal or other remedy, whether within the constitutional court or another organ of public authorities. They are not subject to change by the parliament or the President; however, in Belarus the President rejects the decision of the Constitutional Court and the President's will becomes the binding law.

9 The *Action Popularis* as a Measure to Control the Legal Norms

The abstract control of legal norms, as the main aspect of the activity of constitutional courts for which they were appointed, is supplemented with measures of

53 The essence of presumed compatibility of the reviewed normative act with the constitution is broadly discussed by M. Dąbrowski, *Domniemanie zgodności ustaw z Konstytucją Rzeczypospolitej Polskiej z 1997 roku*, Olsztyn 2017.

specific control of legal norms, i.e. a constitutional complaint and a question of court. The constitutional complaint is possible for an individual (and sometimes for a legal person) to apply directly to a Constitutional Court. Such complaints are especially important from the point of view of one of the functions of constitutional courts, namely the control of the constitutional freedoms and rights of persons and citizens. From the point of view of an individual, it is essential that no regulations incompatible with the constitution should be applied in their case. Politically, equipping the constitutional court with the right to examine a constitutional complaint changes its character from an organ of constitutional arbitration between the organs of public authorities into an organ of the constitutional judiciary which settles disputes taking place between the citizens and the organs of public authorities[54].

It is provided in some countries of the region (except Belarus, Kazakhstan[55], Kyrgyzstan[56], Moldova and Uzbekistan) that – after definite conditions are satisfied – an individual can also apply to the constitutional court with a complaint to find out if their constitutional freedoms or rights have been violated. The circle of entities possessing such a right and the conditions which have to be fulfilled by the complainant before the constitutional court undertakes to examine their complaint are determined in different ways.

The constitutional complaint is another means to protect individual freedoms and rights in Russia. Annually several thousands of entities of private law apply to the federal Constitutional Court under this procedure. Based on complaints about the violation of citizens' constitutional rights and freedoms, the Constitutional Court examined the compatibility of the law applied in a specific case with the Constitution[57]. The subject of constitutional complaints are the citizens, broadly understood as associations of citizens[58] as well as other entities

---

54 Cf. В. Кампо, *Проблемы и перспективы развития украинской модели конституционной юстиции*, "Сравнительное конституционное обозрение" 2011, № 3, p. 156.

55 In Kazakhstan, the citizens possessed and used this means to protect their constitutional freedoms and rights in the period when the Constitutional Court existed.

56 In Kyrgyzstan, the citizens possessed this right till 2003.

57 С.Э. Несмеянова, Т.Я. Хабриева, *Подведомственнось дел*, (in:) М.С. Саликов (ed.), *Конституционный судебный процесс*, Moscow 2004, p. 58.

58 For more on this subject, see: С.В. Нарутто, *Обращение граждан в Конституционный Суд Российской Федерации: Научно-практическое пособие*, Moscow 2011, pp. 174–187. Е. Герасимова, *Конституционная жалоба как полномочие Конституционного Суда России и Федерального конституционного суда Германии: сравнительно-правовой анализ*, "Сравнительное конституционное обозрение" 2010, № 4,

of private law (such as legal persons). Concerning the associations of citizens, the matter refers both to the freedoms and rights of members of those associations and the associations themselves[59]. In the 2002 resolution of the Constitutional Court, local associations (acting via self-governing bodies) were recognized as the subject of a constitutional complaint and treated as territorial associations of citizens[60]. A complaint can be filed both individually and collectively. The complaint filed collectively should refer to the violation of constitutional rights of each of the persons filing it. It is not necessary to exhaust all court proceedings, i.e. it is not necessary to obtain the final court settlement. In Russia, the decision of the court of first instance is sufficient to lodge a constitutional complaint. At the same time, the application of two legal measures simultaneously, namely filing a constitutional complaint to the Constitutional Court and appealing against the sentence of the court to the court of higher instance is not ruled out. The subject of the appeal can only be federal laws (including constitutional ones) as well as the constitutions and laws of the entities of the Russian Federation if they violate the freedoms and rights of the complainant included in the federal Constitution. In practice, within this procedure, the Constitutional Court also examines the constitutionality of normative acts of the President and the Government if there is a direct relation between them and the law and if in a given case they were applied together with the law[61]. For the complaint to be examined by the Constitutional

---

p. 90. П. Блохин, *Двойной юбилей. Конституционное правосудие на службе прав человека*, "Сравнительное конституционное обозрение" 2016, № 2, p. 136.

59 О.С. Хромова, *Индивидуальная жалоба в конституционный суд Российской Федерации: диссертация на соискание ученой степени кандидата юридических наук*, Kemerovo 2006, p. 107.

60 Постановление Конституционного Суда РФ от 02.04.2002 г. N 7-П "По делу о проверке конституционности отдельных положений Закона Красноярского края "О порядке отзыва депутата представительного органа местного самоуправления" и Закона Корякского автономного округа "О порядке отзыва депутата представительного органа местного самоуправления, выборного должностного лица местного самоуправления в Корякскском автономном округе" в связи с жалобами заявителей А. Г. Злобина и Ю.А. Хнаева", Собрание законодательства РФ 2002, № 14, Ст. 1374. This decision of the Constitutional Court is broadly discussed by А.В. Чаптыков, *Субъекты права на обращение в Конституционный суд Российской Федерации: проблемы теории и практики: диссертация на соискание ученой степени кандидата юридических наук*, Abakan 2007, pp. 108–109.

61 Н.А. Марокко, *Функция защиты основных прав и свобод человека и гражданина в контексте реализации полномочий Конституционного Суда Российской Федерации: диссертация на соискание ученой степени кандидата юридических*

Court, the complainant has an obligation to prove that the challenged law is or was applied in their case. While the decision of the Constitutional Court on the unconstitutionality of the reviewed normative acts results in their elimination from the system of the sources of law, the effectiveness of a constitutional complaint towards the protection of the complainant's constitutional rights can be problematic. Even when the Constitutional Court has acknowledged that the complainant is justified, this does not mean an automatic change of the act of law whose application is based on the unconstitutional legal regulation. Such a decision of the Court is the basis for examining it once again before the competent body of public authority, in accordance with the procedure required[62].

In Ukraine, the right to a constitutional complaint belongs to anybody who states that in their finally closed case the court applied a law incompatible with their constitutional freedoms or rights or that the law compatible with the Constitution was applied by the court in a way contradicting the constitutional freedoms or rights of the complainant.

The constitutional complaint was introduced into the Armenian legal order in 2005. At present (after the Constitution was changed in 2015) it can be used by anybody in whose finally closed case the court applied a legal regulation violating their fundamental rights and freedoms (основные права и свободы) guaranteed in Chapter 2 of the Constitution ("Fundamental Rights and Freedoms of the Human Being and the Citizen") or it presented an interpretation of the regulations of law which was incompatible with them.

Citizens, legal persons (as entities of private law) in Tajikistan can appeal to the Constitutional Court against a legal regulation which was applied by a body of public authority (including the court) in their case and which raises constitutional objections.

In Azerbaijan, everybody can appeal to the Constitutional Court against normative acts of the organs of the legislative and the executive powers and acts of the municipal authorities and courts which violate their rights and freedoms with the aim to have the violated human rights and freedoms restored. Prior to this,

---

наук, Moscow 2009, p. 56. Е.В. Герасимова, *Роль Конституционного суда Российской Федерации в системе судебной защиты прав и свобод человека и гражданина: диссертация на соискание ученой степени кандидата юридических наук*, St. Petersburg 2011, pp. 52–53.

62 This aspect is emphasized by Е.В. Батеева, *Законность и конституционная юстиция в современной России: диссертация на соискание ученой степени кандидата юридических наук*, Moscow 2003, p. 118.

they must use the legal measures available in court proceedings and obtain the sentence of the Highest Court[63]. An appeal can be lodged to the Constitutional Court within six months of the sentence of the Supreme Court being delivered, or within three months of the complainant's right to a fair trial being violated. In practice, about 100 constitutional complaints are filed to the Constitutional Court each year.

Constitutional complaint is now allowed by the Belarusian legislators. However, it allows two other procedures to claim the protection of constitutional freedoms or rights of an individual. Firstly, citizens and other entities have the right to turn to the entities competent to file a motion to the Constitutional Court to examine the compatibility of a normative act with the Constitution. To this aim, they must prove that their rights or freedoms are violated by a normative act which – in their opinion – is incompatible with the Constitution. Secondly, when less than a year has passed since the final application of a given normative act towards the complainant. The entity to which the individual applied makes a decision within a month whether it will bring this case to the Constitutional Court. In practice, it happened once (in 2014) that the House of Representatives of the National Assembly of the Republic of Belarus filed a motion to the Constitutional Court to examine the compatibility of definite regulations of the code of criminal proceedings with the Constitution and the Court recognized their incompatibility with the Constitution. In a situation typical of the Belarusian practice, several tens of citizens' requests to apply for proceedings before the Constitutional Court are rejected by the competent organs who refuse to file a motion to the Constitutional Court.

The second procedure known to the Belarusian legislation which can be used by the citizens to attract attention to the incompatibility of the regulations of law with the Constitution is, compared to the first one, more de-formalized and, at the same time has features of the action *popularis* complaint against the violation of the Constitution. The citizens (like the bodies of public authority and social organizations) can apply to the Constitutional Court with information on the occurrence of gaps, contradictions or underspecification. In such a situation, the Constitutional Court is competent to initiate proceedings *ex officio* and settle the matter. It can decree that there is a gap, a contradiction of underspecification in the regulations of law and it can apply to the competent organ to make a legal change. Apart from the obligatory constitutional review of laws before they are

63 К. Макили-Алиев, *Конституционное судопроизводство в Азербайджанской Республике*, "Studia Politologiczne" 2014, No. 32, pp. 195–196.

signed by the President, this is the most frequently applied competence of the Constitutional Court. The Constitutional Court has used it more than 200 times.

A constitutional complaint is also not allowed by the Uzbek legislation. On the other hand, an individual can apply to the Constitutional Court if they believe that their freedoms or rights were violated by way of any normative acts binding in the territory of Uzbekistan, the constitution or a law of the autonomous Karakalpak Republic is inconsistent with the Constitution or a law of Uzbekistan, or they request interpretation of the Constitution's norms or a law. If the Constitutional Court recognizes the individual's appeal as justified, it undertakes the case and settles it[64].

10 The Legal Character and the Legal Force of the Decisions of Constitutional Courts

The legal character of the decisions of constitutional courts is the subject of profound analysis in the doctrine of the states in the region. They are analyzed from the point of view of their normative character, the features characteristic of normative acts and their precedent character. It is emphasized that in this sphere they are not subject to a uniform classification[65]. The decisions of constitutional courts are final. They are not subject to appeal or objection (change)[66]. They are binding directly, and they do not require any confirmation by another entity[67]. In

64 For more on this subject, see: А.В. Чаптыков, *Субъекты права на обращение в Конституционный суд Российской Федерации: проблемы теории и практики: диссертация на соискание ученой степени кандидата юридических наук*, Abakan 2007, pp. 44–46.

65 Eg., see:. А.А. Манасян, *Место решений Конституционного Суда в правовой системе Республики Армени*, "Studia Politologiczne" 2014, Vol. 32 and the literature referred to Н.С. Бондарь, *Судебный конституционализм. Доктрина и практика*, Moscow 2016, pp. 128–169.

66 А. Джагарян, *Вмененная безупречность: решения Конституционного Суда Российской Федерации и правовое качество. Ответ на статью А. Петрова*, "Сравнительное конституционное обозрение" 2014, № 2, p. 116.

67 С.Г. Голубицкая, *Решения Конституционного Суда Российской Федерации в правовой системе России (Теоретические и практические вопросы): диссертация на соискание ученой степени кандидата юридических наук*, Moscow 2002, pp. 121–122; А.М. Кальяк, *Исполнение решений конституционных судов: вопросы теории и практики: на материалах постсоциалистических государств: диссертация на соискание ученой степени кандидата юридических наук*, Томsk 2006, p. 32.

Kazakhstan, a possibility is allowed (which rarely happens in practice) to change the decision of the Constitutional Council on the motion of the President or on the initiative of the Council itself. This can take place in three situations. Firstly, when the provision of the Constitution on the basis of which the decision was taken is changed. Secondly, when new circumstances important for the case appear, and – finally – the decision can be changed (only on the President's initiative) in the interests of the protection of freedoms and rights of citizens and persons, national security as well as the sovereignty and territorial integrity of the state.

Typically, decisions of the Constitutional Court come into effect on the day they are announced (in Kazakhstan and Moldova – on the day they are accepted). In Belarus, on the other hand, the decision comes into effect on the day it is adopted if other acts do not provide for another date.

In Belarus, the decisions of the Constitutional Court are classified by the legislator as normative acts of law. Legal acts and their particular regulations recognized as incompatible with the Constitution do not have legal force.

A simple classification of the decisions of constitutional courts predominates in the countries of the region, namely a division into decisions on compatibility or incompatibility of a normative act or the regulation included in it with the constitution. A more detailed division of the decisions of constitutional courts is provided for in the Armenian legislation. In accordance with the regulations of the law on the Constitutional Court, the Court can also recognize the reviewed normative act or the regulation included in it as compatible with the Constitution in the understanding established by the Constitutional Court in a given sentence. In the given understanding established by the Constitutional Court, this act (respectively: the regulation included in it) is to be applied (interpretative sentences of the Constitutional Court).

In the decision taken, the Ukrainian Constitutional Court can determine the procedure and time of its execution and place an obligation on definite organs of the state's authority to ensure control over the implementation of the decision. Administrative accountability for non-implementation of the decision of the Constitutional Court is also provided for. A mechanism similar to that in Ukraine is applied in Kazakhstan. The Constitutional Council itself can determine the procedure and date of the implementation of its decision. If its decision means increased state expenditures or decreased state incomes, the Constitutional Council establishes the date of implementation of the decision in consultation with the Government.

The problem connected with the effectiveness of constitutional courts in the states of the region (like in the majority of contemporary states) is the procedure of implementing the decisions of constitutional courts[68]. In this context, an important legal solution realized by the states of the region which serves the execution of the decisions of constitutional courts is the implementation of a special procedure of preparing drafts of normative acts to give effect to the decisions of constitutional courts referring to the unconstitutionality of legal regulations. Its application is expected to guarantee that the decisions of constitutional courts are directly reflected in binding legal regulations and that constitutional values are realized in a broad range. In Kyrgyzstan, when the Constitutional Chamber decrees on the incompatibility of a normative act or a regulation included in the latter with the Constitution or when it is necessary, following the decision of the Constitutional Chamber, to remove a gap in the systems of the sources of law, the Government, within four months of the decision of the Constitutional chamber being published, submits to the parliament a draft of a constitutional law or a draft of a law following from this decision. Drafts are subject to examination by the parliament according to a priority procedure. In reference to the other normative acts recognized by the Constitutional Chamber as incompatible with the Constitution, the organ which issued them has an obligation to make them compatible with the Constitution within three months. The organ which abandons making a normative act compatible with the Constitution or performs this duty in an insufficient manner bears legal responsibility.

The Government in Moldova within three months submits a draft law on implementing changes and amendments to the law whose regulations were recognized as incompatible with the Constitution, or on recognizing that they have lost their legal force. If, on the other hand, normative acts of the President or the Government were recognized as unconstitutional, then within two months after the Constitutional Court published the sentence they have an obligation to change their act or adopt a new one. Similar legal solutions were adopted in the Russian Federation. According to them, not later than three months after the decision of the Constitutional Court, the Government must submit to the State Duma a draft of a new law or change, an amendment of the law recognized by the Constitutional Court as incompatible with the Constitution. The draft is examined by the State Duma according to an urgency procedure[69]. In practice,

68 Cf. Ж.В. Начаева, *Эффективносьь исполнения решений Конституционного Суда РФ: проблемы теории и практики: диссертация на соискание ученой степени кандидата юридических наук*, Novosibirsk 2007, p. 162.

69 For more on the specific character of the urgency procedure, see: J. Zaleśny, *Priorytetowe postępowanie ustawodawcze na tle tzw. zwykłego postępowania ustawodawczego. Kilka uwag na tle doświadczeń rosyjskich*, [in:] M. Paździor. B. Szmulik (eds.), *Instytucjonalne*

however, the problem of implementation of decisions is still current (despite the adoption of the proper procedure).

In Kyrgyzstan, recommendations and motions on the improvement of legislation included in the decisions of the Constitutional Council are subject to obligatory examination by the competent state bodies, while the Council must be informed on the activities undertaken by the former. The Belarusian legislator, however, does not provide for any special procedure of giving effect to decisions of the Constitutional Court concerning the implementation of changes into binding normative acts so that they will be coherent with the Constitution and the decision of the Constitutional Court will be fully implemented. This means, and such is usually the practice, that the decisions of the Court remained unimplemented.

11 The Political Significance of Constitutional Courts

The political importance of constitutional courts does not only depend on their legal shape but also on how they are perceived by citizens and their factual position in the state mechanism. Some of the decisions of constitutional courts are not performed in time. Governments may not draft correct laws, and parliaments may not pass them. This reduces the importance of the constitutional court. The constitutional court will be able to fulfill the role it was assigned only if large social groups are convinced about the key importance of the constitution[70] for the functioning of the system of legal, social, political and economic relations. In this understanding, constitutional courts in the states of the region perform differentiated functions in building legally governed power relations and in settling relations between the sources of law. The secondary constitutional review of normative acts is realized in the most efficient way. The control of legislative and presidential acts, on the other hand, is much more entangled in political divisions occurring in the state. Here, one finds deficits in the significance of constitutional courts. They are observed to be susceptible to the expectations and needs of the political power. In a considerable part of the post-Soviet states, constitutional courts are an element strengthening the president's preponderance in the governing system, which takes place at the cost of the violation of constitutional values and rules. The judges themselves, on the other hand, are

gwarancje zasady pluralizmu politycznego w Polsce na tle standardów europejskich, Lublin 2014.

70 Б.С. Эбзеев, *Правовое государство. Конституционный суд. Учебное пособие*, Moscow 1997, p. 135.

treated by large social groups as a part of the system of political power, the same as other segments of public authority, only using different means.

One observes a difference between the constitutional basis of constitutional courts, founded on the solutions of the so-called European model of the constitutional review of law (the French model in Kazakhstan), the doctrine of the states of the region, which refers to the settlements of the European doctrine and practice, which does not fit the practice of a state of law. Constitutional courts do not play any more important role in realizing constitutional values or in building the system of balanced power which does not threaten the rights and freedoms of an individual. It should be borne in mind that the constitutions of some states of the region do not provide for a balanced system of government, but they clearly make the president an organ which is supposed to harmonize and coordinate the activity of other bodies of public authority and this is the direction in which the jurisdiction of constitutional courts is developed. Within the dispute between law and politics taking place in contemporary states, in the post-Soviet states (like in a great majority of contemporary states), politics is the priority, with the policy pursued by the president in particular. The Constitutional Court in Armenia distinguishes itself in this respect as it, more than others, is aimed at the fulfillment of constitutional values.

A significant revolution took place in the constitutional courts of the Russian Federation and Belarus. Following an argument between the President and the Supreme Soviet in Russia in October 1993, the Constitutional Court was dissolved and formed anew, thus becoming a body justifying the President's law-making policy. At the early stage of its existence (1994–1996), the Constitutional Court in Belarus performed an important role in the sphere of building a state of law based on constitutional provisions designating and at the same time stabilizing the political frameworks of Belarus. It made a significant contribution to the protection of constitutional rights and freedoms of Belarusians. As a result of the political changes taking place in the state, since 1997 the Constitutional Court started to lose its influence on the constitutionality of the binding law and it underwent political marginalization. It became an organ affirming the President's political activity and – considering its unconstitutionality – a politically superfluous one. Politically, an organ whose actions are focused on justifying the decisions made by other bodies of public authority is not necessary. Conflicts concerning the election of judges to the Constitutional Court in Ukraine, on the other hand, which result in a lack of quorum, make the performance of its tasks impossible. Consequently, in 2006, for example, the

Court did not examine a single case and in the year 2016 or 2017 it examined just a few cases[71].

Conclusions

The analysis of legal regulation referring to the system of constitutional courts of the post-Soviet states confirmed the hypothesis posed in the present chapter that to a narrower or broader extent it is based on the legal solutions adopted in European countries (the Austrian and French models, respectively). The doctrine of the studied group of countries also refers to the European tradition of the doctrine of constitutional courts. On the other hand, differences are observed between the political model and its doctrinal justification on the one hand, and the political practice in a great majority of post-Soviet states. From the point of view of the protection of the primacy of the constitution, and above all the protection of the rights and freedoms of an individual, this kind of judiciary happens to be ineffective. In this aspect, its application departs from the model solutions and the settlements of the doctrine but – and this must be clearly added – this is a common phenomenon in the contemporary world. Constitutional courts, called to secure the balance of powers and thus the protection of human rights and freedoms, experience a crisis. In practice, the separation of powers breaks down in contemporary states. A permanent struggle is going on between the participants in political relations for priority in the political system of the state and for the imposition of one's standpoint on other participants of political relations. In some countries, the struggle for the superior role in the system of power takes place with the participation of courts. The phenomenon of courtocracy is observed in contemporary countries[72]. A similar process does not occur in any state which arose as a result of the collapse of the USSR. In none of them does the constitutional court show any inclination to dominate over the other participants of power relations. In none of the states of the region has courtocracy appeared. Constitutional courts do not make attempts to trespass the competences assigned to them. They do not impose their interpretation of constitutional regulations on the law-making bodies. They do

---

71 Attention is drawn to this aspect of the political position of the Ukrainian Constitutional Court by А. Евсеев, *Самоограничение в деятельности Конституционного Суда Украины*, "Сравнительное конституционное обозрение" 2018, № 2, p. 51.

72 I write more about it in: Я. Залесны, *Защита доминирующей роли конституции и разделение власти – спор о методах создания права в современных государствах*, "Studia Politologiczne" 2018, No. 48.

not, under the pretext of studying the constitutionality of law regulations, attempt to enforce their subjective political views based on political arguments showing them as an expression of legal reasoning.

The assessment of the application of constitutional judicature in the sphere of the realization of separated and balanced power is more nuanced. In the majority of the states of the region, the role of the law-maker is based on the principle of separated power but does not provide for its balance. In the system of separated power, the dominating political position, which breaks the principle of equality, is granted to presidents. Among others, they perform the role of organs which coordinate and harmonize the activity of other organs of state power. For this reason, if the principle of balanced power is not a constitutional principle, it does not have to be reflected in the jurisdiction of constitutional courts. If, on the other hand, the provisions of constitutions (Azerbaijan, Belarus, the Russian Federation, Kazakhstan, Tajikistan, Uzbekistan) have granted the president the political primacy in relation to the other organs of state power and made him/her responsible for the realization of values which are most important for the state (such as independence, sovereignty or territorial integrity), this primacy cannot be questioned by the constitutional court. The latter must also affirm it, and that does take place.

Devaluation of the importance of constitutional courts is especially noticeable in those post-Soviet states where the constitutional courts decide on the validity of presidential and parliamentary elections. Despite repeated violations of the regulations of the election law (differently affecting the result of the elections), constitutional courts confirm the correctness of the elections, and thus the right of the persons elected in this way to perform definite functions.

In some countries of the region, the system of the constitutional court and its effect on the shape of the binding law have undergone significant changes. At the first stage of its activity (1994–1996), the Constitutional Court in Belarus made a significant contribution to the realization of legal norms included in the Constitution and in the protection of the rights and freedoms of citizens. It played an important role in securing the separation and balance of powers in the state. It fulfilled the tasks assigned to it in an effective way. The status of the Constitutional Court and its political importance was reduced with the consolidation of the political system around the President's office. The President is now the guarantor of the most important values in Belarus (sovereignty, territorial integrity, stability) as well as the guarantor of the Constitution and the rights and freedoms of persons and citizens. The office of the President undertakes comprehensive activities aimed at their realization. The political position of the President does not allow for the existence of a real constitutional review of legal acts issued by him or on his inspiration. The existence of such a body would mean undermining the President's political roles and hence it cannot take place as such.

The motivations to reorganize constitutional courts in Kyrgyzstan were not typical of contemporary states. The Constitutional Court pursued the activity of distorting the idea of an independent body of the constitutional review of law. It took positions which were politically motivated and involved itself in interaction of political provenience and political consequences. In cases pending before it, the court supported the President in office and when the latter – as a result of revolutionary events – fell, it supported the vice-president. A decrease of trust of the participants in political and legal relations to the Constitutional Court working in this way, linked with the recognized need for an independent organ in the legal system controlling the constitutionality of law and serving the protection of the constitutional separation of power and the constitutional rights and freedoms of an individual, caused the dissolution of the Constitutional Court and the establishment of a new organ in its place, namely the Constitutional Chamber of the Supreme Court. Like in Kyrgyzstan, the involvement of the Constitutional Court in strengthening the President's power took place in Ukraine, above all in 2010, the difference being, however, that this did not lead to the dissolution of that organ.

Like in Kyrgyzstan, the Constitutional Court in Kazakhstan was replaced by another organ (Constitutional Council). This took place for radically different reasons than in Kyrgyzstan. Those reasons did not have a situational character. They were connected not only with the negative practice of the existing body of the constitutional review of law. They followed from the President's conviction that the political system of the state needed to be determined in a new way, referring to different political models – not to the so-called European model of the constitutional review of law but to the French solutions. In this way, the Constitutional Council was established on the French model (not only concerning the name of the organ itself, namely the Constitutional Council).

A significant change of the political position of the Constitutional Court took place in 2015 in Armenia. It was connected with an approving assessment of its activity and the belief that the Constitutional Court should be involved in the processes of stabilizing the state's political system in a wider scope than before. It was for this reason that it was equipped with new competences, such as settling conflicts of competence between the constitutional bodies of the state, assessing the compatibility of a draft amendment to the Constitution with the Constitution and the compatibility of issues submitted to a referendum with the Constitution, or the President-initiated preventive control of the constitutionality of laws.

In the post-Soviet states, constitutional courts strengthen the establishment of the state's political system on the basis of constitutional values and principles. They direct the established law, especially of the secondary rank, towards the latter. At the same time, however, as a component of the system of bodies of public power, they are dependent on the processes taking place in the whole system, including the primacy of political solutions over the legal ones shared by the key participants in power relations.

Bibliography

Abdullayev F. S., *Azərbaycan Respublikasında Konstitusiya İcraatının Nəzəri və Praktiki Problemləri*, Bakı 2009.

Aramă E., *Controlul constituţionalităţii legilor: istorie şi actualitate*, Chişinău, Museum 2000.

Barak A., A *Judge on Judging: The Role of a Supreme Court in a Democracy*, "Harvard Law Review" 2002, T. 116.

Blachèr P., *Contrôle de constitutionnalité et volonté generale*, Paris 2001.

Brewer-Carias A., *Judicial Review in Comparative World*, New York 1989.

Bryk A., *The Origins of Constitutional Government. Higher Law and the Sources of Judicial Review*, Kraków 1999.

Cappelletti M., *Judicial Review in the Contemporary World*, Indianapolis 1971.

Dąbrowski M., *Domniemanie zgodności ustaw z Konstytucją Rzeczypospolitej Polskiej z 1997 roku*, Olsztyn 2017.

Delpérée F., *Le renouveau du droit constitutionnel*, „Revue Française de Droit Costitutionnel" 2008, № 2.

Fabbrini S., *Transatlantic Constitutionalism: Comparing the United States and the European Union*, „European Journal of Political Research" 2004, № 4.

Favoreu L., *Constitutional Review in Europe*, (in:) *Constitutionalism and Rights: The Influence of the United States Constitution Abroad*, L. Henkin, A. Rosenthal (eds.), New York 1990.

Favoreu L., *Les cours constitutionnelles*, Paris 1992.

Favoreu L., Philip L., *Les grandes decisions du Conseil Constitutionel*, Paris 1984.

Florczak-Wątor M., *Orzeczenia Trybunału Konstytucyjnego i ich skutki prawne*, Poznań 2006.

Fromont M., *La justice constitutionnelle en France ou l'exception française*, „La Revue Administrative" 1999, numero special 7.

Fromont M., *Justice constitutionnelle comparée*, Paris 2013.

Gamurari V., *Interpretarea tratatelor internaţionale şi a dreptului internaţional de către Curtea Constituţională – o cale de implementare a acestora în ordinea juridică internă a statelor. Materialele Conferinţei* "Rolul Curţii Constituţionale în sistemul protecţiei drepturilor omului şi respectarea CEDO şi jurisprudenţei Curţii Europene a Drepturilor Omului în jurisprudenţa şi legislaţia naţională", Chişinău, 13–14 decembrie 2007.

Garlicki L., *Sądownictwo konstytucyjne w Europie Zachodniej*, Warszawa 1987.

Garlicki L., *The Experience of the Polish Constitutional Court*, (in:) *Constitutional Justice. East and West. Democratic Legitimacy and Constitutional Courts in Post-Communist Europe in a Comparative Perspectives*, F. Laporta, A. Peczenik, F. Schauer (eds.), The Hague 2010.

Ginsburg T., *Judicial Review in New Democracies. Constitutional Courts in Asian Cases*, Cambridge 2003.

Guceac I., *Curs elementar de drept cnstituţional*, Chişinău, Editura Reclama 2001.

Guceac I., *Constituţia la răscruce de mileniu, Ediţia a II-a revăzută şi adăugită*, Bucureşti, Editura Academiei Române 2016.

Hamon F., Wienner C., *La justice constitutionnelle en France et à l'étranger*, Paris 2011.

Jaskiernia J., *Влияние Совета Европы на системные изменения в государствах бывшего Советского Союза*, „Studia Politologiczne" 2014, No. 32.

Kabat-Rudnicka D., *Konstytucjonalizacja Unii Europejskiej a sądownictwo konstytucyjne*, Warszawa 2016.

Kampo W., Sawczyn M., *Legitymizacja orzeczeń sądów konstytucyjnych w kontekście panowania doktryny państwa prawa: aspekt komparatywny i prakseologiczny*, „Zagadnienia Sądownictwa Konstytucyjnego" 2012, № 2 (4).

Koopmans T., *Courts and Political Institutions: A Comparative View*, Cambridge 2003.

Kubas S., *Judicial review: geneza i rozwój*, (in:) *Konstytucja i sądowe gwarancje jej ochrony*, P. Czarny (eds.), Kraków 2004.

Laidler P., *Prawno-polityczny spór wokół wyboru sędziego Sądu Najwyższego USA po śmierci Antonina Scalii*, „Przegląd Sejmowy" 2017, № 3.

Laquieze A., *Le contrôle de constitutionnalite de la loi aux Etats-Unis vu par les penseurs liberaux français u XIXe siècle*, (in:) *Aux origines du contrôle de constitutionnalité XVIIIe-XXe siècle*, D. Chagnollaud (eds.), Paris 2003.

Lever A., *Democracy and Judicial Review: Are They Really Incompatible?*, „Perspectives on Politics" 2009, № 4.

Macejkova I., *Influence of the Constitutional Court of the Slovak Republic on the monism of the Slovak Legal System*, „Конституционное правосудие: Вестник Конференции органов конституционного контроля стран молодой демо кратии" 2009, № 1 (43).

Małajny R. M., *Amerykański prezydencjalizm*, Warszawa 2012.

Manasyan A., *Development of the Constitutional Doctrine and the Stability of the Legal Positions of Constitutional Courts*, Conference Proceedings, Seimas of the Republic of Lithuania. 2015. Lithuania 2015.

Massias J.-P., *Droit constitutionnel des États d'Europe de l'Est*, Paris 2008.

Mikuli P., *Zdekoncentrowana sądowa kontrola konstytucyjności prawa. Stany Zjednoczone i państwa europejskie*, Kraków 2007.

Mocreac V., *Baza juridică şi procedura de soluţionare a recursurilor constituţionale. Materialele Conferinţei "Rolul Curţii Constituţionale în sistemul protecţiei drepturilor omului şi respectarea CEDO şi jurisprudenţei Curţii Europene a Drepturilor Omului în jurisprudenţa şi legislaţia naţională"*, Chişinău, 13–14 decembrie 2007.

Powoływanie sędziów konstytucyjnych w wybranych państwach europejskich, A. Chmielarz-Grochal, A. Michalak, J. Sułkowski (eds.), Warszawa 2017.

Pulbere D., *Controlul constituţionalităţii actelor juridice ale organelor centrale ale puterii de stat – o garanţie a asigurării supremaţiei Constituţiei. Materialele Conferinţei "Rolul Curţii Constituţionale în sistemul protecţiei drepturilor omului şi respectarea CEDO şi jurisprudenţei Curţii Europene a Drepturilor Omului în jurisprudenţa şi legislaţia naţională"*, Chişinău 13–14 decembrie 2007.

Pulbere D., *Cuvânt de salut. Materialele Conferinţei "Rolul Curţii Constituţionale în sistemul protecţiei drepturilor omului şi respectarea CEDO şi jurisprudenţei Curţii Europene a Drepturilor Omului în jurisprudenţa şi legislaţia naţională"*, Chişinău 13–14 decembrie 2007.

Pulbere D., *Alocuţiune rostită în cadrul şedinţei festive consacrate aniversării a 15-a a Curţii Constituţionale a Republicii Moldova. Conferinţa internaţională „Asigurarea supremaţiei Constituţiei, funcţia de bază a Curţii Constituţionale"*, Chişinău 2010.

Puşcaşu V., *Independenţa Curţii Constituţionale în oglinda strmbă a legislatiei. Timpul*, 16 Februarie 2010.

Roussillon H., *Le probléme du contrôle de la constitutionnelité des lois dans les pays socialistes*, „Revue du Droit Publiques et de la Science Politique en France et a l'Étranger" 1977, № 1.

Rouvillois F., *Droit constitutionnel. Fondements et pratiques*, Paris 2005.

Sadurski W., *Prawo przed sądem. Studium sądownictwa konstytucyjnego w postkomunistycznych państwach Europy Środkowej i Wschodniej*, Warszawa 2008.

Shapiro M., *The Success of Judicial Review*, (in:) *Constitutional Dialogues in Comparative Perspectives*, S. J. Kenney, W. M. Reisinger, J. C. Reitz (eds.), New York 1999.

Shapiro M., Stone A., *The New Constitutional Politics of Europe*, „Comparative Political Studies" 1994, № 25.

Smochină A., *Tendinţe actuale în evoluţia jurisdicţiei constituţionale moldoveneşti. Materialele Conferinţei "Rolul Curţii Constituţionale în sistemul protecţiei drepturilor omului şi respectarea CEDO şi jurisprudenţei Curţii Europene a*

Drepturilor Omului în jurisprudența și legislația națională", Chișinău, 13–14 decembrie 2007.

Sokolewicz W., *Sąd Konstytucyjny Federacji Rosyjskiej*, (in:) *Sądy konstytucyjne w Europie. t. IV*, J. Trzciński (eds.), Warszawa 2000.

Szymanek J., *Tradycje konstytucyjne. Szkice o roli ustawy zasadniczej w społeczeństwie demokratycznym*, Warszawa 2006.

Szymanek J., *Ustrój konstytucyjny Kazachstanu*, Warszawa 2013.

Szymanek J., *Emmanuel-Joseph Sieyès, O sądzie konstytucyjnym: tezy projektu ustawy przedstawionego przez Emmanuela-Jospeha Sieyèsa podczas obrad Konwencji w dniu 18 Thermidora roku III* (tłumaczenie, opracowanie i komentarz), „Studia Prawnicze KUL" 2016, № 2.

Szymanek J., *Trybunał Konstytucyjny de lege ferenda – propozycje nowelizacji ustawy w odpowiedzi na opinię Komisji Weneckiej*, „Przegląd Sejmowy" 2017, № 4.

Tănase Al., *Cuvânt de salut. „Rolul justiției constituționale în protecția valorilor statului de drept". Conferința Internațională „Rolul justiției constituționale în protecția valorilor statului de drept": 20 ani: Adoptarea Constituției Republicii Moldova, 8–9 sept. 2014*, Chișinău. Arc 2015.

Tushnet M., *Advanced Introduction to Comparative Constitutional Law*, Cheltenham – Northampton 2014.

Vashkevich A., *The Republic of Belarus: The Road from the Past to the Past*, (in:) *Out of and into Authoritarian Law*, András Sajó (ed.), The Hague, New York, Kluwer Law International 2003.

Vashkevich A., *Judicial Independence in the Republic of Belarus*, (in:) *Judicial Independence in Transition*, A. Seibert-Fohr (ed.), Berlin, Heidelberg, New York: Springer 2012.

Waszkiewicz A., *Sąd Konstytucyjny Republiki Białoruś: przed i po referendum listopadowym 1996 roku*, (in:), *Sądy Konstytucyjne w Europie. Białoruś, Litwa, Łotwa, Rosja, t. IV*, J. Trzciński (ed.), Warszawa 2000.

Zaleśny J., *System konstytucyjny Białorusi*, Warszawa 2011.

Zaleśny J., *Priorytetowe postępowanie ustawodawcze na tle tzw. zwykłego postępowania ustawodawczego. Kilka uwag na tle doświadczeń rosyjskich*, (in:) *Instytucjonalne gwarancje zasady pluralizmu politycznego w Polsce na tle standardów europejskich*, M. Paździor, B. Szmulik (eds.), Lublin 2014.

Zaleśny J., *Zasady podziału władzy w Rosji*, (in:) *Zasady podziału władzy we współczesnych państwach europejskich. t. II*, S. Grabowska, R. Grabowski (eds.), Rzeszów 2016.

Zaporojan V., *„Premisele implementării instituţiei recursului constituţional în Republica Moldova*“, „Justiţia Constituţională în Republica Moldova“ 2005, № 3.

Zaporojan V., *Accesul direct al persoanei la justiţia constituţională (Practica Germaniei)*, „Revista naţională de drept“ 2007, №. 4.

Zubco V., *Probleme şi soluţii privind accesul direct al cetăţenilor la Curtea Constituţională. Materialele Conferinţei "Rolul Curţii Constituţionale în sistemul protecţiei drepturilor omului şi respectarea CEDO şi jurisprudenţei Curţii Europene a Drepturilor Omului în jurisprudenţa şi legislaţia naţională"*, Chişinău 13–14 decembrie 2007.

Абросимова Е.Б., Уметбаева Э.Р., *Ученый совет Института государства и права РАН обсуждает научный доклад Председателя Конституционного Суда РФ*, „Государство и право“ 1992, № 5.

Авакьян С.А., *Конституционное право России: уч. курс. 2-е изд., перераб. и доп.: в 2 т., Т. 2*, Moscow 2006.

Авакьян С.А., *Размышления конституционалиста: Избранные статьи*, Moscow 2010.

Амандыкова С.К., Малиновский В.А., *Роль конституционного суда Республики Казахстан в становлении конституционной доктрины Казахстана*, „Евразийский научный журнал“ 2012, № 10 (53).

Арутюнян Г.Г., *Конституционный Суд в системе государственной власти. Диссертация на соискание ученой степени доктора юридических наук*, Moscow 1999.

Арутюнян Г.Г., *Конституционный мониторинг. Монография*, Yerevan 2016.

Арутюнян Р.Э., *Конституционное правосудие как фактор формирования судебного конституционализма*, „Вестник ПГЛУ“ 2011, № 3.

Бабосов Е.М., *Человек в социальных системах*, Minsk 2013.

Баглай М.В., *Конституционное право Российской Федерации*, Moscow 2007.

Багрій О.І., *Доктрина верховенства Конституції України (за матеріалами практики Конституційного Суду України)*, Uzhgorod 2016.

Барабаш Ю.Г., *Парламентський контроль в Україні (конституційно-правовий аспект)*, Kharkiv 2004.

Барабаш Ю.Г., Селіванов А.О. (eds.), *Конституційна юрисдикція*, Kharkiv 2012.

Басангов Д.А., *Юридическая природа особого мнения Судьи Конституционного Суда Российской Федерации*, „Журнал российского права“ 2006, № 2.

Батеева Е.В., *Законность и конституционная юстиция в современной России: диссертация на соискание ученой степени кандидата юридических наук*, Moscow 2003.

Безруков А.В., *Конституционные основы деятельности судебных органов и прокуратуры в механизме обеспечения правопорядка*, „Конституционное и муниципальное право“ 2016, № 4.

Белкин А.А., *Вопросы юридической силы решений Конституционного Суда Российской Федерации*, „Вестник Конституционного Суда РФ“ 1997, № 2.

Белкин А.А., *Дело о полномочиях судов (Комментарий к Постановлению Конституционного Суда от 16 июня 1998 г.)*, „Уголовное право“ 2000, № 1.

Блохин П.Д., *Двойной юбилей. Конституционное правосудие на службе прав человека*, „Сравнительное конституционное обозрение“ 2016, № 2.

Блохин П.Д., Кряжкова О.Н., *Как защитить свои права в Конституционном суде. Практическое руководство по обращению с жалобой в Конституционный суд России*, Moscow 2014.

Боботов С.В., *Конституционная юстиция*, Moscow 1994.

Богдановская И., *Судебный прецедент и его эволюция*, „Законность“ 2007, № 3.

Бондарь Н., *Конституционное правосудие – универсальный институт разрешения социальных противоречий современного общества*, „Конституционное правосудие: Вестник Конференции органов конституционного контроля стран молодой демократии“ 2007, No 1 (35).

Бондарь Н.С., *Судебный конституционализм. Доктрина и практика*, Moscow 2016.

Боботов С.В., *Конституционная юстиция (сравнительный анализ)*, Moscow 1994.

Бондарь Н.С. Джагарян А.А., *Правосудие: ориентация на Конституцию*, Moscow 2018.

Браун Н.Дж., Уоллер Д.Дж., *Конституционные суды и политическая неопределённость: разрыв конституционной преемственности и «правление судей»*. Часть 1, „Сравнительное конституционное обозрение“ 2017, № 4.

Брежнев О.В., *Судебный конституционный контроль в России: проблемы методологии, теории и практики: дис. … докт. юрид. наук: 12.00.02*, Moscow 2006.

Бринь Т.О., *Конституційний Суд України в механізмі захисту та забезпечення прав і свобод людини і громадянина*, Kharkiv 2010.

Бринце В.Д., *Судовий конституціоналізм в Україні: доктрина і практика ф ормування*, Kharkiv 2013.

Будагова А.Ш., *Конституционный суд Азербайджанской Республики*, (in:) *Конституционный контроль в зарубежных странах*, В.В. Маклаков (ed.), Moscow 2007.

Василевич Г., *Возможности реализации Европейской конвенции о защите прав человека и основных свобод в практике Конституционного Суда Республики Беларусь и национальных судов*, „Белорусский журнал международного права и международных отношений" 2002, № 3.

Василевич, Г.А., *Юридические документы ООН и Совета Европы в практике работы Конституционного Суда Республики Беларусь*, „Право Беларуси" 2005, № 8.

Василевич Г.А., *Послания Конституционного Суда Республики Беларусь о состоянии конституционной законности – реальный вклад в развитие правовой системы*, Minsk 2007.

Василевич Г.А., *Конституционное право Республики Беларусь: Учебник*, Minsk 2010.

Василевич Г.А., *Конституционное правосудие*, Minsk 2012.

Василевич Г.А., *Конституционное правосудие: учебное пособие для студентов учреждений высшего образования по специальности "Правоведение"*, Minsk 2014.

Вашкевич А.Е., *Доступ к конституционной юстиции: европейский опыт и законодательство Республики Беларусь*, (in:) *Актуальные проблемы международного публичного и международного частного права: сборник научных трудов. Выпуск 1*, Minsk 2009.

Вашкевич А., *Конституционный Суд Республики Беларусь: место и роль в системе государственных органов*, (in:) *Судебно-правовая реформа: концепция и пути ее реализации в Республике Беларусь*, Minsk 1992.

Ващенко Ю., *Незалежні регулятори в сфері охорони здоров'я: європейський досвід та перспективи розвитку в Україні*, „Право і громадянське суспі льство" 2014, № 1.

Витрук Н.В., *Конституционное правосудие в России (1990–2001 годы): очерки теории и практики*, Moscow 2001.

Витрук Н.В., *Актуальные проблемы модернизации конституционного право судия в России*, „Журнал российского права" 2011, № 10.

Витрук Н.В., *Конституционное правосудие. Судебное конституционное право и процесс*, Moscow 2011.

Витрук Н.В., *Конституционное правосудие. Учебное пособие*, Moscow 2012.

Волвенко П.В., *Діяльність Конституційного Суду України щодо тлумачення Конституції України: теоретичний аспект*, Kyiv 2006.

Гадельшина Л.И., Гарифуллина А.Р., *Правовые основы взаимодействия Конституционного Суда Российской Федерации с органами государственной власти Российской Федерации*, „Российский Судья" 2017, № 5.

Гаджиев Г.А., *Федеральное Собрание и Конституционный Суд. Партнерство и контроль*, „Российская Федерация" 1994, № 8.

Гаджиев Г.А., *Принципы конституционного права, общие принципы права и конституционные принципы*, (in:) *Конституция и законодательство. По материалам международной научно-практической конференции. Москва, 29 октября 2003 г.*, Ю.А. Тихомиров, Т.Я. Хабриева (eds.), Moscow 2003.

Гаджиев Г.А., *Роль конституционного права и Конституционного Суда должна быть более активна*, „Юридический мир" 2004, № 11.

Гаджиев Г.А., Кряжков В.А., *Конституционная юстиция в Российской Федерации: становление и проблемы*, „Государство и право" 1993, № 7.

Герасимова Е.В., *Конституционная жалоба как полномочие Конституционного Суда России и Федерального конституционного суда Германии: сравнительно-правовой анализ*, „Сравнительное конституционное обозрение" 2010, № 4.

Герасимова Е.В., *Роль Конституционного суда Российской Федерации в системе судебной защиты прав и свобод человека и гражданина: диссертация на соискание ученой степени кандидата юридических наук*, St. Petersburg 2011.

Гергелійник В.О., *Правові проблеми становлення і функціонування конституційної юстиції в Україні*, Kyiv 1999.

Головин А.С., *Правовая природа и юридическая сила актов Конституционного суда Украины // Альманах (Конституционное правосудие в новом тысячелетии)*, Yerevan 2011.

Головин А.С. (ed.), *Питання захисту прав людини і громадянина органами конституційної юрисдикції у сучасних умовах*, Kyiv 2013.

Головистикова А.Н., Дмитриев Ю.А., *Проблемы теории государства и права*, Moscow 2005.

Головін А.С. (ed.), *Захист прав людини органами конституційної юстиції: можливості і проблеми індивідуального доступу*, Kyiv 2011.

Голубицкая С.Г., *Решения Конституционного Суда Российской Федерации в правовой системе России (Теоретические и практические вопросы): д иссертация на соискание ученой степени кандидата юридических наук*, Moscow 2002.

Гордеев И.В., *Конституционная юстиция в государствах-членах СНГ, дисс. на соиск. уч. степ.канд. юрид. Наук*, Moscow 2007.

Гьофе О., *Розум і право. Складові інтеркультурного правового дискурсу*. Kyiv 2003.

Дадиани Л.Я., *К вопросу о сущности, формах и оценке института конституционного надзора*, „Труды Университета дружбы народов им. П. Лумумбы. Т. XX. Экономика и право" 1967, Вып. 2.

Даниелян Г., *Современные проблемы комментария принципа разделения властей*, „Конституционное правосудие: Вестник Конференции органов конституционного контроля стран молодой демократии" 2007, № 4 (38).

Джагарян А., *Вмененная безупречность: решения Конституционного Суда Российской Федерации и правовое качество. Ответ на статью А. Петрова*, „Сравнительное конституционное обозрение" 2014, № 2.

Диноршоев А.М., *Конституционные основы разделения властей в Республике Таджикиста*, Dushanbe 2007.

Диноршоев А.М., Сафаров Д.С., *Процессуальные институты конституционного судопроизводства в Республике Таджикистан*, Dushanbe 2015.

Дробышевский С., Данцева Т., *Формальные источники права*, Moscow 2011.

Евсеев А., *Самоограничение в деятельности Конституционного Суда Украины*, „Сравнительное конституционное обозрение" 2018, № 2.

Едалов Е.В., *Правовой статус президента Российской Федерации как гаранта Конституции России в сфере федерального вмешательства*, „Бизнес в законе" 2009, № 3.

Елеупова А.А., *Осуществление конституционного контроля Конституционным Советом Республики Казахстан: диссертация на соискание ученой степени кандидата юридических наук*, Chelyabinsk 2006.

Енгибарян Р.В., Тадевосян Э.В., *Конституционное право*, Moscow 2017.

Еременко Ю.П., *Нормы советских конституций: автореф. дис…канд. юрид. наук*, Saratov 1968.

Жаркова Л.М., *Содержание и применение юридической конструкции «Послание Конституционного Суда Российской Федерации Федеральному Собранию Российской Федерации»*, (in:) *Конституционные чтения. Выпуск 2. Понятийно-категориальный аппарат для решения научных задач в конституционно-правовой науке*, Т.Д. Зражевской (ed.), Voronezh 2003.

Жучкова Е.В., *Правовые позиции Конституционного Суда Российской Федерации по вопросам уголовного права и уголовного процесса: дис. … канд. юрид. наук: 12.00.02*, Moscow 2009.

Загорье Б., *Нужна ли нам судебная охрана конституции (в порядке обсуждения),* „Вестник сов.юстиции" 1928, № 17 (123).

Залесны Я., *Защита доминирующей роли конституции и разделение власти – спор о методах создания права в современных государствах,* „Studia Politologiczne" 2018, No. 48.

Залесны Я., *Конституционный суд в системе судебной власти Азербайджанской Республики,* „Studia Politologiczne" 2014, No. 32.

Захаров В.В., *Решения конституционного Суда Российской Федерации как источник конституционного права: дис. … канд. юрид. наук: 12.00.02,* Penza 2004.

Зиманов С.З. *Конституция и Парламент Республики Казахстан,* Almaty 1996.

Змиевский Д.В., *Осуществление конституционного судопроизводства на постсоветском пространстве,* „Пробелы в Российском законодательстве" 2008, № 2.

Зорькин В.Д., *Прецедентный характер решений Конституционного Суда Российской Федерации,* „Журнал российского права" 2004, № 12.

Зорькин В.Д., *Конституцию надо менять лишь тогда, когда ее уже нельзя не менять,* „Закон" 2006, № 11.

Зорькин В.Д., *Аксиологические аспекты Конституции России,* „Сравнительное конституционное обозрение" 2008, № 4.

Зорькин В.Д., *Россия и Конституция в XXI веке,* Moscow 2008.

Зорькин В.Д., *Право в условиях глобальных перемен,* Moscow 2013.

Зорькин В.Д., *Конституционный Суд России: доктрина и практика: монография,* Moscow 2017.

Кажлаев С.А., *Генезис правовых позиций Конституционного Суда Российской Федерации,* „Журнал российского права" 2007, № 3.

Казакевич А., *Институт судебной власти Беларуси: политологический анализ,* Kaunas 2009.

Казаклиу А., *Актуальные проблемы конституционной юрисдикции Республики Молдова,* „Сравнительное конституционное обозрение" 2001, № 4.

Калиновский К.Б., *Проблемы использования решений Конституционного Суда Российской Федерации в до Судебном производстве по уголовным делам//Совершенствование деятельности правоохранительных органов по борьбе с преступностью в современных условиях,* Tyumen 2010.

Кальяк А.М., *Исполнение решений конституционных судов: вопросы теории и практики: на материалах постсоциалистических государств:*

диссертация на соискание ученой степени кандидата юридических наук, Tomsk 2006.

Кампо В., *Проблемы и перспективы развития украинской модели конституционной юстиции*, „Сравнительное конституционное обозрение" 2011, № 3.

Караев А.А., *К вопросу об эффективности конституционного контроля*, „Право и государство" 2000, № 3.

Караев А.А., *Конституционный контроль: Казахстан и зарубежный опыт: Учебное пособие*, Almaty 2002.

Караев А.А., *Правовая охрана Конституции: традиции демократического конституционализма и опыт Казахстана: Монография*, Almaty 2010.

Кариева Н., *Конституционный Суд и обращения граждан*, „Вестник Конституционного суда РУз" 2004, Выпуск 10.

Кебец А.А., *Роль Конституционного Суда в обеспечении качества закона*, (in:) *Судебно-правовая реформа: концепция и пути ее реализации в Республике Беларусь*, Minsk 1992.

Кельзен Г., *Судебная гарантия Конституции (конституционная юстиция)*, „Право и политика" 2006, № 8.

Керимов Д.А., Экимов А.И., *Конституционный надзор в СССР*, „Советское государство и право" 1990, № 9.

Кистяковский Б.А., *Социальные науки и право*, Moscow 1916.

Клишас А.А., *Конституционная юстиция в зарубежных странах*, Moscow 2004.

Клишас А.А., *Конституционный контроль и конституционное правосудие в зарубежных странах: дис. … докт. юрид. наук: 12.00.02*, Moscow 2007.

Князев С.Д., *Конституционный Суд в правовой системе Российской Федерации*, „Журнал российского права" 2013, № 12.

Ковешников Е.М., *Основы конституционного права зарубежных стран*, Moscow 2001.

Кодавбович В.А., *Вопросы Конституционного Суда в проекте Конституции Республики Беларусь*, (in:) *Судебно-правовая реформа: концепция и пути ее реализации в Республике Беларусь*, Minsk 1992.

Козлов Л.В., *Роль правовых позиций Конституционного Суда Российской Федерации в обосновании конституционных принципов института собственности: дис. … канд. юрид. наук: 12.00.02*, Moscow 2011.

Козлова Е.И., Кутафин О.Е., *Конституционное право*, Moscow 2017.

Кокотов А.Н., *Насущные вопросы регулирования деятельности Конституционного Суда РФ*, „Российский юридический журнал. Екатеринбург: УрГЮА" 2012, № 2 (83).

Кокотов А.Н., *Право конституции в российском праве*, „Актуальные проблемы российского права“ 2014, № 10.

Корельский В., Перевалов В. (eds.), *Теория государства и права*, Moscow 1998.

Коркмазов М.У., *Защита конституционных прав и свобод человека и гражданина органами Судебного конституционного контроля в Российской Федерации и го Сударствах Центральной и Восточной Европы: автореф. дис. … канд. юрид. наук: 12.00.02*, Moscow 2014.

Кравец И.А., *Конституционная жалоба: традиции и новации в механизме гарантий прав и свобод личности*, „Журнал российского права“ 2003, № 8.

Кравец И.А., *Конституционное правосудие: теория судебного конституционного права и практика судебного конституционного процесса*, Moscow 2017.

Кравченко О.О., *Захист прав і свобод людини та громадянина Конституційним Судом України: доктринальні, прикладні та компаративні аспекти*, Kyiv 2011.

Крусян А.Р., *Сучасний український конституціоналізм: теорія і практика*, Odes 2010.

Кряжков В.А., *Толкование Конституции Российской Федерации Конституционным Судом Российской Федерации*, „Вестник Конституционного Суда РФ“ 1997, № 3.

Кряжков В.А., *Конституционное правосудие в субъектах Российской Федерации*, Moscow 1999.

Кряжков В.А., Лазарев Л. В., *Конституционная юстиция в Российской Федерации*, Moscow 1998.

Кряжков В.А., Митюков М. А., *Конституционный Суд РФ: развитие конституционно-правового статуса*, „Государство и право“ 2011, № 10.

Кряжкова О.Н., *Рассмотрение жалоб граждан о защите прав в Конституционном Суде Российской Федерации*, „Вестник публичного права“ 2004, № 5.

Кряжкова О.Н., *Правовые позиции Конституционного Суда Российской Федерации: теоретические основы и практика реализации судами России*, Moscow 2006.

Кудрявцев Ю.В., *Конституционный Суд России: опыт и проблемы (Международный научный семинар)*, „Государство и право“ 2016, № 1.

Куртов А., *Конституционное правосудие в Республике Казахстан и институт выборов*, „Сравнительное конституционное обозрение“ 2003, № 2.

Курьянович А.В., *Конституция независимой Беларуси: разработка, проекты, принятие. 2-е изд*, Minsk 2011.

Кутафин О.Е., *Предмет конституционного права*, Moscow 2001.

Лазарев Л.В., *Правовые позиции Конституционного Суда России*, Moscow 2003.

Ледях И.А., *Буржуазные конституции в период общего кризиса капитализма*, Москва 1966.

Лунь З.В., *Правова охорона Конституції України*, Kyiv 2003.

Лучин В.О., Доронина О.Н., *Жалобы граждан в Конституционный Суд РФ*, Moscow 1998.

Люхьтерханд О., *Роль и независимость Конституционного Суда в правовом государстве*, (in:) *Роль Конституционного Суда в реализации конституционных прав и свобод граждан: материалы международной конференции*. Минск, 22 сентября 2009 годат Minsk 2010.

Макили-Алиев К., *Конституционное судопроизводство в Азербайджанской Республике*, „Studia Politologiczne“ 2014, No. 32.

Маклаков В.В., *Конституционный контроль в зарубежных странах*, (in:) *Конституционный контроль в зарубежных странах*, В. В. Маклаков (ed.) Moscow 2007.

Малинчев Б.А., *Процессуальные институты в деятельности Конституционного Суда Российской Федерации: дис. … канд. юрид. наук: 12.00.02*, Moscow 2010.

Малюшин А.А., *Вопросы совершенствования юридических форм и механизма реализации конституционно - судебного правотворчества в современных условиях*, „Российский Судья“ 2012, № 11.

Мамедов Э., *Конституционный суд и суды общей юрисдикции в Азербайджане: теоретические и практические проблемы взаимоотношений*, „Кавказ и глобализация“ 2007, № 3.

Манасян А., *Особенности толкования законов при осуществлении конституционного правосудия*, „Евразийский юридический журнал“ 2012, № 12 (55).

Манасян А., *Развитие Конституции Республики Армения как важнейшая предпосылка укрепления армянского конституционализма*, „Сравнительное конституционное обозрение“ 2012, № 3 (88).

Манасян А., *Место решений Конституционного Суда в правовой системе Республики Армения*, „Studia Politologiczne“ 2014, № 32.

Марино И., *Конституционно-правовая школа Института законодательства и сравнительного правоведения при*

Правительстве Российской Федерации в теории и практике российского конституционализма, „Журнал зарубежного законодательства и сравнительного правоведения" 2015, № 1.

Марокко Н.А., О *правовой природе решений Конституционного Суда Российской Федерации*, „Российский Судья" 2006, № 6.

Марокко Н.А., *Функция защиты основных прав и свобод человека и гражданина в контексте реализации полномочий Конституционного Суда Российской Федерации: диссертация на соискание ученой степени кандидата юридических наук*, Moscow 2009.

Марченко М.Н., *Источники права*, Moscow 2008.

Марченко М.Н., *Судебное правотворчество и судейское право*, Moscow 2008.

Маршава Л.А., *Особое мнение Судьи Конституционного Суда РФ как вид неофициального толкования норм Основного закона*, „Вестник Челябинского гос. ун-та" 2012, № 27.

Матеріали круглого столу «Науково-доктринальне забезпечення розвитку конституційної юстиції в Україні», „Вісник Конституційного Суду України" 2015, № 4.

Марокко Н.А., *Функция защиты основных прав и свобод человека и гражданина в контексте реализации полномочий Конституционного Суда Российской Федерации: диссертация на соискание ученой степени кандидата юридических наук*, Moscow 2009.

Машкин В.А., *Конституционный Суд как институт российского правового государства: становление и развитие: диссертация на соискание ученой степени кандидата юридических наук*, Orel 2002.

Медушевский А.Н., *Революция в Киргизии: итоги и перспективы конституционных преобразований*, „Сравнительное конституционное обозрение" 2011, № 1 (80).

Медушевский А.Н., *Революция в Киргизии: итоги и перспективы конституционных преобразований*, „Сравнительное конституционное обозрение" 2011, № 1 (80).

Мельник М., Різник С., *Про межі конституційної юрисдикції та пряму дію норм Конституції України при здійсненні правосуддя*, „Вісник Конституційного Суду України" 2016, № 4–5.

Миклашевич П.П., *Конституционный Суд Республики Беларусь: функции и взаимодействие с другими органами государственной власти*, „Вестник Конституционного Суда Республики Беларусь" 2010, № 4.

Миклашевич П.П., *Развитие конституционного контроля в Беларуси: особенности доктрины и практики*, (in:) *Конституционный контроль: доктрина и практика*, В.Д. Зоркин (ed.), Moscow 2012.

Мирзоев С.Б., *Особенности конституционного нормоконтроля как гарантия нормализации национальных законодательств*, „Вестник ТНУ РТ“ № 3/5 (166).

Мирбобоев Б., *Дальнейшая демократизация взаимоотношений Конституционного суда Республики Узбекистан с другими судами и национальными институтами по правам человека*, „Вестник. Конституционного суда РУз“ 2015, Выпуск 19.

Мироненко О.О., *Препозиційні витоки конституційної юстиції в Україні*, „Вісник Конституційного Суду України“ 1998, № 4.

Митюков М.А., *Акты Конституционного Суда РФ и конституционных (уставных) судов субъектов РФ: общая характеристика и статистический анализ*, „Журнал российского права“ 2001, № 6.

Митюков М.А., *Полномочия Конституционного Суда РФ в его собственной интерпретации*, „Вестн. Том. гос. ун-та“ 2004, № 283.

Митюков М.А., *Судебный конституционный надзор 1924–1933 гг.: вопросы истории, теории и практики*, Moscow 2005.

Митюков М.А., *Предтеча конституционного правосудия: взгляды, проекты и институциональные предпосылки (30-е - начало 90-х годов XX в.): Монография*, Moscow 2006.

Митюков М.А., *Федеральный конституционный закон «О Конституционном Суде Российской Федерации»: правовые дискуссии при разработке и принятии (введение в тему)*, „Конституционное и муниципальное право“ 2006, № 12.

Митюков М.А., *Предтеча конституционного правосудия: взгляды, проекты и институциональные предпосылки (30-е - начало 90-х годов XX в.): Монография*, Moscow 2006.

Митюков М.А., *Методология исследования проблемы послания Конституционного Суда РФ*, „Конституционное и муниципальное право“ 2010, № 12.

Митюков М.А., *Как исполняются решения Конституционного Суда Российской Федерации и конституционных (уставных) Судов субъектов Федерации*, „Журнал российского права“ 2017, № 7.

Мартиненко П., *Місце і роль Конвенції про захист прав людини і основоположних свобод 1950 року в конституційно-правовому механізмі України*, „Вісник Конституційного Суду України“ 2002, № 2.

Морщакова Т.Г., *Принципы и общие правила конституционного правосудия*, (in:) *Российское правосудие в контексте судебной реформы*, Moscow 2004.

Мусабаева А., *О текущем состоянии системы правосудия в Кыргызстане*, http://ipp.kg/ru%3E/news/2239 (accessed: 20.03.2018).

Мырзалимов Р.М., *Конституционный суд Кыргызской Республики (Конституционные основы организации и деятельности): диссертация на соискание ученой степени кандидата юридических наук*, Moscow 2000.

Мырзалимов Р.М., *Вопросы конституционного правосудия в Кыргызстане. Монография*, Bishkek 2001.

Мырзалимов Р.М., *Органы конституционной юстиции в странах Центральной Азии: проблемы теории и практики. Автореферат диссертации на соискание ученой степени доктора юридических наук*, Moscow 2013.

Нарутто С.В., *Обращение граждан в Конституционный Суд Российской Федерации: Научно-практическое пособие*, Moscow 2011.

Насырова Т.Я., *Конституционный контроль*, Kazan 1992.

Начаева Ж.В., *Эффективнось исполнения решений Конституционного Суда РФ: проблемы теории и практики: диссертация на соискание ученой степени кандидата юридических наук*, Novosibirsk 2007.

Нерсесянц В.С., *Суд не законодательствует и не управляет, а применяет право*, (in:) *Судебная практика как источник права*, Moscow 1997.

Несмеянова С.И., *Конституционный Судебный контроль в Российской Федерации: проблемы теории и практики*, Yekaterinburg 2004.

Несмеянова С.Э. Хабриева Т.Я., *Подведомственнось дел*, (in:) *Конституционный судебный процесс*, М.С. Саликов (ed.), Moscow 2004.

Несмеянова С.Э., *Судебная практика Конституционного Суда Российской Федерации с комментариями*, Moscow 2007.

Несмеянова С.Э., *О возможном влиянии Конституционного Суда Российской Федерации на законодателя*, „Журнал конституционного правосудия" 2010, № 3.

Нечкин А.В., *Формы правления в странах Содружества Независимых Государств,* Moscow 2018.

Нудель М.А., *Конституционный контроль в капиталистических странах*, Moscow 1968.

Нуриев Г.Х., *Европеская модель конституционного судопроизводства*, Moscow 2015.

Овсепян Ж.И., *Правовая защита конституций. Судебный конституционный контроль в зарубежных странах*, Rostov-on-Don 1992.

Овсепян Ж.И., *Судебный конституционный контроль в механизме «разделения властей». Ч. 1*, „Правоведение" 1993, № 4.

Овсепян Ж.И., *Становление конституционных и уставных судов в субъектах Российской Федерации (1990–2000 гг.)*, Moscow 2001.

Омаров С.М., *Основные проблемы реализации послания Конституционного Суда Российской Федерации*, „Право. Журнал Высшей школы экономики“ 2011, № 4.

Опря О.В., *Конституционные Суды в постсоциалистических государствах Восточной Европы (на примере Конституционного Суда Республики Болгария): дис. … канд. юрид. наук*: 12.00.02, Moscow 2002.

Остапович И.Ю., *Конституционный Совет Республики Казахстан: вопросы теории и практики: диссертация на соискание ученой степени кандидата юридических наук*, Томск 2005.

Паліюк В.П., *Застосування судами України Конвенції про захист прав людини та основних свобод*, Kyiv 2004.

Парфейников И.С., *Правовые позиции Конституционного Суда Российской Федерации в сфере осуществления правосудия по уголовным делам: дис. … канд. юрид. наук: 12.00.02*, Moscow 2014.

Пастухов М.И., *Конституционная юстиция и судебная власть в Республике Беларусь: законодательство и практика*, „Сравнительное конституционное обозрение“ 2011, № 4.

Пастухов М.И., *Когда слова равны молчанию. Белорусский опыт посланий Конституционного Суда о состоянии конституционной законности*, „Сравнительное конституционное обозрение“ 2014, № 4.

Пастухов М.И., *Конституционное правосудие в Республике Беларусь (1994–2014 гг.)*, „Studia Politologiczne“ 2016, No. 39.

Пастухов М.И., *Особенности судебного конституционного контроля в Республике Беларусь*, „Studia Politologiczne“ 2018, No. 48.

Петров А.А., *Решения Конституционного Суда Российской Федерации в механизме правового регулирования*, Irkutsk 2007.

Петров А.А., *Основания отказа в принятии обращения к рассмотрению Конституционным Судом РФ*, „Журнал российского права“ 2016, № 12.

Петрова Д.В., *Правовые позиции Конституционного Суда Российской Федерации по вопросам его деятельности и конституционного судопроизводства: дис. … канд. юрид. наук: 12.00.02*, Moscow 2008.

Петрова И.В., *Конституционный Суд – орган конституционного контроля в Российской Федераци, Дисс. на соиск. уч. степени. канд. юрид. наук*, Moscow 2004.

Пляхимович И.И., *Комментарий к Конституции Республики Беларусь: в 2 т., Т. 2*, Minsk 2015.

Погорілко В.Ф. (ed.), *Конституційне право України: Академічний курс*, Kyiv 2005.

Подгруша В.В., *Некоторые проблемы инициирования конституционного производства*, (in:) *Конституционное правосудие в Республике Беларусь: пятилетний опыт, проблемы и перспективы. Сборник докладов и материалов*, Minsk 1999.

Подгруша В.В., *Законодательство о конституционном контроле в Республике Беларусь: состояние и перспективы совершенствования*, (in:) *Правовое государство. Конституционный Суд. Материалы международных семинаров*, Minsk 2000.

Пономарев Б.Н. (ed.), *Конституция СССР: Политико-правовой комментарий*, Moscow 1982.

Пряхина Т.М., *Роль юридической охраны Конституции в обеспечении стабильного развития регионов*, (in:) *Правовая реформа и совершенствование управления регионами*, Saransk 1991.

Пугачев А.Н., *Судебный конституционной контроль: учеб.-метод. комплекс для магистрантов юрид. спец.*, Novopolotsk 2009.

Рабінович П., *Правотлумачення і герменевтика (за матеріалами практики Конституційного Суду України)*, „Вісник Академії правових наук України" 2006, № 4.

Рогов И.И., Малиновский В.А. (eds), *Конституционный контроль в Казахстане: доктрина и практика утверждения конституционализма: Монография*, Almaty 2015.

Рустамзаде А., *Конституционный Суд Азербайджанской Республики, Конституційне Та Адміністративне Право*, „Юридичний вісник" 2012, № 4 (25).

Савенко М.В., *Правовий статус Конституційного Суду України*, Kyiv 2000.

Савенко М., *Роль практики Європейського суду з прав людини у конституційному судочинстві України*, „Вісник Конституційного Суду України" 2005, № 6.

Савчин М.В., *Конституційний Суд України як гарант конституційного ладу*, Kyiv 2004.

Савчин М.В., *Становлення конституціоналізму та відповідальне парламентське правління в Україні: криза демократії чи „тиранія" парламентської більшості?*, „Держава і право" 2007, Вип. 36.

Савчин М.В., *Рішення і висновки Конституційного Суду України – специфічне джерело конституційного права*, (in:) *Джерела конституційного права України*, Ю.С. Шемшученко, О.І. Ющик (eds.), Kyiv 2010.

Савчин М.В. *Конституціоналізм і природа конституції: теорія і практика реалізації*, Kyiv 2013.

Савчин М.В., Права людини в Україні в контексті доктрини європейської та української юстиції, (in:) *Права і свободи людини і громадянина в Україні (доктрина Європейського суду з прав людини і Конституційного Суду України)*, П.Ф. Мартиненко (ed.), Kyiv 2013.

Савчин М.В., *Конституційний захист прав людини та проблеми конкуренції юрисдикції*, „Український часопис міжнародного права" 2015, № 1.

Савчин М.В., *Конституційний Суд України та реалізація конкуренції України*, „Публічне право" 2015, № 1.

Савчин М.В., *Конституційні інновації та вірність конституції*, „Віче" 2016, № 7–8.

Савчин М.В., *Современное состояние конституционной юстиции в Украине: вызовы и новые решения*, „Studia Politologiczne" 2018, No. 48.

Савчин М.В., *Сучасні тенденції конституціоналізму у контексті глобалізації та правового плюралізму*, Uzhgorod 2018.

Саликов М.С., *Конституционный Судебный процесс*, Moscow 2003.

Саликов М.С., *Правовые позиции Конституционного Суда Российской Федерации: понятие и система*, „Правоведение" 2003, № 5.

Саликов М.С., *Международные договоры РФ как объекты конституционного контроля*, „Российский юридический журнал" 2014, № 6.

Сапаргалиев Г.С., *Конституционное право Республики Казахстан: Академический курс*, Almaty 2002.

Сапаргалиев Г.С. (ed.), *Конституция Республики Казахстан. Научно-правовой комментарий*, Almaty 2004.

Свистуновой М.А., *Проблемы конституционного контроля в СССР: автореф. дисс. канд. юрид. наук*, Moscow 1971.

Селіванов А.О. Стрижак А.А., *Питання теорії конституційного правосуддя в Україні: актуальні питання сучасного розвитку конституційного правосуддя*, Kyiv 2010.

Сивицкий В.А., *Систематизация конституционно-правовых актов Российской Федерации: дис. … канд. юрид. наук: 12.00.02*, Moscow 1999.

Синюков В.Н., *Российская правовая система: введение в общую теорию*, Moscow 2010.

Скомороха В.Є., *Конституційний Суд України в механізмі державної влади, Автореф. канд. юр. наук*, Kharkiv 2001.

Скомороха В.Є., *Конституційна юрисдикція в Україні: проблеми теорії, методології і практики*, Kyiv 2007.

Скомороха В., *Окремі питання поділу влад і юрисдикція Конституційного Суду України*, „Право України" 1998, № 5.

Скомороха В., *Судовий конституціоналізм в аспекті співвідношення конституційної та конвенційної юрисдикції*, „Вісник Конституційного Суду України" 2015, № 1.

Сліденко І.Д., *Тлумачення конституції: питання теорії і практики в контексті світового досвіду*, Odes 2003.

Сліденко І.Д., *Конституційний контроль в механізмі сучасної правової держави, дисертація доктора юридичних наук*, Kyiv 2010.

Страшун Б.А., *Решения Конституционного Суда Российской Федерации как источник права*, „Конституционное правосудие" 2002, № 4.

Страшун Б.А. (ed.), *Конституционное (государственное) право зарубежных стран. Общая часть*, Moscow 1996.

Стучка П., *СССР и РСФСР. Советская Конституция в вопросах и ответах. 4-е перераб. и доп издание*, Moscow 1924.

Тарасов А.М., *Проблемы законодательного обеспечения государственного контроля*, „Государство и право" 2004, № 10.

Тесленко М., *Конституційна юрисдикція в Україні, Автореф. канд. юр. наук*, Kyiv 2000.

Тихомиров Ю.А., *Курс сравнительного правоведения*, Moscow 1996.

Тихомиров Ю.А., Сухарев А.Я., Демидов И.Ф., *Законность в Российской Федерации*, Moscow 1998.

Ткачук А.П., *Конституційний Суд у механізмі захисту основних прав і свобод людини: модельний підхід*, Kyiv 2012.

Тодика Ю.М., *Тлумачення Конституції і законів України: теорія і практика*, Kharkiv 2001.

Тодика Ю.Н., *Основы конституционного строя Украины*, Kharkiv 1999.

Тодика Ю.Н., Журавський В.С. (eds.), *Конституційне право України*, Kyiv 2002.

Тропер М., *Реалистическая теория толкования*, „Сравнительное конституционное обозрение" 2006, № 1.

Туманов В.А., *Судебный конституционный контроль за конституционностью нормативных правовых актов*, „Советское государство и право" 1988, № 3.

Уваров А.А., *Вопросы адекватного отражения конституционных норм в действующем законодательстве*, „Конституционное и муниципальное право" 2015, № 12.

Филипчик Р.И., *О роли Конституционного Суда в совершенствовании правового регулирования реализации гражданами конституционного права на судебную защиту*, „Весн. Канстытуцыйнага Суда Рэспублікі Беларусь" 2005, № 4.

Хахинова А.А., *Правовые позиции Конституционного Суда Российской Федерации в правовой системе Российской Федерации: дис. … канд. юрид. наук: 12.00.02*, Moscow 2010.

Хабриева Т.Я., *Толкование конституций (уставов) субъектов Российской Федерации: органы и процедура*, (in:) *Теоретические проблемы российского конституционализма*, Moscow 2000.

Хабриева Т.Я. (ed.), *Конституция Российской Федерации: от образа будущего к реальности (к 20-летию Основного Закона России)*, Moscow 2014.

Хабриева Т.Я., Волкова Н.С., *Особенности казуального толкования Конституции Российской Федерации*, (in:) *Теоретические проблемы российского конституционализма*, Moscow 2000.

Хакимова С., *Становление и совершенствование конституционного правосудия в Республике Узбекистан РУз*, „Вестник Конституционного суда РУз" 2005, Выпуск 12.

Холиков К.Н., *Становление и развитие института конституционного надзора в Таджикистане*, Dushanbe 1998.

Холиков К.Н., *Основные направления деятельности Конституционного суда в условиях глобализации//Национальная правовая система стран СНГ в условиях глобализации и региональной интеграции, Матер. Междунар. конф.*, Dushanbe 2007.

Холиков К.Н., *Конституционный суд и конституционное судопроизводство в Таджикистане*, Dushanbe 2014.

Хошимзода Д.Д., *Конституционная юстиция – гарантия законности в Таджикистане*, (in:) *Материалы международной конференции, посвященной 20-летию образования Конституционного суда Республики Таджикистан на тему: «Конституционное правосудие – гарант обеспечения верховенства Конституции» (Душанбе, 17–18 сентября 2015 года)*, Dushanbe 2015.

Хромова О.С., *Индивидуальная жалоба в конституционный суд Российской Федерации: диссертация на соискание ученой степени кандидата юриди ческих наук*, Kemerovo 2006.

Христова Г.О., *Юридична природа актів Конституційного Суду України*, Kharkiv 2004.

Цалиев А.М., Качмазов О.Х., *Правозащитная функция органов конституционной юстиции и прокуратуры*, „Законность" 2010, № 7.

Циппеліус Р., *Юридична методологія*, Kyiv 2004.

Чаптыков А.В., *Субъекты права на обращение в Конституционный суд Российской Федерации: проблемы теории и практики: диссертация на соискание ученой степени кандидата юридических наук*, Abakan 2007.

Чиркин В.Е., *Контрольная власть*, „Государство и право" 1993, № 4.

Чиркин В.Е., *Конституционное право*, Moscow 2015.

Чиркин В.Е. (ed.), *Сравнительное конституционное право. Учебное пособие*, Moscow 2002.

Чудаков М.Ф., *Судебная власть: полномочия в сфере конституционного надзора*, (in:) *Судебно-правовая реформа: концепция и пути ее реализации в Республике Беларусь*, Minsk 1992.

Р.В. Шагиев (ed.), *Актуальные проблемы теории государства и права*, Moscow 2011.

Шаповал В.М., *Зарубіжний парламентаризм*, Kyiv 1993.

Шаповал В.М., *Проблеми розвитку конституційної юрисдикції в Україні*, „Вісник Конституційного Суду України, 1998, № 2.

Шаповал В.М., *Статус Конституционного Суда Украины в контексте принципа разделения властей*, (in:) *Конституционный Суд как гарант разделения властей. Сборник докладов*, Moscow 2004.

Шевчук С.В., *Загальнотеоретичні проблеми нормативності актів судової влади, Дисертація доктора юридичних наук*, Kharkiv 2008.

Шевчук С., *Європейська конвенція про захист прав людини та основних свобод: практика застосування та принципи тлумачення в контексті сучасного українського праворозуміння*, „Практика Європейського суду з прав людини. Рішення. Коментарі" 1999, № 2.

Шевчук С., *Основи конституційної юриспруденції*, Kyiv 2001.

Шевчук С., *Концепція самообмеження суду: доктрина «політичного питання», «політичної діяльності» та «поля розсуду держави»*, „Вісник Академії правових наук України" 2006, № 3.

Шевчук С., *Судова правотворчість: світовий досвід та перспективи в Україні*, Kyiv 2007.

Шевчук С., *Принцип верховенства права та найвища юридична сила Конституції України*, „Право України" 2011, № 5.

Шевчук С., *Узгодженість практики Європейського суду з прав людини та Конституційного Суду України*, „Вісник Конституційного Суду України" 2011, № 4–5.

Шейнин Х., *Конституционный Суд Российской Федерации в системе органов Судебной власти*, „Российская юстиция" 2016, № 3.

Шмавонян Г.А., *Конституционное правосудие Армении в системе разделения властей: диссертация на соискание ученой степени кандидата юридических наук*, Moscow 2000.

Шульженко Ю. Л., *Конституционный контроль в России*, Moscow 1995.

Эбзеев Б.С., *Конституция. Правовое государство. Конституционный Суд*, Moscow 1997.

Эбзеев Б.С., *Правовое государство. Конституционный суд. Учебное пособие*, Moscow 1997.

Эбзеев Б.С., *Конституция, власть и свобода в России. Опыт синтетического исследования*, Moscow 2014.

Єзеров А., *Роль конституційної юстиції в розвитку сучасного українського конституціоналізму*, (in:) *Проблеми сучасної конституціоналістики. Вип. 3. Сучасний український конституціоналізм*, А.Р. Крусян (ed.), Odes 2015.

Эшонов Б., *Становление и развитие Конституционного Суда Республики У збекистан*, „Вестник Конституционного суда Руз" 2001, Выпуск 5.

Ященко А., *Теория федерализма. Опыт синтетической теории права и государства*, Yuriev 1912.

Օհանյան Վ., Իրավունքի աղբյուրների հիմնախնդիրը ՀՀ-ում *(տեսագործնական վերլուծություն)*, Ատենախոսություն, Երևան 2009.

Հարությունյան Գ., Մանասյան Ա., Սահմանադրական վերահսկողություն. Լրամշակված վերահրատարակություն, Ուսում նական ձեռնարկ, Եր.: Իրավունք, 2015.

Վաղարշյան Ա., Իրավունքի աղբյուրների ու իրավական կ արգավորման միջոցների հարաբերակցությունը և h աարակական հարաբերությունների կարգավորման ստորակարգությունը//Պետություն և իրավունք 2006, N 2–3 (32–33).

Notes on Contributors

Kamal Makili-Aliyev, A second-level doctorate degree in law, Visiting Researcher, Law Department, Lund University, Sweden; Chief Researcher of the Academy of Public Administration affiliated at the Office of the President of the Republic of Azerbaijan.

Saule Koshkenovna Amandykova, Doctor of Law, Professor, Eurasian National University named L.N. Gumilyov (Republic of Kazakhstan).

Veniamin Evgenyevich Chirkin, Doctor of Law, Professor, Chief Researcher at the Institute of State and Law of the Russian Academy of Sciences, Principal Researcher at the Institute of Legislation and Comparative Law under the Government of the Russian Federation, Honored Scientist of the Russian Federation, Honored Lawyer of the Russian Federation (Russian Federation).

Davlat Elnazarov, Doctor of Law, Department of State and Legal Disciplines Law Faculty of Russian-Tajik (Slavic) University (Republic of Tajikistan).

Ion Guceac, Doctor of Law, Professor, Vice-President of the Academy of Sciences of Moldova.

Anahit Manasyan, Candidate of Law, Associate Professor of the Department of Constitutional Law of Yerevan State University, Vice-Rector of the Academy of Justice of the Republic of Armenia (Armenia).

Omon Zakirovich Mukhamedzhanov, Doctor of Law, Professor of Tashkent State Law University (Republic of Uzbekistan).

Ruslan Muratbekovich Myrzalimov, Doctor of Law, Professor of Constitutional and Administrative Law Department at Law Faculty of Kyrgyz Jusup Balasagyn National University, Member of Editorial Board for Bulletin of Constitutional Chamber at Supreme Court of Kyrgyz Republic.

Igor Yuryevich Ostapovich, Doctor of Law, Head of the Department of Constitutional and Municipal Law in the Altay Branch of Russian Academy of National Economy and Public Administration under the President of the Russian Federation.

Mykhailo Savchyn, Doctor of Law, professor, Director of the Institute of Comparative Public Law and International Law Studies, Uzhgorod National University (Ukraine).

Jarosław Szymanek, Doctor of Political Sciences, Analytical Department of the Office of the Sejm (Poland).

Alexander Vashkevich, Doctor of Law, Professor, European Humanities University in Vilnius (Lithuania), former judge of the Constitutional Court of the Republic of Belarus.

Jacek Zaleśny, Doctor of Law, Faculty of Political Science and International Studies, University of Warsaw (Poland).

Studies in Politics, Security and Society

Edited by Stanisław Sulowski

Vol.	1	Robert Wiszniowski (ed.): Challenges to Representative Democracy. A European Perspective. 2015.
Vol.	2	Jarosław Szymanek: Theory of Political Representation. 2015.
Vol.	3	Alojzy Z. Nowak (ed.): Global Financial Turbulence in the Euro Area. Polish Perspective. 2015.
Vol.	4	Jolanta Itrich-Drabarek: The Civil Service in Poland. Theory and Experience. 2015.
Vol.	5	Agnieszka Rothert: Power of Imagination. Education, Innovations and Democracy. 2016.
Vol.	6	Zbysław Dobrowolski: Combating Corruption and Other Organizational Pathologies. 2017.
Vol.	7	Vito Breda: The Objectivity of Judicial Decisions. A Comparative Analysis of Nine Jurisdictions. 2017.
Vol.	8	Anna Sroka: Accountability and democracy in Poland and Spain. 2017.
Vol.	9	Anna Sroka / Fanny Castro-Rial Garrone / Rubén Darío Torres Kumbrián (eds.): Radicalism and Terrorism in the 21st Century. Implications for Security. 2017.
Vol.	10	Filip Pierzchalski: Political Leadership in Morphogenetic Perspective. 2017.
Vol.	11	Alina Petra Marinescu: The Discursive Dimension of Employee Engagement and Disengagement. Accounts of keeping and leaving jobs in present-day Bucharest organizations. 2017.
Vol.	12	Jacek Giedrojć: Competition, Coordination, Social Order. Responsible Business, Civil Society, and Government in an Open Society. 2017.
Vol.	13	Filip Ilkowski: Capitalist Imperialism in Contemporary Theoretical Frameworks. 2017.
Vol.	14	Leszek Leszczyński / Adam Szot (eds.): Discretionary Power of Public Administration. Its Scope and Control. 2017.
Vol.	15	Tadeusz Klementewicz: Understanding Politics. Theory, Procedures, Narratives. 2017.
Vol.	16	Tomasz Bichta: Political Systems of the Former Yugoslavia. 2018
Vol.	17	Miroslav Palárik / Alena Mikulášová / Martin Hetényi / Róbert Arpáš: The City and Region Against the Backdrop of Totalitarianism. 2018
Vol.	18	Jolanta Itrich-Drabarek / Stanisław Mazur / Justyna Wiśniewska-Grzelak (eds.): Understanding Politics. Theory, Procedures, Narratives. 2017.
Vol.	19	Jerzy Juchnowski / R. Jan Sielezin / Ewa Maj: The Image of "White" and "Red" Russia in the Polish Political Thought of the 19th and 20th Century. Analogies and Parallels. 2017.
Vol.	20	Roman Kuźniar: Europe in the International Order. 2018.
Vol.	21	Piotr Jaroszynski: Europe - the Clash of Civilisations. 2018.
Vol.	22	Stanisław Filipowicz: Truth and the Will to Illusion. 2018.
Vol.	23	Andrzej Szeptycki: Contemporary Relations between Poland and Ukraine. The "Strategic Partnership" and the Limits Thereof. 2019.

Vol. 24 Sylwester Gardocki / Rafał Ożarowski / Rafał Ulatowski (eds.): The Islamic World in International Relations. 2019.

Vol. 25 Jacek Zaleśny (ed.): Constitutional Courts in Post-Soviet States. Between the Model of a State of Law and Its Local Application. 2019.

www.peterlang.com

www.ingramcontent.com/pod-product-compliance
Ingram Content Group UK Ltd.
Pitfield, Milton Keynes, MK11 3LW, UK
UKHW040857081026
15587UKWH00016B/497

9 783631 793084